MySQL
and Perl
for the
Web

Contents At a Glance

P9-CAS-640

MySQL and Perl for the Web

Paul DuBois

www.newriders.com

201 West 103rd Street, Indianapolis, Indiana 46290
An Imprint of Pearson Education
Boston • Indianapolis • London • Munich • New York • San Francisco

MySQL and Perl for the Web

Paul DuBois

Trademarks

Warning and Disclaimer

Publisher
David Dwyer

Associate Publisher
Al Valvano

Executive Editor
Stephanie Wall

Managing Editor
Kristy Knoop

Development Editor
Chris Zahn

Product Marketing Manager
Stephanie Layton

Publicity Manager
Susan Nixon

Senior Project Editor
Lori Lyons

Copy Editor
Keith Cline

Indexer
Joy Dean Lee

Manufacturing Coordinator
Jim Conway

Book Designer
Louisa Klucznik

Cover Designer
Brainstorm Design, Inc.

Cover Production
Aren Howell

Proofreader
Katherine Shull

Composition
Amy Parker

TABLE OF CONTENTS

About the Author

Paul DuBois began his involvement with MySQL after recoiling in horror at the complexities of dealing with a database from one of the larger commercial vendors, and with its customer support mechanism. Turning to MySQL for relief proved to have unforeseen and unexpected consequences: first, as the opportunity to contribute to the MySQL Reference Manual; then to writing *MySQL* with New Riders; and most recently, to his present employment with NuSphere, a company actively involved in MySQL development, promotion, and training.

Paul's responsibilities and interests have at one time or another involved database development, Web site development and management, mailing list management, system administration, and TCP/IP and AppleTalk networking. He's considered a leader in the MySQL and Open Source communities.

About the Technical Reviewers

These reviewers contributed their considerable hands-on expertise to the entire development process for *MySQL and Perl for the Web*. As this book was being written, these dedicated professionals reviewed all the material for technical content, organization, and flow. Their feedback was critical to ensuring that *MySQL and Perl for the Web* fits our readers' need for the highest-quality technical information.

Bill Gerrard is the Vice-President of Technology at Daze Networks, Inc., a provider of Internet services, including DigitalDaze.com virtual servers with private MySQL database services, and DNSCentral.com, which offers domain name registration, domain name service, Web forwarding, and email forwarding powered in part by MySQL and Perl. Bill lives in Lake Forest, California with his wife Pam and two children.

Jeremy D. Zawodny lives in Silicon Valley and works as an engineer for Yahoo! Finance. He spends his days using Perl, MySQL, Apache, and other great Open Source software so that millions of people can read financial news. In his "spare time," he is also the Executive Editor of *Linux Magazine* and a part-time systems administrator and Web geek for WCNet.org. He is also a slave to his two cats.

Acknowledgments

I'd like to acknowledge my debt to Michael "Monty" Widenius and to the other MySQL developers for creating a database that's been so rewarding to help document, and for being so accessible in responding to questions.

Thanks also to my employers at NuSphere, both for helping to further the development of MySQL and for putting up with my spending so much time writing about it.

My technical reviewers, Bill Gerrard and Jeremy D. Zawodny, contributed valuable comments and criticisms, and, much as I hate to admit it, found a few bugs as well. Their efforts made this a better book for you to read.

The people at New Riders responsible for bringing you this book are Stephanie Wall (Executive Editor), Chris Zahn (Development Editor), Lori Lyons (Senior Editor), Keith Cline (Copy Editor), Joy Dean Lee (Indexer), and Amy Parker (Compositor). You wouldn't be reading this book now if it weren't for Stephanie, by the way—it was her idea.

Thanks to the staff at the Maple Grove Victor Allen's and to the proprietresses of the Sow's Ear in Verona, the coffee shops where the bulk of this book was written. Their establishments provide surroundings conducive to thinking and setting pencil to paper—except during the tumult and din of Celtic Music Sundays at "the Ear!"

Most of all, my love and appreciation to my wife Karen. Her steadfast support of my efforts to write while in the midst of significantly changing life circumstances helped in the completion of this book more than she will probably ever know, and certainly more than I can express.

Tell Us What You Think

As the reader of this book, you are the most important critic and commentator. We value your opinion and want to know what we're doing right, what we could do better, what areas you'd like to see us publish in, and any other words of wisdom you're willing to pass our way.

As an Executive Editor for the Web Development team at New Riders Publishing, I welcome your comments. You can fax, email, or write me directly to let me know what you did or didn't like about this book—as well as what we can do to make our books stronger.

Please note that I cannot help you with technical problems related to the topic of this book, and that due to the high volume of mail I receive, I might not be able to reply to every message.

When you write, please be sure to include this book's title and author, as well as your name and phone or fax number. I will carefully review your comments and share them with the author and editors who worked on the book.

Fax: 317-581-4663
Email: stephanie.wall@newriders.com
Mail: Stephanie Wall
         Executive Editor
         New Riders Publishing
         201 West 103rd Street
         Indianapolis, IN 46290 USA

Introduction

When I wrote *MySQL* for New Riders a year and a half ago, I wondered whether it would receive much of a response, because it wasn't apparent whether the MySQL community was very sizable. I should have known better! MySQL is a very good database, it's easy to use, it's fast, and it's free—all characteristics that help make it deservedly more popular each day. And it's clear now that its users are interested in reading more about it. Consequently, after publishing *MySQL*, the folks at New Riders began to consider how the database community could be served by another MySQL-based title. As we discussed ideas, one that quickly came to mind was the need for substantial coverage on the topic of using MySQL in tandem with Perl and its DBI module for writing Web-based database scripts. This combination is quite widely used, but, oddly enough, only sporadically documented. The result? Many people who see how popular MySQL and Perl are in Web environments decide to try them out, but find themselves without a source that deals at length specifically with these tools.

This book changes that. It contains extensive practical material that will enable you to use MySQL and Perl to bring your Web site to life. It helps you write applications that interact with your visitors and applications that provide dynamic content, freeing you from being tied to static pages that must be updated by hand. The approach used here is based on the belief that learning from examples is one of the most effective ways to gain knowledge and experience. You'll find functional applications that you can modify to suit your own purposes. What you *won't* find is page after page of program listings with little explanation of what's going on. Examples are more meaningful when you understand them, so each application is fully described so that you know not only what it does, but also how and why. This approach emphasizes the following key features:

- **Practicality.** I assume you're interested in working code that does real stuff, so that's what you'll get here. But we'll also discuss the reasons why you do things a certain way, because such understanding will allow you to adapt the material to many more contexts than would any rote-learning approach. We'll discuss the principles that go into designing and implementing the applications, to provide knowledge that will help you modify them more readily or design new ones based on similar principles. If, as is common for Perl, "there's more than one way to do it" and multiple techniques bear consideration, we'll discuss and compare them.

- **Accessibility.** The material here is technical, but not impenetrable. I believe it's possible to present content and substance in a practical way that is also easy to understand and use.

- **Generality.** As we develop a particular application to perform a specific task, I'll point out other types of problems that can be addressed with the general techniques used in the application. That way you can look beyond the code to see how it might be adapted to other purposes—some of which might be of more interest to you than the immediate purpose for which the application is written here.

You'll notice that applications in this book sometimes develop in fits and starts. I'll show one way to do something, and then point out a shortcoming and show how to do it better—occasionally several times. This isn't always the most direct approach, but it provides more latitude to discuss alternatives.

How This Book Is Organized

Chapter 1, "Introduction to MySQL and Perl," provides an overview of what you can expect to accomplish with the combination of MySQL and Perl in a Web-based environment.

Chapter 2, "Getting Connected—Putting Your Database on the Web," shows how to create the database we'll use for the applications developed in this book and provides background material on writing Perl scripts. It introduces the CGI.pm module for Web scripting and the DBI module for interfacing with database servers. It also shows how to write a simple Web application for data entry, editing, and searching.

Chapter 3, "Improving Performance with mod_perl," discusses an Apache module that you can use to dramatically improve the performance of your Perl scripts, as well as issues to be aware of when running scripts in the mod_perl environment.

Chapter 4, "Generating and Processing Forms," discusses how to use CGI.pm to create and initialize forms, and how to extract and interpret information from forms that users fill in and submit.

Chapter 5, "Writing Form-Based Applications," shows several ways to make your scripts more interactive using forms, and how to use MySQL to maintain the information you gather that way. It covers data entry and validation, image uploading and display, and polling. Along the way, it also shows how to create and send email from within scripts, and how to run scripts on a scheduled basis under cron.

Chapter 6, "Automating the Form-Handling Process," shows how to ask MySQL for information about a database table's structure and use that information to automatically generate field elements corresponding to the table's columns. It also describes how that information can help validate contents of submitted forms. Use of lookup tables for form generation and validation is covered as well.

Chapter 7, "Performing Searches," describes how to create search forms, construct database queries based on search parameters that users submit, and display search results.

Chapter 8, "Session Management," discusses state management—how to keep track of information across multiple requests from the same client so they can be treated as a session. It describes various client-side and server-side state management techniques, methods for uniquely identifying clients, and how to use MySQL to store and expire session information.

Chapter 9, "Security and Privacy Issues," discusses how to run a database-backed Web server in a secure fashion. There are a lot of ways to get burned. You should know what they are and what you can do about them. The chapter covers the dangers presented by remote users who use (or abuse) your applications, by other local users who have access to your server host, and by people who spy on your network.

Chapter 10, "E-Commerce Applications," develops a miniature Web site oriented toward commercial activity. It discusses online catalog presentation, ordering techniques, and credit card processing. It also covers how to use transactions, to prevent partial failure of multiple-statement updates from leaving your database in an inconsistent state.

Appendix A, "Obtaining Software," lists the software you need to make effective use of this book, and where to get it.

Appendix B, "References and Further Reading," suggests sources of additional useful information about the topics discussed in this book.

Conventions

The following typographical conventions are used in this book:

Monospaced font indicates Web sites, hostnames, filenames, directory names, commands, and options. Italicized font indicates where you should substitute a value of your own choosing.

Where commands are shown as you enter them, bold indicates the part you type. Non-bold indicates output from the computer. In the following table, the prompt indicates how the command is run:

%	Command is run as a regular UNIX user
#	Command is run as the root UNIX user
C:\>	Command is run under Windows
mysql>	Command is run from the mysql program

In SQL statements, SQL keywords and function names are written in uppercase. Database, table, and column names are written in lowercase. When a SQL statement is shown with a `mysql>` prompt to indicate that you should run it from the `mysql` program, it is terminated with a semicolon ';' because that is `mysql`'s convention for detecting ends of statements. When a SQL statement is not shown with the `mysql>` prompt, no assumption is made about how you might issue it, so no semicolon is shown. If you do happen to run the statement from `mysql`, be sure to add the terminating semicolon.

Where there's something worth noting or some additional information that adds something to the discussion, I'll add a sidebar, which looks like this:

If You Are Not Using `mod_perl`...

You should know one thing about this chapter even if you decide to skip it for now: Most of the rest of this book assumes you'll run your scripts under `mod_perl`. You can recognize such scripts, because they'll be located in the `cgi-perl` directory, not in `cgi-bin`. To use any such script in standalone fashion (assuming it doesn't require `mod_perl`, of course), just put it in your `cgi-bin` directory and adjust the URL accordingly.

Other Information

I maintain a Web site where you can get the source code for the scripts and other support files used in this book. The current list of known errata for the book is available at the site as well, so you may want to check it from time to time for updates:

```
http://www.kitebird.com/mysql-perl/
```

Introduction to MySQL and Perl

1

THIS BOOK SHOWS HOW TO COMBINE THE POWER of relational database technology with the Web to provide information services that neither can deliver alone. A database engine and its support tools provide a variety of ways to extract, analyze, and present information that is important to you. This in itself is a useful asset; but when you connect your database to the Web, you gain several important capabilities and can accomplish even more:

- You can provide database content as Web content to extend the reach of your information. This happens because your Web server acts as an information delivery system that works over the Internet in a relatively platform-neutral fashion. Businesses, for example, can make marketing information available on a global scale to sales personnel who carry with them nothing more than a Web browser. The Web has been available on desktop and laptop computers for several years, and now its use is beginning to spread to handheld devices such as PDAs and cell phones. This means your Web server has the potential to provide the information in your database even to these devices.

- The content you provide through your Web server becomes dynamic because you can draw it from the information residing in your database and tailor it to the interests of individual site visitors. Static pages are fine for unvarying information, such as a list of definitions or a set of instructions. They are unworkable for information that changes frequently, or for situations where visitors need to interact with a Web site to find the information in which they are interested.

- Your Web content is always as current as the information in your database because you're generating your pages directly from that database, not serving up static pages that went stale long ago.
- You can gather information over the Web from clients and store it in a database. In effect, you can make your site act as an interactive data-collection engine.

Some types of dynamic content that use a database are very simple, such as displaying a hit counter in a Web page. Others are more complex, such as presenting a list of today's on-sale specials for a business, conducting an online poll and showing the current results, displaying stock prices, and performing inventory searches or order tracking.

Dynamic content is useful when you cannot anticipate a user's requirements, such as when you want to provide individualized customer support. You can use information in a database to drive and customize that interaction. Consider what happens when you call a help desk for assistance with a product, and you describe the problem you are having to the person on the other end of the phone. How does this person help you? In some cases, by typing in keywords based on your description to perform a search on a help-document database. Some companies have taken this to its logical conclusion and made the database available directly to customers on the corporate Web site. This enables customers to help themselves 24 hours a day without going through phone menus, answering machines, or being put on hold. It also might allow the company to lower support costs.

Another benefit of connecting your database to the Web is a potential reduction in workload. At first you might think that adding dynamic content to your site could only increase work because of the additional programming requirements. It's true that you don't add this capability without effort, but that effort often can save you work in the long run. Consider a scenario where you maintain a Web site in tandem with a database that consists of sports information such as team schedules, game results, league standings, and player statistics. Some of this information is static (the schedules), but the rest changes throughout the season and requires continual updates to your site. One way to accomplish this is by updating your Web pages manually as new information comes in. You can reduce your workload, however, if you go about it properly. Transform the job of updating the site from one of repeatedly modifying a set of static pages to one of writing a few programs that know how to extract the appropriate information from your database and display it to site visitors. The information has to go into the database anyway, so would you rather update the Web pages with the same information manually (in effect entering it twice), or write the programs? In my mind, there's no question: It is always more interesting to write programs than to perform a lot of mindless editing. And you only have to write each program once. Result: less work overall, even when you factor in occasional maintenance modifications to the programs.

Dynamic content doesn't necessarily involve a database. You don't need one to display the current date in a Web page, for example. But databases have so many applications on the Web that you are limited essentially only by your imagination and your technical expertise. If you'll bring the imagination, this book will help you with the technical end by taking you through the process of building useful, highly interactive, and dynamic Web sites from the ground up. As a bonus, this can be done using software that is freely available, so the methods shown in this book can be used by nearly anyone.

What You'll Need

This section describes the primary tools we'll use for building dynamic Web sites and why we're using them. It also discusses the possibilities for adapting the principles and techniques presented here if you prefer to use different tools.

If you need to obtain any of the components discussed in this section, you can find instructions in Appendix A, "Obtaining Software."

Software Requirements

Given the purpose of building database-backed Web sites, we'll need three major components: a Web server, a database management system, and some "glue"—a programming language to connect the Web server to the database so that they can talk to each other. Let's look at each of these components a little more closely:

- **Web server.** For the Web server component, we'll use Apache, an extensible, high-performance server that also happens to be more popular than any other on the Internet.

- **Database management system.** The database is MySQL, a freely available system that is easy to use and administer, and that has good performance. The database engine itself is extremely fast, and the overhead for setting up connections to it is very low. That's an important factor in constructing a responsive Web site; lower overhead translates directly into the capability to handle a higher hit rate and lower hardware requirements. These characteristics make MySQL an excellent choice as a Web development database, which accounts for much of its popularity. (Note that you don't necessarily need to install a MySQL server— you just need access to one. You can write your scripts to connect to databases that are hosted on somebody else's machine, if they've set up access privileges for you.)

- **Programming language.** There are interfaces to MySQL for many languages, so developers have a variety of choices for connecting MySQL to the Web. The glue we'll use to connect the two is Perl, the predominant scripting language on the Web. Perl is popular largely due to its power and versatility, its excellent support for text manipulation, and the number of third-party modules available for it that extend its native capabilities. Two of these are of particular significance for our purposes. The CGI.pm module provides an interface to the Web, making it easy to generate Web pages and to process input gathered from site visitors. The DBI module provides an interface to MySQL and makes it easy to issue database queries from within Perl scripts. An additional integration tool we'll use is mod_perl. This is actually an Apache module, not a Perl module. However, mod_perl makes it possible to embed the Perl interpreter into Apache so that Perl can be executed directly as part of the Web server rather than as a process external to it. This increases performance by eliminating the expense of starting up an additional process each time the server needs to run a Perl script.

In conjunction with the primary components just listed, we'll use other existing packages or applications on occasion rather than writing our own. (One part of effective Web site construction is knowing when to build on the work of others and avoid doing the work yourself.) These packages are secondary tools that will be described further when it comes time to use them.

Many books already address Web site construction and database integration with the Web. There are also plenty of books on Perl programming, including one specifically covering the DBI module, that show how to access databases from Perl. Why one more, and why focus on MySQL?

The answer is actually quite simple. Despite its usefulness, the combination of MySQL and Perl for Web programming has been strangely overlooked. In the Open Source community, for instance, the two most popular Web scripting languages are Perl and PHP. But although Perl has been around longer than PHP, for some reason most MySQL Web coverage has focused on the PHP interface to MySQL. There is relatively little treatment of Perl MySQL applications, even though Perl is just as important. Go into any bookstore and have a look at the many Perl books. Most of them touch on the Web and databases either not at all or devote only a few paragraphs or pages to the topic. Of these, the number that address MySQL is fewer yet. This is unfortunate, because one of MySQL's strengths is its applicability to Web programming.

The lack of coverage of Perl in comparison to PHP is surprising, given Perl's longevity and popularity. Although PHP is often held to be easier to learn than Perl (and thus a better choice for beginners or less-experienced Web developers), Perl has several important advantages: superior text-processing facilities, a richer set of data structures, and a more mature object-processing model. In addition, due to Perl's longer tenure, many more packages that provide capabilities beyond what is built in to the language have been written for Perl, so it has better support for some key technologies such as XML processing.

Perl and MySQL make a strong combination for Web programming, and their use continues to increase. It is important for developers to have a source of information on this topic to which they can turn for assistance. That's what this book gives you.

Hardware and Operating System Requirements

In addition to the Web development components just discussed (Apache, MySQL, Perl), you also need some hardware and an operating system on which to run the site. I'm going to assume that you have access to some kind of UNIX box that is connected to the Internet.[1] You may even find you already have the software you need. Many distributions of UNIX these days include Apache, MySQL, and Perl, and allow you to install them either when you're installing the operating system or later after your system is up and running.

The system you use can be run by yourself or your organization, or a system to which you have access by means of an account with an Internet service provider (ISP). If you have an ISP account (and therefore don't have full control over your machine), you need to pay special attention to some issues. These issues are covered in Chapter 9, "Security and Privacy Issues." Here, too, you may find the software is installed already. Many ISPs provide database and scripting support as part of their Web account services.

If you have yet to acquire the hardware for your system and are still in the evaluation stage, you may be wondering whether you need to make a huge investment to construct a responsive site that has good performance. You probably don't. Many people find that servers running on relatively inexpensive machines are perfectly sufficient. Many sites are based on the combination of a PC and one of the freely available versions of UNIX or Linux. Indeed, several companies have discovered that such systems are sufficiently popular and it is possible to base a viable business venture on selling them as Internet servers and providing support for them. It's not a bad idea to contact some of these companies to see what they have to offer. They will be happy to help you select equipment. If you plan to handle millions of hits a day, however, you need equipment that is more high-powered than what most of us use; but they can help you with that, too.

---

1. Unless indicated otherwise, I generally use the term UNIX to mean Linux and UNIX. As it happens, all our software runs on most of the free versions of Linux or BSD UNIX, as well as on many commercial versions of UNIX. If there is any question, check the installation instructions for each component to see whether there are any issues with the operating system you plan to use.

Adapting This Book for Other Systems

If you are interested in using the material presented in this book but would like to develop and run your Web site on some other kind of system—or use software other than what is used here—this section provides some guidelines and some estimation of the likelihood that you will be successful.

One choice you can make is to run your Web site under Windows rather than under UNIX. Apache, MySQL, and Perl all run under Windows (as do CGI.pm, DBI, and mod_perl).

You should be able to substitute a different database for MySQL. The architecture of the Perl DBI module is designed to make it easy to port an application written for one database so that you can use it with another. DBI does this by providing an abstract interface to database engines. This gives you some leverage should you decide to use (or should a client request that you use) a database other than MySQL. Note that in this book we will use some MySQL-specific constructs; any applications that use these will need some rewriting.

There are means other than mod_perl for improving the performance of Perl scripts run from your Web server. Some alternatives are FastCGI or (if you want to consider commercial software) VelociGen.

You may be able to use another Web server, as long as it has the capability to run Perl scripts. Xitami runs under both UNIX and Windows, for example, and has support for Perl CGI programs. There is no support for embedding the Perl interpreter into Xitami, however. This means you will sacrifice some performance because the server needs to instantiate a separate process to run Perl scripts.

The most difficult part of the example software suite to replace would be the programming language. Virtually every script in this book is written in Perl, so if you want to use another language, you'll have a lot of work to do.

What You Should Know (Reader Requirements)

It's best if you already have some basic familiarity with most of the tools we use throughout this book, because this book is not intended as a beginner's guide. The book won't teach you all the basics of writing SQL queries or Perl programs. If you don't know anything about SQL, HTML, or programming, you'll probably have some difficulty. Despite that warning, however, you should be able to make productive use of this book *if* you have a reasonable amount of determination. If you're hoping to find out how to put together a more interesting or useful Web site, this book can teach you even if you don't know much beyond writing a static HTML page.

If you do happen to be a beginner, here are some words of advice:

- Be sure to read Chapter 2, "Getting Connected—Putting Your Database on the Web." You'll find that chapter of particular importance as a starting point. More experienced readers who are already running a Web site may be able to pass over some or all of the material presented there.

- Supplement your reading here with other material. See Appendix B, "References and Further Reading."
- Join some mailing lists, such as those for MySQL and DBI.

Audience

In general, this book should be of value to anyone who wants to build a Web site, or to make an existing site more interactive, more responsive to visitors in terms of adapting to what they're looking for, and always up to date by drawing on the information currently in a database. This includes individuals, low-budget organizations, businesses both small and large, and academic or government institutions. More specifically, here are a few of the types of people or groups who can use the material presented in this book:

- **Database and Web site developers.** This is the most obvious group of people who stand to benefit from the book. If you're a member of this group, you already may be building the kind of applications we deal with here, but are looking for additional ideas and techniques.

- **Businesses.** Many business people seem to believe they are under the mandate "we have to get our business on the Internet," and that it's no longer possible to survive just as a BAM (brick-and-mortar) organization. (I don't know whether this is true, so I won't try to convince you that a Web presence is an absolute necessity for your business. If you're already motivated to go online, however, this book will help you do it.) We'll cover topics such as product registration, online catalog presentation, and e-commerce. You may not *need* to go online, but you certainly can use the Web to provide better service to your customers and to your own staff.

- **Managers.** You may not know or care about writing programs, but you can use this book to see what kinds of applications can be built and what they can be used for. This can help you focus or articulate your organization's Web strategy and better understand the possibilities for what you can accomplish with your site. (It also can give you some background for communicating with your software developers, who seem to live in a different world and speak a different language than you do!)

- **People who want to share information with others.** If you're tired of exchanging email attachments, you can use the Web to help you collaborate. For example, a group of researchers can construct a repository of shared data that they upload through a Web site and store in a database.

- **People who want to build a personal Web site.** Some people want to build Web-based tools for no better reason than to help them get their own work done more effectively. And that's a perfectly good reason! There's no rule that you have to build a site for use by someone else (such as when a business orients its site toward use by customers). You can target it for your own purposes, often with relatively simple applications. For example, a basic note-taking application is a natural candidate as a Web-based application that uses a database for storing information. By making this information available on the Web, you can access it from anywhere that a browser is available—a client's office, in a hotel room or conference center, and so on. You don't have to be sitting in front of your microcomputer or workstation. And if you want to share the information with others, you can.

The preceding examples illustrate some of the "what you can do" capabilities that result from combining Apache, MySQL, and Perl. There are also certain economic motivations for using this suite of tools:

- The software is freely available, so you can get it with little or no investment.
- You may need to build a site on a shoestring budget. Perhaps you are helping to set up a site for a nonprofit organization that has little in the way of financial resources.
- Some people are just philosophically opposed to using software from large corporations that costs lots of money and is subject to restrictive licensing conditions. (I won't pursue that issue here except to note that for the vast majority of the tools we'll use in this book, you can get them for nothing whenever you want, and you can use them however you please without asking anyone.)

The desire to save money isn't restricted to those with little of it. You may, in fact, be a representative of a large commercial organization, reading this book with the goal in mind of assessing whether it can help your business cut costs without sacrificing performance. I believe it can, but I also recognize that businesses are often deeply ambivalent about free software and have questions about its legitimacy. Like everyone else, they are attracted by the notion of inexpensive tools, but at the same time, suspicious of the term "free." And not without reason, because a lot of free software is junk.

That's not the case with the tools we're using. "Freely available" can mean "free" (no cost), but it doesn't mean "worthless" (no value). It doesn't mean "unprofessional" or "unreliable," either. MySQL, Perl, and Apache are well written and they work. Just because the software is available to anyone, even people or organizations with very limited budgets, doesn't mean it has no value for you.

Nevertheless, if you're running software provided by corporate giants such as Oracle or Microsoft, the thought of switching to software provided by Open Source project teams may give you pause. Let's face it, if you run a business and *don't* perform some kind of preliminary analysis to assess the wisdom of such a move, you're being reckless. Part of your analysis should be to try the software. All this discussion about the value of free software can be taken as propaganda from an author who wants to sell you a book, but you don't need to take my word for it. Anyone can try the software, so put it to the test and see for yourself. If you like it, arrange for support.

Obviously, if you're running a business, you're going to have more stringent requirements than, say, a hobbyist who is running a Web site in the basement on a bargain-bin computer connected to the Internet by something like a cable modem or DSL line. That kind of user probably isn't going to require 24×7 uptime. If the machine blows a disk or memory goes bad, it will just be down until the owner gets around to swapping in a replacement part. (Not to mention that cable and DSL providers rarely make any particular connectivity guarantees for residential service, anyway.)

If you're a business depending on providing continuous access to your Web site for your customers and sales staff, you are going to be concerned about redundant backbone links, backup servers, and support staff. You'd be foolish not to, and you're prepared to make the investment necessary to ensure you get the performance you need.

It's the same way with your software. Most people rely on informal support. MySQL and DBI, for example, have active and helpful user communities available through their mailing lists. Businesses can use the lists, too, but many go further. The software may be free, but professional help is available to help you use it. (This is the point at which free software stops being free!) You can get paid support for MySQL. The MySQL developers are happy to set up formal support agreements. Consultants also are available to help you set up your installation and keep it running.

Using the Applications in This Book

You don't just develop theoretical demonstrations here—we'll develop several complete applications that can actually be used. You might use some of them with little modification, but it's more likely that you'll want to make more significant changes to suit your own purposes. For that reason, when reading about an application, don't take the attitude, "How can I force-fit the problems I want to solve into these applications?" Instead, ask, "How can I adapt this code for my own situation?" It's more important that you understand the code for each example application we develop than that you look at it as a finished product. Think of the programs as not-yet-hardened clay that you can shape to conform to your will.

For concreteness, applications developed in this book typically are presented in a particular context, but they're often usable in other ways. Therefore, don't assume an application cannot help you just because it's presented to solve a problem that doesn't immediately seem to apply to your situation. It's not very productive to ask questions such as "is this a business application?" or "is this a personal application?" What you should concentrate on are the particular techniques an application illustrates and how you might use them. In the next chapter, for instance, we develop a simple application for maintaining a to-do list. If you're setting up an online store, you may not be interested in that—it might seem more applicable to people who want to write notes to themselves, not people who want to conduct business. But one thing the application does is enable you to take input from the Web and store it in a database. When you understand how this works, you can adapt the concept for business purposes, such as an application that enables your customers to submit questions to you asking for product information or price quotes. As another example, later on in the book, we'll deal with online ordering techniques. If you're building a site for a nonprofit organization that serves an educational purpose by disseminating information, you might consider these techniques useless to you on the basis that you are not in business and you are not selling anything. Suppose, however, that your Web site enables people to request printed documents. If so, you're providing a product, just like a "regular" business. You can use shopping-cart techniques to let site visitors request multiple documents while specifying name and shipping address only once (rather than for each document they want). It's true those techniques often are used in commercial contexts, but they can be used for noncommercial purposes, too. You may as well exploit them to make your Web site more useful and convenient for your visitors.

I don't always show the complete source for applications, but you can download the files you need to make it easier for you to try out the applications and to use them as a basis for your own modifications. All the source and data files used here are available from the book's companion Web site:

```
http://www.kitebird.com/mysql-perl/
```

The next chapter discusses the basic issues involved in getting your MySQL and Apache servers configured to work together and how to write Web scripts that access your database. If you're new to Web database programming, you should read that chapter carefully to acquire the background you'll need for the rest of the book. Readers with more experience may prefer to skip directly to later chapters, although it's a good idea to at least skim through Chapter 2, because it describes a number of conventions used throughout the book.

2

Getting Connected—Putting Your Database on the Web

THIS CHAPTER INTRODUCES THE FUNDAMENTAL concepts involved in putting your database on the Web so that you can begin writing and using Web scripts that access MySQL. It deals with techniques on which everything else in the book is built, showing you how to get up and running to do some basic things. For less-experienced readers, it also doubles as a tutorial by providing exposure to concepts you'll need for understanding the material in the following chapters. If you've already been building Web sites, you just may want to skim through to verify that you're familiar with the chapter's material and to acquaint yourself with the conventions used in the book. You can expect to learn the following things in this chapter:

- Basic MySQL and Apache configuration
- General principles involved in writing Perl scripts
- Using DBI from Perl scripts for connecting to the MySQL server and issuing queries
- Using CGI.pm to generate Web pages from Perl scripts
- Putting DBI and CGI.pm together to link MySQL to the Web
- Using Web forms for record entry, editing, and searching
- Error-handling and debugging techniques
- How to put often-used code in a library file

This chapter provides enough information to get you started, and in fact, you'll learn enough to establish a basic Web presence. But the material here really is just a beginning, and later chapters expand on many of the topics. For example, this chapter does not discuss security a great deal, but security is a requirement, not an option. You'd be making a big mistake to think otherwise, and you really shouldn't put sensitive data anywhere near the Web before you've read Chapter 9, "Security and Privacy Issues."

Required Tools

To work through the material in this chapter, you should have the following software installed:

- The MySQL server, if you're going to run a server yourself. If you want to use a server run by someone else, that's okay, too.
- The `mysql` command-line client program. (This is part of the MySQL distribution.)
- The Apache Web server
- Perl 5; make sure you also have the following modules installed as well: CGI.pm, DBI, and `DBD::mysql` (the MySQL-specific driver for DBI). We'll use `mod_perl` later, but it's not necessary for this chapter.

The versions I'm using currently are MySQL 3.23.39, Apache 1.3.19, Perl 5.005_03, CGI.pm 2.74, DBI 1.18, and `DBD::mysql` 1.2216.

The next two sections show how to make sure the database and Web servers are properly set up so that you can access the database we'll be using. This is necessary before we can do more interesting things, such as writing programs that connect your database to the Web. The sections discuss configuration issues only, not installation procedures. I assume that the required software is available, either installed by you or for you by your system administrator. If you need any of the components, see Appendix A, "Obtaining Software," and follow the instructions provided with each distribution that you want to install.

Configuring MySQL

This section describes how to create a new database and set up a MySQL user account that can access it. You could use an existing database and user, of course, but I recommend that you set up new ones specifically for trying out the applications developed in this book. You'll find it easier to keep things straight if they're not mixed up with a database and account you're already using for other purposes. Also, if while you're learning you accidentally expose the username and password used for the example database, that won't put your other databases at risk.

For example purposes, I'm going to assume that you're working on the host www.snake.net and that your MySQL server and Apache server are both running locally on that same host. This means that when you use MySQL, you'll connect to the server by specifying a host name of localhost. I'll also assume that we're going to connect as the user webdev with a password of webdevpass, and that the database is named webdb. If you want to use a different username, password, or database name, you should make the appropriate substitutions in the examples.

Database access must be set up by an existing MySQL user, such as root, who has the ability to grant privileges. To do this for the webdev user, connect to the MySQL server using the mysql program and issue the appropriate GRANT statement. When asked to enter your password, use your MySQL root password.

```
% mysql -h localhost -p -u root
Enter password: ******
mysql> GRANT ALL ON webdb.* TO webdev@localhost IDENTIFIED BY "webdevpass";
mysql> QUIT
```

On the mysql command, the -h option specifies the host where the MySQL server is running, -p tells mysql to prompt for a password, and -u specifies the MySQL user to connect as. If the webdev user account doesn't already exist, the GRANT statement creates it, grants it all privileges on the webdb database, and sets its password. If the webdev account does exist, the GRANT statement simply grants the privileges and sets the password. In the latter case, you may want to grant privileges without changing the webdev user's current password; you can do that by leaving out the IDENTIFIED BY clause:

```
mysql> GRANT ALL ON webdb.* TO webdev@localhost;
```

The GRANT statement sets up privileges for using the webdb database, but doesn't create it. You should do that now. Use mysql to connect to the server as webdev (the user to whom you just granted privileges), and then issue a CREATE DATABASE statement. When asked to enter your password, use your webdev password.

```
% mysql -h localhost -p -u webdev
Enter password: webdevpass
mysql> CREATE DATABASE webdb;
Query OK, 1 row affected (0.01 sec)
mysql> QUIT
```

If you want to run a few sample queries with your new database, try the ones presented here. You should see output similar to what's shown. The mysql command shows how you can connect and specify the database name on the command line to make it the default database for your session. When asked to enter your password, use your webdev password.

```
% mysql -h localhost -p -u webdev webdb
Enter password: webdevpass
mysql> CREATE TABLE test (i INT);
Query OK, 0 rows affected (0.01 sec)
```

continues

continued

```
mysql> SHOW TABLES;
+-----------------+
| Tables_in_webdb |
+-----------------+
| test            |
+-----------------+
1 row in set (0.00 sec)
mysql> DROP TABLE test;
Query OK, 0 rows affected (0.00 sec)
mysql> SHOW TABLES;
Empty set (0.00 sec)
mysql> QUIT
```

If you want to use a database server that's located on a different host, the preceding instructions must be modified, both for creating the webdev account and for connecting as that user. Let's assume that the MySQL server is running on the host db.snake.net. The privileges will need to be set up on that host, but because you'll be connecting to db.snake.net from www.snake.net, the privileges need to be given to webdev@www.snake.net rather than to webdev@localhost. (In other words, you want to associate the privileges with the host from which you'll be connecting to the MySQL server, not the host where the server runs.) To do this, the MySQL root user should run mysql on db.snake.net and issue a GRANT statement like this. When asked to enter your password, use your MySQL root password.

```
% mysql -h localhost -p -u root
Enter password: ******
mysql> GRANT ALL ON webdb.* TO webdev@www.snake.net
    -> IDENTIFIED BY "webdevpass";
mysql> QUIT
```

Note that the mysql command specifies a host of localhost, even though it's being run on db.snake.net, because the server is running locally relative to the host on which mysql is invoked. After the account for webdev@www.snake.net has been created, you should be able to use the webdb database by connecting as webdev from www.snake.net to the server on db.snake.net. To do so, use a mysql command like this:

```
% mysql -h db.snake.net -p -u webdev webdb
Enter password: webdevpass
```

If you have problems setting up a user account or creating a database, see the MySQL Reference Manual or your MySQL administrator.

Configuring Apache

Many people think of a Web server primarily as something that services Web page requests by opening files containing static HTML pages and sending their contents to clients. That is one thing a Web server does, of course, but it's not the only one. Another is to execute programs that generate pages. When you use Apache for this, you're generating dynamic content, because the pages generated by a program can differ each time the program runs. (As a trivial example, consider a program that simply displays the current time of day; it generates different output whenever the time changes.)

Serving dynamic content is more difficult than serving static pages because it involves writing programs to produce the content. It also involves configuring your Web server to know how to find and execute these programs. This section shows how to set up Apache so it knows how to do that, and lays the groundwork for some of the configuration modifications we'll need to make in later chapters.

The examples in this book assume that Apache is laid out using the following set of path names. If the paths on your system are different, just modify the instructions to match.

- `/usr/local/apache`

  The root directory of the Apache layout (the "Web server root").

- `/usr/local/apache/bin`

  The location for executable binary programs. (Actually, this directory doesn't just contain binaries; it contains scripts, too—executable text files.) The most important program here is `httpd` (HTTP daemon), which is what I'm referring to when I say "Apache" (see sidebar). Another important program in the `bin` directory is `apachectl`, a utility used to start and stop the `httpd` server.

- `/usr/local/apache/conf`

  The location for Apache configuration files. The most important file here is `httpd.conf`, the main `httpd` configuration file. Older versions of Apache use three configuration files (`httpd.conf`, `srm.conf`, and `access.conf`). I'm going to assume you're using the current single-file arrangement. If you use all three files, you'll need to decide which ones to modify when you change Apache's configuration.

Why "Apache"?

The program known as Apache is called `httpd` due to its roots in the program of the same name that originated at the National Center for Supercomputing Applications (NCSA). After development of the original NCSA `httpd` stagnated, a group of volunteers took over and directed their efforts into improving it. Because of the numerous patches applied to this version of `httpd` as development continued, it became known as "a patchy server"—hence "Apache."

- /usr/local/apache/htdocs

  The root directory of the Web document tree (the "document root"). This is where you place documents that you want to make available through Apache.

- /usr/local/apache/cgi-bin

  The directory for CGI programs the Web server can execute. This is where the Web scripts written in this chapter will be installed. The cgi-bin directory should be outside the document tree (that is, not anywhere under the document root) so that scripts cannot be requested in plain text. We'll discuss this issue in more detail in Chapter 9. For now, suffice it to say that you don't want remote clients to be able to read your scripts directly, because those scripts may provide clues for hacking your site.

- /usr/local/apache/cgi-perl

  Another program directory. We'll use it specifically for Web scripts that run under mod_perl. We'll get to that in Chapter 3, "Improving Performance with mod_perl," so I won't say much more about it here. The one thing you should know is that most scripts developed from that chapter on will be installed in cgi-perl, because I'll assume you're going to use mod_perl. That means the URLs for those scripts will begin like this:

  ```
  http://www.snake.net/cgi-perl/...
  ```

  If you don't install mod_perl, you should put the scripts in the cgi-bin directory and adjust the URLs to use cgi-bin rather than cgi-perl:

  ```
  http://www.snake.net/cgi-bin/...
  ```

- /usr/local/apache/lib/perl

  The directory for Perl library files. We'll use library files for common operations that are performed by multiple scripts, so that we don't have to write code for them explicitly in each script that uses them. For example, every script that accesses MySQL must connect to the server. Rather than list the connection parameters in each script, we'll make a simple call to a function stored in a library file.

- /usr/local/apache/logs

  The log file directory. The logs are useful when errors occur because they help you figure out what you need to fix. You may also want to analyze the logs to find out how much traffic you're getting and what pages are requested. The default log filenames are access_log (where page requests are written) and error_log (where diagnostic information is written). If you have trouble getting a Web script to run, take a look in the error log to see whether it contains any useful error messages.

You'll notice that most of the directories in the preceding list are grouped under a single parent directory /usr/local/apache. It's possible that the Apache components won't be so centralized on your system. For example, Red Hat Linux distributions like to scatter the pieces around more, putting configuration files under /etc/httpd, the server in /usr/sbin, and so forth. You should poke around on your system or ask your administrator what kind of Apache layout you have. In particular, you'll need to know the locations of the configuration file httpd.conf and the server httpd because you'll need to edit httpd.conf to control Apache's behavior, and you must restart the server to get it to read the modified configuration file. If you cannot edit httpd.conf directly, ask your administrator how to adapt the instructions in this chapter for use on your system.

Configuring Apache for CGI Program Execution

In this section, we'll configure Apache to know how to execute CGI programs located in the cgi-bin directory. A "CGI program" is one with which Apache communicates using the Common Gateway Interface, a protocol that serves as a kind of contract between the program and the Web server and that allows each to know how the other can be expected to behave. The server sets up certain environment variables that provide information about the request received from the client; the CGI program uses this information to figure out how to process the request.

To tell Apache that we want to use the cgi-bin directory for CGI programs, put the following line in your httpd.conf file, if it doesn't already contain such a line:

```
ScriptAlias /cgi-bin/ /usr/local/apache/cgi-bin/
```

The ScriptAlias directive tells Apache to associate a directory with executable programs. Thus, any URL received by the Web server that has /cgi-bin/*xxx* after the host name will be interpreted as a request to execute a program *xxx* in the directory /usr/local/apache/cgi-bin and send its output to the client that sent the request. If the directory named on the ScriptAlias directive does not yet exist, create it:

```
% cd /usr/local/apache
% mkdir cgi-bin
```

If you want to base the association on filename rather than location, you can do that, too. This is useful if you want to put scripts in the document tree (which can be dangerous if it results in remote users being able to read your scripts directly, but you can do that if you really want to).

One typical strategy is to specify that filenames with a certain suffix, such as .pl or .cgi, should be considered CGI programs. For example, the following lines can be used in httpd.conf to identify files in the document tree that have names ending with .pl as CGI scripts:

```
<Files *.pl>
    SetHandler cgi-script
    AllowOverride None
    Options ExecCGI
</Files>
```

Apache's Parent-Child Architecture

The next section describes how to start and stop Apache. For a better understanding of how that works, it's helpful to have some background on Apache's parent-child architecture. When Apache (httpd) starts up, the initial httpd process is the parent process. It reads the configuration file httpd.conf to determine how it should operate. Then it starts forking (spawning) child processes to handle client requests. Each child httpd handles a certain number of requests, and then dies. As each child dies, the parent httpd spawns a new child to take its place.

The number of children spawned initially is controlled by the StartServers configuration directive, and the minimum and maximum number of children the parent tries to keep around are controlled by MinSpareServers and MaxSpareServers. If more simultaneous requests come in than can be handled by the available children, the parent spawns more children, up to the limit specified by MaxSpareServers. As children die, the parent spawns more if the count goes below MinSpareServers. The configuration parameters give you some control over the size of the child pool. Bumping up the maximum value allows more requests to be served simultaneously, but if you put it up too high, you run the risk of allowing too many processes for efficient machine operation. The administrator's task is to find the best balance.

The number of requests served by each child is controlled by the MaxRequestsPerChild directive. Setting it to 1 is inefficient because the parent ends up spawning children at a rate roughly equal to the number of requests. On the other hand, setting the value high (or to 0, which means "unlimited") can have negative consequences. If Apache contains code that has a memory leak, for example, a long-running child may grow large enough over time to take over the machine. The core Apache code isn't likely to do this because it's been pretty well scrutinized, but Apache can be extended with additional modules, and some of these may not have been so well inspected. An additional danger, if you're using mod_perl to allow Apache to execute Perl scripts directly, is that user scripts written in Perl can cause memory leaks (see Chapter 3). Having child httpd processes die after serving a limited number of requests is a safety precaution that guards against such problems. Just as with selecting a server pool size, the administrator's task is to find the proper balance. You want to spawn children relatively infrequently, but not so infrequently that each one gobbles up a huge amount of resources.

Configuring Apache Under Windows

Under Windows, Apache runs as a multithreaded process and does not spawn multiple children. Instead, a single child handles all requests, with each request processed using a separate thread. Consequently, much of the preceding discussion does not apply. You can control the number of simultaneous client connections by controlling the number of threads allowed. To do this, use the ThreadsPerChild directive, which under Windows is equivalent to the StartServers directive. The default value is 50; set it higher if you get a lot of traffic. For MaxRequestsPerChild, the recommended value is 0 because there is just one child. This value causes the child to never exit.

Starting and Stopping Apache Using *apachectl*

The `apachectl` script is a handy utility for checking changes to the Apache configuration file and for starting and stopping Apache itself. It understands several arguments, which are summarized in Table 2.1.

Table 2.1   **Options for** *apachectl*

Option	Effect
configtest	Performs syntax check on configuration file.
start	Starts parent, which spawns children.
stop	Parent and children die immediately.
restart	Children die immediately; parent reinitializes and spawns a new set of children.
graceful	Like restart, but children are allowed to service requests currently in progress before dying.

To start Apache, if it's not running currently, use `apachectl start`. Generally, after the server is running, you leave it alone. If you modify the configuration file, however, you need to restart the server to get it to notice the changes. A sensible precaution before restarting is to run `apachectl configtest` to perform a syntax check on the configuration file. This gives you a way to find errors before using the file with a live server. (If the file contains errors, the server won't restart anyway until you either back out the changes or fix the problem. In the meantime, your Web site will be dead and visitors can't use it.)

To restart a server that is already running, you have three options. The most drastic is to stop it cold by bringing it to a complete halt and starting a new parent. You do this with `apachectl stop` followed by `apachectl start`. A less drastic option is `apachectl restart`, which kills the children but lets the parent continue to run. The parent reinitializes itself, and then spawns a new set of children. The gentlest option is `apachectl graceful`. This is like `apachectl restart`, but any children currently servicing a request are not killed until the request has been satisfied.

A reasonable strategy after you've modified the configuration file and checked it with `apachectl configtest` is to try `apachectl graceful` to restart with the least disruption. However, some configuration changes require a complete shutdown and restart. If your changes don't seem to take effect, try `apachectl stop` followed by `apachectl start`.

Starting and stopping Apache must be done by a user with sufficient privileges, such as `root`. If you don't have the ability to restart the server, you'll need to ask your system administrator to do so.

In addition to being able to control `httpd` manually, you'll want it to start up at system boot time. The boot-time startup mechanism varies between systems, so you should consult your machine's documentation for instructions.

Alternatives to *apachectl* Under Windows

`apachectl` is a shell script, so it doesn't run under Windows. Instead, you can control Apache using the following commands:

`apache`	start Apache
`apache -k shutdown`	stop Apache
`apache -k restart`	restart Apache
`apache -t`	check `httpd.conf` configuration file

Depending on how you installed Apache, you may also be able to start and stop it from the Start menu. For example, the Apache binary distribution installer adds a Start menu item for starting Apache. Other distributions may do this as well; NuSphere MySQL includes Apache, and its installer places a NuSphere group in the Start menu that has items for controlling Apache.

Under Windows NT, you have the additional option of running Apache as a service.

Verifying That Apache Is Serving Pages

When your Apache server is running, you should be able to enter the URL for your site into your browser and view your home page. For example, this URL requests the home page on www.snake.net:

```
http://www.snake.net/
```

Try requesting your own site's home page by substituting its name for www.snake.net. If you don't see the page or you get an error message, check the error log to see what the problem is.

As you begin to install Web scripts later in the book, you'll need to substitute your own host name into the www.snake.net URLs that I use in the examples.

Writing Perl Scripts

Perl scripts are written for a couple of purposes in this book: as programs you invoke yourself from the command line, or as programs that you intend to run from a Web server in response to requests received over the network. (We'll also write some scheduled scripts that are invoked as `cron` jobs, but those are essentially command-line scripts run automatically by the system.) This section shows how to write both kinds of scripts, but instead of starting out by writing something complicated, we'll use the following progression of steps:

1. Verify that Perl works by writing a simple "do nothing" script.
2. Verify that you can access the CGI.pm and DBI modules.
3. Verify that you can get Apache to execute a Perl script to generate a Web page.
4. Verify that you can to connect to MySQL from within a Perl script.
5. Verify that Apache Web scripts can access MySQL.

If you've never written Perl scripts before, you should go through each of the steps. Otherwise, you might want to skim through or skip the material describing the first couple of scripts. Command-line scripts do not need to be put in any special place. You might find it most convenient to create a separate directory under your home directory to use for trying out command-line scripts you write for this book. By contrast, Web scripts need to be installed in your Web server's directory hierarchy. For the scripts in this chapter, that's the `cgi-bin` directory described earlier in the "Configuring Apache" section.

> ### Save Yourself Some Typing
> If you haven't ready done so, you should obtain the software distribution that accompanies this book. It contains the source code for the scripts developed here, as well as any **CREATE TABLE** statements and sample data for the database tables that they use. The distribution is available at the following Web site:
>
>   http://www.kitebird.com/mysql-perl/

Write a Simple Perl Script

To write Perl scripts, you must know where Perl itself is located. Try the following command, which tells your shell (command interpreter) to display the full path name of your Perl program:

```
% which perl
/usr/bin/perl
```

The output you see when you run the `which` command might be different, such as `/usr/local/bin/perl` or `/opt/bin/perl`. Whatever the path name is, make a note of it, because you'll need to substitute that path name wherever you see `/usr/bin/perl` in this book. If `which` doesn't tell you where Perl is, ask your system administrator.

Next, check which version of Perl you have by executing it with the `-v` option:

```
% /usr/bin/perl -v
This is perl, version 5.005_03
```

Perl's version number should be at least 5.005. If you're running Perl 4, the scripts in this book won't work. If you have Perl 5, but it's older than 5.005, some of the scripts may fail.

Now write a simple script using the path name to Perl that you just determined, by using a text editor to create a file named intro1.pl that contains the following lines:

```
#! /usr/bin/perl
# intro1.pl - simple do-nothing Perl script
print "I am a Perl script\n";
exit (0);
```

Be sure to put the correct path to Perl for your system on the first line, and be sure to use double quotation marks (not single) on the line containing the print statement. Then make intro1.pl executable using this command:

```
% chmod +x intro1.pl
```

After making intro1.pl executable, try running it using one of the following commands. You should see the following output:

```
% intro1.pl
I am a Perl script
% ./intro1.pl
I am a Perl script
```

The first form should work if your shell searches your current directory to find commands. If it doesn't, use the second form, where the leading "./" tells the shell explicitly that the script is located in the current directory. [1]

Assuming that you see the proper output for at least one of the commands just shown, you've accomplished a lot. Don't believe me? Then let's discuss a few of the things that could go wrong at this point, even for such a simple script. If you get the Command Not Found error even when you specify the leading "./" on the command name, it's likely that the path name to Perl on the first line of the script is not exactly correct. Check the script and fix the path if necessary.

A different error that might occur is this one:

```
% ./intro1.pl
intro1.pl: Permission denied.
```

If this happens, you forgot to run the chmod +x command. Go back and run it to make the intro1.pl script executable. Of course, it's not very likely that you'll have overlooked this for intro1.pl because I just told you to use it. However, you'll also need to use chmod +x for every other Perl script you write using this book (whether you run it from the command line or from your Web server), and it's easy to forget. In fact, one of the first things you should do if a script refuses to run at all is check its file mode to see whether it's executable. You can do that using ls -l (long listing):

```
% ls -l intro1.pl
-rwxrwxr-x    1 paul      mtp        47 Oct 17 17:00 intro1.pl
```

---

1. I'll assume throughout the rest of the book that the "./" is necessary to run any script located in your current directory.

The x (executable) permissions should be enabled. If they're not, use `chmod +x` to turn them on.

Another possible problem is that the script's output might look like this, with '\n' at end of the line:

```
% ./intro1.pl
I am a Perl script\n
```

If that's what you see, it means you ignored my earlier admonition to use double quotation marks in the `print` statement and used single quotation marks instead. I admire your explorer's spirit in desiring to find out what happens when you do things a different way, but you didn't really follow instructions, so change the single to double quotation marks so that the '\n' prints a newline and not a literal '\n' when you run `intro1.pl`. (This problem occurs, by the way, because Perl treats special characters in single-quoted and double-quoted strings differently. Within double quotes, sequences such as '\n', '\r', and '\t' print as newline, carriage return, and tab. Within single quotes, no such interpretation is done and Perl prints the sequences literally.)

In the course of writing `intro1.pl`, you established a few important things that you should keep in mind as we go along:

- The path to your Perl program
- How to make scripts executable
- Whether you need to invoke a script as `script.pl` or as `./script.pl` when you run it at the command line

Running Perl Scripts Under Windows

Some aspects of the directions in this section for running Perl scripts under UNIX don't apply if you're using Windows. For example, the initial `#!` line that lists the path name of the Perl interpreter is irrelevant (although harmless). Also, you'll want to set up a file association that tells Windows to use Perl to run programs having names that end in `.pl`. If Perl is in your search path, that association enables you to run a Perl script just by typing its name. Therefore, you should be able to run `intro1.pl` from the command prompt like this:

```
C:\> intro.pl
```

These details may be taken care of for you when you install Perl on your system. If you use ActiveState Perl, for instance, its installer should change your path for you and help you establish the filename extension association.

Verify That You Can Access CGI.pm and DBI

intro1.pl serves to ensure that your Perl program is present and can execute scripts. Our second script checks the presence and accessibility of the CGI.pm and DBI modules. Create a script called intro2.pl that contains the following lines:

```
#! /usr/bin/perl
# intro2.pl - verify availability of CGI.pm and DBI modules
use CGI;
use DBI;
$cgi = new CGI;
print "The CGI object was created successfully\n";
@driver_names = DBI->available_drivers ();
print "These DBI drivers are available: @driver_names\n";
exit (0);
```

Make intro2.pl executable, and then try to run it to verify that CGI.pm and DBI can be accessed properly:

```
% chmod +x intro2.pl
% ./intro2.pl
The CGI object was created successfully
These DBI drivers are available: ADO ExampleP Multiplex Proxy mysql
```

The list of driver names may be different on your system, but if you see "mysql" in the list of driver names, you're in good shape. If "mysql" isn't one of the driver names listed, you need to install DBD::mysql, the MySQL-specific DBI driver. If you see error messages to the effect that Perl can't locate either or both of the CGI.pm or DBI modules, most likely they haven't been installed. See Appendix A for instructions on getting and installing any missing software, or ask your system administrator to do so. (Show the administrator your script and the error output to illustrate the problem.)

It's possible when you run intro2.pl that CGI.pm will display a prompt and ask for input parameters. If this happens, just type control-D and the script will proceed:

```
% ./intro2.pl
(offline mode: enter name=value pairs on standard input)
(press control-D here)
The CGI object was created successfully
These DBI drivers are available: ADO ExampleP Multiplex Proxy mysql
```

Under Windows, type control-Z, followed by Return. To suppress this prompt, specify an empty parameter list directly on the command line, as follows:

```
% ./intro2.pl ""
```

Write a Script to Generate a Web Page

In this section, we'll write a script for use from within Apache to generate a Web page. The previous scripts were run from the command line, so you could put them in just about any directory and run them from there. For Web scripts, that's not true; you need to put them in your `cgi-bin` directory because that's where Apache expects programs to be. (At least, that's how we configured it earlier!)

Before writing the script, let's consider what happens when a Web server sends a page to a client's browser, because writing Web scripts differs in some important ways from writing static HTML pages. If you're writing a file containing static HTML, you put some content in the file and install the file in the Web document tree. When a client requests the page, the Web server opens the file, reads it, and writes its contents over the network to the client. But that's actually only part of the process. What really happens is that the Web server sends header lines first—information that precedes the file's contents and that lets the browser know what's coming. Suppose you have a file `mypage.html` that looks like this:

```
<html>
<head><title>My Page Title</title></head>
<body><p>My page body</p></body>
</html>
```

What the Web server sends to the browser may actually look something like this:

```
% lynx -mime_header http://www.snake.net/mypage.html
HTTP/1.1 200 OK
Date: Thu, 26 Oct 2000 20:30:44 GMT
Server: Apache/1.3.17 (Unix) mod_perl/1.25 PHP/4.0.4pl1
Content-Length: 90
Content-Type: text/html

<html>
<head><title>My Page Title</title></head>
<body><p>My page body</p></body>
</html>
```

The example uses `lynx`, a text-based Web browser, to request `mypage.html` from `www.snake.net`. The `-mime_header` option tells `lynx` to display everything it receives from the Web server, not just the contents of the requested page. Notice that the contents of `mypage.html` are preceded by a set of headers and a blank line that signals where they end. The headers tell the browser various things about the server and about what to expect following the blank line. In particular, the `Content-Type:` header tells the browser to expect HTML data. Normally, you don't see these lines because your browser interprets them to see what it can learn from them and then discards them.

What does this mean for you as a script developer? Just this: When you write a static HTML page, the server supplies the headers for you. But when you write a script that generates pages, you have to generate the headers yourself (or at least some of them, such as the `Content-Type:` header). You also write the blank line that signals where the headers end and the page content begins.

Most header lines consist of a header name, a colon, and some additional information. However, the very first header is special. That's the HTTP response header—we don't need to generate it because Apache will do it for us. (There are ways to tell Apache that you want to generate the HTTP header yourself, but we won't do so.)

A simple Perl script that generates the same page as `mypage.html` is shown here. Observe that it generates a `Content-Type:` header and a blank line before putting out the page content:

```
#! /usr/bin/perl
# intro3.pl - script to generate a Web page
print "Content-Type: text/html\n\n";
print <<END;
<html>
<head><title>My Page Title</title></head>
<body><p>My page body</p></body>
</html>
END
exit (0);
```

Put this script in your `cgi-bin` directory, call it `intro3.pl`, make it executable, and then request it using your browser. (Remember to substitute your own Web server's name for `www.snake.net`):

```
http://www.snake.net/cgi-bin/intro3.pl
```

You should see the same page title and text that you'd see for `mypage.html`. If you request the page using `lynx -mime_header`, you should see the page contents preceded by a set of headers similar to those that were sent with `mypage.html`. If `intro3.pl` doesn't work, there are several things you can check:

- Make sure the script is executable. If it's not, you'll likely see an error message in your browser window:

  ```
  You don't have permission to access intro3.pl on this server.
  ```

  Use `chmod +x` to make `intro3.pl` executable if it isn't already.

- Examine the Apache error log to see whether it contains a message about your script. The log often provides useful clues about causes of brokenness in scripts.

- Use the `-wc` flags to tell Perl to perform a syntax check on the script:

  ```
  % perl -wc intro3.pl
  intro3.pl syntax OK
  ```

  If there's a problem, you'll see some kind of diagnostic message rather than the `Syntax OK` message.

intro3.pl generates a Web page "by hand"—that is, the Content-Type: header and HTML markup are written out literally in the script. The next script, intro4.pl, produces the same page content as intro3.pl but does so using the CGI.pm module to generate the header and markup. It looks like this:

```
#! /usr/bin/perl -w
# intro4.pl - generate a Web page using the CGI.pm object-based interface
use strict;
use CGI;
my $cgi = new CGI;
print $cgi->header (),
    $cgi->start_html ("My Page Title"),
    $cgi->p ("My page body"),
    $cgi->end_html ();
exit (0);
```

Install this script in the cgi-bin directory, request it from your browser, and you should see a page that looks the same as the ones produced by mypage.html and intro3.pl. (Actually, if you use your browser's View Source command or use lynx -mime_header to see the raw HTML produced by intro4.pl, you'll notice that CGI.pm doesn't write many newline characters. You may also see capitalized tags, and perhaps a <!DOCTYPE> tag at the beginning of the output. However, none of these things make a difference in the formatted display produced in the browser window.)

As before, we begin the script with a #! line specifying the path to Perl. The -w option is something we haven't used yet. It turns on warning mode, telling Perl to complain about dubious constructs in the script. It's a worthwhile option and we'll use it from now on.

The use strict line instructs Perl to be strict about variable references. Strict mode is valuable because it forces us to declare any variables before we use them. (This actually makes scripts a little more difficult to write initially because they require more programmer discipline, but it helps in the long run because we're less likely to make variable-related errors.)

The intro4.pl script also includes a use statement indicating that we want to use the CGI.pm module. Then it creates a CGI object $cgi that provides access to a bunch of HTML-generating methods (functions). The variable is declared using a my statement, which tells Perl, "I'm going to use this variable, don't complain when I do." (The use strict statement would cause Perl to issue an error had we used the variable without declaring it first.) The print statement strings together calls to several CGI.pm methods, each of which produces a different part of the Web page:

- header() takes care of generating the Content-Type: header. The default type is text/html, but you can pass an argument specifying another type explicitly if necessary. If your program is sending a JPEG image rather than HTML text, for example, you'd specify a type of image/jpeg. Techniques for serving images are described in Chapter 5, "Writing Form-Based Applications."

- The start_html() method sends out the introductory HTML up through the initial <body> tag; the argument to the method indicates the title that should appear within the <title> and </title> tags.
- p() generates a paragraph in the page body. (It produces text surrounded by <p> and </p> tags.)
- The end_html() method produces the closing </body> and </html> tags.

The HTML-generating calls used by intro4.pl are just a few of the methods that CGI.pm provides. Basically, there is a method corresponding to each HTML tag you'd want to write—they are listed in the installed CGI.pm documentation, which you can read using this command:

```
% perldoc CGI
```

For other CGI.pm resources, see Appendix B, "References and Further Reading." I recommend especially *Official Guide to Programming with CGI.pm* by Lincoln Stein, the author of CGI.pm.

intro4.pl uses the object-oriented interface to CGI.pm, where you create a CGI object and then call its methods to generate HTML. CGI.pm also provides a function-based interface. To use it, import the method names into your script's namespace, and then call the methods directly as functions without naming an object. The next script, intro5.pl, looks much like intro4.pl but uses the function-based interface rather than the object-oriented interface:

```
#! /usr/bin/perl -w
# intro5.pl - generate a Web page using the CGI.pm function-based interface
use strict;
use CGI qw(:standard);
print header (),
    start_html ("My Page Title"),
    p ("My page body"),
    end_html ();
exit (0);
```

intro5.pl produces exactly the same output as intro4.pl, but differs from it in the following ways:

- The use CGI line is different. It names the set of methods to be imported into the script's namespace. :standard grabs the most common ones. Another useful set is :html3, which includes the table-generating methods that are part of the HTML 3.2 standard. You can name both sets if you like:

    ```
    use CGI qw(:standard :html3);
    ```

If you just want to import all methods, use the `:all` name set:

```
use CGI qw(:all);
```

`qw()` is a Perl construct for writing single-quoted words without writing the quotes. The previous `use` statement could have been written like this:

```
use CGI ':all';
```

Use whichever format you prefer.

- There's no need to instantiate (create) a CGI object.

- Some CGI.pm method names clash with Perl operators; when these are invoked as functions, you need to use a different letter case. For example, Perl has a `tr` transliteration operator, so the CGI.pm table row method `tr()` must be invoked as `Tr()` or `TR()` when you call it as a function. This problem does not occur with the object-oriented interface because methods are invoked through the CGI object (for example, `$cgi->tr()`), and there is no ambiguity.

- You need to be careful not to name your own functions using names that already are used by CGI.pm. For example, you shouldn't write functions with names that correspond to HTML tags, such as `table()`, `br()`, `h1()`, and so forth. CGI.pm already defines functions with those names.

- Function-based code can be easier to read (and write) because it's less cluttered with instances of "`$cgi->`". For short scripts such as *intro4.pl* and *intro5.pl*, the difference is minimal, but large scripts written using the function-call interface can be significantly easier to read than equivalent object-based scripts.

I'll use the function-based CGI.pm interface from this point on, primarily because I find code written that way easier to read.

Write a Script to Access MySQL

Now we're going to forget about CGI.pm and Web scripts for a while and turn our attention to MySQL instead. (I assume that your server is configured to allow you to access it, as described in the earlier section "Configuring MySQL.") The next script will connect to the MySQL server, perform some simple operations to pull records from a table, and display them. That means we'll need a table to work with, of course. Use the `mysql` program to create a table called `teams` as shown here (substitute the appropriate connection parameters as necessary):

```
% mysql -h localhost -p -u webdev webdb
Enter password: webdevpass
mysql> CREATE TABLE teams (name CHAR(20), wins INT, losses INT);
Query OK, 0 rows affected (0.00 sec)
mysql> INSERT INTO teams VALUES('Fargo-Moorhead Twins',36,16);
Query OK, 1 row affected (0.00 sec)
mysql> INSERT INTO teams VALUES('Winnipeg Maroons',24,26);
Query OK, 1 row affected (0.00 sec)
mysql> INSERT INTO teams VALUES('Minot Why Nots',19,23);
```

continues

continued

```
Query OK, 1 row affected (0.00 sec)
mysql> INSERT INTO teams VALUES('Warren Wanderers',16,30);
Query OK, 1 row affected (0.00 sec)
mysql> SELECT name, wins, losses FROM teams;
+----------------------+------+--------+
| name                 | wins | losses |
+----------------------+------+--------+
| Fargo-Moorhead Twins |   36 |     16 |
| Winnipeg Maroons     |   24 |     26 |
| Minot Why Nots       |   19 |     23 |
| Warren Wanderers     |   16 |     30 |
+----------------------+------+--------+
4 rows in set (0.00 sec)
mysql> QUIT
```

After executing the CREATE TABLE and INSERT statements, you should have a table containing four rows of data, which you display using the SELECT statement. The table happens to represent the Northern League baseball team records for 1917, a year in which the league had only four teams. (The table is deliberately simple to make it easy to use.) To access the teams table from within Perl, create a script intro6.pl that looks like this:

```perl
#! /usr/bin/perl -w
# intro6.pl - connect to MySQL, retrieve data, write plain text output
use strict;
use DBI;
my ($dbh, $sth, $count);
$dbh = DBI->connect ("DBI:mysql:host=localhost;database=webdb",
                     "webdev", "webdevpass",
                     {PrintError => 0, RaiseError => 1});
$sth = $dbh->prepare ("SELECT name, wins, losses FROM teams");
$sth->execute ();
$count = 0;
while (my @val = $sth->fetchrow_array ())
{
    printf "name = %s, wins = %d, losses = %d\n",
                      $val[0], $val[1], $val[2];
    ++$count;
}
print "$count rows total\n";
$sth->finish ();
$dbh->disconnect ();
exit (0);
```

When you run the script, you should see something like this:

```
% ./intro6.pl
name = Fargo-Moorhead Twins, wins = 36, losses = 16
name = Winnipeg Maroons, wins = 24, losses = 26
name = Minot Why Nots, wins = 19, losses = 23
name = Warren Wanderers, wins = 16, losses = 30
4 rows total
```

When Perl sees the `use DBI` statement, it reads in the DBI code to make it available to the script. If DBI isn't installed on your machine, you'll see all kinds of complaints from Perl when it tries to execute this line. That shouldn't happen, however, because we already checked DBI availability using an earlier script (`intro2.pl`).

Assuming the script makes it past the `use DBI` line, we're ready to connect to the database server and run a query. After declaring the variables we'll need using a `my` statement, we establish a connection to the MySQL server by calling the `connect()` method:

```
$dbh = DBI->connect ("DBI:mysql:host=localhost;database=webdb",
                     "webdev", "webdevpass",
                     {PrintError => 0, RaiseError => 1});
```

The `connect()` call returns a database handle that points to a data structure containing information that DBI uses to keep track of the connection. `connect()` takes several arguments: a data source name (DSN), a username and password, and any error-handling attributes you want to specify. The data source name has the following format:

```
DBI:mysql:options
```

The first segment is always `DBI` (not case sensitive). The second segment is `mysql` (case sensitive) for MySQL. This segment indicates the particular database driver to be used. If you were using a different driver, this segment would be different, such as `pg` for PostgreSQL or `InterBase` for InterBase. The syntax of the third segment depends on the particular driver that you're using. For MySQL, it consists of a list of semicolon-separated options, each written in `name=value` format. Therefore, to specify a host name and database name of `localhost` and `webdb`, respectively, the DSN looks like this:

```
DBI:mysql:host=localhost;database=webdb
```

The order of the options in the third segment doesn't matter, and if they're left out, default values may be used. The default host value is `localhost`. (Therefore, we could have omitted this option from the preceding DSN string with no effect.) If the `database` option is omitted, no database is selected when the connection is established.

The final argument to `connect()` enables you to control DBI error-handling behavior. Enabling `RaiseError` rather than `PrintError` tells DBI not just to print a message when a database-related error occurs, but to print a message and terminate the script. This is discussed further in the section "Error Handling and Debugging" later in the chapter.

Following the `connect()` call, the script retrieves and displays records from the `teams` table. The process for doing this involves several steps:

1. Tell DBI what query we're going to issue, using the `prepare()` method. `prepare()` returns a statement handle `$sth` to use for all further operations involving the query. Note that query strings are written in DBI without any special terminator character. This is unlike the `mysql` program, where you indicate the end of each query using a semicolon or '`\g`'.

2. Call `execute()` to send the query to the server and generate a result set (the set of rows selected by the query).

3. Run a loop to fetch each row in the result set and display its contents. DBI has several row-fetching methods. `intro6.pl` uses `fetchrow_array()`, and we'll see others shortly. `fetchrow_array()` returns the next row of the result set as an array, or an empty list when there are no more rows. The `SELECT` query retrieves three columns from the `teams` table, so after fetching a row into `@val`, the elements can be accessed as `$val[0]`, `$val[1]`, and `$val[2]`. Column values are present in the order they are named in the `SELECT` statement; therefore, successive array elements represent `name`, `wins`, and `losses`.

4. Call the `finish()` method to close the result set. This allows DBI to release any resources associated with it. In practice, it's not strictly necessary to invoke `finish()` if you fetch all the rows, because DBI notices when you reach the end of the result set and closes it automatically. If you don't read an entire result set, however, you should invoke `finish()` explicitly. If you execute a query and then read only the first row, for example, you may see a warning message that looks like this when you disconnect from the MySQL server:

   ```
   DBI::db=HASH(0x10150bc0)->disconnect invalidates 1 active statement
   handle (either destroy statement handles or call finish on them
   before disconnecting)
   ```

   That's a sign that you need to call `finish()` explicitly.

After fetching and printing the rows in the result set, `intro6.pl` prints a row count. Notice that the script counts the rows itself while looping through the result set. DBI does provide a `rows()` statement handle method for this purpose. However, its use is problematic, particularly if you plan to use your script with other database engines, because the behavior of `rows()` varies between drivers. Counting the rows yourself works for any driver. (Another approach is to invoke a method that returns the entire result set all at once, and then check the number of rows in the data structure you get back. These calls are described later in "High-Level Retrieval Methods.")

The last thing `intro6.pl` does is shut down the connection to the server by calling `disconnect()`. If you forget to do this, DBI disconnects automatically when a script terminates, but it also prints a message:

```
Database handle destroyed without explicit disconnect.
```

Therefore, it's a good idea to disconnect explicitly. In addition to avoiding the warning message, that allows the MySQL server to perform an orderly shutdown on its end sooner, especially if your script runs for a while after it's done accessing the database. Scripts that are good citizens refrain from holding open connections to MySQL longer than necessary.

It's best to get in the habit of calling `finish()` and `disconnect()` as necessary, because the warnings that result otherwise are not likely to provide any useful information to people who run your scripts. These warnings are particularly confusing when produced by scripts that are run by a Web server on behalf of remote clients. Such users may know only that they're sending a request for a page to your Web server, not that the request triggers execution of a script that performs a database query. A little care in programming leads to less confusion on the part of visitors to your site.

Write a Script to Access MySQL over the Web

Our next script, `intro7.pl`, uses MySQL over the Web. It's really just an adaptation of `intro6.pl`, modified slightly to use CGI.pm. It includes a `use CGI` statement and generates HTML rather than plain text by invoking CGI.pm output methods:

```perl
#! /usr/bin/perl -w
# intro7.pl - connect to MySQL, retrieve data, write HTML output
use strict;
use DBI;
use CGI qw(:standard);
my ($dbh, $sth, $count);
$dbh = DBI->connect ("DBI:mysql:host=localhost;database=webdb",
                     "webdev", "webdevpass",
                     {PrintError => 0, RaiseError => 1});
$sth = $dbh->prepare ("SELECT name, wins, losses FROM teams");
$sth->execute ();
print header(), start_html ("team data");
$count = 0;
while (my @val = $sth->fetchrow_array ())
{
    print p (sprintf ("name = %s, wins = %d, losses = %d\n",
                      $val[0], $val[1], $val[2]));
    ++$count;
}
print p ("$count rows total"), end_html ();
$sth->finish ();
$dbh->disconnect ();
exit (0);
```

Put this script in your `cgi-bin` directory and request it from your browser as follows:

```
http://www.snake.net/cgi-bin/intro7.pl
```

At this point, you've put your database on the Web, at least in a modest way. It's not a very exciting Web presence at this point, but it's a start. (Actually, if you've never done this before, just getting *any* database information to appear in your browser can be kind of exhilarating.)

More About Retrieving Data from MySQL

The intro6.pl and intro7.pl scripts use the fetchrow_array() function to return result set rows as an array, but that's not the only function that DBI provides for fetching rows. There are other row-fetching methods, as well as higher-level methods that perform the entire cycle of result-set processing from prepare() through finish().

Other Row-Retrieval Methods

fetchrow_arrayref() is very similar to fetchrow_array(), but it returns a reference to an array, not the array itself, so you refer to elements of the array as $ref->[i], where i is a column index. Here's an example:

```
$sth = $dbh->prepare ("SELECT name, wins, losses FROM teams");
$sth->execute ();
while (my $ref = $sth->fetchrow_arrayref ())
{
    printf "name = %s, wins = %d, losses = %d\n",
                    $ref->[0], $ref->[1], $ref->[2];
}
$sth->finish ();
```

The third row-fetching method is fetchrow_hashref(). It returns a reference to a hash, and elements of the row are accessed as $ref->{col_name}, where col_name is a column name:

```
$sth = $dbh->prepare ("SELECT name, wins, losses FROM teams");
$sth->execute ();
while (my $ref = $sth->fetchrow_hashref ())
{
    printf "name = %s, wins = %d, losses = %d\n",
                    $ref->{name}, $ref->{wins}, $ref->{losses};
}
$sth->finish ();
```

When there are no more rows available, fetchrow_array() returns an empty list; fetchrow_arrayref() and fetchrow_hashref() return undef.

fetchrow_array() and fetchrow_arrayref() are more efficient than fetchrow_hashref() because it's slower to set up a hash than an array. On the other hand, when a row is stored in an array, you must know the positions of the columns in the row in order to access them properly. The query used in the preceding examples names the columns explicitly:

```
$sth = $dbh->prepare ("SELECT name, wins, losses FROM teams");
```

This enables us to know that names, wins, and losses are in positions 0, 1, and 2. If we rewrote the query to use SELECT * instead, we wouldn't know how to access the columns properly because we wouldn't know for sure the order in which MySQL would return them. (If you're thinking, "I can just run the query manually in mysql to find out the order, and then write my script accordingly," beware that the column order might change if at any point you use ALTER TABLE to modify the structure of the table.)

If you want to use SELECT * queries, fetchrow_hashref() is more suitable because column position doesn't matter; you access column values in the resulting hash by name, not position. If you do that, however, take care not to get bitten by hash element letter-case issues. Perl hash elements are case sensitive, but in MySQL, column names are not. The following queries are all equivalent as far as MySQL is concerned, but each would generate a Perl hash containing a different set of element names than the others:

```
SELECT name, wins, losses FROM teams
SELECT Name, Wins, Losses FROM teams
SELECT NAME, WINS, LOSSES FROM teams
```

To guard against letter-case variations in the way that column names are written in queries, you can force the element names to a particular case. Specify lowercase or uppercase by passing an argument of NAME_lc or NAME_uc to fetchrow_hashref(). The following example uses uppercase:

```
$sth = $dbh->prepare ("SELECT name, wins, losses FROM teams");
$sth->execute ();
while (my $ref = $sth->fetchrow_hashref ('NAME_uc'))
{
    printf "name = %s, wins = %d, losses = %d\n",
                    $ref->{NAME}, $ref->{WINS}, $ref->{LOSSES};
}
$sth->finish ();
```

By forcing column names to a specific letter case, you can access elements of the hash without regard to the letter case used in the query string itself.

High-Level Retrieval Methods

DBI provides a number of methods that perform the entire process of executing a retrieval query, including prepare(), execute(), the fetch loop, and finish(). These methods are selectrow_array(), selectcol_arrayref(), and selectall_arrayref(). (**Note:** Three new calls have been added to recent versions of DBI: selectrow_arrayref(), selectrow_hashref(), and selectall_hashref().)

selectrow_array() is useful when you need to retrieve a single row or a single column value. Invoked in a list context, it returns the first row of a result set as an array:

```
@row = $dbh->selectrow_array (
                "SELECT wins, losses FROM teams WHERE name LIKE 'Fargo%'"
            );
printf "Fargo-Moorhead: %d wins, %d losses\n", $row[0], $row[1] if @row;
```

If you assign the result to a scalar, `selectrow_array()` returns only the first column of the first row. This is especially useful for queries where you're interested only in getting a count:

```
$count = $dbh->selectrow_array ("SELECT COUNT(*) FROM teams");
print "The teams table has $count rows\n";
```

If the query returns no rows, `selectrow_array()` returns an empty list or `undef`, depending on the context in which you invoke it.

`selectcol_arrayref()` returns the first column of a result set, as a reference to an array of values. This array will be empty if the result set is empty. Otherwise, it contains one element per row of the result set:

```
$ref = $dbh->selectcol_arrayref ("SELECT name FROM teams");
print "Teams names are @{$ref}\n" if defined ($ref);
```

`selectall_arrayref()` retrieves the entire result set as a matrix and returns a reference to it. The matrix is empty if the result set is empty. Otherwise, it contains one element per row of the result set, and each of these elements is itself a reference to an array of column values:

```
$ref = $dbh->selectall_arrayref ("SELECT name, wins, losses FROM teams");
if (defined ($ref))
{
    foreach my $row_ref (@{$ref})
    {
        printf "Name = %s, wins = %d, losses = %d\n",
                $row_ref->[0], $row_ref->[1], $row_ref->[2];
    }
}
```

Each of these methods dies when an error occurs if `RaiseError` is enabled. They behave somewhat differently if `RaiseError` is disabled. `selectrow_array()` returns an empty list or `undef`, depending on whether it was invoked in list or scalar context. (Note that returning `undef` in scalar context may also occur if the value retrieved is a `NULL` value, so be careful.) `selectcol_arrayref()` and `selectall_arrayref()` both return `undef` if an error occurs prior to fetching the result set. If an error occurs during the fetch stage, they return whatever data were fetched up to the point of the error.

Queries That Modify the Database

The queries shown so far have been `SELECT` statements, and it's quite probable that the most common operation for which you'll use your database is to retrieve records. But DBI can help you with more than that. This section shows how to issue queries that modify the database in some way. The examples here demonstrate how to empty and repopulate the `teams` table using `DELETE` and `INSERT` statements. In a later section, we'll modify existing records using the `UPDATE` statement.

To issue queries that don't return rows, use the do() method. It executes a statement and returns the number of rows affected, or undef to indicate an error.[2] (If you have RaiseError enabled, you don't have to check for an undef return value, of course.) The following example shows you how to use the do() method to delete and insert records:

```
$count = $dbh->do ("DELETE FROM teams");
print "$count rows were deleted\n";
$count = 0;
$count += $dbh->do ("INSERT INTO teams (name,wins,losses)
                     VALUES('Fargo-Moorhead Twins',36,16)");
$count += $dbh->do ("INSERT INTO teams (name,wins,losses)
                     VALUES('Winnipeg Maroons',24,26)");
$count += $dbh->do ("INSERT INTO teams (name,wins,losses)
                     VALUES('Minot Why Nots',19,23)");
$count += $dbh->do ("INSERT INTO teams (name,wins,losses)
                     VALUES('Warren Wanderers',16,30)");
print "$count rows were inserted\n";
```

If you run the example (it's part of intro8.pl), you should see the following output:

```
% ./intro8.pl
0E0 rows were deleted
4 rows were inserted
```

Notice anything odd about that output? The 4 rows were inserted line makes sense because we inserted four rows. But that initial 0E0 rows were deleted line is strange. There were four rows in the teams table before; why doesn't it say 4 rows were deleted? To understand what's going on here, you need to know one thing about MySQL and one thing about DBI:

- The thing to know about MySQL is that when you issue a DELETE FROM *tbl_name* query to delete *all* the rows of a table, MySQL simply clobbers the table's data file and reinitializes it. This makes for really fast performance, but it's achieved at the cost of not knowing how many rows were in the table originally. Consequently, MySQL returns a row count of zero. If you want to know the number of rows deleted, use a DELETE statement that includes a trivially true WHERE clause like this:

    ```
    DELETE FROM tbl_name WHERE 1>0
    ```

---

2. For MySQL, "affected by" means "changed." For example, the following query returns a rows-affected value of 0, because it doesn't actually change anything:

```
$dbh->do (qq{ UPDATE teams SET wins = wins });
```

For other databases, the number of rows affected by an update generally means the number of rows selected for updating, whether or not the update actually changes any values in the rows. (Therefore, the previous query would return an affected-rows value equal to the number of rows in the table.) If you want MySQL to behave that way, you can add an option to the DSN that enables the mysql_client_found_rows attribute when you connect:

```
$dsn .= ";mysql_client_found_rows=1";
```

In this case, MySQL evaluates the WHERE clause for each row, forcing it to delete rows one by one. You'll get the true row count, at some cost in performance.

- The thing to know about DBI is that do() needs to return distinct values to distinguish the occurrence of an error from the case that no rows were affected, so it uses undef and "0E0". The value undef indicates an error; it evaluates to false in a Boolean context. The string "0E0" indicates that no rows were affected; it evaluates to true in Boolean contexts but is treated as zero in numeric contexts. (It represents zero expressed in scientific or exponential notation). If do() returned 0 to indicate no rows were affected, that evaluates to false in a Boolean context (just like undef) and would be difficult to distinguish from an error. If you want to convert the "0E0" value to a true zero, do this:

```
$count += 0;
```

Alternatively, if you just want to print the value, use printf and a %d format specifier:

```
printf "%d rows were deleted\n", $count;
```

The INSERT statements in the previous example used single quotes around the team names because SQL statements that use single-quoted string data values are more portable to other database systems. For MySQL itself, however, it makes no difference whether you use single quotes or double quotes around string values; MySQL understands them both. For example, the first INSERT statement could have been written using double quotes around the name column value like this:

```
$count += $dbh->do ("INSERT INTO teams (name,wins,losses)
                VALUES(\"Fargo-Moorhead Twins\",36,16)");
```

In this case, the double quotes surrounding the team name are escaped with a leading backslash so that Perl doesn't interpret them as the end of the query string. Another alternative is to use single quotes around the entire query string, in which case the double quotes within the string wouldn't need any escaping:

```
$count += $dbh->do ('INSERT INTO teams (name,wins,losses)
                VALUES("Fargo-Moorhead Twins",36,16)');
```

That's a less suitable method for quoting query strings if you want to embed variable references or special character sequences, such as '\n', '\r', or '\t', within the string. Those are interpreted within double-quoted strings, but not within single-quoted strings, as you can see by running the following program:

```
#! /usr/bin/perl -w
# quotes.pl - demonstrate differing quote behaviors
$var = "I am a string";
print "$var\n";     # print double-quoted string
print '$var\n';     # print single-quoted string
```

The output looks like this:

```
% ./quotes.pl
I am a string
$var\n
```

Yet other ways to quote strings are to use Perl's q{} and qq{} operators, which treat everything between the '{' and '}' characters as single-quoted or double-quoted strings, respectively. These are convenient because you can use whatever kind of quotes you want within the string itself without worrying about escaping them:

```
$count += $dbh->do (q{INSERT INTO teams (name,wins,losses)
                 VALUES('Fargo-Moorhead Twins',36,16)});
$count += $dbh->do (qq{INSERT INTO teams (name,wins,losses)
                 VALUES("Fargo-Moorhead Twins",36,16)});
```

q{} and qq{} are just like using single or double quotes with respect to treatment of embedded variable references and special character sequences.

Using Placeholders

The easiest way to avoid concerns about internal quote characters within queries is to use placeholders. With this mechanism, you put a '?' character in your query string wherever you want to insert a data value, and then supply the value separately. DBI takes the data values and interpolates them into the query string, adding any quotes or backslashes that might be necessary. Using placeholders, the INSERT statements from the previous script could be written like this:

```
$count = 0;
$count += $dbh->do ("INSERT INTO teams (name,wins,losses) VALUES(?,?,?)",
                 undef, 'Fargo-Moorhead Twins',36,16);
$count += $dbh->do ("INSERT INTO teams (name,wins,losses) VALUES(?,?,?)",
                 undef, 'Winnipeg Maroons',24,26);
$count += $dbh->do ("INSERT INTO teams (name,wins,losses) VALUES(?,?,?)",
                 undef, 'Minot Why Nots',19,23);
$count += $dbh->do ("INSERT INTO teams (name,wins,losses) VALUES(?,?,?)",
                 undef, 'Warren Wanderers',16,30);
print "$count rows were inserted\n";
```

Notice that you don't put any quotes around the '?' placeholder characters in the query, not even for the name column value, which is a string. That's because DBI supplies surrounding quotes for you as necessary. The placeholder mechanism also takes care of escaping any quote characters within data values, if there happen to be any, as well as other special characters such as backslashes or null bytes.

The second argument to do() is always undef when you use placeholders. This argument is intended for passing processing attributes to the do() method, but I've never seen anyone actually do that; just pass undef. The arguments following undef are the data values to be bound to the placeholders. These can be numbers or strings. If you want to bind NULL to a placeholder, pass undef.

You may have observed that the query strings for the INSERT statements are all identical in the previous example. When you have a situation like that, you may want to split the do() call into a prepare() call followed by one or more execute() calls. To do this, pass the query to prepare() to get a statement handle $sth. Then, for each row you want to insert, pass the data values to $sth->execute(), which binds the values to the query and sends it to the MySQL server. The preceding example, when rewritten to use that approach, looks like this (note that execute(), unlike do(), requires no undef preceding the data values):

```
$sth = $dbh->prepare ("INSERT INTO teams (name,wins,losses)
                       VALUES(?,?,?)");
$count = 0;
$count += $sth->execute ('Fargo-Moorhead Twins',36,16);
$count += $sth->execute ('Winnipeg Maroons',24,26);
$count += $sth->execute ('Minot Why Nots',19,23);
$count += $sth->execute ('Warren Wanderers',16,30);
print "$count rows were inserted\n";
```

A more common scenario for using prepare() in conjunction with execute() occurs when you're inserting rows within a loop. The following script shows an example of this. It assumes that the input is a file containing tab-delimited values. The script reads each line and trims the trailing newline, and then splits the line at tab characters and passes the resulting values to the execute() method:

```
$sth = $dbh->prepare ("INSERT INTO teams (name,wins,losses)
                       VALUES(?,?,?)");
$count = 0;
while (<>)
{
    chomp;
    $count += $sth->execute (split (/\t/, $_));
}
print "$count rows were inserted\n";
```

Some databases gain a performance benefit from splitting do() into prepare() plus execute() this way. If the database engine constructs a query plan for the statement that is passed by prepare(), it can reuse the plan each time execute() is executed within the loop. If you use do() instead, the query plan must be constructed and executed for each row inserted. None of this pertains to MySQL, which doesn't use query plans, but it may still be a good idea to write a script using prepare() and execute() in the first place rather than do(). If you plan to use a script with other databases at a later date, that may give your script a significant boost when you port it, without a bunch of rewriting.

   Placeholders can be used with any kind of statement, not just INSERT statements. For example, you could prepare a SELECT statement, and then find matching records by prompting the user for the value to be bound to the placeholder by the execute() call:

```perl
$sth = $dbh->prepare (qq{
            SELECT name, wins, losses FROM teams WHERE name = ?
        });
while (1)
{
    warn "Enter team name:\n";  # prompt user
    $name = <>;                 # read response
    chomp ($name);
    last unless $name;          # no name given; exit loop
    $sth->execute ($name);      # bind $name to placeholder
    while (my $ref = $sth->fetchrow_hashref ())
    {
        printf "name = %s, wins = %d, losses = %d\n",
            $ref->{name}, $ref->{wins}, $ref->{losses};
    }
    $sth->finish ();
}
```

Modifying Existing Records

We've seen how to retrieve, delete, and insert records, but not how to change them. The following example shows how to modify existing records using UPDATE. The function takes a database handle argument specifying an open connection to the database server and two team names. It assumes the names represent the winner and loser of a game between the two, and updates the win/loss record of each team appropriately:

```perl
sub update_wins_and_losses
{
my ($dbh, $winner, $loser) = @_;

    $dbh->do (qq{ UPDATE teams SET wins = wins + 1 WHERE name = ? },
              undef, $winner);
    $dbh->do (qq{ UPDATE teams SET losses = losses + 1 WHERE name = ? },
              undef, $loser);
}
```

You might be tempted to use a single query string and employ a placeholder for the name of the column to be updated, like this:

```perl
sub update_wins_and_losses
{
my ($dbh, $winner, $loser) = @_;
my $sth;

    $sth = $dbh->prepare (qq{ UPDATE teams SET ? = ? + 1 WHERE name = ? });
```

continues

continued

```
        $sth->execute ("wins", "wins", $winner);
        $sth->execute ("losses", "losses", $loser);
    }
```

That won't work. Placeholders are for use only with data values, not SQL keywords or operators, or database, table, or column names.

The operation of updating two team records in tandem brings up a question: What if something happens between the two updates, such as the script getting killed or the database server going down? In that case, the win/loss records will be inconsistent. We'll return to this question later when we consider transaction processing in Chapter 10, "E-Commerce Applications."

Specifying MySQL Connection Parameters Using a Library

We've written several scripts now that access MySQL, and we're going to write quite a few more—most of which will use the same connection parameters. Under these circumstances, there's an easier way to connect to the server than writing out the parameters literally in each script: Put the connection code in a library function. We'll do this by writing a module file WebDB.pm and putting it in the lib/perl directory under the Apache server root. (This directory was described earlier in "Configuring Apache.")

The module will contain a connection function that uses the same parameters used in the previous two scripts. While we're at it, we'll also include a function that connects using another common connection mode: Get the name and password from the MySQL option file of the user running the script (the .my.cnf file in the user's home directory). That is useful for command-line scripts that can be run by different users when you want to require those users to supply their own MySQL name and password. A typical .my.cnf file specifies client program connection parameters as follows:

```
    [client]
    user=user_name
    password=user_password
```

As we go along through this book, we'll write several other functions and put them in WebDB.pm. These will be routines for operations that we'll need to perform from multiple scripts; putting them in the library enables us to avoid writing the code in each script. For now, the first version of WebDB.pm looks like this:

```
    package WebDB;

    use strict;
    use DBI;

    my $host_name = "localhost";
    my $db_name = "webdb";
    my $dsn = "DBI:mysql:host=$host_name;database=$db_name";
```

```
# Connect to MySQL server, using hardwired name and password

sub connect
{
    return (DBI->connect ($dsn, "webdev", "webdevpass",
                          {PrintError => 0, RaiseError => 1}));
}

# Connect to MySQL server, using name and password from the current
# user's ~/.my.cnf option file.  The mysql_read_default_file option,
# when added to the DSN, specifies which option file to read.

sub connect_with_option_file
{
    $dsn .= ";mysql_read_default_file=$ENV{HOME}/.my.cnf";
    return (DBI->connect ($dsn, undef, undef,
                          {PrintError => 0, RaiseError => 1}));
}

1;  # return true
```

Install the `WebDB.pm` file in the `/usr/local/apache/lib/perl` directory. Scripts can access it by including the following lines:

```
use lib qw(/usr/local/apache/lib/perl);
use WebDB;
```

The first line adds the directory containing the module to the list of locations Perl searches when looking for module files, and the second line pulls in the code from the module. This allows a script to establish a connection just by invoking the appropriate routine from the library file. A script run from Apache would use the default parameters by connecting like this:

```
$dbh = WebDB::connect ();
```

(You could, in fact, go back and modify the `connect()` call in our earlier scripts to use `WebDB::connect()` and they should still work properly.) If instead you want a script to use the name and password stored in the `.my.cnf` file of the user who runs it, the script should connect like this:

```
$dbh = WebDB::connect_with_option_file ();
```

Here's an example script, `select-user.pl`, that connects that way. It reads the current user's option file, and then runs a SELECT USER() query and displays to the user the name actually found in the file:

```
#! /usr/bin/perl -w
# select-user.pl - user current user's option file to connect
use strict;
use lib qw(/usr/local/apache/lib/perl);
use WebDB;
my($dbh, $user);
$dbh = WebDB::connect_with_option_file ();
$user = $dbh->selectrow_array ("SELECT USER()");
print "You connected as $user\n";
```

continues

continued

```
$dbh->disconnect ();
exit (0);
```

The `select-user.pl` script doesn't have any `use DBI` statement, unlike the earlier scripts that access our database. That's because the `WebDB` module itself includes such a statement, so any script using `WebDB` automatically "inherits" the modules it uses.

The script uses `selectrow_array()` to combine `prepare()`, `execute()`, `fetchrow_array()`, and `finish()` into one operation to generate the first row of the result set. It is useful here because the `SELECT` query returns only one row anyway. In a scalar context, as we've called it here, `selectrow_array()` returns just the first column of the row.

Putting connection routines in a library file has the following advantages:

- MySQL scripts are simpler (and therefore easier to write) when you don't have to specify all the connection parameters in every script.

- Scripts become more portable. If you decide to move your database to another host, for example, just change the host name in `WebDB.pm`, not in all the individual scripts that use the database. If you decide to use a driver for another database such as PostgreSQL, change `mysql` in the `$dsn` value to `pg` in the library file, not in individual scripts.

- Encapsulating connection code is somewhat better for security. If you like to put your scripts in the document tree (rather than in `cgi-bin`), it's possible that if the server is reconfigured, an error will cause the Web server to start sending out your scripts as plain text rather than executing them. If the scripts contain the connection parameters, that's not such a good thing! Putting the connection code in a library file located outside the document tree prevents the Web server from showing it in plain text, even in the event of a configuration error.

  Note that using a library file this way is a security improvement only against *remote clients* discovering the connection parameters. Other users who can log in on the Web server host and install their own Web scripts probably also have permission to read files in the server's library directory. See Chapter 9 for more information.

One disadvantage of libraries is that if you don't install them in a directory that Perl searches by default, your scripts must add the directory to Perl's search list. You'll run into this with scripts written for this book that use the `WebDB` module. If you don't have the `WebDB.pm` file installed in a standard Perl library directory or in `/usr/local/apache/lib/perl`, you'll need to modify the `use lib` statement to reflect where you put the module file.

Error Handling and Debugging

When you write programs, you'll encounter problems, and it's good to know how to get information that can help you pinpoint and resolve those problems. If you don't do something about error checking, your scripts will fail and you won't know why. This section discusses diagnostic and debugging techniques that will be useful to you as you develop MySQL scripts.

One technique that we've already seen is to use the -w option on the #! line that begins your script:

```
#! /usr/bin/perl -w
```

This puts Perl in warning mode, causing it to issue messages when it finds something about the script that doesn't look quite right. You may want to turn on -w while you're developing a script, and then disable it when you put the script into production use. This is particularly true if you've eliminated as many warning messages as possible, but some persist. For example, some warnings may result from code within external modules that you're using, and you can't do anything about those. Other warnings are harmless, but annoying. If you fetch a row that contains columns that are NULL, the corresponding values in the row structure will be undef. Some operations, such as trying to print those values, result in Use of uninitialized value warnings. Removing the -w option silences the warnings. As a general rule, however, I recommend using it if at all possible.

To perform a syntax check on a script without actually executing it, use the following command. Perl will look through the script and issue warnings for errors or other things it doesn't like:

```
% perl -wc script.pl
```

Another helpful debugging technique is one we've already been using:

```
use strict;
```

Turning on strict mode helps you find things such as misspellings of variable names that Perl otherwise would not warn you about. You'll find a use strict statement in the source for almost all the scripts written in this chapter and for every script in the following chapters.

DBI Error-Processing and Tracing Facilities

DBI provides its own mechanism for handling errors, which is controlled through PrintError and RaiseError, two attributes that you can specify when you connect to the MySQL server. If PrintError is enabled, DBI methods print messages using warn() when an error occurs, in addition to returning a status value indicating an error. If RaiseError is enabled, DBI methods print messages using die() when an error occurs. This means that when you enable RaiseError, you don't need to check the return value of DBI calls for an error—if a call returns, you can assume that it succeeded. (`RaiseError` is kind of a blunt tool because scripts just squawk and die on an error when you turn it on. Nevertheless, it has the important virtue of preventing one of the most common problems in database programming—neglecting to check for errors on a uniform basis.)

By default, DBI scripts run with `PrintError` enabled and `RaiseError` disabled. To change the value of either or both, enable or disable them when you invoke `connect()`. For example, you can reverse the default values by disabling `PrintError` and enabling `RaiseError` like so:

```
$dbh = DBI->connect ($dsn, $user_name, $password,
                     {PrintError => 0, RaiseError => 1});
```

If you leave `RaiseError` disabled, you should check the result of DBI method calls. If you also disable `PrintError`, as shown here, you may want to print your own error messages:

```
$dbh = DBI->connect ($dsn, $user_name, $password, {PrintError => 0})
    or die "Cannot connect to server: $DBI::errstr ($DBI::err)\n";
```

The example uses `$DBI::errstr` and `$DBI::err`, two DBI variables that contain the MySQL error message and numeric error code when an error occurs. (If a call succeeds, the variables contain the empty string and 0, respectively, to indicate "no error.") There is also a `$DBI::state` variable that contains a standard five-character SQL error state code, but it's generally not nearly as useful as `$DBI::errstr` and `$DBI::err`. Whichever error variables you want to use, you should retrieve their values immediately after an error occurs. If you invoke another DBI method in the meantime, the error variables will be reset to reflect the result of the more recent call.

Use of *RaiseError* and *PrintError* in This Book

Unless otherwise indicated, scripts in this book run with `PrintError` disabled and `RaiseError` enabled so that errors in DBI calls will cause scripts to terminate automatically with an error message.

Database and statement handles have their own `PrintError` and `RaiseError` attributes. You can use them to modify DBI's error-processing behavior on a handle-specific basis if you like. If you want to change the current database, but not die or print a message if the current MySQL user has no permission to use the database, for example, you could use a function such as the following one. It attempts to select the database, but is silent if an error occurs and indicates by its return value whether the attempt succeeded:

```
sub change_database
{
my ($dbh, $db_name) = @_;
my ($old_pe, $old_re);
my $result;

    $old_pe = $dbh->{PrintError};   # save current attribute values
    $old_re = $dbh->{RaiseError};
```

```
    $dbh->{PrintError} = 0;          # disable both attributes
    $dbh->{RaiseError} = 0;
    $result = $dbh->do ("USE $db_name");
    $dbh->{PrintError} = $old_pe;    # restore attribute values
    $dbh->{RaiseError} = $old_re;
    return (defined ($result));      # return true if USE succeeded
}
```

Another DBI debugging aid is its tracing facility. This can provide a lot of information about what your script is doing. `DBI->trace(1)` turns on tracing with minimal verbosity (the maximum trace level is 9). `DBI->trace(0)` turns off tracing. You can trace individual handles, too. For example, `$sth->trace(n)` sets the statement handle $sth to trace level *n*.

Monitoring Query Execution

A problem that occurs quite often during script development and debugging is that queries generated by the script are malformed. Unfortunately, when you construct queries programmatically, it's not always obvious from looking at the code what is actually being sent to the MySQL server, and that makes it difficult to determine how to fix the problem. You can do several things to obtain query-execution information.

If MySQL logging is turned on and you have access to the server's log file, you can run the following command in a Telnet window to monitor what queries the server is running. Simple inspection of the log file often is sufficient to see what's wrong with queries that are failing:

```
% tail -f mysql_log_file
```

Not everybody has access to the server logs, however. Another way to find out what your queries look like is to print them before executing them:

```
$stmt = qq{ ... your query here ... };
warn "Query: $stmt\n";
$sth = $dbh->prepare ($stmt);
```

That technique isn't so useful if you're using placeholders, though; all you'll see is the string with the '?' placeholder characters intact. You may find it more informative to turn on tracing. Then you'll see the actual query strings that are sent to the server after the data values have been substituted into the query. (You'll need a trace level of at least 2.)

Diagnostic messages normally go to the standard error output, which is your terminal for command-line scripts and the Apache error log for Web scripts. For lines in the error log, it can be difficult to determine which script produced them. You can alleviate this problem by using the `CGI::Carp` module to cause diagnostics to be prefixed with a time stamp and the name of the originating script. Include a statement such as this in your script after the use CGI line:

```
use CGI::Carp;
```

You do have some latitude to modify where diagnostic output goes:

- Trace output (for either command-line or Web scripts) can be sent to a named file by specifying a filename argument when you enable tracing. The following statement specifies that trace output should be written to /tmp/myscript.err:

  ```
  DBI->trace (1, "/tmp/myscript.err");
  ```

  DBI opens trace files in append mode, so any previous contents of the file won't be lost. On the other hand, you need to be careful to remove the trace call from your script when you've eliminated the problem you're trying to solve. If you forget, the trace file becomes larger each time your script runs. Also, if you trace a Web script to a file, be aware that if multiple clients request the script at the same time, the output from the different invocations will be intertwined, making it difficult to tell what's going on.

- Web script diagnostics can be directed to your browser by turning on fatalsToBrowser:

  ```
  use CGI::Carp qw(fatalsToBrowser);
  ```

Here's a short script, fatals.pl, that illustrates how fatalsToBrowser works. Invoke it from your browser to see what happens when it reaches the die() call:

```
#! /usr/bin/perl -w
# fatals.pl - show effect of fatalsToBrowser
use strict;
use CGI qw(:standard);
use CGI::Carp qw(fatalsToBrowser);
print header (),
    start_html ("fatalsToBrowser Demonstration");
    h2("fatalsToBrowser Demonstration");
die "This is an error message\n";
print end_html ();
exit (0);
```

Enabling fatalsToBrowser is useful mostly during script development because it enables you to see error output immediately in your browser window without having to check the Apache error log. When a script goes into production use, it may be best to disable it. At that point, you want any error messages to go to the error log, not to remote clients who most likely would be confused by them.

A Simple Web-Based Application—To-Do List Maintenance

You now know many of the capabilities that the DBI and CGI.pm modules provide you with, but they have been presented in the previous sections relatively separate from each other to allow better focus on each one. In this section, we're going to switch gears and integrate several techniques by developing a little application that illustrates a number of concepts common to Web-based database programs. To keep it small, the application's scope is limited: It just maintains a list of to-do items. You might be thinking, "What good is that? Why wouldn't I just scribble my to-do list on a scrap of paper?" Perhaps you're right. However, although I believe the application can be useful, I'm actually less interested in raw utility than in certain other aspects of it that make for suitable discussion here:

- It's simple and easy to understand.
- It demonstrates many of the concepts we'll use later on and provides further exposure to CGI.pm and DBI facilities. These include such things as form generation, form content processing, database record creation and editing over the Web, and searching based on user input.
- With a little modification, the script can be used as the basis for a variety of related applications.

Furthermore, the application can be developed in a stepwise and modular fashion so that we can add code in sections. Here's the sequence of events we'll follow in writing it:

1. Create a `todo` table in the `webdb` database in which to store the items.
2. Develop an item entry form.
3. Provide a display of existing items.
4. Add the ability to edit items.
5. Add the ability to search for items.

Create the To-Do Table

The first thing we need is a table in which to store the to-do items we want to keep track of. I'll assume each item comprises the following bits of information:

- The date and time when the item was created. This will be a `DATETIME` value rather than a `TIMESTAMP`. A `TIMESTAMP` column does have the advantage that you can have it set automatically to the current date and time when you create a new record (which is convenient for record entry). However, the value also automatically changes whenever the record is modified, at which point it no longer would reflect record creation time. `DATETIME` columns must be set explicitly when records are created, but the values remain stable when other columns in the record are updated. That makes `DATETIME` a more suitable choice for this application.
- The item content (a description of what's to be done). This is a simple `VARCHAR(255)` string column. If you wanted to allow longer items, one of MySQL's `TEXT` column types would be more appropriate.

- The status of the item: open (still unfinished), closed (finished), in progress (started, but not yet finished). An ENUM (enumeration) is a good column type here because values are selected from a small fixed set of choices.

Here's the statement that defines the table, which is called todo rather than to-do. For older versions of MySQL, the hyphen (-) is not a legal character in table names. You can use it in newer versions, but you have to specify the table name within back quotes every time you refer to it (`to-do`), and that's too much bother.

```
CREATE TABLE todo
(
    t       DATETIME NOT NULL,
    content VARCHAR(255) NOT NULL,
    status  ENUM('open','closed','in-progress') NOT NULL,
    INDEX (t)
)
```

Type the preceding statement into the mysql program to create the table (remember to add a semicolon at the end) and you'll be ready to start developing the application that uses it.

Design an Item Entry Form

The initial version of the to-do application, todo1.pl, will be quite rudimentary, allowing only entry of new to-do items. (We'll worry about displaying and editing existing items later). To accomplish the item entry task, the application must do two things:

- Display a form containing a box allowing the text of the item to be entered, and a button for submitting the form.
- Add the new item to the todo table when the Submit button is selected. In this case, after entering the item, another blank entry form should be displayed in case the user wants to add another item.

Because there are two actions to be performed by the application, we should address the question of whether to use one script or two. The usual argument in favor of using multiple scripts is based on being able to split up an application into discrete pieces that don't relate much to each other and that each are simpler than a combined script would be. For example, we might use one script to display the entry form, and another to process submitted items and insert them into the database. However, that analysis doesn't really apply to the to-do application, because the second script also must display an entry form (after adding the new item). Given that both scripts would need to display the form anyway, there's nothing to be gained by decomposing this particular application into multiple scripts.

Having made the decision to use a single script, we're faced with the problem of how to know whether an item was submitted, so that we can tell whether to add a record to the `todo` table before displaying the entry form. Fortunately, it's pretty easy to figure that out. When a CGI script runs, it receives from Apache a number of values in the form of environment variables. CGI.pm allows scripts to extract this information, some of which indicates the values of the elements (parameters) present in any form that might have been submitted. When the script is invoked for the first time, no form parameters will have been set; this tells the script it need only display the entry form. If the user fills in the form and selects the Submit button, the browser sends back the form information to the Web server, which invokes the script again to process the information. This time the CGI environment contains information indicating that the form parameters have been set; the script can detect this and take appropriate action to create a new record in the `todo` table before displaying a new blank form.

Detection of form input is based on the CGI.pm `param()` function, which returns the value of a form parameter given the parameter's name. Therefore, we need to design the form and assign names to its parameters. Here's what it looks like:

```
<form method="post" action="todo1.pl">
To-do item:<br>
<textarea name="content" rows=3 cols=80></textarea><br>
<input type="submit" name="choice" value="Submit">
</form>
```

The `action` attribute of the `<form>` tag names the script that generates the form, `todo1.pl`, because we want that same script to process the form when the user selects Submit and sends it back to the Web server. `todo1.pl` determines what to do based on the values present in the form. Its elements contain two parameters: `content` holds the text of the to-do item, and `choice` provides a Submit button. `choice` is the relevant parameter to use for figuring out whether to create a new item. It will be empty the first time a remote user invokes the script and will have the value `"Submit"` when the user submits the form.

Before we go any further, allow me to digress a bit to discuss a couple of conventions I use in this book for writing applications that contain forms.

Ascertaining the User's Choice

In most cases, I use `choice` as the parameter that indicates what the user wants to do. For the form just shown, that parameter name is used for a single form element (the Submit button). If a form contains several buttons, however, we can name them all `choice` and determine which one the user selected by inspecting the `choice` parameter's value (which happens to be the text displayed in the selected button). For example, we'll add a Search button later, so at that point the form will contain two `submit` elements:

```
<input type="submit" name="choice" value="Submit">
<input type="submit" name="choice" value="Search">
```

The same name is used for both buttons, but we can tell which one a user selects by checking the value of the `choice` parameter, which will be either `"Submit"` or `"Search"`. (This contrasts with the approach of giving each button a different name. In that case, you have to check as many parameters as you have buttons. I prefer to extract the value of a single parameter.)

To simplify name-testing comparisons while allowing for whatever letter-case convention is used for buttons—perhaps you prefer all caps—it's easiest to extract the `choice` parameter value and convert it to a specific case immediately. The form-processing applications in this book convert the value to lowercase, so you'll see a statement like the following one in many of our programs:

```
$choice = lc (param ("choice"));
```

The `lc()` function also has the effect of converting `undef` to the empty string. That means we don't have to test `$choice` with `defined()`; we can just go ahead and use it without worrying about whether we'll trigger warnings in the error log about use of an uninitialized variable.

Acting on the User's Choice

After extracting the `choice` value, we need to examine it and dispatch to the proper actions that implement the user's intent. For the logic of our to-do application, its dispatch code could be structured as follows:

```
if ($choice eq "submit")            # form was submitted
{
    # ... insert new item
}
# ... display entry form
```

However, looking ahead to the fact that we'll be adding other choices in upcoming versions of the application, I'll use a different dispatch format that is more extensible and also includes a clause to handle "can't happen" choices. The revised code looks like this:

```
if ($choice eq "")                  # initial script invocation
{
    # ... display entry form
}
elsif ($choice eq "submit")         # form was submitted
{
    # ... insert new item
    # ... display entry form
}
else                                # hmm, we don't recognize the value!
{
    # ... print warning message
}
```

This dispatch code tests for the initial script invocation first, based on the fact that the choice parameter is empty when the user first requests the script. The middle clause tests for the "submit" choice indicating that the user selected the Submit button. The final clause handles the "can't happen" case.

The structure of the code is such that the middle part can be extended easily by adding elsif clauses to handle other choices as we revise the application. The final clause comes in handy as a safety net for situations such as when you modify a form to add a button for an additional choice but forget to add code to the dispatcher to handle the button. The "can't happen" clause prints an error message that notifies you about the omission the first time you try to use the new button.

Here's the main body of the first version of our application:

```perl
#! /usr/bin/perl -w
# todo1.pl - initial version of to-do application

use strict;
use lib qw(/usr/local/apache/lib/perl);
use CGI qw(:standard);
use WebDB;

print header (),
    start_html (-title => "To-Do List", -bgcolor => "white"),
    h2("To-Do List");

# Dispatch to proper action based on user selection

my $choice = lc (param ("choice")); # get choice, lowercased

if ($choice eq "")                 # initial script invocation
{
    display_entry_form ();
}
elsif ($choice eq "submit")
{
    insert_item (param ("content"));
    display_entry_form ();
}
else
{
    print p ("Logic error, unknown choice: $choice");
}

print end_html ();
```

The script puts out the page headers, title, and initial heading. Then it determines what to do based on the user's choice and finishes the page. The call to start_html() shows something we haven't used before: a named-argument list, where arguments are specified in *-name* => *value* format. CGI.pm supports this because several of its methods take so many optional arguments. Using named arguments enables you to specify just the ones you want, in any order. For the start_html() call shown, the title argument specifies the text of the page title and the bgcolor argument sets the background color of the page.

After writing out the initial part of the page, todo1.pl examines the choice parameter to see what to do. When the script is invoked for the first time, choice is empty. If the user fills in the form and selects the Submit button, choice will be "submit", so the script knows it should add a new todo table record. The insert_item() function takes care of this. The only information passed to the function is the item content, because the item's creation time ("now") and its initial status ("open") can be provided automatically. insert_item() does take some trouble to avoid entering items with empty content, because the user might select the Submit button without entering any text or after entering just whitespace. The function also doesn't bother connecting to MySQL unless there is really something to insert:

```
sub insert_item
{
my $content = shift;
my $dbh;

    $content =~ s/^\s+//;    # strip leading whitespace
    $content =~ s/\s+$//;    # strip trailing whitespace
    if ($content ne "")      # if content is non-empty, add to table
    {
        $dbh = WebDB::connect ();
        $dbh->do (qq{
            INSERT INTO todo SET t = NOW(), status = 'open', content = ?
                }, undef, $content);
        $dbh->disconnect ();
    }
}
```

Whether or not a new item is created, todo1.pl displays an entry form, using the following function:

```
sub display_entry_form
{
    print start_form (-action => url ()),
        "To-do item:", br (),
        textarea (-name => "content",
                    -value => "",
                    -override => 1,
                    -rows => 3,
                    -columns => 80),
        br (),
        submit (-name => "choice", -value => "Submit"),
        end_form ();
}
```

Put `todo1.pl` in the `cgi-bin` directory and make it executable. (Web scripts must be executable, just like command-line scripts.) Then invoke `todo1.pl` from your browser to see how it works:

```
http://www.snake.net/cgi-bin/todo1.pl
```

There are a couple of subtle points about the form-generation code in the `display_entry_form()` routine. The first concerns the action argument to the `start_form()` that determines what script to invoke when the form is submitted. The `url()` function evaluates to the script's own URL, which is how you get a script to invoke itself without hardwiring its name into the code. (Hardwiring the name is a bad idea; if you rename your script, it breaks.)

The second point involves the `textarea()` call. CGI.pm is designed to let you carry form values from one invocation of a script to the next, so that you can more easily set up a form with its previous values without initializing each element explicitly. For your item entry form, that means when you submit an item, the text of the item would carry over and be displayed in the next page automatically. That's extremely useful for many applications. (If you're presenting a product registration form that a user submits after filling in only some of the required fields, for example, you can present in response another form already filled with the supplied values along with a reminder to fill in the other fields.) However, for our to-do manager, that behavior is undesirable. Having the text of an item carry over to the next page means you'd have to delete the text before entering the text of the next item. To defeat this carryover behavior for the text box, we pass the `override` parameter to the `textarea()` function that generates it. Setting `override` to `1` tells CGI.pm to use the value of the `value` argument (that is, the empty string) no matter what was in the previous form. You can see the effect of this for yourself by removing the `override` argument from the `textarea()` call and then entering a few items. Notice that to enter the second and subsequent items, you now have to clear out the value that carried over into the form from the previous one. Restore `override` and you'll see that this no longer occurs.

Display Existing Items

At this point, we have a simple application that enables us to enter new records into our `todo` table over the Web. But how do we see our items? The item entry page doesn't show them to us. One way to see the records is to run a query using `mysql`:

```
mysql> SELECT * FROM todo;
+---------------------+-------------------------------------------+--------+
| t                   | content                                   | status |
+---------------------+-------------------------------------------+--------+
| 2001-03-12 19:54:38 | Finish ch. 6 before the editor kills me   | open   |
| 2001-03-13 09:23:09 | Fix ch. 5 code examples                   | open   |
| 2001-03-15 15:27:55 | Revise ch. 10 outline                     | open   |
+---------------------+-------------------------------------------+--------+
```

Given that we are entering records using a browser, however, it would be nice to see them that way, too. The next version of the script, todo2.pl, will do just that. It will take information from the Web and put it in the database, and it will take information from the database and send it to the Web. The modification means the script will make greater use of MySQL because it will not only create new records, it also will retrieve existing ones. This requires a change to the application's connect and disconnect behavior. Currently, it connects to the server only if there is a record to insert, establishing the connection immediately before the INSERT statement and disconnecting immediately after. After we add item-display capability, that's no longer appropriate. The script will always need a connection because it will check for existing records every time it runs. Consequently, we'll move the connect and disconnect code out of the insert_item() function and into the main logic of the application and pass the database handle $dbh to each function that needs it. We'll also add calls to display the current items. With these changes, the body of todo2.pl is as follows (leaving out the initial lines that haven't changed):

```perl
print header (),
    start_html (-title => "To-Do List", -bgcolor => "white"),
    h2("To-Do List");

my $dbh = WebDB::connect ();

# Dispatch to proper action based on user selection

my $choice = lc (param ("choice")); # get choice, lowercased

if ($choice eq "")                      # initial script invocation
{
    display_entry_form ();
    display_current_items ($dbh);
}
elsif ($choice eq "submit")
{
    insert_item ($dbh, param ("content"));
    display_entry_form ();
    display_current_items ($dbh);
}
else
{
    print p ("Logic error, unknown choice: $choice");
}

$dbh->disconnect ();

print end_html ();
```

To display the existing to-do items, `display_current_items()` runs a `SELECT` query and processes the results. The code shown here displays the most recent items first (`ORDER BY t DESC` sorts items in time-descending order):

```perl
sub display_current_items
{
my $dbh = shift;
my ($sth, $stmt, $count);

    print hr (), strong ("Current items:");
    $stmt = qq { SELECT * FROM todo ORDER BY t DESC };
    $sth = $dbh->prepare ($stmt);
    $sth->execute ();
    $count = 0;
    while (my $row = $sth->fetchrow_hashref ())
    {
        print br (), br (),
                "$row->{t} $row->{status}",
                br (),
                $row->{content};
        ++$count;
    }
    $sth->finish ();
    print p ("No items were found") if $count == 0;
}
```

These modifications take care of displaying the current items. Here's an example of what they look like when displayed in the browser window:

```
2001-03-12 19:54:38 open
Finish ch. 6 before the editor kills me

2001-03-13 09:23:09 open
Fix ch. 5 code examples

2001-03-15 15:27:55 open
Revise ch. 10 outline
```

You can run `todo2.pl` to see how the page display now includes existing items. Unfortunately, after we enter a lot of items, the page becomes longer and takes more time to load into our browser with each additional item, so we need some way to restrict how many items to show at once. One simple way to throttle the displayed-item list is to add a `LIMIT` clause to the `SELECT` query. `LIMIT` is a MySQL-specific option that enables you to tell the server to return only a portion of the selected rows. Suppose we want to display no more than five items. This can be accomplished by changing the `SELECT` query from this:

```
SELECT * FROM todo ORDER BY t DESC
```

to this:

```
SELECT * FROM todo ORDER BY t DESC LIMIT 5
```

LIMIT 5 limits the query to the first 5 rows of the result. If there aren't yet that many items in the table, MySQL returns them all. (The number 5 is arbitrary; the point of using a small value is that you won't have to add many entries to see the effect of the LIMIT clause on item display.) Call the script todo3.pl, and then run it a few times to see how it works.

You may be thinking that LIMIT isn't really a very good solution to the problem of restricting the item display to a manageable length, and you're right. It's a simple strategy, but also simple-minded: after we add more than five items, we don't see the first items again! Other possible solutions, such as displaying a section of the available items, with "next" and "previous" links to other sections of the list, are discussed further in Chapter 7, "Performing Searches."

Add Item-Editing Capabilities

After using the application for a while, presumably we'll actually complete some of the tasks that we've entered into our to-do list, and then we'll want to mark them as done or delete them. (You would mark them as done if you want to keep a record of what you've accomplished, or just delete them if you want to keep the list short.) Also, the ability to edit the text of existing items would be handy: You might decide an item's content needs revision, or you might want to allow other people to use the application to add annotations or other comments to your items. Let's write the next version of the application, todo4.pl, to include the ability to edit items. How does this change the application, compared to the previous version?

- We'll need an unambiguous way to select an item for editing. However, none of the columns in the table is suitable for that purpose. The t column that indicates the item creation time comes close, but not close enough. (Suppose you and your spouse both use the application; it's conceivable that you'd both add an item within the same second.) Therefore, we'll need a column in the table with values that are guaranteed to be unique so that each item has a distinct ID.

- In the current-item display part of the page, we'll need to add links to each item so that they can be selected for editing or deletion.

- We'll need not just an entry form, but an item-editing form. The entry form is unsuitable for editing purposes because it allows only the item text to be specified, and the form comes up blank. An editing form has different requirements. It must come up with the item's current text displayed, and it needs an additional element allowing the item status to be displayed and modified.

One way of providing unique ID values for the todo table is to use a sequence number column. Most databases have a way of generating sequences; MySQL's method is the integer AUTO_INCREMENT column. We can even add the column to the table without destroying its existing contents using MySQL's ALTER TABLE statement. Enter the following query in mysql to add an id column to the todo table:

```
mysql> ALTER TABLE todo ADD id INT NOT NULL AUTO_INCREMENT PRIMARY KEY;
```

The way an `AUTO_INCREMENT` column works is that if you enter a new record without specifying a value for the column (or if you enter a value of `NULL` explicitly), MySQL automatically sets the column to the next sequence number. ("Next" means the largest value that has already been used, plus one.) That works well to assign sequence numbers to new items, but how do we assign them to rows that already are in the todo table? As it happens, we don't have to. When MySQL adds an `AUTO_INCREMENT` column to a table, it automatically numbers any existing rows in the table. You can see this for yourself. After issuing the `ALTER TABLE` statement, try the following query and you'll see the ID values that were added:

```
mysql> SELECT * FROM todo;
```

Now we should consider whether adding the id column requires any changes to the queries currently used by the to-do manager:

- Does it change the `INSERT` statement that adds new items? No, because if we don't specify a value for the id column in the statement, MySQL automatically sets its value to the next sequence number. That's exactly what we want to happen.
- Does it change the `SELECT` statement used to retrieve items for the current item display? The answer would be yes if we had named columns explicitly in that statement. But we used `SELECT *` to select all columns, and we used `fetchrow_hashref()` to fetch rows into a hash structure. After changing the table, that structure will contain a new id member automatically. We don't have to fetch it explicitly.

What does change is the current-item display code, because we need to add Edit and Delete links for each item. The `display_current_items()` function looks like this after we modify it to add the links:

```
sub display_current_items
{
my $dbh = shift;
my ($sth, $stmt, $count);

    print hr (), strong ("Current items:");
    $stmt = qq { SELECT * FROM todo ORDER BY t DESC LIMIT 5 };
    $sth = $dbh->prepare ($stmt);
    $sth->execute ();
    $count = 0;
    while (my $row = $sth->fetchrow_hashref ())
    {
        my $edit_url = sprintf ("%s?choice=edit;id=%d", url (), $row->{id});
        my $delete_url = sprintf ("%s?choice=delete;id=%d", url (),
                                  $row->{id});
        print br (), br (),
                "$row->{t} $row->{status}",
                " [", a ({-href => $edit_url}, "Edit"), "]",
                " [", a ({-href => $delete_url}, "Delete"), "]",
```

continues

continued

```
                        br (), "\n",
                        "$row->{content}\n";
            ++$count;
        }
        $sth->finish ();
        print p ("No items were found") if $count == 0;
    }
```

We construct the URLs using `url()` to get the script's base URL, and then add `choice` and `id` parameters that specify what action to perform and to identify which item the user selected. We pass these URLs to the CGI.pm `a()` function to generate anchors for hyperlinks that the user can click. When one of these Edit or Delete links is selected, the browser sends back to the Web server a URL something like the following:

```
http://www.snake.net/cgi-bin/todo4.pl?choice=edit;id=14
http://www.snake.net/cgi-bin/todo4.pl?choice=delete;id=3
```

Note how we're extending the use of the `choice` parameter. Up until now, we've used it only for buttons, recovering its value using `param()`. But that function also provides access to parameters passed in URLs (that is, access to information present as *name=value* pairs after the '?' in the URL). That means we don't need to know or care whether a `choice` value arrives as part of a form or in the URL—a very nice feature indeed. `param()` tells us the user's choice whether the user clicks a button or selects an Edit or Delete link. If the user selects a link, `param()` also tells us the `id` value that indicates which item to operate on.

Now you need to write the code that handles the Edit and Delete choices and that modifies the `todo` table accordingly. Let's cover deleting an item first, because that's easier than editing an item. The clause in the dispatch logic that handles the choice is pretty simple:

```
    elsif ($choice eq "delete")
    {
        if (!delete_item ($dbh, param ("id")))
        {
            print p ("No record with id ". param ("id"). " was found");
        }
        display_entry_form ();
        display_current_items ($dbh);
    }
```

The clause calls `delete_item()` to clobber the item with the appropriate ID number, and then displays a fresh entry form and list of current items. `delete_item()` looks like this:

```
    sub delete_item
    {
    my ($dbh, $id) = @_;
```

```
    return ($dbh->do (qq{ DELETE FROM todo WHERE id = ? },
                undef,
                $id));
}
```

Item editing is a bit more involved because it's not a single-step operation. First, we display an edit form initialized with the item's current values, along with an Update button for submitting the modified item. (In addition, we'll provide a Cancel button in case the user decides not to modify the item after all.) Second, we process the updated item when the Update button is selected. The dispatch logic needs several new clauses to handle these choices:

```
elsif ($choice eq "edit")
{
    if (my $row = select_item ($dbh, param ("id")))
    {
        display_edit_form ($row);
    }
    else
    {
        print p ("No record with id ", param ("id"), " was found");
        display_current_items ($dbh);
    }
}
elsif ($choice eq "update")
{
    update_item ($dbh, param ("id"), param ("content"), param ("status"));
    display_entry_form ();
    display_current_items ($dbh);
}
elsif ($choice eq "cancel")
{
    display_entry_form ();
    display_current_items ($dbh);
}
```

select_item() runs a simple SELECT query to retrieve the item with the given id value and returns the row as a hash reference.

```
sub select_item
{
my ($dbh, $id) = @_;
my ($sth, $row);

    $sth = $dbh->prepare (qq{ SELECT * FROM todo WHERE id = ? });
    $sth->execute ($id);
    $row = $sth->fetchrow_hashref ();
    $sth->finish ();
    return ($row);
}
```

The row returned by `select_item()` is passed to `display_edit_form()` so that the form can be initialized to the item's current state:

```
sub display_edit_form
{
my $row = shift;

    print strong ("Item Editing Form"),
        start_form (-action => url ()),
        hidden (-name => "id", $row->{id}),
        "To-do item $row->{id}:", br (),
        textarea (-name => "content",
                    -value => $row->{content},
                    -override => 1,
                    -rows => 5,
                    -columns => 100),
        br (),
        radio_group (-name => "status",
                    -values => ["open", "closed", "in-progress"],
                    -default => $row->{status}),
        br (),
        submit (-name => "choice", -value => "Update"),
        submit (-name => "choice", -value => "Cancel"),
        end_form ();
}
```

The editing form differs from the entry form in the following ways:

- It has a different title (a cosmetic difference).

- The item ID is displayed in the form for the user to see, but that value is just static text and won't be returned when the user selects the Update button. We'll need the value when the form is submitted so that we can tell which item to update, so the form also includes the id value as a hidden form value. This instance of the value is not displayed to the user, but will be transmitted back to the Web server when the edited item is submitted.

- The content field is initialized to `$row->{content}`. That makes the form come up with the item's current text displayed and ready for modification.

- A set of radio buttons is provided for setting the item's status, and the current status value is used to set the default button. (The possible values for the status buttons are hardwired into the code based on your knowledge of the table structure. In Chapter 6, "Automating the Form-Handling Process," we'll see how to generate a radio button list automatically by examining a table's structure directly to pull out the legal enumeration values.)

- The `choice` button for submitting the modified item is labeled `"Update"` rather than `"Submit"` to prevent the application from confusing it with the Submit button in the item entry form.

- The form includes a Cancel button to give the user the option of returning to the item entry form without making any changes.

If a modified item is submitted, we call `update_item()`. This function needs four parameters: the database handle, the item ID (to identify which item to update), and the new content and status of the item (the item creation date remains unchanged):

```
sub update_item
{
my ($dbh, $id, $content, $status) = @_;

    $content =~ s/^\s+//;    # strip whitespace
    $content =~ s/\s+$//;
    $dbh->do (qq{ UPDATE todo SET content = ?, status = ? WHERE id = ? },
              undef,
              $content, $status, $id);
}
```

Add Item-Searching Capabilities

We're almost done building the to-do list manager. All that remains is to add searching capability, so that items can be selected by content based on a word or phrase. There are different ways to enable users to perform searches, but we'll use a simple strategy: Add a Search button to the item entry form. To enter new items, you can use the form as before. To search for items, enter a word or phrase and select Search rather than Submit. The only modification we need to make to the `display_entry_form()` function is to change this line:

```
submit (-name => "choice", -value => "Submit"),
```

To this:

```
submit (-name => "choice", -value => "Submit"),
submit (-name => "choice", -value => "Search"),
```

To handle the new button, add another clause to the dispatch code. The search string arrives as the value of the `content` parameter, so we pass that to the search function:

```
elsif ($choice eq "search")
{
    display_entry_form ();
    display_search_hits ($dbh, param ("content"));
}
```

The function for displaying search hits will need to display individual items, just like the function that displays the current items. Therefore, we'll move the item-display code from `display_current_items()` into a function `display_item()` and call the latter function from within `display_search_hits()` as well. `display_search_hits()` searches for and displays matching items as follows:

```
sub display_search_hits
{
my ($dbh, $str) = @_;
my ($sth, $stmt, $count);

    print hr (), p ("Search Results");
    $str =~ s/^\s+//;   # strip whitespace
    $str =~ s/\s+$//;
    if ($str eq "")     # cancel search if there's nothing to search for
    {
        print p ("No search term was entered");
        return;
    }
    print hr (), strong ("Items matching \"$str\":");
    $stmt = qq { SELECT * FROM todo WHERE content LIKE ? ORDER BY t DESC };
    $sth = $dbh->prepare ($stmt);
    $sth->execute ("%$str%"); # search for wildcard form of string
    $count = 0;
    while (my $row = $sth->fetchrow_hashref ())
    {
        display_item ($row);
        ++$count;
    }
    $sth->finish ();
    print p ("No matching items were found") if $count == 0;
}
```

The SELECT query uses a WHERE clause based on LIKE rather than on = to perform a pattern match rather than a literal match. Note the use of `"%$str%"` as the search string, rather than `$str`. If we searched just for `$str`, we'd find only records where the content value is exactly that string. By using the SQL "match anything" wildcard character '%' on both ends of `$str`, we'll find items that contain the string anywhere in the content value—that's the more useful thing to do here.

The helper function `display_item()` looks like this:

```
sub display_item
{
my $row = shift;
my ($edit_url, $delete_url);

    $edit_url = sprintf ("%s?choice=edit;id=%d", url (), $row->{id});
    $delete_url = sprintf ("%s?choice=delete;id=%d", url (), $row->{id});
    print br (), br (),
            "$row->{t} $row->{status}",
            " [", a ({-href => $edit_url}, "Edit"), "]",
```

```
              " [", a ({-href => $delete_url}, "Delete"), "]",
              br (), "\n",
              "$row->{content}\n";
     }
```

Install this script as `todo5.pl` in the `cgi-bin` directory to try it out.

Shortcomings of the To-Do Application

The to-do application we've just built performs several functions now. You can enter new items, see existing ones, edit or delete items, and search for items that match a string. That need not stop us from critiquing the application, however. Some of the ways it could be improved are described here:

- The application doesn't perform much verification of field input. It makes sure items are not blank, but there's no check that the item is within the 255 character limit of the content field in the `todo` table. Nor does it complain if you remove all the text when you modify an item. (Take a look at the `update_item()` function; how could the update operation be made better?)

- Searches are very rudimentary. It doesn't allow searching for results that fall within a given date range or that have a particular status. For example, you can't search for items that were entered within the last month that now are marked "done."

- The item display format could be better. For example, dates are displayed to full resolution down to the second. It's perhaps not very likely you really care about the seconds part of the item creation time. The script could chop off the seconds, either using `DATE_FORMAT()` in the `SELECT` query or by chopping the end of already retrieved values.

- There is no security. Anyone who can connect to your Web server can see or change items in your list. That's okay if you want to allow other people access to your list, but my guess is that it's unlikely you want the whole world to use it.

- It's useful for managing only one person's to-do list. A more general application might provide a front end that allows users to sign in, and then chooses the appropriate list to edit.

You can probably think of other ways the application might be improved or extended to be more useful. If so, that's good. It's usually a worthwhile exercise to consider ways to make an application better. Naturally, you want to give some thought to this during the design stage before you spend a lot of time building the thing, but there's certainly no rule you can't keep an eye out for ways to improve the design later.

Adapting the To-Do Application for Other Uses

The to-do list maintenance application implementation involves a number of concepts that come up in several related contexts. With a little modification, you could use the application as the basis for any of the following types of programs:

- **Note-taking application.** This actually is simpler than a to-do list manager; you need to record only the text of items, not manage status values.

- **Scheduler.** Add a field to the forms allowing the date to be specified or edited, modify the script accordingly, and the application becomes a rudimentary scheduling manager.

- **Guest book.** For this type of application, the entry display component can be made optional (depending on whether you want to display previous entries), and you'd remove the entry editing and searching functions

- **Customer feedback help desk application.** Here you'd remove the entry display, editing, and searching functions. Alternatively, you could modify the form so that those functions become accessible if an administrator signs in to use the application. If the entry form were modified to include a field for an email address, the application could allow the administrator to send back replies to people submitting questions. The item-editing function might allow email responses to be generated, perhaps saving the response in the table along with the original question.

Some of the applications just described require the ability to do things that we haven't covered yet, such as date verification, email generation, user authentication, and session support. We'll get to these topics in later chapters.

What You Have Achieved

By working through the material in this chapter, you have learned how to do the following things from within Perl scripts:

- How to use DBI to connect to and disconnect from the MySQL server
- How to run queries to add new records, or retrieve, delete, or modify existing records
- How to generate dynamic Web pages using CGI.pm to produce HTML
- How to perform basic Web form-processing operations
- How to perform simple searching

Web servers were initially conceived as a means of transferring files easily to users on remote hosts. Generating dynamic pages as you've done in this chapter produces a Web serving environment that is fundamentally different. We're still providing information to users, and they're still viewing what appear to be pages in their browsers. But those pages don't originate as static files on the Web server host, they're generated on demand by programs that actively respond to user requirements. In the to-do application, for example, information goes both ways. The user sends information to be stored into the database, and the application pulls information from the database for display to the user. This is a much different, more flexible, and more interactive environment than can be provided using only static HTML pages.

It's also more taxing on the Web server, which becomes responsible not just for opening files and shoving their contents out through network sockets, but for executing programs on behalf of the client. If the server has to execute these programs frequently, the result can be a significant drain on your host's resources. In the next chapter, we'll discuss how to reduce a good deal of this resource consumption.

3

Improving Performance
with *mod_perl*

THE PRIMARY GOAL IN CHAPTER 2, "GETTING CONNECTED—Putting Your Database on the Web," was to take care of the basic aspects of getting your MySQL server to work with Apache. The important thing there was just to get data in and out of your databases over the Web, without any particular regard for performance. In this chapter, we'll consider a simple method for improving performance that can help you throughout the rest of this book: use the Apache mod_perl module. In other words, the chapter isn't so much about how to write scripts as about how to make them run faster. I'll describe what mod_perl is and how it changes the way Apache handles scripts to make them execute more quickly. Then we'll see what configuration changes are necessary for using mod_perl and discuss some guidelines for making sure your scripts run properly.

For more information about mod_perl, see Appendix B, "References and Further Reading." You'll probably want to consult the mod_perl Guide as a general reference. Several other mod_perl documents make informative reading, too.

What *mod_perl* Is and How It Works

When Apache receives a request for a static HTML file, it can serve the request directly by opening the file and writing it out over the network to the client. This is not true for programs, such as the Perl cgi-bin scripts we wrote in Chapter 2. Those scripts aren't processed by Apache itself. Instead, Apache starts up Perl as an external process and returns its output to the requesting client. This works well for extending Apache's capabilities, but invoking an external program taxes the Web server host and also introduces some delay into serving the request. This overhead is incurred repeatedly as script requests arrive because Apache starts up a new Perl process to handle each one.

An alternative to running scripts using external processes is to make the script handler part of Apache itself. In the case of Perl scripts, we can use the mod_perl module to embed the Perl interpreter into Apache. The result is that Apache gains the capability to execute Perl scripts directly. This approach has several advantages:

- Apache can execute Perl scripts more quickly because it need not start up or wait for standalone external processes.

- A given Apache process can serve many script requests because it doesn't terminate when a script finishes; it just waits for the next request. This allows Apache to perform caching for scripts that are requested repeatedly, which results in a further performance improvement. (The script-execution process involves examining the script and compiling it to an internal form, and then running that form. When Perl runs as part of Apache, the compiled script remains loaded in memory and is immediately available for execution. It need not be recompiled if the server receives another request for it.)

- Because the Perl interpreter doesn't just exit when the script terminates the way it does when Perl is executed as a standalone process, the script-execution environment persists across scripts. This makes possible some things that can't be done when scripts are executed individually by independent Perl processes. One of these is persistent database connections (connections to a database server that can be shared over successive scripts, minimizing overhead for setup and teardown).

These benefits do come at a price, of course. There are also some disadvantages to using mod_perl:

- Apache installation and configuration becomes more involved.

- The script-execution environment persists across scripts. (Yes, I included this in the preceding list of advantages, but persistence of the Perl interpreter's internal state also can cause problems if a script is a bad citizen that contaminates the environment of its successors.) Such scripts require some tweaking to behave better.

- Embedding the Perl interpreter into Apache causes `httpd` processes to become larger and take more memory. You may find it prudent or necessary to perform some configuration tuning.

- `mod_perl` scripts always run under the user and group IDs of the `httpd` process. You can't execute them with the privileges of another user or group using the suEXEC mechanism the way you can with standalone scripts.

I've listed more disadvantages than advantages, which you may find alarming. However, most of the disadvantages are one-time issues. Apache configuration is more complicated with `mod_perl`, but after you get things set up the way you want them, you usually can leave your configuration alone. A script that needs some modification to run as a good citizen under `mod_perl` generally needs to be fixed once, not multiple times.

The benefits, on the other hand, are continuous. Having scripts run faster with `mod_perl` than when executed as standalone programs is a benefit you enjoy for as long as you continue to use Apache. The amount of improvement varies from site to site, but the `mod_perl` Guide indicates that developers report scripts running anywhere from 2 to 20 times faster than the equivalent standalone versions. See Appendix B for other reports of user experiences.

Should You Use *mod_perl*?

Now, having made an effort to convince you that `mod_perl` is a good thing, allow me to point out that you do not have to use it if you don't want to. Indeed, if you run a low-traffic site, performance may be adequate as is, response time for clients may be perfectly satisfactory, and you may never experience any compelling reason to use `mod_perl`. If you don't want to deal with `mod_perl` now, just skip ahead to the next chapter. If your site's activity increases, however, you may find performance becomes an issue about which to be concerned. In that case, you can always return to this chapter and reconfigure Apache for `mod_perl` when you need it.

If you decide to use `mod_perl` and do find that it's useful (as I expect you will), there are other Apache modules you may want to consider. Perl isn't the only language that can be embedded into Apache as a module; languages such as PHP, Python, Ruby, and Java also can be used in module form for writing Web scripts, with advantages similar to those offered by `mod_perl`.

If You Are Not Using `mod_perl`...

You should know one thing about this chapter even if you decide to skip it for now: Most of the rest of this book assumes you'll run your scripts under mod_perl. You can recognize such scripts, because they'll be located in the `cgi-perl` directory, not in `cgi-bin`. To use any such script in standalone fashion (assuming it doesn't require mod_perl, of course), just put it in your `cgi-bin` directory and adjust the URL accordingly.

Other Uses for *mod_perl*

As described thus far, mod_perl is a means for improving performance of Perl scripts on a Web site, and in fact, that's the main reason we use it in this book. mod_perl actually is more than that, however, and the performance boost can be viewed as something of a side effect of its primary purpose.

Apache is written in C and provides a C application programming interface (API). Developers can extend Apache's capabilities by writing modules in C that communicate through that API. But not everybody wants to write C code. This is where mod_perl comes in. Its principal function is to provide an alternative to writing in C by mapping the Apache API onto a Perl API so that you can extend Apache by writing Perl programs. That's why mod_perl embeds the Perl interpreter into Apache—it provides a bridge between the Apache C API and programs written in Perl. The primary effect of this is to make Apache internals available through the Perl language. The secondary side effect (the one we're actually more interested in here) is that because Perl is available immediately and has already been started up, Perl scripts execute significantly faster.

Perl programs that exploit the Perl API can do some clever things. For example, packages such as Embperl, ePerl, and Mason provide you with the ability to write HTML pages that contain embedded Perl code. They use the Perl API to access Apache's page-processing mechanisms, which allows them to look for bits of embedded code, run the Perl interpreter to evaluate the code, and use the results in producing the page. A related module, AxKit, uses mod_perl to process XML pages. mod_perl allows AxKit to combine the power of the Apache API with Perl's XML support to transform XML pages containing embedded Perl into a variety of formats. From the same XML source, for example, you can produce an HTML page for browser display, a printer-friendly version for hard copy, or a minimal-text version for handheld wireless devices.

Alternatives to *mod_perl*

mod_perl isn't the only mechanism available for speeding up Perl script execution. Others, such as FastCGI and VelociGen, can be used instead of mod_perl or in tandem with it. You can configure Apache to use mod_perl for some scripts and FastCGI or VelociGen for others. For more information, visit www.fastcgi.com and www.velocigen.com.

mod_perl Configuration

Apache uses a standard protocol, the Common Gateway Interface (CGI), to communicate with externally executed scripts such as those we put in the cgi-bin directory in the preceding chapter. When a CGI script begins executing, it can assume that Apache has set up certain environment variables. For example, REMOTE_ADDR and REQUEST_URI indicate the client's host IP number and the request path. When Apache uses mod_perl to execute a script directly, it doesn't set up the CGI environment. In principle, there is no need, because a script that has direct access to Apache's internals obviously can extract that information itself if it wants. But the practical implication of this is that Perl CGI scripts won't function properly under mod_perl unless they are rewritten to use the Apache API or unless something else sets up the CGI environment for them.

Obviously, the latter alternative is preferable. If you already have a bunch of CGI scripts, you don't want to rewrite them all specifically for mod_perl. Fortunately, there is an easy solution to this problem. mod_perl includes an Apache::Registry module that sets up the CGI environment for you. If we use it to run our CGI scripts, mod_perl becomes transparent to them so that (for the most part) they don't need to know or care whether they're being run by a standalone Perl process or by mod_perl. This enables you to move your scripts between the standalone and mod_perl execution environments easily.[1]

Oh, you noticed that "for the most part" in the preceding paragraph, did you? That disclaimer was necessary because scripts containing certain constructs need modification for mod_perl. We'll get to this in the section titled "Writing mod_perl Scripts."

The rest of this section describes how to configure Apache to use mod_perl and Apache::Registry for running Perl scripts. The steps are as follows:

1. Create a directory for mod_perl scripts.
2. Verify that mod_perl is installed.
3. Configure httpd.conf to tell Apache how to execute mod_perl scripts.
4. Test your configuration.
5. Set up a mod_perl startup file (optional, but useful).

Before following these instructions, verify that you have recent enough versions of Perl and CGI.pm. You should have Perl 5.005 or later. You should also have CGI.pm 2.36 or later, because earlier versions don't work with mod_perl. If your versions aren't recent enough, you'll need to upgrade. See Appendix A, "Obtaining Software," for instructions.

Create a Directory for *mod_perl* Scripts

Chapter 2 covered general Apache directory layout issues, including how to configure Apache to execute scripts found in the server's cgi-bin directory. Here we'll use a different directory for scripts that we intend to be executed by mod_perl. The examples in this chapter assume the use of cgi-perl under your Apache server's root, so the first thing you need to do is create that directory:

```
% cd /usr/local/apache
% mkdir cgi-perl
```

---

1. Clearly, I'm making an argument for being able to write scripts that run whether or not you have mod_perl installed, so that readers who can't install mod_perl or who elect not to will be able to run most of the scripts in this book without modification. There is a counterargument, which is that if you know you're going to use mod_perl, you can get even better performance by dispensing with Apache::Registry and interacting more directly with Apache.

If you're using a different layout, make the appropriate substitutions in these commands and in the configuration instructions throughout the rest of this section.

Verify That *mod_perl* Is Installed

To use mod_perl, it needs to be compiled into the Apache httpd binary or loaded as an Apache dynamic shared object (DSO). Try running httpd -l to get a list of compiled-in modules. If mod_perl is among them, it's already installed. If mod_perl isn't compiled in, check whether it's available as a DSO. (Look in the modules directory under the server root directory to see whether there's a file with mod_perl in its name.) If not, you'll need to install mod_perl before proceeding to the next step. For instructions, refer to Appendix A.

Configure *httpd.conf*

If you're using a DSO version of mod_perl, you need to tell Apache where to find it by adding a LoadModule directive to your httpd.conf file. (If the name of the file is different from mod_perl.so on your system, make the appropriate adjustment to the line shown here.)

```
LoadModule perl_module modules/mod_perl.so
```

Next (for both compiled-in and DSO installations), tell Apache to associate mod_perl with scripts located in the cgi-perl directory by adding the following lines to httpd.conf:

```
Alias /cgi-perl/ /usr/local/apache/cgi-perl/
<Location /cgi-perl>
    SetHandler perl-script
    PerlHandler Apache::Registry
    PerlSendHeader on
    Options ExecCGI
</Location>
```

The Alias line specifies that when a URL begins with /cgi-perl/ after the host name part (for example, http://www.snake.net/cgi-perl/myscript.pl), Apache should look in the /usr/local/apache/cgi-perl/ directory to find the script. (You must use Alias; don't use ScriptAlias, because it won't work with mod_perl.)

The <Location> block provides the specifics about how to handle scripts found in the cgi-perl directory. The SetHandler and PerlHandler directives specify that we want to run them using Apache::Registry so that a CGI environment gets set up before they start executing. PerlSendHeader tells Apache that we want it to generate the HTTP header that precedes script output sent to the client. The Options line turns on CGI script-execution capability for the cgi-perl directory.

It's also possible to associate mod_perl with scripts based on their filenames rather than on their location. (You might do this if you want to put scripts in the document tree rather than in the `cgi-perl` directory.) To execute scripts having names ending in `.pl` as mod_perl CGI scripts, for example, add these lines to `httpd.conf`:

```
<Files *.pl>
    SetHandler perl-script
    PerlHandler Apache::Registry
    PerlSendHeader on
    Options ExecCGI
</Files>
```

One drawback to associating `.pl` scripts with `mod_perl` this way is that the association will apply not only to new scripts that you write, but also to scripts that are already present in your document tree—scripts that may not have been written with `mod_perl` in mind. If that's a problem, you might want to consider using a `mod_perl`-specific extension such as `.mpl` instead. (Don't forget to change the `<Files>` line from `*.pl` to `*.mpl` if you do this.)

As long as you're modifying `httpd.conf`, add the following lines, too. They provide access to `Apache::Status`, a handler that displays all kinds of diagnostic information about your `mod_perl` setup when you send a `perl-status` request to Apache. Add the lines as shown, except that you should change the IP number on the `allow from` line to the name or IP number of the host on which you run your Web browser:

```
<Location /perl-status>
    SetHandler perl-script
    PerlHandler Apache::Status
    order deny,allow
    deny from all
    allow from 192.168.1.15
</Location>
```

Test Your *mod_perl* Configuration

Each time you modify the configuration file, as in the preceding section, you must restart Apache. (See Chapter 2 for instructions on doing so.)

Do that right now, and then you'll be ready to test your setup. To begin, request the `perl-status` "page" from your site:

```
http://www.snake.net/perl-status
```

In your browser, you should see something similar to Figure 3.1, where the initial part of the display shows some overall configuration information and the items below the line provide links to pages listing more specific information about `mod_perl` itself. Select a few of the links to get a feel for the kinds of information they provide.

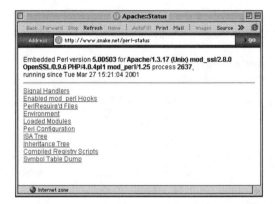

Figure 3.1   Output from the perl-status handler.

Next, create the following short script in the cgi-bin directory (that's right, cgi-bin, not cgi-perl):

```
#! /usr/bin/perl
print "Content-Type: text/html\n\n";
print "<html><head><title>Script Environment</title></head><body>\n";
print map { "$_ = $ENV{$_}<br>\n" } sort (keys (%ENV));
print "</body></html>\n";
```

Name the script perltest.pl, make it executable, and request it through your browser (http://www.snake.net/cgi-bin/perltest.pl). The script should print the names and values of its environment variables. One of the output lines will show the value of the GATEWAY_INTERFACE environment variable, which should begin with CGI:

```
GATEWAY_INTERFACE = CGI/1.1
```

Now copy perltest.pl to the cgi-perl directory and request http://www.snake.net/cgi-perl/perltest.pl so that the script is executed by mod_perl rather than by a standalone Perl process. The output should be similar, but the value of GATEWAY_INTERFACE should begin with CGI-Perl, not CGI. This indicates that the CGI environment has been set up by the mod_perl Apache::Registry module. In addition, the output should show a variable MOD_PERL containing your mod_perl version number:

```
GATEWAY_INTERFACE = CGI-Perl/1.1
MOD_PERL = mod_perl/1.24
```

This exercise with perltest.pl shows how you can run a script either as a standalone CGI program or using mod_perl. It also shows what you need to do if you have a script that needs to know whether it's running under mod_perl—that is, you can use either of the following tests:

```
if (exists ($ENV{MOD_PERL})) { print "mod_perl yes\n"; }
if ($ENV{GATEWAY_INTERFACE} =~ /^CGI-Perl/) { print "mod_perl yes\n"; }
```

Set Up a *mod_perl* Startup File

The `Apache::Registry` handler automatically sets up the CGI environment for your Perl scripts. You can augment the information that `Apache::Registry` provides by setting up a `mod_perl` startup file to be read during Apache's initialization process. (The file is written in Perl, of course.) To do this, use a `PerlRequire` directive. If you want to call the file `startup.pl` and put it with the other Apache configuration files in the `conf` directory under the server root, for instance, add this line to `httpd.conf`:

```
PerlRequire conf/startup.pl
```

If you want to put the startup file in `lib/perl` with the other Perl library files, use this line instead:

```
PerlRequire lib/perl/startup.pl
```

After configuring `httpd.conf` to specify the location of the startup file, what should you put in it? That's up to you. One way to use the file is to set up additional information in the standard environment under which you want your scripts to run. If many of your scripts include a `use lib pathname` line to add a given directory to the Perl search path, you can add the directory to the path in the startup file instead. Then it's added automatically, and your scripts don't need to do it for themselves.

Another use for the startup file is to preload common Perl modules to improve performance. When Apache starts up, it reads and processes its configuration file (which includes processing the `mod_perl` startup file). Then it spawns a bunch of child `httpd` processes to handle client requests. In general, the more work you can get done in the parent `httpd` process before it starts spawning children, the more efficient your system will be. This is true not only for script execution speed, but also for system resource consumption, particularly memory use. Let's see why this is.

Each child `httpd` begins executing as a copy of the parent, and, due to the way virtual memory works, it shares the address space of the parent rather than doubling the amount of memory used. As the processes run, the amount of shared address space tends to decrease. (If the child changes a data structure, for instance, any memory pages containing that data can no longer be shared with the parent. The system duplicates those pages and marks them as unshared—unique to and owned by the child.) Nevertheless, a large amount of address space generally continues to be shared between the parent and its children; this is a big win for memory management and for system performance in general.

You can use the `mod_perl` startup file to influence your system's performance by exploiting the address space sharing provided by virtual memory. If you tend to use certain Perl modules in many of your scripts, you can name them in the startup file to preload them into the parent `httpd` process. The code of these modules then becomes part of that process and thus part of its address space that can be shared with the child processes. The parent process becomes larger, but overall memory use goes down, compared to having those modules loaded by each individual child and becoming part of their unshared address space.

An additional benefit of code preloading is that the code is compiled only once, by the parent. The children receive the code precompiled. Any module that isn't preloaded must be loaded and compiled by each child individually when scripts that are run by the child request it; therefore more processor time is used.

With the preceding discussion in mind, let's look at an example startup file. Suppose you want to give your scripts access to Perl library files in the /usr/local/apache/lib/perl and /var/lib/perl directories without having to put use lib statements for those directories in every single script. Suppose also that most of your scripts use the CGI.pm and DBI modules, so you want to preload them. You can accomplish these goals by writing your startup file as follows:

```
use strict;
use lib qw(/usr/local/apache/lib/perl);
use lib qw(/var/lib/perl);
use CGI ();
CGI->compile (':all');
use DBI ();
use DBD::mysql ();
1;    # return true
```

Here are some things to note about this startup file, because they aren't particularly obvious:

- You might not actually need to include the use lib line for the lib/perl directory. Recent versions of mod_perl search that directory automatically.

- The () after the names of the modules that are preloaded prevents method names from being imported. This saves a little memory during Apache startup, and importing the names can wait until your scripts execute.

- The call to CGI->compile() forces preloading of the CGI.pm methods that otherwise are autoloaded on demand. Without this call, these methods won't be loaded until later, and the code will go into the unshared address space of individual httpd children.

- Normally DBI locates and loads the DBD::mysql driver when you're using the DBI module to access MySQL. But that doesn't happen until later, when you actually attempt to connect to the MySQL server. To get the advantage of preloading for the driver and not just the main DBI module, you have to load the driver explicitly at startup time.

- The final line is required; don't leave it out. When Perl reads the startup file, it expects a return value of true or false to indicate whether the file executed successfully. The final line evaluates to 1 (true), which becomes the return value. If you omit the line, Apache startup fails after writing a line like this to the error log:

```
[error] conf/startup.pl did not return a true value
```

You must restart Apache each time you modify the startup file, just as when you modify `httpd.conf`. However, there's a slight complication in that the startup file won't be read under certain circumstances. If `mod_perl` is loaded as a DSO, it's torn down completely and reloaded from scratch whenever Apache restarts. In this case, you don't have anything to worry about; the startup file will be reread when `mod_perl` is reinitialized. On the other hand, if `mod_perl` is compiled in to `httpd`, Apache doesn't reread the startup file by default. You have a couple of options here. First, you can restart with `apachectl stop` followed by `apachectl start`. That brings the server all the way down and starts a new one, causing the entire initialization sequence to be performed. Alternatively, you can add the following directive to `httpd.conf`:

```
PerlFreshRestart on
```

`PerlFreshRestart on` explicitly tells Apache to reread the `mod_perl` startup file when it restarts, even for `apachectl restart` and `apachectl graceful`. However, the `mod_perl` Guide cautions that `PerlFreshRestart` can cause problems on some systems. Before deciding whether to use it, read the section in the Guide titled "Evil Things Might Happen When Using `PerlFreshRestart`." If you decide against it, you'll need to go the route of using `apachectl stop` and `apachectl start` to restart the server after startup file changes.

After restarting Apache, you can check whether it reloaded the startup file by requesting the `perl-status` page described in the section "Test Your `mod_perl` Configuration." If you change the Perl search path, for example, this should be reflected in the value of the `@INC` array at the bottom of the `perl-status` "Loaded Modules" page.

Alternatives to the Startup File

Some of the work that you do in the `mod_perl` startup file can be accomplished directly in `httpd.conf`. You can add directories to Perl's search path using a `PerlSetEnv` directive in `httpd.conf` to set the `PERL5LIB` variable. The value can be a single directory pathname or a list of colon-separated pathnames:

```
PerlSetEnv PERL5LIB /usr/local/apache/lib/perl:/var/lib/perl
```

However, this is less efficient than using the startup file because it adds a little overhead for each script run by `mod_perl`. When you set the path in the startup file, it's done once and affects all scripts automatically.

You can preload Perl modules using the `PerlModule` directive. This is equivalent to loading the modules in the startup file. One or more modules can be named:

```
PerlModule CGI DBI DBD::mysql
```

Writing *mod_perl* Scripts

In general, writing CGI scripts to run under `mod_perl` doesn't differ much from writing them for execution under a standalone Perl process. Therefore, if you create a standalone script in the `cgi-bin` directory, you often can expect that moving it to the `cgi-perl` directory won't cause problems, the script will just run faster. The `perl-test.pl` script we used earlier to test the `mod_perl` configuration was an example of this: It functioned properly whether run from `cgi-bin` or from `cgi-perl`. You can try this with other scripts as well. For example, you can move the scripts developed in Chapter 2 from `cgi-bin` to `cgi-perl` to see whether they work properly.

That's not to say that there are never any problems using CGI scripts under `mod_perl`. This section describes things to guard against so your scripts don't cause problems for themselves, other scripts, or your Web server. It discusses the issues you should be aware of for the applications in this book. You might trip over others in your own scripts, however; so for additional information, check the `mod_perl_to_cgi` and `mod_perl_traps` documents listed in Appendix B.

Script-Writing Shortcuts

When you write scripts for `mod_perl`, you can use certain shortcuts as compared to writing them for standalone execution:

- A `mod_perl` script must be executable, just like its standalone counterpart, but you don't need to include the initial `#!` line that specifies the pathname to the Perl interpreter.
- For any directory added to the Perl search path with a `use lib` statement in the startup file, you don't need to add it in any of your scripts.

Of course, if you take advantage of these shortcuts, you'll need to add the `#!` and `use lib` lines back in if you decide later to use your scripts as standalone CGI programs (for example, to use them on a host that supports only that execution mode). In this book, scripts written for `mod_perl` will begin with the `#!` line and will include any necessary `use lib` line, even though they don't strictly need them. That way you'll more easily be able to use them even if you don't install `mod_perl`, by moving them to the `cgi-bin` directory instead.

Diagnostic Output Generation

It's often useful to tell Perl to generate error messages that help you determine that your scripts have problems and what to do about it. You may find the following techniques useful for getting diagnostic information and debugging your scripts:

- Use the `-w` option on the `#!` line at the beginning of your scripts to tell Perl to emit warnings for questionable constructs:

    ```
    #! /usr/bin/perl -w
    ```

    `mod_perl` doesn't use the pathname, but it will notice the `-w` option and turn on warning mode.

- Include a use diagnostics line to tell Perl to print suggestions about the causes of problems:

  ```
  use diagnostics;
  ```

- Install the Apache::DBdebugger module and preload it in the mod_perl startup file. This module isn't included with Apache or mod_perl by default, but you can get it from http://cpan.perl.org/.

Output resulting from these techniques will go to the Apache error log, so you'll need to look there for diagnostic messages. Naturally, you should try to write your scripts to eliminate warnings if possible. If you use the -w option on the #! line, the error log can become useless if you have so many warnings being produced that it becomes difficult to tell what's important and what isn't. Try to modify your scripts to make the warnings go away.

Script Environment Contamination

With a standalone script, the environment provided by the external Perl process that executes the script goes away when the script terminates. The processes are independent and don't affect each other. With mod_perl, this is not true, because a given httpd process can run several scripts over the course of its lifetime, and there is state information in the Perl interpreter that persists from request to request. This is essential behavior for implementing some kinds of services such as persistent database connections, but it can lead to problems as well. If you're sloppy in your programming, one script can pollute the environment for subsequent scripts. Here's a simple example:

```
#! /usr/bin/perl -w
print "Content-Type: text/html\n\n";
print $x++, "\n";
```

Put this script in your cgi-bin directory as increment.pl, and then request it several times in quick succession. You'll see the value 0 in your browser window each time. Then move it to cgi-perl and request it from there several more times. Now you'll see a series of numbers that is "sort of" random but generally increasing. (The order depends on the order in which the httpd children are selected to process your requests.) The reason this occurs is that $x is a global variable but is never initialized. The first time any given child executes increment.pl, the value of $x is 0. The next time, the script inherits the previous value and increments that.

Don't use variables as global variables without declaring them as such or without initializing them first. The increment.pl script doesn't follow this principle, so it needs some modification to be a better citizen. Fortunately, that's easy to do. Just declare $x to be global explicitly with use vars, and then initialize it:

```
#! /usr/bin/perl -w
use strict;
use vars qw($x);
$x = 0;
```

```
print "Content-Type: text/html\n\n";
print $x++, "\n";
```

The use strict line isn't actually required to make the script yield consistent results (0 each time it's invoked); it's just good programming practice to use it.

When you initialize a variable, make sure it's initialized every time your script executes. The following bit of code sets $x to 1, but only if some_test() succeeds:

```
use vars qw($x);
$x = 1 if some_test ();
```

The problem is that $x remains set to 1 even if some_test() fails on every subsequent invocation of the script. Suppose what some_test() does is check a user-supplied password and return true if the password is okay. After $x gets set, it remains set, even if the next person to come along provides an incorrect password! The following code handles the situation properly:

```
use vars qw($x);
$x = 0;
$x = 1 if some_test ();
```

So does this:

```
use vars qw($x);
$x = some_test () ? 1 : 0;
```

The basic principle here is that you don't want to start making decisions based on variable values until you know they've been initialized properly.

When you're trying to determine the cause of problems due to shared script environments, you may find it useful to stop Apache and restart it using httpd -X. The -X option tells Apache to run as a single process rather than in the usual parent-children configuration. That makes shared-environment problems show up more quickly. (You should do this only on a development server, not a production server.)

Variable Scope Effects

mod_perl runs scripts by wrapping them inside a function (one reason for this is that it can assign each script its own unique namespace). This can cause problems due to variable scope. Here is a simple program that illustrates the effect:

```
#! /usr/bin/perl -w
print "Content-Type: text/html\n\n";
my $x = 0;
f ();
exit (0);

sub f
{
    print $x++, "\n";
}
```

If you request this script several times from your browser, the script doesn't print 0 each time as you would expect. Instead, the values increase. This occurs even though the variable $x is explicitly initialized to 0. A clue that something is wrong here will be found in the Apache error log:

```
Variable "$x" will not stay shared at line 5.
```

(The line number is off due to the script being executed inside the wrapper function.) The difficulty here is that when the script is run inside a wrapper by mod_perl, your entire script becomes a single function, and any functions in the script become inner subroutines. That means f() is an inner subroutine that references a lexically scoped my() variable belonging to its parent subroutine and that isn't passed to it as an argument. As a result, the inner subroutine sees $x with the correct value the first time the script runs. After that, the variable becomes unshared and the inner subroutine continues to use its own unshared value of $x on subsequent invocations. This issue is discussed in more detail in the mod_perl Guide, along with various solutions to the problem. One way to avoid the difficulty is to change the declaration of $x to be global:

```perl
#! /usr/bin/perl -w
print "Content-Type: text/html\n\n";
use vars qw($x);
$x = 0;
f ();
exit (0);

sub f
{
    print $x++, "\n";
}
```

You can declare a variable using my if you want to, *as long as* you pass it as an argument to any subroutine that needs it, instead of accessing it directly from the subroutine as a global variable. (That's actually the way I prefer to write scripts, which is why you won't see many instances of use vars in this book.) If you want to modify the variable inside the subroutine, pass it by reference:

```perl
#! /usr/bin/perl -w
print "Content-type: text/html\n\n";
my $x = 0;
f (\$x);
exit (0);

sub f
{
my $x_ref = shift;

    print ++${$x_ref}, "\n";
}
```

Code Caching Effects

Recall that mod_perl caches compiled scripts. This helps it run scripts faster, but what happens if you change a script? Does mod_perl continue to execute the cached version? Nope. Apache::Registry keeps track of the scripts that it has run and checks the modification date of the original file when a script is requested again. If the date has changed, it recompiles the script and the new version is used instead. You can verify this for yourself. Request a script, and then change it and click the Reload button in your browser. You should see the changed output. Then change the script back and click Reload again. You should see the original output. That's what you expect and want to happen.[2]

However, this behavior doesn't apply to modules pulled into your script via use or require. If you change those files, the changes won't be noticed until you restart the server. Another workaround for this problem is to use the Apache::StatINC module, which forces Apache to check the last modification time even for modules referenced from use or require statements. This is a technique best used on a development server, because it slows down Apache. Run perldoc Apache::StatINC from the command line for more information.

Script caching also is responsible for another mysterious problem. If you use or require a library file, that file's code is pulled in to your script, compiled, and cached, as usual. If the file doesn't contain a package declaration to specify a namespace, however, the code goes into your script's own namespace. This is main when you run scripts in standalone mode, but scripts run in their own unique namespace under mod_perl. If your script is called script.pl, for example, the namespace might be &Apache::ROOT::cgi_2dperl::script_2epl. Normally, having unique namespaces per script is a good thing, because it helps keep scripts that are run under a given httpd child from colliding with each other in the main namespace. But it causes a problem for unpackaged library code. Here's why: Suppose you run your script script.pl that uses a library file MyLib.pm containing a function lib_func(). script.pl will execute properly. Now suppose you have a second script, script2.pl, that wants to use MyLib.pm, too. When the second script executes, mod_perl sees the use or require line for the library file, notices that the file has already been processed and cached, and doesn't bother to recompile it. Then when script2.pl calls lib_func() from the library file, an error occurs:

```
[error] Undefined subroutine
&Apache::ROOT::cgi_2dperl::script2_2epl::lib_func called
```

---

2. If you're watching the Apache error log while you make changes to a script, you'll probably notice messages that say subroutine *xxx* redefined, where *xxx* is some function in the script. You can make these go away by restarting Apache.

This happens because functions in the library file have been compiled, but they're in the namespace for `script.pl`, not `script2.pl`. To fix this problem, make sure the library file includes a `package` declaration, and then invoke its functions using the `package` identifier. `MyLib.pm` can be written like this:

```
package MyLib;

sub lib_func
{
    ...
}
...
```

After making that change, your scripts should invoke `MyLib::lib_func()` rather than `lib_func()`.

Persistent Database Connections

Normally, scripts that use MySQL open a connection to the MySQL server, access the database, and close the connection. Such connections are non-persistent. You can use persistent database connections instead if you want to share connections among database scripts and minimize connection setup overhead. However, you don't actually make any changes to your scripts to do this. Instead, preload the `Apache::DBI`module from your `mod_perl` startup file:

```
use Apache::DBI ();
```

Alternatively, use a `PerlModule` directive in `httpd.conf`:

```
PerlModule Apache::DBI
```

(In either case, if you preload both `Apache::DBI` and DBI, you should load `Apache::DBI` first.) After you restart Apache to make the change take effect, each child `httpd` process will manage a pool of open connections to the MySQL server. This happens transparently to your scripts. DBI's `disconnect()` method is overridden to become a no-op, and the `connect()` method is overridden with one that checks whether the database you're connecting to is already open. If so, the connection is reused. For more information, run `perldoc Apache::DBI` from the command line.

Running Scripts with Special Privileges

You can invoke a standalone Perl script under Apache's suEXEC mechanism to run them under a particular user ID if the script needs higher security or greater privileges. This isn't possible with `mod_perl` scripts because they run within Apache, and Apache can't change its own user ID (unless you run it as `root`, which is a huge security risk). A workaround for this in some cases is to run a helper application using suEXEC for that part of your script's task that requires special privileges. Or, if your script doesn't actually require `mod_perl`, put it in the `cgi-bin` directory and launch it with suEXEC as a standalone script.

You should now be able to install mod_perl if you want to. And by bearing in mind the discussion just presented concerning mod_perl-related issues to watch out for, you should be able to write scripts that run properly whether or not they run under mod_perl. Of course, none of the programs shown in this chapter really do much of anything; they are intended only to illustrate various aspects of mod_perl's behavior. In the next chapter we'll discuss the design of form-based scripts, an extremely common type of Web application that enables you to accomplish real work.

4

Generating and Processing Forms

I N CHAPTER 2, "GETTING CONNECTED—PUTTING YOUR DATABASE on the Web,"
we constructed a simple form-based application (the To-Do list manager) where we
discussed topics related to form generation and processing, as we needed them. This
chapter takes a more systematic approach. It lays out the structure of forms, describes
the various kinds of elements you can use within forms, and discusses general techniques for extracting the contents of forms after they've been submitted by users. In
Chapter 5, "Writing Form-Based Applications," we'll use the material presented here
to build several different kinds of applications.

This chapter is the most "MySQL-less" of the book; nevertheless, everything
discussed here is intended for the sole purpose of helping you use MySQL more
effectively. Forms have many uses in a database context:

- The data-entry capability afforded by forms enables you to collect commentary.
  Basic versions of this type of application just solicit information, such as a bare-
  bones guestbook that lets people tell you they visited your site. More elaborate
  versions involve taking some action based on the information submitted. An
  application that provides a form for customer complaints generates database
  records that must each be given attention for resolution of the issues raised. Or
  you might gather information as a means of constructing a searchable database
  for other people to use. If you have an application that collects and stores restaurant reviews, for example, you can provide a search interface so that visitors can
  look for information about a given restaurant to see how customers rate it.

- Forms provide a natural interface for registration applications. You can use them to register conference attendees, to allow people to apply for accounts on an online auction site, to submit loan or credit card requests, and so forth. All of these generate records that you can store in your database.

- "Sign up for more information" forms enable people to submit an address that you store and use later to send news or notifications when information on a topic of interest becomes available. This includes all kinds of things, such as mailing lists, daily weather reports, sports news, real-estate listings, and political campaign updates.

- You can provide record-editing capabilities allowing table contents to be modified. Suppose you have an organization that maintains membership records. A form-based interface can be used to enable members to update their personal information: Your application would retrieve the appropriate membership record from the database and use its contents to initialize an editing form so that the member can modify the information.

- Forms make it easy to implement polling and voting applications where you ask users to choose from a set of alternatives. Many such applications also offer access to the most recent up-to-the-minute results. The database enables you to store vote tallies and retrieve them to display current results.

- Questionnaires and surveys map well onto forms, which provide a structured environment for presenting lists of questions and capturing responses. In some ways, a questionnaire is just a generalization of a poll from a single question to multiple questions. However, questionnaires often contain items that allow free text entry rather than just presenting a fixed set of alternatives.

- Online ordering scenarios involve searching and selecting, two activities that typically are form based.

- Forms enable users to specify actions that you perform on their behalf. For an auction site, you can let people submit profiles for items they're interested in, and then notify them when such items come up to bid. If you're out of stock on an item that a customer wants to buy, offer to let the customer know when the item becomes available and provide a form to collect an address or telephone number by which to contact the customer. You can collect specifications of stock market conditions that should generate email alerts ("the price of Acme Birdseed, Inc. has dropped below $14 a share"). An application that enables users to construct greeting cards generates email to card recipients, and later enables those recipients to retrieve cards that have been designed for them.

- Search engines typically operate using a form-based front end that enables users to enter search parameters to describe what they want to see so that you can run searches for them.

You can probably come up with many other examples. Just think of all the paper forms you deal with in daily life, and consider how they might be handled via electronic submission and processing.

The preceding examples involve collecting information from the user and either storing it in the database or using it to construct a query to search for information already in the database. They illustrate the potential for treating your Web site as a front end that enables you to use your database more effectively. But information flows the other way, too. You can use your database to help you create your Web site. For example, you can take information from the database to automate certain aspects of form construction. If you associate a set of radio buttons in a form with the possible values of an ENUM column in a table, you can generate the button set automatically by reading the column definition directly from the table structure to see what the legal values are. You don't need to hardwire the possible choices into your script. You also can use table information to help automate form-input validation. (A simple example: If a form field corresponds to a table column that has an integer type, you know that values entered into the field must contain numeric values.) You can use this kind of information to reduce the amount of form-related programming you do. You may even decide to use tables to store entire form descriptions. If you do this, you can create forms completely automatically, an approach that also increases the likelihood that you can perform automated validation of responses without special-purpose programming. We'll take a look at some of these techniques in Chapter 6, "Automating the Form-Handling Process."

Form Anatomy

Forms simplify the process of collecting information by offering a structured mechanism for visitors to interact with your site. To a limited extent, you can solicit information from users by having them make choices from lists of hyperlinks, but that quickly turns into the Web equivalent of automated telephone answering-system menus. Forms are more effective.

For structured types of information, such as a list of choices, forms enable you to spell out the options explicitly for the user and provide a convenient way for the user to make a selection. Form elements such as check boxes, radio buttons, pop-up menus, and scrolling lists make it easy to display lists or sets such as colors, sizes, age or salary ranges, number of people per household, state names, and so forth. That way users don't have to type so much; they just select the proper item.

For situations where it won't do to use elements that provide only prespecified options, you can allow users to enter free text. If you're providing a form through which customers request product information, you can include a text field so that they can say exactly what they want to know. In a help desk application, you must let clients describe what problem they're having. If you're an elected official and you provide your constituents with a feedback form, you must let them express their concerns. You also can use text input in conjunction with structured elements such as a set of radio buttons. (Label the last button "Other" and put a text box next to it to handle cases not covered by the other buttons in the set.)

This section provides a description of the elements that make up forms. It discusses both the HTML syntax for these elements and the CGI.pm calls that generate that HTML for you so that you don't have to write it out yourself. For example, a submit button named `choice` can be written in HTML like this:

```
<input type="submit" name="choice" value="Done">
```

The button also can be generated by printing the result of a call to the CGI.pm `submit()` function:

```
print submit (-name => "choice", -value => "Done");
```

CGI.pm enables you to specify function parameters in named fashion, using *-paramname* => *paramvalue* format. This format provides a great deal of flexibility, because you can omit optional parameters, and you can specify parameters in any order.

Each CGI.pm function returns a string value, which you can print, assign to a variable, pass to a function, and so forth. The examples in this chapter use `print` statements. In later chapters, we'll see scripts that construct forms in memory and pass the resulting strings around before printing them.

The discussion here is descriptive rather than exhaustive—that is, I describe typical use of the CGI.pm calls, not every possible parameter to every possible call. For more comprehensive background on form syntax, consult a good HTML reference. For information about CGI.pm in particular, consult Lincoln Stein's *Official Guide to Programming with CGI.pm* or the online CGI.pm documentation. Appendix B, "References and Further Reading," lists these and other suggested sources. Also, you can read the installed CGI.pm documentation by running the following command:

```
% perldoc CGI
```

Beginning and Ending a Form

Forms begin and end with <form> and </form> tags, which are produced by calling `start_form()` and `end_form()`. A typical way to generate a form is as follows:

```
print start_form (-action => url ());
# ... generate form elements ...
print end_form ();
```

`start_form()` takes several optional parameters—`action`, `method`, and `enctype`—that determine the attributes written into the <form> tag and that affect how the form is processed. The `action` parameter indicates the action that the Web server should perform when the user submits the form to send its contents back to the server. Normally this is the URL of the script that processes the form's contents. Often this URL is that of the script that generated the form in the first place; it's idiomatic in CGI.pm programming for a script both to generate a form and to process the contents of the form when the user submits it. This technique is carried out using two principles:

- When a script generates the form, it specifies itself as the form's action so that it is reinvoked when the user submits the form.

- The script detects whether it is being invoked for the first or subsequent time by examining the information in the CGI environment. The initial invocation will find no form information present in the environment; subsequent invocations will find the contents of a submitted form.

The use of self-referencing scripts may be idiomatic but it's not required; there is no rule that a form must be generated and processed by the same script. A script can generate a form with an action that names a different script—or even an action that is not a script at all. For example, the `action` parameter might be something like `mailto:address` if you want the form contents to be encoded and sent as an email message to the given address.

If you specify no `action` parameter, the default is `self_url()`, which expands to the URL that was sent by the browser to invoke your script in the first place. If that URL included any parameters (a '?' after the script name, followed by *name=value* pairs), `self_url()` includes those parameters as well. If you want just the path of the script itself without any parameters, use `url()` instead. Generally, when you use a script to generate a form as well as to process it, it's best not to specify the `action` parameter by writing the script's URL literally into the script. By using `self_url()` or `url()` instead, CGI.pm determines the URL when the script runs. That way, your script will always generate the proper self-referencing `action` value even if you rename or move your script, something that is not true if you write the URL literally.

The `method` parameter controls how form contents are transmitted back to the Web server when the user submits the form. Its value can be `POST` or `GET`. With `POST`, the contents are sent in the body of the request, separate from the URL. With `GET`, the form contents are appended to the end of the URL sent back to the Web server. `GET` involves some risk of hitting URL length limitations and possible silent truncation, so generally `POST` is a better choice. Scripts in this book use `POST`, which is also the default if you specify no method parameter.

`enctype` controls how form contents are encoded for transmission. If you don't specify an encoding method, the default is `application/x-www-form-urlencoded`. This suffices for most situations, with one important exception: If your form includes a file upload field, you should use `multipart/form-data` instead or files will not upload properly. These encoding type values are available as the constants `$CGI::URL_ENCODED` and `$CGI::MULTIPART`. The default for `start_form()` is `$CGI::URL_ENCODED`; if you want to generate a multipart form, you can call `start_multipart_form()` instead. It accepts the same arguments as `start_form()`, but uses a default encoding type of

$CGI::MULTIPART. This means that in practice you need never specify an encoding explicitly—just call the function that defaults to the type of encoding you want.

Form Components

Forms generally consist primarily of special elements that enable the user to interact with the form, such as buttons, lists, or text-input fields. These elements often are interspersed with static text or HTML markup. For example, it's often useful to display a text caption such as "Your name:" next to an input field to indicate what should be entered into the field. HTML markup can be used to control layout of the form elements; techniques range from inserting <br> tags to force line breaks between elements to placing elements within an HTML table to achieve a particular spatial configuration.

Interactive form elements can be grouped into several categories:

- Form-submission elements
- Text-input elements
- File-upload elements
- Hidden field elements
- Multiple-choice elements

The following sections discuss the particular HTML structure of these element types and show how to generate them using CGI.pm functions, but most elements have several things in common. Every form element begins with some tag, which includes one or more attributes, each written in *attrname=attrvalue* format. The most common attributes are name and value. These identify the element and specify its default value (that is, the value it has when the form is displayed initially). For example, a text-input field named telephone with initial contents of 555-1212 might be written like this:

```
<input type="text" name="telephone" value="555-1212">
```

When you generate a form element by calling a CGI.pm function, it's important to specify the name and value attributes by passing like-named parameters to the function. For example, the preceding <input> tag would be produced by calling textfield() like this:[1]

```
print textfield (-name => "telephone", -value => "555-1212");
```

---

1. Actually, if you examine the output of the print statement, you'll see that it looks like this if you have CGI.pm 2.69 or higher:

```
<input type="text" name="telephone" value="555-1212" />
```

Why the extra slash at the end of the tag? That's an XHTML convention. XHTML is a transition step between HTML and XML; the slash is evidence of the current trend toward an

continues

Another common parameter to CGI.pm functions is `override`. This doesn't correspond to an attribute of the HTML generated by CGI.pm. Rather, it's used to control CGI.pm's "sticky" form behavior, which works as follows: When you generate a form element, CGI.pm looks for the element's value in two places. One is the `value` parameter in the function call. The other is the CGI environment. (The environment won't have any value for the element when your script is invoked initially, but it will when the user fills in the element and submits the form.) By default, any value present in the CGI environment takes precedence, *even if* you include a `value` parameter in the function call that generates the element. CGI.pm does this to make it easier for an application to generate a form that contains whatever values the user submitted in the previous form. This is useful behavior, for example, if a user fills in some but not all of the required fields in a form: You can print an error message and redisplay the form with all the information the user did provide. For situations in which this sticky behavior is undesirable, you can specify `-override => 1` in the parameter list of the element-generating call to force CGI.pm to ignore the CGI environment and use the `value` parameter for the element's value.

To examine the environment yourself, call CGI.pm's `param()` function. Pass it the name of a field, and it returns the value of that field:

```
$val = param ("telephone");
```

This is how a script finds out what information is present in a form that has been submitted. We'll cover `param()` in more detail in the later section "Recovering Values of Form Elements."

Form Submission Elements

Most forms provide a button for sending the contents of the form to the Web server. Typically this button is labeled Submit, Send, Continue, or something similar. These buttons are created using `<input>` tags that have a `type` attribute of `submit`. To present a submission button named `choice` and labeled `Done`, for instance, the HTML looks like this:

```
<input type="submit" name="choice" value="Done">
```

XML-enabled Web. XML is a markup language that has some similarities to HTML, but has stricter rules. One of these rules is that every opening tag `<xxx>` must have a corresponding closing tag `</xxx>`. If there is no text between the opening and closing tags, a single-tag shortcut of `<xxx />` is allowed to serve as both the opening and closing tag. XHTML shares the property with XML that closing tags are required, and CGI.pm produces XHTML-compliant tags by default, which is why you get the extra slash. If you want to generate plain HTML tags, specify `-no_xhtml` in your `use CGI` statement. For example:

```
use CGI qw(-no_xhtml :standard);
```

The label displayed in the button is controlled by the `value` attribute; if there is no such attribute, the default label is the button's name. The label also becomes the element's value when the user selects the button. To generate a form-submission button using CGI.pm, call the `submit()` function:

```
print submit (-name => "choice", -value => "Done");
```

Another kind of button is a reset button, which causes form elements to revert to the values they had when the browser first displayed the form. It can be written like this:

```
<input type="reset" value="Reset Form">
```

The corresponding CGI.pm call is `reset()`, which takes a single argument indicating the text to be displayed in the button:

```
print reset ("Reset Form");
```

You do not have to specify an element name for reset buttons; if a user selects such a button, the reset action is handled entirely by the browser without transmitting anything to the Web server.

To display an image that acts as a form-submission button (thus making the image "clickable"), use an `<input>` tag that specifies the image location, such as the following one:

```
<input type="image" name="my_img" src="/images/my_img.gif" attributes...>
```

The attributes for an image button should include at least `name` to identify the button and `src` to specify the image URL. Another useful attribute is `alt`, which provides text for the browser to display if the image cannot be found or if the user has image loading turned off. (If you're thinking that `src` and `alt` seem familiar, you're right. They are attributes commonly used in `<img>` tags for displaying images. You can also include other `<img>` tag attributes in an image button, such as `height`, `width`, or `align`.) To generate an image button using CGI.pm, call `image_button()`:

```
print image_button (-name => "my_img",
                     -src => "/images/my_img.gif",
                     -alt => "[click me to submit]");
```

When a user selects an image button, the x and y coordinates of the image are sent to the Web server and can be recovered using `param()`. For a button name of `my_img`, the parameter names will be `my_img.x` and `my_img.y`. These coordinates enable you to respond to button clicks differently depending on where they occur (if you want to).

> **Should You Include a Form–Submission Element?**
>
> Sometimes you don't need to include a submission button. Browsers often will submit a form if you just press the Return or Enter key. Generally, however, it's less confusing to users if there is an explicit submission element that they can select. Another problem is that if you have multiple forms in a page, Return or Enter may do nothing—or may even submit the wrong form! Also, be cautious about having multiple forms that share submission element names. (For example, you might have a button named submit in each form.) You need some way to determine which form was submitted. One way to do so is to make sure each button has a unique label. Another is to include a hidden field in each form, each having the same name but a unique value. The value of this field tells you which form was submitted.

Text-Input Elements

Text fields enable users to enter arbitrary text. They're useful for capturing input when you have no reasonable means of providing a fixed set of alternatives. If a user is ordering a shirt, you can provide pop-up menus listing all the sizes and colors in which the shirt is available. If you want to know the user's name or telephone number, however, a pop up is no good; you must provide a text field that enables the user to enter the correct value.

Text fields come in three types: single-line fields, password fields, and multiple-line fields. These are written using HTML as follows:

```
<input type="text" attributes ...>
<input type="password" attributes ...>
<textarea attributes...>...</textarea>
```

<input> elements of the text and password types both are single-line fields, so the following remarks about text fields apply also to password fields. The only difference between them is that when you type into a password field, the browser displays bullets or asterisks, not the characters you're really typing.

Text fields take the usual name and value attributes. Any value given becomes the text displayed in the element as its initial contents; otherwise, it comes up blank. You can also specify a size attribute to control the length of the field (in characters), and a maxlength attribute to limit the number of characters that a user can enter into the field. For example, you might specify a maxlength value of 2 for a field in which you want users to enter a two-character state abbreviation:

```
<input type="text" name="state" size="2" maxlength="2">
```

You might also use maxlength if you're paranoid that some jerk will try to paste a 10MB core dump file into your form and submit it to see whether your Web server crashes. Unfortunately, anyone who wants to do that probably knows how to subvert your form to remove the maxlength parameter. So you should consider maxlength as advisory only, and applicable primarily to well-behaved users.

To produce a multiple-line text-input field, use <textarea>. You must also supply a closing </textarea> tag; any text between the tags displays as the field's initial contents. (This differs from the way you specify the initial value for other elements using a value attribute.) Other useful <textarea> attributes besides name are rows and cols to indicate the size of the field (both are required), and wrap to control word-wrap behavior. Allowable wrap values are off (no word wrapping), virtual (the browser performs word wrap but does not transmit line endings), and physical (the browser displays and transmits text exactly as it was typed by the user). soft and hard are synonyms for virtual and physical.

To generate text-input elements using CGI.pm calls, use the textfield(), password_field(), and textarea() functions. Here are some examples:

```
print textfield (-name => "age",
                     -size => 10,
                     -maxlength => 10);
print password_field (-name => "password");
print textarea (-name => "comment",
                -value => "ENTER COMMENT HERE",
                -rows => 5,
                -cols => 80,
                -wrap => "virtual");
```

File-Upload Elements

To enable a user to select a file and upload it to the Web server when the form is submitted, use a file-upload field:

```
<input type="file" attributes...>
```

The browser will display a text-input field and a Browse button for browsing the local client's file system. Allowable attributes are name, size, and maxlength (with the same meaning as for single-line text input fields). The corresponding CGI.pm call is filefield(), which is just like textfield() except that no value parameter is accepted. (CGI.pm does this to discourage you from doing the naughty thing of initializing the field to the name of a file likely to contain sensitive information in hopes that the user will upload it accidentally.)

```
print filefield (-name => "upload", -size => 60);
```

When you include a file-upload element in a form, you must use an encoding type of $CGI::MULTIPART. The easiest way to do this is to generate the form by calling start_multipart_form() rather than start_form().

There are security dangers inherent to the use of file-upload fields. These dangers and some precautions you can observe to minimize them are discussed in Chapter 9, "Security and Privacy Issues."

Hidden Field Elements

Hidden fields enable you to specify form elements that have a name and value and that are returned to the Web server when the user submits the form, but that are not displayed to the user. The HTML for a hidden field looks like this:

```
<input type="hidden" attributes...>
```

A hidden field should have at least a `name` attribute so that you can identify it to obtain its value when the form is processed. Normally, you'll also include a `value` attribute, although it's possible for the value to be empty and still be meaningful.

To generate a hidden field using CGI.pm, call the `hidden()` function:

```
print hidden (-name => "id", -value => "34");
```

You can assign multiple values to a hidden field; just specify the `value` parameter as a reference to an array:

```
print hidden (-name => "rgb", -value => ["red", "green", "blue"]);
```

Alternatively:

```
@values = ("red", "green", "blue");
print hidden (-name => "rgb", -value => \@values);
```

Hidden fields are useful for passing information back and forth between your script and the client's browser because they allow one invocation of your script to communicate with the next. This enables you to tie together multiple pages. For example, we used this technique for the item-editing feature of the To-Do list manager in Chapter 2 to allow the application to track the ID of the item being edited. One invocation of the script generates the page with the form containing the item to be edited. The next invocation receives the item ID along with the item contents and uses the ID to figure out which record to update in the `todo` table.

Regardless of how useful hidden fields are, you shouldn't be lulled into supposing that they provide the slightest measure of security. The values are hidden only with respect to the browser's display window. The user can expose any hidden field values easily using the browser's View Source command to examine the raw HTML for your form. That's not to say you should never use hidden fields, just that you shouldn't use them for applications where security is paramount. See Chapter 9 for more discussion on how hidden fields can be exploited by hackers and for alternatives that provide better security.

Multiple-Choice Elements

Multiple-choice elements provide a group or list consisting of a fixed set of alternatives from which you can choose. Some of these are single-pick elements enabling you to select only one item from the group, such as radio button sets, pop-up menus, and scrolling lists. Others elements are multiple-pick, enabling you to select any or all (or perhaps even none) of the available choices. Multiple-pick elements include check box sets and scrolling lists. (Scrolling lists are listed for both categories because you can use them either way, to allow a single choice or multiple choices.)

Radio buttons and check boxes usually are implemented using groups consisting of multiple elements. The following HTML illustrates how to write a two-element radio button group and a three-element check box group:

```
<input type="radio" name="yesno" value="yes">Yes!
<input type="radio" name="yesno" value="no" checked>No!

<input type="checkbox" name="accessories" value="floppy">Floppy disk drive
<input type="checkbox" name="accessories" value="sound">Sound card
<input type="checkbox" name="accessories" value="pad">Mouse pad
```

For radio buttons, all elements within the group must have the same name. Otherwise, browsers will treat them as belonging to different groups and will enable the user to select more than one of the buttons. However, each button within a group should have a unique value so that you can distinguish which one the user selected. When the form is submitted, the value of the selected button is returned to the Web server. For the yesno group just shown, this value will be either yes or no. You can use the checked attribute to mark a button as the one to be selected by default when the browser first displays the form. (In the preceding example, the No! item is the default.)

For checkbox groups, it's not strictly necessary that you give all boxes within a group the same name, but it is more convenient. If you give each one a different name, you'll have to make several tests when the form is submitted to determine which ones are turned on. If you give all check boxes in a group the same name, CGI.pm can return to you in a single operation the values of all those that are selected. To obtain an array containing the values of all selected check boxes in the preceding accessories check box list, call param() in an array context like this:

```
@accessories = param ("accessories");
```

The default value for a check box if you don't specify one is on; clearly you should give each check box in a group a unique value if you expect to be able to tell them apart. Otherwise, you'll be left in the position of trying to discern which on value came from which check box—an impossible task.

To generate a radio button set with CGI.pm, use radio_group():

```
print radio_group (-name => "yesno",
                   -values => ["yes", "no"],
                   -labels => {"yes" => "Yes!", "no" => "No!"});
```

The name parameter is a single string; CGI.pm automatically assigns each button in the group the same name. values is a reference to an array that provides the values for successive buttons within the group. labels is a reference to a hash that maps button values onto the captions to be displayed with each button. (If you don't specify any labels, CGI.pm uses the values as the labels.) The `radio_button()` call just shown indicates the label hash directly in the parameter list. You can also set up the hash beforehand like this:

```
%yesno_labels = ("yes" => "Yes!", "no" => "No!");
print radio_group (-name => "yesno",
                   -values => ["yes", "no"],
                   -labels => \%yesno_labels);
```

By default, the first radio button in a group will be selected. (That is, CGI.pm adds the `checked` attribute to the HTML for that button.) To select a particular button explicitly, pass a `default` parameter that specifies the value of the appropriate button. This call selects the no button:

```
%yesno_labels = ("yes" => "Yes!", "no" => "No!");
print radio_group (-name => "yesno",
                   -values => ["yes", "no"],
                   -labels => \%yesno_labels,
                   -default => "no");
```

To prevent any button from becoming the default, pass a `default` parameter listing a value that doesn't appear in the `values` array. (The value must be non-empty; the empty string or `undef` do not suppress selection of a default button.) For example, you could select no default by writing the `default` parameter in the previous example as follows, because `[NO DEFAULT]` is not the value of any of the buttons:

```
-default => "[NO DEFAULT]"
```

Why might you not want a default button? One situation where this is useful is for conducting an online poll. If you present the form with one of the alternatives already selected, you might bias the results toward that choice.

Generating check boxes is similar to generating radio buttons, except that you call `checkbox_group()` rather than `radio_group()`:

```
%acc_labels = (
               "floppy" => "Floppy disk drive",
               "sound" => "Sound card",
               "pad" => "Mouse pad"
              );
print checkbox_group (-name => "accessories",
                      -values => ["floppy", "sound", "pad"],
                      -labels => \%acc_labels);
```

The `name`, `values`, and `labels` parameters are used the same way for `checkbox_group()` as for `radio_group()`, but the behavior for default buttons is different. Unlike radio button sets, where the first button is selected by default, no check box is turned on unless you specify explicitly that you want it on. Therefore, in the preceding example, none of the check boxes is selected by default. The next example causes the `sound` check box to be selected:

```
print checkbox_group (-name => "accessories",
                      -values => ["floppy", "sound", "pad"],
                      -labels => \%acc_labels,
                      -default => "sound");
```

To select multiple check boxes in a group, use the default parameter to pass a reference to an array of values. The following example selects both the floppy and pad buttons:

```
print checkbox_group (-name => "accessories",
                      -values => ["floppy", "sound", "pad"],
                      -labels => \%acc_labels,
                      -default => ["floppy", "pad"]);
```

Radio buttons always should be created in groups of two or more, but it sometimes makes sense for a check box group to consist of a single element. This is appropriate when you just want to present a yes/no or on/off item such as "Are you satisfied with our service?" or "With or without fries?" or "Check here if you wish to receive new product announcements." To generate a single check box, call checkbox():

```
print checkbox (-name => "happy",
                -value => "yes",
                -label => "Are you happy?",
                -checked => 1);
```

In this call, the checked parameter causes the check box to be selected by default. Omit that parameter to leave the check box turned off.

radio_group() and checkbox_group() both accept other parameters that you may find useful. The linebreak parameter forces a line break between buttons, causing them to stack vertically. Alternatively, you can place buttons within an HTML table to arrange them nicely. If either or both of the rows and cols parameters are specified, they are taken as table dimensions. (If you specify only one of these parameters, the other defaults to 1.) When you place radio buttons or check boxes within a table, several other options become useful. You can use rowheaders and colheaders to specify labels for rows and columns. Each parameter should be passed as a reference to an array containing the appropriate number of header strings. If the headers supply all the labeling that you need, you can suppress display of any labels next to the buttons themselves by passing the nolabels parameter.

Here's a full-blown example that places a set of radio buttons within a 3 × 2 table, complete with headings. It enables the user to select a combination of size and color. In this case, the headings provide sufficient labeling, so a nolabels parameter is included to turn the labels off.

```
print radio_group (-name => "size_color",
                   -values => # column 1 values, then column 2 values
                       ["small_black", "medium_black", "large_black",
                        "small_white", "medium_white", "large_white"],
                   -cols => 2,
                   -rows => 3,
```

```
                -colheaders => ["Black", "White"],
                -rowheaders => ["Small", "Medium", "Large"],
                -nolabels => 1);
```

Radio button and check box groups display a set of items using one form element per item. You can also create list elements, which present a set of items using a single form field. List elements include pop-up menus and scrolling lists. Both have an HTML syntax that uses `<select>` and `</select>` tags to enclose `<option>` tags that specify the items in the list. Here is an example pop-up menu that presents a list of animals from which to choose:

```
<select name="animal">
<option value="dog">dog</option>
<option value="cat">cat</option>
<option value="turkey">turkey</option>
<option value="snake">snake</option>
<option value="mouse">mouse</option>
</select>
```

To turn this into a scrolling list, add a `size` attribute to the `<select>` tag; the value indicates the number of rows to display in the list. (If the list contains more elements than that, the browser will display a scrollbar enabling users to move through the list.) If you want users to be able to select multiple items from the scrolling list, add the `multiple` attribute as well:

```
<select name="animal" size="3" multiple>
<option value="dog">dog</option>
<option value="cat">cat</option>
<option value="turkey">turkey</option>
<option value="snake">snake</option>
<option value="mouse">mouse</option>
</select>
```

To generate a pop-up menu using CGI.pm, call `popup_menu()`:

```
print popup_menu (-name => "animal",
                  -values => ["dog", "cat", "turkey", "snake", "mouse"]);
```

By default, the item values are used as the labels to be displayed to the user. (The labels are the strings between pairs of `<option>` and `</option>` tags.) To specify your own labels, pass a reference to a hash that maps values to labels. You can also specify which item is displayed as the default. (Normally, the first item is used.) The following call uses the same values as in the preceding example, but displays animal sounds as the captions and uses the `turkey` item as the default:

```
%animal_sounds = (
          "dog" => "Bow wow",
          "cat" => "Meow",
          "turkey" => "Gobble, gobble",
          "snake" => "Hissss",
          "mouse" => "Squeak"
     );
```

```
print popup_menu (-name => "animal",
                  -values => ["dog", "cat", "turkey", "snake", "mouse"],
                  -labels => \%animal_sounds,
                  -default => "turkey");
```

To generate a scrolling list, use `scrolling_list()`. This function takes the same parameters as `popup_menu()`, but also accepts `size` and `multiple` parameters, enabling you to set the display size and to indicate that the list allows multiple selections. In addition, you can specify multiple default values if you want more than one item to be selected when the list first displays. To do this, pass a `default` parameter as a reference to an array of values. The following example displays the animal sound list as a multiple-pick list with three items visible, with the `cat` and `mouse` items selected as the initial defaults:

```
print scrolling_list (-name => "animal",
                      -values => ["dog", "cat", "turkey", "snake", "mouse"],
                      -labels => \%animal_sounds,
                      -size => 3,
                      -multiple => 1,
                      -default => ["cat", "mouse"]);
```

Recovering Values of Form Elements

The preceding sections describe the CGI.pm functions you can call to generate form elements. Of course, creating a form for display is only part of the story. You'll want to process its contents after the user fills it in and submits it. The most convenient way to obtain this information is by calling CGI.pm's `param()` function, which examines the CGI environment and returns the values of form elements. `param()` can be invoked several ways:

- If you call `param()` with the name of a parameter as the argument, it returns the value of that parameter:

  ```
  $val = param ("telephone");
  ```

  If the element is not present in the environment, `param()` returns `undef`. (Note that a parameter may be present but have an empty value if the user left it empty. This means you'll often need to check not only that a value is defined but also that it has a non-empty value.)

- For elements that might have multiple values (such as a set of check boxes for which more than one box is checked), `param()` can return all the values. Just call it in an array context:

  ```
  @val = param ("animal");
  ```

- If an element has multiple values but you call `param()` in a scalar context, it returns just the first value. This is an important difference from many list-valued

Perl functions that return a count of the number of elements in the list if called in scalar context. If you want the count instead, you can do this:

```
@val = param ("animal");
$count = @val;
```

- To get a list containing the names of the parameters that are present in a submitted form, call `param()` with no argument:

```
@names = param ();
```

Be aware that you cannot assume that this list names all the elements in the form. Browsers may send back values only for non-empty elements. If you don't select any members of a group of check boxes, for example, the browser won't return any value for the group. This has a very important implication: You cannot deduce what fields a form contains from the submitted form contents; you must know in advance what they are. Suppose you call `param()` to get a list of field names and run a loop using the names so that you can verify their values. If one goal of your verification process is to test whether fields that are required to have a value do in fact have one, the loop won't help you achieve that goal, because the list of names might not contain all fields in the form.

You can also use `param()` to assign values to form elements:

```
param (-name => "comment", -value => "Enter your comment here");
param (-name => "animals", -value => ["chicken", "horse", "cow"]);
```

If you issue these calls and then generate a form that contains elements named `comment` and `animals`, those elements will be set to the assigned values (unless you specify `-override => 1` when you generate them, of course).

The ability to set form parameters this way can also be advantageous in situations where you want to process values in stages without creating global variables to store them. For example, you can call `param()` to extract a parameter into a temporary variable, perform some processing on it, and then call `param()` again to store the variable's resulting value back into the environment. When you need to refer to the value again later, extract it again. The electronic greeting card application developed in Chapter 5 is one example that demonstrates how to use this technique.

Displaying Text in Forms

Forms need not consist entirely of interactive elements that enable users to enter information and select items. You can display static text as well to enhance the appearance of your form. For example, the following code generates a form that includes a caption indicating what to enter into the text box. Without the caption, users would have no idea what to enter into the box:

```
print start_form (-action => url ()),
       p ("Please enter your name:"),
       textfield (-name => "name"),
       submit (-name => "choice", -value => "Submit"),
       end_form ();
```

When you mix text and form elements this way, be aware that CGI.pm performs HTML escaping for you, but only for calls specifically related to form generation. This means that for calls such as submit() or popup_menu(), you can pass strings containing characters that are special in HTML ('<', '>', '&', and '"'), and they will be converted to the proper HTML entities (<, >, &, and "). If these characters occur in arguments to other calls such as p() or td(), however, you must escape them yourself. You can do this by calling escapeHTML():

```
print start_form (-action => url ()),
       p (CGI::escapeHTML ("Please enter your first & last name:")),
       textfield (-name => "name"),
       submit (-name => "choice", -value => "Submit"),
       end_form ();
```

In this example, I wrote the function as CGI::escapeHTML() because its name is not imported into your script's namespace unless you do so explicitly. If you want to invoke escapeHTML() without referring to it through the CGI:: prefix, list its name in your use CGI statement. For example:

```
use CGI qw(:standard escapeHTML);
```

```
print start_form (-action => url ()),
       p (escapeHTML ("Please enter your first & last name:")),
       textfield (-name => "name"),
       submit (-name => "choice", -value => "Submit"),
       end_form ();
```

Including HTML Markup in Forms

Sometimes it's useful to include HTML markup in a form to affect the appearance or layout of text or form elements. The following example uses strong() to emphasize the form title, and an HTML table to organize element captions and fields so that they line up nicely. Without using a table, the left edges of the text fields won't line up and will as a result appear ragged.

```
print start_form (-action => url ()),
       p (strong (escapeHTML ("Please enter your first & last name:"))),
       table (
           Tr (
               td ("First name:"),
               td (textfield (-name => "first_name")),
           ),
           Tr (
               td ("Last name:"),
```

```
        td (textfield (-name => "last_name")),
    ),
  ),
  submit (-name => "choice", -value => "Submit"),
  end_form ();
```

In this example, it's important to call escapeHTML() to perform character escaping on the title before calling strong(). If you call strong() to emphasize the title first, and then pass the result to escapeHTML(), you'll end up escaping the special characters in the <strong> tags, with the result that those tags will display literally in the browser window!

URL Encoding

The <form> tag includes a URL as the value of the action attribute, and URLs have their own special characters, just like HTML text. If you want to use any of these characters literally, you'll need to perform some encoding to avoid generating a malformed URL. Suppose you're generating a form that is processed by a script, my script.pl, that has a space in its name:

```
print start_form (-action => "my script.pl");
```

When you submit the resulting form from your browser, you may get an error such as this:

```
The requested URL /cgi-perl/my was not found on this server.
```

Note that everything in the script name to the right of the space has been lost. This happens because literal spaces are not legal in URLs and must be encoded. However, URL values are encoded differently than regular HTML, because the set of special characters differs. (It includes not only a space, but ':', '/', '?', ';', and others.) To accomplish this, use the escape() function. It is similar to escapeHTML(), but performs URL encoding rather than HTML encoding:

```
print start_form (-action => escape ("my script.pl"));
```

That's a somewhat unusual case, because script names normally don't include spaces. However, URL encoding also applies to other values that are used as hyperlinks, such as the href attribute of <a> tags and the src attribute of <img> tags. These values often contain parameters, and it's quite common for parameter values to require encoding. Suppose you want to generate a link that automatically triggers a search for low-priced office chairs, using an item parameter to name the type of item and restriction to indicate any special search restrictions. You might try writing the link like this:

```
$url = "search.pl?item=office chair;restriction=price<100";
print a ({-href => $url}, "Search for economy office chairs");
```

That won't work: spaces cannot be used in URLs, and the '<' character is special. The resulting output looks like this:

```
<a href="search.pl?item=office chair;restriction=price&lt;100">
Search for economy office chairs</a>
```

The a() function performs HTML encoding on the href value, which takes care of the '<' character in the price<100 part. But that's not good enough because it leaves the space unchanged. To generate the URL properly, use escape():

```
$url = sprintf ("search.pl?item=%s;restriction=%s",
                          escape ("office chair"),
                          escape ("price<100"));
print a ({-href => $url}, "Search for economy office chairs");
```

escape() encodes each special character as a '%' followed by two hexadecimal digits representing the character's ASCII value. The resulting hyperlink looks like this:

```
<a href="search.pl?item=office%20chair;restriction=price%3C100">
Search for economy office chairs</a>
```

Note that you do *not* want to pass the entire URL to escape() because that turns off the special meaning of characters that should remain special. Don't use escape() this way:

```
$url = escape ("search.pl?item=office chair;restriction=price<100");
print a ({-href => $url}, "Search for economy office chairs");
```

That encodes the space and '<' characters. But it also encodes '?' and ';' characters that are supposed to indicate where the URL parameters are. The result is that those characters lose their special meaning:

```
<a href="search.pl%3Fitem%3Doffice%20chair%3Brestriction%3Dprice%3C100">
Search for economy office chairs</a>
```

Like escapeHTML(), escape() must be imported into your script's namespace with the useCGI statement if you want to refer to it without a leading CGI:: prefix:

```
use CGI qw(:standard escapeHTML escape);
```

URL Shortcuts

If you write a script that generates a page containing links to other pages, it's always correct to write the links using an absolute URL that includes the host name and full pathname to the page:

```
<a href="http://www.snake.net/cgi-perl/somescript.pl">A script</a>
<a href="http://www.snake.net/projects/index.html">Project index</a>
```

However, it's often possible to use shortcuts by providing relative URLs. If you're referring to a page that is located on the same server, you can omit the initial part of the URL up through the host name:

```
<a href="/cgi-perl/somescript.pl">A script</a>
<a href="/projects/index.html">Project index</a>
```

Furthermore, if you're referring to a page located in the same directory as your script, you can even leave out the pathname leading to the page. If two links are generated by a script installed in the cgi-perl directory, for example, the link for somescript.pl need not include the leading path because it's in the same directory. index.html is not located there, so we still need the path. Therefore, the minimal URLs we can use are as follows:

```
<a href="somescript.pl">A script</a>
<a href="/projects/index.html">Project index</a>
```

URL References and Mirror Hosts

Be careful when using URL shortcuts if some of your pages are mirrored (replicated) onto another host but contain links to pages that are not mirrored. You should refer to the non-mirrored pages using absolute URLs. If you use relative links, when someone visits the mirror host and clicks a link to a non-mirrored page, the browser will look for that page on the mirror host and an error will result.

A related issue concerning security occurs if you're mirroring a secure page that is accessed using absolute URLs beginning with the https prefix rather than http. If you reference embedded content (such as images) from a secure page, be sure that their URLs also begin with https or the referencing page will become insecure.

A Short Form Element Demonstration

Let's write a short script, elt_demo.pl, that shows how to use the material discussed in the earlier part of this chapter. The script is simple but does several things:

- It generates a form that includes an instance of each type of element we've discussed so far. You can select or fill in elements and then submit the form.

- The script is self-referential; it not only generates the form, it also processes it by causing itself to be invoked when you select the Submit button.

- elt_demo.pl examines its CGI environment using param() to determine whether information for a submitted form is present. If so, it extracts and displays that information to enable you to see how various types of fields are received by the Web server.

- The script demonstrates a few rudimentary techniques for processing information received from the form. If the single-line text field contains information, it characterizes the value. If a file was uploaded, it prints some information about the file such as its name and size.

- It shows how CGI.pm's sticky form behavior enables you to generate a form that is initialized using values from the previous form. The form includes a check box that enables you to turn this behavior on or off so you can see its effect.

You may find it useful to install the script from the book's source distribution so that you can play with it. Modify the parameter lists for the various form element–generating calls to see what effect your modifications have.

The elt_demo.pl script begins with a fairly predictable preamble:

```
#! /usr/bin/perl -w
# elt_demo.pl - form element demonstration

# This script shows how to generate form elements using CGI.pm calls.
# It also shows how to recover form element values from submitted forms.

use strict;
use CGI qw(:standard escapeHTML);

print header (),
    start_html (-title => "Form Element Demonstration", -bgcolor => "white");
```

The code that generates the form first determines whether to use sticky form behavior, so that we can tell whether to populate the form with its previous values. The default is "off," of course, because the value is controlled by a check box in the form itself, and the first time you invoke the script, no form elements have any values:

```
my $sticky = defined (param ("sticky"));
```

Next, we generate the form using a long print statement. The form begins with start_multipart_form() rather than start_form() because the form includes a file-upload field. Note how each call to generate an element within the form includes an override parameter that reflects the current state of the sticky check box. The exceptions to sticky behavior are: The sticky check box itself, which is deliberately always sticky so that it always retains its previous setting; the file upload field, because CGI.pm won't initialize it anyway; and the Submit and Reset buttons.

```
print start_multipart_form (-action => url ()),
        hidden (-name =>"hidden field",
                -value => "hidden value",
                -override => !$sticky),
        p ("Text field:"),
        textfield (-name =>"text field", -override => !$sticky),
        p ("Password field:"),
        password_field (-name =>"password field", -override => !$sticky),
        p ("Text area:"),
        textarea (-name =>"text area",
                    -rows => 3,
                    -cols => 60,
                    -wrap => "virtual",
                    -override => !$sticky),
```

```
# no override parameter here; CGI.pm wouldn't initialize it anyway
p ("File upload field:"),
filefield (-name =>"file field", -size => 60),
p ("Radio button group:"),
radio_group (-name => "radio group",
                -values => ["a", "b", "c"],
                -labels => {
                    "a" => "Button A",
                    "b" => "Button B",
                    "c" => "Button C"
                    },
                -override => !$sticky),
p ("Checkbox group:"),
checkbox_group (-name => "checkbox group",
                -values => ["a", "b", "c"],
                -labels => {
                    "a" => "Box A",
                    "b" => "Box B",
                    "c" => "Box C"
                    },
                -override => !$sticky),
p ("Popup menu:"),
popup_menu (-name => "popup menu",
            -values => ["a", "b", "c", "d", "e", "f"],
            -labels => {
                "a" => "Item A", "b" => "Item B", "c" => "Item C",
                "d" => "Item D", "e" => "Item E", "f" => "Item F"
                },
            -override => !$sticky),
p ("Single-pick scrolling list:"),
scrolling_list (-name => "scrolling list single",
                -size => 3,
                -values => ["a", "b", "c", "d", "e", "f"],
                -labels => {
                    "a" => "Item A", "b" => "Item B", "c" => "Item C",
                    "d" => "Item D", "e" => "Item E", "f" => "Item F"
                    },
                -override => !$sticky),
p ("Multiple-pick scrolling list:"),
scrolling_list (-name => "scrolling list multiple",
                -size => 3,
                -multiple => 1,
                -values => ["a", "b", "c", "d", "e", "f"],
                -labels => {
                    "a" => "Item A", "b" => "Item B", "c" => "Item C",
                    "d" => "Item D", "e" => "Item E", "f" => "Item F"
                    },
                -override => !$sticky),
br (), br (),
# this checkbox is deliberately always sticky
checkbox (-name => "sticky", -label => "Use sticky fields"),
```

continues

continued

```
            br (), br (),
            submit (-name => "choice", -value => "Submit"),
            " ",    # separate buttons with a space
            reset ("Reset form"),
            end_form ();
```

The elt_demo.pl script also includes code that checks to see whether a form was submitted. If so, it displays the information that it finds. escapeHTML() is used extensively here. The values we're printing might contain special characters, but CGI.pm won't automatically escape them for us because we're not generating form elements at this point:

```
# Determine which form elements are present from previous form

print hr (), p ("Form element names and values submitted in previous form:");
my @names = param ();  # get list of parameter names
if (!@names)        # initial script invocation
{
    print p ("(no elements present)");
}
else                # subsequent script invocation
{
    # present a general display of the information from the submitted form
    my @item = ();
    foreach my $name (@names)
    {
        my @val = param ($name);
        # if element is multiple-valued, display as "[val1, val2, ...]"
        $val[0] = "[" . join (", ", @val) . "]" if @val > 1;
        push (@item, escapeHTML ("$name: ($val[0])\n"));
    }
    print ul (li (\@item)); # print values within <ul> ... </ul> list

    # perform a couple of field-specific checks

    if (my $val = param ("text field"))     # check single-line text field
    {
        print p ("The text field contains a value '"
                . escapeHTML ($val)
                . "'. This value satisifies the following conditions:");
        $val =~ s/^\s+//;       # trim leading/trailing whitespace
        $val =~ s/\s+$//;
        @item = ();
        # is it empty?
        push (@item, "empty: " . ($val eq "" ? "yes" : "no"));
        # is it an integer?
        push (@item, "integer: " . ($val =~ /^[+-]?\d+$/ ? "yes" : "no"));
        # is it a date? (this is a very WEAK date check!)
        push (@item, "date: " . ($val =~ /^\d+\D\d+\D\d+$/ ? "perhaps" : "no"));
```

```
        print ul (li (\@item)); # print list showing test results
    }
    if (my $file = param ("file field"))    # check file upload field
    {
        print p ("A file was chosen for uploading.  Its name is '"
            . escapeHTML ($file)
            . "', and its size is " . (stat ($file))[7] . " bytes."
            . " The upload attributes are:");
        @item = ();
        for my $attr (keys (%{uploadInfo ($file)}))
        {
            push (@item, escapeHTML ("$attr: " . uploadInfo ($file)->{$attr}));
        }
        print ul (li (\@item)); # print list showing upload attributes
    }
}
print hr ();
```

After printing the list of the parameter names and values, the script demonstrates some simple tests of the input. If there is a value in the single-line text field, `elt_demo.pl` performs some simple characterization of the value:

- Is it empty? (Yes, unless it contains a non-whitespace character.)
- Is it an integer? (Yes, if it's all digits, optionally preceded by a plus or minus sign.)
- Does it look like a date? (Yes, if it contains three numeric components separated by non-numeric characters; the script prints "perhaps" rather than "yes" because this test is not very rigorous.)

The code that checks whether or not the text field value looks like an integer actually contains a bug, which you can demonstrate by entering a value consisting of a single digit 0. In this case, `elt_demo.pl` doesn't even recognize that the field contains a value! The reason this happens is that the string `"0"` evaluates to false in a Boolean context. The following test does not have this problem:

```
if (defined (my $val = param ("text field"))) ...
```

Be sure to perform the proper test when you write your own form-processing code, to avoid falling prey to this problem.

If a file was uploaded, the script prints the file's name, its size, and the upload attributes. The value of the file-upload field contains the filename, so we can treat it as a string for printing purposes, and we can pass it to `uploadInfo()`, a function provided by CGI.pm that provides information about the file. `uploadInfo()` returns a reference to a hash of attribute names and values, so we iterate through the hash keys to get the values.

The value returned by CGI.pm for a file-upload parameter actually has a dual purpose. Not only can you treat the value as a string containing the filename, you also can use it as a file handle to read the file or to pass to other file-related functions. That being so, we pass the handle to stat() to access an array of values describing the file. (We're interested only in the eighth element, which indicates the file size.) We don't do anything with the file itself, but that's harmless; the contents are stored in a temporary file, and the Web server automatically deletes it when the script terminates.

Form Design Issues

The material in this chapter showed how to create the elements that make up a form. When you're designing a form-based application, you need to apply this knowledge in the context of the task you're trying to accomplish to determine how to present and process your form. Here are some general issues to consider when you're writing such an application:

What kind of information do you want to collect? What's the easiest way for the user to provide it? In theory, you could construct practically any form using nothing but text fields, because almost any kind of information can be gathered that way. If a field is allowed to have only a fixed number of legal values, however, it might be preferable to use a more highly structured multiple-choice element such as a pop-up menu. This makes it easier for users to select a value without typing it explicitly, and with no possibility of entering an incorrect value.

What are the default values? Do you want to display the form with default values filled in? If you do, you risk having users be lazy by assuming those values are good enough. Or do you want to display empty fields, possibly supplying default values for those fields that users leave empty?

What kind of input validation is necessary? Do some fields require a value? Do values have to be supplied in a particular format (such as a number, a two-character state abbreviation, or an email address)? Are you prepared to handle bad input? This can take the form of missing or mistaken values (in free text fields, for example), or deliberately malicious and malformed information designed as an attempt to hack your site. If the input turns out to be unsuitable, can you redisplay the form showing the values that were submitted, along with feedback indicating clearly what must be added or modified to make the form acceptable? (It's better not to say "click the Back button" if possible, because some browsers may not present the form properly under some circumstances. For example, a browser might erase a form entirely when you go back to it.)

How much display space is available? Some elements are functionally equivalent, but have different properties that make them suitable for different situations. Consider, for example, the tradeoff between convenience and amount of window real estate required for radio buttons, pop-up menus, and single-pick scrolling lists. Each of these presents a list of alternatives from which you select one item. If you have the space, radio buttons can be better because each option is visible in the browser window at all times. With a pop-up menu, you must click the menu to see the options. However, the amount of space a set of radio buttons takes is proportional to the number of items, so it's not a good choice when there are many items. In this case, a pop-up menu can be superior because it's more compact and takes a fixed amount of layout space regardless of the number of items. But even here, a pop-up menu may not be suitable if the number of options is so large that the menu can't fit on the screen. You run into the problem that the user must scroll the menu to see all the items. If scrolling will be necessary, it's better to use a navigational item designed for that purpose—a scrolling list. The user can move up and down in the list easily without having it disappear when the pointer is moved out of the list or if the button is released. A list uses a little more space than a pop up, but you get to decide how much.

What kind of confirmation or feedback do you provide for successful submissions? Do you just thank the user? Reformat the form contents for display as a confirmation page? Send an email message as confirmation? Some combination of methods?

In Chapter 5 we'll develop several applications for which these issues come into play. We'll keep them in mind and explore various options. For example, we'll use a number of form-validation techniques and provide several kinds of form submission confirmation.

5

Writing Form-Based Applications

CHAPTER 4, "GENERATING AND PROCESSING FORMS," covered the general techniques involved in creating forms. In this chapter, we'll use those techniques to write several types of form-based applications, and in Chapter 6, "Automating the Form-Handling Process," we'll discuss how you can use information in your database to help you handle forms automatically.

Web programming includes such a diverse range of applications that we can't hope to cover more than a fraction of the possibilities. Nevertheless, there are several recurring issues, and the applications in this chapter illustrate a number of useful techniques that you should be able to apply to many of your own projects. Therefore, although useful in their own right, these applications are not just ends in themselves—they serve an illustrative purpose as well. The projects we'll tackle, and some of the techniques they involve, are as follows:

- A product-registration script that enables customers to register purchases online by visiting your Web site rather than by mailing in a paper form. It shows how to generate and validate a form on the basis of specifications stored in a data structure.

- A guestbook. I guess every Web programming book has to have a guestbook, so this one does, too. However, our version serves only as a means by which to demonstrate how to incorporate email capabilities into your scripts. The guestbook itself uses email to help keep you apprised of new entries, and we'll cover other ways you can use mail capabilities in your applications. The section also discusses how to set up jobs that execute according to predetermined schedule.

- A giveaway contest application that enables visitors to your site to submit contest entries. This section covers some basic fraud-detection techniques to help combat ballot-box stuffing, selection of random entries to choose contest winners, and entry summary and expiration methods.

- A simple poll. We'll develop a script that uses a form to present candidates users can vote for, and that displays a results page showing the current vote totals. The application uses MySQL to count the votes, and the results page uses the current totals in the database so that the results shown are always up to date.

- Image-storage and image-display scripts. Images are an integral part of many Web applications, which necessitates a method for getting them to your server host and accessing them from within your scripts. To provide support for image use, we'll illustrate how to load images into MySQL two ways: over the Web using a form containing a file-upload field, and from the command line. In addition, this section shows how to display images in Web pages by pulling them from your database.

- An application that enables you to construct an electronic greeting card interactively and notify the recipient that it's waiting. The card is stored as a database record so that it can be retrieved and displayed later for the recipient. The application also notifies you when the recipient views the card. This application incorporates image-display capabilities and shows how to implement multiple-stage record construction, how to trigger a notification when a record's status changes, and how to handle removal of expired cards.

The applications in this chapter have very different purposes, but share certain common characteristics. Generally, you'll find that form-based programs involve the following steps, although the steps vary in complexity from application to application, depending on your goals and requirements:

- Generate a form to solicit the information you want to collect from the user. Some forms are relatively trivial: Our polling application presents a form containing nothing more than a set of radio buttons listing the candidates and a Submit button. The user clicks one time to pick a candidate, a second time to submit the vote, and that's it. Other forms are more extensive: The product-registration application has many fields because we need to gather information about both the product being registered and the user who's registering it.

- Validate the form's contents when the user fills it in and submits it. Form validation can be minimal or quite extensive. You may have fields that are required but were left blank by the user, or fields that must contain a certain kind of information but were filled in incorrectly. In such cases, the user must submit additional or revised information. You'll find it necessary to inform the user that the form cannot be processed, as well as what should be done to correct any problems. We'll demonstrate several feedback techniques over the course of the chapter.

- Store the form submission. Some applications store form information in a file or mail it somewhere for further processing. This being a book on MySQL, we will of course focus on using a database as the primary storage mechanism for each application.

- Generally, you provide some kind of feedback to the user after a form submission has been received and processed. This can be quite simple, such as a thank you message expressing appreciation for the user's participation in a poll or survey, or a brief acknowledgement that the submission was received. Or you may redisplay the information to provide confirmation to the user that it was received properly.

A small reminder before you proceed: You'll find the source code for the scripts developed here in the `webdb` software distribution that accompanies this book. You can get it at the following Web site:

```
http://www.kitebird.com/mysql-perl/
```

You may find it useful to install each script and try it out first before you read the section that describes how it works.

Product Registration

Registration applications serve many purposes. You can use them to allow people to register products they have purchased, sign up for conferences, request a catalog, add themselves to a mailing list, and so forth. The obvious advantage over paper forms for you when you receive a registration from someone is that you needn't re-key the information to get it into your database—the Web application inserts it for you. An advantage for users is instant transmission of their registration information without having to dig up a stamp or put the registration form in the mail.

In this section, we'll write a script, `prod_reg.pl`, that collects product registrations over the Web. Generally, this kind of registration form has, at a minimum, fields to identify the product and the customer, and our application will confine itself to gathering that kind of information. Many registration forms have additional fields for demographic information such as household income, type of employment, or how the product will be used. We'll skip that stuff; you can add it later if you like.

To process registrations, we need a database table in which to store registration records and an application that collects information from customers and inserts records into the table. The table we'll use looks like this:

```
CREATE TABLE prod_reg
(
    # record identification information: unique record ID and time of
    # creation
    id          INT UNSIGNED NOT NULL AUTO_INCREMENT PRIMARY KEY,
    t           TIMESTAMP,

    # product identification information: serial number, purchase date,
    # where purchased
    serial      VARCHAR(30),
    purch_date  VARCHAR(20),
    store       VARCHAR(30),

    # customer identification information: name (last, first, middle
    # initial), postal address, telephone, email address
    last_name   VARCHAR(30),
    first_name  VARCHAR(30),
    initial     VARCHAR(5),
    street      VARCHAR(30),
    city        VARCHAR(30),
    state       CHAR(2),
    zip         VARCHAR(10),
    telephone   VARCHAR(20),
    email       VARCHAR(60)
)
```

The prod_reg table contains columns that serve to identify the record itself as well as the product and the customer. The first two columns, id and t, provide a unique identification number for each record and indicate when records are created. We can have MySQL supply values for these columns automatically when we create new records; therefore, they need not be represented in the product-registration form.[1] The rest of the columns describe the product (serial number, purchase date, place of purchase) or the customer (all the other columns). The user must supply these product and customer values, so the form will contain corresponding fields for all of them.

---

1. Using a TIMESTAMP enables us to have MySQL fill in the time automatically when we create new records. If you expect to edit records later, however, it wouldn't be an appropriate choice because MySQL would update the value whenever you change a record. In that case, you should pick DATE or DATETIME and set the t column to CURRENT_DATE or NOW() at record-creation time.

Our application fits into the product-registration process as follows:

- When a customer purchases one of our products, it will include a paper registration form that can be filled in and mailed the traditional way. However, the form also will have a note:

```
If you prefer to register online, visit our Web site at:
http://www.snake.net/cgi-perl/prod_reg.pl
```

- When the customer goes to the Web site (assuming a preference for registering online rather than completing a paper form), the application presents a form for collecting registration information that reflects the structure of our `prod_reg` table. (The form will contain fields corresponding to each of the table's columns except `id` and `t`.) The customer completes the registration by filling in the form, and then selects the Submit button to send the information back to the Web server.

- The application examines the form to make sure all required fields (such as the product serial number) have been provided. If not, we display some feedback to the user indicating that additional information is necessary and redisplay the form so that the customer can complete it properly. Otherwise, we use the form contents to create a new record in the `prod_reg` table and display a confirmation page to the customer indicating that the registration was received.

From this description, we can see that our application needs to generate a form, extract and validate the contents of the submitted form, insert registration information into the database, and display confirmation to the user. (Not coincidentally, these activities correspond to the steps I mentioned earlier in the chapter as those that are common to many form-based applications.)

Designing the Form

For the `prod_reg.pl` application, we'll use a form that consists entirely of plain-text input fields. That's a pretty regular field structure, so instead of writing out a lot of separate `textfield()` calls to generate the fields, let's try a different approach. We can specify form information as an array of field descriptions:

```
my @field_list =
(
    { name => "serial", label => "Serial number:", size => 30, req => 1 },
    { name => "purch_date", label => "Purchase date:", size => 20, req => 1 },
    { name => "store", label => "Where purchased:", size => 30 },
    { name => "last_name", label => "Last name:", size => 30, req => 1 },
    { name => "first_name", label => "First name:", size => 30, req => 1 },
    { name => "initial", label => "Initial:", size => 5 },
    { name => "street", label => "Street:", size => 30 },
    { name => "city", label => "City:", size => 30 },
    { name => "state", label => "State:", size => 2 },
    { name => "zip", label => "Zip code:", size => 10 },
```

continues

continued

```
            { name => "telephone", label => "Telephone:", size => 20 },
            { name => "email", label => "Email address:", size => 60 }
    );
```

Each item in the `@field_list` array is a hash that describes a single field. This array serves multiple purposes:

- It helps us generate the entry form. The `name`, `label`, and `size` attributes specify a field name, the label to display next to it (so the user knows what to enter into the field), and a field size. Field names correspond to the names of the underlying table columns, to make it easy to associate form values with the appropriate table columns at record-creation time.

- The array helps us validate submitted form contents when a user sends in a registration: We'll determine whether any given field is required to have a value by checking its `req` attribute.

Because the `@field_list` array applies to both generation and validation of the registration form, we'll pass it as a parameter to multiple functions in the main dispatch logic of our `prod_reg.pl` script:

```
my $choice = lc (param ("choice")); # get choice, lowercased

if ($choice eq "")                        # initial script invocation
{
    display_entry_form (\@field_list);
}
elsif ($choice eq "submit")
{
    process_form (\@field_list);
}
else
{
    print p (escapeHTML ("Logic error, unknown choice: $choice"));
}
```

Generating the Form

The `display_entry_form()` function generates the registration form by iterating through the field list and using the information contained in each list element to construct a call to `textfield()`. Then it adds a Submit button at the end:

```
sub display_entry_form
{
my $field_ref = shift;      # reference to field list
```

```
    print start_form (-action => url ());
    print p ("Please enter your product registration information,\n"
            . "then select the " . strong ("Submit") . " button.");
    foreach my $f (@{$field_ref})
    {
        print escapeHTML ($f->{label}), " ",
              textfield (-name => $f->{name}, -size => $f->{size}),
              br (), "\n";
    }
    print submit (-name => "choice", -value => "Submit"),
              end_form ();
}
```

It isn't necessary to use `escapeHTML()` to encode values passed to `textfield()` because CGI.pm automatically encodes parameters to functions that generate form elements. However, the labels displayed next to the input fields are just static text, so we need to encode them in case they contain any special characters.

One problem with the preceding code is that it produces a visually distracting form. The labels have different lengths, so the input fields that appear to the right of the labels won't line up vertically. We can provide a more regular layout by arranging labels and input fields within columns of an HTML table. Here's a modified version of `display_entry_form()` that produces a table:

```
sub display_entry_form
{
my $field_ref = shift;       # reference to field list
my @row;

    print start_form (-action => url ());
    print p ("Please enter your product registration information,\n"
            . "then select the " . strong ("Submit") . " button.");
    foreach my $f (@{$field_ref})
    {
        push (@row, Tr (
                td (escapeHTML ($f->{label})),
                td (textfield (-name => $f->{name}, -size => $f->{size}))
            ));
    }
    print table (@row),
            submit (-name => "choice", -value => "Submit"),
            end_form ();
}
```

Another improvement would be to give the user a hint about which fields are required to have a value. We can use the `req` attribute for this, but first it's necessary to decide how to indicate "this field is required" to the user. There are different ways to accomplish this:

- Print the labels for the required fields differently than for non-required fields. One common technique is to use red text or bold text. Personally, I don't like red text very much, because it doesn't look much different from black text to me. (I have defective color vision.) Printing field labels in bold can be problematic if the user has selected a display font for which bold and plain text don't look much different. For example, I find that if I set the font to Arial 10-point, bold and plain text don't look any different in browser windows. Under these circumstances, making the text bold communicates no information.

- Add some kind of image next to missing fields. This is visually distinctive but doesn't work very well if the user has image loading turned off. Also, it requires more complicated logic in generating the form.

- Use an asterisk next to the label for required fields.

We'll settle on the simplest technique (putting an asterisk next to the label of each required field). It's also a good idea to modify the introductory text that precedes the form, to indicate what the asterisks signify:

```
sub display_entry_form
{
my $field_ref = shift;        # reference to field list
my @row;

    print start_form (-action => url ());
    print p ("Please enter your product registration information,\n"
           . "then select the " . strong ("Submit") . " button.");
    print p ("(Fields with an asterisk next to the name are required.)\n");
    foreach my $f (@{$field_ref})
    {
        my $label = $f->{label};
        $label .= "*" if $f->{req};     # add asterisk for required fields
        push (@row, Tr (
                td (escapeHTML ($label)),
                td (textfield (-name => $f->{name}, -size => $f->{size}))
            ));
    }
    print table (@row),
            submit (-name => "choice", -value => "Submit"),
            end_form ();
}
```

Processing Form Submissions

After the user fills in and submits the form, prod_reg.pl handles the submission by calling process_form(). A minimal version of this function might just look through the field list to make sure that the user actually provided values in all the required fields. We can do this by checking the req attribute for each element in our list that describes form fields:

```perl
sub process_form
{
my $field_ref = shift;       # reference to field list

    foreach my $f (@{$field_ref})
    {
        next unless $f->{req};        # skip test if field is not required
        my $value = param ($f->{name}); # get value
        if (!defined ($value) || $value eq "")
        {
            print p ("Hey, you didn't fill in all the required fields!");
            return;
        }
    }

    # add registration to database and display confirmation page
    insert_record ($field_ref);
}
```

As noted, that's a minimal approach. It doesn't tell the user which fields were missing. It also gets fooled if the user just types spaces in the required fields. We certainly can do a better job. Some of the possible improvements here are to trim extraneous whitespace from the fields before checking them, tell the user which elements are required, and redisplay the form if it's incomplete.

How should we handle the problem of providing feedback to the customer about which fields are missing? Here's one approach:

1. Loop through the fields, checking each of them until we find one that's missing.

2. Announce which field is missing and redisplay the form so that the customer can enter the value and resubmit the form.

3. Repeat until all required fields have been supplied.

Here's another:

1. Check all the fields.

2. Announce which fields are missing and redisplay the form so that the customer can correct all the problems and resubmit the form.

The first method of form validation is simpler to implement, but leads to an application that's extremely tedious to use because the user finds out about only one problem at a time. The second method provides more information. To implement it, we need to save up the error messages as we check the fields. Here is a modified version of process_form() that does this:

```perl
sub process_form
{
my $field_ref = shift;       # reference to field list
my (@errors);

    foreach my $f (@{$field_ref})
    {
        next unless $f->{req};          # skip test if field is not required
        my $value = param ($f->{name}); # get value
        $value = "" unless defined ($value);    # convert undef to empty string
        $value =~ s/^\s+//;             # trim leading/trailing whitespace
        $value =~ s/\s+$//;
        push (@errors, $f->{label}) if $value eq "";    # it's missing!
    }
    if (@errors)
    {
        print p ("Some information is missing."
                . " Please fill in the following fields:");
        s/:$// foreach (@errors);   # strip colons from end of labels
        print ul (li (\@errors));
        display_entry_form ($field_ref);    # redisplay entry form
        return;
    }

    # add registration to database and display confirmation page
    insert_record ($field_ref);
}
```

To validate the form, process_form() loops through each field and checks its req attribute. If the field is not required, no further test is necessary. Otherwise, we have a look at the field value. First, it's converted to an empty string if the value is undef.[2] Then any whitespace at the ends of the value is removed so that we don't think a value is present if it contains only spaces.[3] If the result is empty, a required value is missing and we add a message to the @errors array.

---

2. The purpose of converting undefined values to empty strings is just to suppress warnings that would otherwise be triggered by the presence of the -w flag on the script's initial #!/usr/bin/perl line. Otherwise, attempting to operate on such values results in messages in the error log.

3. I'm actually a bit ambivalent about pointing out that whitespace removal helps us perform better validation. By doing so, I'm giving away one of my own techniques for dealing with intrusive form-based applications that insist on requiring information that I consider private. I find that just entering a space into a field often will fool an application into thinking that I've given it real information!

If @errors is non-empty after the loop terminates, the form is incomplete. process_form() responds by showing the user which fields must be filled in, and then redisplays the form by calling display_entry_form(). Here is an instance where CGI.pm's sticky form behavior is quite valuable. None of the form element-generating calls in display_entry_form() include an override parameter, so when that function redisplays the form, CGI.pm automatically fills in the fields with whatever values the customer just submitted. That enables us to easily display the form in the same browser window as the error messages. The customer can determine from the error messages at the top of the window which fields still need to be filled in, and can enter the required values without clicking the Back button to return to the entry form. (It's of little value to display error messages if we then require the customer to click Back; as soon as the customer does so, the error messages disappear!)

Before we move on to discuss the insert_record() function that actually adds a new record to the prod_reg table, let's make one more change. One thing process_form() does while checking field values is to trim extraneous whitespace. We'd like to use these tidied-up values when inserting the new registration record, but unfortunately they are just discarded because we used a temporary variable for field checking. If we save the values, we can use them later when adding the record. One easy way to do this is based on the fact that Perl enables us to create new hash attributes on the fly: We can create a new value attribute in each field information hash and stuff the trimmed value into it. The resulting field-checking loop follows. Note that we want to save all values (not just the required ones), so the test of the req attribute must be moved from the beginning of the loop to the end:

```
foreach my $f (@{$field_ref})
{
    my $value = param ($f->{name}); # get field value
    $value = "" unless defined ($value);   # convert undef to empty string
    $value =~ s/^\s+//;              # trim leading/trailing whitespace
    $value =~ s/\s+$//;
    $f->{value} = $value;           # save trimmed value
    push (@errors, $f->{label}) if $value eq "" && $f->{req};
}
```

Storing the Registration Record

After a form has been received that passes the form validation process, insert_record() stores the record and displays a confirmation message to the customer. There are a number of ways to construct an INSERT statement. One source of variation is that MySQL supports different syntaxes for INSERT:

```
INSERT INTO prod_reg SET col1 = val1, col2 = val2, ...
INSERT INTO prod_reg (list of columns) VALUES(list of values)
```

Another source of variation is that DBI supports different ways of specifying data values for a query. We can either insert the values directly into the query string or use placeholders.

To use the first INSERT syntax just shown and insert the values into the query string, you could do something like this:

```
$stmt = "";
foreach my $f (@{$field_ref})
{
    next if $f->{value} eq "";        # don't bother with empty fields
    $stmt .= "," if $stmt;            # put commas between assignments
    $stmt .= $f->{name} . " = " . $dbh->quote ($f->{value});
}
$stmt = "INSERT INTO prod_reg SET $stmt";   # complete the statement
$dbh->do ($stmt);                           # and execute it
```

The loop ignores empty fields; we'll just let MySQL supply whatever default values the corresponding columns have. If a field is not empty, we place its value into the string to assign it to the appropriate column—after processing it with quote() to perform any quoting and escaping that may be necessary, of course.

To use placeholders instead, we still walk through the fields, but this time we put '?' placeholder characters into the query string and save the column values so that we can pass them to the do() method:

```
$stmt = "";
@placeholder = ();
foreach my $f (@{$field_ref})
{
    next if $f->{value} eq "";        # don't bother with empty fields
    $stmt .= "," if $stmt;            # put commas between assignments
    $stmt .= $f->{name} . " = ?";     # add column name, placeholder
    push (@placeholder, $f->{value}); # save placeholder value
}
$stmt = "INSERT INTO prod_reg SET $stmt";   # complete the statement
$dbh->do ($stmt, undef, @placeholder);      # and execute it
```

Functionally, there isn't much difference between the two ways of constructing the query, and I doubt whether there is much reason to prefer one over the other in terms of performance, either. Take your pick. (If you expect to be issuing zillions of INSERT statements, however, you might want to run a few benchmarks to gather some empirical performance numbers.)

Regardless of how you construct the INSERT query, it's a good idea after executing it to present some sort of confirmation to the customer. We'll discuss confirmation pages in more detail later, but for now we'll just present a short message and thank the user:

```
print p ("We have received your product registration. Thank you.");
```

The application doesn't check whether the registration record actually was inserted properly. If we want to warn the customer about problems creating the registration record, we should check the return value from do(), and then display an appropriate message:

```
$rows = $dbh->do ($stmt, undef, @placeholder);
if ($rows)
{
    print p ("We have received your product registration. Thank you.");
}
else
{
    print p ("Sorry, we were unable to process your product\n"
            . "registration. Please try again later.");
}
```

Another potential problem is that a serial number might be submitted multiple times. This can occur different ways. The customer might click the Back button and then select Submit again mistakenly. Or a customer might enter the serial number incorrectly, duplicating a number already entered by another customer. What then? As written, the prod_reg.pl script does nothing special. It just inserts the record as usual. The theory behind this cavalier behavior is that a customer can't really do much about these problems anyway, so why say anything? On the other hand, you might want to expend a little extra effort to provide yourself with information about possible problems. For example, you could run a query periodically to find duplicate serial numbers so that you can examine the appropriate records. Here's a query that finds serial numbers that appear multiple times in the prod_reg table:

```
SELECT serial, COUNT(serial) AS count FROM prod_reg
GROUP BY serial HAVING count > 1
```

Enter a registration record, and then click your browser's Back button and the form's Submit button a few times to generate some duplicate records. Then run the preceding query from the mysql program to see what kind of output it produces. If you adopt the approach of looking for duplicate values using this query, you'll find that it becomes much slower as your table accumulates more records. That's because the table doesn't have any indexes on it. Use ALTER TABLE to add an index on the serial column and the query will run much more quickly:

```
ALTER TABLE prod_reg ADD INDEX (serial)
```

Checking for Empty Value Lists

The insert_record() function constructs an INSERT statement, but doesn't bother to check whether the list of column assignments following the SET keyword is empty. We know it won't be, because our form has several required fields and insert_record() isn't called unless they've been filled in. If for some reason you have a form for which no fields are required, however, you should check for an empty column assignment list. Why? Because if the form is empty and you don't check, you'll find yourself constructing and trying to execute an INSERT statement that looks like this, which is syntactically invalid:

```
INSERT INTO tbl_name SET
```

If you're determined to insert a new record even when there are no values, you might want to consider using an INSERT syntax, which does allow an empty value list:

```
INSERT INTO tbl_name () VALUES()
```

This "empty" INSERT syntax is understood by MySQL 3.23.3 and later versions.

Suggested Modifications

process_form() displays all the error messages together at the top of the browser window if there are problems with a form submission. Modify the application to display each message immediately below the field to which it applies, to put the messages in closer proximity to the offending fields. You can do this by creating an error attribute in @field_list elements, and changing display_entry_form() to check for and display that attribute. If you want to display a warning icon as well, what would you need to do?

If you have independent information about your products, you may be able to use it to improve the integrity of product registrations. Suppose you have a product-listing table that contains a record of each item that you've manufactured, including its serial number. You could have the prod_reg.pl application present an initial "gatekeeper" page that displays a form containing only an input field for the product serial number. When the customer supplies the number, check your product listing to verify that the number is valid, and proceed to the main entry form if so. Otherwise, you know the serial number was entered incorrectly and you can ask the user to double-check the number on the product.

prod_reg.pl isn't very rigorous in its validation, other than to make sure required fields aren't missing. Modify it to perform field-specific validation. Make sure the state abbreviation is legal, for example, or verify that if the email field is filled in that the value looks like a valid address. For extra fun, check the purchase date to make sure it looks like a date. (Because dates can be specified many ways, however, you probably should display a note indicating the format you expect date values to follow.)

Using text boxes for all the input fields makes it easy to describe the form using a data structure so that we can generate it and validate it automatically. But some of the fields might be easier for the user to fill in if we had used other field types. For example, the field for entering the state could be represented by a scrolling list containing the possible state abbreviations. (This would also help make sure that users don't enter an incorrect state value.) How would you modify the @field_list array and the form-generation code to handle this? Is it worth it?

The application pretty much assumes the postal address style used in the United States. (For example, we have a field for Zip Code, which is hardly a worldwide convention.) How would you generalize the form to be less U.S.-centric?

Modify insert_record() to present a more informative confirmation page that shows the customer what information was stored. (You might be surprised how often people recognize that they've entered one or more values incorrectly if you just reformat the information and show it to them again.) If you make this change, you should also provide information about whom the customer should contact to report any errors. An alternative to storing the record in the database before displaying it in a confirmation page is to present the information along with an "Are you sure?" button. If the customer is sure, store the record in the database; otherwise, allow the customer to edit the information further and resubmit it.

Using Email from Within Applications

When I began to outline which applications to discuss in this book, I considered whether to include a guestbook that visitors to your site can "sign" by filling in a form. A guestbook is simple, so it makes a good introductory form-based application that you can write without a lot of work. Also, you can store the comments in a database, which gives it some relevance to MySQL. But guestbooks have been covered in so many books on Web programming that they've become standard fodder, and my initial gut reaction to writing about them was "ugh."

What to do? I went back and forth from one horn of this dilemma to the other several times. Eventually, I decided to include a guestbook application (right here, in fact), but primarily as an excuse to cover something else: how to add email capabilities to scripts. The guestbook is so simple that we don't have to pay much attention to it, yet it provides a meaningful context for discussing email-generation techniques. Dilemma resolved.

Here is the scenario: You want to provide a guestbook so that people who visit your site can comment on it, and you'll allow people to view comments from previous visitors. But you're concerned about people submitting comments that are unsuitable. If someone writes something that contains foul or libelous language, for instance, you'll want to remove it. That means the guestbook needs to be monitored—but you don't want to be bothered having to check it all the time for new entries, or it becomes a burden. One solution to this problem is to have the guestbook itself tell you when it gets a new entry, by sending you an email message containing the content of the entry. That way you receive updates as new entries arrive, just by reading your mail as you normally do. You don't have to keep remembering to visit the guestbook to check for recent additions.

To hold guestbook comments, we'll use the following table. Visitors will provide the `name`, `email`, and `note` columns; we'll provide the `id` and `date` values:

```
CREATE TABLE guest
(
    id      INT UNSIGNED NOT NULL AUTO_INCREMENT PRIMARY KEY,
    date    DATE NOT NULL,
    name    VARCHAR(50),
    email   VARCHAR(60),
    note    VARCHAR(255)
)
```

The `guest.pl` script that handles the guestbook has three functions: display an entry form, process new entries, and show previous entries. Accordingly, the main program looks like this:

```
print header (),
    start_html (-title => "Sign or View My Guestbook", -bgcolor => "white"),
    h2("Sign or View My Guestbook");

my $choice = lc (param ("choice")); # get choice, lowercased

if ($choice eq "")                     # initial script invocation
```

continues

continued

```
{
    display_entry_form ();
}
elsif ($choice eq "submit")
{
    process_form ();
}
elsif ($choice eq "view comments")
{
    display_comments ();
}
else
{
    print p (escapeHTML ("Logic error, unknown choice: $choice"));
}

print end_html ();
```

The `display_entry_form()` function presents a simple form for entering comments and a button that allows previous comments to be viewed:

```
sub display_entry_form
{
    print start_form (-action => url ()),
        table (
            Tr (
                td ("Name:"),
                td (textfield (-name => "name", -size => 60))
            ),
            Tr (
                td ("Email address:"),
                td (textfield (-name => "name", -size => 60))
            ),
            Tr (
                td ("Note:"),
                td (textarea (-name => "name", -cols => 60, -rows => 4))
            ),
        ),
        br (),
        submit (-name => "choice", -value => "Submit"),
        " ",
        submit (-name => "choice", -value => "View Comments"),
        end_form ();
}
```

If the user selects the View Comments button, the script calls `display_comments()` to look up all the previous comments and display them:

```
sub display_comments
{
my $dbh;
my $sth;
```

```
    $dbh = WebDB::connect ();
    $sth = $dbh->prepare ("SELECT * FROM guest ORDER BY id");
    $sth->execute ();
    while (my $ref = $sth->fetchrow_hashref ())
    {
        print p (escapeHTML ("ID: $ref->{id} Date: $ref->{date}")),
                p (escapeHTML ("Name: $ref->{name}")),
                p (escapeHTML ("Email: $ref->{email}")),
                p (escapeHTML ("Note: $ref->{note}")),
                hr ();
    }
    $sth->finish ();
    $dbh->disconnect ();
}
```

If the visitor fills in the form and selects the Submit button, we extract the form contents, add a new record to the database, and send the guestbook administrator an email message:

```
sub process_form
{
my $dbh;
my $sth;
my $ref;

    # Add new entry to database, then reselect it so we can get the
    # id and date values to use for the mail message.
    $dbh = WebDB::connect ();
    $dbh->do ("INSERT INTO guest (date,name,email,note) VALUES (NOW(),?,?,?)",
                undef,
                param ("name"), param ("email"), param ("note"));
    $sth = $dbh->prepare ("SELECT * FROM guest WHERE id = LAST_INSERT_ID()");
    $sth->execute ();
    $ref = $sth->fetchrow_hashref ();
    $sth->finish ();
    $dbh->disconnect ();

    # display confirmation to user
    print p ("Thank you.");

    # send the entry to the administrator via email
    mail_entry ($ref);
}
```

In the interest of making the application as simple as possible, process_form() performs no validation whatsoever. It just adds whatever information the user provided, even if there isn't any. Then, after adding the new entry, the application needs to mail a copy of it to you. However, this information must include the ID number of the entry (you'll need that value so you can specify which record to remove if it's found to be objectionable), and we might as well present the date, too. To look up the record just inserted, we identify it using LAST_INSERT_ID(). That function returns the most recent `AUTO_INCREMENT` value created during the current session with the MySQL server, which just happens to be the `id` value of the record just inserted. After we have the record, we're ready to send some email by calling `mail_entry()`. Before describing that function, I'll discuss the general technique for sending mail from a script, because we'll be doing that several places in this book. Then we'll adapt that technique for `guest.pl` and use it within the context of mailing guestbook entries.

Sending Email from Scripts

To send mail from within a Perl script, it's pretty common on UNIX systems to open a pipe to the `sendmail` program and write the message into it like so:

```
open (OUT, "| /usr/lib/sendmail -t")
    or die "Cannot open pipe to sendmail: $!\n";
print OUT "From: $sender\n";
print OUT "To: $recipient\n";
print OUT "Subject: I'm sending you mail\n";
print OUT "\n";    # blank line between headers and message body
print OUT "This is the message body.\n";
close (OUT);    # close pipe to send message
```

There are other mail-sending alternatives. The Perl CPAN provides several modules for this purpose; the one we'll use is `Mail::Sendmail`. One of its advantages is that it doesn't require `sendmail` and therefore works under both UNIX and Windows.[4]

Here is a short script, `testmail.pl`, that illustrates how to use `Mail::Sendmail`:

```
#! /usr/bin/perl -w
# testmail.pl - Send mail using the Mail::Sendmail module

use strict;
use Mail::Sendmail;

my $recipient = "black-hole\@localhost";    # CHANGE THIS!
my $sender = "black-hole\@localhost";       # CHANGE THIS!

# Set up hash containing mail message information
my %mail = (
    From    => $sender,
    To      => $recipient,
    Subject => "I'm sending you mail",
    Message => "This is the message body.\n"
);
sendmail (%mail) or die "sendmail failure sending to $mail{To}: $!\n";

exit (0);
```

---

4. If `Mail::Sendmail` isn't available on your system, you should obtain and install it before proceeding. (See Appendix A, "Obtaining Software.") You can use one of the other mail modules in the CPAN if you like, but you'll have to adapt the scripts in this book that assume the use of `Mail::Sendmail`.

The script accesses Mail::Sendmail by including the appropriate use statement. Then it sets up a hash containing keys for various parts of the message and passes the hash to the sendmail() function. From, To, Subject, and Message are the most useful attributes, but sendmail() understands others, too. (You should change the $recipient and $sender addresses before you try out this script on your system. However, note that the addresses should include a host name, or sendmail() may reject the message.) For further information, you can read the documentation using this command:

```
% perldoc Mail::Sendmail
```

Based on the preceding discussion, we can write a mail_entry() function for guest.pl that takes care of sending new entries to the administrator. The argument passed to it is the new entry record from the guest table, supplied as a hash reference. mail_entry() uses the contents of the entry to format a simple message body and mails it out. (You'll want to change the To and From addresses before trying out the script on your own site.)

```
sub mail_entry
{
my $ref = shift;
my %mail =
(
    From => "black-hole\@localhost",           # CHANGE THIS!
    To => "black-hole\@localhost",             # CHANGE THIS!
    Subject => "Exciting New Guestbook Entry",
    Message => "
id:     $ref->{id}
date:   $ref->{date}
name:   $ref->{name}
email:  $ref->{email}
note:   $ref->{note}
"
);

    sendmail (%mail);
}
```

Removing Guestbook Entries

Eventually, guest.pl may mail an entry to you that you deem unworthy of inclusion in your guestbook. How do you remove it? One way to delete the entry is to use the mysql program and issue the appropriate query manually:

```
mysql> DELETE FROM guest WHERE id = 37;
```

But it would be more convenient to have a command that requires you to provide only the ID for the entry (or entries) you want to delete:

```
% ./guest_clobber.pl 37 81 92
```

Here's a script you can use for that. There's not much to it, because all it needs to do is construct and run one or more DELETE statements:

```
#! /usr/bin/perl -w
# guest_clobber.pl - remove guestbook entries; name IDs on the command line

use strict;
use lib qw(/usr/local/apache/lib/perl);
use WebDB;

die "No arguments given\n" unless @ARGV;
my $dbh = WebDB::connect ();
$dbh->do ("DELETE FROM guest WHERE id = ?", undef, shift (@ARGV)) while @ARGV;
$dbh->disconnect ();

exit (0);
```

Dealing with High Guestbook Traffic

If your guestbook turns out to be quite popular, you may find that it's sending you more mail messages than you care to deal with. In that case, you can employ a different approach: Generate a single "digest" message once per day containing all the entries from the previous day. That means there will be more of a delay before you receive notification about new entries, but you'll get one larger message rather than a bunch of smaller ones. If you want to do this, modify guest.pl by ripping out the code that generates email, and then set up a program that runs on schedule each day to identify the relevant entries and mail them to you.

Job scheduling under UNIX involves adding an entry to your crontab file that specifies a program you want run by the cron program.[5] Details vary slightly among systems; use the following commands to get the particulars for your system about the cron program and about crontab file editing:

```
% man cron
% man crontab
```

On some systems, a separate command describes the crontab file format:

```
% man 5 crontab
```

---

5. Under Windows, you can use one of the cron clones that are available; there are freeware, shareware, and commercial versions. (Appendix A lists where you can obtain these products.)

To schedule a job, add a line to your crontab file that specifies when the job should run. If I have a script guest_digest.pl installed in my bin directory, I can specify that I want it to run each day at 1:00 a.m. with a crontab line like this:

```
0 1 * * * /u/paul/bin/guest_digest.pl
```

The first four fields indicate the minute, hour, day, and month the job should run. A '*' character indicates execution every applicable interval (for example, the '*' characters in the third and fourth fields mean "every day of every month"). The fifth field is used for day-of-week scheduling, with values of 0 through 6 meaning Sunday through Saturday.

Now that we have set up scheduled execution of the guest_digest.pl script, I suppose we'd better write it:

```perl
#! /usr/bin/perl -w
# guest_digest.pl - produce digest of yesterday's guestbook entries

use strict;
use lib qw(/usr/local/apache/lib/perl);
use WebDB;

my $prelude = "Yesterday's guestbook entries:";

my $dbh = WebDB::connect ();
my $sth = $dbh->prepare (
            "SELECT * FROM guest
            WHERE date = DATE_SUB(CURRENT_DATE,INTERVAL 1 DAY)
            ORDER BY id");
$sth->execute ();
while (my $ref = $sth->fetchrow_hashref ())
{
    # print introductory text, but only before the first
    # record, and only if there are any records
    if (defined ($prelude))
    {
        print "$prelude\n";
        undef $prelude;
    }
    print <<EOF;
-------------------------------------------
id:     $ref->{id}
date:   $ref->{date}
name:   $ref->{name}
email:  $ref->{email}
note:   $ref->{note}
EOF
}
$sth->finish ();
$dbh->disconnect ();

exit (0);
```

In the `crontab` entry, I indicated that `guest_digest.pl` is in the `/u/paul/bin` directory, so that's where I'd install the script. For testing, we can run `guest_digest.pl` manually at the command line:

```
% /u/paul/bin/guest_digest.pl
Yesterday's guestbook entries:
-----------------------------------------------
id:     57
date:   2001-01-24
name:   Joe Visitor
email:  joev@joevis.net
note:   Here's my pithy comment!
...
```

The script figures out yesterday's date using MySQL's `DATE_SUB()` function and displays all the entries created on that date. You'll notice that `guest_digest.pl` doesn't reference `Mail::Sendmail` and it doesn't call `sendmail()`. So, you may be wondering how it sends you a daily mail message when it runs under `cron`. The answer is that `guest_digest.pl` itself doesn't, but `cron` does. When `cron` runs a program specified in a `crontab` file, it mails any output produced by the program to the `crontab` owner. Therefore, we're still generating email—we're just not doing so explicitly from the script. If your `cron` doesn't behave that way and just throws away any job output, you should of course modify `guest_digest.pl` to mail its output explicitly. In fact, you might decide to do that anyway, because the `Subject:` header for `cron`-generated mail isn't especially informative—as you'll see when it sends you a message for the first time.

Suggested Modifications

The guestbook application could stand some improvement. The most obvious short-coming is that `process_form()` doesn't perform even the most rudimentary form validation, such as making sure the visitor provided at least a name. Add some code to do that.

As written, when you submit a comment, you cannot view comments by other visitors except by returning from the confirmation page to the entry-form page. Improve the application's navigation options by putting a View Comments button in the confirmation page so that visitors can go right to the past comments page from there.

The page generated by `display_comments()` will become quite large after your guestbook receives a number of entries. Rewrite that function to either limit the display to the *n* most recent entries, or to present a multiple-page display with each page limited to *n* entries.

Other Uses for Email

Email can be used in many different ways from your scripts. For example, you can email a message to people who fill in a form. This can be useful if you want to provide additional confirmation to users from whom you've received a form submission, in a way that's more permanent than displaying a message in a browser window. (Any information in the window disappears as soon as the user closes it or visits another page.) Suppose a customer uses the product-registration application developed earlier in the chapter and happens to fill in the email field in the form. You could use the address to mail a copy of the registration record to that customer. To provide this capability, add this line to the end of the insert_record() function in the prod_reg.pl script:

```
mail_confirmation ($field_ref);
```

Then add the following function to the script; it checks whether the email address is present and sends a message to that address if so:

```
sub mail_confirmation
{
my $field_ref = shift;       # reference to field list
my %mail =
(
    From => "black-hole\@localhost",        # CHANGE THIS!
    Subject => "Your product registration information"
);

    # Determine whether or not the email field was filled in
    foreach my $f (@{$field_ref})
    {
        if ($f->{name} eq "email")
        {
            return unless $f->{value};  # no address; do nothing
            $mail{To} = $f->{value};
            last;
        }
    }
    $mail{Message} = "Thank you for registering your product.\n";
    $mail{Message} .= "This is the information we received:\n\n";
    foreach my $f (@{$field_ref})
    {
        $mail{Message} .= "$f->{label} $f->{value}\n";
    }
    sendmail (%mail);
}
```

Note that the mail_confirmation() function verifies that the email field is filled in before attempting to send mail, but it doesn't check whether the value actually looks like a valid address. We'll see how to perform that kind of test when we write our next application.

Another way to use email within the application would be to have it send you notification if it notices that a user submits a registration with a serial number that duplicates a number already in the table. This probably indicates a typo on some user's part.

Some uses for email apply not at the time you collect information from your visitors, but later. It's fairly common to put a field in a form allowing a user to sign up to receive announcements. You'd store the address when the form is submitted, and then retrieve all addresses later each time you have an announcement to send.

Running a Giveaway Contest

Some Web sites are fairly stable, with content that doesn't change very much. Suppose, however, that you operate a site that provides frequently changing information, such as a news site for a radio or television station. You probably want people to visit often to see new material, and you may be looking for some sort of attraction to lure them to the site on a recurring basis. Then it hits you: Offer a periodic giveaway contest, where people can enter their name once for each giveaway. This serves multiple purposes:

- It encourages people to visit your site regularly.
- You get people to divulge information that you can use later to send them annoying junk mail telling them how wonderful your site is and urging them to visit even *more* frequently!

Okay, I'm just kidding about that second purpose. I don't condone gathering information and then misusing it, although that is often the reason giveaways are held. (Ever notice how you end up on a new mailing list after you put your business card into one of those "Win a Free Dinner!" fishbowls at a restaurant? Now you know why; those things are really a trap for the unwary.)

There are several aspects to running a giveaway contest such as this:

- Obviously, you have to have prizes to give away. I leave this part up to you.
- You need to collect entries. This can be done using a form-based script.
- You have to perform periodic drawings to determine who the winners are. Initially, we'll write our application to handle a daily giveaway, because the queries are simpler to write. Later we'll consider the issues involved in modifying the application for longer periods of time, such as weekly or monthly.
- You must notify the winners of their good fortune.
- You may want to run summary queries to provide you with information about the popularity of your contest, or perhaps delete old entries.
- When you're ready to retire the application, remember to remove it from the Web site. Otherwise, you'll have one of those hideous "Most recent winner: Jane Doe, February 13, *XXXX*" situations, where *XXXX* is about 10 years ago. A good way to disgust your visitors is to awaken their interest in a contest and then have them realize that it's an ancient promotion that you're no longer maintaining.

We'll discuss how to implement each of these phases of the contest shortly (except for acquiring the prizes and deleting the application), but first we should consider something else: fraud.

Detecting Fraud

One issue to be concerned about when you develop this kind of application is the potential for ballot-box stuffing. You don't want people to submit multiple entries to gain an unfair advantage over other contestants. Detection of fraudulent entries is a very difficult problem to solve in general, because in a Web environment it's difficult to uniquely identify visitors to your site. Fortunately, one thing you have working for you in a giveaway situation is that contestants have an incentive to submit correct information. (Only a silly or stupid contestant would submit an entry containing fake information, because you'd have no way to contact the contestant if you drew that entry as a winner.) You can use this fact to help you determine whether one entry duplicates another.

One general "bad guy" strategy for submitting multiple entries is to enter information each time that is correct yet slightly different from earlier entries. Conversely, a general strategy for defeating these attempts is to remove variation by converting values to a single standard format before storing them. This gives you a better chance of detecting duplicates. The following list discusses some of these techniques:

- Trim leading and trailing whitespace to prevent people from attempting to submit multiple entries using values that differ only in the amount of whitespace:[6]

```
$val =~ s/^\s+//;
$val =~ s/\s+$//;
```

- Convert sequences of multiple whitespace characters to single spaces. This defeats attempts to make values unique that are based on putting differing numbers of spaces between words:

```
$val =~ s/\s+/ /g;
```

- Don't be fooled by letter-case variations. "Paul", "PAUL", and "paul" are all the same name, and you'd want to recognize them as such. To that end, don't store text values in case-sensitive table columns, or else convert values to a known case before storing them. For example, you can convert strings to uppercase or lowercase like this:

```
$val = uc ($val);
$val = lc ($val);
```

CHAR and VARCHAR columns are not case sensitive. CHAR BINARY and VARCHAR BINARY are case sensitive, as are TEXT and BLOB columns. If you do use a column type that is case sensitive, you should force values to a given case before storing them.

---

6. We used this whitespace-removal technique earlier, but for another reason: to prevent our applications from thinking that a field containing only tabs or spaces has a real value in it.

- Remove punctuation if you can. The following pattern removes all characters but letters and spaces, which converts differing values, such as "John A. Smith" and "John A Smith", to the same value:

```
$val =~ s/[^ a-zA-Z]//g;
```

- Convert values that are partially numeric to strictly numeric form when possible. A user might attempt to submit three entries by using variant forms of the same telephone number, such as "123-4567", "123 4567", and "1234567". A string comparison would consider these all different, even though you'd easily recognize them as the same. By stripping out the non-digit characters, all three forms become the same value "1234567". You can do this by performing the following substitution:

```
$val =~ s/\D//g;
```

The same kind of conversion can be useful with other types of values, such as credit card or social security numbers.

We'll use several of these techniques in our giveaway application. They aren't a complete solution to the duplicate-entry problem, but they do help make entries more uniform. These value-transformation operations are likely to be useful in other scripts as well, so we'll add them as utility functions to our WebDB.pm module file (see Chapter 2, "Getting Connected—Putting Your Database on the Web"). For example, a function to trim whitespace from the ends of a value can be written like this:

```
sub trim
{
my $str = shift;

    return "" if !defined $str;
    $str =~ s/^\s+//;
    $str =~ s/\s+$//;
    return ($str);
}
```

trim() is likely to be the first transformation we apply to field values, so we also can have it convert undef to the empty string. That way it takes care of two value-checking operations automatically. To use trim(), invoke it as follows:

```
$val = WebDB::trim ($val);
```

The other functions are written in similar fashion; we'll call them collapse_white-space(), strip_punctuation(), and strip_non_digits(). You'll find all these functions in the version of WebDB.pm provided in this book's webdb source distribution.[7]

---

7. If you decide to add other validation functions to WebDB.pm and you're using mod_perl, remember that you'll need to restart Apache. mod_perl notices only changes to scripts that are invoked directly, not changes to library modules.

Making entries more uniform helps us in two ways. First, we can attempt to eliminate as many duplicate entries as possible at the time they are submitted. To do this, we'll require contestants to provide some piece of information that makes entries unique. If you consider telephone numbers unique and want to allow only one entry per person per day, for example, you can construct a unique index on the contestant record table that consists of the entry date and the telephone number. Then if someone attempts to enter twice on the same day, we can toss the second entry by noticing that an entry with the same phone number has already been received. (There are at least three problems with this strategy: A person might have multiple phone numbers and could submit one entry per number; a person might enter once with the area code specified and once without; and people who legitimately share the same phone number, such as household members, are prevented from each submitting separate entries. However, I'm going to ignore these problems and just observe that they illustrate the difficulty of arriving at bulletproof uniqueness criteria. You will of course want to determine specific fraud-detection guidelines for your own situation.)

Second, entries that are more uniform help us each time we draw a winning entry. When we select a specific contestant record, we can use it to locate other entries that are near matches and examine them to see whether they look suspiciously similar to the winning entry.

Designing the Contestant Table

The table for storing contestant entries is not complicated. As usual, we'll have an AUTO_INCREMENT column named `id` to which MySQL will assign unique identifier numbers, and a column to record the record-creation time. We'll also have a few columns that identify the contestant:

```
CREATE TABLE contestant
(
    id          INT UNSIGNED NOT NULL AUTO_INCREMENT PRIMARY KEY,
    entry_date  DATE NOT NULL,
    name        VARCHAR(50) NOT NULL,
    email       VARCHAR(60) NOT NULL,
    telephone   VARCHAR(20) NOT NULL,
    UNIQUE (entry_date, telephone)
)
```

The `contestant` table includes a unique index composed of values in the `entry_date` and `telephone` columns. This enforces the constraint that only one entry per day can be submitted for any given phone number. The date can be assigned by our application, `giveaway.pl`, when it receives an entry. The telephone number must be provided by the contestant, but might be entered using varying formats, so we'll perform some preprocessing on it to increase our chances of duplicate detection.

Collecting Contest Entries

The main logic of the giveaway.pl script is pretty much identical to that of prod_reg.pl, so it need not be shown here. Basically, it checks the choice parameter to see whether it's empty or submit, and then displays the entry form or processes a submitted form accordingly.

The contestant entry form contains only three text-input fields (contestant's name, email address, and telephone number) and a Submit button. Here again, as with the product-registration application, we can use a hash to describe each field, and then pass the hash array to the form-generating and record-entry functions. The field array looks like this:

```
my @field_list =
(
    { name => "name", label => "Name:" },
    { name => "email", label => "Email address:" },
    { name => "telephone", label => "Telephone:" }
);
```

The array contains field hashes that differ slightly from those we used for the product-registration form. First, there is no req hash attribute to indicate which fields must be non-empty. We're going to require all fields to be filled in, so the form-validation code can enforce that requirement uniformly for all fields. Second, we'll make all fields the same length, so there's no need for a size attribute, either. The code to generate the entry form ends up much like that for product registrations, with some small modifications:

```
sub display_entry_form
{
my $field_ref = shift;      # reference to field list
my @row;

    print start_form (-action => url ()),
            p ("Please complete the following form to submit your\n"
              . "entry for our giveaway contest. Please, only\n"
              . "one entry per person per day.");
    foreach my $f (@{$field_ref})
    {
        push (@row, Tr (
                td (escapeHTML ($f->{label})),
                td (textfield (-name => $f->{name}, -size => 60 ))
            ));
    }
    print table (@row),
            submit (-name => "choice", -value => "Submit"),
            end_form ();
}
```

When a contestant submits an entry, we'll perform some tests on it. If the entry is unsuitable, we'll redisplay the form with appropriate feedback indicating how to fix the problems. Otherwise, we'll use the form contents to create a new contestant table record and thank the user for participating:

```perl
sub process_form
{
my $field_ref = shift;       # reference to field list
my @errors;
my ($name, $email, $telephone);
my $dbh;

    # First, make sure all fields have a value
    foreach my $f (@{$field_ref})
    {
        my $val = WebDB::trim (param ($f->{name})); # get trimmed field value
        push (@errors, $f->{label}) if $val eq "";  # it's empty!
        # put modified value back into environment
        param (-name => $f->{name}, -value => $val);
    }
    if (@errors)
    {
        print p ("Some information is missing."
            . " Please fill in the following fields:");
        s/:$// foreach (@errors);   # strip colons from end of labels
        print ul (li (\@errors));              # print column names
        display_entry_form ($field_ref);    # redisplay entry form
        return;
    }

    # Re-extract the modified values from the environment and perform some
    # field-specific checks.  Also, transform values to more uniform format
    # to make it easier to catch duplicates.

    $name = param ("name");
    $email = param ("email");
    $telephone = param ("telephone");

    # Collapse runs of white space, eliminate punctuation in the name field
    $name = WebDB::collapse_whitespace ($name);
    $name = WebDB::strip_punctuation ($name);

    # Check the email value using a rudimentary pattern that requires
    # a user name, an @ character, and a hostname containing at least
    # two components.

    if (!WebDB::looks_like_email ($email))
    {
        push (@errors, "Email address must be in user\@host.name format");
    }
```

```
# Strip non-digit characters from telephone number
$telephone = WebDB::strip_non_digits ($telephone);
if (length ($telephone) < 7)
{
    push (@errors, "Telephone number must contain at least seven digits");
}

if (@errors)
{
    print p ("Your entry could not be processed. Please\n"
            . "correct the following problem(s) and resubmit the entry:");
    print ul (li (\@errors));          # print error messages
    display_entry_form ($field_ref);   # redisplay entry form
    return;
}

# Everything looks okay.  Insert record, thank user.
# Use INSERT IGNORE to ignore attempts to enter twice.
# (If an entry contains entry_date and telephone values
# that duplicate an existing record, it will be rejected.)

$dbh = WebDB::connect();
$dbh->do ("INSERT IGNORE INTO contestant (entry_date,name,email,telephone)
        VALUES(CURRENT_DATE,?,?,?)",
    undef,
    $name, $email, $telephone);
$dbh->disconnect ();

print p ("We have received your entry. Thank you.");
print p ("We will notify you if you are a winner!");
}
```

The test to verify that each field has been filled in is similar to what we've done before: Trim whitespace from the ends and check whether the result is empty. To avoid having to strip whitespace again later when performing more specific tests, the loop stores the modified value back into the environment:

```
# put modified value back into environment
param (-name => $f->{name}, -value => $val);
```

That way, when we extract the values again later, we get the already-stripped versions. In effect, we're treating the parameter space as a global clipboard that can be used to pass data around between different phases of an application.[8]

---

8. We could also have used the technique of storing the stripped variable values in a `value` attribute of the field information hashes, the way we did for the product-registration application. I'm using `param()` here to illustrate another technique that accomplishes the same end without modifying the field hashes.

For fields found to be missing, we collect error messages and display them if the form is not complete. If values were supplied for all fields, further processing is performed on each field according to the type of information it's expected to contain. The field-specific operations are designed to verify that the content matches some expected format and to put values into a standardized format that will help us identify duplicate entries.

For the name, we collapse runs of whitespace characters to single spaces and eliminate punctuation. This isn't necessary for validation of the entry, but it's useful for fraud detection later: After we pick a winning entry, standardizing the name values will help us find possible duplicates on the name field.

For the email value, we call looks_like_email(), a utility routine that checks whether a value looks like an email address in user@host.name form. Email address validation can be a really complicated task to perform in any exhaustive sense. For example, Friedl (*Mastering Regular Expressions*, by Jeffrey E. F. Friedl) shows a regular expression that works for the general case, but it's 6598 characters long! I prefer something a bit less complex that just weeds out obvious clunkers. We'll require a string containing a username, an '@' character, and a domain name consisting of at least two components separated by periods:

```
sub looks_like_email
{
my $str = shift;

    return ($str =~ /^[^@]+@[^.]+\.[^.]/);
}
```

As an explanation of the pattern, here it is again, this time expressed using Perl's /.../x pattern notation that allows embedded comments:

```
return ($str =~ /
        ^           # match beginning of string
        [^@]+       # match non-empty sequence of non-@ characters
        @           # match literal @ character
        [^.]+       # match non-empty sequence of non-period characters
        \.          # match literal period
        [^.]        # require at least one more non-period character
    /x);
```

The pattern match passes correct addresses and flunks several forms of malformed addresses:

```
fred@user-surly.com                  okay
fred@central.user-surly.com          okay
fred.rumblebuffin@user-surly.com     okay
fred@user-surly                      bad; domain name has only one component
fred@                                bad; no domain name
@user-surly.com                      bad; no user name
@                                    bad; no user name or domain name
```

looks_like_email() is the kind of routine that's likely to be useful in several scripts, so I put it in WebDB.pm to make it easily accessible. Putting the address-checking test in a function also is beneficial if you decide at some point that you prefer to use a different pattern for checking addresses—perhaps one that's stricter. Just modify looks_like_email() and all your scripts that use it immediately become more strict in what they consider a valid address. You don't need to modify each script individually.[9]

Telephone numbers are one of those types of information that can be specified different ways, so we strip non-digit characters to convert the value to a standard format before storing it. Also, it's a good idea to check the result to make sure it contains at least seven digits, because anything shorter is sure to be malformed:

```
$telephone = WebDB::strip_non_digits ($telephone);
if (length ($telephone) < 7)
{
    push (@errors, "Telephone number must contain at least seven digits");
}
```

If the @errors array is non-empty after the field-specific tests, one or more problems were found, so process_form() displays the error messages and shows the form again so that the user can correct the problems. Otherwise, everything looks okay and the entry can be added to the contestant table. The query uses INSERT IGNORE rather than just INSERT. The IGNORE keyword is a MySQL-specific extension to the INSERT statement that's very helpful in this case. It causes the new entry to be discarded silently if it contains the same telephone number as an existing record entered on the same day. Without IGNORE, the script would abort with an error if the entry happens to duplicate an existing record.

An alternative to INSERT IGNORE is REPLACE (another MySQL extension), which would kick out any earlier entry that matches the new one. However, INSERT IGNORE seems a bit fairer in this case. It keeps the existing record, which gives precedence to the earliest entry.

process_form() could test whether the new entry was inserted or ignored, by checking the row count returned by the do() call. If the result is zero, the record was a duplicate and was discarded. However, we don't bother checking. What for? If someone really is attempting to submit multiple entries, why provide any feedback about the success or failure of the attempt? Letting such users know they failed only serves to alert them that they need to try harder. The principle here is to provide as little information as possible to the bad guys.

---

9. One caveat: Remember that in a mod_perl environment, you'd need to restart Apache to get it to notice that the library file containing the function has been changed.

Picking Winning Entries

It's necessary to pick a winning entry for each contest period. Our giveaway is a daily one, so picking an entry is a matter of selecting a random row from the entries submitted on a given day. For example, the contest for January 17, 2001 closes at the end of the day, so as of January 18, 2001 on, we can pick a winner any time, like this:

```
mysql> SELECT * FROM contestant WHERE entry_date = '2001-01-17'
    -> ORDER BY RAND() LIMIT 1;
+-----+------------+------------+---------------+-----------+
| id  | entry_date | name       | email         | telephone |
+-----+------------+------------+---------------+-----------+
| 97  | 2001-01-17 | Paul DuBois | paul@snake.net | 5551212   |
+-----+------------+------------+---------------+-----------+
```

The WHERE clause in the query identifies the candidate rows from which you want to make a selection, ORDER BY RAND() "sorts" the rows into a random order, and LIMIT 1 restricts the result set to the first of these rows. The effect is to pick one of the given day's rows at random.

You cannot use RAND() in an ORDER BY clause prior to MySQL 3.23.2. However, there is a workaround available for older versions. It involves selecting an additional column containing random numbers and sorting the result on that column. This randomizes the result set with respect to the other columns:

```
mysql> SELECT *, id*0+RAND() AS rand_num
    -> FROM contestant WHERE entry_date = '2001-01-17'
    -> ORDER BY rand_num LIMIT 1;
+-----+------------+------------+---------------+------------+--------------+
| id  | entry_date | name       | email         | telephone  | rand_num     |
+-----+------------+------------+---------------+------------+--------------+
| 53  | 2001-01-17 | Paul DuBois | paul@snake.net | 6085551212 | 0.2591492526 |
+-----+------------+------------+---------------+------------+--------------+
```

The inclusion of id*0 in the expression defeats the query optimizer, which would otherwise think that the additional rand_num column contains constant values and "optimizes" the ORDER BY rand_num clause by eliminating it from the query.

Now that we have a query for selecting a random row, we can begin picking winning entries. To do so manually, you can run one of the SELECT queries just shown, substituting the appropriate date. Or the computer can do the work automatically if you use a cron job that runs each day to choose a winner from among the preceding day's entries. For example, I might put the following entry in my crontab file to run a script named pick_winner.pl at 5 a.m. every day:

```
0 5 * * * /u/paul/bin/pick_winner.pl
```

Assuming that cron is of the variety that automatically mails job output to the crontab file owner, pick_winner.pl can select a winning entry and display its contents using normal print statements. We can test the script easily by running it from the command line, yet receive the results by mail when the script runs under cron.

`pick_winner.pl` begins by connecting to the database (not shown), and then determines whether there are any relevant entries for the contest date:

```
# default date is "yesterday"
my $contest_date = "DATE_SUB(CURRENT_DATE,INTERVAL 1 DAY)";
# select date in CCYY-MM-DD form
my $date = $dbh->selectrow_array ("SELECT $contest_date");
my $count = $dbh->selectrow_array (
                "SELECT COUNT(*) FROM contestant
                WHERE entry_date = $contest_date");
print "Giveaway contest results for $date:\n";
print "There were $count entries.\n";
```

The DATE_SUB() expression evaluates to the date for "yesterday" no matter what the current date is, so we don't need to figure it out ourselves. However, the output from pick_winner.pl should indicate which date it's picking a winner for, and printing a DATE_SUB() expression literally isn't very useful for that, to say the least. The first SELECT query solves this problem.[10] MySQL evaluates DATE_SUB() and returns the resulting date in standard CCYY-MM-DD format that will be more meaningful for display purposes. (You could put the DATE_SUB() expression inside a call to DATE_FORMAT() if you want a different output format, of course.)

Next, pick_winner.pl counts the number of entries for the given date and reports the date and entry count. If there are any entries, it picks one at random and displays its contents:

```
if ($count > 0)     # don't bother picking winner if there are no entries
{
    my ($id, $name, $email, $telephone) = $dbh->selectrow_array (
                "SELECT id, name, email, telephone FROM contestant
                WHERE entry_date = $contest_date
                ORDER BY RAND() LIMIT 1");
    # Paranoia check; this shouldn't happen
    die "Error, couldn't select winning entry: $DBI::errstr\n"
                                    unless defined ($id);
    print "The winning entry is:\n";
    print "id: $id\n";
    print "name: $name\n";
    print "email: $email\n";
    print "telephone: $telephone\n";
}
```

Run the script from the command line to make sure it works:

```
% /u/paul/bin/pick_winner.pl
Giveaway contest results for 2001-01-17:
There were 4 entries.
The winning entry is:
id: 397
name: Wendell Treestump
email: wt@stumpnet.org
telephone: 1234567
```

---

10. Some database engines require that a SELECT statement always use at least one table. MySQL does not, so we can use SELECT as a calculator that evaluates expressions without reference to any table.

If you have more than one entry, you can run the script several times to verify that it doesn't always pick the same entry.

To make `pick_winner.pl` more useful, we can modify it slightly to accept an optional date from the command line. That way we can override the default date and pick winners for any day. (And, as it happens, by specifying today's date, we can use `pick_winner.pl` to see how many entries have been submitted for the current date so far. In this case we ignore the "winner" entry, of course, because other entries might still arrive.) The modification is quite trivial. Following the line that sets the default date, add another line that checks the `@ARGV` array for a command-line argument:

```
# default date is "yesterday"
my $contest_date = "DATE_SUB(CURRENT_DATE,INTERVAL 1 DAY)";
$contest_date = "'" . shift (@ARGV) . "'" if @ARGV;
```

Now we can invoke the script with an explicit date:

```
% /u/paul/bin/pick_winner.pl 2001-1-15
```

With a little more work, we can have `pick_winner.pl` recognize "dates" such as `-n` to mean "*n* days ago." Add the following lines after the `@ARGV`-checking line:

```
if ($contest_date =~ /^'-(\d+)'$/)  # convert -n to n days ago
{
    $contest_date = "DATE_SUB(CURRENT_DATE,INTERVAL $1 DAY)";
}
```

That makes it easier to specify dates on the command line. To pick a winner for three days ago or to see how many entries have been submitted today, use the following commands:

```
% /u/paul/bin/pick_winner.pl -3
% /u/paul/bin/pick_winner.pl -0
```

We attempted to eliminate exact duplicates at record-entry time by standardizing the telephone number that forms part of the unique table index. If you like, you can also look for duplicates at winner-picking time by modifying `pick_winner.pl` to produce additional information that may be helpful for assessing whether your winner is legitimate or fraudulent. To do this, run some queries that look for near matches to the winning entry. If these queries produce any output, you can investigate further. (These results should be considered advisory only; you should examine them manually to evaluate for yourself whether you think something funny is going on.)

One approximate-matching technique can be used to locate questionable entries based on telephone numbers. The number is supposed to be unique among all entries for a given day, but we can eliminate duplicates at entry-submission time only if the number is *exactly* the same as the number in an existing entry. How about the following entries; do they look like duplicates to you?

```
+------+------------+-----------------+----------------------+------------+
| id   | entry_date | name            | email                | telephone  |
+------+------------+-----------------+----------------------+------------+
|  407 | 2001-01-17 | Bill Beaneater  | bill@beaneater.net   | 5551212    |
|  413 | 2001-01-17 | Bill Beaneater  | bill@beaneater.net   | 6085551212 |
|  498 | 2001-01-17 | Bill Beaneater  | bill@beaneater.net   | 16085551212|
|  507 | 2001-01-17 | Fred Franklin   | fred@mint.gov        | 4145551212 |
+------+------------+-----------------+----------------------+------------+
```

The telephone numbers in the second and third entries aren't exact matches to the number in the first entry, so our `giveaway.pl` script didn't reject them. But as humans, we can easily see that they represent the same telephone number (assuming that 608 is the local area code). The contestant just used the country and area codes to construct phone numbers that are valid but not exactly the same. We can also see that the fourth entry comes from a different area code, so it's not a duplicate—which illustrates why we need to examine approximate-match query output manually.

To find entries with a telephone number that is close to the number in the winning entry, use the following query (`$id` represents the `id` value of the winning entry):

```
SELECT contestant.*
FROM contestant, contestant AS winner
WHERE winner.id = $id
AND contestant.entry_date = winner.entry_date
AND contestant.id != winner.id
AND RIGHT(contestant.telephone,7) = RIGHT(winner.telephone,7)
```

The query involves a self-join. It locates the winning entry in the `contestant` table (under the alias `winner`), and then compares that entry to all others submitted on the same day, looking for a match on the rightmost seven digits of the telephone number. (As with all self-joins, we must refer to the table two different ways to make it clear to MySQL which instance of the table we mean at each point in the query.)

Use the `name` column instead if you want to see whether the winner submitted several entries under the same name. (Perhaps the winner has several phone numbers and submitted one entry per number.) The query is similar to the preceding one except that it looks for matches in the `name` value:

```
SELECT contestant.*
FROM contestant, contestant AS winner
WHERE winner.id = $id
AND contestant.entry_date = winner.entry_date
AND contestant.id != winner.id
AND contestant.name = winner.name
```

The query to look for duplicates on the email address is the same except that both references to the `name` column in the last line should be changed to `email`.

If you decide that a contest winner should be disqualified, just rerun `pick_winner.pl` manually to choose another winner for the appropriate date. (This was in fact one of the reasons for writing it to take an optional date on the command line: That enables you to run the script whenever you want and tell it the day for which you want it to pick a winner.)

> **Other Uses for Near-Match Detection**
>
> The techniques discussed for finding similar records in the contestant table can be adapted for other contexts. Suppose you use your database to generate mailing labels from a list of newsletter subscribers or people to whom you send advertising flyers. If you want to cut down on postage costs, you might try modifying these queries to find instances where you're sending multiple mailings to the same person.

Other more general queries can be used to help you assess the extent to which duplicates are present over the entire table (not just for the winning entry). The following queries attempt to identify duplicates for each day, based on the three contestant-supplied values:

```
SELECT entry_date, name, COUNT(*) AS count
FROM contestant
GROUP BY entry_date, name HAVING count > 1

SELECT entry_date, email, COUNT(*) AS count
FROM contestant
GROUP BY entry_date, email HAVING count > 1

SELECT entry_date, RIGHT(telephone,7) AS phone, COUNT(*) AS count
FROM contestant
GROUP BY entry_date, phone HAVING count > 1
```

Notifying the Winner

If you want to contact a contest winner by telephone, you can do that by looking at the phone number in the winner's contestant table entry. Of course, that doesn't involve any programming, so it's not very interesting! Let's assume, therefore, that you want to issue the "you're a winner!" notification by email, using the email value in the entry. We'll write a notify_winner.pl script that uses the Mail::Sendmail module discussed earlier in the chapter ("Using Email from Within Applications"). The only piece of information this script needs from us is the winning entry ID number. notify_winner.pl can look up the appropriate record and determine from its contents where the message should be sent:

```
#! /usr/bin/perl -w
# notify_winner.pl - Notify giveaway contest winner, given winning entry ID

use strict;
use lib qw(/usr/local/apache/lib/perl);
use Mail::Sendmail;
use WebDB;

# Make sure there's a command-line argument and that it's an integer
@ARGV or die "Usage: $0 winning_entry_id\n";
my $id = shift (@ARGV);
$id =~ /^\d+$/ or die "Entry ID $id is not an integer.\n";
```

continues

continued

```
# Retrieve winning entry from database
my $dbh = WebDB::connect();
my ($entry_date, $name, $email, $telephone) = $dbh->selectrow_array (
                "SELECT entry_date, name, email, telephone FROM contestant
                WHERE id = ?",
                undef, $id);
$dbh->disconnect ();
die "Sorry, there's no entry number $id\n" unless defined ($entry_date);

# Construct mail message and send it (use login name of the user who's
# running the script for the From: address)
my $login = getpwuid ($>) or die "Cannot determine your user name: $!\n";
my %mail =
(
    To => $email,
    From => "$login\@localhost",
    Subject => "Congratulations, you're a winner!",
    Message => "
Congratulations, $name!  You are the winner of our giveaway
contest for the date $entry_date.  To claim your fabulous prize,
please follow these instructions:

<insert instructions for claiming fabulous prize here>."
);

sendmail (%mail) or die "Attempt to send mail failed\n";

exit (0);
```

The script constructs the From: address using the login name of the person running it. You might want to change that. (You should also modify the message body to provide appropriate instructions for claiming the prize.)

Dealing with Old Entries

Eventually the contestant table may grow quite large. That might not bother you if you want to maintain the entries for statistical purposes. For example, you can run queries such as the following ones to generate a summary of submission activity to assess how popular the giveaway is. The first produces a daily summary, and the second summarizes by month:

```
SELECT
    entry_date,
    COUNT(*) AS count
FROM contestant GROUP BY entry_date

SELECT
    YEAR(entry_date) AS year,
    MONTH(entry_date) AS month,
```

```
        COUNT(*) AS count
    FROM contestant GROUP BY year, month
```

The `webdb` distribution accompanying the book includes a script `giveaway_summary.pl` that you can install in your Web server's script directory and invoke to display the result of these queries in a browser window.

You may prefer to delete rather than retain old entries. The following query clobbers all submissions from before January 1, 2001:

```
mysql> DELETE FROM contestant WHERE entry_date < '2001-01-01';
```

It's likely you'd want this kind of query to be run automatically so that you don't have to remember to do it yourself. Here's a script, `expire_contestant.pl`, that does so. (To retain old entries for a different number of days, change the `$days` value):

```
#! /usr/bin/perl -w
# expire_contestant.pl - clobber old contestant entries

use strict;
use lib qw(/usr/local/apache/lib/perl);
use WebDB;

# how long to keep entries (in days)
my $days = 30;

my $dbh = WebDB::connect();
$dbh->do (
        "DELETE FROM contestant
        WHERE entry_date < DATE_SUB(CURRENT_DATE,INTERVAL ? DAY)",
        undef, $days);
$dbh->disconnect ();

exit (0);
```

Now, set up an entry in your `crontab` file to run `expire_contestant.pl` as a `cron` job. The format of the entry depends on how often you want expiration to occur. The following entries all run the job at 4 a.m., but vary in the frequency of expiration—choose the form you prefer. The first runs daily, the second each Sunday, and the third on the first day of each month:

```
0 4 * * * /u/paul/bin/expire_contestant.pl
0 4 * * 0 /u/paul/bin/expire_contestant.pl
0 4 1 * * /u/paul/bin/expire_contestant.pl
```

Suggested Modifications

The `contestant` table contains no information indicating who the winners are, so you'll have to remember whom you pick each day. Add a column to the table and modify `notify_winner.pl` to update the appropriate entry by marking it as a winner.

Consider what modifications you'd need to make to change the drawing period from daily to weekly or monthly. Changing the period of time over which contestants are allowed a single entry affects several things:

- What you'd use for the unique key in the contestant table
- How often you draw entries, and the date range you use to select candidate rows
- The notification message in `notify_winner.pl`
- Any approximate-match duplicate detection queries you may be using
- cron job scheduling for `pick_winner.pl` and `expire_contestant.pl`

In general, these changes will follow from any changes you make to the `contestant` table to determine the unique key. If you want to conduct a monthly giveaway, for example, you could add `year` and `month` columns to the `contestant` table, and change the unique index from `entry_date` and `telephone` to `year`, `month`, and `telephone`. Then, at entry submission time, use `YEAR(CURRENT_DATE)` and `MONTH(CURRENT_DATE)` to insert the current year and month values. That way, you can continue to use `INSERT IGNORE` to discard duplicate records automatically at entry submission time. Other queries later on in the contest process would select records based on year and month rather than `entry_date`.

Use MySQL to provide you with information about how your Web site is being used and to help you evaluate its effectiveness: Log apparent attempts at submitting duplicate entries. (Check whether the row count returned by the `INSERT IGNORE` query in `giveaway.pl` is zero, and log the entry if so.) This gives you information that might indicate widespread abuse attempts and that can help you decide to implement stricter entry requirements, or perhaps just to terminate the contest altogether.

The `INSERT IGNORE` statement in `giveaway.pl` uses the MySQL-specific `IGNORE` extension. If you want to make the script more portable so that it runs under other databases, yet doesn't die with an error on attempts to enter duplicate entries, how do you do it?

Conducting a Poll

In this section, we'll take a look at polling, a common activity on the Web:

- News organizations often conduct polls on current events: Which candidate do you plan to vote for? How would you assess the president's handling of foreign policy? Is the economy in good shape?

- Sports sites ask for predictions: Who will win the World Series? the Super Bowl? the World Cup? Who's the best athlete of the last decade? Do you think the designated hitter rule should be eliminated?

- Polls enable you to gather feedback about your site or your organization: How easy was it to find what you needed on our Web site? How would you grade our customer service? Do you think our news coverage is objective or biased?

- Ratings are a natural use for polls: How would you rate this restaurant? How much did you enjoy this movie?

Most polls have a fairly standard format: Pose a question to the user and present a set of answers from which to choose, along with a submission button for casting the vote. Poll applications also commonly show the user the current results after a vote is cast. Sometimes a link is provided on the voting form that goes directly to the results page, for users who prefer not to vote or who have voted in the past and just want to see where the vote stands now.

As a simple poll, we'll ask people to vote for their favorite Groundhog's Day celebrity using a script groundhog.pl. The two prime candidates are Jimmy the Groundhog in Sun Prairie, Wisconsin, and Punxsutawney Phil in Punxsutawney, Pennsylvania. (This is about the most basic poll you can have—there are only two choices.) The poll script will handle the following operations:

- When first invoked, the script displays a page containing a form that presents the candidate groundhogs using a set of radio buttons, and a button for casting the vote. The page also includes a "see current results" link, in case the user wants to see the vote totals without actually submitting a vote.

- After the user submits a vote, the script adds it to the lucky groundhog's tally, thanks the user for voting, and displays the current results.

- If the user selects the "current results" link rather than casting a vote, the script just displays the results.

The main logic for the groundhog.pl script is as follows:

```perl
my %groundhog_map =      # hash that maps groundhog names to labels
(
    "jimmy" => "Jimmy the groundhog (Sun Prairie, Wisconsin)",
    "phil" => "Punxsutawney Phil (Punxsutawney, Pennsylvania)"
);

print header (),
    start_html (-title => "Vote for Your Favorite Groundhog",
                -bgcolor => "white");

# Dispatch to proper action based on user selection

my $choice = lc (param ("choice")); # get choice, lowercased
```

continues

continued

```
if ($choice eq "")                    # initial script invocation
{
    display_poll_form (\%groundhog_map);
}
elsif ($choice eq "submit")           # tally vote, show current results
{
    process_vote (\%groundhog_map, 1, param ("name"));
}
elsif ($choice eq "results")          # just show current results
{
    process_vote (\%groundhog_map, 0);
}
else
{
    print p (escapeHTML ("Logic error, unknown choice: $choice"));
}

print end_html ();
```

In a sense, this part of the script is similar to the corresponding parts of the
prod_reg.pl and giveaway.pl scripts: It encodes information about the form in a data
structure that it passes to the form-generation and form-processing functions. However, the data structure is different because we're going to present a set of radio
buttons, not a set of text-input fields. Accordingly, we set up a hash map that associates
groundhog names with descriptive labels. We use the names as the values of our radio
buttons on the polling form and in the database table used to store the votes. The
descriptive labels are more meaningful for users and are used for display in the polling
form and results pages.

The map gets passed to each function that needs it (display_poll_form() and
process_vote()). The process_vote() routine has a dual purpose; it handles the cases
when the user submits a vote or just selects the "see current results" link. The second
argument indicates whether a vote is expected; if so, a third argument contains the
selected groundhog name.

display_poll_form() presents a form containing a radio button for each groundhog and a Submit button:

```
sub display_poll_form
{
my $map_ref = shift;    # groundhog name/label map

    print start_form (-action => url ()),
        p ("Which groundhog is your favorite?"),    # pose question
        radio_group (-name => "name",
                     -values => [ sort (keys (%{$map_ref})) ],
                     -default => "[NO DEFAULT]",
                     -override => 1,
                     -labels => $map_ref,
                     -linebreak => 1),    # display buttons vertically
```

```
            br (),
            submit (-name => "choice", -value => "Submit"),
            end_form ();
        # add link allowing user to see current results without voting
        print hr (),
            a ({-href => url () . "?choice=results"}, "See current results");
    }
```

$map_ref refers to the hash that associates the groundhog names with their descriptive labels. This hash can be used as is to supply the labels parameter to the radio_group() function, but we also need to extract the names for the values parameter. However, values requires a reference to an array, not an array, so we can't pass the list of names directly:

```
    -values => sort (keys (%{$map_ref}))        # incorrect
```

Putting the list inside [ ] creates a reference:

```
    -values => [ sort (keys (%{$map_ref})) ]    # correct
```

The default value for the radio buttons is chosen explicitly not to be equal to either of the groundhog names. This causes the form to be displayed with no button selected, to avoid swaying the vote. Setting the linebreak parameter to non-zero causes the buttons to display vertically.

Of course, we're jumping ahead of ourselves here a little bit. What do we do with a vote when it's submitted? We need a table in which to store the vote counts for each candidate. Here's a simple table to hold groundhog names and vote counters:

```
CREATE TABLE groundhog
(
    name    CHAR(10) NOT NULL,              /* groundhog name */
    tally   INT UNSIGNED NOT NULL DEFAULT 0 /* number of votes */
)
```

Initializing the table is trivial; all we need is an INSERT statement that adds rows naming each groundhog (we need not set the tally column explicitly because its default value is zero):

```
INSERT INTO groundhog (name) VALUES ('jimmy'), ('phil')
```

Now that we have a table, we can use it to tally votes and display results. The process_vote() function takes care of this. Its $tally_vote argument indicates whether to tally a vote or just display results. However, we need to check whether a vote actually was submitted even if $tally_vote is non-zero. (The voting form comes up with no radio button selected; if the user just selects the Submit button, the form's name parameter that contains the name of the selected groundhog will be empty.) Therefore, we update the current tally for the appropriate groundhog and thank the user for voting only if we find a legal vote. Then we display the current results:

```perl
sub process_vote
{
my ($map_ref, $tally_vote, $name) = @_;
my ($dbh, $rs_ref, $row_ref, $sum, @table_row);

    $dbh = WebDB::connect ();
    if ($tally_vote)
    {
        # make sure name was given and that it's one of the legal names
        if (defined ($name) && defined ($map_ref->{$name}))
        {
            $dbh->do ("UPDATE groundhog SET tally = tally + 1 WHERE name = ?",
                        undef, $name);
            print p ("Thank you for voting!");
        }
        else
        {
            print p ("No vote was cast; did you make a choice?");
        }
    }

    print p (" The current results are:");
    # retrieve result set as a reference to a matrix of names and tallies
    $rs_ref = $dbh->selectall_arrayref ("SELECT name, tally FROM groundhog");
    $dbh->disconnect ();

    # compute sum of vote tallies
    $sum = 0;
    map { $sum += $_->[1] } @{$rs_ref};
    if ($sum == 0)  # no results!
    {
        print p ("No votes have been cast yet");
        return;
    }

    # Construct table of results: header line first, then contents.
    # For each groundhog, show votes as a tally and as a percentage
    # of the total number of votes.  Right-justify numeric values.
    push (@table_row, Tr (th ("Groundhog"), th ("Votes"), th ("Percent")));
    foreach $row_ref (@{$rs_ref})
    {
        my $label = $map_ref->{$row_ref->[0]};  # map name to descriptive label
        my $percent = sprintf ("%d%%", (100 * $row_ref->[1]) / $sum);
        push (@table_row, Tr (
                td (escapeHTML ($label)),
                td ({-align => "right"}, $row_ref->[1]),    # tally
                td ({-align => "right"}, $percent)          # % of total
            ));
    }
    print table (@table_row);
}
```

To display the current vote totals, we run a query to retrieve the names and vote tallies from the groundhog table. `selectall_arrayref()` returns a result set as a reference to a matrix (specifically, as a reference to an array, each element of which is a reference to an array containing one row from the table).[11] After retrieving the result set, we sum the `tally` values to determine the total number of votes cast. This has two purposes. First, we can tell from the total whether any votes have been cast yet. Second, the total allows us to calculate the percentage of votes each groundhog has received when we generate the rows of the vote display table. The name-to-label map gives us the descriptive label from the groundhog name, which is HTML-encoded using `escapeHTML()` in case it contains any special characters. (In fact, neither of the labels do, but this approach prevents surprises if we decide to change the labels at a later date.) No encoding is needed for the tally or the percentage values because we know they're numeric and therefore contain no special characters.

Suggested Modifications

Our poll just counts votes. It doesn't tell you when votes were cast. Modify the application to log each vote and when it occurred so that you can perform time-based analysis of poll activity. Write some summary queries that show the number of votes cast each day (week, month, and so on) that your poll is open.

Suppose you hear about another famous groundhog that lives in the city of Bangor, Maine. Consider what you'd need to do to change the set of candidates presented by the poll:

- The current vote counters should be set back to zero to eliminate any head start by the existing candidates.
- You'd need another row in the `groundhog` table for the new candidate.
- You'd need to add another entry to the hash map that associates ground hog names and descriptive labels.

That's not actually too much work. But now suppose you want to conduct a second poll. The `groundhog.pl` script is adequate if groundhog voting is the only poll you'll ever run, but it has some shortcomings for multiple poll presentations. Using our present poll implementation, you'd need to write a script specifically for each poll you want to carry out. You'd also need a separate vote-tallying table for each one. These problems arise because the script is intimately tied to knowledge about this particular poll. It knows precisely what the choices are, what labels should be associated with the names, and the title for the poll form. In Chapter 6, we'll consider a more general polling implementation that eliminates these shortcomings. It's more work to implement, but more flexible.

---

11. The `selectall_arrayref()` function is useful here to get the entire result set into a data structure because we need to iterate through the result set twice. If we used a row-at-a-time fetch loop, we'd have to run the query twice to process the results twice.

Storing and Retrieving Images

Images are used in many Web applications. This section describes a couple of small scripts that provide you with the ability to load images into MySQL over the Web or from the command line. It also discusses a script that serves images over the Web by pulling them from the database. My reason for placing a section on image storage and retrieval at this point in the chapter is that we'll need image-serving capability for the next section, which demonstrates how to write an electronic greeting card application. One feature of that application is that it enables users to select a picture to display with the card when the recipient views it.

Obviously, to implement that capability, we'll need to be able to send images to the client's browser. And we'll need to supply the application with some images first so that it has something to send! So, here we are.

Images Aren't Special! (Part I)

Although the scripts presented in this section show how to perform storage and retrieval using images, the techniques can be adapted easily for working with any kind of data, not just images. The information here can help you construct a database of sound or video clips, PDF files, compressed data, and so forth.

For storing the images, we'll use a table called `image` that contains a descriptive name for the image, the image itself, a thumbnail (small version) of the image, and the image MIME type:

```
CREATE TABLE image
(
    name        VARCHAR(60) NOT NULL,   # descriptive name for image
    UNIQUE (name),
    image       BLOB NOT NULL,          # image data
    thumbnail   BLOB NOT NULL,          # thumbnail data
    mime_type   VARCHAR(20) NOT NULL    # image MIME type
)
```

The scripts we'll develop refer to images by name. The `name` column has a unique index so that we don't give the same name to two different images. `image` and `thumbnail` are `BLOB` columns, the usual type for binary data. (`VARCHAR` isn't really suitable for such data, because it has a maximum length of just 255 characters.) The `mime_type` column contains values that identify the image format. These will be values such as `image/gif`, `image/jpeg`, `image/png`, and so forth. The image type value applies to both the image and its thumbnail.

To populate the `image` table, we'll write an image-loading script (`upload_image.pl`) that allows images stored on your local disk to be uploaded using your browser for storage into MySQL. It works as follows:

- The initial page presents a form containing a file-upload field for specifying the image file you want to transfer and a field for giving the image a descriptive name. If you have an image of the U.S. flag in a file named `us_flag.jpg`, for example, you might give it a descriptive name of "Stars & Stripes."

- When you submit the form, your browser will send the field values back to the Web server, including the contents of the image file. `upload_image.pl` receives this information, creates a thumbnail version of the image, and stores everything into the database. It also presents a confirmation page that reports the status of the upload operation and displays the image so that you can see that it really was received properly.

Where Should Images Be Stored?

One of the ongoing debates about images and databases is whether to store images in the database or whether to store them in the file system and store only the pathname in the database. `upload_image.pl` shows how to store images in the database so that you'll know how to do it if you want to, but I'm not going to try to settle the debate. If you want more information about the pros and cons of each approach, search the MySQL mailing list archives.

The dispatch logic for `upload_image.pl` is similar to that of several previous applications, so I won't show it here. It invokes `display_upload_form()` to present the entry form and `process_form()` to handle submitted images.

`display_upload_form()` generates the image-selection form. The important thing you should notice about the code is that it uses `start_multipart_form()` rather than `start_form()`. File uploads require form contents to be encoded differently from "regular" forms (otherwise the file content transfer won't work properly):

```
sub display_upload_form
{
    print start_multipart_form (-action => url ()),
            "Image file: ", br (),
            filefield (-name => "image", -size => 60),
            br (),
            "Descriptive name for image: ", br (),
            textfield (-name => "name",
                        -value => "",
                        -override => 1,
                        -size => 60),
            br (), br (),
            submit (-name => "choice", -value => "Submit"),
            end_form ();
}
```

When the user submits an image, `process_form()` is called. This function makes sure the name and image file were both supplied, creates the thumbnail from the image, stores everything in the database, and displays a confirmation page:

```
sub process_form
{
my $name = param ("name");          # image name
my $image = param ("image");        # image file
```

continues

continued

```perl
my @errors = ();
my $dbh;
my $mime_type;
my ($full, $thumb);
my $serve_url;

    $image = "" unless defined ($image);# convert undef to empty string
    $name = WebDB::trim ($name);        # trim extraneous whitespace from name

    # check for required fields
    push (@errors, "Please supply an image name") if $name eq "";
    push (@errors, "Please specify an image file") if $image eq "";
    if (@errors)
    {
        print p ("The following errors occurred:");
        print ul (li (\@errors));
        print p ("Please click your Browser's Back button to\n"
                . "return to the previous page and correct the problem.");
        return;
    }

    # Form was okay; get image type and contents and create new record.
    # Use REPLACE to clobber any old image with the same name.

    $mime_type = uploadInfo ($image)->{'Content-Type'};
    ($full, $thumb) = read_image_file ($image);
    $dbh = WebDB::connect ();
    $dbh->do (
            "REPLACE INTO image
            (name,image,thumbnail,mime_type)
            VALUES(?,?,?,?)",
                undef,
                $name, $full, $thumb, $mime_type);
    $dbh->disconnect ();

    # Image was stored into database successfully.  Present confirmation
    # page that displays both the full size and thumbnail images.

    print p ("The image upload was successful.");
    # encode the name with escape() for URL, but with escapeHTML() otherwise
    $serve_url = sprintf ("serve_image.pl?name=%s", escape ($name));
    $name = escapeHTML ($name);
    $mime_type = escapeHTML ($mime_type);
    print p ("Image name: $name"),
            p ("MIME type: $mime_type"),
            p ("Full size image:"),
            img ({-src => $serve_url, -alt => $name}), "\n",
            p ("Thumbnail image:"),
```

```
            img ({-src => "$serve_url;thumbnail=1", -alt => $name}), "\n";
    # Display link to main page so user can upload another image
    print hr (), a ({-href => url ()}, "Upload next image");
}
```

process_form() validates the form by making sure that both the descriptive image
name and the file pathname are present. We do the usual thing of trimming extraneous
whitespace from the descriptive name. However, we don't do that for the pathname
because that value legitimately could begin or end with spaces, and trimming it would
change the name. (CGI.pm makes the file contents and information about the file
available through the pathname; changing it would render the script unable to access
the file.)

If any errors occur during validation, we indicate what they are and instruct the
user to return to the preceding page to correct the problems. You may recall that in
the discussion of form validation for the product-registration application, I discouraged
the approach of having users click the Back button, favoring instead the method of
redisplaying the form on the same page as the error messages. Aren't I contradicting
that advice here? Yes, I am; and before you read the footnote that explains why, I invite
you to consider why this might be.[12]

If the form contents check out okay, we get the image's MIME type using
uploadInfo(), a CGI.pm function that provides information about the uploaded file,
given the filename as an argument. (This function is described in Chapter 4,
"Generating and Processing Forms," in the section that discusses the sample form
application.) The return value is a reference to a hash of file attributes and values. One
of these attributes, Content-Type, gives us the image's MIME type.

Next, we read the image from the temporary file in which it is stored.
read_image_file() (discussed shortly) reads the image file, creates the thumbnail, and
returns both values. At this point, we have all the information we need to create a new
image table record. The statement that adds the record uses REPLACE rather than INSERT
to make it easy to overwrite an existing image with a new one. (INSERT would generate an error, and INSERT IGNORE would keep the old image and discard the new one.
Neither behavior is desirable here.)

---

12. The reason I don't follow my own advice here is that CGI.pm won't initialize the value
of file-upload fields. This prevents script writers from trying to trick users into uploading specific files, but it also means you can't take advantage of CGI.pm's sticky form behavior for file
fields. In fact, this isn't just a CGI.pm behavior; browsers themselves may refuse to honor a
value attribute for a file-upload field, even if your script includes one by writing the HTML
directly. This means we can't properly redisplay the form with the values submitted by the user,
and therefore really don't have much choice but to ask the user to return to the previous page.

Images Aren't Special! (Part II)

I have the feeling that I should write a headline in GREAT BIG LETTERS that the do() statement used in the process_form() function answers the often-asked question, "How, oh how, do I insert images into my database? What's the special trick?" Well, actually, there isn't one. Images are inserted the same way as any other kind of data: Use placeholders or the quote() function. The usual thing that gives people trouble putting images in a database is the failure to properly escape the special characters that images usually contain. Images consist of binary data, so attempting to put an image directly into the query string without properly escaping its content almost certainly will fail. If you use a placeholder, or insert the image data into the query string after calling quote(), you'll have no problems.

If images seem special compared to text values, due to the need to escape special characters, that's a sign you're probably not processing text properly, either. With text values, you can often get away with not using placeholders or quote(), but that doesn't mean it's correct to do so. Text can contain special characters that cause problems, too—such as quote characters. It's important to use placeholders or quote() for *all* data, not just images or other binary data. If you do that consistently, you'll likely find that the magic conceptual distinction between text and images disappears.

With the image safely stored away in the database, we can present a confirmation page to the user. Given that we're working with images, we may as well make this a graphical page. Therefore, we'll not only inform the user that the upload succeeded, but we'll also display the image and its thumbnail as well.

The image parts of the confirmation page are nothing more than <img> tags that reference an image stored in the database. If the image's name is "My Image," for instance, the tags will look like this:

```
<img src="serve_image.pl?name=My%20Image" alt="My Image">
<img src="serve_image.pl?name=My%20Image;thumbnail=1" alt="My Image">
```

When your browser sees each of these tags in the page, it will send requests to the Web server to retrieve the corresponding images. As the tags show, these requests are handled by another script, serve_image.pl. (We have yet to write this script, but we'll get to it soon.) serve_image.pl yanks an image out of the database and turns it into a valid image transfer to the browser. The <img> tags refer to the script without a leading pathname; we can get away with that if we install serve_image.pl in the same directory as upload_image.pl. The name parameter specifies which image serve_image.pl should return to the browser, and the absence or presence of the thumbnail parameter indicates whether it should return the full-size image or the thumbnail.

The last thing process_form() displays in the confirmation page is a link to the main upload_image.pl page so that the user can transfer another image if desired.

We still have to see how to read the contents of the uploaded image file from the temporary file where it's stored and how to produce a thumbnail from it. Let's return to read_image_file(), the function that actually does this. This function uses some of the capabilities of Image::Magick, a Perl module that allows sophisticated image manipulations to be performed. (You should obtain Image::Magick from the CPAN and install it if you don't already have it.)

We pass read_image_file() the value of the image parameter from the upload form. That parameter contains the name of the file. However, CGI.pm performs a little trick that also allows it to be treated as an open file handle pointing to the uploaded file, so we can use it to read and process the file:

```perl
use Image::Magick;

sub read_image_file
{
my $fh = shift;                  # filename/file handle
my $img = new Image::Magick;
my ($full, $thumb);
my $err;

    # read full-size image directly from upload file
    (read ($fh, $full, (stat ($fh))[7]) == (stat ($fh))[7])
        or error ("Can't read image file: $!");
    # produce thumbnail from full-size image
    $err = $img->BlobToImage ($full);
    error ("Can't convert image data: $err") if $err;
    $err = $img->Scale (geometry => "64x64");
    error ("Can't scale image file: $err") if $err;
    $thumb = $img->ImageToBlob ();
    return ($full, $thumb);
}
```

To handle the image, we create a new Image::Magick object, then invoke a few of its methods after reading the contents of the file containing the full-size image. BlobToImage() converts the raw image data to a form that Image::Magick can use, and Scale() resizes the image to produce the thumbnail. The 64x64 argument to Scale() does not indicate the final pixel size of the resulting image; it indicates the boundary within which the resized image must fit. (That is, Scale() does not change the aspect ratio of the image, only its size.) After scaling the image, we call ImageToBlob() to retrieve the thumbnail as a string.[13]

read_image_file() uses error(), a small utility function that just displays an error message, closes the page, and exits:

```perl
sub error
{
my $msg = shift;

    print p (escapeHTML ("Error: $msg")), end_html ();
    exit (0);
}
```

---

13. Here's something that may or may not affect you: I find that Image::Magick often crashes in read_image_file() at the ImageToBlob() call if the image is in GIF format and uses transparency.

Security and File Uploads

File-uploading operations have the potential to cause some security problems. See Chapter 9, "Security and Privacy Issues," for a discussion of these problems and what you might want to do about them.

upload_image.pl is complete at this point, so you can install it and try it out right now if you like. Note that although the script should upload images properly, the confirmation page won't yet display the uploaded images. That's because we haven't yet written serve_image.pl, the script that handles requests to display images from the image table.

Before we create serve_image.pl, I want to take a slight detour, because I personally find it really tedious to upload image files one by one over the Web. That's convenient for occasional transfers; but when I have a pile of images, I'd rather transfer them to a UNIX box and run a command-line script that loads them. Here's a command-line equivalent to the upload_image.pl script called load_image.pl:

```perl
#! /usr/bin/perl -w
# load_image.pl - load an image file into the image table

use strict;
use lib qw(/usr/local/apache/lib/perl);
use Image::Magick;
use WebDB;

# Determine image file and image name.  Use basename of filename if no image
# name is given.

die "Usage: $0 image_file [ image_name ]\n" unless @ARGV >= 1 && @ARGV <= 2;
my $image_file = shift (@ARGV);
my $image_name = shift (@ARGV);
($image_name = $image_file) =~ s|.*/|| if !defined $image_name;

# determine MIME type of image file from filename extension

my %mime_map = (
    "gif" => "image/gif",
    "jpg" => "image/jpeg",
    "jpeg" => "image/jpeg",
    "jpe" => "image/pjpeg",
    "png" => "image/png"
);
my $mime_type = $mime_map{lc ($1)} if $image_file =~ /\.([^.]+)$/;
die "Cannot determine image MIME type\n" if !defined $mime_type;

# Read image file and generate thumbnail from image

my $img = new Image::Magick;
my ($err, $image_data, $thumbnail_data);
```

```
$err = $img->Read ($image_file);
die "Can't read image file: $err\n" if $err;
$image_data = $img->ImageToBlob ();
$err = $img->Scale (geometry => "64x64");
die "Can't scale image file: $err\n" if $err;
$thumbnail_data = $img->ImageToBlob ();

# Insert new record into the database image table

my $dbh = WebDB::connect ();
$dbh->do (
        "REPLACE INTO image
        (name,image,thumbnail,mime_type)
        VALUES(?,?,?,?)",
            undef,
            $image_name, $image_data, $thumbnail_data, $mime_type);
$dbh->disconnect ();
warn "$image_name loaded\n";      # announce success of image storage operation

exit (0);
```

load_image.pl expects to find either one or two arguments on the command line.
The first is the image filename. The second, if present, is the descriptive name to give
to the image. (If not present, the filename itself is used as the descriptive name.) The
script determines the image type from the filename suffix.

Of course, I don't really want to type in a bunch of load_image.pl commands at
the shell prompt any more than I want to upload images over the Web one by one. So
I FTP the images to a directory Images on my UNIX box, and then log in there and
write a shell script load_images.sh that looks like this:

```
#! /bin/sh
./load_image.pl Images/blackcat.jpg "Black Cat"
./load_image.pl Images/flowers.jpg "Flower Bouquet"
etc.
```

The basis of this script can be created using just a few commands:

```
% ls Images > load_images.sh
% chmod +x load_images.sh
% vi load_images.sh
:1,$s/.*/.\/load_image.pl Image\/&/
```

All that needs to be added is the #! line at the beginning of the script and the
descriptive names at the end of the command lines, and then I can load all the images
easily by running load_images.sh. This is particularly useful when moving all the
images to another machine, because the same script can be used there. (In other
words, writing the script creates a repeatable action.)

If you don't have a shell account, you can't use this command-line approach. If you
do have one, however, to my mind this method is much preferable to uploading
images individually or typing a bunch of individual commands. If you're setting up the
image table using the webdb distribution that accompanies this book, you'll find that its

image directory includes the `load_images.sh` script and an `Images` subdirectory containing a set of sample images to use.

Serving Images

Now that we can get images into the database, how do we get them out again? This section shows how to write `serve_image.pl`, the script that retrieves an image from the `image` table and displays it in a Web page. We need this script so that the confirmation page generated by `upload_image.pl` can properly show the uploaded images. We'll also use `serve_image.pl` for image display in the electronic greeting card application developed later in this chapter.

Before we write this script, let's briefly go over the mechanism used to transfer images over the Web to browsers. Images are referenced from Web pages using `<img>` tags. Typically, the tag refers to a static file on the Web server host. For example, the following tag refers to the "Powered by Apache" image file located in the top directory of the document tree on the host `www.snake.net`:

```
<img src="http://www.snake.net/apache_pb.gif">
```

A browser retrieves the image by sending the URL named in the `src` attribute to the Web server. The server in turn satisfies the request by opening the file and sending it to the browser, preceded by some header information that allows the browser to make sense of the data. Typical headers are `Content-Type:` to specify the MIME type for the image format (`image/gif`, `image/jpeg`, and so forth), and `Content-Length:` to let the browser know how many data bytes to expect.

However, images can be served from sources other than files. If we use a script to duplicate the kind of output the Web server sends when it transfers a static image file, the browser won't care. The script can do this easily by reading a record from the `image` table and using it to generate a request response. The `mime_type` column value indicates what kind of `Content-Type:` header to send and the length of the image data provides a value for the `Content-Length:` header. We write the headers followed by the image data, and we're done. (Now you see why we store the MIME type in the `image` table.)

Naturally, we don't want to write a different script for each image, so we'll have `serve_image.pl` accept a `name` parameter at the end of the URL specifying the name of the image to display. Additionally, if the URL also includes a `thumbnail` parameter, we'll serve the thumbnail image rather than the full-size version. And as a final touch, let's give the script the capability to present a gallery page if we invoke it with a `gallery` parameter rather than an image name. In this case, the script will look up all the image names and descriptions and write an HTML page that includes an `<img>` tag for the thumbnail version of each one. The thumbnails will be clickable so that you can select any of them to see the corresponding full-size image. (In other words, `serve_image.pl` will write an HTML page that causes itself to be invoked in its image-serving capacity.) The URLs for invoking `serve_image.pl` in these various ways look like this:

```
http://www.snake.net/cgi-perl/serve_image.pl?name=image_name
http://www.snake.net/cgi-perl/serve_image.pl?name=image_name;thumbnail=1
http://www.snake.net/cgi-perl/serve_image.pl?gallery=1
```

The dispatch logic for `serve_image.pl` extracts the URL parameters and determines what to do as follows:

```
if (defined (param ("name")))
{
    display_image (param ("name"), param ("thumbnail"));
}
elsif (defined (param ("gallery")))
{
    display_gallery ()
}
else
{
    error ("Unknown request type");
}
```

The image-serving code really is pretty trivial. It checks whether to use the full-size image or the thumbnail, and then looks up the appropriate record from the `image` table, determines the image length from the image data, and writes the headers followed by the data:

```
sub display_image
{
my ($name, $show_thumbnail) = @_;
my $col_name = (defined ($show_thumbnail) ? "thumbnail" : "image");
my ($dbh, $mime_type, $data);

    $dbh = WebDB::connect ();
    ($mime_type, $data) = $dbh->selectrow_array (
                "SELECT mime_type, $col_name FROM image WHERE name = ?",
                undef, $name);
    $dbh->disconnect ();
    # did we find a record?
    error ("Cannot find image named $name") unless defined ($mime_type);

    print header (-type => $mime_type, -Content_Length => length ($data)),
            $data;
}
```

By default, the `header()` function writes a `Content-Type:` header with a value of `text/html` if you don't specify any `type` parameter. We need to override that with the MIME type of the image, otherwise the browser may misinterpret the output and try to display the image data as text. (You can see whether your browser makes a mess of images by removing the type parameter from the header() call and then requesting an image from your browser.)

If the gallery parameter is present in the URL, serve_image.pl generates an HTML page that displays the thumbnails for all the images in the image table:

```
sub display_gallery
{
my ($dbh, $sth);

    print header (), start_html ("Image Gallery");

    $dbh = WebDB::connect ();
    $sth = $dbh->prepare ("SELECT name FROM image ORDER BY name");
    $sth->execute ();
    # we're fetching a single value (name), so we can call fetchrow_array()
    # in a scalar context to get the value
    while (my $name = $sth->fetchrow_array ())
    {
        # encode the name with escape() for the URL, with escapeHTML() otherwise
        my $url = url () . sprintf ("?name=%s", escape ($name));
        $name = escapeHTML ($name);
        print p ($name),
            a ({-href => $url},      # link for full size image
                # embed thumbnail as the link content to make it clickable
                img ({-src => "$url;thumbnail=1", -alt => $name})
            ),
            "\n";
    }
    $sth->finish ();
    $dbh->disconnect ();

    print end_html ();
}
```

For each image, display_gallery() displays the image name and an <img> tag for the thumbnail. The <img> tag is embedded within a hyperlink that takes the user to the full-size image; you can click any thumbnail to see the larger version.

The error() utility routine handles any problems by presenting a short error page. It differs from the version used in upload_image.pl slightly because it generates a complete HTML page:

```
sub error
{
my $msg = shift;

    print header (),
            start_html ("Error"),
            p (escapeHTML ($msg)),
            end_html ();
    exit (0);
}
```

Suggested Modifications

upload_image.pl doesn't check whether the uploaded file really is an image. Is that a problem? If so, can you fix it?

It's possible to load into the image table images that some browsers may be unable to display. For example, older browsers likely won't know what to do with images in PNG (Portable Network Graphics) format. Modify the display_gallery() function of serve_image.pl to exclude images except those in formats the browser understands.

If you load lots of images into the image table, you'd probably want to modify the gallery display code in serve_image.pl to split up the gallery into a multiple-page display. Techniques for multiple-page presentations are described in Chapter 7, "Performing Searches."

serve_image.pl assumes that it is supposed to read images from the image table. If you use it to serve images on behalf of many different applications, you may find it limiting to share the image table among them all. Modify serve_image.pl to accept a table parameter on the URL so that applications can specify which table to use. To preserve compatibility with its original behavior, have the default table be image if no table parameter is present.

Modify upload_image.pl and load_image.pl to store image files in the file system and reference them from the database by storing the pathname in the image table. When you do this, can you toss serve_image.pl in the trashcan?

Electronic Greeting Cards—Send a Friend a Greeting

Our next application enables users to construct electronic greeting cards and send them to friends. You use your browser to create a card, and the recipient uses a browser to view it. This is a more ambitious (and complex) undertaking than any of our previous applications because it has to do a whole bunch of stuff:

- When you first visit the application, you see a card information form into which you enter the name and email address for the recipient and for yourself, as well as the text of the greeting you want to send.

- If you want to select a picture to be displayed with the card, the application switches to a page that displays a gallery of images. After you pick one, the application switches back to the original information form. If you decide to select a different picture, the process repeats.

- After you've finished constructing the card, the application assigns it an expiration date and generates an email message to the recipient indicating that a card is waiting and the URL to use for viewing it.

- When the recipient issues a request for the card, the application retrieves the appropriate record from the database, generates a Web page that displays it, and updates the record to indicate that the recipient has seen the card. If you asked to be notified when the recipient views the card, the application sends you an email message to that effect.
- The application removes old cards from the database periodically.

In effect, the application enables one person to communicate asynchronously with another by means of email and the Web, and it uses MySQL to provide the persistent storage that makes this possible. The application consists of several scripts that handle the various tasks involved:

- `make_ecard.pl` manages the card-creation process. It presents the card information form and the picture gallery page.
- When the recipient requests the card, `show_ecard.pl` displays it, updates the record as having been seen, and notifies the card sender.
- We need a supply of images and a means of displaying them to be able to present pictures with cards. `make_ecard.pl` and `show_ecard.pl` rely for this on the image table and the `serve_image.pl` script developed in the preceding section, "Storing and Retrieving Images." If you haven't yet read that section, it would be a good idea to do so.
- `expire_ecard.pl` removes old cards from the database. It runs periodically as a cron job that checks card expiration dates.

Card construction can take place across the span of several page requests, so we may need to store and retrieve the card to and from the database many times before it's completed. If the user switches from the card information form to the image gallery page, for example, the contents of the form are saved to the database before presenting the gallery. After the user selects a picture, we pull the information back out of the database and use it to initialize the form before redisplaying it. Because we need to tie together multiple page requests (so that we can associate them all with the same card), we'll create a unique ID when a user begins the card-creation process, and carry that ID along at each stage until the card is finished.

The ecard table for storing card records looks like this:

```
CREATE TABLE ecard
(
    id              INT UNSIGNED NOT NULL AUTO_INCREMENT,   # card ID number
    PRIMARY KEY (id),
    recip_name      VARCHAR(255),   # recipient name and email address
    recip_email     VARCHAR(255),
    sender_name     VARCHAR(255),   # sender name and email address
    sender_email    VARCHAR(255),
    sender_notify   ENUM('N','Y'),  # notify sender when recipient views card?
    message         TEXT,           # card message
    picture         VARCHAR(40),    # name of picture to show with card
```

```
      expiration      DATE,          # when to expire card
      viewed          DATE           # when recipient first viewed card
)
```

The `id` column specifies the unique identification number that is used to track each card throughout the card-construction process. We'll also include it as part of the URL that is sent to the recipient so that when a recipient requests a card, we can figure out which one to display.

The recipient name and email address allow us to notify the recipient. (Strictly speaking, notification requires only the email address, but a name allows the application to generate messages that are more personal.)

The sender name and email address are needed so that we can inform the recipient who's responsible for sending the message, and also for generating a notification message if the sender wants to be told when the recipient views the card. `sender_notify` is a two-value column indicating whether the card sender desires this kind of notification.

The `message` and `picture` fields comprise the content of the greeting. `message` contains the text of the greeting, and `picture` indicates which image from the `image` table to display with the message. (A `picture` value of NULL indicates "no picture.")

The `ecard` table also contains two DATE columns. `expiration` is NULL until the sender completes the card, and then it is set to indicate the date when the card can be deleted from the `ecard` table. We'll have the application refuse to modify any card that already has the expiration date set. This convention prevents accidental duplicate card submissions if the card sender clicks the browser's Back button after sending the card and then selects the Send Card button again. This same convention is also a modest security enhancement; it prevents someone else from coming along later and modifying a card that's already been completed. The `viewed` column indicates when the recipient asked to see the card. It's NULL until such a request is received.

Many of these columns are mandatory. Before a card can be sent, we'll enforce the constraint that the names and email addresses all must be supplied, as well as the message text. Because a card may be created in several steps, however, the point at which this information is required does not occur until the user finally indicates the card is finished. That means we must enforce the "fields required" rule only when the user selects the Send Card button and not before.

Card Storage and Retrieval Utility Routines

Our card-creation script `make_ecard.pl` needs to perform several types of operations on card records. The script itself represents card information internally as a hash with key names that are the same as columns in the `ecard` table. However, we'll need to exchange that information back and forth with the client's Web browser, and we'll need to store the hash into and retrieve it from the corresponding database record:

- When the card information form is displayed, we look up any information about the card that exists in the database and use it to initialize the form that the user sees.

- When the user switches to the image gallery page or indicates that the card is complete, we extract the contents of the information form using CGI.pm's param() function and save the card to the database.

To do all this, we'll use three functions: extract_card_params() to get card values from the script environment, lookup_card_record() to retrieve a card from the database, and update_card_record() to store a card in the database. All three functions require the card's id value so they can tell which card to operate on. As we'll see shortly, the main logic of the application makes sure this value is known before any of these utility routines are called.

extract_card_params() looks in the script parameter environment for values that the user can specify. This does not include the expiration or viewed dates because the user has no control over them, and they don't come into play until the card has been completed, anyway. The function extracts the relevant card values from the parameter space, constructs a hash from them, and returns a reference to the hash. We create a slot for each parameter to make sure each one is defined and trim the values to eliminate any extraneous spaces:

```
sub extract_card_params
{
my $card_ref = {};

    $card_ref->{id} = param ("id");
    foreach my $param ("recip_name", "recip_email", "sender_name",
                        "sender_email", "sender_notify", "message", "picture")
    {
        $card_ref->{$param} = WebDB::trim (param ($param));
    }
    return ($card_ref);
}
```

lookup_card_record() fetches a card from the database given the card ID number and returns it as a hash reference:

```
sub lookup_card_record
{
my ($dbh, $id) = @_;
my ($sth, $ref);

    $sth = $dbh->prepare ("SELECT * FROM ecard WHERE id = ?");
    $sth->execute ($id);
    $ref = $sth->fetchrow_hashref ();
    $sth->finish ();
    return ($ref);  # undef if card doesn't exist
}
```

To update a card, we shove it back into the database by converting the card hash to an UPDATE statement. Again, the ID number identifies the proper card:

```
sub update_card_record
{
my ($dbh, $card_ref) = @_;
```

```
my ($stmt, @placeholder);

    # don't store an empty value in this column
    $card_ref->{sender_notify} = "N" if $card_ref->{sender_notify} ne "Y";

    # Construct the SET clause listing the column values to be updated.
    # Skip the id element here (it's used in the WHERE clause, not the
    # SET clause).
    foreach my $key (keys (%{$card_ref}))
    {
        next if $key eq "id";
        $stmt .= "," if $stmt;              # separate assignments by commas
        $stmt .= "$key = ?";                # construct placeholder reference
        push (@placeholder, $card_ref->{$key}); # save placeholder value
    }
    return unless @placeholder; # do nothing if there's nothing to update

    # complete the statement, then execute it
    $stmt = "UPDATE ecard SET $stmt WHERE id = ?";
    push (@placeholder, $card_ref->{id});
    $dbh->do ($stmt, undef, @placeholder);
}
```

Now that we have these support routines in place, we can see how they fit into the overall architecture of the card construction process.

Card Construction Main Logic

When you invoke make_ecard.pl, it needs to know whether you're beginning a new card or are already in the middle of creating one. This is accomplished using the card ID number, which exists during the card-making process, but not before. The first part of the script therefore checks for an id parameter prior to executing the dispatch code:

```
my $card_ref;                     # card information hashref
my $dbh = WebDB::connect ();      # connect to database

# Determine whether to begin a new card or continue working
# on an existing one by checking for a card ID value.

my $id = param ("id");
if (!defined ($id) || $id !~ /^\d+$/)
{
    # ID is missing (or is not an integer, and is therefore malformed).
    # Create new ecard record; this generates a new ID number
    $dbh->do ("INSERT INTO ecard SET id = NULL");
    $id = $dbh->{mysql_insertid};         # retrieve ID number
    param (-name => "id", -value => $id);  # place ID in parameter space
    $card_ref = extract_card_params ($id); # construct standard card hash
}
```

continues

continued

```
else
{
    # ID was found, so the card should already exist in the database.
    # Make sure it does and that the expiration date hasn't been set.
    # (If that date has been set, the card has already been sent!)
    $card_ref = lookup_card_record ($dbh, $id);
    if (!$card_ref || $card_ref->{expiration})
    {
        # error - disconnect and close the page; we need proceed no further
        $dbh->disconnect ();
        print p ("No card with ID $id exists, or card has already been sent");
        print end_html ();
        exit (0);
    }
}
```

If `make_ecard.pl` finds no ID number, it begins a new card by creating a new record in the ecard table. The `INSERT` statement causes MySQL to create a new ID number; id is an `AUTO_INCREMENT` column and setting it to `NULL` generates the next number in the sequence. This number is available as the value of the `mysql_insertid` database handle attribute after executing the `INSERT`. (We could also determine the value by issuing a `SELECT LAST_INSERT_ID()` query, but `mysql_insertid` provides the same information without the overhead of a second query.) Then we put the id value into the parameter space and construct a standard hash structure. At this point, all elements of the hash except id are empty.

If `make_ecard.pl` does find an id value, that means the user is working on an existing card, so there should already be a record for it in the database. We look up the record to make sure it really exists, and then check the expiration date to verify that it hasn't already been set. (The expiration value remains `NULL` until the user sends the card; if it's set, that indicates the user is probably accidentally sending the card again or that someone else is attempting to modify it. Either way, we refuse to continue any further.)

After the preceding initial code executes, we know that we have a database record representing the current contents of the card. We may also have new information in the script's parameter space, if the user has just submitted the card information form or chosen an image from the picture gallery. The dispatch code determines what to do, based as usual on the value of the `choice` parameter. This code is structured around the choices the user can make on the form page and the gallery page:

- The information form has two buttons—Select Picture (or Change Picture if an image has already been chosen) and Send Card.
- The gallery page shows a set of images, any of which many be selected. There is also a Continue button if the user decides not to select any picture.

If the value of choice is empty or continue, we populate the card form with whatever information has already been specified and display it. (The value will be continue if the user was just viewing the gallery page but decided not to choose a picture.) If choice is select picture or change picture, we switch to the image gallery page. If choice is add_picture, the user just chose a picture. Finally, if the value of choice is send card, the user has completed the card and we can save it for good and notify the recipient.

```perl
my $choice = lc (param ("choice")); # get choice, lowercased

if ($choice eq "" || $choice eq "continue")
{
    # New card or user declined to choose a picture from the
    # gallery page.  Just redisplay the card information form.
    display_entry_form ($card_ref);
}
elsif ($choice eq "select picture" || $choice eq "change picture")
{
    # display image gallery (but save form info first)
    $card_ref = extract_card_params ($id);
    update_card_record ($dbh, $card_ref);
    display_gallery ($dbh, $id);
}
elsif ($choice eq "add_picture")
{
    # User chose a picture from the gallery page. Extract the picture
    # name and add it to the card hash, then redisplay card form.
    $card_ref->{picture} = param ("picture") if param ("picture");
    update_card_record ($dbh, $card_ref);
    display_entry_form ($card_ref);
}
elsif ($choice eq "send card")  # all done; send the card
{
    $card_ref = extract_card_params ($id);
    send_card ($dbh, $card_ref);
}
else
{
    print p (escapeHTML ("Logic error, unknown choice: $choice"));
}
```

Displaying the Card Information Form

The code for displaying the form is a bit different from most of those we've written so far. Each field-generating call is passed a value parameter and override is turned on so that the value becomes the field's default value. Normally we might rely on CGI.pm's sticky behavior to initialize a form with any previous values. That doesn't work for make_ecard.pl, because sometimes the values come from the database rather than the parameter space. (This is the case if the user was just viewing the gallery page, for example.) At any rate, $card_ref always points to the card's current contents, whether they come from the database or the parameter space, so we can use it to provide the form's default values.

```
sub display_entry_form
{
my $card_ref = shift;   # reference to card hash

    if ($card_ref->{picture} ne "") # If the card has a picture, display it
    {
        my $img_url = sprintf ("serve_image.pl?name=%s",
                               escape ($card_ref->{picture}));
        print img ({-src => $img_url,
                    -alt => escapeHTML ($card_ref->{picture})});
    }

    print start_form (-action => url ()),
        hidden (-name => "id",
                -value => $card_ref->{id},
                -override => 1),
        hidden (-name => "picture",
                -value => $card_ref->{picture},
                -override => 1),
        p ("Use this form to send an electronic greeting card to a friend."),
        "Person to whom you're sending the card:",
        table (
            Tr (
                td ("Name:") ,
                td (textfield (-name => "recip_name",
                               -value => $card_ref->{recip_name},
                               -override => 1, -size => 60))
            ),
            Tr (
                td ("Email address:"),
                td (textfield (-name => "recip_email",
                               -value => $card_ref->{recip_email},
                               -override => 1, -size => 60)),
            )
        ),
        br (), br (), "Message to send to recipient:",
        br (),
        textarea (-name => "message",
                  -value => $card_ref->{message},
                  -override => 1,
                  -rows => 3,
                  -cols => 60,
                  -wrap => "virtual"),
```

```
        br (), br (),
        "Please identify yourself (the person from whom the card is sent):",
        table (
            Tr (
                td ("Name:") ,
                td (textfield (-name => "sender_name",
                               -value => $card_ref->{sender_name},
                               -override => 1, -size => 60))
            ),
            Tr (
                td ("Email address:"),
                td (textfield (-name => "sender_email",
                               -value => $card_ref->{sender_email},
                               -override => 1, -size => 60)),
            )
        ),
        br (),
        p ("Would you like to be notified when the recipient views the card?"),
        # Note: if $card_ref->{sender_notify} is empty, the default
        # becomes the first radio button ("N"), which is what we want.
        radio_group (-name => "sender_notify",
                     -values => [ "N", "Y" ],
                     -labels => { "N" => "No", "Y" => "Yes" },
                     -default => $card_ref->{sender_notify},
                     -override => 1),
        br (), br (),
        submit (-name => "choice",
                -value => ($card_ref->{picture} ne "" ?
                           "Change" : "Select") . " Picture"),
        " ",
        submit (-name => "choice", -value => "Send Card"),
        end_form ();
}
```

The form display code adapts to the presence or absence of a picture selection in two ways. First, if the card has a picture, we display it above the form so that the user can see it. (The code generates an `<img>` tag that invokes our `serve_image.pl` script to obtain the image.) Second, the picture selection button title is Select Picture if no picture has been chosen, and Change Picture otherwise.

The form also includes a couple of hidden fields. We need the `id` value to identify the card. But we also carry along the `picture` value. That's not something the user can specify in the form, but we don't want to lose the value by not including it here. (Otherwise `param("picture")` will be empty when the user submits the form and we update the card record in the database using the information in that form.)

Presenting the Picture Gallery

When the user selects the Select Picture/Change Picture button, `make_ecard.pl` calls `display_gallery()` to present a gallery page that shows thumbnails of the images in the `image` table. This is preferable to displaying the full-size images because thumbnails require less bandwidth to transfer, load more quickly, and result in a more compact display. (Full-size image display is better limited to showing the card itself, which involves only one picture.)

We'll display each thumbnail with its name and make both of them hyperlinks so that the user can click either one to select an image for the card. To reduce the length of the gallery page, we'll arrange the images into a table and present several images per row. Six images per row significantly reduces the amount of vertical scrolling the user must do to see the entire gallery, without making the table so wide that the user likely would need to scroll horizontally to see all the images in a given row. (This is a fairly arbitrary choice, tied to my decision to use 64×64 for the thumbnail size when we built the `image` table. If you wanted to get fancier, you could modify the `image` table to store the dimensions of the thumbnails, and then attempt to determine from those values what a reasonable column count would be for the gallery table.)

What if the user takes a look at the gallery and decides not to select any of them? We could provide instructions to click the Back button, but another way to handle this issue and provide the user a sense of continuing to move forward through the card-creation process is to put a Continue button on the page along with a caption "select Continue to choose no image." Thus, `display_gallery()` presents a page that consists of a table of images followed by a short form containing only the Continue button.

```
sub display_gallery
{
my ($dbh, $id) = @_;
my ($image_list_ref, $nimages, $nrows, $ncols);
my @table_row;

    print start_form (),
        # include card ID so next page knows which card to use
        hidden (-name => "id", -value => $id, -override => 1);

    # Select the names of all images available in the gallery
    $image_list_ref = $dbh->selectcol_arrayref (
                "SELECT name FROM image ORDER BY name");
    if (!$image_list_ref || @{$image_list_ref} == 0)
    {
        print p ("Sorry, there are no pictures available at this time"),
            submit (-name => "choice", -value => "Continue"),
            end_form ();
        return;
    }
    print p ("To make a picture selection, click on the picture or\n"
```

```perl
                . "on its name. To continue without choosing a picture,\n"
                . "select the Continue button at the end of the page.\n");

    # Determine the number of images available. Then, given the
    # number of columns to display in the table, figure out how
    # many rows there will be.
    $nimages = @{$image_list_ref};
    $ncols = 6;
    $nrows = int (($nimages + $ncols - 1) / $ncols);
    for my $row (0 .. $nrows - 1)
    {
        # construct a string containing the cells in the row
        my @cell;
        for my $col (0 .. $ncols - 1)
        {
            if (($row * $ncols) + $col < $nimages)  # display image in cell
            {
                my $name = $image_list_ref->[$row * $ncols + $col];
                # URL for displaying the image thumbnail
                my $img_url = sprintf ("serve_image.pl?name=%s;thumbnail=1",
                                                    escape ($name));
                # URL for selecting this picture and adding it to the card
                my $select_url = url ()
                        . sprintf ("?choice=add_picture;id=%d;picture=%s",
                                    $id, escape ($name));
                # display image name and thumbnail; make each one a hyperlink
                # that adds the picture to the card
                push (@cell,
                        a ({-href => $select_url}, escapeHTML ($name))
                        . br ()
                        . a ({-href => $select_url},
                            img ({-src => $img_url,
                                    -alt => escapeHTML ($name)}))
                        );
            }
            else                                    # display empty cell
            {
                # this happens on last row when there aren't
                # enough images to fill the entire row
                push (@cell, " "); # put non-breaking space in cell
            }
        }
        push (@table_row,
            Tr (td ({-valign => "top", -align => "center"}, \@cell)));
    }
    print table ({-border => 1}, @table_row),
        p ("Select Continue to return to main card form\n"
            . "without making a picture selection.\n"),
        submit (-name => "choice", -value => "Continue"),
        end_form ();
}
```

If the user selects the Continue button, `display_gallery()` posts a form containing a `choice` value of `Continue` and an `id` parameter that identifies the card. (The `id` value is contained in the form as a hidden value to make sure it gets communicated back to `make_ecard.pl`.) The script processes the Continue button by just redisplaying the form to show the current contents of the card.

On the other hand, if the user selects a picture name or thumbnail, each of those is linked to a URL that contains the appropriate parameters for adding the picture to the card. Each URL contains a `choice` value indicating that a picture was chosen, the ID number of the card, and a `picture` parameter indicating which picture to add:

```
make_ecard.pl?choice=add_picture;id=n;picture=name
```

The dispatch code for the `add_picture` choice sets the `picture` attribute of the card hash using the value of the `picture` parameter from the URL. (If there was already a `picture` value in the card hash, it will be replaced by the picture named in the URL. This way we don't lock the user into a given picture.) Then we store the modified card information in the database and redisplay the card information form:

```perl
elsif ($choice eq "add_picture")
{
    # User chose a picture from the gallery page. Extract the picture
    # name and add it to the card hash, then redisplay card form.
    $card_ref->{picture} = param ("picture") if param ("picture");
    update_card_record ($dbh, $card_ref);
    display_entry_form ($card_ref);
}
```

We're making progress, but we still need to take care of the code to store the final card and send the notification email.

Sending the Card

When the user selects the Send Card button to complete the card, `make_ecard.pl` must take the following steps:

- Extract the card information from the form and make sure all the required fields are present.
- Assign an expiration date. (As a side-effect, this marks the card as "done," a convention we use to prevent double submissions or attempts to tamper with the card.)
- Store the card in the database.
- Send email to the recipient containing instructions for viewing the card.
- Send email to the user who's sending the card noting that it's been sent and also containing instructions for viewing it.
- Display a confirmation page to the user.

Extracting the card from the form is just a matter of calling `extract_card_params()` to construct the card hash. This is done in the main dispatch logic. The other steps are handled by the `send_card()` function:

```perl
sub send_card
{
my ($dbh, $card_ref) = @_;
my @errors;
my %req_field_map =
(
    "recip_name" => "Recipient's name",
    "recip_email" => "Recipient's email address",
    "message" => "The message to send to the recipient",
    "sender_name" => "Your name",
    "sender_email" => "Your email address"
);
my $card_life = 30;         # how long to retain the card, in days
my ($iso_date, $desc_date);
my ($url, $recip_url, $sender_url);
my %mail;

    # Make sure required fields are filled in
    foreach my $key (keys (%req_field_map))
    {
        # if field is required but missing, it's an error
        if (defined ($req_field_map{$key}) && $card_ref->{$key} eq "")
        {
            push (@errors, $req_field_map{$key} . " must be filled in");
        }
    }

    # Perform additional constraint checking: email fields must look
    # like addresses.

    if ($card_ref->{recip_email} ne ""
        && !WebDB::looks_like_email ($card_ref->{recip_email}))
    {
        push (@errors,
            "Recipient email address is not in user\@host.name format");
    }
    if ($card_ref->{sender_email} ne ""
        && !WebDB::looks_like_email ($card_ref->{sender_email}))
    {
        push (@errors,
            "Your email address is not in user\@host.name format");
    }

    if (@errors)
    {
        print p ("The following problems were found in the card form:");
        print ul (li (\@errors));         # print error messages
```

continues

continued

```
        display_entry_form ($card_ref);    # redisplay form
        return;
    }

    # Get expiration date in ISO and descriptive formats
    ($iso_date, $desc_date) = get_card_expiration ($card_life);
    # Assign expiration date and store final card in database
    $card_ref->{expiration} = $iso_date;
    update_card_record ($dbh, $card_ref);

    # Get full URL of current script and convert last component to name
    # of card-display script. Then add card ID and viewer role parameters.

    $url = url ();
    $url =~ s/[^\/]+$/show_ecard.pl/;
    $recip_url = $url . sprintf ("?id=%d;recip=%s",
                        $card_ref->{id}, escape ($card_ref->{recip_email}));
    $sender_url = $url . sprintf ("?id=%d;sender=%s",
                        $card_ref->{id}, escape ($card_ref->{sender_email}));

     # Send email to card recipient

    $mail{To} = $card_ref->{recip_email};
    $mail{From} = $card_ref->{sender_email};
    $mail{Subject} = "An electronic greeting card for you!";
    $mail{Message} = "
Hello, $card_ref->{sender_name} ($card_ref->{sender_email}) has sent you
an electronic greeting card.

You can view the card with your Web browser at the following address:

$recip_url

The card will be available for $card_life days (until $desc_date).
";
    sendmail (%mail);

    # Send email to card sender

    $mail{To} = $card_ref->{sender_email};
    $mail{From} = $card_ref->{sender_email};
    $mail{Subject} = "Your card to $card_ref->{recip_name}";
    $mail{Message} = "
This message is for your records.  You sent an electronic greeting card to:
$card_ref->{recip_name} ($card_ref->{recip_email})

You can view the card with your Web browser at the following address:

$sender_url
```

```
    The card will be available for $card_life days (until $desc_date).
";
    sendmail (%mail);

    # display confirmation page
    print p ("Your card has been sent. Thank you for using this service.");
}
```

The send_card() function first validates the form by checking for required fields and making sure the values in the email fields actually look like email addresses. (The test for required fields cannot be done earlier in the card-construction process because we enable the user to leave any of the fields blank up to the point when the card is to be sent.) It's unnecessary to trim whitespace here like we did in the validation procedure for most of the applications developed earlier in the chapter; that already has been done by the extract_card_params() function. looks_like_email() is one of the utility routines in the WebDB module. It runs a pattern test on a string to verify that it looks like a legal email address.

If any errors are found, we show the error messages and redisplay the form so that the user can correct the problems. Otherwise, the card checks out okay, so we assign it an expiration date and update the record in the database:

```
# Get expiration date in ISO and descriptive formats
($iso_date, $desc_date) = get_card_expiration ($card_life);
# Assign expiration date and store final card in database
$card_ref->{expiration} = $iso_date;
update_card_record ($dbh, $card_ref);
```

get_card_expiration() calculates the expiration date, given the number of days the card should "live." The date can be obtained from either MySQL or Perl, but however we get it, we'll need it in two formats. The date must be in ISO 8601 format (CCYY-MM-DD) for storage into MySQL. For display in the email messages, we'll use a more descriptive format—for example, January 23, 2001 rather than 2001-01-23.

To get the expiration date from MySQL, we can use CURRENT_DATE to get today's date and DATE_ADD() to perform date arithmetic. That returns the expiration date in ISO format. To get the descriptive format, we do the same thing but pass the result to DATE_FORMAT(). Here's a query to retrieve the expiration date in both formats, where $card_life represents how many days to retain the card in the database:

```
($iso_date, $desc_date) = $dbh->selectrow_array (
    "SELECT
        DATE_ADD(CURRENT_DATE,INTERVAL $card_life DAY),
        DATE_FORMAT(DATE_ADD(CURRENT_DATE,INTERVAL $card_life DAY),'%M %e, %Y')");
```

Alternatively, we can get the expiration date from Perl using `time()` and `localtime()`. `time()` returns the current time in seconds. We can add to that value the number of seconds in 30 days, and then pass the result to `localtime()` to convert it to an eight-element array containing the various parts of a date. (Month, day, and year are contained in elements 3 through 5 of the array.) The `year` value represents the number of years relative to 1900, so we add 1900 to get the absolute year. The `month` is a numeric value in the range 0 to 11; we can use it as is to index into an array of month names to get the month name, or add one to get the actual month number. The code looks like this:

```
@monthname = (
    "January", "February", "March", "April", "May", "June",
    "July", "August", "September", "October", "November", "December"
);
($day, $month, $year) = (localtime (time () + (60*60*24*$card_life)))[3..5];
$year += 1900;      # convert year to 4-digit form
$iso_date = sprintf ("%04d-%02d-%02d", $year, $month+1, $day);
$desc_date = "$monthname[$month] $day, $year";
```

Which method of calculating the expiration date is preferable? Personally, I prefer the SELECT version because we can get both `date` values using a single `selectrow_array()` call. But that method incurs the overhead of a round trip over the network to the MySQL server. Getting the date directly from Perl does not, so it's more efficient.

After calculating the expiration date and using it to update the card record in the database, the only thing left to do is send email to the card recipient and the sender. These notification messages can be simple or fancy. On the fancy side, you'll notice when you create a card at one of the big e-card sites is that they include lots of extra stuff in their email, much of it related to advertising. That's the kind of thing you'll have to customize for yourself. For our purposes here, we'll confine the message content to the essentials related only to the card content. The message sent to the recipient will look like this:

> To: *recipient*
> From: *sender*
> Subject: An electronic greeting card for you!
> Hello, *sender* has sent you an electronic greeting card.
> You can view the card with your Web browser at the following address:
> *URL*
> The card will be available for *n* days
> (until *expiration date*).

The message for the sender looks like this:

> To: *sender*
> From: *sender*
> Subject: Your card for *recipient*
> This message is for your records. You sent an electronic greeting card to:
> *recipient*

You can view the card with your Web browser at the following address:
URL
The card will be available for *n* days
(until *expiration date*).

The sender and recipient names and email addresses are contained in the card hash, and `$desc_date` indicates the expiration date in descriptive form. But what address should we use in the `From:` header, and what should the URL for requesting the card look like?

The `From:` address should be some valid address in case the person receiving the message attempts to reply to it. One choice is to have the message appear to come from the card sender, which is what `make_ecard.pl` does. (An alternative would be to have messages appear to come from your card-sending service, using an address such as `e-cards@snake.net`. If you use a special address, you'll have to set up an account to receive mail sent to it, or alias it to someone else.)

The more difficult thing is figuring out what kind of URL to include in the messages so that the card sender and recipient can view the card. We'll use another script, `show_ecard.pl`, for retrieving and displaying the card, so the initial part of the URL has to name that script. If we assume that `make_ecard.pl` and `show_ecard.pl` are both installed in the same directory on your Web server, `make_ecard.pl` can get its own URL and use it to figure out the URL for `show_ecard.pl` by replacing the last component (everything after the last slash) with "show_ecard.pl":

```
$url = url ();
$url =~ s/[^\/]+$/show_ecard.pl/;
```

We'll also need to add some information to the URL that identifies the card. The ID number does this, but we really need something more than just the ID by itself. Remember that we want to be able to tell when the recipient requests the card for the first time so that we can mark the card record in the database as having been viewed. We also may need to notify the sender when that happens. That means we need to know who is requesting the card. Also, we want to discourage casual card browsing by people other than the sender or recipient. (That is, we don't want other people sending requests for arbitrary card ID numbers, to see what cards people are sending. We're not guaranteeing that cards are private, but the intent isn't really to provide each card as a completely public resource, either.)

One simple way to tell whether the sender or the recipient is requesting a card and to discourage browsing by outsiders is to use card-retrieval URLs that identify the role and address of the requester. If card 407 was sent by the U.S. President to the First Lady, the URLs that would be provided to each of them for viewing the card would look like this:

```
.../show_ecard.pl?id=407;sender=president@whitehouse.gov
.../show_ecard.pl?id=407;recip=first.lady@whitehouse.gov
```

These URLs are constructed from the base URL by appending the appropriate parameter values:

```
$recip_url = $url . sprintf ("?id=%d;recip=%s",
                    $card_ref->{id}, escape ($card_ref->{recip_email}));
$sender_url = $url . sprintf ("?id=%d;sender=%s",
                    $card_ref->{id}, escape ($card_ref->{sender_email}));
```

With the URLs in hand, we have all the information we need to generate the email messages and send them. `make_ecard.pl` does so using the `sendmail()` function from the `Mail::Sendmail` module discussed earlier in the chapter.

Retrieving Cards for Display

Requests to see cards are handled by the `show_ecard.pl` script. For purposes of reading a card from the database, the script needs only the card ID number:

```
SELECT * FROM ecard WHERE id = n
```

Given that we want only the card sender and recipient to view the card, however, we'll also require that the email address in the URL match the appropriate email address in the card record. If the recipient requests the card, for example, the query looks like this:

```
SELECT * FROM ecard WHERE id = n AND recip_email = 'address'
```

For the sender, the query checks the `sender_email` column rather than the `recip_email` column. Given this mechanism, `show_ecard.pl` acts as follows:

- Look in the URL for the `id` parameter that identifies the card, and either a `sender` or `recip` parameter that identifies the role and email address of the person who wants to see it.

- Look up the record that matches the `id` value and the email address from either the `sender_email` or `recip_email` column (depending on which one was specified in the URL). This way casual attempts to view cards will fail. (To hack in, you would have to know not only a card's ID number, but also who sent it or to whom it was sent.)

- Display the card. `show_ecard.pl` generates a page containing the text of the card and, if there is a picture, an `<img>` tag that is handled by `serve_image.pl`.

- If the card's `viewed` column is `NULL` and the requester is the recipient, this is the first time the recipient has asked to see the card. Set the `viewed` value to the current date and, if the sender has requested notification, send an email message confirming that the recipient has taken a look at the card.

The first part of show_ecard.pl checks the URL parameters, determines whether they're valid, and displays the card if so:

```perl
print header (),
    start_html (-title => "View Your Electronic Greeting Card",
                -bgcolor => "white");

my $id = param ("id");
my $sender = param ("sender");
my $recip = param ("recip");
my $valid = 0;

if (defined ($id))          # got the card ID, look for sender or recipient
{
    if (defined ($sender))
    {
        $valid = 1;
        show_ecard ($id, $sender, "sender_email");
    }
    elsif (defined ($recip))
    {
        $valid = 1;
        show_ecard ($id, $recip, "recip_email");
    }
}
if (!$valid)
{
    print p ("Missing or invalid e-card parameters specified.\n"
            . "Please check the URL that was sent to you.");
}

print end_html ();
```

Assuming the card ID value and an email address are present in the URL, show_ecard() looks up the card from the database and displays it:

```perl
sub show_ecard
{
my ($id, $email, $col_name) = @_;
my $dbh = WebDB::connect ();
my ($sth, $ref);

    $sth = $dbh->prepare (
                "SELECT * FROM ecard
                WHERE id = ? AND $col_name = ?");
    $sth->execute ($id, $email);
    $ref = $sth->fetchrow_hashref ();
    $sth->finish ();
    if (!$ref)
    {
        $dbh->disconnect ();
        print p ("Sorry, card was not found; perhaps it has expired.");
        return;
    }
```

continues

continued

```
# Print recipient name and email.  If a picture was selected,
# generate an <img> tag for it.  Then display the message text and
# sender information.

print p (escapeHTML ("To: $ref->{recip_name} ($ref->{recip_email})"));
if ($ref->{picture} ne "")
{
    print img ({-src => "serve_image.pl?name=" . escape ($ref->{picture}),
                -alt => escapeHTML ($ref->{picture})});
}
print p (escapeHTML ($ref->{message}));
print p (escapeHTML ("This message was sent to you by: "
                . "$ref->{sender_name} ($ref->{sender_email})"));

# If this is a request by the recipient, set the "viewed" date if
# it hasn't yet been set; notify the sender that the recipient has
# viewed the card if the sender requested notification. Also,
# display some links for replying to to sender by email or for
# generating a reply card.

if ($col_name eq "recip_email")
{
    my $mail_url = sprintf ("mailto:%s?subject=%s",
                            escape ($ref->{sender_email}),
                            escape ("Thanks for the e-card"));
    print hr ();
    print a ({ -href => $mail_url }, "Send mail to sender") , br ();
    print a ({ -href => "make_ecard.pl" }, "Create your own e-card");

    if (!$ref->{viewed})
    {
        $dbh->do ("UPDATE ecard SET viewed=CURRENT_DATE WHERE id = ?",
                undef, $ref->{id});
        notify_sender ($ref) if $ref->{sender_notify} eq "Y";
    }
}
$dbh->disconnect ();
}
```

The notify_sender() function generates email to let the sender know the recipient has looked at the card:

```
sub notify_sender
{
my $ref = shift;        # card record
my %mail;
```

```
    $mail{To} = $mail{From} = $ref->{sender_email};
    $mail{Subject} = "Your e-card for $ref->{recip_name}";
    $mail{Message} = "
Your card to $ref->{recip_name} ($ref->{recip_email})
has been viewed by the recipient.";
    sendmail (%mail);
}
```

Expiring Old Cards

The expiration column is present in the ecard table to allow old cards to be removed; there's no need to keep them around forever. Cards won't delete themselves, however, so we need to set up a mechanism to handle that task. This can be done by setting up a cron job to identify and delete cards whose expiration date has passed. If I want to expire cards at 1:15 a.m. each morning using a script expire_ecard.pl installed in my bin directory, for example, I'd add a line like this to my crontab file:

```
15 1 * * * /u/paul/bin/expire_ecard.pl
```

The expiration script itself can be written different ways. The following version deletes the expired records, but also prints a message indicating how many records were deleted. (As usual, I'm assuming that cron will mail to me the output of any programs it runs on my behalf.)

```
#! /usr/bin/perl -w
# expire_ecard.pl - remove greeting cards that have expired

use strict;
use lib qw(/usr/local/apache/lib/perl);
use WebDB;

my $dbh = WebDB::connect ();     # connect to database
my $count = $dbh->do ("DELETE FROM ecard WHERE expiration < CURRENT_DATE");
$count += 0;     # convert string to number, in case it's "0E0"
print "$count e-cards have expired and were deleted\n";
$dbh->disconnect ();
exit (0);
```

Suggested Modifications

Our card-sending application is the most complex of the chapter. Nevertheless, it's relatively unsophisticated, compared to some of the big sites devoted to electronic greeting cards, and there are a lot of things you could add to it. A couple of obvious additions would be to allow delivery to multiple recipients, or to allow the delivery date to be set. As written, the card is sent to a single recipient, and it's sent as soon as the user selects the Send Card button. You could also implement card categories such as "get well," "sympathy," "good luck", "birthday," or "wedding." If you had such categories, you could add a SET column to the image table that would indicate which card categories each image applies to, enabling you to present category-specific image galleries. Other modifications could focus on enhancing the existing features in various ways. If you have lots of images, for example, you'd probably want to present the picture gallery using multiple pages instead of displaying all pictures on the same page.

When a visitor first begins to create a card, make_ecard.pl generates a new ID number so the card can be tracked through each part of the process. At the end of the process, we assign an expiration date. If the user never completes the card, however, the expiration date remains NULL. That's a problem: The expiration mechanism is based on the value of the expiration date, so uncompleted cards never get expired. How would you address this problem, making sure not to remove records for cards that visitors currently are working on?

After a visitor completes the card construction process, it's not possible for someone else to come along and modify the card. (make_ecard.pl will notice that the expiration date has been set, which indicates that the card is finished.) However, card hijacking is possible while the card is being built, between the time that the card ID generated and the time the expiration date is assigned. How might you deal with this?

Modify expire_ecard.pl to provide information that indicates how many of the expired cards actually were viewed by the recipient.

In this chapter, you've seen how to build several interactive applications that run from your browser. For some of these applications, we attempted to reduce the amount of work involved in generating and processing the form by storing information about it in a data structure. In the product-registration script at the beginning of the chapter, for example, we used an array to list the names, labels, and sizes of the text-input fields, as well as whether each field had to have a non-empty value at form-submission time. In Chapter 6, we'll further explore the potential for deriving information about forms in a way that can be used automatically. For applications that are tied to tables in your database, one good source of information that can be used in relation to form processing is the knowledge that MySQL itself has about the structure of the tables in your database. As we'll see, this information can be used in several ways to make your Web programming tasks easier.

6

Automating the Form-Handling Process

Four phases of form processing were identified in Chapter 5, "Writing Form-Based Applications": generating the form for display to the user, validating the contents of the form when the user submits it, storing the contents of the form in the database, and presenting confirmation to the user. For the form-based applications that we've built thus far, MySQL has come into play primarily during the third phase (as a means of storing form responses). The role of MySQL in each application has thus been to serve as a repository—a box in which to save information collected from people who visit our site.

In this chapter, we'll examine the potential for using MySQL not just as a storage bin for information obtained through form submissions, but also as a more active participant in the form-handling process. In particular, we'll focus on pulling information from the database and using it to generate forms and evaluate the responses that users submit. In other words, this chapter explores some of the ways to use your database to help you process fields or entire forms on an automatic basis. This is possible because MySQL can provide you with several useful sources of information:

- **You can use table structure metadata.**

   When you're using a form containing fields that correspond to the columns in a database table, it's often possible to use information about the table's structure (also known as *metadata*) to help you create elements of the form. For example, you can ask MySQL for a description of a column's characteristics so that you can figure out how long to make a text-input field that corresponds to the column. You can determine the list of legal values for an ENUM or SET column, and then use the list to construct a form field such as a set of radio buttons for an ENUM or a set of check boxes for a SET. You can also use information about a table's structure to validate values submitted for form elements. For example, if a column has an integer type, the value of the corresponding field must also be an integer.

- **You can generate field elements from the results of queries.**

  Although an application may present a form designed to gather information for entry into a particular table, forms often can be improved by referring to the contents of other tables. Suppose you have an entry form for creating personnel table records, where each record includes a department code. If you have a department table that lists the names and codes of each department, you can use its contents to make the personnel form more understandable: Have your application display department names (which are more meaningful than codes to people), and then map the name selected by the user to the code when adding the record to the personnel table. Other kinds of information are so commonly used that you may as well store them in the database instead of repeating the information in multiple scripts. A State Name field in a form that gathers address information typically has about 50 legal values. If you put the states into your database, any script can run a query to look them up and create a pop-up or scrolling list.

- **You can set up tables designed specifically to store form descriptions.**

  If you have occasion to present several forms that are similar to each other, you may be able to store descriptions for them in the database. Then you can write a routine that queries the tables and generates the entire form, and others that validate form responses and store their contents, all on a completely automated basis. An example that we'll explore in this chapter is construction and validation of forms for online polls.

By automating certain aspects of the form-generation and form-processing cycle using the information that MySQL can provide to you from your database, you reduce the amount of application-specific code in your scripts. In effect, your database becomes a development tool for writing code that is more general and reusable. In the process of discussing the techniques described in this chapter, we'll develop code for a couple of Perl modules that live in the WebDB namespace and that can be reused for multiple applications.

Obtaining Database and Table Information

You can ask MySQL for several kinds of information about the databases and tables that it supports. It's possible to get lists of databases and tables, and you can get descriptions about each of the columns in a table. Much of this information is available using various forms of the SHOW statement, a MySQL-specific query that we'll examine in some detail in the next few sections.

Listing Databases and Tables

To get a list of databases hosted by a MySQL server, use the SHOW DATABASES query. If you want to know what tables are in a particular database, use SHOW TABLES FROM *db_name*. If you're writing an interactive query builder, for example, you might let the user first pick a table from the current database, then specify query conditions for selecting records from that table. A full-blown application for doing that is more involved than I want to get into here, but the following short script, pick_table.pl, illustrates the concept of getting a list of table names from MySQL and converting it into a pop-up menu:

```perl
#! /usr/bin/perl -w
# pick_table.pl - present a list of tables from the current database as
# a popup menu.

use strict;
use lib qw(/usr/local/apache/lib/perl);
use CGI qw(:standard escapeHTML);
use WebDB;

print header (), start_html (-title => "Pick a Table", -bgcolor => "white");

# Get reference to list of tables, convert it to an array
my $dbh = WebDB::connect ();
my @list = @{ $dbh->selectcol_arrayref ("SHOW TABLES") };
$dbh->disconnect ();

# Display table-selection form
unshift (@list, "Select a table");  # put a title at head of popup menu
print start_form (-action => url ()),
    popup_menu (-name => "table", -values => \@list, -override => 1),
    br (), br (),
    submit (-name => "choice", -value => "Submit"),
    end_form ();

# Display table selection from previous script invocation, if any
my $table = param ("table");
$table = "" if !defined ($table);
```

continues

continued

```
print hr (), p (escapeHTML (
                    $table eq "" || $table eq "Select a table"
                       ? "No table has been chosen."
                       : "You chose this table: $table"
            ));

print end_html ();
exit (0);
```

Note how the script puts a `"Select a table"` item at the head of the pop-up to serve as the default value, and then checks for that string later when determining whether the user actually picked a table. If you want to display a set of radio buttons instead, you might change the body of the script to something like this:

```
# Display table-selection form
print start_form (-action => url ()),
    radio_group (-name => "table",
                    -values => \@list,
                    -default => "[NO DEFAULT]",
                    -linebreak => 1,
                    -override => 1),
    br (), br (),
    submit (-name => "choice", -value => "Submit"),
    end_form ();

# Display table selection from previous script invocation, if any
my $table = param ("table");
$table = "" if !defined ($table);
print hr (), p (escapeHTML (
                    $table eq ""
                       ? "No table has been chosen."
                       : "You chose this table: $table"
            ));
```

Listing Table Structure Information

In addition to simple lists of databases and tables, MySQL also can provide more detailed information about the structure of a table's columns. Suppose we have a table named `coffee` that is used for recording orders at a coffee shop:

```
CREATE TABLE coffee
(
    id      INT NOT NULL AUTO_INCREMENT PRIMARY KEY, # record ID/timestamp
    ts      TIMESTAMP,
    qty     TINYINT UNSIGNED NOT NULL DEFAULT 1,     # quantity
    size    ENUM('S','M','L') NOT NULL DEFAULT 'M',  # serving size
    extras  SET('cream','sugar'),                    # extra ingredients
    remark  VARCHAR(30)                              # special instructions
)
```

The table contains rows that look like this:

```
+----+----------------+-----+------+-------------+---------------+
| id | ts             | qty | size | extras      | remark        |
+----+----------------+-----+------+-------------+---------------+
|  1 | 20010227060327 |   1 | L    | cream       | LOTS of cream |
|  2 | 20010227061749 |   1 | M    | sugar       | 2 lumps       |
|  3 | 20010227064232 |   2 | M    | NULL        | NULL          |
|  4 | 20010227070751 |   1 | L    | cream       | NULL          |
|  5 | 20010227071006 |   3 | S    | cream,sugar | NULL          |
...
```

If we're using a form-based application, coffee.pl, to enter these records, we might use the following function to generate the entry form, which includes text-input fields for the qty and remark values, a set of radio buttons for specifying the serving size, and a set of check boxes for the extras:

```
sub display_form
{
    print start_form (-action => url ()),
        p ("Quantity:"),
        textfield (-name => "qty"),
        p ("Serving size:"),
        radio_group (-name => "size",
                        -values => [ "S", "M", "L" ],
                        -default => "M"),
        p ("Extras:"),
        checkbox_group (-name => "extras", -values => [ "cream", "sugar" ]),
        p ("Special instructions:"),
        textfield (-name => "remark", -size => "30"),
        br (), br (),
        submit (-name => "choice", -value => "Submit"),
        end_form ();
}
```

The function relies heavily on our knowledge about the structure of the coffee table and how form submissions will be processed:

- We name the fields after the corresponding table columns.
- We know the possible legal values for the size and extras fields. We also know which values should be selected by default (M for size, nothing for extras).
- We know the size of the remark column—30 characters.
- We didn't include any fields for the id or ts columns because we know that both of them have types for which MySQL will supply values automatically when we enter new records. (id gets the next AUTO_INCREMENT value, ts gets the current date and time.)

I haven't shown any code to validate submitted forms, but any such code would enforce certain constraints, and these also would be based on our knowledge of the table definition:

- The `qty` field value must be numeric, but it shouldn't be allowed to be negative.
- We could either require the quantity to be filled in, or use the default value (1) if it's left blank.
- The `size` and `extras` fields should have values that are legal members of the corresponding table columns. (We'd like to hope that will always be true because the only values that we're presenting to the user are those known to be valid in the first place. However, it's always possible that someone might attempt to submit a hacked form to see how bulletproof the application is, so to be sure that submitted values are legal, it's best to check them.)

As it happens, a lot of the information needed for generating the form and processing submissions is directly available from MySQL itself as the output from the SHOW COLUMNS statement. Let's see what that information is and how to use it.

The *SHOW COLUMNS* Statement

To find out about the columns in a given table, issue a SHOW COLUMNS query.[1] If you run a few instances of this statement from the `mysql` program, you'll see what kinds of things MySQL can tell you about your tables. The following example shows the output of SHOW COLUMNS for our `coffee` table:

```
mysql> SHOW COLUMNS FROM coffee;
+--------+----------------------+------+-----+---------+----------------+
| Field  | Type                 | Null | Key | Default | Extra          |
+--------+----------------------+------+-----+---------+----------------+
| id     | int(11)              |      | PRI | NULL    | auto_increment |
| ts     | timestamp(14)        | YES  |     | NULL    |                |
| qty    | tinyint(3) unsigned  |      |     | 1       |                |
| size   | enum('S','M','L')    |      |     | M       |                |
| extras | set('cream','sugar') | YES  |     | NULL    |                |
| remark | varchar(30)          | YES  |     | NULL    |                |
+--------+----------------------+------+-----+---------+----------------+
```

If you want to know only about some of the columns, use a LIKE clause. Then SHOW COLUMNS will produce an output record only for each column with a name that matches the string following the LIKE keyword. The string is treated as a SQL pattern; for example, '%r%' matches any column name that contains an 'r' character:

```
mysql> SHOW COLUMNS FROM coffee LIKE '%r%';
+--------+----------------------+------+-----+-------------+-------+
| Field  | Type                 | Null | Key | Default     | Extra |
+--------+----------------------+------+-----+-------------+-------+
| extras | set('cream','sugar') | YES  |     | cream,sugar |       |
| remark | varchar(30)          | YES  |     | NULL        |       |
+--------+----------------------+------+-----+-------------+-------+
```

---

1. SHOW FIELDS is a synonym for SHOW COLUMNS.

To display information about a single column, use a LIKE clause and specify the column's name literally as a string:

```
mysql> SHOW COLUMNS FROM coffee LIKE 'size';
+-------+-----------------+------+-----+---------+-------+
| Field | Type            | Null | Key | Default | Extra |
+-------+-----------------+------+-----+---------+-------+
| size  | enum('S','M','L') |    |     | M       |       |
+-------+-----------------+------+-----+---------+-------+
```

You may find that SHOW COLUMNS produces more output columns than the six shown here, depending on your version of MySQL, but these six should always be present. You may also find that SHOW COLUMNS prints very long lines that wrap around and are difficult to read in a terminal window. You can deal with this by using '\G' at the end of the query (rather than ';' or '\g') to print output columns stacked vertically:

```
mysql> SHOW COLUMNS FROM coffee LIKE 'size'\G
*************************** 1. row ***************************
  Field: size
   Type: enum('S','M','L')
   Null:
    Key:
Default: M
  Extra:
```

You can probably see immediately how the output from SHOW COLUMNS might be useful for generating our entry form. For example, we can use it to get the names of the table's columns, from which the field names are determined. The information for the qty and remark columns tells us how long to make the corresponding text-input fields. The legal values for the ENUM and SET columns can be used to construct list elements in the form such as radio buttons and check boxes.

I'll give a general description of the types of information that SHOW COLUMNS provides, and then discuss how to use it with reference to the coffee table in particular. Note that although my convention is to write type and attribute keywords such as TINYINT and AUTO_INCREMENT using uppercase letters, SHOW COLUMNS prints much of its output in lowercase. Be sure to take that into account when using output from this statement in your scripts. Note also that this discussion probably will seem abstract unless you run SHOW COLUMNS on some of your own tables to see for yourself what kind of result it produces for various column types. I encourage you to do that before reading further.

The output from SHOW COLUMNS includes information about several aspects of table columns:

- Field

  The name of the column. You can use this information by itself to find out what columns a table contains, or in conjunction with the other SHOW COLUMNS output to determine the characteristics of each column.

- Type

  This value always begins with the name of the column's type. It may also include additional information:

    - For many types, the size or display width is indicated in parentheses. For example, `char(10)` indicates a 10-character string column, `tinyint(3)` signifies a tiny integer with a display width of 3 characters, and `decimal(10,2)` indicates a floating-point column that can have up to 10 digits, with 2 of them after the decimal point.

    - `ENUM` and `SET` column `Type` values include the list of legal elements in parentheses as a set of single-quoted values separated by commas.

    - Some types include additional attributes, such as `zerofill` for numeric types, `unsigned` for unsigned integer types, and `binary` for case-sensitive character columns.

- Null

  This value is `YES` if the column can have `NULL` values, empty otherwise.

- Key

  The `Key` value provides rudimentary information about the table's index structure. The possible values are `PRI` (`PRIMARY KEY`), `UNI` (`UNIQUE` index), `MUL` (non-unique index), or empty (not indexed).

- Default

  Indicates the column's default value. For a string column, an empty `Default` value means that the default is the empty string. The word "NULL" means the column's default is the `NULL` value. Actually, for string columns, it could also mean that the `default` value is the literal word "NULL," but how likely is that? In any case, the word "NULL" appears only when you run `SHOW COLUMNS` from the `mysql` program or when you use the `mysqlshow` command. When you read the output from within a DBI script, a `NULL` default value is returned as `undef`, which eliminates any ambiguity between the string "NULL" and a true `NULL` value.

- Extra

  This value provides miscellaneous extra information. At the moment, MySQL uses it for only one purpose: to display the word `auto_increment` for `AUTO_INCREMENT` columns.

There are a couple of instances where `SHOW COLUMNS` output is somewhat unintuitive. First, `Null` is always `YES` for a `TIMESTAMP` column, because you can set such a column to NULL no matter how it is declared (the result being that the column gets set to the current time and day). Second, integer columns with the AUTO_INCREMENT attribute and TIMESTAMP columns always have a Default value of NULL, because the way you get the special auto-generated values for these kinds of columns is to set them to NULL when you insert a new row.[2]

Using *SHOW COLUMNS* Output to Build Forms

Let's look further at the output produced by SHOW COLUMNS for the coffee table and see what we can determine based solely on that information. Here it is again:

```
mysql> SHOW COLUMNS FROM coffee;
+--------+---------------------+------+-----+---------+----------------+
| Field  | Type                | Null | Key | Default | Extra          |
+--------+---------------------+------+-----+---------+----------------+
| id     | int(11)             |      | PRI | NULL    | auto_increment |
| ts     | timestamp(14)       | YES  |     | NULL    |                |
| qty    | tinyint(3) unsigned |      |     | 1       |                |
| size   | enum('S','M','L')   |      |     | M       |                |
| extras | set('cream','sugar')| YES  |     | NULL    |                |
| remark | varchar(30)         | YES  |     | NULL    |                |
+--------+---------------------+------+-----+---------+----------------+
```

Given this information, we can make the following deductions:

- The id column contains auto_increment for the Extra value. This is a tipoff that the column's value will be provided automatically by MySQL when a new record is inserted, so we don't need to include it in the entry form at all. TIMESTAMP columns are typically initialized automatically as well, so we can omit the ts column from the form, too.

- The qty column is an integer, so values would be gathered using a text-input field. According to the Type information, we'd need a field three characters long to collect quantity values. The fact that the column is unsigned is not of consequence for generating the entry form. (It can be used for validating values submitted by users, but we're not at that point yet.) If we wanted to initialize the qty field in the entry form, we could do so by consulting the Default column and using the value found there (1).

- The information for the size column tells us that it's an enumeration, which means we can display it as some kind of list element: a set of radio buttons, a pop-up menu, or a single-pick scrolling list. The Type information indicates the legal values to include in the list, and Default indicates that we should initialize the element with M as the default value.

---

2. Prior to MySQL 3.23, the Default value for AUTO_INCREMENT columns is displayed as zero.

- The output for the `extras` column is similar to that for `size`. However, this column is a `SET` rather than an `ENUM`, so we'd display it using a set of check boxes or a multiple-pick scrolling list.
- The `Type` information for the `remark` column says `varchar(30)`, so it's a string; we'll need a text-input field 30 characters long for the corresponding form element.

The preceding discursive narrative discussing the relevance of `SHOW COLUMNS` output to form generation makes sense to you as a human (I hope!), but it doesn't help a Perl script much. How do we actually exploit this information in a program, and to what extent should we do so? There are several possibilities. You could try to automate form generation as much as possible, or you could decide you're willing to make some assumptions about the fields and use the information from `SHOW COLUMNS` in a more limited way. What you'll generally find when dealing with this tradeoff is that the more you want your program to figure out for itself, the more difficult it will be to teach it how to do that. If you want to get the code written more quickly, make some assumptions on behalf of your script.

To generate the `coffee` table entry form, for example, you could write the script to figure out every field type, based on the corresponding table column types. It would have to determine that `id` and `ts` don't appear in the form at all, that the `qty` and `remark` columns should be represented by text-input fields, and that the `size` and `extras` columns should be represented by list fields of some sort. Or, you can begin by using `SHOW COLUMNS` output in a more modest way, and then expand your use of it later. That's what we'll do here. We'll start by "just knowing" what kind of field each column is represented by, and use only information about the size of the `qty` and `remark` text-input fields, and about the member lists for the `size` and `extras` fields for constructing the radio buttons and check boxes. After that, we'll get information about default values and use them to initialize form elements.

In each case where we use `SHOW COLUMNS` output to generate a field, we can begin by extracting into an array the information for the column in which we're interested. For example, the query to do that for `qty` looks like this:

```
# get row describing the desired column
@val = $dbh->selectrow_array ("SHOW COLUMNS FROM coffee LIKE 'qty'");
```

For this column, we want to know the length of column values. That's contained in the `Type` information (`$val[1]`), which looks like this:

```
tinyint(3) unsigned
```

To obtain the length (the number in parentheses) and use it to generate a text-input field, the following code suffices:

```
($len) = ($val[1] =~ /\(((\d+)\)/);
print textfield (-name => "qty", -size => $len);
```

We may as well put the length-extraction code in a function to make it easy to use. We'll pass the database handle, and the table and column names, and expect to get back the column length in return. Before writing any code to extract the length, however, there's actually one additional detail to be aware of when retrieving information about a column. Remember that the string following the LIKE keyword is interpreted as a SQL pattern. Therefore, to match the column name literally, you need to turn off the special meaning of any SQL pattern characters ('_' and '%') that occur within the name by escaping them with a backslash. This is easy in Perl:

```
$col_name =~ s/([_%])/\\$1/g;
```

The get_column_length() function returns the column length. It uses a helper function, get_column_info(), also shown:

```
sub get_column_length
{
my ($dbh, $tbl_name, $col_name) = @_;
my @val;

    @val = get_column_info ($dbh, $tbl_name, $col_name);
    ($val[1] =~ /\((\d+)\)/)
            or die escapeHTML ("No length found for $tbl_name.$col_name\n");
    return ($1);
}

sub get_column_info
{
my ($dbh, $tbl_name, $col_name) = @_;
my ($esc_col_name, @val);

    # escape SQL pattern characters to force literal column name match
    ($esc_col_name = $col_name) =~ s/([_%])/\\$1/g;
    @val = $dbh->selectrow_array (
                "SHOW COLUMNS FROM $tbl_name LIKE '$esc_col_name'"
            );
    @val or die escapeHTML ("No information found for $tbl_name.$col_name\n");
    return (@val);
}
```

get_column_length() assumes that you'll call it only for columns that actually have a length present in the Type information, and dies an unceremonious death if that's not true. That assumption is true for our qty and remark columns, so we're safe. Whew.

> **Passing a Database Name to *get_column_length()***
>
> There is no database name argument in the definition of get_column_length(). What if you want to get the length of a column from a table in a different database? No problem. Pass a value of *$tbl_name* that is fully qualified with the database name in *db_name.tbl_name* form:
>
> ```
> $len = get_column_length ($dbh, "other_db.my_tbl", "my_col");
> ```
>
> This same principle applies to other functions written later in this chapter that take a table name argument.

Extracting the element lists for the size and extras columns is more work than getting a column length because the information is more complex than a string of digits. The Type values for these columns look like this:

```
enum('S','M','L')
set('cream','sugar')
```

To process a value in this format, convert it to a set of individual member values by trimming off the leading word and the parentheses from the ends of the string, breaking it into individual values at the commas, and stripping the quotation marks from the ends of each value. The result is an array that we can use to produce a list element for the entry form. The following function, get_column_members(), takes a database handle, a table name, and a column name as arguments, and returns a list of legal column members:

```
sub get_column_members
{
my ($dbh, $tbl_name, $col_name) = @_;
my @val;

    @val = get_column_info ($dbh, $tbl_name, $col_name);
    # strip "enum(" or "set(" from beginning and ")" from end of "Type" value
    $val[1] =~ s/^[^(]*\((.*)\)$/$1/;
    # split on commas, then trim quotes from end of each word
    @val = split (/,/, $val[1]);
    s/^'(.*)'$/$1/ foreach (@val);
    return (@val);
}
```

If we modify our original display_form() function in coffee.pl to use our new functions that look up column information for us from the database, it will automatically size the text-input fields and determine the correct choices for the list elements:

```
sub display_form
{
my ($dbh, $qty_len, $remark_len, @size, @extras);

    $dbh = WebDB::connect ();
    $qty_len = get_column_length ($dbh, "coffee", "qty");
    $remark_len = get_column_length ($dbh, "coffee", "remark");
    @size = get_column_members ($dbh, "coffee", "size");
    @extras = get_column_members ($dbh, "coffee", "extras");
    $dbh->disconnect ();

    print start_form (-action => url ()),
        p ("Quantity:"),
        textfield (-name => "qty", -size => $qty_len),
        p ("Serving size:"),
        radio_group (-name => "size",
                        -values => \@size,
                        -default => "M"),
```

```
        p ("Extras:"),
        checkbox_group (-name => "extras", -values => \@extras),
        p ("Special instructions:"),
        textfield (-name => "remark", -size => $remark_len),
        br (), br (),
        submit (-name => "choice", -value => "Submit"),
        end_form ();
    }
```

You could use get_column_members() to generate other kinds of list elements. To generate a pop-up menu or a scrolling list rather than radio buttons, for example, call popup_menu() or scrolling_list() rather than radio_group().

We didn't specify any labels argument when we generated our radio buttons and check boxes, so CGI.pm uses the values for both the values and labels. Without additional external information, there's little else we can do, based just on the list of legal column members. One possibility is to present labels that have the initial letter capitalized. That's one more statement; the following example shows how to do this for the extras check boxes:

```
@val = get_column_members ($dbh, "coffee", "extras");
%labels = map { $_ => ucfirst ($_) } @val;
print checkbox_group (-name => "extras",
                      -values => \@val,
                      -labels => \%labels);
```

The map function takes each element name and turns it into a key/value pair consisting of the name and the name with the first character capitalized. The result is a hash that is indexed on the element names. By specifying labels this way, the HTML produced by checkbox_group() looks like this:

```
<input type="checkbox" name="extras" value="cream">Cream
<input type="checkbox" name="extras" value="sugar">Sugar
```

If you examine the modified display_form() function more closely, you may notice a couple of problems. First, we left the radio button default value (M) hardwired in. That's information we could have gotten from SHOW COLUMNS, but didn't. Second—and more serious—we're issuing four separate queries to the database each time we generate the form! Maybe we should grab the output for the entire table with a single query and save it in a data structure so that we can use the information as much as we want with no need for additional queries. And if we provide an object-oriented interface for that information and put it in its own module, we can use the same code in a variety of applications. If we name the module WebDB::TableInfo to place it in the WebDB namespace, for example, coffee.pl would be able to extract the table information for field sizes and member lists something like this:

```
use WebDB::TableInfo;

$dbh = WebDB::connect ();                          # connect to database
$tbl_info = WebDB::TableInfo->get ($dbh, "coffee"); # get table information
$dbh->disconnect ();                               # done with database
```

continues

continued

```
$qty_len = $tbl_info->length ("qty");           # get column lengths
$remark_len = $tbl_info->length ("remark");     # for text fields

@size = $tbl_info->members ("size");            # get members for
@extras = $tbl_info->members ("extras");        # list fields
```

This approach also has the advantage of better encapsulation. The SHOW statement is a MySQL-specific query, and putting it inside the module is a step toward hiding database-specific details from our applications.

To create a module that can be accessed as just shown, several things are necessary:

- The module file should begin with a package statement that specifies its name:

    ```
    package WebDB::TableInfo;
    ```

- The file should be placed in an appropriate location. The module name WebDB::TableInfo indicates that the module filename will be TableInfo.pm and it must be installed as WebDB/TableInfo.pm[3] under some directory in the search path used by your scripts. The easiest way to do this is to move into the directory where you installed WebDB.pm, and then create a subdirectory, WebDB, and install TableInfo.pm in the subdirectory.

If your scripts are set up to be able to find WebDB, the preceding strategy also allows them to find WebDB::TableInfo with no additional modification. If the module files are installed under /usr/local/apache/lib/perl, for example, you can reference both WebDB and WebDB::TableInfo like this:

```
use lib qw(/usr/local/apache/lib/perl);
use WebDB;
use WebDB::TableInfo;
```

The general outline of the TableInfo.pm file is as follows. It includes a package line containing an appropriate package identifier, references the other modules that it requires, defines the methods that it provides, and ends with the conventional 1; statement that returns true to the Perl interpreter:

```
package WebDB::TableInfo;

use strict;
use CGI qw(:standard escapeHTML);
use DBI;

sub get ...          # define get() method

sub length ...       # define length() method

sub members ...      # define members() method

1;                   # return true from module file
```

---

3. If you're using this module under Windows, the filename would be WebDB\TableInfo.pm rather than WebDB/TableInfo.pm.

The first method any script will call from this module is get(), which saves the table name for use in error messages by other module methods, issues a SHOW COLUMNS query, and returns a reference to an object that contains the information returned by the query about the table's columns:

```
sub get
{
my ($class, $dbh, $tbl_name) = @_;
my $self = {};                          # table information hashref

    $self->{table} = $tbl_name;     # save table name
    $self->{data} = $dbh->selectall_arrayref ("SHOW COLUMNS FROM $tbl_name")
        or die escapeHTML ("No information found for $tbl_name\n");

    # Construct a row map that associates each column name with the
    # row of SHOW COLUMNS output for that column, to make it easier
    # to find information by column name later.
    $self->{row} = {};
    foreach my $row_ref (@{$self->{data}})
    {
        $self->{row}->{$row_ref->[0]} = $row_ref;
    }

    # bless object into class, return reference to it
    return (bless ($self, $class));
}
```

The first argument that get() receives is the class name, even though you don't pass that name in the argument list when you call the method. That's because you invoke get() through the class name, like this:

```
$tbl_info = WebDB::TableInfo->get ($dbh, "tbl_name");
```

Perl notices this and puts the class name at the head of the argument list, where we can access it and use it in the **bless()** call to place the object into the appropriate class.

get() constructs a lookup map allowing information for any given column to be accessed by name. That's the kind of thing we'll need to do fairly often, so we can write a helper method, _column_info(), that returns the array of SHOW COLUMNS information for a column, given its name:[4]

```
sub _column_info
{
my ($self, $col_name) = @_;

    return (@{$self->{row}->{$col_name}})
        if exists ($self->{row}->{$col_name});
    die escapeHTML ("No information found for $self->{table}.$col_name\n");
}
```

---

4. The leading underscore in the name of _column_info() is a Perl convention indicating that the method should be considered private to other methods of the class. The convention is a loose one, however; there's nothing to stop your scripts from calling it. You could make the method really private by defining it within a closure in the definition of the get() method, but I don't see any particular reason to do that.

To get the column length or the list of legal column members, invoke `length()` or `members()`. These are similar to our earlier non–object–oriented functions `get_column_length()` and `get_column_members()`:

```
sub length
{
my ($self, $col_name) = @_;
my $len;

    $len = ($self->_column_info ($col_name))[1];
    ($len =~ /\(((\d+)\)/)
        or die escapeHTML ("No length found for $self->{table}.$col_name\n");
    return ($1);
}

sub members
{
my ($self, $col_name) = @_;
my @val;

    @val = $self->_column_info ($col_name);
    # strip "enum(" or "set(" from beginning and ")" from end of "Type" value
    $val[1] =~ s/^[^(]*\((.*)\)$/$1/;
    # split on commas, then trim quotes from end of each word
    @val = split (/,/, $val[1]);
    s/^'(.*)'$/$1/ foreach (@val);
    return (@val);
}
```

For each of these methods, the first argument passed to them is the object itself. This is similar to the way that Perl passes the class name when you invoke the `get()` class method. The difference is that `length()`, `members()`, and `_column_info()` are invoked through an object that is an instance of the class, so Perl passes the object rather than the class name. This provides us with a convenient means of referring to the object in question so that we can access its data or call other object methods.

With this interface, only one query to the database is needed to obtain all the available information about a table's columns; you can use the information as little or as much as you want without incurring the cost of another query. At the moment, `coffee.pl` uses the information only to determine field lengths and member lists. However, there are other column attributes it could take advantage of, such as default values. Let's rectify that situation by writing a new method, named `default()`, that we can use to initialize fields in the form.

Writing `default()` is a little trickier than you might think at first. The value we want is in the `Default` column of the output produced by SHOW COLUMNS, so we could just return that value:

```
sub default
{
my ($self, $col_name) = @_;

    return (($self->_column_info ($col_name))[4]);
}
```

In fact, that works perfectly well for most column types. For example, the default for the `size` column is a simple string, which we can extract like this:

```
$size_default = $tbl_info->default ("size");
```

However, for a SET column, the version of `default()` just shown doesn't work so well. It's possible for a SET column to have a default value consisting of multiple set members. If we were to notice that most of our customers want cream and sugar added to their coffee, for example, we might change the `extras` column in the `coffee` table to reflect this by using an ALTER TABLE statement to set the default value to `'cream,sugar'`:

```
ALTER TABLE coffee ALTER extras SET DEFAULT 'cream,sugar'
```

In this case, we'd also want `coffee.pl` to select both `extras` check boxes by default when presenting the entry form. But for that to work, we need to pass a `default` parameter to `checkbox_group()` that points to an array of values. (Passing the string `'cream,sugar'` wouldn't work, because CGI.pm has no idea that it should interpret the string as a comma-separated list of individual check box values.) Therefore, for SET columns, it would be more helpful for `default()` to split the default value string and return an array. Let's write `default()` to work either way, so that you can get a scalar or an array depending on how you call it:

```
$size_default = $tbl_info->default ("size");      # get default as scalar
@extras_default = $tbl_info->default ("extras");  # get default as array
```

Perl's `wantarray()` function is what we need here, because it indicates whether a function is called in a context that requires an array. This allows `default()` to determine what kind of value to return:

```
sub default
{
my ($self, $col_name) = @_;
my $default;

    $default = ($self->_column_info ($col_name))[4];
    return ($default) unless wantarray ();
    return (defined ($default) ? split (/,/, $default) : ());
}
```

`default()` is cognizant of the possibility that a SET column default might be NULL (undef); in this case, `default()` returns the empty list when called in an array context.

Now we can write a version of `display_form()` that uses the WebDB::TableInfo module. It's more comprehensive than earlier versions because it automatically initializes list element defaults in addition to specifying the set of possible values:

```
sub display_form
{
my ($dbh, $tbl_info, $qty_len, $remark_len, @size, @extras);
my ($qty_default, $size_default, @extras_default);
```

continues

continued

```
$dbh = WebDB::connect ();                          # connect to database
$tbl_info = WebDB::TableInfo->get ($dbh, "coffee"); # get table information
$dbh->disconnect ();                               # done with database

$qty_len = $tbl_info->length ("qty");              # get column lengths
$remark_len = $tbl_info->length ("remark");        # for text fields

@size = $tbl_info->members ("size");               # get members for
@extras = $tbl_info->members ("extras");           # list fields

$qty_default = $tbl_info->default ("qty");
$size_default = $tbl_info->default ("size");
@extras_default = $tbl_info->default ("extras");

print start_form (-action => url ()),
    p ("Quantity:"),
    textfield (-name => "qty",
                 -size => $qty_len,
                 -default => $qty_default),
    p ("Serving size:"),
    radio_group (-name => "size",
                   -values => \@size,
                   -default => $size_default),
    p ("Extras:"),
    checkbox_group (-name => "extras",
                      -values => \@extras,
                      -default => \@extras_default),
    p ("Special instructions:"),
    textfield (-name => "remark", -size => $remark_len),
    br (), br (),
    submit (-name => "choice", -value => "Submit"),
    end_form ();
}
```

So what does all this messing around gain us? The primary advantages are that your applications become more flexible and adaptive to the structure of your database, and you reduce your workload:

- When your applications determine for themselves what your tables look like, they are less dependent on your own knowledge about the characteristics of those tables. To the extent that an application uses the information available, it becomes adaptive with respect to changes in your database. Consider what happens to coffee.pl if your marketing people decide to engage in that scurrilous technique of trying to make servings seem larger by relabeling the sizes S, M, and

L as M, L, and XL. You could implement the change in the database by modifying the definition of the `size` enumeration column:

```
# first add the new element XL
ALTER TABLE coffee MODIFY size ENUM('S','M','L','XL') NOT NULL
# map existing values in the table to the next size up
UPDATE coffee SET size = ELT(FIELD(size,'S','M','L'),'M','L','XL')
# delete the now-extraneous element S and bump the default from M to L
ALTER TABLE coffee MODIFY size ENUM('M','L','XL') NOT NULL DEFAULT 'L'
```

But now you'd have a problem if you wrote the size choices literally into the function that generates the entry form. There is a mismatch between the new column definition and the values listed in the script. You must change your script or the form will include one value that is no longer valid for the column (S) and will be missing another value that users cannot select at all (XL). This difficulty can be avoided by using the information available from SHOW COLUMNS, because then the script can always determine the proper values to display. (In fact, one reason to use ENUM columns is precisely because you can convert the column descriptions from SHOW COLUMNS automatically to generate form elements that enable the user to select only correct values.)

- Adding flexibility is more work initially; but if you write general library functions, you need to write them only once, and you can use them over and over from multiple applications. The end result is an overall reduction in programming effort.

These are not unalloyed benefits, of course. They come at a price, because you're pounding your database harder. If your site already has a lot of traffic, that may be a price you're not willing to pay. You'll have to decide how to balance the tradeoff between hard-coding form information for performance and running queries to gain flexibility.

One technique that can be useful in this situation is to implement some type of caching. When the script needs to present the form, check the cache. If the form isn't there, generate it and save it in the cache before displaying it to the user. If the form does exist in the cache, just display it. If you change the structure of the underlying table, remove the cache entry to force it to be regenerated the next time the script runs. This approach requires that you set up some kind of coordination between the administrator who manages the table and the Web scripts that use it. However, the performance benefits can be considerable because you greatly reduce the number of queries issued in connection with constructing the form.

Other Ways to Initialize Forms

In the versions of display_form() shown earlier in the chapter for displaying the
coffee table entry form, we provided default values for form fields by passing a
default parameter to field-generating calls. CGI.pm also allows field values to be initialized using the param() function. If you invoke param() to load values into your
script's parameter environment, CGI.pm will find the values and use them to initialize
the fields when you generate the form. We can take advantage of this behavior to
write a method that examines a table description, and for each column extracts the
default value and uses it to initialize the corresponding form parameter:

```
sub load_column_defaults
{
my $self = shift;
my ($col_name, $default);

    foreach my $row_ref (@{$self->{data}})
    {
        $col_name = $row_ref->[0];
        # for SET columns, treat default as a reference to an array,
        # otherwise as a scalar
        if ($self->typename ($col_name) eq "set")
        {
            $default = [ $self->default ($col_name) ];
        }
        else
        {
            $default = $self->default ($col_name);
        }
        param (-name => $col_name, -value => $default);
    }
}
```

With load_column_defaults(), you can set up field defaults with a single call, and
then generate the form as usual, except that you don't need to pass a default parameter to any field-creation calls:

```
$tbl_info->load_column_defaults ();
print start_form (-action => url ()),
    p ("Quantity:"),
    textfield (-name => "qty", -size => $qty_len),
    p ("Serving size:"),
    radio_group (-name => "size", -values => \@size),
    p ("Extras:"),
    checkbox_group (-name => "extras", -values => \@extras),
    p ("Special instructions:"),
    textfield (-name => "remark", -size => $remark_len),
    br (), br (),
    submit (-name => "choice", -value => "Submit"),
    end_form ();
```

You'll notice that load_column_defaults() handles SET columns specially, because in that case, the default value might actually consist of multiple individual values. The helper method typename() used by load_column_defaults() pulls out a column's type name from the Type value returned by SHOW COLUMNS. The type is always the initial word of that value, so it can be determined like this:

```
sub typename
{
my ($self, $col_name) = @_;
my $type;

    # strip Type information beginning at first non-word character
    ($type = ($self->_column_info ($col_name))[1]) =~ s/\W.*//;
    return ($type);
}
```

load_column_defaults() is most useful when you're presenting an entry form used to collect data that will be inserted into the database as a new record. If you want to use a form for updating existing records, a different approach is more appropriate; you typically present to the user a form that is initialized using the contents of the record to be modified. Then the column values in the record will be used as field initializers when you generate the form. To handle this situation, the following method, load_record(), stores the contents of a record into the parameter environment. You can call load_record() in either of two ways. First, you can pass the record as a hash reference, in which case load_record() determines the column names from the keys of the hash. Second, you can pass the record as a reference to an array of column values. In this case, the column names aren't implicit in the array, so you must pass a second reference that points to an array containing the names of the columns in the value array:

```
sub load_record
{
my ($self, $rec_ref, $name_ref) = @_;
my ($col_name, $val);

    # Determine whether record was passed as hash or array reference.
    # In the latter case, an array of column names must also be given.

    if (ref ($rec_ref) eq "HASH")
    {
        foreach $col_name (keys (%{$rec_ref}))
        {
            $val = $rec_ref->{$col_name};            # column value
            if ($self->typename ($col_name) eq "set")
            {
                # convert SET values to array reference
                $val = (defined ($val) ? [ split (/,/, $val) ] : []);
```

continues

continued

```
                }
                param (-name => $col_name, -value => $val);
            }
        }
        elsif (ref ($rec_ref) eq "ARRAY" && ref ($name_ref) eq "ARRAY")
        {
            for (my $i = 0; $i < @{$rec_ref}; $i++)      # for each column...
            {
                $val = $rec_ref->[$i];                   # get column value
                $col_name = $name_ref->[$i];             # get column name
                if ($self->typename ($col_name) eq "set")
                {
                    # convert SET values to array reference
                    $val = (defined ($val) ? [ split (/,/, $val) ] : []);
                }
                param (-name => $col_name, -value => $val);
            }
        }
        else
        {
            die escapeHTML ("load_record() was called with illegal arguments\n");
        }
    }
```

The following code shows how to load a record into a form if you fetch the record as a hash reference. After loading the record into the parameter environment, you can generate the editing form and display it to the user with the field values initialized from the column values:

```
$sth = $dbh->prepare ("SELECT * FROM coffee WHERE id = 5");
$sth->execute ();
$tbl_info->load_record ($sth->fetchrow_hashref ());
$sth->finish ();
print start_form () ...    # generate editing form
```

Alternatively, you can fetch the record as an array reference and load it before you create the editing form. When you do this, you must also get a reference to the array of column names and pass it to load_record() as well:

```
$sth = $dbh->prepare ("SELECT * FROM coffee WHERE id = 5");
$sth->execute ();
$name_ref = $sth->{NAME};   # get column names
$tbl_info->load_record ($sth->fetchrow_arrayref (), $name_ref);
$sth->finish ();
print start_form () ...    # generate editing form
```

Initializing Enumeration Fields to "No Value"

If you initialize a set of radio buttons from the value of an ENUM column, you may run into a problem when the value is NULL. Suppose you have a table that records sales for appliance items that can be purchased with service (maintenance) plans having a duration of 12, 24, or 60 months. The table includes a service_plan column declared as follows, where NULL is an allowable value, and also the default:

```
service_plan ENUM('12 month','24 month','60 month') NULL DEFAULT NULL
```

The idea here is that NULL represents "no plan." In this case, you may want to display three radio buttons corresponding to the service plan lengths, but have none of them selected by default. Unfortunately, if you pass undef to radio_group() as the value of the default parameter, CGI.pm thinks that you just haven't specified any default at all, so it goes ahead and uses the first button as the default anyway. One way to handle this is to call load_column_defaults() (or load_record()), and then override the setting for the enumeration field with a value that's not a legal ENUM member:

```
$tbl_info->load_column_defaults ();      # or load_record ()
param (-name => "service_plan", -value => "[NO DEFAULT]");
```

That would work for radio buttons, but not if you map the ENUM to a pop-up menu, because some element of the menu must always be selected. In that case you may be better off to override both the enumeration values and the default. You can do this by prepending a "title" element to the head of the member list:

```
$tbl_info->load_column_defaults ();      # or load_record ()
@val = $tbl_info->members ("service_plan");
unshift (@val, "Please select a service plan");
param (-name => "service_plan", -value => \@val);
```

If you use this strategy, you must take care to treat the value "Please select a service plan" as a special case that means "no plan" when you process submitted forms.

Alternatively, you could avoid this whole mess by making None an explicit member of the enumeration, using it as the default, and disallowing NULL values in the column:

```
service_plan ENUM('None','12 month','24 month','60 month') NOT NULL
```

Limitations of Automatic Form Construction

Given that having an application look up table information for itself increases its form-generation flexibility, it's reasonable to ask how far you can carry this idea. Can you generate a complete form entirely on the basis of SHOW COLUMNS output? Yes and no. You may be able to, but it's not always clear that you really want to. There are some things MySQL cannot tell you. For example, it can't tell you what labels you want to display next to the fields in the form. You could use the column names as the labels, but column names often are insufficiently descriptive to make a form meaningful to the people who use it. There are also other limitations of automatic form generation that you have to deal with:

- You can determine a column's length from the column description, but the length may not be useful for the purpose of sizing a text-input field. Suppose you want to present a 300-character text field. You can't store field values in a VARCHAR column, because that type has a limit of 255 characters. A TEXT field can be used instead; it has a maximum length of 65,535 characters, and thus is easily large enough to hold the values. However, a script that tries to autosize text-input fields on the basis of the column type knows nothing about your intent to allow only 300 characters. For a type of TEXT, it would deduce that the field should be 65,535 characters long!

- For some column types, a script can't necessarily determine for itself what kind of field to use for the column. Should an ENUM column be presented as radio buttons, a pop-up menu, or a scrolling list? Should a SET column map to check boxes or a scrolling list? Sometimes you can use an adaptive approach based on the number of members in the column description. (For example, you could decide to represent an ENUM with radio buttons if it has five or fewer elements and with a pop-up menu otherwise.) But that's not a general solution that works in all cases.

- Table structure information doesn't help you much with form layout issues. Do you want radio buttons to line up horizontally or vertically? Should text fields go next to the caption, or underneath? If you have a long string column, should it be represented by a multiple-row text box? If so, how long should each line be?

- Dates are a problem. MySQL can't tell what format you intend to use in a date-valued field. Your application may enable users to enter date values in a format such as MM/DD/CCYY, and then perform a conversion to ISO format (CCYY-MM-DD) on the user's behalf before storing the record. Or you may prefer to use separate year, month, and day fields, and then combine them when entering the record. Those are things no script can determine just by looking at the table structure.

Despite these limitations, in some situations you can process forms in a completely automated fashion, and we'll see an instance of this in the section "Automating Poll Processing" later in the chapter. Generally, however, a middle-of-the-road approach is likely to be more useful. Write the application to use whatever table structure information is unambiguous, and give it the benefit of your own knowledge for the rest. coffee.pl is an illustration of this approach. It determines some aspects of the entry form for itself, but we supplied the field captions and decided for it what the field types would be.

One way to discover some of the limitations of automated form construction is to push the approach and see what barriers you encounter. Here's an example where we'd run into problems with the `coffee.pl` script: The qty column of the `coffee` table is an unsigned integer type. If you want to constrain the range of possible quantities to a small number of values, you might decide to change it to an ENUM instead:

```
ALTER TABLE coffee
MODIFY qty ENUM('1','2','3','4','5','6','7','8','9','10') NOT NULL DEFAULT '1'
```

That would make it possible to use the column description to generate a radio button set or pop-up menu automatically that would contain only legal values for the column. As `coffee.pl` is presently written, however, it wouldn't actually notice whether you changed qty from a TINYINT to an ENUM. That's because we've built in the assumption that quantities will be collected using a text-input field. For the script to automatically adapt to a change of column type, it would have to check those types and determine on the fly what kind of field to generate for each column. Unfortunately, then we run into one of the limitations described in the preceding list: Three different field types can be used to represent ENUM columns. How would the script figure out which is most appropriate? That's something you'd have to decide. (Later in the chapter, we'll see how to use a lookup table to solve the problem of limiting the valid quantity values without changing the qty column from an integer to an enumeration.)

Using *SHOW COLUMNS* Output to Validate Form Submissions

SHOW COLUMNS output can help you do more than generate forms. It's also useful for validating the contents of a form after the user fills it in and submits it. This section describes some kinds of validation that can be performed automatically based on table descriptions. As is true for generating forms, you may need to add your own knowledge for validating them. For example, the qty column of the `coffee` table is an unsigned integer. A script can tell from this at validation time that it should disallow non-numeric values as well as numeric values that are negative. However, zero is a non-negative number that would pass such a test, even though it's highly unlikely you'd want to allow zero as a valid quantity. That's something you'd need to check for explicitly, based on the specific quantities you intend to allow. One general strategy that allows for both automatic and special-purpose validation tests is as follows:

- Check all the fields, applying some battery of automatic tests.
- If any errors are detected, notify the user and redisplay the form.
- If all the fields pass the tests, run any special-purpose tests that may be necessary to handle conditions not covered by the automatic tests.

As a demonstration of this strategy, we'll write a set of automated tests, packaged as a `validate()` method for the `WebDB::TableInfo` module, and then apply this method to validation of entries obtained from the form presented by `coffee.pl`. To write `validate()`, let's consider what kinds of things it can check for based purely on the information produced by SHOW COLUMNS (as well as some things it should *not* check for):

- If a column cannot contain NULL values, it's reasonable to assume that the corresponding field must be filled in. (If you want to provide default values, you could do so by calling `load_column_defaults()` or `load_record()` prior to generating and displaying the form.)

- For integer columns, the field value must be a string of digits, optionally preceded by a sign character. If the column has the `unsigned` atrribute, negative values should be disallowed.

- For integer, CHAR, and VARCHAR columns, the column length constrains the length of field values.

- For ENUM columns, the field value must be one of the members listed in the column definition.

- For SET columns, the corresponding field may consist of multiple values, each of which must be listed in the column definition.

- When testing whether a field is empty, we can trim whitespace from the end of the value. Trimmed values can be put back in the parameter environment so that if additional tests need to be performed, the value can be extracted later without needing to be trimmed again. The exceptions to this strategy are fields that correspond to SET or ENUM columns. It's legal for members of those column types to be declared with leading or trailing whitespace; trimming would cause spurious results when checking for a match.

- No checking should be done for fields that contain dates. When you store a value into a DATE column, it must be in ISO format (CCYY-MM-DD), but that's not a constraint that `validate()` can enforce in a general way, because you may well want users to enter values in some other format, such as MM/DD/CCYY.

Here's an implementation of the `validate()` method based on the preceding discussion. For each column in the table associated with a form, it uses the column name to extract a parameter value from the script environment, and then performs tests on the value based on the column description. If any errors are found, messages describing them are accumulated in an array, which becomes the return value. If `validate()` finds no problems, it returns an empty list.

```
sub validate
{
my $self = shift;
my @errors;

    foreach my $col_name (keys (%{$self->{row}}))
```

```
{
    my $typename = $self->typename ($col_name);
    my ($val, $err);

    # For a SET column, allow multiple values; this test is done BEFORE
    # the empty field test because it's allowable for sets to be empty.

    if ($typename eq "set")
    {
        my @val = param ($col_name); # use array to allow multiple values
        push (@errors, $err)
            if $err = $self->check_set_value ($col_name, @val);
        next;
    }

    # all other columns should have a scalar value

    $val = param ($col_name);

    # Check for blank fields.
    # if the value is missing but the column is not nullable, it's
    # an error (exception: for timestamp columns and auto_increment
    # columns, it's assumed they won't even be represented in the form.)

    if ((!defined ($val) || $val eq "") &&
            !$self->has_attr ($col_name, "nullable"))
    {
        push (@errors, "$col_name must have a value")
            if !$self->has_attr ($col_name, "auto_increment")
                && $typename ne "timestamp";
        next;
    }

    if ($typename eq "enum")
    {
        push (@errors, $err)
            if $err = $self->check_enum_value ($col_name, $val);
        next;
    }

    $val = WebDB::trim ($val);                  # trim whitespace
    param (-name => $col_name, -value => $val); # return to environment

    if ($typename =~ /int$/)        # one of the integer types
    {
        push (@errors, $err)
            if $err = $self->check_integer_value ($col_name, $val);
    }
    elsif ($typename =~ /char$/)    # char or varchar
    {
        push (@errors, "$col_name is too long")
```

continues

continued

```
                    if CORE::length ($val) > $self->length ($col_name);
        }

        # Add any additional tests here ...
    }

    return (@errors);       # empty list if no errors
}
```

In the course of performing its tests, the `validate()` method invokes a number of subsidiary methods, several of which have not yet been described. The `has_attr()` method checks for various attributes in the column description:

```
sub has_attr
{
my ($self, $col_name, $attr_name) = @_;
my @val = $self->_column_info ($col_name);

    # Look in Null value for YES to see if column is nullable
    return ($val[2] eq "YES") if $attr_name eq "nullable";
    # Look in Extra value for auto_increment
    return ($val[5] eq "auto_increment") if $attr_name eq "auto_increment";
    # Look for other attributes (unsigned, zerofill, binary) in Type value
    # (split, then shift off type name to leave attribute words)
    @val = split (" ", $val[1]);
    shift (@val);
    return (grep (/^$attr_name$/, @val));
}
```

Other methods check values for various column types. Each of them returns an empty string if the value is okay, or an error message otherwise. `check_integer_value()` verifies that a value is an integer, that it is non-negative if the column is unsigned, and that the value doesn't exceed the column's display width:[5]

```
sub check_integer_value
{
my ($self, $col_name, $val) = @_;

    return ("$col_name must be an integer") if $val !~ /^([-+])?\d+$/;
    return ("$col_name cannot be negative")
        if $self->has_attr ($col_name, "unsigned") && $val < 0;
    return ("$col_name is too long")
        if CORE::length ($val) > $self->length ($col_name);
    return ("");
}
```

---

5. Note that `validate()` and `check_integer_value()` both invoke Perl's built-in `length()` function as `CORE::length()` to distinguish it from the `length()` method of the `WebDB::TableInfo` module itself.

check_enum_value() tests a scalar to make sure it's one of the valid members of an ENUM column. check_set_value() is similar, but more involved. It must check array values, each of which must be a valid member of a SET column. Both of these methods use the i modifier for the pattern match because ENUM and SET columns are not case sensitive:

```perl
sub check_enum_value
{
my ($self, $col_name, $val) = @_;
my @members = $self->members ($col_name);

    # use //i test; ENUM is not case sensitive
    return ("$col_name cannot have a value of $val")
        if !grep (/^$val$/i, @members);
    return ("");
}

sub check_set_value
{
my ($self, $col_name, @val) = @_;
my @members = $self->members ($col_name);
my @illegal;

    foreach my $val (@val)
    {
        # use //i test; SET is not case sensitive
        push (@illegal, $val) if !grep (/^$val$/i, @members);
    }
    return ("$col_name cannot contain " . join (",", @illegal)) if @illegal;
    return ("");
}
```

Here's how to use validate() in the context of the coffee.pl application, which invokes a process_form() function when the user submits an entry form. validate() runs the automatic tests, and if those succeed, we run any additional tests not handled automatically:

```perl
sub process_form
{
my ($dbh, $tbl_info, @errors);

    $dbh = WebDB::connect ();
    $tbl_info = WebDB::TableInfo->get ($dbh, "coffee");

    # Perform automated tests.  If they succeed, perform the field-specific
    # tests (only one such test is needed here).

    @errors = $tbl_info->validate ();
    if (!@errors)
    {
```

continues

continued

```
            # we know the qty value is numeric and non-negative
            # at this point; make sure it isn't zero
            push (@errors, "Quantity must be greater than zero")
                if param ("qty") == 0;
    }

    # If any errors occurred, display messages, return failure.

    if (@errors)
    {
        $dbh->disconnect ();
        @errors = map { escapeHTML ($_) } @errors;
        print p ("The following errors occurred:"),
                ul (li (\@errors));
        return (0);
    }

    # Record is okay; insert into table, display confirmation, return true.

    $tbl_info->insert_record ($dbh);

    $dbh->disconnect ();

    print p ("Record was inserted successfully"),
        p (a ({-href => url ()}, "Enter next record"));

    return (1);
}
```

The insert_record() method used near the end of process_form() constructs and executes an INSERT statement to create a new record, based on the table structure and the contents of the form. We'll discuss how it works in the next section, along with a method, update_record(), that can be used to issue UPDATE statements when you're editing existing records.

validate() works best if you define your tables with a couple of points in mind:

- Declare your columns NOT NULL if the corresponding form fields must be filled in.
- Specify an explicit display width for integer fields if you want validate() to enforce a specific length constraint on field values.

Even with these assumptions, however, validate() is subject to several limitations:

- validate() doesn't know anything about the labels you display in a form, so error messages can refer only to column names, not descriptive field labels.
- Form parameters are checked only if they have the same name as a column in the table. If your form contains fields that don't map onto table columns, validate() won't check them.

- There are several column types that `validate()` doesn't check very well. For example, we could add tests to make sure that fields for DECIMAL, FLOAT, or DOUBLE columns contain numeric values. We could also check lengths for DECIMAL, FLOAT/DOUBLE, and BLOB/TEXT. (Although to do that, we'd need to make the `length()` method smarter, because it too knows nothing about these types.)

The nature of these limitations may make `validate()` unsuitable for use with a given application. However, you may still find it useful to apply some of the individual value-checking techniques that it illustrates. Or you might choose to extend it. For example, as `validate()` is written, the error messages that it generates refer to column names. To get better messages, you might rewrite `validate()` to accept and use a hash argument that maps column names to descriptive field labels, something like this:

```
@errors = $tbl_info->validate ($dbh, {
            "qty" => "Quantity",
            "size" => "Serving size",
            "extras" => "Additional ingredients"
        });
```

Using *SHOW COLUMNS* Output to Insert or Update Records

After you've validated the contents of a submitted form, you store the information in the database. Table information from SHOW COLUMNS comes in handy for this phase of form processing (just as it does for earlier phases), although it's necessary to make a distinction between the issues involved in inserting new records and those for updating existing ones.

Inserting New Records

To gather information for the purpose of creating a new record, the process is as follows:

1. Generate the entry form, initialized with empty values. (Alternatively, to fill the form with the default values listed in the table description, call `load_column_defaults()` before creating the form.)

2. Display the form to the user.

3. Validate the form when the user submits it.

4. Insert the form contents as a new record, specifying in the INSERT statement only those fields that are non-empty.

We've discussed the first stages of this process earlier in the chapter. Now we can consider how we might use table description information to help us construct the INSERT statement for storing the form contents into the table. As it turns out, table information doesn't actually tell us much. We can use it to determine whether a field maps onto a SET column, but that's about it. Nevertheless, that's important because a set field might contain multiple values that need to be converted to a single string.

Here is a method, `insert_record()`, that takes a database handle, looks through the columns in a table, extracts the corresponding form parameter value for each one, and adds it to the INSERT statement:

```
sub insert_record
{
my ($self, $dbh) = @_;
my $assign;
my @placeholder;
my (@val, $val);

    # construct assignments for SET clause using all non-empty fields

    foreach my $col_name (keys (%{$self->{row}}))
    {
        my $typename = $self->typename ($col_name);
        @val = param ($col_name);        # field value for column
        if ($typename eq "set")
        {
            $val = join (",", @val);     # convert multiple values to scalar
        }
        else
        {
            $val = shift (@val);
        }
        # don't bother with empty fields
        next unless defined ($val) && $val ne "";
        $assign .= "," if $assign;       # put commas between assignments
        $assign .= $col_name . " = ?";   # add column name, placeholder
        push (@placeholder, $val);       # save placeholder value
    }
    $dbh->do ("INSERT INTO $self->{table} SET $assign", undef, @placeholder);
}
```

`insert_record()` assumes that field values are stored in the parameter environment and can be accessed by calling `param()`. It doesn't bother adding any *name=value* assignment to the INSERT statement for any field that is empty. This is advantageous for two reasons. First, although you could provide a default value for an empty field by looking up the column's default value in the table description, MySQL will set the column to its default automatically if you just omit it from the INSERT statement (and it's more efficient to let MySQL do so than to list the default explicitly). Second, skipping assignments for columns with no corresponding parameter values gives `insert_record()` an easy way to pass over TIMESTAMP and AUTO_INCREMENT columns. That's generally what you want, because these are rarely represented in entry forms. They are special kinds of columns and it's much more common to let MySQL assign them values automatically. (TIMESTAMP columns end up with the current time and day, and AUTO_INCREMENT columns are assigned the next sequence number.)

A limitation of insert_record() is that it skips not only empty fields, but also fields that don't have the same name as a table column. In forms that collect a date value from users, for example, a common strategy for making dates easier to validate is to represent them as three separate integer-valued fields. Suppose you have a DATE column named entry_date in a table. You might represent it using three fields named day, month, and year. insert_record() would expect to find an entry_date field corresponding to the entry_date column, and would ignore the day, month, and year fields entirely. The result is that your entry_date column wouldn't be assigned any value in the INSERT statement.

Sometimes you can work around this lack of correspondence between table columns and form fields pretty easily, by manipulating the parameter environment before invoking insert_record(). If you have validated the date-part fields and know they form a legal date value, you could synthesize a parameter value for the entry_date column like this:

```
param (-name => "entry_date",
       -value => sprintf ("%04d-%02d-%02d",
                   param ("year"), param ("month"), param ("day")));
```

If you do this before calling insert_record(), that method will find a "field" value named entry_date, properly written in ISO format, and will happily add it to the INSERT statement.

You can use this same technique if you have a DATE column that you want to set to the current date when the record is created, but that has no corresponding field in the form. Extract the current date from Perl and install it into the parameter environment like this:

```
($day,$month, $year) = (localtime (time ()))[3..5];
param (-name => "entry_date",
       -value => sprintf ("%04d-%02d-%02d", $year + 1900, $month + 1, $day));
```

In both cases, the idea is the same: insert_record() is limited to using only those values it can find by calling param(), but there's nothing to stop you from putting your own values into the parameter space for insert_record() to discover.

Updating Existing Records

The process for editing an existing record differs somewhat from that for inserting new records. There are a couple of possible approaches. One way to perform record editing is to display a blank entry form and have the user fill in those values that need to be changed. Then when the form is submitted, construct an UPDATE statement that modifies the values only for those columns corresponding to non-empty fields in the form. This is easier for you as the application writer, but it's not very helpful for users:

- The user doesn't see the record's current contents and can't tell which fields need to be changed, at least not without consulting some external source of information.

- There is no way to delete a column value, because this approach treats an empty field as signifying "leave this column alone" rather than "delete this column value."

A better method is to display the editing form with all the fields filled in from the record's current contents. Then the user can see what value each column contains easily and can tell which ones need to be revised. Also, a column's value can be deleted just by clearing the corresponding field in the editing form. To implement this approach, use the following general procedure:

- Retrieve from the database the record that is to be modified.

- Generate the editing form, using the contents of the record to initialize the fields. The form should include a hidden field that contains the value of some unique index to allow the record to be identified later when the user submits the form. (If the unique index comprises multiple columns, use multiple hidden fields.)

- Display the form to the user.

- Validate the form when the user submits it.

- Use the form contents to update the record indicated by the value of the unique key specified by the hidden field (or fields). The UPDATE statement should assign a value to every column in the table corresponding to an editable form element.

It's more work to fill in the fields for an editing form, because you must look up the record first. (The effort required to load the record into the form can be reduced by using the load_record() method from the WebDB::TableInfo module.) It's also more work to generate an UPDATE statement than an INSERT statement. For one thing, you need to identify which record to update. (This can be done using a WHERE clause based on the unique key value.) For another, you must assign values to all the other columns, even those that are empty. (A column might have had a non-empty value that the user now wants cleared.) For an empty field, however, you can set the corresponding column to two possible values: the empty string or NULL. Which should you choose?

Here's where it's helpful to have information about the characteristics of the table's columns. It's generally better to use NULL if the table column allows NULL, because that corresponds better than the empty string to the "no value" case. Consider what happens if you have an INT or DATE column that can be NULL. If you set the column to NULL, that's what gets stored in the record. If you store an empty string, MySQL will perform type conversion and you'll get a 0 for an INT or 0000-00-00 for a DATE; that's probably not what you want.

Using this information, we can write a method, update_record(), that takes arguments for a database handle and the name of the column (or columns) that make up the unique key. (The key values are those you will have represented using hidden fields.) If `coffee.pl` had a record-editing capability, you'd update a record like this, because `id` is the unique key column:

```
$tbl_info->update_record ($dbh, "id");
```

The implementation of `update_record()` is as follows:

```
sub update_record
{
my ($self, $dbh, @key) = @_;
my ($assign, $where);
my @placeholder;
my (@val, $val);

    # Construct assignments for SET clause using all non-empty non-key columns

    foreach my $col_name (keys (%{$self->{row}}))
    {
        next if grep (/^$col_name$/, @key); # skip key columns
        my $typename = $self->typename ($col_name);
        @val = param ($col_name);            # field value for column
        if ($typename eq "set")
        {
            $val = join (",", @val);     # convert multiple values to scalar
        }
        else
        {
            $val = shift (@val);
        }

        # If the field has no value, determine whether to insert
        # undef or an empty string into the column based on whether
        # or not the column can take NULL values.

        if (!defined ($val) || $val eq "")
        {
            $val = ($self->has_attr ($col_name, "nullable") ? undef : "");
        }

        $assign .= "," if $assign;       # put commas between assignments
        $assign .= $col_name . " = ?";   # add column name, placeholder
        push (@placeholder, $val);       # save placeholder value
    }

    # Construct WHERE clause using all key columns to identify record.
    # All keys are assumed to be scalars and non-NULL.

    foreach my $col_name (@key)
    {
        $val = param ($col_name);
        $where .= " AND " if $where;     # put AND between assignments
        $where .= $col_name . " = ?";    # add column name, placeholder
```

continues

continued

```
        push (@placeholder, $val);      # save placeholder value
    }

    $dbh->do ("UPDATE $self->{table} SET $assign WHERE $where",
            undef, @placeholder);
}
```

Generating Form Elements from Lookup Tables and Query Results

Up to this point in the chapter, we've concentrated on ways to automate form processing by consulting the information that MySQL provides in table descriptions. In
this section, we'll discuss how to generate form elements from table contents rather
than table structure. This technique is used most commonly to generate list elements
corresponding to enumerations and to sets—that is, lists for which you must pick a
single value and lists from which you are allowed to pick multiple values.

Using Lookup Tables for Enumerations

Here's a simple example where you might want to use a lookup table to generate a
form element. Suppose you have several applications that each present a form containing a pop-up menu element for specifying a salutation ("Mr.", "Mrs.", and so on). But
you don't want to write out all the salutations literally in every script. One way to
avoid this is to declare the salutation column as an ENUM in the underlying table associated with each form:

```
salutation ENUM('Mr.','Mrs.','Miss','Ms.','None') NOT NULL DEFAULT 'None'
```

Then you can create the pop-up menu automatically from the column description in
the table information. But you don't want to do that, either; because if you decide to
add a new salutation (such as "Dr."), you'd need to change the ENUM definition in all
tables affected by the change.

In this situation, another way to deal with the problem is to list your salutations in
a separate lookup table. This allows your scripts to generate the pop-up menu automatically from the contents of this table (we'll see how shortly), but it also enables you
to change the list of salutations easily. To add a new salutation, just add a row to the
table, and all the scripts that use the table automatically adjust to the change with no
additional programming. You can also rename or delete values from the lookup table
with no need to update your scripts.

Lookup tables can be used to present enumeration-type fields even for columns
that you may not represent using an ENUM. Earlier, we discussed the possibility of
converting the qty column in the coffee table from a TINYINT to an ENUM, to allow a
specific set of quantity values to be listed explicitly in the column specification and

converted automatically to a list element such as a pop-up menu. Another way to address this issue is to continue representing qty as a TINYINT, but list the valid quantities in a separate lookup table.

Using Lookup Tables for Form Generation

Let's see how lookup tables work for generating form elements by writing a script, coffee2.pl, for entering coffee orders that is similar to coffee.pl but that uses lookup tables qty_value and size_value for the qty and size fields. The table for quantity values can be very simple, because it needs only one column. To create the table and initialize it, execute the following statements:

```
CREATE TABLE qty_value
(
    value   TINYINT UNSIGNED NOT NULL
)

INSERT INTO qty_value (value) VALUES(1),(2),(3),(4),(5),(6),(7),(8),(9),(10)
```

The INSERT statement creates rows with values from 1 to 10. It uses the syntax that allows multiple VALUES() lists, so that you can insert multiple rows with a single statement. If your version of MySQL is older than 3.22.5, you'll need to insert the values one at a time:

```
INSERT INTO qty_value (value) VALUES(1)
INSERT INTO qty_value (value) VALUES(2)
INSERT INTO qty_value (value) VALUES(3)
...
```

After you have the qty_value table initialized, the quantity values can be selected from it using a simple query:

```
SELECT value FROM qty_value ORDER BY value
```

If we assume the existence of a get_lookup_values() function that takes a database handle and a query as arguments and returns the looked-up values, we can generate a pop-up menu for the qty field as follows:

```
$qty_val_ref = get_lookup_values (
                    $dbh,
                    "SELECT value FROM qty_value ORDER BY value");
print popup_menu (-name => "qty", -values => $qty_val_ref);
```

Note the ORDER BY clause in the query. The function can't possibly read your mind to know how to sort the values, so it's up to you to specify what the order is. get_lookup_values() returns a reference to an array that can be passed to popup_menu() to provide the list of values displayed in the menu.

For the serving size lookup table, one possibility is to create and initialize a size_value table that lists the valid sizes like this:

```
CREATE TABLE size_value
(
    value   CHAR(3) NOT NULL
)

INSERT INTO size_value (value) VALUES('S'),('M'),('L')
```

However, this table actually is not very useful, because there is no natural way to sort the rows into the proper order (S, M, L). We can't just omit the ORDER BY clause when we select the rows from the table and hope that they come out in the right order, but ORDER BY value won't return the rows in correct order, either.[6] To deal with this, we'll add a sequence number column that enables you to specify the value order explicitly. In addition, a third column containing a more descriptive label for each size will enable you to generate a couple of different styles of lookup lists. Here are the resulting table-creation and table-initialization statements:

```
CREATE TABLE size_value
(
    seq     TINYINT UNSIGNED NOT NULL PRIMARY KEY,
    value   CHAR(3) NOT NULL,
    label   CHAR(6) NOT NULL
)

INSERT INTO size_value (seq,value,label)
    VALUES(1,'S','Small'),(2,'M','Medium'),(3,'L','Large')
```

With this version of the size_value table, we can get the size values in the proper order and use them to generate radio buttons like this:

```
$size_val_ref = get_lookup_values (
                    $dbh,
                    "SELECT value FROM size_value ORDER BY seq");
print radio_group (-name => "size", -values => $size_val_ref);
```

Furthermore, if we write get_lookup_values() to be smart enough, it can return not only a reference to the list of field values, but a reference to a map for associating values with the labels. This allows a different style of labels to be presented. For example, we could call it like this for the serving sizes to be able to display labels like Small, Medium, and Large rather than S, M, and L:

```
($size_val_ref, $size_label_ref) = get_lookup_values (
                    $dbh,
                    "SELECT value, label FROM size_value ORDER BY seq");
print radio_group (-name => "size",
                    -values => $size_val_ref,
                    -labels => $size_label_ref);
```

---

6. You may object that if you add DESC to sort the column in reverse (ORDER BY value DESC) the values do indeed sort into the order S, M, L, but that's just coincidence. (Add a row containing XL to the size_value table and see what happens.)

Note the differences from the way we previously generated the size element in the form. We're now passing to get_lookup_values() a query that retrieves two columns (value and label) rather than one, and we're getting back two references as a result. The first points to the list of values, as before; the second points to a value-to-label hash that we can pass as a labels parameter to radio_group().

This illustrates something you can do with lookup tables easily that you can't do at all when you generate form elements by reading table descriptions. The description for an ENUM column lists the values of the column, and you can use that to create a form element. If you want to associate particular labels with the values, however, that isn't possible using the column description alone.

Of course, we still have to write get_lookup_values(), and we have to enable it to know whether to construct the value-to-label map. That's actually not very difficult, because when DBI executes a query, it can tell how many columns are in the result set. If there is a second column, we'll assume it contains labels and use it to construct a value-to-label map:

```
sub get_lookup_values
{
my ($dbh, $query) = @_;
my ($sth, @val, $label_ref);

    $sth = $dbh->prepare ($query);
    $sth->execute ();
    # check whether or not query returns a label column
    $label_ref = {} if $sth->{NUM_OF_FIELDS} > 1;
    while (my @row = $sth->fetchrow_array ())
    {
        push (@val, $row[0]);
        $label_ref->{$row[0]} = $row[1] if $label_ref;  # add label map entry
    }
    $sth->finish ();
    return (wantarray () ? (\@val, $label_ref) : \@val);
}
```

You can see that although it takes a little more work to create a lookup table, you gain some flexibility in terms of the kinds of displays you can generate. This approach offers a number of possibilities you can exploit. For example, it can help you generate forms in different languages. If you add a column indicating the language of a label, you can store rows for several different languages in a lookup table and retrieve the rows for the appropriate language at form-generation time.

Now that we have our lookup tables set up, one more thing we'll do for coffee2.pl is to create a new table, coffee2. It's identical to the coffee table except that the size column is a VARCHAR rather than an ENUM:

```
CREATE TABLE coffee2
(
    id      INT NOT NULL AUTO_INCREMENT PRIMARY KEY, # record ID/timestamp
    ts      TIMESTAMP,
```

continues

continued

```
qty     TINYINT UNSIGNED NOT NULL DEFAULT 1,    # quantity
size    VARCHAR(10) NOT NULL DEFAULT 'M',       # serving size
extras  SET('cream','sugar'),                   # extra ingredients
remark  VARCHAR(30)                             # special instructions
)
```

Why this difference between `coffee` and `coffee2`? Because we're listing the possible serving sizes in the lookup table `size_values`. There's no need to list them *again* in the coffee record table, and in fact doing so may cause you problems. For our initial version of `size_value`, the only sizes it will contain are S, M, and L, which matches the sizes we've been using all along. If you add, modify, or delete values from `size_value`, however, you'd create a mismatch between an `ENUM` version of the `size` column and the values in the lookup table. This problem goes away if we use a `size` column that is a simple character string.

We still need to consider the problem of getting the field defaults initialized. That really isn't much of a problem, because we can get them from the `coffee2` table description and load them into the parameter environment like this:

```
$tbl_info = WebDB::TableInfo->get ($dbh, "coffee2");
param (-name => "qty", -value => $tbl_info->default ("qty"));
param (-name => "size", -value => $tbl_info->default ("size"));
```

Putting this all together, we can generate the entry form using lookup tables like this:

```
sub display_form
{
my ($dbh, $tbl_info, $qty_val_ref, $size_val_ref, $size_label_ref, $remark_len);
my (@extras, @extras_default);

    $dbh = WebDB::connect ();                        # connect to database
    $tbl_info = WebDB::TableInfo->get ($dbh, "coffee2");# table information

    # Look up values for qty field
    $qty_val_ref = get_lookup_values (
                    $dbh,
                    "SELECT value FROM qty_value ORDER BY value");
    # Look up values and labels for size field
    ($size_val_ref, $size_label_ref) = get_lookup_values (
                    $dbh,
                    "SELECT value, label FROM size_value ORDER BY seq");

    $dbh->disconnect ();                             # done with database

    # set defaults for qty and size fields
    param (-name => "qty", -value => $tbl_info->default ("qty"));
    param (-name => "size", -value => $tbl_info->default ("size"));

    # ditto for extras field
    @extras_default = $tbl_info->default ("extras");
    param (-name => "extras", -value => \@extras_default);
```

```
    # get length for remark field, value for extras field
    $remark_len = $tbl_info->length ("remark");
    @extras = $tbl_info->members ("extras");

    print start_form (-action => url ()),
        p ("Quantity:"),
        popup_menu (-name => "qty", -values => $qty_val_ref),
        p ("Serving size:"),
        radio_group (-name => "size",
                    -values => $size_val_ref,
                    -labels => $size_label_ref),
        p ("Extras:"),
        checkbox_group (-name => "extras", -values => \@extras),
        p ("Special instructions:"),
        textfield (-name => "remark", -size => $remark_len),
        br (), br (),
        submit (-name => "choice", -value => "Submit"),
        end_form ();
}
```

Another way to specify default values is to store them in the lookup table itself. First, use ALTER TABLE to add a defval column to the qty_value and size_value tables:

```
ALTER TABLE qty_value ADD defval TINYINT DEFAULT 0
ALTER TABLE size_value ADD defval TINYINT DEFAULT 0
```

Then specify the initial default values with these two statements:

```
UPDATE qty_value SET defval = 1 WHERE value = 1
UPDATE size_value SET defval = 1 WHERE value = 'M'
```

Note that the defval column doesn't contain the default value; it indicates which row contains the default value. In the size_value table, for example, all rows have a defval value of 0, except the row where the value column is M, which has defval set to 1.

To use the defaults within our script, we read them and load them into the parameter environment like so:

```
$qty_default = get_lookup_default ($dbh, "qty_value", "value", "defval");
$size_default = get_lookup_default ($dbh, "size_value", "value", "defval");
param (-name => "qty", -value => $qty_default);
param (-name => "size", -value => $size_default);
```

The get_lookup_default() function used here looks in the given table and extracts the value of the specified column for the row where value of the default value column is 1:

```
sub get_lookup_default
{
my ($dbh, $tbl_name, $col_name, $def_col_name) = @_;
my $default;

    $default = $dbh->selectrow_array (
            "SELECT $col_name FROM $tbl_name WHERE $def_col_name = 1");
    return ($default);
}
```

This approach makes the default value explicit in the lookup table. You can also change the default just by modifying the contents of the table. Suppose you want to change the serving size default from M to S. Here's one way to do it:

```
UPDATE size_value SET defval = 0 WHERE value = 'M'
UPDATE size_value SET defval = 1 WHERE value = 'S'
```

Or you can accomplish the same end with a single statement:

```
UPDATE size_value SET defval = IF(value='S',1,0)
```

MySQL evaluates the expression specified in the first argument of the IF() function. If the expression is true (that is, not 0 or NULL), the value of IF() becomes the value of the second argument. If the expression is false, IF() returns the third argument. The result is to set defval to 1 for the row with S in the value column, and to 0 for all other rows.

One limitation to be aware of when you store the default value indicator in the lookup table is that this approach doesn't work if the table is shared among different applications that want to have different default values.

Using Lookup Tables for Validation

When a user submits a form containing an element that was generated by means of a lookup table, you can also use the table to validate the element. The following function, check_lookup_value(), runs a query to determine whether a particular value can be found in a lookup table. It returns true if the value is present, and false otherwise:

```
sub check_lookup_value
{
my ($dbh, $tbl_name, $col_name, $val) = @_;
my $result;

    $result = $dbh->selectrow_array (
                "SELECT COUNT(*) FROM $tbl_name WHERE $col_name = ?",
                    undef, $val);
    return ($result > 0);
}
```

You might use the function like this to perform field validation:

```
push (@errors, "Quantity is illegal")
    unless check_lookup_value ($dbh, "qty_value", "value", param ("qty"));
push (@errors, "Serving size is illegal")
    unless check_lookup_value ($dbh, "size_value", "value", param ("size"));
```

Other Ideas for Using Lookup Tables

Enumeration list lookup tables have myriad uses in data entry applications:

- Keep a list of state abbreviations and names in a table and use it for presenting the state field in forms that collect address information. Sometimes you can use it multiple times in the same form, such as when you collect both a shipping address and a billing address.

- Forms that enable users to indicate the specifications for build-to-order items are a natural application for lookup tables. Every part of the specification for which multiple choices exist can be represented by a list element constructed from the contents of a lookup table. If you're selling computers, for example, you can use lookup tables to present the options for processor speed, hard drive capacity, amount of memory, and so forth.

- A lookup table can help you in any situation involving a primary underlying table in which you store a code value for efficiency, but for which you have a secondary table that lists more meaningful labels for the codes. If you're collecting medical records for surgeries that are stored by code number, use a lookup table to present a descriptive string for each kind of surgery to the user, and then map the string to the code when storing the record. If you have a `department` table that lists department titles and codes, use it to present a list of titles to users for a personnel entry form application that stores codes in the `personnel` table.

Lookup tables are useful in search applications, too. For real estate offerings, you can present a list of property types (such as retail, office, industrial, residential), locations, and so forth. For inventory searches, you can allow the user to limit the search by selecting a particular item category. For example, if you have listings of furniture items, you can present a category pop-up menu containing items such as dining area, kitchen, living room, and bedroom.

If you're using a lookup table to allow you to display specific labels to users in an entry or editing form, you may also want to use the table later for purposes such as report generation. Let's say you want to create a summary that shows your coffee sales per month, categorized by serving size. A basic query that displays sizes as S, M, and L is as follows:

```
mysql> SELECT YEAR(ts) AS year, MONTH(ts) AS month, size,
    -> SUM(qty) AS quantity
    -> FROM coffee2
    -> GROUP BY year, month, size;
+------+-------+------+----------+
| year | month | size | quantity |
+------+-------+------+----------+
| 2001 |     1 | L    |      118 |
| 2001 |     1 | M    |      197 |
| 2001 |     1 | S    |       74 |
| 2001 |     2 | L    |      173 |
| 2001 |     2 | M    |      229 |
| 2001 |     2 | S    |       82 |
| 2001 |     3 | L    |      198 |
| 2001 |     3 | M    |      243 |
| 2001 |     3 | S    |      125 |
+------+-------+------+----------+
```

However, you can display the more meaningful labels found in the `size_value` table by using a join:

```
mysql> SELECT YEAR(c.ts) AS year, MONTH(c.ts) AS month, s.label AS size,
    -> SUM(c.qty) AS quantity
    -> FROM coffee2 AS c, size_value AS s
    -> WHERE c.size = s.value
    -> GROUP BY year, month, size
    -> ORDER BY year, month, s.seq;
+------+-------+--------+----------+
| year | month | size   | quantity |
+------+-------+--------+----------+
| 2001 |     1 | Small  |       74 |
| 2001 |     1 | Medium |      197 |
| 2001 |     1 | Large  |      118 |
| 2001 |     2 | Small  |       82 |
| 2001 |     2 | Medium |      229 |
| 2001 |     2 | Large  |      173 |
| 2001 |     3 | Small  |      125 |
| 2001 |     3 | Medium |      243 |
| 2001 |     3 | Large  |      198 |
+------+-------+--------+----------+
```

Note how this second query takes advantage of the `seq` column in the lookup table so that you can sort size values properly. (If you have a `GROUP BY` clause in a query, the output normally is sorted on the columns named in that clause. The second query needs to sort on a different set of columns, necessitating an explicit `ORDER BY` clause that includes the `seq` column.)

Using Lookup Tables for Sets

You may be curious why we converted form generation in `coffee2.pl` to use lookup tables for the `qty` and `size` fields, but not for the `extras` field. The reason is that the underlying `extras` column in the database table is a `SET`. Recall that we converted the `size` column from an `ENUM` to a `VARCHAR` column because an `ENUM` would go out of correspondence with the rows in the `size_value` table if we added, changed, or deleted rows in that table. Similarly, if you want to use a lookup table for the `extras` field, you'd have to change the `extras` column to a `VARCHAR`. In this case, however, there's an additional issue. Unlike the `size` field, for which only one value can be chosen, it's allowable to select several `extras` values. This means the `extras` column would have to be wide enough to accommodate a string listing all the values if they are all selected. Currently the longest value would be `'cream,sugar'`; but if you started adding other options such as chocolate syrup, sprinkles, and whipped cream, you could end up needing a rather long column.

To convert a SET column to use a lookup table, you really should use a different approach, outlined here:

- Create the lookup table `extras_value` and put one row in it for each applicable value. Probably you'd want a `seq` column (as with `size_value`) so that you can sort the rows into a specific order:

```
CREATE TABLE extras_value
(
    seq     TINYINT UNSIGNED NOT NULL PRIMARY KEY,
    value   CHAR(10) NOT NULL
)

INSERT INTO extras_value (seq,value) VALUES(1,'cream'),(2,'sugar')
```

- Create a table, `coffee3`, that is like `coffee2` except that it has no `extras` column at all:

```
CREATE TABLE coffee3
(
    id      INT NOT NULL AUTO_INCREMENT PRIMARY KEY, # record ID/timestamp
    ts      TIMESTAMP,
    qty     TINYINT UNSIGNED NOT NULL DEFAULT 1,     # quantity
    size    VARCHAR(10) NOT NULL DEFAULT 'M',        # serving size
    remark  VARCHAR(30)                              # special instructions
)
```

- Create another table, `extras`, with an `id` column for linking the record to the "parent" record in the `coffee2` table, and a `value` column declared the same way as the `value` column in the `extras_value` table:

```
CREATE TABLE extras
(
    id      INT NOT NULL,              # parent record ID
    INDEX   (id),
    value   VARCHAR(10)
)
```

- When you store an order, create one row in the `extras` table for each selected extra ingredient. Each row should be given the same `id` value as the corresponding row in the `coffee2` table.

Automating Poll Processing

In the preceding chapter, we developed a script to conduct an online poll ("vote for your favorite groundhog"). After writing that script, we discussed several of its shortcomings, primarily having to do with the amount of information about the poll that was hardwired into the script: the number of choices, the labels to display for those choices, the internal names used in the vote tallying table, the poll title, and so forth. Putting all these things into the polling script makes it efficient, but also very special purpose. You might expect an application to be highly specialized and tailored to your particular requirements if it's something like a customized order-processing system, but online polls are fairly stereotyped. Specialization in a polling application is a limitation, because it forces you to write a different script for each poll.

If we remove some of this specialization by moving it out of the poll-processing code and into the database, we'll make the code more generalized and reusable for handling multiple polls. We can do quite a bit to parameterize poll form generation and processing. For example, why not store the candidate names and descriptive labels in the database? If we do that, we can dissociate the form-generation code from knowledge about the content of any specific poll. The code need not care what the poll is about, it need only understand the structure of the poll table. Then we should be able to create the form automatically and use the same code to conduct any number of polls.

To carry out this more general approach to poll administration, we need several kinds of information:

- As before, we need to store the poll candidates in a vote tally table so that we can associate a counter with each candidate.

- We also need to store some descriptive text for each candidate. This becomes the label displayed for that choice in the poll form. For the groundhog poll you conducted before, the labels for `jimmy` and `phil` would be "Jimmy the Groundhog (Sun Prairie, Wisconsin)" and "Punxsutawney Phil (Punxsutawney, Pennsylvania)."

- The `groundhog` table that was used to store groundhog vote totals contained two rows, with each row storing one groundhog's name and vote tally. As such, it's useful only for one specific poll. To store the results of multiple polls, we'll need a more general table design. For example, we'll need to give each poll a name or number so we can tag each candidate with the appropriate poll identifier. Otherwise, we won't be able to tell which candidates are part of each poll.

- The groundhog polling program "knew" the order in which to display the choices. A general-purpose polling routine won't have any such knowledge. We might use a heuristic like "display choices in alphabetic order," but that won't always work. For example, polls that ask for ratings often list items using an order such as "very good," "good," "average," "poor," and "very poor," which is not alphabetic. Similarly, polls that ask the question "what political party are you affiliated with?" typically list the major parties first and the minor parties last, which may not be alphabetic, either. To deal with this difficulty, we can assign sequence numbers to poll choices to determine the display order.

- A poll contains other information that needs to be parameterized, such as the poll caption (that is, the question that appears in the form preceding the choices). Also, we might want to specify the text of the submission button, and perhaps the thank-you message to present to users after they've voted. If we want to present a "view past polls" link, then we'll probably want to display them by date, so it'll be useful to include the date when the poll begins. In fact, an end date would also be useful so that we can specify a point beyond which votes will no longer be accepted or that we can use to expire old polls if we want.

It appears that we'll need to store some pieces of information that apply to the poll as a whole (the caption, submission button text, thank-you message, and dates), as well as some that apply only to individual poll candidates (the name, descriptive label, and vote tally). This can be handled by using two tables, which we can tie together using a poll ID number. The first table, `poll`, maintains the general information about each poll:

```
CREATE TABLE poll
(
    id            INT UNSIGNED NOT NULL AUTO_INCREMENT,   /* poll ID (unique) */
    PRIMARY KEY (id),
    name          VARCHAR(40) NOT NULL,          /* name for poll (also unique) */
    UNIQUE (name),
    title         VARCHAR(255) NOT NULL,         /* descriptive title */
    question      VARCHAR(255) NOT NULL,         /* question posed by poll */
    submit_title  VARCHAR(20) DEFAULT NULL,      /* submit button title */
    thank_you     VARCHAR(255) DEFAULT NULL,     /* thank-you message */
    begin_date    DATETIME,                      /* begin/end dates of poll */
    end_date      DATETIME DEFAULT NULL
)
```

The id value is an `AUTO_INCREMENT` column. MySQL assigns a unique number to this column whenever we create a new `poll` record. id values must be unique so we can refer unambiguously to specific polls. To make it easier to refer to polls by more meaningful labels, however, the `poll` table also includes a `name` column that should be set to a string value that provides a name for the poll. The `name` values also must be unique because we don't want two polls to have the same name.

The `title` and `question` columns provide the title to display for the poll and the question that potential voters are asked. `submit_title` is the label to use for the vote-submission button and `thank_you` is the message to display after a user submits a vote.

Either of these can be NULL, in which case, we'll supply appropriate defaults ("Submit" and "Thank you for voting").

The begin_date and end_date column values indicate when voting for the poll begins and ends. The begin_date column must be given a value, but end_date value can be NULL to indicate that the poll has an open end date. These two columns have type DATETIME. DATE might be good enough under some conditions, but if you have very short polls that last less than a day, DATE won't have sufficient granularity and DATETIME is better. (An example would be a poll conducted during a television show and that lasts only as long as the show, so that the results can be announced at the end of the broadcast.)

The poll_candidate table is a companion to the poll table; it contains information about each choice presented to voters:

```
CREATE TABLE poll_candidate
(
    id      INT NOT NULL,                           /* poll ID */
    seq     TINYINT DEFAULT 0,                      /* display sequence number */
    name    VARCHAR(30) NOT NULL,                   /* internal candidate name */
    label   VARCHAR(255) DEFAULT NULL,              /* label displayed to users */
    tally   BIGINT UNSIGNED NOT NULL DEFAULT 0,     /* current vote tally */
    UNIQUE (id, name)
)
```

The id column identifies the poll table record with which each poll_candidate record is associated. For any given id value, there will be one poll record and multiple poll_candidate records.

name is the internal name used to identify each candidate (it becomes associated with a particular radio button) and label is the descriptive text displayed for the candidate. In the groundhog poll, for example, we could use jimmy as a name value and "Jimmy the groundhog (Sun Prairie, Wisconsin)" as a label value. If a label is the same as the name, we'll allow the label value to be NULL in the table to save space.

The seq column is used to solve the problem, "in what order should poll items be displayed?" For the candidates in a given poll, you should set the values of this column to appropriate sequential values to order them the way you want. You'll recognize this use of a sequence number column from the earlier section in this chapter on lookup tables. For the polling application, however, we'll add a small twist by retrieving records sorted by both sequence number and label, to allow easy display of candidates in alphabetic order. That way, you can set all the seq values for a set of candidates to the same value (such as zero); in effect, this causes the poll choices to be sorted by the labels.

The tally column records the vote count for a given poll candidate. It's a BIGINT to allow for polls where you expect a very large number of votes.

The poll_candidate table index is a unique multiple-part key on id and name. The index serves two purposes, one for inserting records and one for retrieving them. When we insert records, the index prevents creation of duplicate records that have the same name for a given poll, to ensure that each candidate name is unique. For retrieval, the index allows all records for a poll with a given id value to be retrieved quickly, even when we don't specify a name value. That's because id is a leftmost prefix of the index (see the following sidebar).

Leftmost Prefixes of Indexes

When you create a multiple-column index (or key), MySQL can use the index in a query if you specify values for all the index columns. However, the index may also be used if you specify values only for some of its columns, as long as they form some leading part of the key. This is called a leftmost prefix of the key. If you manufacture a medical product that is packaged in individually numbered vials that are grouped for sale into boxes, cases, and lots, for example, you might have a multiple-column index that comprises columns named lot, case, box, and vial. You gain the benefits of the index if you specify values for all four columns in a query. But the index is useful even if you specify just lot, case, and box, to find all vials in a box. In this case, you've specified the leftmost three columns of the index. Other leftmost prefixes are lot and case, or just lot. However, the combination of lot and box does not form a leftmost prefix, because it skips the case column.

Under our revised layout for storing poll data, we can load the information needed for the groundhog poll using the following statements:

```
INSERT INTO poll (name,title,question,begin_date)
    VALUES('groundhog','Groundhog Poll','Who is your favorite groundhog?',
        NOW())
INSERT INTO poll_candidate (id,seq,name,label)
    VALUES
        (LAST_INSERT_ID(),1,'jimmy',
            'Jimmy the groundhog (Sun Prairie, Wisconsin)'),
        (LAST_INSERT_ID(),2,'phil',
            'Punxsutawney Phil (Punxsutawney, Pennsylvania)')
```

While we're at it, let's go ahead and load another poll, too. This one asks users to vote for their favorite composer:

```
INSERT INTO poll (name,title,question,begin_date)
    VALUES('composer','Composer Poll','Which composer do you like best?',
        NOW())
INSERT INTO poll_candidate (id,seq,name,label)
    VALUES
        (LAST_INSERT_ID(),1,'jsbach','Johann Sebastian Bach'),
        (LAST_INSERT_ID(),2,'beethoven','Ludwig Van Beethoven'),
        (LAST_INSERT_ID(),3,'mozart','Wolfgang Amadeus Mozart'),
        (LAST_INSERT_ID(),4,'wagner','Richard Wagner')
```

For both of these polls, the poll table record has the begin_date column set to the current date and time using the NOW() function. The end_date column is not specified, so MySQL sets it to the default value of NULL, meaning the poll is still open. We've also left the id column unspecified because we want MySQL to assign an ID automatically: id is an AUTO_INCREMENT column, so MySQL generates new unique ID values for us. Each time MySQL creates a new `AUTO_INCREMENT` value, it can be accessed by calling the `LAST_INSERT_ID()` function. Thus, by inserting each poll's `poll_candidate` records immediately after creating the corresponding `poll` record, we can get the proper `id` column value without even knowing what that value is. (This technique would not work if you inserted the two `poll` table records first and then the six `poll_candidate` table records. In that case, all six `poll_candidate` records would be assigned the ID number of the second `poll` record.)

Here's a third poll that asks people to describe their head shape. It is set up a little differently than the other two polls because it relies on some of the conventions that we'll use. First, the candidate names will also be used as the labels displayed in the poll form, so we can leave the labels `NULL`. Second, the candidate `seq` values are unspecified, so MySQL will assign them the default value (zero); the result is that candidates will be displayed alphabetically in the poll form.

```
INSERT INTO poll (name,title,question,begin_date)
    VALUES('head','Head Shape Poll','What shape best describes your head?',
           NOW())
INSERT INTO poll_candidate (id,name)
    VALUES
        (LAST_INSERT_ID(),'round'),
        (LAST_INSERT_ID(),'egg'),
        (LAST_INSERT_ID(),'block'),
        (LAST_INSERT_ID(),'without form and void')
```

Now that we have our poll tables set up, we need to write some code to use them. Let's put the code to manage poll processing into a separate library module and provide an object-oriented interface to it. Then we can create a poll as an object that we manipulate by calling object methods. The module needs to perform several tasks for us:

- New poll object creation
- Poll form generation
- Vote tabulation
- Poll result display

If we put this code into its own module, `WebDB::Poll`, we can write a general-purpose polling script, `poll.pl`, that looks like this:

```
#! /usr/bin/perl -w
# poll.pl - present a poll using the generalized tables.

use strict;
use lib qw(/usr/local/apache/lib/perl);
use CGI qw(:standard escapeHTML);
use WebDB;
use WebDB::Poll;
```

```perl
# Get poll name or ID number and set up poll object
my $poll_name = param ("poll");
if (!defined ($poll_name))
{
    print header(), p ("No poll name was specified");
    exit (0);
}
my $dbh = WebDB::connect ();
my $poll = WebDB::Poll->new ($dbh, $poll_name);
if (!$poll)
{
    $dbh->disconnect ();
    print header(),
        p (escapeHTML ("No information for poll $poll_name was found"));
    exit (0);
}

print header (),
    start_html (-title => escapeHTML ($poll->{data}->{title}),
                -bgcolor => "white");

# Dispatch to proper action based on user selection

my $choice = lc (param ("choice")); # get choice, lowercased

if ($choice eq "")                                      # initial invocation
{
    print $poll->generate_form ();  # display the voting form
}
elsif ($choice eq lc ($poll->{data}->{submit_title}))   # a vote was submitted
{
    print $poll->tally_vote (param ("candidate"));  # tally vote
    print $poll->text_result ();                    # show current results
}
elsif ($choice eq "results")                            # just show results
{
    print $poll->text_result ();
}
else
{
    print p (escapeHTML ("Logic error, unknown choice: $choice"));
}

$dbh->disconnect ();
print end_html ();

exit (0);
```

The `poll.pl` script determines which poll to present based on the value of the `poll` parameter, which means that we can invoke it as follows to present each of the polls in our poll tables:

```
http://www.snake.net/cgi-perl/poll.pl?poll=groundhog
http://www.snake.net/cgi-perl/poll.pl?poll=composer
http://www.snake.net/cgi-perl/poll.pl?poll=head
```

Note that we can't print the page until we look up the poll information. (For example, we need to defer printing the page title until after we fetch poll data from the tables, because the title is stored in one of the tables.) Because of this, we'll write methods that generate HTML so they return results as strings. That allows the HTML to be printed immediately or saved for later, depending on an application's requirements.

If you compare `poll.pl` to our earlier `groundhog.pl` script that presented only the groundhog poll, you'll see a big difference in that `poll.pl` contains no information specific to any given poll. The poll name is obtained as a parameter from the script environment, and the information about that poll comes from the database tables.

The `poll.pl` script is based on the assumptions that the `poll` parameter identifies the poll to administer and that the `choice` parameter value indicates what to do. The script interprets `choice` values as follows:

- If `choice` has no value, the script is being invoked for the first time, so we just display the voting form.
- If `choice` has a value equal to the `submit_title` column value, the user just submitted a vote. We process the vote and display the current results.
- If `choice` is `results`, the user wants to see the current results without voting, so the script just displays the results.

The file `Poll.pm` that contains the polling module code is constructed using guidelines like those used earlier for writing `WebDB::TableInfo` earlier in the chapter. It should begin with an appropriate `package` statement that specifies the module name and `use` statements that reference the modules it needs, and it must be installed as `WebDB/Poll.pm` under some directory in Perl's search path.

The general outline of `Poll.pm` looks like this:

```
package WebDB::Poll;

use strict;
use CGI qw(:standard escapeHTML);
use DBI;

sub new ...            # definition for new() method

sub generate_form ...  # definition for generate_form() method

# ... definitions for other methods ...

1;                     # return true from module file
```

The new() method creates a new poll object, given a database handle and a poll name:

```
$poll = WebDB::Poll->new ($dbh, $poll_name);
```

It reads the information for the named poll from the database, creates a data structure to store the information, and returns a reference to the structure. If the poll cannot be found, new() returns undef. The implementation looks like this:

```
sub new
{
my ($class, $dbh, $poll_name) = @_;
my $self;
my ($col_name, $sth, $data);

    # If $poll_name is an integer, look for a match in the id
    # column. Otherwise look in the name column.
    $col_name = ($poll_name =~ /^\d+$/ ? "id" : "name");
    # select record value, and active value indicating whether or
    # not the poll still is accepting values
    $sth = $dbh->prepare (
                "SELECT *, IF(begin_date <= NOW()
                        AND (end_date >= NOW() OR end_date IS NULL),1,0)
                        AS active
                FROM poll
                WHERE $col_name = ?");
    $sth->execute ($poll_name);
    $data = $sth->fetchrow_hashref ();  # no loop; only one record is expected
    $sth->finish ();
    return (undef) unless $data;    # no record found

    # supply defaults for missing fields
    $data->{submit_title} = "Submit" unless $data->{submit_title};
    $data->{thank_you} = "Thank you for voting." unless $data->{thank_you};

    # Look up poll's candidate records using poll ID value.  Retrieve them
    # using the seq and label values to put them in the proper display order.
    # Fetch each one as a reference to a hash, storing them in an array.
    # If label is blank or NULL, use the name as the label.
    $sth = $dbh->prepare (
                "SELECT
                    name,
                    IF(label IS NULL || label = '',name,label) AS label,
                    tally
                FROM poll_candidate WHERE id = ?
                ORDER BY seq, label");
    $sth->execute ($data->{id});
    $data->{candidate} = [];
    while (my $ref = $sth->fetchrow_hashref ())
    {
        push (@{$data->{candidate}}, $ref);
    }
    $sth->finish ();
```

continues

continued

```
        # Paranoia check: if there are no poll_candidate records, the
        # poll information is incomplete.
        return (undef) unless @{$data->{candidate}};

        # We have all the information.  Create a new poll object, save the
        # poll data and the database handle into it for later, bless the
        # object into the appropriate class, and return it.
        $self = {};
        $self->{results_link} = 1;
        $self->{data} = $data;
        $self->{dbh} = $dbh;
        return (bless ($self, $class));
    }
```

The new() method is written to handle a $poll_name value that is either an integer poll ID or a poll name. If the value is an integer, we look for it in the id column. Otherwise, the value cannot match any id value, so we assume that it's a poll name and look for it in the name column.

After determining the column to check for a match, we construct a query to retrieve all columns from the matching record, as well as one additional column, active, that indicates whether the poll is currently active. The active value is determined using the following expression in the query selection list:

```
IF(begin_date <= NOW() AND (end_date >= NOW() OR end_date IS NULL),1,0)
```

The point of this IF() in the SELECT query is to determine whether the value of NOW() lies within the date range specified by begin_date and end_date in the appropriate poll table record. The test against end_date has to account for the case where the value may be NULL to indicate an open-ended poll.

It's up to individual applications to determine what to do with the active value. The WebDB::Poll module itself doesn't enforce any requirement in the new() method that a poll must be active. If it did, we wouldn't be able to retrieve poll information for closed polls, which would prevent us from finding out their final results! On the other hand, putting the burden of checking active on application scripts has its own drawbacks. If you look back to poll.pl, for example, you'll see that it has an apparent bug. It doesn't check whether a poll is active, so it would accept votes even for closed polls. We'll address this problem later in the section "Closing a Poll."

After constructing the appropriate SELECT query, we execute it and fetch the result. Because there are unique indexes on both the id and name columns, we should get back at most one row, regardless of whether we're looking for a poll ID number or a name. If the SELECT statement doesn't return any rows, the poll doesn't exist and new() returns undef. Otherwise, we check a couple of the column values and supply defaults if they're missing, and then go on to retrieve the associated poll_candidate records using the id column value to identify them. This second SELECT has two notable features. One is the column selection list, which uses IF() to implement the convention that if a label is missing (NULL or blank), we'll use the name for the label:

```
IF(label IS NULL || label ='',name,label) AS label,
```

The other is the ORDER BY clause, which implements our convention for allowing candidates to be displayed in alphabetic order. Sorting is done on two columns, seq and label. If the seq values differ, they control the sort order, and therefore the order in which candidates display in the poll form. If seq values are identical, the label values control the sorting, so that candidates display in alphabetic order.

Internally, poll objects are represented as hashes. The database handle passed to new() becomes one hash element named dbh. (It's remembered for further operations on the poll—which means you shouldn't close the connection until you're done with the poll object.) The information pulled from the database becomes another element, data, which is itself a hash. The data hash contains one element for each column in the record from the poll table (plus the active element that indicates whether the poll is still open). It also contains a candidate element containing candidate information as an array. This array has an element for each row from the poll_candidate table. Here are some examples showing how to access various types of poll information:

```
$poll->{dbh}                              poll database handle
$poll->{data}->{title}                    title column from poll table
$poll->{data}->{active}                   whether poll is active
$poll->{data}->{candidate}                poll candidate records
$poll->{data}->{candidate}->[0]->{tally}  vote tally for first candidate
```

new() also defines a results_link hash element. By default, this is true, meaning that the poll form should include a link allowing the user to go directly to the poll results page without voting. An application can set this attribute to 0 (false) to disable this link.

Assuming that new() returns a poll object and not undef, we can use the object to perform various operations. The first thing a script is likely to do with a poll object is to invoke its generate_form() method, which returns a string containing the HTML for the form. The way you use this will depend on how you're presenting the poll. If the poll is the main thing on the page, you'll want to print the rest of the supporting page structure around the poll:

```
print header (),
    start_html (-title => escapeHTML ($poll->{data}->{title}),
                -bgcolor => "white");
print $poll->generate_form ();
print end_html ();
```

If the poll is a small part of a more complex page, you'd print the poll at the appropriate point in page generation, and the supporting structure would be different.

The code for the generate_form() method looks like this:

```
sub generate_form
{
my $self = shift;
my $data = $self->{data};
my $str;        # string to hold HTML for form
my @name;       # candidate names
my %labelmap;   # candidate name -> label map

    $str = start_form (-action => url ());

    # identify poll
    $str .= hidden (-name => "poll", -value => $data->{id}, -override => 1);

    # ask the question
    $str .= p (escapeHTML ($data->{question}));

    # generate candidate name list and name -> label map for radio buttons
    foreach my $candidate (@{$data->{candidate}})
    {
        push (@name, $candidate->{name});
        $labelmap{$candidate->{name}} = $candidate->{label};
    }
    $str .= radio_group (-name => "candidate",
                         -values => \@name,
                         -labels => \%labelmap,
                         # we assume no candidate has this value...
                         -default => "[NO DEFAULT]",
                         -override => 1,
                         -linebreak => 1);

    # add the submission button
    $str .= br ()
            . submit (-name => "choice", -value => $data->{submit_title});
    $str .= end_form ();

    # add link allowing user to see current results without
    # voting, unless that has been suppressed
    if ($self->{results_link})
    {
        $str .= hr ();
        $str .= a ({-href => url () . "?choice=results;poll=$data->{id}"},
                    "Show current results");
    }

    return ($str);
    }
```

The form is fairly typical. The form action parameter is the current script's URL, to cause it to be self-referencing. For identification purposes, we write the poll id value into the form as a hidden poll parameter so that the next time the script is invoked we'll be able to tell which poll to work with. Then we present the text of the poll question (the question the user answers by casting a vote), the list of candidates, and the submission button. The last thing added is a link that enables the user to see the results without voting, unless it has been suppressed.

To generate the radio buttons that show each of the candidates, we need to get the candidate names and labels. These are available as the `name` and `label` attributes in each of the candidate records stored in the `candidate` array, so we walk through that array to construct an array of names and a hash that maps names to descriptive labels. The resulting structures contain the information needed for the `values` and `labels` parameters to the `radio_group()` function.

The last element of the form is a submission button named `choice` and labeled using the value stored in the `submit_title` attribute of the poll data. (This also becomes the value of the button when it is selected. If you look back at the dispatch logic of `poll.pl`, you'll see that it determines whether a vote needs to be processed by comparing the `choice` parameter to this string rather than to `submit`.)

When the form submission button is selected, a vote may have been cast. The `tally_vote()` method should be invoked to process it and add the vote to the chosen candidate's tally:

```perl
sub tally_vote
{
my ($self, $name) = @_;
my $dbh = $self->{dbh};
my $data = $self->{data};
# default return value
my $message = "No vote was submitted; did you make a choice?";

    if (!$data->{active})
    {
        $message = "Sorry, the poll has closed."
    }
    elsif ($name)
    {
        # make sure the vote matches one of the legal candidate names
        for my $i (0 .. @{$data->{candidate}}-1)
        {
            if ($name eq $data->{candidate}->[$i]->{name})
            {
                # update tally in database table
                $dbh->do ("UPDATE poll_candidate SET tally = tally + 1
                        WHERE id = ? AND name = ?",
                    undef, $data->{id}, $name);
                # update tally in the in-memory structure
                ++$data->{candidate}->[$i]->{tally};
                # return value is the thank-you message
                $message = $data->{thank_you};
            }
        }
    }
    return ($message);
}
```

`tally_vote()` processes the vote and returns a string that can be displayed to the user to indicate what action was taken. The string can take three forms. First, if the poll is not active, no action is taken and we return a string indicating that the poll is closed.

Second, if the `name` parameter is empty, no vote actually was cast. (This happens when the user selects the submission button without choosing any candidate's radio button.) In this case, we take no action and return a message saying no vote was found. The same message also is returned if the `name` parameter is not empty but doesn't match any of the legal candidate names. (Presumably a result of a form-hacking attempt.)

Third, if a vote is cast for a legal candidate, we update that candidate's vote tally and return the poll's thank-you message to indicate success. To count a vote, we update the counter for the appropriate row in the `poll_candidate` table as well as the in-memory poll information. The in-memory structure is updated on the assumption that after processing the vote you'll likely want to display the current results. By updating this structure, it becomes possible to present the results without having to query the database again to get the proper tally values.

The simplest way to display poll results is in text form. The `text_result()` method is used for this. It generates an HTML table and returns it as a string. The code is much like that from our original poll implementation in the `groundhog.pl` script:

```
sub text_result
{
my $self = shift;
my $data = $self->{data};
my ($str, $sum, @table_row);

    $str = p (" The current results are:");
    # compute sum of vote tallies
    $sum = 0;
    map { $sum += $_->{tally} } @{$data->{candidate}};
    if ($sum == 0)   # no results!
    {
        $str .= p ("No votes have been cast yet");
        return ($str);
    }
    # Construct table of results, header line first, then contents.
    # For each candidate, show votes as a tally and as a percentage
    # of the total number of votes.  Right-justify numeric values.
    push (@table_row, Tr (th (""), th ("Votes"), th ("Percent")));
    for my $i (0 .. @{$data->{candidate}}-1)
    {
        my $candidate = $data->{candidate}->[$i];
        my $percent = sprintf ("%d%%", (100 * $candidate->{tally}) / $sum);
        push (@table_row, Tr (
                td (escapeHTML ($candidate->{label})),
                td ({-align => "right"}, $candidate->{tally}),
                td ({-align => "right"}, $percent)
```

```
          ));
    }
    $str .= table (@table_row);
    return ($str);
}
```

Closing a Poll

To close a poll, all you need to do is assign a non-NULL value to the end_date column. To close the head-shape poll as of "right now" or as of a specific date, for example, the queries look like this:

```
UPDATE poll SET end_date = NOW() WHERE name = 'head'
UPDATE poll SET end_date = '2001-04-01' WHERE name = 'head'
```

To make this a little easier, we can write a short script, close_poll.pl, that takes a poll name (or number) as an argument and sets the end date to NOW(). It also accepts a second argument if you want to specify the end date explicitly:

```perl
#! /usr/bin/perl -w
# close_poll.pl - set the end_date for a poll

# The date defaults to "NOW()" if not given; if given it must be in
# ISO format.

use strict;
use lib qw(/usr/local/apache/lib/perl);
use WebDB;

@ARGV or die "Usage: close_poll.pl poll_name_or_id [date]\n";
my $poll_name = shift (@ARGV);
my $date = (@ARGV? shift (@ARGV) : undef);

# If $poll_name is an integer, look for a match in the id
# column. Otherwise look in the name column.
my $col_name = ($poll_name =~ /^\d+$/ ? "id" : "name");

my $dbh = WebDB::connect ();
my $rows = $dbh->do (
                "UPDATE poll SET end_date = IFNULL(?,NOW())
                WHERE $col_name = ?",
                    undef, $date, $poll_name);
warn "Warning: no poll $poll_name was found\n" if $rows == 0;
$dbh->disconnect ();

exit (0);
```

The IFNULL() function returns its first argument if that argument is not NULL and returns the second argument otherwise. It's used in the UPDATE query because we can't pass the string "NOW()" using a placeholder (it would end up as a literal string, not as a function call). By using IFNULL(), we can pass an explicit date to the query if one was given and have it be used as a literal string. Otherwise, we pass `undef` and the current value of `NOW()` is used.

Earlier, I mentioned that `poll.pl` had a bug in that it would accept votes for a poll that is closed. In a sense that's not strictly true, because the `tally_vote()` method in the `WebDB::Poll` module does check whether a poll is active before it adds a vote. However, that means the user will find out that a poll is closed only after casting a vote. It'd be better for `poll.pl` to check a poll's status and let the user know earlier that the poll is closed. To effect this change, modify the clause in the dispatch logic that presents the polling form from this:

```
if ($choice eq "") # initial invocation
{
    print $poll->generate_form ();  # display the voting form
}
```

to this:

```
if ($choice eq "")                    # initial invocation
{
    if ($poll->{data}->{active})
    {
        print $poll->generate_form ();  # display the voting form
    }
    else
    {
        print p ("Sorry, the poll has closed.");
        # add link allowing user to see current results without voting
        print hr (),
            a ({-href => url () . "?choice=results;poll=$poll->{data}->{id}"},
                "Show current results");
    }
}
```

The modification displays the form only if the poll is active; otherwise, it tells the user that the poll is closed, but also presents a link for checking the current results.

Displaying Results of Multiple Polls

I've noticed that polls on Web pages often have a link you can follow to view results of past polls. If you want to do that, too, it's fairly easy. The procedure goes like this:

1. Run a query to pull information for each of the polls
2. Display a page containing links to each poll. You could either present links to the respective results pages, or, if some polls are still open, present links to the voting pages as well.

The following simple script, `show_polls.pl`, lists all available polls and the relevant links for each:

```
#! /usr/bin/perl -w
# show_polls.pl - present a list of polls
```

```
use strict;
use lib qw(/usr/local/apache/lib/perl);
use CGI qw(:standard escapeHTML);
use WebDB;

print header (),
    start_html (-title => "Polls Available", -bgcolor => "white");

my $dbh = WebDB::connect ();

my $sth = $dbh->prepare (
                "SELECT *, IF(begin_date <= NOW()
                        AND (end_date >= NOW() OR end_date IS NULL),1,0)
                        AS active
                FROM poll
                ORDER BY id");
$sth->execute ();
while (my $ref = $sth->fetchrow_hashref ())
{
    # display only date part of begin_date (strip the time)
    print substr ($ref->{begin_date}, 0, 10), br (), "\n";
    print escapeHTML ($ref->{title} . ": " . $ref->{question}), br (), "\n";
    print a ({-href => "poll.pl?poll=$ref->{id}"}, "[vote]"), " "
                                            if $ref->{active};
    print a ({-href => "poll.pl?choice=results;poll=$ref->{id}"},
                "[results]"),
            br (), "\n";
    print br ();
}
$sth->finish ();

$dbh->disconnect ();
print end_html ();

exit (0);
```

To list only open polls, use this query instead:

```
SELECT * FROM poll
WHERE begin_date <= NOW() AND (end_date >= NOW() OR end_date IS NULL)
```

If you want to use the script to keep tabs on your site's polling activity, you'd likely find it helpful to modify it to present other information such as the date range for each poll, the total number of votes cast, and so forth. If you want to know the number of votes cast, you must perform a more complex query that runs a join between the poll and poll_candidate tables. For example, you can retrieve poll table columns along with total votes cast in each poll like this:

```
SELECT poll.*, SUM(poll_candidate.tally) AS "total votes"
FROM poll, poll_candidate
WHERE poll.id = poll_candidate.id
GROUP BY id
ORDER BY begin_date DESC, id DESC
```

Suggested Modifications

Write a graphic_results() method that is like text_results() but that displays poll results in graphical form.

Modify the WebDB:Poll module so the methods take additional parameters for controlling their behavior. For example, you could modify generate_form() to display radio buttons with or without linebreaks, or to enable you to generate a pop-up menu or scrolling list rather than a set of radio buttons.

As an alternative to modifying the existing methods to accept additional parameters, write methods for setting options. Such methods could store information in the poll object itself, and that information could be consulted later by generate_form().

Add some fraud detection to prevent ballot-box stuffing.

We don't log each vote, we just count them. Modify the application to keep a record of each vote and when it occurred. You could use this to track day-by-day activity, for example.

In this chapter, we've examined several ways you can use information in your database to help you create forms, as well as to validate form contents and to generate the queries for storing the contents. These techniques can help you write reusable code for your data-entry applications. They're useful in any context involving forms, however; one important application of forms is to provide front ends to search engines so that users can specify search parameters. The next chapter deals with issues involved in performing searches; as you might expect, some of the techniques discussed in this chapter will make an appearance in that chapter as well.

7

Performing Searches

THE WEB PROVIDES A LIMITED NUMBER OF WAYS THAT enable users to select what they're interested in seeing. A lot of Web sites start out as a collection of pages containing static information with embedded hyperlinks that guide visitors to various places within the site. This is standard hypertext navigation and it probably accounts for the majority of user activity on the Web. It's a useful way to direct people, but it only goes so far. As you add more content to your site, sooner or later you'll need to provide some other way for visitors to find what they want. Links have a limited usefulness in this respect, because although they are very easy to provide (just put a bunch of `<a href>` tags into your pages), they are also more limiting to the user. They express the choices you want to provide or that you can anticipate in advance, and these are not necessarily what the visitor wants.

As an alternative, search forms can be used to give your visitors capabilities that are difficult to provide using hyperlinks. You can allow users to specify directly what they want by filling in the form to indicate what kind of information is of interest and submitting it (sending it back to the Web server) to have the request acted on. This means more work for you as a Web developer because you have to set up or write some kind of program to process the form. But it enables users to say explicitly what they want, and helps you to take them directly to the information in which they're interested.

Search applications are a natural context in which to use your database on the Web, because searching is one of the things databases are designed to do well. Coupling a Web-based front end with a database back end is an extremely popular way to make all kinds of information available to visitors without trying to figure out in advance what data they might want to look for. By keeping your information in the database and generating results on-the-fly, your Web pages are always up-to-date—something not true for sites that consist of static pages.

This chapter shows you how to build search applications for which you provide a search form and tie it to your database to give your visitors the ability to get at the information in which they're interested. In so doing, you move from deciding for site visitors what their options are to allowing them a measure of control over what content they see. There's an important concept here; namely, that you can use your database to let users help themselves.

Search applications of this type vary widely in scope and capability, ranging from simple things such as finding a word in an online dictionary to more complex searches based on multiple parameters—for example, "all used minivans more than three years old with less than 100,000 miles, with a V-6 engine, cruise control, air conditioning, and a luggage rack." Regardless of the complexity of the search, however, most such applications have several things in common. Obviously, you always must run some kind of query on behalf of the user, but implementing user-directed search applications actually involves quite a bit more than that. You're responsible for each of the following things:

- Designing a form that enables users to specify what they are interested in. This is the primary interface to your search engine, so the form must include fields for every aspect of the search over which you want the user to have control. (For example, cars may come in different colors—but unless you provide an appropriate element in the search form, users can't ask for cars in a particular color.)

- Identifying the search parameters when the form is submitted and constructing an appropriate SELECT query from them. The main issue here is constructing the proper WHERE clause—the part that indicates which records to retrieve. The clause may be simple or complex, depending on the number of parameters the user can specify. There may be other issues as well. If you let the user choose the sort order, the search parameters affect how you construct the ORDER BY clause. If you allow the user to select from among alternative display formats, the choice may affect the amount or type of information that you retrieve. (One common example: Allowing the user to specify how many hits to display per page affects how many records you retrieve at a time.)

- Issuing the query and presenting the results. In this phase of the application, you deal with issues such as how many records are returned by the query (which may affect whether you display a single page or multiple pages), the complexity of individual records, and the destination to which you send the information.

(It's most common to display results in a browser window, but you might provide the information in other formats, such as a downloadable tab-delimited file, or a reduced-content display for handheld devices.)

These phases sometimes interact, which makes it more difficult to design your application (or more interesting, depending on how you look at it). If you present search results in a standard sort order, you can build the order into your script and apply it uniformly regardless of the search parameters entered by the user. On the other hand, if you give the user some control over how to sort search results, that affects the design of the search form because you must provide a field for selecting the order. It also affects query construction because the ORDER BY clause must be built on-the-fly based on user input.

In the next section, we'll begin by writing a search application that is moderately complex, but still simple enough to understand easily. The particular scenario is that of an application designed for use by realtors and their customers: It presents a form enabling people to search through a database of listings for residential properties. The form provides fields for a number of different parameters such as location, architectural style, and price. (I list location first based on the realtor's axiom, "location, location, location.") This scenario is specific for concreteness, but the techniques we'll cover are more general and can be used in many types of search applications. As you read, think about how you'd apply the material here to the tables in your own database.

After building the initial version of this application, we'll create a revised version that adds other features such as the capability to deal with a large number of hits by presenting multiple-page results that include "next page" and "previous page" links. The revised version also will show pictures with the results, enable the user to search additional fields, send listings to other people by email, and more.

Finally, we'll switch gears a bit and consider when it's reasonable to present information via the "search by clicking links" paradigm—that is, when it can be useful to present a set of pages by using indexes that consist of link lists. Despite my earlier disparagement of link-based navigation as a means of allowing users to search for information, in some situations this is a helpful way to provide access to data. A typical kind of scenario to which this technique applies is when you have some type of organization, such as a business with many staff members. To help visitors find people by name, it's easy to provide an index consisting of letters of the alphabet that are links to different sections of the directory that list people whose names begin with the corresponding letter. Naturally, we'll generate the links dynamically using information in the database so that they remain current without a lot of manual editing. Sometimes people implement directories using static pages, but it's really a headache to maintain this kind of list if the information changes very often. A database-backed solution makes it much easier to keep the information up-to-date; changes to the database translate immediately into updated content if you generate the indexes by querying the database.

Writing a Form-Based Search Application

In this section, we'll develop res_search.pl, the initial version of an application designed for searching residential real estate listings. The section describes how to set up the underlying tables, generate the search form, interpret parameters when users submit searches so that we can construct appropriate queries, and display the results.

The application relies heavily on functions in the WebDB and WebDB::TableInfo modules that were written in Chapter 6, "Automating the Form-Handling Process," so you probably will need to take a look at that chapter if you haven't already read it. Specifically, we're going to construct a number of search form elements by asking MySQL to provide information about the structure of a residence table that contains home listings, and by reading the contents of lookup tables. This helps to provide some flexibility in the application because it enables you to store search form options in the database instead of coding them into your application. (For example, one lookup table lists the various locations in which users can look for matching records. The locations aren't wired into the script.) By using this strategy, you can change many of the options that the search form presents to users by updating your database rather than by rewriting your script.

Setting Up the Database Tables

The res_search.pl script uses a number of tables to do its work. The primary table is residence, which contains the listings of homes for sale. This is the base table—that is, the table we'll be searching. Other tables are used to hold the allowable values for several of the search parameters that users can specify. These are res_location, res_price, res_bedrooms, and res_bathrooms, which list the values for location, price, and the number of bedrooms and bathrooms, respectively.

The residence table used to store home listings looks like this:

```
CREATE TABLE residence
(
    id            INT UNSIGNED NOT NULL,        # listing identifier
    location      VARCHAR(25) NOT NULL,         # general locality
    style         ENUM('Condominium','Duplex',  # type of house
                  'Ranch','Split-level') NOT NULL,
    price         BIGINT UNSIGNED NOT NULL,     # asking price
    bedrooms      TINYINT UNSIGNED NOT NULL,    # number of bedrooms
    bathrooms     DECIMAL(4,1) NOT NULL,        # number of bathrooms
    built         SMALLINT UNSIGNED NOT NULL,   # year when built
    features      SET('heated garage','deck',   # additional amenities
                  'pool','basement') NOT NULL,
    description VARCHAR(255),                    # descriptive blurb
    PRIMARY KEY (id),
    INDEX       (location),
    INDEX       (style),
    INDEX       (price),
    INDEX       (bedrooms),
    INDEX       (bathrooms),
    INDEX       (built),
    INDEX       (features)
)
```

The `id` is the listing identifier. This column should have unique values. However, it's not an `AUTO_INCREMENT` column, because I'm assuming that the values come from an external source and that we cannot generate them automatically. (For example, in the area where I live, the identifiers consist of 6–digit numbers that are assigned by a central registry service used by all realtors.) `location` is the general geographic locality of the residence, such as "Downtown." (I haven't included any fields for the specific street address, although clearly you would do so for a production application.) `style` is the architectural style of the home. `price` is the seller's asking price. `bedrooms` and `bathrooms` indicate the number of each type of room. `bedrooms` is an integer because they are measured in whole units. `bathrooms` is a `DECIMAL(4,1)` to allow for fractions, as in "two and a half baths." `built` indicates the year the home was built. The `residence` table doesn't store age because age values change over time. The year a home was built is fixed, so it's better to store that instead. Besides, if we need age, we can compute it from the `built` value. (MySQL happens to have a built–in `YEAR` type, but its range begins with the year 1900. The `residence` table uses `SMALLINT` for the `built` column, to accommodate older homes.) `features` lists any additional features or amenities the residence includes. This column is a `SET` so that a record can list as few or as many features as are applicable. The `description` column provides for a string in which to store general descriptive information about the residence. `description` values should, of course, be taken with a grain of salt. For example, "nice fixer-upper" is realtor-speak for "this place is a dump," and "cozy" generally means "tiny and cramped beyond belief."

Each column that will be searchable by `res_search.pl` is indexed so that we can find values quickly. They are also declared `NOT NULL`, which should help if you have a version of MySQL earlier than 3.23 that does not allow `NULL` values in an index. (Also, columns can be processed more quickly and require less space if you declare them `NOT NULL`, regardless of your version of MySQL.)

Generating Sample Search Data

The webdb source distribution contains a directory `search` in which you'll find the programs described in this chapter. You'll also find a number of SQL scripts, which you should feed to the `mysql` program to create and initialize the tables you'll need. For example, `cr_res_tbls.sql` creates the residence-related tables and creates a number of records for you to search so that you don't have to create them yourself. Here's some illustrative sample data for the `residence` table, to give you an idea of the kind of records it contains:

```
INSERT INTO residence (id,location,style,price,bedrooms,bathrooms,built,
                       features,description)
    VALUES
    (397428,'Downtown','Condominium',174900,3,2,1998, 'deck,pool',
        'Elegant living for the senior circuit, many amenities, no pets'),
    (386298,'Bradford Heights','Ranch',374900,4,3,1988,
        'deck,heated garage,basement',
        'Spacious quarters, quiet neighborhood, woods nearby'),
    (402942,'Bradford Heights','Ranch',224900,3,2.5,1992,'deck,basement',
        'Quiet neighborhood, woods nearby'),
    (400129,'South Side','Duplex',95900,2,1,1982,'basement',
        'nice fixer-upper; cozy!')
```

Several columns in the `residence` table have a limited number of values, and as such would be good candidates for being represented as ENUM columns. These include the `style`, `location`, `bedrooms`, and `bathrooms` columns. ENUM columns are useful in that we can convert column descriptions to list elements in the search form automatically, using the techniques shown in Chapter 6. As you can see from the CREATE TABLE statement, however, I've used an ENUM type only for the `style` column. In most cases, we'll use lookup tables to store the possible search form options. If you use a lookup table rather than an ENUM, you can add new options just by adding rows to the table. With an ENUM, you must use ALTER TABLE to modify the structure of the `residence` table. (For that reason, I'd have used a lookup table for `style`, too, except that I needed an excuse to show how to perform searches against an ENUM column!)

Each lookup table consists of a single column named `value`. However, the declaration for this column in each table depends on the kind of information to be stored. For example, in the `residence` table, `location` is a VARCHAR(25) column, so the `value` column in the `res_location` lookup table is a VARCHAR(25) as well:

```
CREATE TABLE res_location
(
    value   VARCHAR(25) NOT NULL
)
```

`res_location` contains the following location names:

```
INSERT INTO res_location (value)
    VALUES ('Bradford Heights'),('Downtown'),('South Side'),
        ('Delford Creek'),('Fieldstone Meadows')
```

The lookup tables associated with the `bedrooms` and `bathrooms` columns are created and initialized similarly. In each case, the `value` column type is the same as the type for the corresponding column in the `residence` table:

```
CREATE TABLE res_bedrooms
(
    value   TINYINT UNSIGNED NOT NULL
)
INSERT INTO res_bedrooms (value)
    VALUES(1),(2),(3),(4),(5),(6),(7)

CREATE TABLE res_bathrooms
(
    value   DECIMAL(4,1) NOT NULL
)
INSERT INTO res_bathrooms (value)
    VALUES(1),(1.5),(2),(2.5),(3),(3.5),(4)
```

`res_location`, `res_bedrooms`, and `res_bathrooms` each correspond to columns in the `residence` table that have a small number of values. However, lookup tables can be used even for columns that are not so constrained. For example, `price` can have a wide range of values, but we can use a lookup table for the purpose of segmenting the possible range of values into a small set of price points. This provides a convenient way for users to select a value, because picking an item from a list generally is easier than typing in a number manually. The res_price table in which we'll store price points looks like this:

```
CREATE TABLE res_price
(
    value   BIGINT UNSIGNED NOT NULL
)
INSERT INTO res_price (value)
    VALUES(100000),(150000),(250000),(500000),(750000),(1000000)
```

Setting Up the Main Logic

Before writing any of the functions that implement specific phases of the search process, let's consider the application's overall operation and set up the dispatch code accordingly. Initially, the application presents a form that enables the user to specify what type of listings are of interest. When the user selects the form's Search button, res_search.pl looks up listings based on the search parameters and presents a result page that shows the matching listings. The page also will contain a new search form so that the user can enter another search directly without having to return to the preceding page. (This new form will be filled in with the same values that were submitted, to make it easy for the user to modify the parameters and resubmit it.)

The main part of the program looks like this:

```
#! /usr/bin/perl -w
# res_search.pl - search residential real estate listings

use strict;
use lib qw(/usr/local/apache/lib/perl);
use CGI qw(:standard escapeHTML);
use WebDB;
use WebDB::TableInfo;

print header (),
        start_html (-title => "Residence Search", -bgcolor => "white");

my $dbh = WebDB::connect ();

# Dispatch to proper action based on user selection

my $choice = lc (param ("choice")); # get choice, lowercased

if ($choice eq "")                      # initial invocation
{
    display_form ($dbh);
}
```

continues

continued

```
elsif ($choice eq "search")        # perform search
{
    display_form ($dbh);           # redisplay the form
    perform_search ($dbh);         # present the results
}
else
{
    print p (escapeHTML ("Logic error, unknown choice: $choice"));
}

$dbh->disconnect ();

print end_html ();

exit (0);
```

Creating the Search Form

The search form is generated by the `display_form()` function and contains fields in which the user can specify values for the following aspects of the residence listings: location, architectural style, price point (maximum price the user is willing to pay), minimum number of bedrooms and bathrooms, and additional features the user wants. That's a lot of stuff, and these parameters correspond to several kinds of information: strings, numbers, `ENUM` values, and `SET` values. However, it turns out not to be difficult to generate the form because almost all the information we need is stored in the database already. The values for the architectural style and additional features are present in the column definitions for the `ENUM` column `style` and the `SET` column `features`, and the values for the other parameters are listed in the lookup tables. We'll present each list of options as a pop-up menu, except for the additional features list, which we'll display as a set of check boxes.

Let's cover the pop-up menus first. For each of these, we need to collect the information necessary for a call to `popup_menu()`. (If you prefer to generate radio buttons or scrolling lists, the following discussion applies without modification except that you'd call `radio_group()` or `scrolling_list()`.) Each pop-up menu is constructed as a list of specific values, plus we'll add an `Any` item so that the user doesn't have to pick a particular value. If the user picks `Any` from the list of locations, for example, we'll interpret that to mean "any location is okay." (In other contexts, similar types of generic items might be labeled "All," "None of the above," and so forth, depending on your purposes.) When you provide a generic or "no choice" item such as `Any` in a pop-up menu, there are several issues to consider:

- If you're using a lookup table to generate the menu, you might store the `Any` item as a row in the table, just like the other items. Similarly, if you're using an `ENUM` column, you might make `Any` a legal member of the enumeration.

However, I don't like to do this. I prefer instead to obtain the non-Any values from the database, and then add Any to the list before generating the pop-up menu. There are two reasons for this. First, if you are using the column definition or lookup table for other scripts, Any may have no meaning to those scripts and would have to be removed from the list of options. If you have a data-entry application for creating new `residence` table records, for example, it doesn't make any sense to allow users to select Any as a particular home's location or style—those columns should have some specific non-generic value. Therefore, in such an application, you'd have to filter out the Any item for form generation and validation purposes. Second, you can't store Any in the list of options anyway if you're using a lookup table that contains non-string values. `res_bedrooms` is an example of this; it contains numbers, not strings. Any wouldn't be a legal value in the table.

- If you want the Any item to be the default value for a list, it's easiest if you make it the first item in the list, because radio button sets and pop-up menus will display with the first item selected by default. If you add the Any item to the end of the list, you must specify its value as the default explicitly when you generate the field. (Scrolling lists display with no item selected by default, so you must specify Any explicitly as the default value no matter its position in the list.)

- If you pass only a `values` parameter to the field creation call, you need to add Any only to the list of values. If you're mapping values to labels by passing a `labels` parameter, too, make sure to add an entry for Any to the map as well.

- When the user submits the search form, be sure to interpret the proper value as your generic item. If you decide to change Any to All in the form generation code, for example, remember to look for All in the code that interprets form submissions.

With these points in mind, we can proceed to generate the pop-up menus for our search form. The list of locations is stored in the `res_location` lookup table, so we can get the list, add the Any item to the head of the list, and generate a pop-up menu from it like this:

```
$location_val_ref = WebDB::get_lookup_values (
                    $dbh,
                    "SELECT value FROM res_location ORDER BY value");
unshift (@{$location_val_ref}, "Any");
print "Location: ",
        popup_menu (-name => "location", -values => $location_val_ref);
```

If you wanted to put Any at the end of the list and make it the default, you'd do so by using `push` rather than `unshift` after calling `get_lookup_values()`. In this case, Any no longer would be the first item, so you'd have to specify it as the default explicitly:

```
$location_val_ref = WebDB::get_lookup_values (
                    $dbh,
                    "SELECT value FROM res_location ORDER BY value");
```

continues

continued

```
    push (@{$location_val_ref}, "Any");
    print "Location: ",
            popup_menu (-name => "location",
                            -values => $location_val_ref,
                            -default => "Any");
```

The pop-up menus for the `bedrooms` and `bathrooms` fields are generated in much the same way as for the `location` field, so I won't show the code here. Creating the list of price points is a little more complicated. The values in the `res_price` table are just numbers, but the pop-up menu should display labels that are more descriptive (such as "Up to $100,000" for the value `100000`). In this case, we need a list of values as well as a hash that maps the values to labels. We can ask MySQL to format the labels for us, and if our lookup query returns two columns, `get_lookup_values()` will return references to both the value list and the label map.[1] Those references give us the `values` and `labels` parameters for the `popup_menu()` call:

```
    ($price_val_ref, $price_label_ref) = WebDB::get_lookup_values (
                        $dbh,
                        # use q{ ... } so Perl leaves the $ alone
                        q{ SELECT value, CONCAT('Up to $',FORMAT(value,0))
                        FROM res_price ORDER BY value });
    unshift (@{$price_val_ref}, "Any");
    $price_label_ref->{Any} = "Any";
    print "Maximum price: ",
            popup_menu (-name => "price",
                            -values => $price_val_ref,
                            -labels => $price_label_ref);
```

`FORMAT(value,0)` formats the value with commas every three digits (the `0` argument means "no decimal places"), and we use `CONCAT()` to glue the "Up to $" part to the front of the formatted value. After obtaining the value list and label map, we add `Any` entries to both the list and the map, and then print the pop-up menu.

For the list of architectural styles, a different approach is necessary because the values are stored in the `ENUM` definition for the `style` column, not in a lookup table. We read the table description using the `WebDB::TableInfo` module and extract from that information the list of legal style values:

```
    $tbl_info = WebDB::TableInfo->get ($dbh, "residence");
    @style = $tbl_info->members ("style");
    unshift (@style, "Any");
    print "Architectural style: ",
            popup_menu (-name => "style", -values => \@style);
```

1. This behavior of `get_lookup_values()` is explained in Chapter 6.

The additional features stored in the `features` column is a `SET` rather than an enumeration list. Thus, any number of features may be selected, not just one, and there is no need for an `Any` item. The legal values are found in the `features` column definition, so we refer to the table information again to get the list of members, and then use it to construct a set of check boxes:

```
@features = $tbl_info->members ("features");
print "Required additional features:",
        checkbox_group (-name => "features",
                        -values => \@features,
                        -linebreak => 1);
```

Here is the entire function `display_form()` that generates the search form. The code is similar to what I've just described, except that it prints the form elements in tabular format to make them line up better:

```
sub display_form
{
my $dbh = shift;
my $tbl_info;
my ($location_val_ref, $bed_val_ref, $bath_val_ref);
my ($price_val_ref, $price_label_ref);
my (@style, @features);

    $tbl_info = WebDB::TableInfo->get ($dbh, "residence");

    # Generate the popup menus for the option lists. Add an "Any" item
    # to the head of each list to serve as the default value.

    # Values for architectural styles are in the style column definition

    @style = $tbl_info->members ("style");
    unshift (@style, "Any");

    # Values for locations, prices, and numbers of bedrooms and bathrooms
    # are in lookup tables.  For prices, there are labels that differ from
    # the values.

    $location_val_ref = WebDB::get_lookup_values (
                    $dbh,
                    "SELECT value FROM res_location ORDER BY value");
    unshift (@{$location_val_ref}, "Any");

    # Look up values and labels for price range.  For a value of
    # 100000, generate a label of "Up to $100,000".
    ($price_val_ref, $price_label_ref) = WebDB::get_lookup_values (
                    $dbh,
                    # use q{ ... } so Perl leaves the $ alone
                    q{ SELECT value, CONCAT('Up to $',FORMAT(value,0))
                    FROM res_price ORDER BY value });
```

continues

continued

```
        unshift (@{$price_val_ref}, "Any");
        $price_label_ref->{Any} = "Any";

        $bed_val_ref = WebDB::get_lookup_values (
                        $dbh,
                        "SELECT value FROM res_bedrooms ORDER BY value");
        unshift (@{$bed_val_ref}, "Any");

        $bath_val_ref = WebDB::get_lookup_values (
                        $dbh,
                        "SELECT value FROM res_bathrooms ORDER BY value");
        unshift (@{$bath_val_ref}, "Any");

        # Get additional features list from the features column definition
        @features = $tbl_info->members ("features");

        print start_form (-action => url ()),
            p ("Please select the characteristics for the type of home in\n"
               . "which you're interested, then select the Search button."),
            table ({-border => 1},
                Tr (
                    td ("Location:"),
                    td (popup_menu (-name => "location",
                                -values => $location_val_ref))
                ),
                Tr (
                    td ("Maximum price:"),
                    td (popup_menu (-name => "price",
                                -values => $price_val_ref,
                                -labels => $price_label_ref))
                ),
                Tr (
                    td ("Architectural style:"),
                    td (popup_menu (-name => "style",
                                -values => \@style))
                ),
                Tr (
                    td ("Minimum number of bedrooms:"),
                    td (popup_menu (-name => "bedrooms",
                                -values => $bed_val_ref))
                ),
                Tr (
                    td ("Minimum number of bathrooms:"),
                    td (popup_menu (-name => "bathrooms",
                                -values => $bath_val_ref))
                ),
                Tr (
                    td ("Required additional features:"),
                    td (checkbox_group (-name => "features",
```

```
                           -values => \@features,
                           -linebreak => 1))
            )
        ),
        br (), br (),
        submit (-name => "choice", -value => "Search"),
        end_form ();
    }
```

Interpreting Search Parameters and Constructing the Query

The next step is to write `perform_search()`, which interprets the contents of the search form when the user submits it. What we want to end up with is a query that includes an appropriate WHERE clause that reflects the conditions the user specified in the form. (We'll also have an ORDER BY clause to sort the listings, but for now we'll hardwire that in. In the section "Extending the Search Application," one of the modifications we'll make is to give the user some control over the sort order, at which point we'll have to build both the WHERE and ORDER BY parts of the query from the contents of the form.)

As we examine the form parameters, we'll collect a set of conditions that qualifying listings must satisfy. However, for any parameter that is set to Any, we can skip the test on the corresponding residence table column. If the bathrooms value is 2.5, for example, the query must include a bathrooms >= 2.5 condition, but if the value is Any, no bathrooms test is needed at all. This means the number of conditions can vary from search to search. An easy way to deal with this is to collect the tests in a @condition array, and then use join() to glue them together with AND in between. Any values referenced by placeholder markers in the conditions can be collected in a @placeholder array. That gives us the information needed to build the query and run it:

```
sub perform_search
{
my $dbh = shift;
my $tbl_info;
my $val;
my @condition;        # conditions for WHERE clause
my @placeholder;      # values for placeholders
my ($sth, $stmt, $col_list, $where);
my $count;

    # Collect conditions corresponding to the
    # parameters specified in the search form.

    $val = param ("location");
    if (defined ($val) && $val ne "Any")
    {
        push (@condition, "location = ?");
        push (@placeholder, $val);
```

continues

continued

```perl
    }
$val = param ("price");
if (defined ($val) && $val ne "Any")
{
    push (@condition, "price <= ?");         # specified price is a maximum
    push (@placeholder, $val);
}
$val = param ("style");
if (defined ($val) && $val ne "Any")
{
    push (@condition, "style = ?");
    push (@placeholder, $val);
}
$val = param ("bedrooms");
if (defined ($val) && $val ne "Any")
{
    push (@condition, "bedrooms >= ?");      # value is a minimum
    push (@placeholder, $val);
}
$val = param ("bathrooms");
if (defined ($val) && $val ne "Any")
{
    push (@condition, "bathrooms >= ?");     # value is a minimum
    push (@placeholder, $val);
}

# Figure out the numeric value of the selected features so that
# we can use it in comparisons against the features SET column.

$tbl_info = WebDB::TableInfo->get ($dbh, "residence");
$val = $tbl_info->get_list_numeric_value ("features");
if ($val > 0)                                # are any features required?
{
    push (@condition, "((features + 0) & ?) = ?");
    push (@placeholder, $val, $val);    # need value *twice*
}

# List of columns to select (format price with commas and
# a leading dollar sign)
$col_list = "id, location, CONCAT('\$',FORMAT(price,0)) AS price,"
            . "style, bedrooms, bathrooms, built, features, description";
# WHERE clause listing the conditions
$where = "WHERE " . join (" AND ", @condition) if @condition;
$where = "" unless $where;
# complete query
$stmt = "SELECT $col_list FROM residence $where"
        . " ORDER BY location LIMIT 100";
```

```
$sth = $dbh->prepare ($stmt);
$sth->execute (@placeholder);
$count = 0;
while (my $ref = $sth->fetchrow_hashref ())
{
    display_listing ($ref);
    ++$count;
}
$sth->finish ();

print ("Sorry, no qualifying listings were found.") if !$count;
}
```

That's the entire function. It's a mouthful, so let's examine how various parts of it work.

Testing Single-Valued Parameters

The perform_search() function begins by checking the single-valued parameters corresponding to the pop-up menu fields and constructing appropriate column tests from them. All of these can be handled pretty much the same way: Extract the value and add a condition to the query if the value isn't Any. For example, the price parameter represents the maximum price the user is willing to pay, so we want listings with price values no greater than the selected value:

```
$val = param ("price");
if (defined ($val) && $val ne "Any")
{
    push (@condition, "price <= ?");        # specified price is a maximum
    push (@placeholder, $val);
}
```

On the other hand, the bedrooms and bathrooms parameters represent the minimum number of each type of room that homes must have, so the tests go in the other direction:

```
$val = param ("bedrooms");
if (defined ($val) && $val ne "Any")
{
    push (@condition, "bedrooms >= ?");     # value is a minimum
    push (@placeholder, $val);
}
$val = param ("bathrooms");
if (defined ($val) && $val ne "Any")
{
    push (@condition, "bathrooms >= ?");    # value is a minimum
    push (@placeholder, $val);
}
```

The location and style parameters are exact-valued parameters, so the tests that involve them use the = operator.

Testing Multiple-Valued Parameters

Processing the set of required features is more difficult (that is, more interesting!) than checking the pop-up menus, because multiple features might be selected, not just one of them. If fact, it might even be that none of them is selected, in which case no test is needed. The easiest and most obvious way to find records that match the features values is to concatenate the selected options into a comma-separated list of values, treat the resulting string as a SET value, and compare it to the features column:

```
if (@val = param ("features"))
{
    push (@condition, "features = ?");
    push (@placeholder, join (",", @val));
}
```

Thus, if the user were to select features such as deck, pool, and basement, the result would be a condition in the WHERE clause that looks like this:

```
features = 'deck,pool,basement'
```

Unfortunately, although that's the easy thing to do, it's also incorrect. The intent of the features element is to allow the user to indicate the minimum set of features considered acceptable. If a residence has additional features, that's okay. If a home has a heated garage in addition to a deck, pool, and basement, for example, all the required features are present and it should be considered a match. The test just shown fails to find such a residence because it looks only for exact matches.

For situations in which you consider a SET value to match even if it contains other options in addition to the required ones, the condition on the SET column must be an "at least" test. That is, the column value must contain at least a given set of members, but is allowed to contain others. One way to perform that kind of test is to generate a complicated condition based on MySQL's FIND_IN_SET() function:

```
@val = ();
foreach my $val (param ("features"))
{
    push (@val, "FIND_IN_SET(?,features)");
    push (@placeholder, $val);
}
push (@condition, join (" AND ", @val));
```

The resulting test looks like this:

```
FIND_IN_SET('deck',features)
AND FIND_IN_SET('pool',features)
AND FIND_IN_SET('basement',features)
```

That'll work, but another approach is possible that uses a single comparison no matter how many options must be matched. This method is based on the fact that MySQL represents SET columns internally as numbers, with successive member values corresponding to successive bits in the number (in other words, corresponding to powers of two). For example, the features column has four members, each of which is represented internally using the following values:

Member Name	Decimal Value	Binary Value
heated garage	1	0001
deck	2	0010
pool	4	0100
basement	8	1000

Any value in the features column is represented internally as the sum of the individual members present in the value. For example, 'deck,pool,basement' is represented as 2 + 4 + 8, or 14. (In binary, this is 0010 + 0100 + 1000, or 1110.) It's useful to know this because if you refer to a SET column in a numeric context within an expression, MySQL treats the value as a number rather than as a string, and you can manipulate it using bit arithmetic. That makes it possible to process a set of options in a form by mapping each option onto the appropriate numeric value to determine the composite value, and then using the result as a bit mask to find features values that have at least those bits turned on. For example, we know that the value 'deck,pool,basement' corresponds to 14, so we can find records that have at least those elements present in the features column using the following condition:

```
((features+0)&14) = 14
```

In this expression, +0 acts to convert the value of the features column to a number (this is how you tell MySQL, "treat this SET value as a number, not a string"), and &14 performs a bitwise AND (intersection) operation. The result consists of all bits that are present both in the features value and in the value 14. If the three requested features are present in a listing's features value, the result is 14 and we have a match. If other features are present as well, the result is still 14 and we have a match. However, if some required features are missing from the features value, the result will be less than 14 and there is no match.

The preceding process may seem like a lot of work, but actually can be represented in relatively little code. The biggest problem is to convert the options selected in the search form to the appropriate numeric value. That's something we can do by referring to the SET members listed in the residence table description, so let's write a function to perform this conversion as a method of the WebDB::TableInfo module.

The method takes an argument that is assumed to be the name both of the table column and the corresponding parameter in the form, converts any options that are selected in the form to numeric values, and returns the sum:

```
sub get_list_numeric_value
{
my ($self, $col_name) = @_;
my @members;
my (@val, $val);

    # Get the SET members listed in the column description
    @members = $self->members ($col_name);
    # Get the elements actually selected in the corresponding form field
    @val = param ($col_name);

    # March through the SET members.  For each one selected in
    # the form, add its numeric value (a power of two) to the
    # total. This constructs a bit mask with bits turned on for
    # the selected SET members.

    $val = 0;
    for (my $i = 0; $i < @members; $i++)
    {
        $val += (1 << $i) if grep (/^$members[$i]$/i, @val);
    }
    return ($val);
}
```

By invoking this method, we can determine the condition that finds records containing the proper features relatively easily:

```
$tbl_info = WebDB::TableInfo->get ($dbh, "residence");
$val = $tbl_info->get_list_numeric_value ("features");
if ($val > 0)                           # are any features required?
{
    push (@condition, "((features + 0) & ?) = ?");
    push (@placeholder, $val, $val);    # need value *twice*
}
```

Note that because the bitmask value is referenced twice in the condition, it's necessary to shove it onto the @placeholder array two times. Also note that the SET column need not be represented by a set of check boxes for this approach to work. It can be used with multiple-pick scrolling lists as well.

Should Search Parameters be Validated?

The perform_search() function doesn't perform much validation of the form contents, which may seem curious in light of the emphasis placed on validation in Chapter 6. My rationale for this is that validation is more important when you're creating or updating information in the database than when you're just searching for it. In an application that inserts or modifies records, validation is necessary to prevent creation of records with incorrect information (either by accident on the part of innocent users or by intent on the part of malicious ones). For searching, validation is not always required. For example, in the res_search.pl application, the only options available to users are the ones we provide, so any values a user submits should be legal. In other search applications, validation can be useful or desirable. If you have the user enter a state name or abbreviation using a text field, for example, you may wish to verify that the field has a legal value before using it in a query.

But what if a malicious user submits bad input? The most probable scenario is that your unfriendly visitor will supply input intended to subvert your query. This shouldn't be a problem, so long as you're properly adding form input to the query by using placeholders (as we have done in res_search.pl) or by using quote(). If you do this, your query won't be malformed no matter what input the user submits. If the user supplies bad values, it's most likely to result in a query that fails to match anything. In this sense, hack attempts are self-defeating because they make the query useless. (Note that this applies only to data values. You can't use placeholders or quote() for parts of the query such as column names, keywords, or expression operators. If you have fields in a form that correspond to those kinds of query components, you *must* validate them.)

Presenting the Search Results

After examining all the relevant parameters in the search form and collecting the conditions that need to be satisfied, we have all the information necessary to construct and execute the query. This happens at the end of the perform_search() function:

```
# List of columns to select (format price with commas and
# a leading dollar sign)
$col_list = "id, location, CONCAT('\$',FORMAT(price,0)) AS price,"
        . "style, bedrooms, bathrooms, built, features, description";
# WHERE clause listing the conditions
$where = "WHERE " . join (" AND ", @condition) if @condition;
$where = "" unless $where;
# complete query
$stmt = "SELECT $col_list FROM residence $where"
        . " ORDER BY location LIMIT 100";
```

continues

continued

```
$sth = $dbh->prepare ($stmt);
$sth->execute (@placeholder);
$count = 0;
while (my $ref = $sth->fetchrow_hashref ())
{
    display_listing ($ref);
    ++$count;
}
$sth->finish ();

print ("Sorry, no qualifying listings were found.") if !$count;
```

perform_search() just displays all the listings returned by the query, subject to the
constraint that it won't show more than 100 records. (The query includes a LIMIT 100
clause as a simple precaution against returning a huge number of listings.) If the user
were to run a search that matches hundreds of records, that would result in a very long
result page—not good. One way to deal with large result sets is to display them over
multiple pages; that issue is dealt with in the section "Extending the Search
Application." For now, we'll produce a single page display but limit its length. In the
absence of more sophisticated methods that require more work to implement, LIMIT is
a simple but effective way to prevent a script from swamping client browsers with
gigantic amounts of information.

perform_search() passes each entry to display_listing() to handle the details of
showing individual listings. display_listing() prints the information in tabular form.
However, it avoids writing out a long table() invocation that lists calls to produce
each table row and cell explicitly. Instead, it uses a @col_name array that lists the order
in which to display columns and a %label hash that maps column names onto labels
to display with the corresponding values:

```
sub display_listing
{
my $ref = shift;
my @row;        # array to hold display table rows
my @col_name = # columns to display, in the order they should be displayed
(
    "id", "location", "price", "style", "bedrooms", "bathrooms",
    "built", "features", "description"
);
my %label =     # labels for each column
(
    "id"            => "Residence ID",
    "location"      => "Location",
    "price"         => "Asking price",
    "style"         => "Architectural style",
    "bedrooms"      => "Number of bedrooms",
    "bathrooms"     => "Number of bathrooms",
    "built"         => "Year built",
```

```
    "features"      => "Additional features",
    "description"   => "Other information"
);

    # Generate table rows; each one contains a label and a value

    foreach my $col_name (@col_name)
    {
        push (@row, Tr (
                td ($label{$col_name} . ":"),       # label
                td (escapeHTML ($ref->{$col_name})) # value
            ));
    }

    print hr (), table ({-border => 1}, @row);
}
```

We now have a working search application. Try it out and see how it works. But instead of being happy with it, we can think a bit about how to improve it. That's the subject of the next section.

Extending the Search Application

Although res_search.pl serves to provide a Web-based interface into the contents of our residence table so that users can search it for themselves, we can make a number of modifications to produce a more capable application. Some of the possibilities (the ones we'll actually implement) are as follows:

- The price selection field needs some improvement. It allows you to specify the top end of the price range you're looking for, but not the bottom. This means that the higher a price range you select, the more listings will be found as matches. That's somewhat counterintuitive, because you'd expect that as you look for homes that are more and more expensive, you'd find fewer and fewer matches. We could interpret the price points in the other direction ("$100,000 and up" rather than "Up to $100,000"), but that still has the problem that you can match a lot of listings at prices you're really not interested in. To deal with this, we'll change the price pop-up menu to present prices as ranges that have both a minimum and a maximum. That changes the way in which we generate the menu, and also the way we interpret its value when users submit searches.

- We'll add an option for sort order to give the user control over that aspect of the result display. The effect of this is that the ORDER BY clause no longer can be hardwired into the script. Instead, it must be determined based on user preference as expressed in the search form.

- The application currently can search a number of the columns in the `residence` table, looking for values that are strings (`location`), numbers (`price`, `bedrooms`, `bathrooms`), enumeration elements (`style`), or sets (`features`). It does not allow the `description` column to be searched. That column may contain important information, so we'll add the ability to search for keywords in descriptions. Along with this, we'll provide an option to specify whether the `description` value must contain all the words (if multiple words are entered) or just some of them.

- The `built` column indicates when homes were built. We'll make this column searchable so that searches can eliminate residences that are older than a certain age. On the face of it, this is just another pop-up menu in the search form, and as such may not seem to serve any additional purpose for our narrative. However, we'll construct the list of possible values for this field not by using a lookup table, but by retrieving the `built` values directly from the `residence` table. This means the pop-up menu will display only those values actually present in the current listings. It also means the values shown in the menu may vary somewhat, depending on the listings available from day to day.

- We'll add image-display capability. If pictures of a residence are available, we'll show them so that the user can see what the home looks like. However, adding pictures has the potential for making search result pages extremely image-heavy and very slow to load, so we'll also change the default display format to a summary table that lists the most important characteristics of each matching listing. Each item in the table will include a link to see the complete listing, including pictures. This way the user gets a brief overview of matching residences via the summary table, but has access to more complete information, should that be desired.

- To allow for the possibility that the user is searching residence listings on behalf of someone else, we'll allow listings to be sent by email. This enables you to do such things as mail listings for homes that might be suitable for a friend who is relocating to your area. If you're a realtor, you could use this feature to notify customers of homes they might like to take a look at.

- An issue in the original `res_search.pl` was that for searches that matched many listings, the result page could become quite long. Changing to a summary format alleviates the problem but does not eliminate it. Therefore, we'll split the result display into several pages if the number of hits goes above a certain threshold.

- The `features` column currently contains only four items that the user can select: `heated garage`, `deck`, `pool`, and `basement`. We'll add several more items to this column and assess what effect this has on the way the application handles the change.

In the previous section, discussion of the development of res_search.pl took place on a stage-by-stage basis, describing in turn how to generate the search form, how to interpret submitted searches, and how to present search results. For the revised version, res_search2.pl, the discussion proceeds by describing how to add each additional capability, and its impact on the various stages of the application. Consequently, I generally won't show entire listings for display_form(), perform_search(), and so forth. Instead I'll show just the changes to these functions that pertain to a given capability. For example, we'll begin by examining the changes needed to modify the price pop-up menu and how this affects form generation and interpretation, and then go on to add the option for controlling sort order. You'll probably find it helpful to have a copy of res_search2.pl on hand to refer to as you progress through this discussion.

Changing the Price Points

res_search.pl enables the user to choose home listings that satisfy a price constraint by presenting a price pop-up menu that contains items such as this:

```
Any
Up to $100,000
Up to $150,000
Up to $250,000
Up to $500,000
Up to $1,000,000
```

As noted in the introduction to this section, however, those options are fairly non-specific because the price ranges are bounded only on the bottom end. A different approach is to present ranges bounded on each end, so that we have items with both a minimum and a maximum. This changes the items in the pop-up menu as follows:

```
Any
Up to $100,000
$100,001 to $150,000
$150,001 to $250,000
$250,001 to $500,000
$500,001 to $1,000,000
$1,000,001 and up
```

It's trickier to generate items such as these from the lookup table, but they enable the user to be more specific. This approach also enables the user to select only homes costing more than a million dollars, something that's not possible under the first approach. We can still use the contents of the res_price table to get the necessary information, but our formatting and display requirements are more complex. That means we'll have to forego using get_lookup_values() and process the table values ourselves. The query we'll use looks like this:

```
SELECT value, FORMAT(value,0), value+1, FORMAT(value+1,0) FROM res_price
```

The first two columns selected by the query represent the maximum value for a given price range (both without and with commas). The next two columns represent the value that's one greater; this indicates the minimum of the next price range. As we process each row returned by the query, we'll remember this minimum value so we can use it with the next row. To represent pop-up item values that go along with the labels, we'll use strings of the form "*min,max*" to indicate the endpoints of the range. For the first range, the minimum will be 0 (as in "Up to $100,000"). For the last range, *max* will be missing, which we'll interpret as "no limit" (as in "$1,000,001 and up"). The code in `display_form()` that queries the `res_price` table and generates the list of items looks like this:

```
# Generate values and labels for the price range popup.
# First, add "Any" as the first item in the list.

@price_val = ( "Any" );
%price_label = ( "Any" => "Any" );

# Run query to get price range information

$sth = $dbh->prepare (
            "SELECT value, FORMAT(value,0), value+1, FORMAT(value+1,0)
             FROM res_price");
$sth->execute ();
@prev_row = ();
while (my @row = $sth->fetchrow_array ())
{
    if (!@prev_row)          # this is the first row (implicit min = 0)
    {
        $val = "0,$row[0]";
        $label = "Up to \$$row[1]";
    }
    else                     # not first row: min, max are both known
    {
        $val = "$prev_row[2],$row[0]";
        $label = "\$$prev_row[3] to \$$row[1]";
    }
    push (@price_val, $val);
    $price_label{$val} = $label;
    @prev_row = @row;
}
$sth->finish ();
if (@prev_row)               # last row (no explicit max)
{
    $val = "$prev_row[2],";
    $label = "\$$prev_row[3] and up";
    push (@price_val, $val);
    $price_label{$val} = $label;
}
```

Then we generate the menu with a call to popup_menu() that includes the values and labels that we've created:

```
popup_menu (-name => "price",
                    -values => \@price_val,
                    -labels => \%price_label)
```

The HTML produced by popup_menu() looks like this:

```
<select name="price">
<option  value="Any">Any</option>
<option  value="0,100000">Up to $100,000</option>
<option  value="100001,150000">$100,001 to $150,000</option>
<option  value="150001,250000">$150,001 to $250,000</option>
<option  value="250001,500000">$250,001 to $500,000</option>
<option  value="500001,750000">$500,001 to $750,000</option>
<option  value="750001,1000000">$750,001 to $1,000,000</option>
<option  value="1000001,">$1,000,001 and up</option>
</select>
```

Now the price ranges are more specific, and the value attribute for each option is in a format that we can use easily to delimit the search when processing the price parameter in perform_search():

```
$val = param ("price");
if (defined ($val) && $val ne "Any")
{
    my ($min, $max) = split (/,/, $val);
    if ($max ne "")                    # min, max both known
    {
        push (@condition, "(price >= ? AND price <= ?)");
        push (@placeholder, $min, $max);
    }
    else                             # no explicit max
    {
        push (@condition, "price >= ?");
        push (@placeholder, $min);
    }
}
```

Giving the User Control over Sort Order

The original version of res_search.pl knows only how to present search results in a single sort order. (It sorts using the location column.) Because of that, the ORDER BY clause was written literally into the query. To afford the user more flexibility, we can add another option to the search form in display_form() for controlling sort order:

```
Tr (
    td ("Sort results by: "),
    td (radio_group (-name => "order_by",
                -values => [ "location", "price", "style" ],
                -labels =>
```

```
                        {
                            "location" => "Location",
                            "price" => "Price",
                            "style" => "Style",
                        }))
    )
```

This changes the way we construct the ORDER BY clause in perform_search(); we can no longer write it literally, but must construct it based on the order_by parameter:

```
$order_by = "location";              # default sort order
$val = param ("order_by");
if (defined ($val))
{
    $order_by = "location" if $val eq "location";
    $order_by = "price" if $val eq "price";
    $order_by = "style" if $val eq "style";
}
$order_by = "ORDER BY $order_by";
```

This gives us an $order_by variable that we can use in the query string when we're ready to issue the query (which we're not, yet.)

The code that generates the order_by field uses radio buttons to present the sort options. Arguably, it would be more consistent to use a pop-up menu, given that pop-up menus and not radio buttons are used elsewhere in the form. One difference is that for those elements, the options come from lookup tables, and therefore we don't necessarily know how many of them there will be. If there can be a lot of options, radio buttons can take up a lot of space, and a pop-up menu may be a better choice. However, that's not the case with the order_by options. We know how many values there are and that it's a small number. Radio buttons are useful under these conditions because they make all the options visible at a glance. With a pop-up menu, you have to click it to see the options that are available.

Searching for Keywords in Text

This section discusses how to look for substrings in the description column of residence records. It's true that the original res_search.pl already performs string searches (such as when it looks for matches on location values), but queries constructed by that script look only for exact matches on the column, and only for a single value. Adding the ability to look for keywords in the description column involves another kind of text-based search that differs from the previous ones in a couple of ways:

- We'll be looking for substring matches, not exact matches—that is, we'll consider a keyword to match a description if the word appears in the description anywhere.

- We'll allow the user to specify multiple words. This complicates things a little, because there are two ways to consider a record as matching the words. It can match only if the description contains all the words, or if it contains any of them. (Basically, this boils down to whether we connect tests for the words with AND or with OR when constructing the query.) To let the user to have it either way, the form will provide a field that includes "Match all words" or "Match any word" options.

Adding the description-related items to the search form is a matter of adding a text-input field for the keywords, and a field with the match type options. For the latter field, I'll use a set of radio buttons, for the same reason I used buttons to present the sort order field (it has a small fixed number of options). The code to generate these fields goes into display_form() as another row of the table() call that writes the form:

```
Tr (
    td ("Keywords:"),
    td (textfield (-name => "description", -size => 40),
        br (),
        radio_group (-name => "desc_match_type",
                     -values => [ "all", "any" ],
                     labels => {
                         "all" => "Match all words",
                         "any" => "Match any word"
                     }))
)
```

To process these new fields for query construction in perform_search(), we must determine which words the user wants to find, and how to connect the tests that look for the words. The condition for finding any given word is based on a substring match, so the operator is LIKE rather than =, and we'll add the '%' SQL pattern-match character to both ends of the word so that it matches no matter where in the description it occurs. Also, if there are multiple words, we must join the conditions together with AND or OR, depending on the type of match to perform. This means we'll end up with conditions that look like this:

```
(description LIKE '%word1%' AND ... AND description LIKE '%wordn%')
(description LIKE '%word1%' OR ... OR description LIKE '%wordn%')
```

The parentheses around the entire clause are necessary only for the OR form of the condition (to prevent the query from being misinterpreted if there are other conditions), but it's easiest just to add them in either case. The text-matching condition is generated like this:

```
$val = WebDB::trim (param ("description"));
if ($val ne "")                          # any keywords to look for?
{
    my @word = split (/\s+/, $val);
    $val = lc (param ("desc_match_type"));
```

```
    my $bool_op = "AND";    # determine boolean connective (default = AND)
    $bool_op = "AND" if $val eq "all";
    $bool_op = "OR" if $val eq "any";
    # create one test per word; join tests with $bool_op;
    # enclose entire string in parentheses
    push (@condition,
          "("
        . join (" $bool_op ", ("description LIKE ?") x @word)
        . ")");
    # convert each word xxx to %xxx% before adding to @placeholder
    push (@placeholder, map { "%$_%" } @word);
}
```

Most of this code is fairly straightforward, except perhaps the `join` and `map` calls. The second argument to `join` creates one `LIKE` test for each word. It uses Perl's `x` "string multiplier" operator to create an array of `description LIKE ?` strings, one string for each element in the `@word` array. The `map` call modifies the words before they are added to the `@placeholder` array; it converts them to patterns by adding '%' to the ends of each word.

Allowing the `description` column to be searched may create a performance problem because `LIKE` matches can be slow. The `CREATE TABLE` statement for the `residence` table didn't include any index on the `description` column, but even if we add one, it wouldn't help. We're looking for word matches anywhere in the description, and MySQL can use an index for `LIKE` comparisons only if the pattern for the word you're looking for is anchored to the beginning of the column value (as in `WHERE description LIKE 'word%'`).

The effect of keyword searches on performance may not be noticeable if the user happens to enter constraints for any of the other searchable columns. In that case, MySQL optimizes the query to find matches based on the indexed columns, and then uses the matching records to test the condition on the non-indexed `description` column. To the extent that the matches on the indexed columns produce a small intermediate result set, the substring matches won't slow a query down much. However, if you have lots of records in the `residence` table and the user searches only for description keywords, searches may become slow, particularly when many keywords are given. If this becomes an issue, you may want to consider other strategies for performing keyword matches. One possibility is to maintain a separate table that contains a row for each word of each `description` value. This table must be updated whenever a `residence` table record is created or its `description` value is modified, but the table can be indexed and searched using exact string matches. Another possibility is to use MySQL's `FULLTEXT` index type (if you have MySQL 3.23.23 or later). This involves creating an index on the `description` column:

```
ALTER TABLE residence ADD FULLTEXT (description)
```

With the index in place, you can replace the LIKE conditions in the query with conditions that look like this:

```
MATCH(description) AGAINST('word')
```

MATCH()/AGAINST() returns a relevance ranking value, which will be zero if the word isn't present.

Adding Search-by-Age Capability

Next, we'll incorporate a field in the search form that displays a list of ages so that the user can exclude homes older than a given age. This is obviously something that could be done easily by means of a lookup table analogous to the other lookup tables we've been using. To illustrate an alternative technique, however, we'll generate this form element a little differently: We'll look up all the unique built values directly from the residence table and use them to construct a pop-up menu.

With regular lookup tables that are separate from your base table, the list of values in the table tends to be fairly stable. (It's easy to modify the lookup table by adding or deleting rows, but typically you don't do so very often.) When you derive the values directly from the contents of a base table that may change fairly often, there's a certain instability that you must be prepared to contend with. In the case of the residence table, the particular year-built values depend on the listings available at the time of any given search. It's possible that there will be no values or a single value when the residence table is new; it's also possible that there will be many values when the table becomes large. To accommodate this flux in the number of possible built values, we can write the application to be adaptive. If there are fewer than two values, it won't present any age pop-up menu at all; and if there are a large number, it will present a scrolling list rather than a pop-up menu.

We also need to consider what kind of values to present as labels to the user. It would be easiest to write the code to present built values directly, but those represent absolute years. People seem to prefer thinking about houses in terms of how old they are rather than the particular year they were built. Fortunately, it's easy to compute an age from the year by subtracting the year from the current year:

```
SELECT YEAR(CURRENT_DATE)-built FROM residence
```

We can avoid having to convert ages back to years when we process searches by selecting both the year and the age. By using ages for the pop-up item labels, we make the field easier for users to understand, and by using the years for the item values, we make it easier for the script to use them in queries. The values and labels can be obtained like this:

```
# Generate a popup for "year built", but display values to users
# as age in years.

($built_val_ref, $built_label_ref) = WebDB::get_lookup_values (
                    $dbh,
```

continues

continued

```
"SELECT DISTINCT
        built, CONCAT(YEAR(CURRENT_DATE) - built,' years')
    FROM residence ORDER BY built");
```

The query uses `SELECT DISTINCT` rather than just `SELECT`, because we want only unique values; without `DISTINCT`, we'd get back a value for every row in the `residence` table! Next, we determine how many values we actually have. If there are fewer than two distinct values, there really isn't any choice to make, so we don't want to produce any age field at all. We'll also try to avoid creating a really long pop-up menu by using a scrolling list if there are more than 20 values:

```
if (@{$built_val_ref} <= 1)       # don't bother with a by-age element
{                                 # if there's no real choice
    $by_age_element = "";
}
else                              # generate either a popup or a list
{
    unshift (@{$built_val_ref}, "Any");
    $built_label_ref->{Any} = "Any";
    if (@{$built_val_ref} <= 20)        # use a popup menu
    {
        $by_age_element = popup_menu (-name => "built",
                                      -values => $built_val_ref,
                                      -labels => $built_label_ref);
    }
    else                          # use a scrolling list
    {
        $by_age_element = scrolling_list (-name => "built",
                                          -values => $built_val_ref,
                                          -labels => $built_label_ref);
    }
}
```

After determining the value of `$by_age_element`, we can refer to it somewhere in the call to `table()` that generates the search form. The following code places it after the field for architectural style. If `$by_age_element` is the empty string, nothing gets printed. Otherwise, we generate a row with the proper caption and either a pop-up menu or a scrolling list containing the allowable values:

```
Tr (
    td ("Architectural style:"),
    td (popup_menu (-name => "style",
            -values => \@style))
),
# generate the row for the by-age element, if there is one
($by_age_element eq ""
    ? ""
    : Tr (td ("Oldest age to consider:"), td ($by_age_element))),
)
```

Processing the `built` element when the form is submitted is pretty much the same as for most of the other pop-up menus. If there's a non-Any value present, we construct the appropriate test and add it to the `@condition` array:

```
$val = param ("built");
if (defined ($val) && $val ne "Any")
{
    push (@condition, "built >= ?");          # value is a minimum
    push (@placeholder, $val);
}
```

There is one more rather important detail that needs to be taken care of to help the application to run better. At the moment, the `residence` table has no index on the `built` column; we should create one in order to make the `SELECT` query that looks up values more efficient. To do this, use the following `ALTER TABLE` statement:

```
ALTER TABLE residence ADD INDEX (built)
```

"Wait a minute," you say. "The lookup tables we've been using to generate the other pop-up menus don't have any indexes on them. If we index the `built` column of the `residence` table because we're going to use it to look up option values, shouldn't we index the `value` column of the lookup tables that we're already using?" Strictly speaking, I suppose we should. However, those tables are so small that the performance difference will be negligible. Nevertheless, if you want to index the lookup tables, here are the index creation statements to do so:

```
ALTER TABLE res_location ADD INDEX (value)
ALTER TABLE res_price ADD INDEX (value)
ALTER TABLE res_bedrooms ADD INDEX (value)
ALTER TABLE res_bathrooms ADD INDEX (value)
```

Our by-age field is constructed on-the-fly by reading a table for values. That is similar to the way we construct other lookup-based fields, but differs in that we're not getting the values from a table created specifically to hold element options. Instead, the values come from the base table that we're searching (`residence`). The implementation is similar either way, but there are some implications you should consider before generating form elements from the base table in your own applications:

- With a lookup table, the set of options is more consistent and stable. By contrast, when you draw the values from the table that you're searching, the values vary according to the table's current contents. If the table is modified often, the values presented in the form may vary often as well. Consider the difference between approaches in another context. If you have an online store and you're presenting a search form that enables visitors to query your product inventory, you may want to list all the categories for items you sell, not just categories for items you have in stock at the moment. The latter might give visitors the impression you don't carry a very wide variety of merchandise if your inventory happens to be low at the moment. On the other hand, if you're using a search form for an application that produces summaries or reports, you may well want to list only values that are present in the base table. Suppose you provide a form in which to enter parameters for sales reports that are generated from a `sales` table. If the form has a `state` field so that you can get reports for a particular state, it makes sense to display the names only of those states in which you have customers— that is, those states actually represented in the `sales` table.

- The base table will almost always be much larger than a lookup table, so the query to pull values from it generally will be more expensive, even with indexing.

- Using values from the base table is not a good technique for columns that have a large number of distinct values. For example, presenting a field based on the `resident` table's `price` column probably would generate a long list of values as the table becomes large. The use of a few discrete price ranges is a better approach in this case.

If you really want to look up values from your base table, but you don't want to run a potentially expensive query each time you generate the search form, consider using the base table to generate a lookup table. For example, you could create a table for `built` values like this:

```
CREATE TABLE res_built
(
    value   SMALLINT UNSIGNED NOT NULL
)
```

Then you can load the table using the values present in the `residence` table:

```
INSERT INTO res_built (value) SELECT DISTINCT built FROM residence
```

This gives you a small table that can be used efficiently to generate a pop-up menu without searching the `residence` table. There's a downside, however: The `res_built` table will exactly reflect the `built` values present in the `residence` table at the time that you create it, but will go out of date somewhat as you modify records in the `residence` table. Because of this, you'll probably want to purge and reload the lookup table periodically. The rate of divergence between the two tables depends on the amount of update activity on the `residence` table. This rate, together with the amount of divergence you want to tolerate, influences the frequency at which you should reload the `res_built` table. A reasonable strategy is to reload it once a day for a while, and then assess whether that seems to be suitable. If not, modify the reload frequency up or down. (Or, as they say in cookbooks, "season to taste.") To avoid the possibility of having other applications accessing the `res_built` table while it's being reloaded, lock the tables while you're using them:

```
LOCK TABLE res_built WRITE, residence READ
DELETE FROM res_built
INSERT INTO res_built (value) SELECT DISTINCT built FROM residence
UNLOCK TABLES
```

Alternatively, if you have a version of MySQL that supports transactions, and your tables are the proper type for transaction processing, you can reload the `res_built` table as a multiple-statement transaction. (Transactions are discussed in Chapter 10, "E-Commerce Applications.")

Adding Pictures, Changing the Display Format, and Emailing Listings

Up to this point, we've dealt with residence listings entirely as text-based records. However, for items such as we're dealing with here (homes), their suitability to potential buyers depends heavily on appearance, and search results often are more meaningful to users if descriptive information is accompanied by a picture. It can be a very useful thing for your visitors to be able to see what candidate homes look like. To that end, we'll create a new table `res_picture` for storing pictures. At the same time, we'll change the display format from one that shows each listing in full to one that displays a summary table. The reason for this is that if we show the entire set of full listings, including pictures, the result page likely will become image laden and quite slow to load. The summary table will display several important characteristics of the listings and make each ID value a hyperlink that the user can select to see a complete listing. Another addition we'll make in this section is the ability to send listings by email. If you search the available listings and come across one you think a friend might be interested in, or if you're a realtor that uses the search application to find listings for clients, it can be useful to be able to send a message containing information about the listing.

To accommodate these changes, I'll make a couple of architectural modifications to the `res_search2.pl` application, compared to `res_search.pl`:

- The query execution and result display code will be moved out of `perform_search()` and into a separate function, `display_summary()`. This isn't strictly necessary, but it helps keep `perform_search()` from getting so large that it becomes difficult to discuss.

- The code to present complete listings will be moved into another script, `res_display.pl`, which will handle both the text and pictures, if there are any. `res_display.pl` also handles the task of mailing listings to people. The most likely time you'd think about mailing a listing to someone is when you're looking at the complete information for it—that is, when you're viewing a page generated by `res_display.pl`. Therefore, it makes more sense to add email capability to that script rather than to `res_search2.pl`.

The first thing we need is a table in which to store any pictures that might be available for residences. We could just include a `picture` column in the `residence` table if we knew there never would be more than one picture per home. But using a separate table gives us more flexibility, because it allows a `residence` record to be associated with as many pictures as you want. The res_picture table shown here holds the necessary information:

```
CREATE TABLE res_picture
(
    res_id      INT NOT NULL,                           # ID of parent record
    INDEX (res_id),
    picture_id  INT UNSIGNED NOT NULL AUTO_INCREMENT,   # picture ID
    PRIMARY KEY (picture_id),
    picture     BLOB NOT NULL,                          # image data
    caption     VARCHAR(60),                            # optional caption
    mime_type   VARCHAR(20) NOT NULL                    # image MIME type
)
```

res_id indicates which residence record a picture is associated with. This column is indexed so that we can find all pictures for any given residence quickly. However, the index on this column is not unique. (A residence might have multiple pictures, all of which should be assigned the same res_id value.) picture_id assigns a unique value to each picture so that we can refer unambiguously to any res_picture record. picture holds the actual image data; caption, if not NULL, provides a label to display with the picture. mime_type enables us to determine the proper Content-Type: header to use when transferring the image over the network to the client.

Where to Get Sample Pictures

The webdb distribution for the book includes some sample images under the search directory, as well as a script you can use to load them into the res_picture table. Check the README file there for instructions. I won't describe the script; it's very similar to the load_image.pl script developed in Chapter 5, "Writing Form-Based Applications," but tailored to the structure of the res_picture table.

Generating the Summary Table

When we move the query execution and result display code into a separate function, the last part of perform_search() no longer does these things. Instead, it just passes query information to display_summary():

```
display_summary ($dbh, $where, $order_by, @placeholder);
```

display_summary() determines which columns to retrieve, and then issues the query and generates an HTML table to show the results:

```
sub display_summary
{
my ($dbh, $where, $order_by, @placeholder) = @_;
my $col_list = # list of columns to retrieve in SELECT statement
    "id, location, CONCAT('\$',FORMAT(price,0)) AS print_price,"
    . "style, bedrooms, bathrooms";
my @col_name = # columns to display in the summary table, in the order
               # they should be displayed (id is not listed here, it's
               # handled specially)
```

```
(
    "location", "print_price", "style", "bedrooms", "bathrooms"
);
my %label =      # labels for each column of summary table
(
    "location"      => "Location",
    "print_price"   => "Price",
    "style"         => "Style",
    "bedrooms"      => "Bedrooms",
    "bathrooms"     => "Bathrooms",
);
my ($stmt, $sth);
my $count = 0;
my @row;               # summary table row array
my $str;

    $stmt = "SELECT $col_list FROM residence $where $order_by LIMIT 100";
    $sth = $dbh->prepare ($stmt);
    $sth->execute (@placeholder);

    # Column display order is determined from @col_name, except that ID is
    # special because it becomes the hyperlink for displaying a full listing.

    # Construct table headers

    $str = th ("Residence ID");
    foreach my $col_name (@col_name)
    {
        $str .= th (escapeHTML ($label{$col_name}));
    }
    push (@row, Tr ($str));

    # Construct each table row

    while (my $ref = $sth->fetchrow_hashref ())
    {
        # ID column is a hyperlink to display the complete listing
        $str = td (a ({-href => "res_display.pl?id=$ref->{id}"}, $ref->{id}));
        # Other columns are just static text
        foreach my $col_name (@col_name)
        {
            $str .= td (escapeHTML ($ref->{$col_name}));
        }
        push (@row, Tr ($str));
        ++$count;
    }
    $sth->finish ();

    if ($count == 0)
    {
        print p ("Sorry, no qualifying listings were found.");
```

continues

continued

```
    }
    else
    {
        print table (@row);
    }
}
```

One of the columns we're allowing users to sort on is `price`. This has a certain implication for the way we construct our query. To sort by price, we need a numeric sort. However, we display prices in the result page using values such as $123,456, which MySQL treats as strings due to the dollar sign and commas. These values don't sort in the same order as numbers. (For example, $99,999 sorts lexically after $100,000 even though it's a smaller number.) To handle this case, the script uses the `price` column for sorting, but retrieves the formatted price under the name `print-price` for display.

The display itself is presented in tabular form as a row of labels describing what's in each column of the summary, followed by one row of information per listing. `display_summary()` turns each residence ID into a hyperlink the user can select to see the complete listing and any pictures there might be.

Displaying or Emailing Individual Listings

The summary table produced by `res_search2.pl` includes links for displaying full listings. These links invoke another script, `res_display.pl`, that presents the complete text of a listing and causes itself to be reinvoked to display any pictures associated with the listing. `res_display.pl` also has a third function, which is to enable the user to email listings.

The initial part of `res_display.pl` is written to handle either an `id` or `picture` parameter and to display text or image data accordingly:

```
#! /usr/bin/perl -w
# res_display.pl - display a residence listing or picture

# Interprets URLS of the following forms:
# .../res_display.pl?id=n            show listing n
# .../res_display.pl?picture=n       show picture n

use strict;
use lib qw(/usr/local/apache/lib/perl);
use CGI qw(:standard escapeHTML);
use WebDB;
use WebDB::TableInfo;
use Mail::Sendmail;

my $id = WebDB::trim (param ("id"));
my $picture_id = WebDB::trim (param ("picture"));
my $email = WebDB::trim (param ("email"));
if ($id ne "")
```

```
{
    display_listing ($id, $email);
}
elsif ($picture_id ne "")
{
    display_picture ($picture_id);
}
else
{
    error ("No recognizable action was requested. ($id)");
}

exit (0);
```

The script also checks for an `email` parameter and passes it along to `display_listing()` in case the user requested that an email message be sent. (The preamble includes a `use Mail::Sendmail` statement to give the script access to email support. See Chapter 5, "Writing Form-Based Applications," for more information about the `Mail::Sendmail` module).

`display_listing()` is invoked when an `id` parameter is received indicating which listing to show. This function uses the ID to look up the proper `residence` table record, displays it, and then checks whether there are any pictures of the residence. If so, for each one it displays the caption (if there is one) and generates an `<img>` tag referring to the image so that the browser will issue an additional request to fetch the image. The `src` attribute of each `<img>` tag is written to cause `res_display.pl` to invoke itself again, this time with a `picture` parameter indicating which picture to send to the client browser:

```
<img alt="[picture]" src="res_display.pl?picture=n">
```

The `display_listing()` function displays the text of the listing in much the same way as the original `res_search.pl`, except that it produces output only for a single record. It also sends the listing by email if there is an `email` parameter, and presents a short form at the end of the page (which is where you enter an address in the first place). The way this works is that if you fill in the recipient field and submit the email form, `res_display.pl` sends the message to the recipient and then redisplays the same listing you were looking at before.

```
sub display_listing
{
my ($id, $email) = @_;
my ($dbh, $sth, $ref);
my @col_name =  # columns to display, in the order they should be displayed
(
    "id", "location", "price", "style", "bedrooms", "bathrooms",
    "built", "features", "description"
);
my %label =     # labels for each column
(
```

continues

continued

```
            "id"            => "Residence ID",
            "location"      => "Location",
            "price"         => "Asking price",
            "style"         => "Architectural style",
            "bedrooms"      => "Number of bedrooms",
            "bathrooms"     => "Number of bathrooms",
            "built"         => "Year built",
            "features"      => "Additional features",
            "description"   => "Other information"
    );
    my $pictures = 0;

        print header (),
                start_html (-title => "Residence Listing", -bgcolor => "white");

        # Look up the listing

        $dbh = WebDB::connect ();
        $sth = $dbh->prepare ("SELECT * FROM residence WHERE id = ?");
        $sth->execute ($id);
        $ref = $sth->fetchrow_hashref ();
        $sth->finish ();

        if (!defined ($ref))
        {
            $dbh->disconnect ();
            print p ("Sorry, no residence with ID $id was found"),
                end_html ();
            return;
        }

        # Send the listing by email if an address is present.
        # Then display the listing in the browser window.  email_text()
        # and display_text() both use the same set of values and labels,
        # though they format the information differently.

        email_text ($email, $ref, \@col_name, \%label) if $email ne "";
        display_text ($ref, \@col_name, \%label);

        # Display captions and <img> links for any pictures associated
        # with the listing

        $sth = $dbh->prepare (
                    "SELECT picture_id, caption FROM res_picture
                    WHERE res_picture.res_id = ?");
        $sth->execute ($id);
        while (my ($picture_id, $caption) = $sth->fetchrow_array ())
        {
            # don't need escape() -- we know $picture_id is a number
```

```
        my $url = url () . "?picture=$picture_id";
        print p ("Pictures:") if $pictures == 0;
        print p (escapeHTML ($caption)) if $caption;
        print img ({-src => $url, -alt => "[picture]"});
        ++$pictures;
    }
    $sth->finish ();

    $dbh->disconnect ();

    print p ("No pictures of this residence are available") if !$pictures;

    # Print a little form allowing the user to email the listing

    print hr (), start_form (-action => url ()),
        p ("Email this listing to a friend!"),
        # include id so next invocation knows which record to redisplay
        hidden (-name => "id", -value => $id, -override => 1),
        p ("Recipient's email address:"),
        # clear the field to prevent accidental duplicate mailings
        textfield (-name => "email", -size => 60,
                    -value => "", -override => 1),
        br (),
        submit (-name => "choice", -value => "Mail It"),
        end_form ();

    print end_html ();
}
```

The `email_text()` and `display_text()` functions used by `display_listing()` are very similar. They both format the contents of a `residence` record. `display_text()` is the simpler of the two functions. It produces an HTML table for display in the browser window:

```
sub display_text
{
my ($rec_ref, $col_name_ref, $label_ref) = @_;
my @row;        # array to hold display table rows

    foreach my $col_name (@{$col_name_ref})
    {
        push (@row,     # add label and column value to table
            Tr (
                td ($label_ref->{$col_name} . ":"),
                td (escapeHTML ($rec_ref->{$col_name}))
            ));
    }

    print table ({-border => 1}, @row);
}
```

`email_text()` validates the email address first, and then formats the listing as plain text, attempts to send it, and indicates whether or not the attempt was successful. As part of the message, it also includes the URL for viewing the listing on the Web, in case the recipient wants to see it that way:

```
sub email_text
{
my ($email, $rec_ref, $col_name_ref, $label_ref) = @_;
my %mail = (    # Hash containing mail message information
    From    => $email,
    To      => $email,
    Subject => "Residential Listing Information For You",
    Message => ""
);

    # Perform some validation of the email address

    if (!WebDB::looks_like_email ($email))
    {
        print p (escapeHTML ("$email is an invalid email address."));
        return;
    }

    # Generate the message, then send it

    foreach my $col_name (@{$col_name_ref})
    {
        $mail{Message} .= "$label_ref->{$col_name}: $rec_ref->{$col_name}\n";
    }
    $mail{Message} .= "\nYou can also view this listing at:\n"
                        . url () . "?id=$rec_ref->{id}\n";
    if (sendmail (%mail))
    {
        print p (escapeHTML ("The listing has been mailed to $email"));
    }
    else
    {
        print p (escapeHTML ("An error occurred while attempting to\n"
                        . "mail the listing to $email"));
    };
}
```

Each `<img>` link produced by `display_listing()` reinvokes `res_display.pl` with a picture parameter indicating which `res_picture` table image to display. The dispatch logic sees this parameter and calls `display_picture()` to take care of yanking the image out of the table and shoving it over the network:

```
sub display_picture
{
my $picture_id = shift;
my ($dbh, $sth, $mime_type, $data);
```

```
$dbh = WebDB::connect ();
($mime_type, $data) = $dbh->selectrow_array (
            "SELECT mime_type, picture FROM res_picture
            WHERE picture_id = ?",
            undef, $picture_id);
$dbh->disconnect ();
# did we find a record?
error ("Cannot find picture ID $picture_id") unless defined ($mime_type);

print header (-type => $mime_type, -Content_Length => length ($data)),
        $data;

$dbh->disconnect ();
}
```

Presenting Multiple-Page Search Results

Earlier in this chapter, we prevented searches from returning a huge stack of records to the client using the simple expedient of adding a `LIMIT 100` clause to the query. In this section, we'll tackle the problem a different way, by presenting the search result using multiple pages if the number of hits goes above a certain threshold. There are a couple of issues to consider when you want to accommodate the possibility of large result sets by splitting the result display into multiple pages:

- We need to present just part of the result set on each page, not the entire thing. This involves adding an appropriate `LIMIT` clause to the record-selection query.
- We need to make it possible for the user to navigate to pages that display the other parts of the result set. This involves adding a set of links to each result page.

When presenting the first page for a given result set, the search parameters will have come from the form that the user just submitted. The user arrives at subsequent pages by selecting navigation links. These links have the potential to become somewhat complex, because they must include two kinds of information:

- The search parameters the user submitted that determine the `WHERE` clause and the `ORDER BY` clause. These define the basic result set containing the records the user wants to see, and the order in which they should be presented.
- The parameters that control which records to display on a given page. I'll call these the page control parameters; they include at least the starting position within the result set and the number of records to display on the page. These two values translate directly into the values that go into the `LIMIT` clause.

In other words, each navigation link must include sufficient information to allow `res_search2.pl` to re-create the search and to determine which part of the result set to display. The script itself need not care whether the parameters it receives come from a form submitted by the user or as part of the URL. In either case, we can extract the necessary information by calling `param()`, which works just as well for URL parameters as for forms.

The particular set of page control parameters you use depends on the navigation style you provide in the result set pages. A simple style presents just "next page" and "previous page" links:

```
[previous] [next]
```

Another style presents these links, but also a set of page numbers as links that can be selected to go directly to individual pages of the result:

```
[previous] [1] [2] [3] [4] [5] [next]
```

If you want to provide pages that contain only next-page and previous-page links, the only thing you need to know is whether there actually are next and previous pages. It's trivial to determine the latter, based on the current starting position within the result set: If the first record you're displaying on a page isn't the first record in the set, then clearly there is at least one previous page. Determining whether there is a next page is more difficult, because you must know whether any records follow the ones you're displaying on the page. You can do this in two ways:

- When you retrieve the records for each page, use a `LIMIT` clause that fetches one more record than you actually intend to display. If you want to present 10 records per page, for example, use `LIMIT` clauses that fetch 11 records. The queries look like this:

  ```
  SELECT ... LIMIT 0, 11
  SELECT ... LIMIT 10, 11
  SELECT ... LIMIT 20, 11
  ...
  ```

  For each page, display the first 10 records that you get back from the query; if you also get an 11th record, you can discard it but its presence tells you there is a next page.

- Alternatively, before displaying any records at all, execute a preliminary query that uses `COUNT(*)` to determine the size of the result set. Then as you display each page of the result, you can tell that there is a next page if you haven't yet reached the maximum record number.

If you present only the next-page and previous-page links, the required page control parameters include only the starting record number and the number of records per page. If you want to present the more informative navigation display that includes links to each individual page of the result, you must also know the total number of records so that you can figure out how many pages there are. Therefore, you begin by issuing a `COUNT(*)` query to determine the result set size.

The navigation style that provides only next-page and previous-page links is simpler to implement, but less informative and less helpful to users. For `res_search2.pl`, we'll implement the style that includes individual page links. To do this, we'll need all three page control parameters, which I'll denote as follows:

- `start_pos`, the starting position within the result set that indicates the first record to display on a page.
- `page_size`, the number of records to display per page.
- `max_rec`, the total size of the result set. Together with `page_size`, `max_rec` determines how many pages there are.[2]

The first stage in implementing multiple-page output is to identify the search parameters. This is what the `perform_search()` function does. It was written originally for the purpose of determining the contents of the WHERE and ORDER BY clauses from the contents of the search form. However, this function does its work by calling `param()` to get the parameters, and `param()` also works for parameters passed in URLs. That's very convenient, because it means `perform_search()` needs no modification at all. It can figure out the WHERE and ORDER BY clauses without regard to whether the user invoked the script by submitting a search form or by selecting a navigation link.

After we know the parameters we need to fetch records for display, we must determine which part of the result set to present. This is where the page control parameters come in. They're needed to construct the proper LIMIT clause that allows the appropriate part of the result to be retrieved and presented in the summary table.

For `res_search2.pl`, all the modifications to enable multiple-page result set display take place in `display_summary()`. When you reach this point in the chapter, you'll need to modify the version of `res_search2.pl` provided in the `webdb` distribution. Take a look at the source for `res_search2.pl`; you'll see some comments describing how to disable the single-page version of `display_summary()` and enable the multiple-page version.

The revised version of the function isn't completely different (the format in which the summary table is displayed doesn't change, for example), but there are several new sections of code. The new `display_summary()` is shown in its entirety here, followed by explanations of the new parts:

```
sub display_summary
{
my ($dbh, $where, $order_by, @placeholder) = @_;
my $col_list =    # list of columns to retrieve in SELECT statement
    "id, location, price, CONCAT('\$',FORMAT(price,0)) AS print_price,"
    . "style, bedrooms, bathrooms";
my @col_name =    # columns to display in the summary table, in the order
                  # they should be displayed (id is not listed here, it's
                  # handled specially)
(
```

continues

---

2. It's not strictly necessary to pass the total result set size from page to page. You could run the COUNT(*) query for each page. However, it's more efficient to run that query once to get the count, and then pass the value in the navigation links.

continued

```
     "location", "print_price", "style", "bedrooms", "bathrooms"
);
my %label =     # labels for each column of summary table
(
     "location"      => "Location",
     "print_price"   => "Price",
     "style"         => "Style",
     "bedrooms"      => "Bedrooms",
     "bathrooms"     => "Bathrooms",
);
my ($start_pos, $page_size, $max_rec);
my @nav_link;      # navigation link array
my $limit;         # LIMIT clause
my @row;           # summary table row array
my ($stmt, $sth);
my $str;

     # Get the page control parameters.  If they're not present, this is
     # the first time we're running this search.  In that case, run a query
     # to determine the result set size and initialize the page parameters.

     $start_pos = param ("start_pos");
     $page_size = param ("page_size");
     $max_rec = param ("max_rec");
     if (!defined (param ("start_pos")))
     {
         $start_pos = 0;
         $page_size = 5;     # change this to change #hits/page
         $stmt = "SELECT COUNT(*) FROM residence $where";
         $max_rec = $dbh->selectrow_array ($stmt, undef, @placeholder);
         # We don't need to do much if there aren't any records...
         if ($max_rec == 0)
         {
             print p ("Sorry, no qualifying listings were found.");
             return;
         }
         # put values into environment so gen_nav_link() can find them
         # (except for start_pos, which isn't constant across links)
         param (-name => "page_size", -value => $page_size);
         param (-name => "max_rec", -value => $max_rec);
     }

     # $start_pos = number of initial records to skip
     # $page_size = number of records to retrieve

     $limit = "LIMIT $start_pos, $page_size";

     print p ("$max_rec matching listings were found.");
```

```
$stmt = "SELECT $col_list FROM residence $where $order_by $limit";
$sth = $dbh->prepare ($stmt);
$sth->execute (@placeholder);

# Column display order is determined from @col_name, except that ID is
# special because it becomes the hyperlink for displaying a full listing.

# Construct table headers

$str = th ("Residence ID");
foreach my $col_name (@col_name)
{
    $str .= th (escapeHTML ($label{$col_name}));
}
push (@row, Tr ($str));

# Construct each table row

while (my $ref = $sth->fetchrow_hashref ())
{
    # ID column is a hyperlink to display complete listing
    $str = td (a ({-href => "res_display.pl?id=$ref->{id}"}, $ref->{id}));
    # Other columns are just static text
    foreach my $col_name (@col_name)
    {
        $str .= td (escapeHTML ($ref->{$col_name}));
    }
    push (@row, Tr ($str));
}
$sth->finish ();

print table (@row);

# Generate and print navigational links (if there actually are multiple
# pages).  Generate a prev-page link, numbered page links, and a
# next-page link.  prev-page/next-page indicators are just static text
# if not applicable.  Numbered link for current page is static, too.

if ($max_rec > $page_size)
{
    if ($start_pos == 0)                    # first page: no predecessor
    {
        push (@nav_link, "previous");
    }
    else
    {
        push (@nav_link, gen_nav_link ("previous", $start_pos-$page_size));
    }

    for (my $i = 0; $i < $max_rec; $i += $page_size)
    {
```

continues

continued

```
            my $page_no = int ($i / $page_size) + 1;
            if ($start_pos == $i)                # this is the current page
            {
                push (@nav_link, $page_no);
            }
            else
            {
                push (@nav_link, gen_nav_link ($page_no, $i));
            }
        }

        if ($start_pos+$page_size > $max_rec)   # last page: no successor
        {
            push (@nav_link, "next");
        }
        else
        {
            push (@nav_link, gen_nav_link ("next", $start_pos+$page_size));
        }

        # Put square brackets around each link/label, then print them

        @nav_link = map { "[$_]\n" } @nav_link;
        print hr (), @nav_link;
    }
}
```

The multiple-page version of `display_summary()` first checks the values of the page control parameters that determine which part of the result set to display and how many navigation links we'll need to generate. These values are the starting position, page size, and size of the result set. When we first begin to run the search (that is, when the script is invoked as a result of the user submitting the search form), none of these parameters will have values, so it's necessary to initialize them. On subsequent pages, we'll have received the parameter values via the URL of the navigation link used to invoke the script, so we can just extract them from the script environment. This means we can tell whether or not to initialize the parameters by checking whether they're already available in the environment:

```
$start_pos = param ("start_pos");
$page_size = param ("page_size");
$max_rec = param ("max_rec");
if (!defined (param ("start_pos")))
{
    $start_pos = 0;
    $page_size = 5;     # change this to change #hits/page
    $stmt = "SELECT COUNT(*) FROM residence $where";
    $max_rec = $dbh->selectrow_array ($stmt, undef, @placeholder);
    # We don't need to do much if there aren't any records...
    if ($max_rec == 0)
```

```
    {
        print p ("Sorry, no qualifying listings were found.");
        return;
    }
    # put values into environment so gen_nav_link() can find them
    # (except for start_pos, which isn't constant across links)
    param (-name => "page_size", -value => $page_size);
    param (-name => "max_rec", -value => $max_rec);
}
```

If it turns out that the parameters must be initialized, we need to find out the size of the result set by running a preliminary query that uses COUNT(*). This query uses the WHERE clause conditions from the search parameters submitted by the user. However, you don't use any LIMIT clause (you want to count all the records), and you don't need an ORDER BY clause, either. (The query returns only one row; there's no need to sort it.) After the query has been run, we know whether the result set will be empty. If so, we can short circuit the entire display operation by informing the user no records were found.

Assuming the result set isn't empty, the starting position is initialized to 0. (In MySQL, rows are numbered from 0 for the LIMIT clause). The page size is somewhat arbitrary; res_search2.pl uses a value of 5. Notice that after initializing the page parameters, we put their values into the script environment. That's because our link generator (discussed shortly) will expect to find them there; in effect, we're using the parameter space as a clipboard.

Now we're ready to fetch some records and display them. The starting position and the page size determine the appropriate LIMIT clause to add to the query that retrieves the records to be displayed on the page. The summary table format is the same as before, although we add one extra bit of information: the total number of records matched by the search parameters. (Hey, we had to determine the size of the result set, anyway. Why not provide that information to the user?)

Following the summary table, we generate and display the navigation links, but only if they're necessary. If the result set size doesn't exceed the number of records per page, we don't need multiple pages, and consequently no links are displayed. Otherwise, we generate a set of numbered page links preceded by a previous-page link and followed by a next-page link. The code generates static text rather than a link for nonexisting pages and for the numbered link that corresponds to the current page, because there's little point in sending the user to a page that doesn't exist or that is already displayed in the browser window. For example, the previous-page indicator is static text if we're currently on the first page, because in that case there is no previous page:

```
    if ($start_pos == 0)                    # first page: no predecessor
    {
        push (@nav_link, "previous");
    }
    else
    {
        push (@nav_link, gen_nav_link ("previous", $start_pos-$page_size));
    }
```

Each link is generated by calling gen_nav_link() to create the proper URL for rein-voking res_search2.pl to display a particular part of the result set. gen_nav_link() takes two arguments: the label to use for the link ("next," "previous," or a page num-ber), and the starting record number for the page:

```
sub gen_nav_link
{
my ($label, $start_pos) = @_;
my @param =      # parameters to extract from environment
(
    # page control parameters
    "max_rec", "page_size",
    # search parameters
    "location", "price", "style", "bedrooms", "bathrooms", "features",
    "description", "desc_match_type", "order_by"
);
my $url;

    # tell the script to continue the search and which record to start with
    $url = url () . "?choice=search;start_pos=$start_pos";

    # add other page control and search parameters
    foreach my $name (@param)
    {
        my @val = param ($name);
        # if a parameter has multiple values, add it multiple times
        foreach my $val (@val)
        {
            $url .= ";$name=" . escape ($val);
        }
    }
    return (a ({-href => $url}, escapeHTML ($label)));
}
```

gen_nav_link() encodes into the URL a choice value of search to tell the script to keep searching, and adds the page control parameters that indicate which part of the result set to display and the search parameters needed to reconstruct the search. Most of these values are already present in the script's environment, so they are obtained by calling param(). The only value that is not available this way is the starting position, which varies from page to page and must be passed to gen_nav_link() as an argu-ment. If a search parameter has multiple values (as may be the case for the features parameter), the name is added to the URL several times, once for each value.

The amount of new code needed to implement multiple-page result set display really isn't that extensive. (Compare the sizes of the single-page and multiple-page ver-sions of display_summary() in the source for res_search2.pl.) However, trying to understand how the parts work together to pass information around from page to page can be confusing, so you really should try out the script at this point and see what kind of URLs the script generates for the navigation links.

Extending the *features* Column to Include More Items

When we created the residence table, the features column included only four items:

```
features SET('heated garage','deck', 'pool','basement') NOT NULL
```

There are many other kinds of things that could be listed here that people would be interested in knowing about, and SET columns can hold up to 64 members, so let's take advantage of that by modifying the column to contain some more items. We can do that with an ALTER TABLE statement that lists all the old items and adds several new ones:

```
ALTER TABLE residence MODIFY
    features SET('heated garage','deck','pool','basement','central air',
                 'patio','jacuzzi','fireplace','ethernet','wooded lot',
                 'lakefront','pond/stream','near school','near park',
                 'near bus line','near shopping','central vacuum') NOT NULL
```

This statement modifies the structure of the table that we're searching, so it's reasonable to ask what effect the change might have on res_search2.pl and whether we'll need to make any compensatory revisions. As it turns out, you don't *have* to make any changes:

- Changing the number of members in the features column has no effect on the capability of display_form() to generate the check boxes corresponding to each feature, because we used WebDB::TableInfo to get the member list, and that module doesn't depend on the specific contents of the column.

- Similarly, no changes are necessary to the code in perform_search() that generates a bitmask from the selected features to use in the WHERE clause of the selection query, or in display_summary() to encode the features in the URLs for the navigation links. Like display_form(), those functions are written with no reference to any specific knowledge about the features column other than that it's a SET.

Nevertheless, you might *want* to make a few changes. One modification that is optional but useful concerns the layout of the feature check boxes in the search form. display_form() generates those boxes by calling checkbox_group() and passing it a linebreak parameter to display the boxes as a vertical list. As you add more features, that list can become fairly long. checkbox_group() has the capability to display check boxes in tabular form with several items per row, so you might want to take advantage of that to generate a more compact feature display.

Another display-related change you might want to make is to sort the items alphabetically. The original items weren't alphabetic, and the ALTER TABLE statement just shown doesn't add the new items in any particular order, either. When there are only four items, the order in which they're displayed doesn't matter so much, but with a larger number, the display can be much easier to read if you sort the items. There are a couple of ways to accomplish this. Either redefine the column so that the items are listed in order, or else sort the list of items after you extract them from the column description and before generating the form. I prefer the latter method, because then you don't have to remember to make sure the members are in order when you issue an ALTER TABLE statement.

To implement these changes, sort the list of `features` members when you extract it from the table description, like this:

```
@features = sort ($tbl_info->members ("features"));
```

Then generate the check boxes by calling `checkbox_group()` with no `linebreak` parameter but with a `cols` parameter indicating how many columns to use for a tabular check box display:

```
Tr (
    td ("Required additional features:"),
    td (checkbox_group (-name => "features",
                        -values => \@features,
                        -cols => 4))
)
```

These modifications make the script a bit more adaptive with respect to future changes you might make to the `features` column. (If you're wondering whether sorting the items for display will affect the script's capability to properly construct the bitmask for the query in `perform_search()`, it won't. The bitmask is constructed by looking for matches based on feature name rather than on position within the column description.)

Suggestions for Modification

Allow the user to select a set of listings from the summary table by adding a check box to each line in the table and including a button that sends a request to `res_display.pl` to show the complete information for multiple listings. This can help eliminate some of the back and forth between search result pages and pages that show full listings. (This modification would require changes both to `res_search2.pl` and to `res_display.pl`.)

Modifying the `price` menu in the search form to use ranges rather than maximum price makes result sets more specific, but each item in the menu specifies both endpoints of the range. The application would be more flexible if it allowed the user to specify the top and bottom of the range independently. You could do this with two pop-up menus, although then you might also want to add some kind of check that the minimum the user selects actually is lower than the maximum.

Reimplement multiple-page search result display to use a session for storing search parameters rather than passing tons of information in the navigation links. (You'll need to read Chapter 8, "Session Management," for the necessary background information on doing this.)

Add a "sender" field to the email form presented by `res_display.pl`. That way you can identify yourself when you mail a listing to someone. As that script is written currently, recipients have no idea who sent the information.

Providing Link-Based Navigation

Near the beginning of the chapter, I mentioned that link-based navigation has certain limitations that search forms circumvent by enabling you to help your users find what they're looking for more directly. However, I also pointed out that link navigation can be useful sometimes, and this section discusses the kind of situation for which that is true.

My primary objection to link navigation earlier was that it enables users to move through your documents only in ways you can think of to provide in advance. If your document set has a regular and highly structured organization, however, you know perfectly well what the navigation options are, and it may be quite reasonable to provide links to all of them. If you have information about a list of people, for example, you can provide a nicely organized set of links that enable visitors to quickly get to any particular item in the list. If your information is stored in your database, that's even better; you can generate the links dynamically as people visit your site and they'll always be up-to-date without endless manual tweaking and editing when the information changes.

Let's apply this concept to a situation in which you want to maintain an online staff directory for your organization: Each person has an entry in a `staff` table in your database, and you want to make it easy to find any given person by name. To do this, we'll provide an index consisting of a set of links, with each link pointing to an individual `staff` table entry. The links will be sorted alphabetically so that they can be scanned easily. We'll also separate the index into sections by letter (all names beginning with "A," all names beginning with "B," and so forth), and provide a navigation bar listing the letters as links to each section of the index. Thus, to find the entry for Joe Smith, you select "S" from the navigation bar to get to the section of "S" names, scan that section to find Joe's name, and then select the name to see the information in Joe's `staff` table record.

We'll implement this directory two ways: once using a single-page index and once using a multiple-page index. The single-page index will provide a navigation bar and list the names of all staff members on a single page. The multiple-page index will consist of two tiers. The lower tier provides separate pages for each letter, with each page listing only names beginning with the corresponding letter. The upper tier is a single page that contains a navigation bar pointing to the lower-level pages.

These methods have in common the need to know how to present the entry for a given staff person (which is what your visitors actually are interested in seeing, after all), and they need to know how to construct indexes based on the contents of the `staff` table. Where they differ is in the particular form of the indexes (one-tier versus two-tier) and on the scope of the items listed on a page (all items versus items only for a given letter). The scope of the single-page index comprises all records, and therefore is suitable primarily for smaller record sets. Otherwise, you end up generating a page that is quite long, takes a long time to load, and is cumbersome to use. A multiple-page index accommodates larger numbers of items, because the scope of each subindex page is limited to just a part of the record set. This makes the individual pages easier to manage. It's also less work for the database and your application, because you retrieve only part of the directory for each subindex page.

To present the single-page and multiple-page versions of the staff directory, we'll write two applications, `staffs.pl` and `staffm.pl`. They both use the same underlying `staff` table, which looks like this:

```
CREATE TABLE staff
(
    id          INT UNSIGNED NOT NULL AUTO_INCREMENT,   # record identifier
    PRIMARY KEY (id),
    lname       VARCHAR(30) NOT NULL,                   # last name
    fname       VARCHAR(30) NOT NULL,                   # first name
    position    VARCHAR(30) NOT NULL                    # job
)
```

This table is quite minimal, containing only an `id` column that provides a unique record identifier, the first and last names, and staff position. It's simple because the purpose of this section is to show how to provide structured access to the table's records, not how to display them. Besides, the basic principles for displaying link-based index pages are quite similar for more complex forms of information, so you can adapt them to many different kinds of tables without much modification.

The general form of the queries used by both `staffs.pl` and `staffm.pl` are similar, so I'll describe them here before moving on to the specifics for each application. Each script needs to determine appropriate entries for the navigation bar, which means figuring out which letters are represented by records in the `staff` table. This can be done using the following query:

```
SELECT DISTINCT UPPER(LEFT(lname,1)) AS letter FROM staff ORDER BY letter
```

`LEFT(lname,1)` extracts the first letter of each staff member's last name, `ORDER BY` sorts them, and `DISTINCT` makes sure we get back each letter only once. You could just generate a set of 26 links and avoid running this query, but then you might end up with links that point nowhere. (There's no point in having a link for "X" if nobody has a last name beginning with "X.") The query enables us to avoid generating dead links in the navigation bar. Also, the query makes the navigation bar somewhat less language dependent (perhaps your alphabet doesn't have 26 letters).

To pull out names and format them for display in the single-page index, we can use a query of this form:

```
SELECT id, CONCAT(lname,', ',fname) AS name FROM staff ORDER BY name
```

For the multiple-page directory with a subindex page per letter, the query is similar but limited to entries for names beginning with a specific letter. For example, the following query retrieves names beginning with "W":

```
SELECT id, CONCAT(lname,', ',fname) AS name FROM staff
WHERE lname LIKE 'W%' ORDER BY name
```

In both cases, the query also selects the id column. That value is needed to make the links in the item list point to the proper record associated with the name, because we'll be generating hyperlinks from the query results. The name becomes the label that's visible to the user in the index page, and the ID is used to construct a URL that invokes the application again and tells it to display a particular staff entry.

Presenting a Single-Page Directory

The script staffs.pl that presents the staff directory using a single page handles only two tasks: displaying the index page and displaying individual entries. The URLs for these two cases look like this:

```
.../staffs.pl          present index page
.../staffs.pl?id=n     present record number n
```

The main part of the program containing the dispatch logic is correspondingly simple:

```perl
#! /usr/bin/perl -w
# staffs.pl - staff directory, single-page index

use strict;
use lib qw(/usr/local/apache/lib/perl);
use CGI qw(:standard :netscape escapeHTML);
use WebDB;

print header (), start_html (-title => "Staff Directory", -bgcolor => "white");

my $dbh = WebDB::connect ();

my $id = WebDB::trim (param ("id"));
if ($id ne "")                # ID is present, display that entry
{
    display_entry ($dbh, $id);
}
else                         # no ID given, display index page
{
    display_index ($dbh);
}

$dbh->disconnect ();

print end_html ();

exit (0);
```

Note that the use CGI statement includes the :netscape group. That's because the index page generation code uses the center() function, which is part of that group.

It's easier to format an individual entry for display than to construct the index (particularly because our staff table is so pathetically minimal!), so let's get that out of the way first. display_entry() takes arguments for the database handle and entry ID. It looks up the entry, prints its contents, and also provides a link back to the index page:

```perl
sub display_entry
{
my ($dbh, $id) = @_;
my ($sth, $ref);

    $sth = $dbh->prepare ("SELECT * FROM staff WHERE id = ?");
    $sth->execute ($id);
    $ref = $sth->fetchrow_hashref ();
    $sth->finish ();
    if (!$ref)
    {
        print p (escapeHTML ("No record for ID $id was found."));
        return;
    }

    # Display contents of record

    print p (escapeHTML ("ID: $ref->{id}"));
    print p (escapeHTML ("Name: $ref->{lname}, $ref->{fname}"));
    print p (escapeHTML ("Position: $ref->{position}"));

    # Display a link back to the index page

    print hr (), p ("[" . a ({-href => url ()}, "index") . "]");
}
```

Index page construction is the more interesting part. For a single-page index, the elements of the navigation bar point to other locations within the same page. The per-letter sections of the page to which the bar elements point can be marked with anchor tags of the following form, where c is a letter of the alphabet:

```html
<a name="c">c</a>
```

To refer to these markers, the elements of the bar consist of hyperlinks like this:

```html
<a href="#c">c</a>
```

The '#' character indicates a relative link to a location within the same page. The function gen_nav_bar() creates these links by determining the letters for which there are applicable staff table records and turning them into hyperlinks that point to each section of the index page:

```perl
sub gen_nav_bar
{
my $dbh = shift;
my ($letter_ref, @bar);
```

```
    # Get reference to array of letters represented by staff entries

    $letter_ref = $dbh->selectcol_arrayref (
                        "SELECT DISTINCT UPPER(LEFT(lname,1)) AS letter
                        FROM staff ORDER BY letter");
    return () if !$letter_ref || !@{$letter_ref};    # error or empty result?

    # Turn each letter into a relative link to the corresponding
    # section of index page

    return (map { "[" . a ({-href => "#$_"}, $_) . "]\n" } @{$letter_ref});
}
```

The index page itself is generated by `display_index()`, which calls `gen_nav_bar()` to construct the navigation bar, and then displays it above and below the list of names:

```
sub display_index
{
my $dbh = shift;
my ($sth, @nav_bar, @item_list);
my $cur_letter = "";

    @nav_bar = gen_nav_bar ($dbh);
    if (!@nav_bar)
    {
        print p ("The directory has no entries.");
        return;
    }
    print p (a ({-name => "top"},
                "Select a letter to go to that part of the directory:"));
    print hr (), center (@nav_bar), hr ();

    # Retrieve and display the list of items, grouped by initial letter

    $sth = $dbh->prepare (
                    "SELECT id, CONCAT(lname,', ',fname) AS name
                    FROM staff ORDER BY name");
    $sth->execute ();
    while (my ($id, $name) = $sth->fetchrow_array ())
    {
        # If we've arrived at a new letter, begin a new list
        if ($cur_letter ne uc (substr ($name, 0, 1)))
        {
            # Print any cached list for previous letter
            print ul (li (\@item_list)) if @item_list;
            # Set up for new list
            @item_list = ();
            $cur_letter = uc (substr ($name, 0, 1));
            print p (strong (a ({-name => "$cur_letter"}, $cur_letter))
```

continues

continued

```
                            . " [" . a ({-href => "#top"}, "index") . "]");
        }
        # Save current item in list
        push (@item_list,
                a ({-href => url () . "?id=$id"}, escapeHTML ($name)));
    }
    $sth->finish ();

    # Print final cached list
    print ul (li (\@item_list)) if @item_list;

    # Display navigation bar again
    print hr (), center (@nav_bar), hr ();
}
```

The entry list is displayed in sections, grouped by letter. Each section displays the letter as a caption, together with a link to the top of the page so that the user can get to the navigation bar easily. Within each section of the index, names are displayed using a bullet list.

Generating this kind of display requires us to notice while processing the entries when we begin each new section of the list, so that we can display appropriate caption letters at the beginning of each section. display_index() uses $cur_letter to track the section. Each time a mismatch occurs between $cur_letter and the initial letter of the name in the current record, we've gotten to a new section of the index.

That's all there is to it. Use the cr_staff_tbl.sql script provided in the webdb distribution to create the staff table and populate it with some sample data. Then install staffs.pl in your script directory, request it from your browser, and click away to navigate through the staff directory.

Presenting a Multiple-Page Directory

The script staffm.pl presents the multiple-page version of the staff directory. It has to handle three tasks: generating the main index page, generating the subindex pages, and displaying individual entries. The URLs for these tasks look like this:

```
.../staffm.pl              present main index page
.../staffm.pl?letter=c     present subindex page for letter c
.../staffm.pl?id=n         present record number n
```

The main part of the application is quite similar to that of staffs.pl; the only difference is that it also checks for a letter parameter and invokes display_subindex() if it's present:

```
#! /usr/bin/perl -w
# staffm.pl - staff directory, multiple-page index
```

```
use strict;
use lib qw(/usr/local/apache/lib/perl);
use CGI qw(:standard :netscape escapeHTML);
use WebDB;

print header (), start_html (-title => "Staff Directory", -bgcolor => "white");

my $dbh = WebDB::connect ();

my $id = WebDB::trim (param ("id"));
my $letter = WebDB::trim (param ("letter"));
if ($id ne "")                  # ID is present, display that entry
{
    display_entry ($dbh, $id);
}
elsif ($letter ne "")           # index letter is present, display subindex
{
    display_subindex ($dbh, $letter);
}
else                            # no params given, display main index page
{
    display_index ($dbh);
}

$dbh->disconnect ();

print end_html ();

exit (0);
```

display_entry() is the same for staffm.pl as for staffs.pl; no need to show it here.
display_index(), on the other hand, is much simpler than the staffs.pl version. It
needs only a navigation bar pointing to the subindex pages. You could pretty this page
up a little with some descriptive text, but staffm.pl doesn't get too fancy in this
regard. It just prints a short paragraph, the navigation bar, and a count indicating the
number of entries in the directory:

```
sub display_index
{
my $dbh = shift;
my (@nav_bar, $count);

    @nav_bar = gen_nav_bar ($dbh, "");
    if (!@nav_bar)
    {
        print p ("The directory has no entries.");
        return;
    }

    print p ("Welcome to the staff directory.\n"
            . "Entries are listed by last name.\n"
            . "Please select a letter below to find the person\n"
            . "you're looking for.");
```

continues

continued

```
    print hr (), center (@nav_bar), hr ();

    # Show how many entries the directory contains

    $count = $dbh->selectrow_array ("SELECT COUNT(*) FROM staff");
    print p ("The directory contains $count entries.");
}
```

The real work happens in display_subindex(), which, given a letter, retrieves the corresponding records for that letter and displays them. This is tantamount to displaying a single section of the single-page index:

```
sub display_subindex
{
my ($dbh, $letter) = @_;
my ($sth, @nav_bar, @item_list);

    @nav_bar = gen_nav_bar ($dbh, $letter);
    if (!@nav_bar)
    {
        print p ("The directory has no entries.");
        return;
    }

    print p ("Staff directory entries for the letter '$letter'");
    print hr (), center (@nav_bar), hr ();

    # Retrieve and display the list of items for a specific letter

    $sth = $dbh->prepare (
                    "SELECT id, CONCAT(lname,', ',fname) AS name
                    FROM staff WHERE lname LIKE ? ORDER BY name");
    $sth->execute ($letter . "%");
    while (my ($id, $name) = $sth->fetchrow_array ())
    {
        # Save current item in list
        push (@item_list,
                a ({-href => url () . "?id=$id"}, escapeHTML ($name)));
    }
    $sth->finish ();

    # Print list
    print ul (li (\@item_list)) if @item_list;

    # Display navigation bar again
    print hr (), center (@nav_bar), hr ();
}
```

The version of gen_nav_bar() in staffm.pl is a little more complex than for the single-page index. The URLs reinvoke staffm.pl to display a particular page of the directory. It also takes some care to generate static text rather than a link, if the link would point to the current page (that's why display_subindex() passes a letter to it as an argument):[3]

```
sub gen_nav_bar
{
my ($dbh, $letter) = @_;
my $letter_ref;

    # Get reference to array of distinct letters represented by staff entries

    $letter_ref = $dbh->selectcol_arrayref (
                        "SELECT DISTINCT UPPER(LEFT(lname,1)) AS letter
                        FROM staff ORDER BY letter");
    return () if !$letter_ref || !@{$letter_ref};   # error or empty result?

    # Turn each letter into a relative link to corresponding section
    # section of index page. If the link would point to the current page
    # (indicated by $letter), generate static text instead.

    return (map { "["
            . ($letter eq $_ ? $_ : a ({-href => url () . "?letter=$_"}, $_))
            . "]\n" } @{$letter_ref});
}
```

Suggested Modifications

Modify staffs.pl or staffm.pl to provide multiple indexing styles. For example, the application could provide the option of displaying entries grouped not just by name but by position. (Don't forget to index position to make lookups on that column more efficient.)

The two-tier index approach employed by staffm.pl can be extended to more levels. If your organization is quite large, for example, you could add another level that organizes the directory into departments and contains links that take you to named-based indexes for the staff members in each department. What you have to balance here is the size of the lowest-level index pages versus the number of levels. You can add levels to achieve a finer subdivision of records at the lowest level, but then it takes longer to navigate down through the index. One way to help users when you add levels is to combine link-based navigation with a search form. You can use the techniques described earlier in this chapter to provide a form for finding staff members by name or position, for example.

---

3. display_index() also passes a second argument, but the value is the empty string. This matches none of the link letters, so all the links are active—exactly what we want for the main index page.

The material in this chapter has covered search capabilities provided by means of search forms and by means of link–based navigation techniques. The examples shown here should give you lots of ideas for writing applications that provide search access to your own tables. However, I should point out before you dive in and start coding that you may want to have a look at Chapter 8. In that chapter, we'll cover the topic of preserving application information from one invocation of a script to another, including techniques for doing so without sending it all over the network for each request. If you're implementing search applications that manage multiple-page result set displays, you can use sessions as an alternative method for storing information associated with navigation links, rather than passing a lot of information in the URLs for those links.

8

Session Management

I N THIS CHAPTER, WE'LL CONSIDER VARIOUS WAYS that applications can keep track of "state," a term that refers to the current condition or characteristics of an object or activity. For a shopping cart, state consists of the items that you've chosen so far. If you're taking an online quiz, the state information includes the current question and perhaps a running total of the number of questions you've answered correctly or incorrectly. A survey may be so long that it's conducted using several smaller pages rather than one long page that involves a lot of vertical scrolling. State for a survey presented in this fashion indicates the page you're currently at and your responses to the questions you've already answered. State information also allows your responses for the various pages to be grouped properly so that they don't get mixed up with those from other users.

These activities take place over a series of pages that are logically grouped and considered parts of a larger unit—a unit called a *session*. Unfortunately, HTTP is not very good for session management because it's a stateless protocol that makes no provision for allowing a Web server to associate one request with any other request. Statelessness helps make HTTP a simple protocol, but it causes problems when you're trying to write applications that need to keep track of what the user is doing. Without state information, a shopping cart forgets each of your items as you pick the next, a quiz won't remember your current score, and a multiple-page survey can't figure out which page to present when you select the Continue button to go to the next page.

All these types of activities do successfully take place on the Web, of course, so obviously there are ways of coping with the stateless nature of HTTP. It's just that you have to take care of managing state information yourself. One common technique is for the client to send an ID value to the server with each request that takes place during a session. That's what we did in Chapter 5, "Writing Form-Based Applications," for our electronic greeting card application that allows a card to be constructed across the course of several pages. Each card is associated with an ID value that gets carried along from one request to another, transmitted either as a hidden field in a form or as a parameter in a URL. We'll explore that technique and others in more detail throughout this chapter.

As just described, state information is useful for conducting sessions that tie together requests that occur one after the other (as for the shopping cart, the quiz, and the survey). You can also use state to implement resumable activities such as an online chess game that you can suspend when you're tired of playing, and then continue playing where you left off at a later date. Another use for state is to affect a set of requests that don't necessarily make up what you'd normally think of as a session. For example, a news site might allow you to create a user profile where you specify the article categories in which you're most interested. ("Skip the current events and society page, just show me the sports and editorials.") The profile influences how the Web server at that site responds to you on all subsequent visits to the site.

State maintenance and session management often are used in conjunction with security and authentication techniques. For example, a state-maintaining application may gather information such as a credit card or taxpayer ID number that needs to be kept private. In this case, you may want to establish a secure connection before having the user provide any sensitive information. Or an application may require that you authenticate at the beginning of a session by providing a username and password, and then use your name to figure out which user profile applies to any requests you issue after that. Security and authentication are important topics, but we'll defer consideration of them until Chapter 9, "Security and Privacy Issues."

State Maintenance Techniques

Several techniques have been developed to cope with the stateless nature of HTTP so that applications can provide a measure of continuity across requests. Some of these methods use the client for storing the information; others keep the information on the server.

Client-Side State Maintenance

For client-side techniques, the state information is maintained by the client and submitted to the server. These methods are described here, using the online quiz scenario to illustrate how each one might be used to keep track of state information:

- Hidden fields enable you to embed information in a form that is sent to the client, where it remains stored in the page displayed by the browser until the user transmits it back to the Web server. For the quiz, you can generate a form that includes hidden fields that indicate the current numbers of correct and incorrect responses received so far. Each time the user submits an answer to a question, you update the totals and include the new values in the next form sent to the user's browser.

- You can include state information as part of a URL. For example, the `action` parameter for each form that presents a quiz question could include in the URL the number of correct and incorrect responses received from the user for the previous questions. If you specify that the form contents should be returned as a `GET` request, then when the user answers the current question and submits the form, the browser will encode the values of fields in the form and add them to the URL. For example, the URL that returns the response for the twenty-second question might look something like this after the browser adds a parameter to indicate the user's answer:

  ```
  http://www.snake.net/cgi-perl/quiz.pl?correct=18;incorrect=3;answer=b
  ```

- Cookies are a client-side mechanism invented specifically to allow state maintenance.[1] Cookies are transmitted back and forth in the headers of requests and responses exchanged by the client and server. When the server wants the browser to store a value, it sends the information using a `Set-Cookie:` header. For example, the quiz scores could be initialized by sending the client a `Set-Cookie:` header like this one along with the page that presents the first question:

  ```
  Set-Cookie: quiz-scores=incorrect&0&correct&0
  ```

  Each time the user submits an answer to a question, the browser returns the `quiz-scores` cookie in the request headers using a `Cookie:` header. The server extracts the cookie value, updates the totals, and sends back a new `Set-Cookie:` header with the next page so that the browser can update the `quiz-scores` values it is storing. For more information about the cookie specification, see Appendix B, "References and Further Reading."

---

1. If a worse name than "cookie" was ever invented for nomenclature purposes, I don't know what it is.

For each of these techniques, the server sends the client the initial state information to be stored. The client returns this information with each subsequent request in the session, possibly receiving in return updated information from the server after the server processes the request. The server need never remember the state values because they are stored on the client. It needs to know only how to handle information received from the client (which includes the current state data and the new response). As the server processes the request, it updates the state information and returns it to the client, where it remains until the client submits the next request.

Because information is stored by the client when you use these techniques, they require no reconfiguration of the Web server. However, client-side state maintenance is subject to certain drawbacks:

- You might accumulate large amounts of information, all of which is sent back and forth for each request. If you implement a shopping cart that stores the currently chosen items on the client end, the amount of information grows with each new selection. This can be a problem, because if you store information in the URL or using hidden fields in a form that's sent to the server using the GET method rather than POST, you may find the information being truncated silently. Cookies often have a size limitation as well (about 4KB in many implementations).

- Some kinds of information really shouldn't be sent back to the client at all, such as personal or private information. Suppose you require a user to supply a password to gain access to a form for editing a preferences profile. If you put the password in a hidden field so that the user need not enter it again when the editing form is submitted, you expose the password to additional snooping as it makes another round trip over the network.

- Information stored on the client end is subject to modification by the user and therefore not necessarily trustworthy. If you include a value in the state data that indicates the user's access privilege level for the information in your database, the user could change the value to a higher level by editing this information. Hidden fields can be seen easily using the browser's View Source command, and the form contents can be modified easily. (The method is described in Chapter 9.) Cookies can be viewed and modified by using an editor to open the cookie file created by the browser. The more data you store on the client side, the worse the problem becomes.

- Use of cookies is subject to variation in client capabilities. You can't use them to handle requests from a client browser that is so old it doesn't support the cookie protocol. Cookies also require cooperation on the part of the user. Browsers that can handle cookies typically enable the user to indicate whether to receive them; many users are suspicious of cookies and refuse to accept them.

- Information stored on the client side can be extremely transient. If the user closes the browser window in the middle of a session, any state information stored in hidden fields is lost and the user must start over. The same is true for state information included in URLs, with the exception that it's possible to set a bookmark to retain the link. (This can be good or bad. One use for bookmarking is to allow the user to suspend a session and return to it later. On the other hand, if the user sets a bookmark to a page generated by an application that has time-limited sessions, and then returns to the bookmarked page only to find the session has expired, the result is frustration over the now-invalid link.) Normally, if you want to maintain state information for an extended time on the client side, hidden fields and URLs are unsuitable. Cookies work better for long-term data because they can be given a specific lifetime.

Despite these drawbacks, client-side techniques are easy to use, and you'll probably find them perfectly suited for some applications, especially simpler ones. For applications where client-side state storage isn't good enough, however, it's necessary to manage state data on the server.

Server-Side State Maintenance

An alternative to client-side techniques is to store state information on the server side. In this case, the client announces itself to the server on each request using some kind of client identifier, and the server associates the ID with the appropriate state information that it maintains on the client's behalf. Some techniques you can use for server-side state maintenance are as follows:

- You can take advantage of the existence of the Web server as a long-running process. If your Web server allows it, you can ask it to store information for you in its own memory, and then access that information on subsequent requests.

- You can store state information in more traditional repositories such as a file or a database.

Use of server memory is applicable primarily for storing small amounts of information; it's not a good technique when you need to maintain potentially large amounts of data. If your storage requirements are significant, files or databases offer much greater capacity.

Server memory also is unsuitable if you need durable or persistent information that exists until you delete it explicitly. Under Windows, for example, Apache runs as a single process, and server memory is lost each time the server is restarted. Under UNIX, Apache runs using a multiple-process architecture involving several children. This means you can't rely on getting the same child for each request issued during a session, but the children can use shared memory to communicate with each other. (You can use the Perl IPC::Shareable module to implement a shared storage area.) State information stored this way survives the termination of any given child process, but still is lost across machine restarts. If you need persistence of state data, you should use files or a database.

Several characteristics of server-side state maintenance techniques distinguish them from client-side methods:

- With client-side state storage, the client provides all the state data on each request, so requests are self-identifying. When you store information on the server side, you must have some way to uniquely identify each client so that you can associate requests from a given client with the appropriate state data.

- Server-side storage reduces the amount of information sent back and forth. For session-tracking purposes, the client need not provide all state information on each request, just a session ID and whatever new information is specific to a given request. In a shopping cart, for example, the client need only transmit each item as it is selected, not the entire contents of the cart.

- Server-side storage is more secure, because clients cannot tamper with it; they cannot see or modify state information except what you allow to be seen or modified. It's also more secure in terms of exposure to other users; the fewer times you send information back and forth over the network, the better. (Of course, if you must be really secure against snooping, you should use an encrypted connection.)

- Server-side state management requires more complex server support. If you want to use a file as a state container, you must be concerned about using locking protocols to keep multiple processes from writing to the file at the same time. It's also necessary to institute storage and retrieval procedures. A database eliminates these problems, because it handles locking issues for you, and storage and retrieval is a matter of writing the correct SQL statements. But of course, if you want to use a database to store state information, you must set one up first. In either case, state maintenance consumes more processing, memory, and disk resources on the server host compared to client-side methods.

- If you want permanent storage, server-side techniques make this easy because you can put the information in a file or a database. On the other hand, if you don't want a session record to be permanent, you have to provide a mechanism for identifying and deleting expired sessions. Expiration of state information is easy for client-side methods, because the server need not keep track of when to dispose of it. With hidden fields or URLs, information expires automatically if the user closes the browser window or moves on to visit another site. With cookies, you have two options: Set an expiration date in the cookie and let the browser delete it when that time arrives; or specify no explicit expiration date, in which case the browser deletes the cookie when it exits.

- Server-side techniques may result in orphan sessions—sessions that users begin but never complete. A person who starts adding items to their shopping cart at your online store and then decides to leave without buying anything creates an orphan session. Here, too, you must be concerned about identifying and expiring sessions that are no longer of value.

- Server-side storage enables you to do some things you just cannot do with client-side techniques, at least not without some horrendous hackery. One of these is coordination of state data among multiple clients. If you're trying to implement a game that enables people to play each other over the Internet, client-side storage requires you to store state in multiple clients, leading to synchronization problems. Server-side methods enable you to centralize state information so that multiple clients can access it more easily. You can also synthesize shared resources using state data gathered from multiple clients, such as a high scores list based on all previous player sessions.

The preceding comparison is summarized in Table 8.1. In general, it's more work to manage state information on the server side, but it's also more secure and reliable. We'll concentrate on server-side methods for the rest of this chapter. Of these techniques, storage of state information in the Web server's memory doesn't provide persistence, so we won't discuss that further. That leaves storage of state data in files or a database. If you don't want to worry about locking protocols or inventing storage and retrieval conventions, however, that rules out files. The only remaining choice for server-side management of state information is to store it in a database. It is, of course, a complete coincidence that we arrive at this conclusion in a book about MySQL! Funny how that works.

Table 8.1   **Comparison of Client-Side and Server-Side Session Information Storage Methods**

	Client-Side Methods			Server-Side Methods		
	Hidden Field	*URL Parameter*	*Cookie*	*Server Memory*	*File*	*Database*
Suitable for Long-Term Storage			x		x	x
Survives Server Restarts	x	x	x	Perhaps	x	x
Survives Host Restarts	x	x	x		x	x
Automatic Expiration	x	x	x			
Hackable by Client	x	x	x			
Potential for Exposure to Other Clients	High	High	High	Low	Low	Low

Client Identification

To use server-side state maintenance, you must be able to uniquely identify each client. Otherwise, you have no way of grouping requests from a given client. But just how *do* you identify the client? The problem is a difficult one, because browsers don't provide any information that is guaranteed to be both unique and persistent. This section describes some techniques you can use to identify clients, classified into two general categories: passive and active. Passive methods use some form of information that is intrinsic to the client itself, such as the IP number of the host from which the request is received. For active methods, the server generates an ID and sends it to the client when the session begins, and the client returns the ID with each subsequent request until the session ends.

Passive Client Identification Methods

I'm going to describe passive identification techniques briefly, but only for the purpose of disparaging them. The main point you should take away from this discussion is that passive identification is unreliable.

One way to identify clients passively is to use their IP number. When the Web server sets up the CGI environment for a script, some of that information characterizes the client. For example, the REMOTE_ADDR variable indicates the client host's IP number. It's tempting to use this variable in your scripts to distinguish one client from another, but unfortunately client IP numbers are not necessarily unique or stable:

- On a host such as a UNIX box that allows multiple users to log in, many users can run browsers at the same time. Requests from all these users originate from the same IP address, which therefore does not serve as a unique client identifier.

- Some Internet services route requests from their users through a proxy server. All such requests appear to come from the same host, regardless of the real point of origin. The same is true for sites that use NAT or other forms of address translation to map multiple client machines onto the same IP number. (This is an increasingly common situation in homes and small offices that have multiple machines but pass all traffic through a router that serves as the single point of connection to the Internet.)

- It's possible for a client's IP number to change periodically, causing any IP-based check to fail. Client hosts that obtain their IP number from a DHCP server may undergo address changes each time their IP lease expires and they obtain a new number from the server. If a service runs multiple proxy servers that handle users in round-robin fashion, a client's IP address changes as it cycles through these servers.

The same limitations also apply to client identification attempts based on host names, which are closely tied to IP numbers.

Is IP-Based Client Identification Completely Worthless?

IP numbers and host names are of no use for applications that serve the Internet at large. However, they may be of some value in more highly constrained situations. If your organization exercises complete control over an intranet consisting entirely of single-user hosts with static IP addresses, for example, it may be reasonable to assume for identification purposes that each client's IP number or host name is unique and provides a reliable indicator of request origin.

Another way to attempt passive identification is to use the time of a client's initial connection. Each moment in time is distinct from every other, after all. Unfortunately, that property of the natural universe does not translate well into the world of computers that divide time into discrete slices. There's no way to guarantee that two requests won't arrive so close together as to occur during the same time slice. If this happens, two clients assume the same identity. A further problem with time-of-connection identification is that it allows an imposter to claim "my initial connection was at time t," and gain access to any session that happened to begin at that time.

Conclusion: Passive techniques for identifying clients don't work very well.

Active Client Identification Methods

The alternative to passive client identification is to play an active role on the server end. The procedure goes like this:

1. When a client begins a session, generate an identifier on the server side and remember it for later so that you can associate it with the state data you're maintaining for the session.

2. Give the identifier to the client and require that the client return it with all subsequent requests that are part of the session.

3. Each time a request arrives that contains the identifier, look up the associated session and interpret the request in the context of the session's current state.

4. When the session ends, forget the identifier or mark it inactive to cause any additional use of the identifier by the client to fail.

One way to assign client identifiers to new sessions is to use a sequence generator such as an `AUTO_INCREMENT` column. This is easy to implement, because MySQL manages for you the details of making sure each request for an identifier is satisfied with a unique value. Another active identification method is to require users to begin a session by providing a username and password. If the name and password check out okay, you can use the name as the client ID value. But do these techniques provide good client identifiers? To answer this question, we must ask what characteristics distinguish good client identifiers from bad ones. Here are a couple that are important:

- Each identifier should be unique, so that you don't mix up clients with each other.

- Identifiers should not be guessable. You want the ID that you give to a client to be used only by that client, not by someone else who is trying to hijack sessions and just happens to be able to guess a valid identifier. Basically, this means your identifiers should be random and chosen from a large pool of possibilities.

When assessed against these characteristics, how do `AUTO_INCREMENT` values and login names stack up as client identifiers? In both cases, the values are unique, so they satisfy the first criterion of good identifiers. However, both methods involve easily guessable values. `AUTO_INCREMENT` values form a linear sequence, so they're extremely predictable. Usernames don't form a sequence, but they're still much more easily guessed than random values. If you're using a login phase in an application, it's a good idea to generate a random value after a successful login and use that rather than the username for the client identifier.

Implementing Session Support

For the remainder of this chapter, we'll discuss how to provide session support that uses active client identification and server-side storage of session records in a database. We'll also write a few applications that demonstrate how to implement sessions, using the following general procedure:

1. When a user connects initially, generate a random session ID, send it to the client, and initialize a session record in the database.

2. As each subsequent request arrives from the user, extract the session ID and use it to retrieve the session record. Update the record as necessary using any new information in the request.

3. At the end of each request, take one of two actions: Close the session if you still need it for future operations, or delete it if you don't. If a customer adds an item to a shopping cart but is not done shopping, for example, you'd just close the session. After the customer has finished shopping and you've stored the final order, you'd delete the session.

The mechanism for transmitting the session ID between the client and server from request to request is application-specific. Common techniques propagate identifiers in cookies, hidden fields, or URLs. (Those methods should sound familiar; they're the client-side methods discussed earlier in the chapter. In other words, even though server-side storage of state data reduces the amount of information transmitted with each request, you still need a bit of client-side information to hold the session ID.)

What to Include in the Session Record

There are certain standard kinds of information you may want to include in the session record. Most obviously, the record must contain a session ID, otherwise you cannot identify the session. In addition, a couple of other values can be helpful for administrative purposes. You might want to include a timestamp indicating session creation time or last modification time for expiration purposes. If you share a session table between applications, you may want to include an application identifier as well, so that you can identify which application each session record belongs to. (If you use a separate session table per application, this is not a problem.)

The session record generally also will include application-specific data, the content of which depends on individual application requirements. In a multiple-page survey application, for example, you might store the intermediate responses in the session record until the user completes the survey. If you have an application that enables people to request an insurance policy quote online, you may guide the user through a series of forms to gather the information you need. A session record can be useful for storing this information until the request has been completed.

If you design a session table for a particular application, you can include columns in the table specifically for the types of session information you want to record. This is also true when you share a session table among applications, as long as they all store the same kind of state data. If you want to share a session table among applications that have differing requirements, however, you need a uniform storage mechanism that will work for each application that uses the table. This can be accomplished by using a `BLOB` or `TEXT` column large enough to accommodate all your data and storing everything in that column. One way to do this is to serialize your state information (and that's what we'll do in this chapter). Serialization converts information to a single string value that can be unserialized later to recover the original data. If you want to access the session table using programs written in several languages, however, you may encounter compatibility issues between different serialization algorithms. A way around this problem is to store your session data using some representation that is neutral with respect to the programming languages you're using. For example, XML can be used to represent arbitrary session data—assuming you can find a suitable XML processor for each of the languages you're using to write scripts.

The *Apache::Session* Module

We could implement all the session management code ourselves using the guidelines discussed so far, but an alternative is to use the `Apache::Session` module, which already does much of what we need. This module has the following characteristics:

- It uses an algorithm based on MD5 (Message Digest #5) to generate random session IDs that are not easily guessable by intruders.

- It uses server-side storage so that clients cannot modify session information directly.

- The module can use either files or a database, which provides persistent storage for session data that survives server and machine restarts. We'll use MySQL to store session records, but `Apache::Session` also supports several other database engines such as Postgres and Sybase. This may be helpful if you need to port your code to another database.

- Session records are represented as hash structures, and `Apache::Session` ties these hashes to database access methods. This makes it easy to store and access session data just by referring to hash members.

- Session values are stored in the database using serialization. In this way, `Apache::Session` imposes little constraint on the type of data you can store in session records.

- `Apache::Session` handles locking issues for you; while one client has a session open, no other client can modify it.

Setting Up to Use *Apache::Session*

You should get and install the `Apache::Session` module from the CPAN if you don't already have it. `Apache::Session` relies on `Storable` to serialize session data, so make sure you have that module, too. If you need other modules that are missing, `Apache::Session` should tell you what they are when you try to build it.

After you've installed `Apache::Session`, use the following commands to read its general and MySQL-specific documentation:

```
% perldoc Apache::Session
% perldoc Apache::Session::MySQL
% perldoc Apache::Session::Lock::MySQL
% perldoc Apache::Session::Store::MySQL
```

The information provided by the last of these commands shows that to use `Apache::Session` with MySQL, you must create a table named `sessions` that contains the following columns:

```
CREATE TABLE sessions
(
    id          CHAR(32) NOT NULL PRIMARY KEY,   # session identifier
    a_session   TEXT                             # session data
)
```

Whenever `Apache::Session` creates a new session record, it generates a unique identifier and stores it in the `id` column. Any session values you add to the record are stored in the `a_session` column after being serialized. (You need not worry about creating the ID or storing the data; those operations are handled transparently for you.) `Apache::Session` itself manipulates only the two columns shown; although you can add other columns to the table if you like, they'll be ignored unless you provide your own mechanism for manipulating the additional columns externally to `Apache::Session`.

The table used by `Apache::Session` must be named `sessions`; there is no provision for specifying an alternative name.[2] You can put a `sessions` table in any database you like, but for our applications, I'll assume here that it's in the `webdb` database. Make sure that the table is both readable and writable to the MySQL account that your scripts use for connecting to the MySQL server.

Opening a Session

To use `Apache::Session` with MySQL, include the appropriate use statement in your scripts and declare a hash structure in which to store your session data:

```
use Apache::Session::MySQL;
my %session;
```

When you're ready to open a session, invoke `tie` and pass it several arguments: the session hash, the name of the submodule that `Apache::Session` should use for managing sessions, a session identifier, and attributes that indicate how to communicate with MySQL. The attributes can take two forms, because `Apache::Session` can use the database handle associated with an existing connection, or it can establish a new MySQL connection. To use an existing database handle, open the session like this:

```
$dbh = WebDB::connect ();   # get a database handle
tie %session, "Apache::Session::MySQL", $sess_id,
        {
            Handle => $dbh,
            LockHandle => $dbh
        };
```

If you don't use an existing connection, you must supply the appropriate parameters, to allow `Apache::Session` to establish the connection itself:

```
tie %session, "Apache::Session::MySQL", $sess_id,
        {
            DataSource => "DBI:mysql:host=localhost;database=webdb",
            UserName => "webdev",
            Password => "webdevpass",
            LockDataSource => "DBI:mysql:host=localhost;database=webdb",
            LockUserName => "webdev",
            LockPassword => "webdevpass"
        };
```

In either case, the value of `$sess_id` indicates the session record you want to use. To create a new session, pass a value of `undef`. Otherwise, the value should be the ID of an existing session record.

---

2. This means the table will be shared among applications. If you really want multiple **sessions** tables, you must put them in different databases.

If you pass the handle for an existing connection to `tie`, `Apache::Session` leaves the connection open when you close or delete the session. You should close the connection yourself when you're done with it. If `Apache::Session` itself establishes a connection to the MySQL server when you open a session, it also closes the connection when you close or delete the session. An implication of this behavior is that if you intend to manage multiple simultaneous sessions from within the same script, it's probably better to open the connection yourself and pass the resulting database handle to all the session-initiation calls. Otherwise, you will have a separate connection to MySQL open for each session.

An additional point to keep in mind when you open a session using a handle to an existing connection: Don't close the connection while the session is still open. If you do, `Apache::Session` won't be able to save the session contents to the database!

Accessing Session Data

After you've successfully opened a session, you store values in it by creating them as hash values. To store a username in your session, for example, assign it to an appropriately named hash element:

```
$session{user_name} = $user_name;
```

To retrieve the value, access the same element:

```
$user_name = $session{user_name};
```

As a more involved example, another way to use a session record is to store and retrieve form elements. To load a set of form values into the hash, you can use the following loop. It calls `param()` to get the names of the parameters that are present, and then extracts the value of each one and stuffs it into the session record. The trick here is that you can't store multiple-value elements (such as a set of check box values) as a scalar, so they must be converted to array references:

```
foreach my $name (param ())
{
    my @val = param ($name);
    $session{$name} = (@val > 1 ? [ @val ] : shift (@val));
}
```

Conversely, to install the contents of a session record into the parameter environment, do this:

```
foreach my $name (keys (%session))
{
    param (-name => $name, -value => $session{$name});
}
```

Then you can generate and display a form, and those elements having names corresponding to session hash keys will be filled in automatically. (This assumes that you take advantage of CGI.pm's sticky form behavior and don't specify the `override` parameter when you call functions that generate form fields.)

When you choose key names for session hash values, they can be whatever you like, except that they shouldn't begin with underscores. Such names are reserved by Apache::Session for its own purposes, although the only one it actually uses currently is _session_id for the session identifier.

Closing or Terminating a Session

When you're done using a session object in a script, you can release (close) it by calling untie():

```
untie (%session);
```

If you made any changes to the session, Apache::Session normally saves it back to the database automatically when you close it; you don't have to take any explicit action. This behavior is subject to one caveat: A change may not be noticed if a session object references a more complex structure such as an array and you change an element of the structure. (This happens because you're not actually changing the value of the session hash element itself, you're changing the value of the thing the element points to.) To handle this situation, you can force an update using a trivial assignment, such as the following one:

```
$session{_session_id} = $session{_session_id};
```

That's a harmless way of making the session manager think the session has been modified, causing it to save the record to the database when you close the session. You can use this technique with any session element, not just _session_id.

If you have a session open that you no longer need at all, remove it by deleting the session object:

```
tied (%session)->delete ();
```

untie() and delete() affect the underlying session record differently. When you close a session by calling untie(), you can reopen it later by specifying the appropriate session ID. If you delete a session by invoking delete(), the corresponding session record is removed from the sessions table and cannot be used again.

The *WebDB::Session* Module

To avoid repeating the session-opening code in each script that uses session management, let's encapsulate it into a module called WebDB::Session that acts as a front end to Apache::Session. The module also provides some other convenience routines. It has the following interface:

- Any script that needs the WebDB::Session module should reference it by including the following use statement:

    ```
    use WebDB::Session;
    ```

You need no use statement for Apache::Session, because all the details requiring that module will be handled internally by WebDB::Session.

- To open a session and obtain a reference to the session object, invoke the open()
  method:

      $sess_ref = WebDB::Session->open ($dbh, $sess_id);

  The first argument, $dbh, indicates the database handle to use. It should be a
  handle to an open connection to MySQL, or undef if you want open() to contact the MySQL server using built-in connection parameters. The $sess_id
  argument should be either the ID of an existing session or undef to create a
  new session.

- open() returns a reference to the session object, or undef to indicate an error. In
  the latter case, you can access the global variable $WebDB::Session::errstr to
  get the error message.

- To close a session or destroy it, use the close() or delete() methods:

      $sess_ref->close ();
      $sess_ref->delete ();

  These object-oriented methods are analogous to the corresponding untie() and
  delete() operations in Apache::Session that close and remove sessions.

- Because open() returns a reference to the hash that represents the session (not
  the hash itself), the syntax for setting or getting session values requires that you
  dereference the session object:

      $sess_ref->{user_name} = $user_name;   # set session value
      $user_name = $sess_ref->{user_name};   # get session value

  To make access to session data more generic, however, WebDB::Session provides
  an attr() accessor method as the preferred interface:

      $sess_ref->attr ("user_name", $user_name);   # set session attribute
      $user_name = $sess_ref->attr ("user_name");   # get session attribute

  Why bother doing this? Because setting and getting values this way is more
  abstract; it decouples session data access from the fact that the session is represented by a hash. That makes it easier to replace the underlying session mechanism if some day you decide to reimplement WebDB::Session without using
  Apache::Session at all.

  Another accessor method, session_id(), can be used to get the session ID from
  the record. This is a read-only method, because the session ID value is generated
  and assigned inside the module and should not be changed by your application.

Implementation of the WebDB::Session module is not very complicated. The module begins with a package statement, some use statements that reference the modules it needs, and a declaration for the global variable used to hold the error message if open() cannot open a session:

```
package WebDB::Session;

use strict;
use DBI;
use Apache::Session::MySQL;

# global variable for error message

$WebDB::Session::errstr = "";
```

The open() method initiates a session after examining its $dbh argument to determine whether to use an existing MySQL connection or to connect using the built-in default parameters. (You can change the defaults; those shown here are the same as the ones we used for the WebDB::connect() call.)

```
sub open
{
my ($type, $dbh, $sess_id) = @_;
my %session;    # session hash
my %attr;       # connection attributes
# default connection parameters
my $dsn = "DBI:mysql:host=localhost;database=webdb";
my $user_name = "webdev";
my $password = "webdevpass";

    # Set up connection attributes according to whether
    # or not we're using an existing connection

    if (defined ($dbh))      # use existing connection
    {
        %attr =
        (
            Handle => $dbh,
            LockHandle => $dbh
        );
    }
    else                     # use default connection parameters
    {
        %attr =
        (
            DataSource => $dsn,
            UserName => $user_name,
            Password => $password,
            LockDataSource => $dsn,
            LockUserName => $user_name,
            LockPassword => $password
```

continues

continued

```
            );
    }
    eval            # open session, putting tie within eval to trap errors
    {
        tie %session, "Apache::Session::MySQL", $sess_id, \%attr;
    };
    if ($@)         # session establishment failed
    {
        $WebDB::Session::errstr = $@;    # save error message
        return undef;
    }

    # get reference to session hash, bless it into class, and return it
    return (bless (\%session, $type));
}
```

For the most part, `WebDB::Session` behaves similarly to `Apache::Session` when opening a session. One thing that differs is handling of errors. If `Apache::Session` cannot
open a session, you get a noisy error message in your browser window and your script
dies. (This can occur, for example, if a user tries to resume a session for a record that
has been deleted.) We avoid this by wrapping the `tie` call within an `eval` block and
returning `undef` to indicate an error. Your scripts should check the return value of
`open()` and take appropriate action. The following example calls `open()` and prints a
message to indicate the cause of the problem if an error occurs:

```
defined ($sess_ref = WebDB::Session->open (undef, undef))
    or print p ("Could not create session: $WebDB::Session::errstr");
```

In practice, you'll probably find that `$WebDB::Session:errstr` contains technical information more useful to you as a developer than to end users of your applications. It
may be best to print its value using code that is enabled only during an application's
development cycle to help you see what's going on. You can disable it before deploy-
ing the application for production use.

The `close()` and `delete()` methods map onto the corresponding `Apache::Session`
calls for closing and destroying session objects:

```
sub close
{
my $self = shift;

    untie (%{$self});
}

sub delete
{
my $self = shift;

    tied (%{$self})->delete ();
}
```

The `attr()` accessor method through which you set or get session values takes either one or two arguments. The first argument names the data value you're referring to. If that is the only argument, `attr()` just returns the appropriate session value by extracting the corresponding hash element. If there is a second argument, `attr()` uses it to set the session value first before returning it:

```
sub attr
{
my $self = shift;

    return (undef) unless @_;           # no arguments
    $self->{$_[0]} = $_[1] if @_ > 1;   # two arguments; set value first
    return ($self->{$_[0]});            # return current value
}
```

If you access a session element that does not exist, `attr()` returns `undef`. If you want to store an array or a hash, you should store it by reference. When accessing it later, dereference the value to recover the original array or hash.

The `session_id()` method that returns the session identifier is nothing more than a call that invokes `attr()` for you with the name of the session ID key. This hides from your applications the magic name that `Apache::Session` uses for the ID and exposes its value using a public method instead:

```
sub session_id
{
my $self = shift;

    return ($self->{_session_id});
}
```

The `WebDB::Session` module file should be installed under some directory that is in the Perl search path used by your scripts, and should be named `WebDB/Session.pm` (or `WebDB\Session.pm` under Windows). On my system, I install it as `/usr/local/apache/lib/perl/WebDB/Session.pm`.

Passing Session IDs in URLs

As a demonstration of how `WebDB::Session` is used, this section describes a script, `stages_url.pl`, that manipulates sessions. To keep it simple, each session contains only one piece of state data: a `counter` value that keeps track of the stage the session is at, where "stage" is defined as the number of pages the script has displayed so far during the current session. `stages_url.pl` stores the counter on the server in the session record and uses the URL to pass the session ID from page to page so that script invocations can determine which session to use. This script illustrates the following session-related techniques:

- How to determine whether to begin a new session or continue an existing one
- How to retrieve session records and manipulate their contents

- How to terminate a session
- How to detect errors for cases when a session record cannot be created or cannot be found.

When you first invoke `stages_url.pl`, it creates a new session and initializes the stage counter. Then it displays a page that shows the session ID, the stage counter, a link for progressing to the next page, and another for terminating the session. The page looks like this (the ID varies from session to session):

```
Session ID: 341cbe58daa5da95f9ced74b7bf7726e
Session stage: 1

Select [this link] to continue to the next stage.
Select [this link] to quit.
```

If you select the first link to continue the session, the script presents another page that looks the same, except that the `Session stage` value increments by one. This happens as long as you keep selecting the "continue" link. When you select the "quit" link, the script displays a page that shows the final number of stages and a link enabling you to begin a new session:

```
Session ID 341cbe58daa5da95f9ced74b7bf7726e has ended after 4 stages.

Select [this link] to start a new session.
```

`stages_url.pl` determines what parameters are present in the URL and uses them to figure out what to do. Initially you invoke the script with no parameters using this URL:

```
http://www.snake.net/cgi-perl/stages_url.pl
```

The continue-session and terminate-session URLs are generated by the script itself and displayed as links so you can select them. Both URLs contain the session ID, and the terminate-session URL contains a `quit` parameter as well:

```
http://www.snake.net/cgi-perl/stages_url.pl?sess_id=xxx
http://www.snake.net/cgi-perl/stages_url.pl?sess_id=xxx;quit=1
```

`stages_url.pl` begins with a preamble that references the necessary modules. Then it checks the URL parameters, opens the session, and prints the appropriate type of page:

```
use strict;
use lib qw(/usr/local/apache/lib/perl);
use CGI qw(:standard escape escapeHTML);
use WebDB::Session;

my $sess_id;     # session ID
my $sess_ref;    # reference to session record

# Determine whether or not there is a session ID available.  If not,
# create a new session; otherwise, read the record for an existing session.

$sess_id = param ("sess_id");   # undef if no param (initial connection)
```

```
if (!defined ($sess_id))          # create new session
{
    defined ($sess_ref = WebDB::Session->open (undef, undef))
        or error ("Could not create new session: $WebDB::Session::errstr");
}
else                              # retrieve existing session
{
    defined ($sess_ref = WebDB::Session->open (undef, $sess_id))
        or error ("Could not retrieve session record for ID $sess_id: "
                   . $WebDB::Session::errstr);
}

# If this is a new session, initialize the stage counter

$sess_ref->attr ("count", 0) if !defined ($sess_ref->attr ("count"));

print header (),
    start_html (-title => "Session Stages", -bgcolor => "white");

if (!defined (param ("quit")))       # continue existing session
{
    display_next_page ($sess_ref);  # display page for first/next stage
    $sess_ref->close ();            # done with session; close it
}
else                                # terminate session
{
    display_last_page ($sess_ref);  # display termination page
    $sess_ref->delete ();           # destroy session for good
}

print end_html ();
```

stages_url.pl determines whether a session ID is available by looking for a sess_id parameter, and then creates a new session or retrieves an existing one accordingly. The session-opening code checks each case and prints error messages specific to the problems that might occur. The tests used by stages_url.pl are more elaborate than your applications may need: You may not care whether you're opening a new or existing session, or about displaying such specific error messages. For such instances, you may be able to reduce the session-opening code to the following statement:

```
$sess_ref = WebDB::Session->open (undef, param ("sess_id"))
    or error ("Could not open session");
```

After opening the session, we initialize the stage counter if necessary. (The session's count value will be undefined if we just created the session.) This initialization code could have been put into the preceding if statement, where the new session actually was created. However, it can be a good thing to separate the session opening and initialization operations. Code to open a session tends to be fairly stereotypical, whereas session initialization depends heavily on the type of state data you're using, and varies from application to application. Keeping the two separate makes it easier to copy and paste session-opening code between applications without having to tweak it.

For a new or continuing session, `stages_url.pl` calls `display_next_page()`. This routine increments the stage counter and displays a page showing the session ID, the current stage, and links for continuing or terminating the session. Incrementing the counter changes the state data; this will cause the session record to be saved to the database automatically when we close the session.

```perl
sub display_next_page
{
my $sess_ref = shift;

    # increment stage counter
    $sess_ref->attr ("count", $sess_ref->attr ("count") + 1);

    # display current session information
    print p (escapeHTML ("Session ID: " . $sess_ref->session_id ())),
            p ("Session stage: ", $sess_ref->attr ("count"));

    # display links for continuing or terminating session
    my $url = sprintf ("%s?sess_id=%s", # URL for continuing session
                        url (), escape ($sess_ref->session_id ()));
    print p (sprintf ("Select %s to continue to the next stage.",
                        a ({-href => $url}, "this link")));
    $url .= ";quit=1";                  # URL for quitting session
    print p (sprintf ("Select %s to quit.",
                        a ({-href => $url}, "this link")));
}
```

For a session that is to be terminated (which is the case when the `quit` parameter is present), the script calls `display_last_page()` to generate a page that displays the session ID, the final stage count, and a link for beginning a new session:

```perl
sub display_last_page
{
my $sess_ref = shift;

    # display final session state
    print p (escapeHTML (sprintf ("Session %s has ended after %d stages.",
                        $sess_ref->session_id (),
                        $sess_ref->attr ("count"))));

    # display link for starting new session
    print p (sprintf ("Select %s to start a new session.",
                        a ({-href => url ()}, "this link")));
}
```

The `error()` utility routine prints a message when a problem is detected:

```perl
sub error
{
    print header (),
```

```
            p (escapeHTML ($_[0])),
            end_html ();
    exit (0);
}
```

To test `stages_url.pl`, invoke it with no parameters in the URL, and then select the various links in the pages that it generates. There is no explicit MySQL activity in the script itself, because all that is handled behind the scenes automatically as `WebDB::Session` invokes `Apache::Session` operations for you. If MySQL logging is enabled and you have access to the log file, however, you may find it instructive to watch the queries that `Apache::Session` issues as you progress through the stages of this application:

```
% tail -f logfile
```

I've described the `stages_url.pl` script in terms of a session through which you move linearly by selecting links in successive pages, but users don't always behave that way. To get an idea of how this script responds when you don't just proceed from page to page, try some of the following actions and observe what happens:

- Begin a session to get the initial page, and then reload the page.
- Begin a session, select the "continue" link to go to the next page, and then reload the page.
- Begin a session, select the "quit" link to go to the last page, and then reload the page.
- Select your browser's Back button after reaching various session stages, and then reload the page or select one of its links.
- Invoke the script with a fake `sess_id` parameter:

  ```
  http://www.snake.net/cgi-perl/stages_url.pl?sess_id=X
  ```

- Invoke the script without a `sess_id` parameter but with a `quit` parameter:

  ```
  http://www.snake.net/cgi-perl/stages_url.pl?quit=1
  ```

When you try these things, do you find any of the behaviors that result to be unacceptable? If so, what can you do about them? Also, consider the fact that if you just close a page when a session is in progress, the session record in the database is not destroyed—resulting in an orphaned session. Can you do anything about that?

Passing Session IDs in Hidden Fields

`stages_url.pl` uses a URL parameter to pass the session ID from page to page. If you're displaying a page containing a form, you can use a hidden field to pass the ID by calling the `hidden()` function when you generate the form:

```
print hidden (-name => "sess_id", -value => $sess_id);
```

After the user submits the form, you can retrieve the ID by calling `param()`, just as you do when the ID is passed as part of the URL:

```
$sess_id = param ("sess_id");
```

This method of passing session identifiers is fairly straightforward, so I won't discuss it further. The webdb distribution includes a script, `stages_hidden.pl`, that demonstrates an implementation of this technique.

Passing Session IDs in Cookies

A third ID-propagation technique is to use a cookie (assuming that the user has cookies turned on, of course.) Let's see how to do this with a script, `stages_cookie.pl`. On the surface, this script presents pages that are the same as those displayed by `stages_url.pl`, the script written in "Passing Session IDs in URLs." However, the underlying details for setting and getting the session ID are quite different. The cookie script also behaves differently than `stages_url.pl` in some subtle ways, as we'll see shortly.

`stages_cookie.pl` relies on CGI.pm's cookie-handling interface to create and retrieve cookies. This interface is provided through the `cookie()` function.[3] For example, a cookie with a name of `"my cookie"` and a value of `"my value"` can be created like this:

```
$cookie = cookie (-name => "my name", -value => "my value");
```

The `name` and `value` parameters are required, but there are others you can use to specify additional cookie attributes. The full set of parameters that `cookie()` understands for creating cookies is as follows:

- `name` is the name of the cookie. It should be a scalar value.
- `value` indicates the cookie's value, which can be a scalar or a reference to an array or a hash.
- `domain` indicates the hosts to which the browser should return the cookie. If no `domain` value is specified, the browser returns the cookie only to the host from which it came. If the value names a host or domain, the browser returns the cookie to that host or to any host in the domain. Domain names should begin with a dot to distinguish them from host names. A domain name also is required to contain at least two dots (to keep you from trying to match top-level domains). Therefore, to specify a domain of `"snake.net"`, you should specify it as `".snake.net"`.

---

3. You can also create cookies using the `CGI::Cookie` module. It has an interface quite similar to that of the `cookie()` function, which in fact uses the module internally. To read the `CGI::Cookie` documentation, use this command:

```
% perldoc CGI::Cookie
```

- **path** associates a cookie with specific documents at a site; the browser returns the cookie to the current server for any request having a URL that begins with a given **path** value. For example, "**/**" matches all pages on the site (in effect creating a site-wide cookie). This is the default if no path is specified. A cookie with a **path** value of "**/cgi-perl**" is more specific; the browser will return the cookie only with requests for scripts in or under the /cgi-perl directory. To associate a cookie only with a specific script, pass the script's full pathname. Any CGI.pm script can get its own pathname without hardwiring it in by calling the url() function as follows:

    ```
    $path = url (-absolute => 1);
    ```

    Site-wide cookies are useful for associating a client with state information that applies to all pages, such as a preferences profile that affects how your site interacts with the user. For such cookies, try to pick a unique name to keep your application's cookie from being clobbered by cookies sent by other applications that run on your site. More specific **path** values can be used to limit network traffic (the client browser will return the cookie with fewer requests) and to reduce the probability of cookie name clash between applications.

- **expires** sets an expiration date for the cookie. If you specify no expiration, the browser remembers the cookie only until it exits. For a cookie to have a specific lifetime, you must assign it an explicit expiration date. For a date in the future, the browser remembers the cookie until that date is reached. If the date is in the past, the browser deletes the cookie. This is useful if you associate a session with a cookie: When you destroy a session, tell the browser to destroy the corresponding cookie that it's holding by sending a new cookie with an expiration date in the past. That way the browser won't try to reuse the session.

    Expiration values can be given literally as GMT dates, but it's more convenient to specify them using shortcut values relative to the current time. For example, expiration values of +1d and -1d indicate one day in the future and in the past. The shortcut suffix letters are 's' (seconds), 'm' (minutes), 'h' (hours), 'd' (days), 'M' (months), and 'y' (years). Be careful about specifying relative values far into the future, such as +1000y; you may find that you end up with a cookie containing a date in the past! I assume this is due to some sort of arithmetic wraparound problem.

- **secure** can be set to any **true** value (such as 1) to tell the browser to return the cookie only if the connection is secure, to protect its contents from snooping.

After creating a cookie, you can send it to the browser by calling header(). Suppose you want to create a cookie named sess_id to use for session-identification purposes. If the variable $sess_id contains the session ID value, the cookie can be created and sent in the headers as follows:

```
$cookie = cookie (-name => "sess_id",              # cookie name
                  -value => $sess_id,              # cookie value
                  -path => url (-absolute => 1),   # use only with this script
                  -expires => "+7d");              # expire in 7 days
print header (-cookie => $cookie);
```

The cookie parameter to header() causes the appropriate Set-Cookie: header to be sent, based on the contents of $cookie. The particular cookie shown here is associated only with the current script (so as not to interfere with any other cookies sent from our site), and will expire seven days. No secure parameter was specified, so a secure connection is not required. If you want to send multiple cookies (which is legal, and sometimes useful), specify them using a reference to an array:

```
print header (-cookie => [ $cookie1, $cookie2 ]);
```

header() sends cookies to the browser, but that's only half the job. You also need to retrieve them from the browser in future requests, so your application can figure out what to do next. If you want the names of all available cookies, call cookie() with no arguments; to get the value of a specific cookie, pass its name to cookie():

```
@name = cookie ();                # get names of all available cookies
$sess_id = cookie ("sess_id");    # get value of cookie named "sess_id"
```

cookie() returns undef if you call it with the name of a cookie that doesn't exist. This is generally how you distinguish when your script is being invoked for the first time from when it's being invoked again after you've already sent the client the cookie:

```
$sess_id = cookie ("sess_id");
if (!defined ($sess_id))
{
    # ... it's the first invocation
}
else
{
    # ... it's a subsequent invocation
}
```

Choosing a Cookie Name and Path

When you use cookies to store session IDs, choose the name and path parameters that you pass to cookie() appropriately. If a script uses its full pathname for the path value to make the cookie apply only to itself, you can choose any name you want without worrying about the name conflicting with cookies generated by other applications. If you're applying a session to a wider range of pages, the name of the associated cookie becomes more important. If you're using a path of "/" to create a site-wide cookie for a display preferences profile, for example, a generic name value such as sess_id would be ill advised. Names such as display_prefs or viewing_prefs would be better for reducing the probability of conflict with other cookies. In general, the less specific your path value, the more specific your cookie name should be.

Now we're all set to write the `stages_cookie.pl` script. It needs to perform the following operations:

- Detect an existing cookie or create a new one, and open the corresponding session.
- Initialize the session if it's new.
- Present a page appropriate to the current state of the session.

The first step is to figure out whether a session ID cookie was sent by the browser and what its value is, so that we can determine whether to create a new session or look up an existing one. The following code shows one approach, based on the assumption that the cookie containing the session ID is named `sess_id`:

```
# If the cookie containing the session ID is not present, create a new
# session and prepare a cookie to send to the client that contains the
# session ID.  Otherwise, use the ID to look up an existing session.
# If all attempts to open a session fail, we can't continue.

$sess_id = cookie ("sess_id");  # get value of sess_id cookie if it's present

if (!defined ($sess_id))        # create new session and cookie
{
    defined ($sess_ref = WebDB::Session->open (undef, undef))
        or error ("Could not create new session: $WebDB::Session::errstr");
    $cookie = cookie (-name => "sess_id",
                      -value => $sess_ref->session_id (),
                      -path => url (-absolute => 1));
}
else                            # retrieve existing session
{
    defined ($sess_ref = WebDB::Session->open (undef, $sess_id))
        or error ("Could not retrieve session record for ID $sess_id: "
                . $WebDB::Session::errstr);
}
```

If the cookie doesn't exist, `$sess_id` will be undefined. This indicates a first-time invocation, so we must create a new session. It's also necessary to create a cookie containing the session ID and send it to the browser, so the browser can return it with subsequent requests. On the other hand, if the cookie does already exist, its value is the ID for an existing session. In this case, we don't have to create a new cookie. (Clearly, the browser must already have one, or it wouldn't have sent it to us.)[4]

---

4. In some situations you'll want to issue a new cookie even when the browser already has one. If you extend the cookie's expiration time each time your script is requested, for example, you'll need to return a new cookie to tell the browser to update the one it's holding. If you destroy a session, you should tell the browser to delete the cookie associated with the session by sending a new cookie with an expiration date in the past.

The preceding code is fairly straightforward, but subject to an ugly problem if your application creates sessions that have a limited lifetime. Suppose a visitor starts using your application, and then goes on vacation and doesn't use the application again until after the session has expired. On the user's next visit, when the browser sends the cookie, the code will attempt to look up the corresponding session. Because the session is no longer there, the script prints an error message and quits. In fact, for the code just shown, there is now no way for the user to start over except by deleting the cookie on the browser end somehow so that the browser can't send it. There are various approaches to dealing with this problem:

- Fail inexplicably with a cryptic error message that confuses and annoys the user.
- Begin a new session and send the browser a new cookie to replace the old one.
- Tell the user that the session has expired and send the browser a cookie that tells it to delete the old one.

Clearly the first option is the least desirable, although it's what actually happens with the preceding code. The last two options share the characteristic that they cause the browser to get rid of its old cookie, and that's something you should do regardless of the method you use to handle a cookie that has gone out of sync with the session it used to be associated with.

The following code handles the difficulty using the second option. It assumes that a session with a given ID has become unavailable if an error occurs trying to open it, and that a new session should be started. It also generates a new cookie to go with the session. This can be sent to the browser to replace the cookie it currently has, preventing it from sending the bad cookie again in the future:

```
# If the cookie containing the session ID is present, use the ID to look up
# an existing session. If the attempt fails or there was no cookie, create
# a new session and prepare a cookie to send to the client that contains
# the session ID. If all attempts to open a session fail, we can't continue.

$sess_id = cookie ("sess_id");  # get value of sess_id cookie if it's present

$sess_ref = WebDB::Session->open (undef, $sess_id) if defined ($sess_id);

if (!defined ($sess_ref))       # no cookie or couldn't retrieve old session
{
    defined ($sess_ref = WebDB::Session->open (undef, undef))
        or error ("Could not create session: $WebDB::Session::errstr");
    $cookie = cookie (-name => "sess_id",
                      -value => $sess_ref->session_id (),
                      -path => url (-absolute => 1));
}
```

This second approach is the one used by stages_cookie.pl (and by the remaining applications in this chapter). If you like, you could modify it to notify the user when an error occurs (for example, by pointing out that the old session has expired and that you've created a new one).

After we check for a cookie as just outlined, `$cookie` has a value if we've just created a new cookie to be sent to the browser, and `undef` otherwise. We can pass it as the `cookie` parameter to the `header()` function either way, because `header()` is smart enough not to generate a `Set-Cookie:` header if `$cookie` is `undef`. But should we call `header()` at this point? It depends. Keep in mind that for cookie-based applications, any cookies must be sent prior to writing any page content. On the other hand, you may not always know whether you have to send a cookie until after you've started executing the code that generates the page! As it happens, in our current script, the cookie-detection code isn't the only place where we may need to create a cookie. If the user selects a "quit" link to terminate the session, we'll need to delete the session record and present the "session terminated page," and we'll also need to tell the browser to delete the session cookie by sending a new cookie with an expiration date in the past. Unfortunately, if we've already started printing the page content, it's too late to send the cookie.

One way to deal with the problem of writing headers and page content in the proper order is to defer output: Save the contents of any page you generate in a string, and then print the string after you know what headers must be sent. `stages_cookie.pl` does this using a `$page` variable to hold the HTML for the page content:

```
my $page;

# If this is a new session, initialize the stage counter

$sess_ref->attr ("count", 0) if !defined ($sess_ref->attr ("count"));

if (!defined (param ("quit")))   # continue session
{
    $page .= display_next_page ($sess_ref); # display page for first/next stage
    $sess_ref->close ();                     # done with session; close it
}
else                             # terminate session
{
    $page .= display_last_page ($sess_ref); # display termination page
    $sess_ref->delete ();                    # destroy session for good
    # Create cookie that tells browser to destroy the one it's storing
    $cookie = cookie (-name => "sess_id",
                      -value => $sess_ref->session_id (),
                      -path => url (-absolute => 1),
                      -expires => "-1d");     # "expire yesterday"
}

# Send headers, including any cookie we may have created.
# Then send page contents.

print header (-cookie => $cookie);

print start_html (-title => "Session Stages", -bgcolor => "white"),
```

continues

continued

```
        $page,
        end_html ();
```

The `display_next_page()` and `display_last_page()` functions are similar to the functions with the same names in `stages_url.pl`, but they return any HTML they generate as a string rather than printing it immediately. They also create slightly different URLs for continuing and terminating the session. `stages_url.pl` wrote URLs that included the session identifier:

```
http://www.snake.net/cgi-perl/stages_url.pl?sess_id=xxx
http://www.snake.net/cgi-perl/stages_url.pl?sess_id=xxx;quit=1
```

In `stages_cookie.pl`, we're passing the session ID in a cookie, so the URLs don't need any `sess_id` parameter:

```
http://www.snake.net/cgi-perl/stages_cookie.pl
http://www.snake.net/cgi-perl/stages_cookie.pl?quit=1
```

The revised versions of `display_next_page()` and `display_last_page()` used by `stages_cookie.pl` look like this:

```
sub display_next_page
{
my $sess_ref = shift;
my $page;

    # increment stage counter
    $sess_ref->attr ("count", $sess_ref->attr ("count") + 1);

    # display current session information
    $page .= p (escapeHTML ("Session ID: " . $sess_ref->session_id ()))
            . p ("Session stage: ", $sess_ref->attr ("count"));

    # display links for continuing or terminating session
    my $url = url ();                       # URL for continuing session
    $page .= p (sprintf ("Select %s to continue to the next stage.",
                    a ({-href => $url}, "this link")));
    $url .= "?quit=1";                      # URL for quitting session
    $page .= p (sprintf ("Select %s to quit.",
                    a ({-href => $url}, "this link")));

    return ($page);
}

sub display_last_page
{
my $sess_ref = shift;
my $page;

    # display final session state
    $page .= p (escapeHTML (sprintf ("Session %s has ended after %d stages.",
```

```
                    $sess_ref->session_id (),
                    $sess_ref->attr ("count"))));

    # display link for starting new session
    $page .= p (sprintf ("Select %s to start a new session.",
                    a ({-href => url ()}, "this link")));

    return ($page);
  }
```

If you try out stages_cookie.pl at this point, you'll see that it behaves much the same
as stages_url.pl. In fact, its behavior is *exactly* the same as long as you proceed
through a session by selecting links in successive pages. To see where the two scripts
differ, go back to the end of the discussion of stages_url.pl, where I gave a list of
things to try to see how that script acts when you don't go through pages in sequence.
Try those same things with stages_cookie.pl; you should notice several differences
between the behaviors of the two scripts. When a session ID is propagated in the
URL, for instance, the ID disappears if you just close the window. The result is an
orphaned session. With a cookie, closing the window doesn't orphan the session that
way; if you issue a new request for the script, the cookie gets sent again, and the script
can determine what to do.

That's not to say that it's not possible to strand a session when you use cookies. If
you quit and restart your browser, the cookie disappears. Then if you invoke
stages_cookie.pl again, you get a new session (and the previous one becomes
orphaned). This happens because we assigned the cookie no expiration value, so the
browser remembers the cookie only as long as it continues to run.

Now that you have some experience with sessions, your head is probably brimming
with ideas about using them to eliminate some of the shortcomings in the applications
developed in earlier chapters. For example, our electronic greeting card application is
in fact session based (although we didn't discuss it in those terms), but the implementation leaves something to be desired:

- We generated card IDs using an AUTO_INCREMENT column to make sure each card
  had a unique value. Unfortunately, because these IDs are sequential, they are easy
  to guess. An intruder can visit our site, begin a new card, examine its ID, and
  then try other ID values near to it as likely candidates for other cards that are
  still in the process of being constructed and that can be hijacked. If we used random session IDs instead (such as those generated by Apache::Session), intruders
  would have a much more difficult time guessing the ID of an in-progress card
  and card stealing would become more difficult.

- If a visitor begins a card but never finishes it, the expiration date for the corresponding record in the ecard table never gets set. This was a problem for the
  expiration program expire_ecard.pl, which is able to determine whether to
  expire a card only if that date is set. One solution to this problem would be to
  store a card in a session record while it's being constructed, and then move the

card to the `ecard` table only after the card has been completed. That way, records never appear in the `ecard` table until the expiration date is known, and the expiration process can always tell whether any given card record should be deleted. Unfortunately, this is an example of solving one problem by creating another. We would only transfer the expiration problem to another table, namely, the `sessions` table. If cards are stored in the session table while they are being constructed, how do we know when to expire a session record for a card that the user never finishes? The answer is to assign the session record itself an expiration date that is distinct from the expiration used for the card. Some ideas for solving this type of problem are discussed in "Expiring Sessions" later in this chapter.

- If you were to modify `make_ecard.pl` to track session records using cookies, you'd create a problem for the user who has second thoughts about sending a card in the middle of the card-construction process. As long as the card ID is propagated by means of hidden fields and URLs, it's possible to forget a card just by closing the window or visiting another site. When the ID is stored in a cookie, that doesn't work because the browser continues to remember it. The user would find that returning to the card-making script would cause the old card to reappear! Fortunately, this is easy to solve. Provide a Forget Card button and have `make_ecard.pl` respond to it by forgetting the session and telling the browser to delete the cookie that holds the ID.

Another use for cookies would be the `res_search2.pl` script described in Chapter 7, "Performing Searches." In that application, we implemented display of multiple-page search results by using a set of links to each of the pages, where each link included a lot of information. However, much of that information was constant across links, such as the search parameters needed to derive the result set. An alternative implementation might use a cookie to store all the information that remains constant from page to page, and then include in the URLs only those values that vary between pages.

Expiring Sessions

Server-side state storage is, in general, a better approach than storing state information on the client. However, client-side techniques do have one particular advantage over server-side state management: When your scripts don't store any state on the server, they don't have to be concerned about removing it or expiring it. That becomes the client's problem. Clients handle this in various ways. Passive expiration occurs for state information stored on the client side in URLs or in hidden fields automatically when the user closes the window or goes to a different page. Client-side information stored in a cookie can be more persistent because cookies can be given an expiration date—but even so, expiring the cookie is something you get to let the browser worry about.

By contrast, when you manage state data on the server side, you must think about how long you want that information to stick around. Although it's perfectly possible to create longstanding sessions that you intend to allow to exist indefinitely, in other cases, sessions should have a definite lifetime. Sometimes you can take care of this by associating a user action such as Quit or Log Out with session destruction. Unfortunately, there is no guarantee all users will remember to quit or log out, so you may end up with a lot of dead or orphaned sessions in your sessions table. This section explores some techniques for identifying and getting rid of extraneous sessions.

Adding a Timestamp to Session Records

One method for recording the time showing when session records were last modified is to let MySQL do it automatically. To accomplish this, include a TIMESTAMP column in your sessions table:

```
CREATE TABLE sessions
(
    t           TIMESTAMP,
    id          CHAR(32) NOT NULL PRIMARY KEY,
    a_session   TEXT
)
```

With this addition, MySQL will update the t column of any session record that is updated. Apache::Session won't do anything with the column (it manages only id and a_session), but you can examine sessions table records yourself. To delete records that haven't been changed in a year, for example, use this query:

```
DELETE FROM sessions WHERE t < DATE_SUB(NOW(),INTERVAL 1 YEAR)
```

This provides a very simple mechanism for expiring sessions. The drawback is that it assumes you can tell when to delete a session purely on the basis of its last modification date, independent of the content of the session data. That's an invalid assumption under some circumstances, particularly for applications that create state data that may not change frequently. If you store user preferences in a session record, for example, a visitor may set up preferences once and then never change them again. In this case, even if the visitor returns to the site often, the preferences session's modification date doesn't change and the session record expires a year after it was created.

Storing Expiration Values in Session Data

An alternative to using a TIMESTAMP column is to store an expiration time explicitly in the session data under some session attribute name that applications agree to by convention. This approach has the disadvantage that the expiration time is serialized with the other session data, and therefore not directly visible to MySQL. To check a session's expiration date, you must open the session, and then access the appropriate session value. The countervailing advantage is that this approach enables you to write a program that can expire session records without knowing anything about their contents other than the name of the expiration attribute.

If we write an expires() method for setting and getting expiration values, we can hide the details of their representation inside WebDB::Session. Those details are as follows:

- What name should we use for the key (attribute) associated with the expiration value?
- How should we represent expiration times?

We know that the key name shouldn't begin with an underscore, because Apache::Session reserves names of that form. But the name also shouldn't be something likely to be used for other purposes by applications that use WebDB::Session. (That means that names such as expiration or expires are probably bad choices.) I'll use the name #<expires># under the assumption that adding non-alphanumeric characters reduces to near zero the probability that an application will use the same name for some other purpose.

Choosing a name gives us an easy way to implement expires()—namely, as a call to attr() that supplies the proper attribute name:

```
sub expires
{
my $self = shift;

    return ($self->attr ("#<expires>#", @_));
}
```

Then you can set or get an expiration value like this:

```
$sess_ref->expires ($expires_time);    # set value
$expires_time = $sess_ref->expires ();  # get value
```

The expiration value will be undef if a session has no expiration assigned.

We also must decide how to represent expiration time values. One possibility is to use Perl's time() function, which returns the number of seconds since some reference date (known as "the epoch"). Thus, you could do something like this to open a session and assign it an expiration time of three days in the future:

```
defined ($sess_ref = WebDB::Session->open (undef, $sess_id))
    and $sess_ref->expires (time () + 3*60*60*24);
```

Unfortunately, time() values are relative to a reference date, and the reference varies among different platforms. For example, the epoch is typically January 1, 1970 under UNIX and January 1, 1904 under Mac OS. This is a problem if you have Web servers on different platforms that share a common MySQL database to store session records. Scripts that run on the various platforms won't necessarily use the same time reference, with the result that expiration values won't have a consistent baseline.

To solve this problem, we can convert `time()` values to a non-relative GMT date before storing them, and convert them back to seconds when retrieving them. This allows scripts to use `time()` but have values stored in the database using a consistent baseline. To implement this mechanism, we can pass `time()` values to `gmtime()` to obtain a GMT date as an array containing elements for second, minute, hour, day, month, and year. The inverse transformation is performed by calling `timegm()` to convert the array back to a `time()` value. After making these changes, the implementation of `expires()` is as follows:

```
use Time::Local;    # this module is needed because it contains timegm()

sub expires
{
my $self = shift;
my $expires;

    # If an argument was given, interpret it as a local time() value in
    # seconds; convert the value to an absolute GMT date array and store
    # a reference to it.
    $self->{"#<expires>#"} = [ gmtime ($_[0]) ] if @_;

    # Return current expiration value (if there is one) by converting the
    # GMT date array back to a local time() value in seconds.  Return undef
    # if there is no expiration.
    $expires = $self->{"#<expires>#"};
    $expires = timegm (@{$expires}) if defined ($expires);
    return ($expires);
}
```

To hide the fact that we're using `time()`, we can provide a `now()` method that scripts can use to get the current time. This helps if you decide later to change the expiration implementation, because you just need to change the `expires()` and `now()` methods, not the scripts that call them:

```
sub now
{
    return (time ());
}
```

With these changes, `expires()` compensates for variations in time reference dates among platforms, and scripts will interoperate properly even if you set the expiration date from a script running on one platform and test it later from a script running on another platform.[5]

---

5. Actually, this solution is still subject to some variation between Web server hosts: It assumes those hosts all have the time set correctly, relative to their own time zone.

Now that we have expiration support in place, it's relatively easy to write a little
script, expire_session.pl, that scans the sessions table looking for and deleting
expired sessions. It fetches the session ID values, and then opens each one and examines its expiration value:

```perl
#! /usr/bin/perl -w
# expire_session.pl - destroy session records that contain an expiration time
# older than current time.

use strict;
use lib qw(/usr/local/apache/lib/perl);
use WebDB;
use WebDB::Session;

my $count = 0;          # number of session records
my $permanent = 0;      # number of records with no expiration value set
my $expired = 0;        # number of records that have expired and were deleted

my $sess_ref;
my $dbh = WebDB::connect ();
my $sth = $dbh->prepare ("SELECT id FROM sessions");
$sth->execute ();
while (my $id = $sth->fetchrow_array ())
{
    ++$count;
    next unless defined ($sess_ref = WebDB::Session->open ($dbh, $id));
    if (!defined ($sess_ref->expires ()))   # session never expires
    {
        ++$permanent;
    }
    elsif ($sess_ref->expires () < $sess_ref->now ())
    {
        $sess_ref->delete ();
        undef $sess_ref;
        ++$expired;
    }
    $sess_ref->close () if defined ($sess_ref);
}
$sth->finish ();
$dbh->disconnect ();
print "$count sessions, $permanent permanent, $expired expired\n";
exit (0);
```

expire_session.pl does not expire sessions for which expires() returns undef (that
is, sessions that have no expiration value). This is important for several reasons:

- It enables you to create permanent sessions that never expire.
- It avoids creating a race condition whereby a new session might get clobbered
  inadvertantly if the expiration process happens to examine the session between
  the time it is created and the time its expiration value is assigned.

- It leaves sessions intact that are created by applications that don't follow the convention of assigning an expiration date.

You can run `expire_session.pl` manually from the command line whenever you want; to run it on a regular basis, install it as a `cron` job.

> ### Apache::Session Does Not Require Apache
>
> Although the `Apache::Session` module lives in the `Apache` namespace, it doesn't actually require Apache and can be used in standalone fashion (for example, by command-line scripts or `cron` jobs that need access to session records). `expire_session.pl` is an example of this. It uses `WebDB::Session` (and therefore `Apache::Session`), even though you don't run it under Apache.

Let's do something to see session expiration in action. Make a copy of `stages_cookie.pl` called `stages_cookie2.pl`. Then change the session-initialization code from this:

```
# If this is a new session, initialize the stage counter

$sess_ref->attr ("count", 0) if !defined ($sess_ref->attr ("count"));
```

To this:

```
# If this is a new session, initialize the stage counter and the expiration.

$sess_ref->attr ("count", 0) if !defined ($sess_ref->attr ("count"));
$sess_ref->expires ($sess_ref->now () + 60) if !defined ($sess_ref->expires ());

# Display when expiration will occur

$page .= p (sprintf ("Expiration occurs in %d seconds.",
                         $sess_ref->expires() - $sess_ref->now ()));
```

The new code adds a session expiration of 60 seconds and prints the number of seconds until the session expires. Invoke `stages_cookie2.pl` and click the "continue" link several times. You'll notice the expiration value decreasing each time. Finally, it reaches zero and then…goes negative! Hmmm. Shouldn't the session expire? Yes, but remember we're handling removal of expired sessions externally using `expire_session.pl`. Run that program manually and it should remove your session. Then select the "continue" link in your browser window again. `stages_cookie2.pl` should discover your session to be missing and generate a new one with a fresh 60-second expiration.

We could modify the `WebDB::Session` module's `open()` method to check a session when you open it and delete it automatically if its expiration time has been reached. However, that would enforce a constraint making it impossible for an application to open expired sessions, should it want to do so for some reason (for example, to gather statistics on the expiration dates of records in the `sessions` table). Another approach that provides some flexibility to applications is to leave `open()` unchanged and write another method, `open_with_expiration()`, that is like it but performs the expiration check. This method can be implemented rather simply as a call to open() followed by a test of the expiration value:[6]

```
sub open_with_expiration
{
my $self = &open (@_);

    # If session exists and has an expiration time that
    # has passed, clobber it.

    if (defined ($self) && defined ($self->expires ())
        && $self->expires () < $self->now ())
    {
        $WebDB::Session::errstr = sprintf ("Session %s has expired",
                                            $self->session_id ());
        $self->delete ();
        $self = undef;
    }
    return ($self);
}
```

For any session that has not expired, open_with_expiration() is functionally equivalent to open(). Otherwise, it deletes the session and returns undef.

Now modify stages_cookie2.pl to use the new method. The line that tries to open an existing session looks like this:

```
$sess_ref = WebDB::Session->open (undef, $sess_id) if defined ($sess_id);
```

Change it to invoke open_with_expiration() instead:

```
$sess_ref = WebDB::Session->open_with_expiration (undef, $sess_id)
                                        if defined ($sess_id);
```

When you try the modified stages_cookie2.pl and select the "continue" link repeatedly, you should see that as the current session reaches its expiration time, it gets deleted automatically and a new session begins.

Expiring sessions this way doesn't eliminate the need for an external program that scans the sessions table periodically, because automatic expiration takes place only for sessions that you open by calling open_with_expiration(). On the other hand, an expiration scan becomes a bit simpler, because you can let WebDB::Session do the actual work of deleting the sessions. All you need to do is sweep through the sessions table, opening each session and closing those for which open_with_expiration() doesn't return undef. Here's how you'd write the loop for a script, expire_session2.pl, that is similar to expire_session.pl, but uses the new session-opening method:

---

6. open_with_expiration() calls &open() rather than open() due to an ambiguity with Perl's built-in function of the same name. Adding & resolves the name to the version in our module file.

```
while (my $id = $sth->fetchrow_array ())
{
    ++$count;
    $sess_ref = WebDB::Session->open_with_expiration ($dbh, $id);
    if (!defined ($sess_ref))
    {
        ++$expired;    # session has expired
        next;
    }
    # session never expires if there's no expiration value
    ++$permanent if !defined ($sess_ref->expires ());
    $sess_ref->close ();
}
```

One problem with running an expiration scan is that it locks the table while you're reading the set of session ID values. Then it locks the table again while reading each session record, and again if you delete the record. That's a lot of locking, and it may have a negative impact on your site's performance if you have heavy session activity going on. This problem will be greatly alleviated when MySQL gains the capability to perform row-level locking rather than table locking (a capability that is under development as I am writing this).

In the meantime, to alleviate locking problems, you could incorporate other techniques into the table scan such as putting a delay between session reads or splitting the scan into segments. Slowing a script down deliberately isn't something you do with very many scripts, because normally you want your scripts to execute quickly. However, an expiration scan has a much lower priority than servicing page requests, so preventing it from interfering with page requests is more important than having it run fast. And it's very easy to implement a delay: Just put a `sleep()` call into the session-checking loop. The following statement at the beginning or end of the loop puts a one-second delay between the processing for each session:

```
sleep (1);
```

Make sure you don't issue the `sleep()` call while the session is open, however. You want the script to hold sessions open for as brief a time as possible.

If your `sessions` table is large, splitting a scan into segments is one way to keep MySQL from returning a huge session ID result set, so that you can process the table in smaller, more manageable pieces. The following is the main part of a script, `expire_session3.pl`, that segments the scan into 100-record pieces using MySQL's `LIMIT` clause:

```
$chunk_size = 100;
$count = $dbh->selectrow_array ("SELECT COUNT(*) FROM sessions");
$offset = $count;
while ($offset > 0)
{
    $offset -= $chunk_size;
    if ($offset < 0)    # final chunk is only partial
    {
```

continues

continued

```
        $chunk_size += $offset;
        $offset = 0;
    }
    $offset = 0 if $offset < 0;
    my $sth = $dbh->prepare (
                "SELECT id FROM sessions LIMIT $offset, $chunk_size");
    $sth->execute ();
    my $sess_ref;
    while (my $id = $sth->fetchrow_array ())
    {
        $sess_ref = WebDB::Session->open_with_expiration ($dbh, $id);
        if (!defined ($sess_ref))
        {
            ++$expired;       # session has expired
            next;
        }
        # session never expires if there's no expiration value
        ++$permanent if !defined ($sess_ref->expires ());
        $sess_ref->close ();
    }
    $sth->finish ();
}
```

The loop reads sections of the table from the end to the beginning to avoid a problem that occurs if you read from the beginning to the end. Suppose you read the first 100 session records and expire 50 of them. That causes 50 of the following records in the table to "shift down" into the first 100 records, so that when you read the next 100 records, you miss those 50. (Of course, any kind of scan that reads a table in sections may be affected by record-shifting when there are other programs modifying the table, such as scripts that create new sessions. There's not much we can do about that, but we may as well at least keep the script from interfering with itself!)

Adding an Expiration Column to Session Records

Another way to perform expiration, which I'll just outline rather than showing an implementation, would be to add an expires column to the sessions table, and then modify WebDB::Session to store expiration values in that column rather than in the session data. This change can be implemented inside the expires() method such that it wouldn't be visible to applications that use WebDB::Session.

Storing expiration values this way would require issuing queries to MySQL (because Apache::Session won't manipulate the expires column for you). However, putting values in a separate column would make it much easier for the expiration scan to do its job. It wouldn't need to open sessions to find out expiration values; it could examine the expires column directly.

Strategies for Using Expiration Dates

When you associate each session record with the appropriate client by means of a cookie that contains the session identifier, you can use several expiration strategies:

- Assign an expiration to a session and the cookie only when the session is first opened. This causes the session and the cookie to have a fixed lifetime. They both expire when the given date is reached, regardless of whether and how often the user visits your site in the meantime.

- Assign an expiration to a session and the cookie each time the session is opened. This extends the expiration date each time the user visits. As long as the visits occur at intervals shorter than the expiration period, the session and the cookie both remain active. Under this strategy, your applicatin must resend the cookie to the browser in the response to each request, not just when the session is created. Otherwise, the browser won't know the cookie lifetime has been extended.

- Assign no expiration at all. In this case, the session and the cookie behave quite differently. The session doesn't expire at all, but the cookie expires (is deleted by the browser) when the browser exits. If you want a "permanent" session, you need the cookie to have a long lifetime as well. Assign it an explicit expiration date as far as possible in the future.

Storing User Preferences

In this section, we'll write an application, `prefs.pl`, that uses sessions to manage user profiles. The particular scenario involves management of page-display preferences, although for simplicity we'll limit the scope of these preferences to a block of text displayed in the pages generated by the application itself. At the end of this section, you'll find a few suggestions for other ways to use profiles by making a few changes to the concepts presented here.

The script `prefs.pl` is designed to keep track of page-display preferences stored in a session record: You can select a font size (small, medium, large), and `text` attributes (bold, italic). It presents a page that shows some sample text displayed using your current preferences, and a form that enables you to change those preferences. In addition, to demonstrate the fact that sometimes you want users to be able to delete their profiles, the application also provides a Log Out operation that causes the session containing the preferences to be destroyed.

The script also demonstrates how to move information in both directions between a form and a session record, with special attention to the fact that form elements may have non-scalar values. This enables you to store form values in a session record, and to initialize a form from the contents of the session.

The script begins with some code that checks for a cookie and opens a session. This is much like we've done before, except that it assigns an explicit expiration date to the cookie to cause the browser to remember it across restarts. User profiles tend to be the sorts of things that have a long lifetime. This means the cookies associated with them also must be long-lived, so it's necessary to assign each session cookie an explicit expiration date to make sure the browser remembers it well into the future. (If we give a user a cookie that contains no explicit expiration value, it will be forgotten when the browser exits. That is undesirable for this application.)

```
$sess_id = cookie ("sess_id");  # get value of sess_id cookie if it's present

$sess_ref = WebDB::Session->open (undef, $sess_id) if defined ($sess_id);

if (!defined ($sess_ref))        # no cookie or couldn't retrieve old session
{
    defined ($sess_ref = WebDB::Session->open (undef, undef))
        or error ("Could not create session: $WebDB::Session::errstr");
    $cookie = cookie (-name => "sess_id",
                        -value => $sess_ref->session_id (),
                        -path => url (-absolute => 1),
                        -expires => "+1y");     # expire in one year
}
```

After opening the session, we check to see whether it needs to be initialized. The font size always has a value for an existing session, so we can assume that the session is new if size is undefined:

```
if (!defined ($sess_ref->attr ("size")))
{
    $sess_ref->attr ("size", "3");       # medium size
    $sess_ref->attr ("style", undef);    # plain style
}
```

The font size value is a simple scalar. The possible values we'll allow are 1, 3, and 5, where 3 is the value for "medium." The text style can be empty or have up to two values, but at the moment we'll set it to undef to signify "plain text" (neither bold nor italic).

After the session is ready to go, we can use it to interpret the user's instructions:

- If this is the first invocation, just display the sample text and preferences form.
- If the user submitted new preferences, save them in the session record, and then display the sample text and the form, updated to reflect the modified preferences.
- If the user wants to log out, destroy the session record and the cookie. This causes the preferences to be forgotten.

Each of these actions is handled by the dispatch code:

```
my $choice = lc (param ("choice"));  # get choice, lowercased

if ($choice eq "")                   # initial invocation
{
    $page .= display_prefs_form ($sess_ref);   # display sample text and form
    $sess_ref->close ();
}
elsif ($choice eq "submit")          # user submitted new preferences
{
    process_form ($sess_ref);                  # modify preferences
    $page .= display_prefs_form ($sess_ref);   # display sample text and form
    $sess_ref->close ();
}
elsif ($choice eq "log out")         # destroy session and cookie
{
    $sess_ref->delete ();
    $page .= p ("The session has been terminated.");
    # Create cookie that tells browser to destroy the one it's storing
    $cookie = cookie (-name => "sess_id",
                      -value => $sess_ref->session_id (),
                      -path => url (-absolute => 1),
                      -expires => "-1d");      # "expire yesterday"
}
else
{
    error ("Logic error, unknown choice: $choice");
}
```

Any HTML generated within the dispatch code is saved in a string, not printed immediately. That technique is one we've used before, to defer output until after we know for sure whether a cookie needs to be sent in the headers that precede the page content:

```
print header (-cookie => $cookie),
      start_html (-title => "Prefs Demo", -bgcolor => "white"),
      $page,
      end_html ();
```

`display_prefs_form()` displays the sample text and the form that enables you to change your preferences:

```
sub display_prefs_form
{
my $sess_ref = shift;
my (@style, $page, $sample);

    # Generate some sample text

    $sample = <<EOF;
Now is the time for all good men to come to the aid of their
```

continued

```
        quick brown foxes that jump over lazy sleeping dogs.
        EOF

            # Apply the current preferences to the sample text.  The font is
            # a single scalar value.  The style might have no value, a single
            # value, or multiple values.  In the latter case it must be accessed
            # by reference rather than as a scalar.

            $sample = font ({-size => $sess_ref->attr ("size")}, $sample);

            if (!defined ($sess_ref->attr ("style")))        # undef
            {
                @style = ();                                 # empty list
            }
            elsif (ref ($sess_ref->attr ("style")) ne "ARRAY")  # bold OR italic
            {
                @style = ( $sess_ref->attr ("style") );      # list of one element
            }
            else                                             # bold AND italic
            {
                @style = @{$sess_ref->attr ("style")};       # list of two elements
            }
            $sample = b ($sample) if grep (/^bold$/, @style);
            $sample = i ($sample) if grep (/^italic$/, @style);

            $page .= p ("Here is some text displayed using your current preferences:")
                    . hr () . p ($sample) . hr ();

            # Extract preferences from session record and stuff them into the
            # parameter environment so they initialize the fields in the
            # preference-changing form.

            foreach my $name ("size", "style")
            {
                param (-name => $name, -value => $sess_ref->attr ($name));
            }

            $page .= start_form (-action => url ())
                    . p ("To modify your preferences, make the changes below.\n"
                        . "Your choices will be applied on the next page\n"
                        . "when you select the Submit button.")
                    . p ("Font size:")
                    . radio_group (-name => "size",
                                    -values => ["1", "3", "5"],
                                    -labels => {
                                            "1" => "small",
                                            "3" => "medium",
                                            "5" => "large"
                                            }
                            )
```

```
              . p ("Text style:")
              . checkbox_group (-name => "style", -values => ["bold", "italic"])
              . br () . br ()
              . submit (-name => "choice", -value => "Submit")
              . " "
              . submit (-name => "choice", -value => "Log Out")
              . end_form ();

      return ($page);
}
```

`display_prefs_form()` uses the session record two ways: to determine the format of the sample text and as a source of values for initializing the form elements. The font is easy to pull from the session record and apply to the sample text, because it always has a single scalar value. Handling the `style` value is trickier. Either or both of the bold and italic values can be enabled, so the `style` value in the session record might be `undef`, a scalar, or an array reference. The value is extracted and converted to an array no matter what form it takes in the session, so that whatever `style` attributes are present can be ascertained easily using `grep()`. The code shown in `display_prefs_form()` explicitly sets the `@style` array to the empty list for the `undef` case, to make the action for the "no style value" case explicit. That's not strictly necessary, because `@style` is initialized to the empty list by default. Here's a simpler way to convert the `style` values to an array:

```
if (ref ($sess_ref->attr ("style")) eq "ARRAY")
{
    @style = @{$sess_ref->attr ("style")};
}
elsif (defined ($sess_ref->attr ("style")))
{
    @style = ( $sess_ref->attr ("style") );
}
```

After displaying the text, `display_prefs_form()` extracts the preferences from the session record again and loads them into the script's parameter space. The purpose of this is to exploit CGI.pm's sticky form behavior that allows parameter values in the environment to be used to initialize form elements. CGI.pm correctly handles parameter values whether they are scalars or references, so we don't have to do any special messing around in the parameter initialization loop.

Each time the user submits new preference selections, `process_form()` examines the form's field values and saves them in the session record:

```
sub process_form
{
my $sess_ref = shift;

    # Extract form values and save them to the session record
    foreach my $name ("size", "style")
    {
```

continues

continued

```
            my @val = param ($name);
            # store multiple-valued elements by reference,
            # and empty or single-valued elements as scalars
            $sess_ref->attr ($name, (@val > 1 ? [ @val ] : shift (@val)));
    }
}
```

The primary issue here is that arrays cannot be stored directly in a session record. They must be stored by reference, so the loop determines whether any given field value is a scalar or an array, and then stores a scalar or an array reference accordingly. If you select both bold and italic style values, param() returns an array of two values for the style parameter. The code in process_form() converts this to an array reference and stores that in the session record.

Try out prefs.pl by invoking it and changing your preferences a few times to verify that it displays the sample text appropriately. You can see from this the immediate effect of modifications you submit on the contents of the session record. You also can test the script's behavior in other ways:

- Invoke prefs.pl and submit some changes to your preferences. Then close the browser window and reinvoke the script. Your changed preferences should be remembered.

- Quit and restart your browser, and then reinvoke prefs.pl. Your preferences still should be remembered. This happens because we assigned an expiration date to the session cookie. Had we not done so, the browser would have deleted the cookie and the script would have started a new session for you, initialized to the default display preferences. (The original session would have become orphaned as well.)

- If you select Log Out, and then invoke the script again, you should get a new page showing the sample text and form displayed using the default preferences. This happens because Log Out destroys your session, so the next invocation needs to generate a new one.

Other Applications for User Profiles

Sessions that contain profile or preference information can be used for many purposes, including the following:

- Create a profile to remember name, address, and phone number when a user visits your online store. Then use the information to automatically initialize form fields when the user visits your store later. This makes it easier for your customers to order products from your store.

- Let your visitors tell you which kinds of news items they're most interested in seeing. Use this interests profile on your "current news" page to display headlines only for items in those categories they want to see. The same idea applies to auction sites; you can provide information about new items in categories a user happens to be interested in.

- For an online help desk, remember the last several documents a user asked to look at. When the user next visits, present a short menu allowing those documents to be recalled easily, on the assumption that they are still the ones of most immediate interest.

Remember that `prefs.pl` generates a cookie that specifically applies only to itself by using the script's full pathname as the `path` value. To manage profiles that apply to a wider range of pages, you'll need to generate a cookie with a less-specific `path` value, such as `"/"` to create a site-wide cookie, and you should pick a more-specific cookie name that is less generic than `sess_id`!

Implementing Resumable Sessions

One benefit provided by sessions is that they enable you to implement activities that can be suspended for a while and then resumed later when the user is ready to continue. This is a common thing to do with long-running games that users may play over the course of several days. Resumable sessions are also useful for presenting an activity in discrete segments: The user completes the activity one piece at a time, but can break off at any point and continue later. If you're asking users to complete a lengthy survey, for example, you can make the experience more palatable by not requiring that the entire thing be completed in a single sitting. The user who is interrupted or needs to do something else while answering questions can suspend the survey and then return to it later at a more convenient time. (Of course, some users may forget to complete their form. You might want to solicit an email address at the beginning of the process and store it along with a timestamp in the session record so that you can send a reminder message to users who seem not to have made any progress on their surveys for a while.)

In this section, we'll implement an application `survey.pl` that presents a survey conducted over several pages. For simplicity, we'll present only three pages and ask only one question per page, where each page contains a multiple-choice question and two buttons, Continue and Finish Later. The user selects Continue to submit the answer for the current question and continue on to the next page. Finish Later suspends the survey; if the user selects this button, the script presents a page containing instructions that indicate how to resume the survey later.

survey.pl uses a session record to track the progress of the survey. As the user submits answers to questions, the application adds them to the session record. When the user completes the survey, the script prints a thank-you message, moves the answers from the session record to a survey table designed to record completed surveys, destroys the session, and tells the browser to delete the session cookie.

To represent the survey questions, survey.pl uses the following array, where each question corresponds to a hash with three elements. In each hash, the question element is the question to present to the user, answers lists the possible alternatives the user can choose from, and name indicates the column in the database table where we'll store the results when the user has finished:

```
my @question =
(
    {
        question => "Which of these foods do you like best?",
        answers => ["hamburgers", "hot dogs", "bratwurst"],
        name => "food"
    },
    {
        question => "Do you put ketchup on your %food%?",
        answers => ["yes", "no", "sometimes", "I prefer tabasco sauce"],
        name => "ketchup"
    },
    {
        question => "How many %food% do you usually eat at one sitting?",
        answers => ["1", "2", "3", "more than 3!"],
        name => "quantity"
    }
);
```

The survey table used to hold completed surveys looks like this:

```
CREATE TABLE survey
(
    id          INT NOT NULL AUTO_INCREMENT PRIMARY KEY,
    food        CHAR(25),
    ketchup     CHAR(25),
    quantity    CHAR(25)
)
```

For this application, the questions are coded right into the script, and the layout of the survey table is tightly tied to the questions. For greater flexibility, you'd probably want to use the database to store information about the questions to be asked, generate the question forms on the basis of table lookups, and store completed survey responses using a more general table structure.

Our application uses a simple mechanism for tailoring questions according to the responses to previous questions. When a question contains a sequence of the form %xxx%, survey.pl looks for another question with a name value of xxx, and then replaces %xxx% with the answer to that question. Thus, when the script asks the second and third questions, it replaces the instances of %food% in those questions with the user's answer to the first question. If the user answers "bratwurst" to the first question, for example, the second question becomes "Do you like ketchup on your bratwurst?"

As usual, our script begins by checking for a session-identifier cookie and opens the corresponding session. The code is similar to that used for earlier applications; there's no need to show it here. Then we initialize the session if it's a new one:

```
if (!defined ($sess_ref->attr ("index")))
{
    $sess_ref->attr ("index", 0);
    $sess_ref->attr ("answers", { });    # hash to hold answers
    $sess_ref->attr ("suspended", 0);
}
```

The session record has several elements. index indicates how many questions the user has answered so far; the script uses this value to figure out which question to present on any given page. answers is a reference to a hash that holds the answers that the user has submitted. suspended is something of a frill. We'll set it to a non-zero value if the user selects the Finish Later button, to indicate that the session is being suspended. When the user resumes the survey, we'll notice the non-zero value and add a little "Welcome Back" message to the page:

```
if ($sess_ref->attr ("suspended"))
{
    $page .= p ("Welcome Back.");
    $sess_ref->attr ("suspended", 0);
}
```

The dispatch logic checks which question is current and performs the appropriate action. For a session that is just beginning (or that has been resumed after having been suspended), we just display the current question. If the user submitted an answer, we record it and advance to the next question (or finish up if the user has completed the survey). If the user wants to finish the survey later, we mark the session suspended and display some instructions indicating how to resume the survey later:

```
my $choice = lc (param ("choice")); # get choice, lowercased

my $cur_q = $question[$sess_ref->attr ("index")];    # info for current question

if ($choice eq "")                    # present question
{
    $page .= display_question ($sess_ref, $cur_q);
    $sess_ref->close ();
}
elsif ($choice eq "submit")      # record answer, present next question
{
    $page .= process_answer ($sess_ref, $cur_q);
    if ($sess_ref->attr ("index") < @question)  # any more questions?
    {
        $cur_q = $question[$sess_ref->attr ("index")];
```

continues

continued

```
            $page .= display_question ($sess_ref, $cur_q);
            $sess_ref->close ();
    }
    else                                        # no more questions
    {
        # store responses in database, destroy session, create cookie
        # that tells browser to delete the one it's storing, and thank
        # the user
        save_answers ($sess_ref);
        $sess_ref->delete ();
        $cookie = cookie (-name => "sess_id",
                          -value => $sess_ref->session_id (),
                          -path => url (-absolute => 1),
                          -expires => "-1d");     # "expire yesterday"
        $page .= p ("Hey, thanks for participating.");
    }
}
elsif ($choice eq "finish later")       # suspend session
{
    $sess_ref->attr ("suspended", 1);    # mark session as suspended
    $sess_ref->close ();
    $page .= p ("To be continued.")      # give user instructions for resuming
            . p ("You can resume by selecting\n"
                    . a ({-href => url ()}, "this link")
                    . ", or by visiting the following URL: ")
            . p (url ());
}
else
{
    error ("Logic error, unknown choice: $choice");
}
```

The `display_question()` function generates the pages that present each question to the user. The most noteworthy thing here is that the answers to previous questions are consulted as necessary to resolve any references to them that appear in the question string:

```
sub display_question
{
my ($sess_ref, $question) = @_;
my ($answers, $str, $page);

    # Get question to ask, then substitute in previous answers
    # if sequences of the form %xxx% are found, where xxx is
    # the name associated with the answer.

    $answers = $sess_ref->{answers};
```

```
        $str = $question->{question};
        $str =~ s/%([^%]+)%/$answers->{$1}/ while $str =~ /%[^%]+%/;

        $page .= start_form (-action => url ())
            . p (($sess_ref->attr ("index") + 1) . ". $str")      # question
            . radio_group (-name => "answer",                     # possible answers
                            -values => $question->{answers},
                            -default => "[NO DEFAULT]",
                            -linebreak => 1)
            . br () . br ()
            . submit (-name => "choice", -value => "Submit")
            . " "
            . submit (-name => "choice", -value => "Finish Later")
            . end_form ();

        return ($page);
    }
```

Each time the user submits an answer by selecting the Continue button, process_answer() checks the form contents. If the user didn't actually select one of the alternatives, we issue a reminder and leave the index counter unchanged so that display_question() will present the same question again. Otherwise, we add the new answer to the session record and increment the counter to go to the next question:

```
sub process_answer
{
my ($sess_ref, $question) = @_;
my $answer = WebDB::trim (param ("answer"));
my $page;

    if ($answer eq "")  # user didn't select any answer; display reminder
    {
        $page .= p ("Please answer the question.");
    }
    else
    {
        # Add new answer to those that already have been recorded; each
        # answer is keyed to the name of the "survey" table column in
        # which it will be stored at survey completion time.  Then
        # increment question index so next question gets displayed.

        my $answers = $sess_ref->attr ("answers");
        $answers->{$question->{name}} = $answer;
        $sess_ref->attr ("answers", $answers);
        # go to next question
        $sess_ref->attr ("index", $sess_ref->attr ("index") + 1);
    }
    return ($page);
}
```

Finally, after the user has completed the survey, we call save_answers() to extract the responses from the session record and store them in the survey table:

```
sub save_answers
{
my $sess_ref = shift;
my $answers = $sess_ref->attr ("answers");  # the user's answers
my ($dbh, $stmt, @placeholder);

    # the keys of the answers hash are the column names in the "survey"
    # table in which to store the answers

    foreach my $key (keys (%{$answers}))
    {
        $stmt .= "," if $stmt;      # put commas between assignments
        $stmt .= "$key = ?";        # add column name, placeholder
        push (@placeholder, $answers->{$key});  # save placeholder value
    }
    $stmt = "INSERT INTO survey SET $stmt"; # complete the statement
    $dbh = WebDB::connect ();
    $dbh->do ($stmt, undef, @placeholder);
    $dbh->disconnect ();
}
```

Suggested Modifications

Implement a Start Over button that forgets all the previous answers and begins again with the first question.

Implement a Go Back button that enables the user to back up and change the answers to previous questions.

When Sessions Aren't Enough

Sessions in this chapter have consisted of a set of requests originating from a given client. When the session ID is stored in a cookie, a session is further limited implicitly to requests from a single browser, because any given cookie belongs to a specific browser. This approach works well for many applications, but sometimes you need additional capabilities. One limitation is that you can't access a session from multiple machines. For example, you can't suspend a session-based activity while at work, and then go home and resume it. When you need "mobile" session capability, other techniques can be used such as putting a front end on the session lookup process: Have the user log in using a name and password, and then use the name to associate the session with the user. These kinds of techniques lead us into consideration of security and authentication issues, which we'll take up in the next chapter.

9

Security and Privacy Issues

AT SEVERAL POINTS IN THE EARLIER CHAPTERS, I've alluded to various security-related concerns such as the need to check the contents of forms to make sure submitted information is valid. In this chapter, we'll pull these threads together to survey some of the security issues with which you should be concerned when you develop and run a Web site, and to discuss what you can do to address the dangers. In many cases, the purpose of security measures is to protect the integrity of your own data. But security also comes into play with regard to the collection and use of information that you obtain from visitors to your site, which brings up the topic of privacy. You should respect the privacy of people who use your site, so the chapter also discusses ways to avoid compromising the information they provide to you. Trust is a valuable commodity that you don't want to lose.

The discussion in this chapter is specific to security as it relates to Web development, but you should also be concerned about general system security. Even if you run a little-known site that doesn't receive much traffic, don't think that you're safe merely because of your relative obscurity. The bad guys are continually running scanners looking for machines with vulnerabilities. These scans are not based on how well known you are. They're automated, and they sweep the entire Internet address space. You *will* be found and probed.

One thing I want to emphasize at the outset is that good security is *difficult* to achieve, and there is no simple recipe you can follow to make your site safe and secure forever. New exploits are discovered on an ongoing basis, so I encourage you to adopt a security-conscious mindset in which you're continually on the lookout for new information that can help you ward off the bad guys. Security is not just a matter of acquiring tools; it's also a frame of mind from which springs the desire to understand why the tools are necessary and how to use them effectively. If you use the techniques shown here, they will *help* make your site secure; they will not guarantee no one can find an exploit. Computer security is a very large topic served by an extensive literature. For more information, I've suggested some additional resources in Appendix B, "References and Further Reading," that you might find helpful.

Know Your Cryptography Regulations

This chapter includes some material related to cryptographic techniques. Cryptography is regulated in some countries. I'm assuming here that you'll write and use cryptography-related software in accordance with your country's legal policies.

Channels of Information

Web applications involve the flow and storage of information, and the goal of security is to protect that information so that it can't be seen or modified except by the appropriate parties. For a typical database-backed Web application, information travels through several conduits, all of which are points of attack that are subject to inspection or subversion. Opportunities for compromise present themselves in many ways:

- One information channel goes over the network between the Web server and the clients that access it. Potential insecurities include having the connection wiretapped by a third party or having the client himself submit false information or excessive amounts of information in an attempt to mislead or overwhelm your application.

- Information flows between Apache and the MySQL server. Traffic over this channel may be subject to snooping.

- The Apache server executes Web scripts and those scripts in turn may read and write files or connect to the MySQL server. By default, all Web scripts run with the privileges of the user and group IDs under which Apache itself runs. This means that if several people have permission to install scripts for the Web server to execute, one person's script may gain access to another person's Web-related files.

- People sometimes store MySQL connection parameters (such as usernames and passwords) in files. Failure to protect these files from inspection by other users can lead to unauthorized database access.

- MySQL itself stores information in database tables that are represented by files. These files should be accessible only to the MySQL server. In a poorly administered installation, other people with login accounts on the server host may be able to bypass the server and access database files directly.

The dangers related to these various sources of information interact, such that a weakness in one area can lead to exploits in another area. If you have scripts that perform database operations, you might store MySQL connection parameters in a file for use by those scripts. Another person who has no MySQL access but can install Web scripts may be able to write a script that, when run by Apache, gains access to your parameter file and uses its contents to access your databases. In this way, file system access translates into database access. This issue may concern you particularly if you have a Web-hosting account with an ISP on a server shared by many other users about whom you know nothing and have little reason to trust.

Feeling nervous yet? You should. Nevertheless, there are a number of techniques for dealing with such problems:

- To guard against the dangers posed by clients who submit bad data to an application (either deliberately or just by mistake), the application should validate anything it cannot afford to take for granted.

- Keeping Web scripts and files secure involves proper file ownerships and access permissions. It also helps to keep executable scripts outside the Web server document tree. However, file security is difficult to achieve if multiple users have access to the Web server. Under some circumstances you may need to consider moving your installation to a different provider.

- Managing access to the MySQL server's data directory is a matter of properly setting up file permissions and user ID under which the server runs, and of keeping the MySQL account names and passwords secure.

- To protect information from being intercepted and inspected as it travels over a network connection, you can use an encrypted channel.

The following sections discuss these issues in more detail and outline your options for preventing problems.

Dangers Presented by Remote Users

Web applications typically respond to information provided by clients. However, writing an application that is driven by client input allows the client to control, at least to some extent, how the application works. This is one basis for Web attacks—a client provides input that makes your application behave in a way you did not anticipate and did not intend. Generally, the input will be something designed to cause you to expose more information than you want disclosed, or something designed to cause your Web or database server to malfunction or crash.

Effective prevention of such attacks requires that you be aware of how they can occur so that you can prepare for them in advance. Bad input doesn't just come from malicious clients trying to make your life miserable. It can also come from innocent users who simply enter the wrong thing by mistake, Nevertheless, if you're not prepared, the result is the same either way: a misbehaving application that does something other than what you want.

Sources of Client Input

Input presented by clients to your applications is not necessarily trustworthy, no matter what form it takes. These forms are as follows:

- **Information supplied through cookies.** Normally, cookies are an invisible part of the client-server interaction as far as the user is concerned. However, cookies are maintained by the browser on the user's local disk in a file. The file can be edited to manipulate cookie contents, so cookies are just as subject to compromise as any other kind of information received from the client.

- **Parameters supplied in a URL.** For example:

  ```
  http://www.snake.net/cgi-perl/some_app.pl?param1=x;param2=y;param3=z
  ```

  Applications often generate these URLs themselves. (For example, the real-estate search applications in Chapter 7, "Performing Searches," generate URLs for going to different pages of a search result or for displaying individual listings.) But obviously anyone can invoke your script by entering a URL into their browser manually and typing whatever they want for the parameter values. You cannot therefore assume the parameters will contain only sane values such as your application itself might provide.

- **Parameters received from a form.** These are subject to mischief through a procedure that I'll describe shortly. A malicious user can use this procedure to subvert fields that normally cannot be modified (such as hidden fields) or fields that otherwise provide only the choices you supply when you generate the form (such as radio buttons or check boxes). This means you can't trust the value of any field to be what you expect.

Illegitimate Manipulation of Input Data

To demonstrate the point that you have reason to be suspicious of any information you receive from a client, I'll describe briefly how to subvert a form. This will demonstrate that the only thing you really know about a form is what you send to the client. You know nothing about what happens in the interval between your sending the form to the client and the client returning it with the fields filled in, and it's possible to get back something quite different than what you expect.

When you send a form to a browser, your expectation is that the user will fill in text fields, make selections from radio buttons, check boxes, or lists, and so forth. You may also include hidden fields containing information that the client is not supposed to modify. When the user submits the form, you obviously wouldn't trust text fields of a form to contain only legal values, because users can type whatever they want into them. That's why you routinely verify such fields against content or length constraints. Other types of fields seem to offer better security prospects. Hidden fields have values that are assigned by you when you generate the form, not by the user. And structured form elements such as radio buttons, check boxes, and lists enable the user to select only those choices you provide explicitly when you create the form. Therefore, you might think, "Do I need to check such fields, given that their values are guaranteed to be legal?" If there really were any such guarantee, you wouldn't. But the assumption inherent in that question is flawed; there is no guarantee. These types of form elements are useful for users because they make it more convenient to fill in forms, but they provide no assurance about the integrity of the data you receive back. The sense of security these fields offer script writers is entirely illusory. They are no less subject to modification than text fields.

To illustrate, suppose you have an application that conducts an online shopping session. Near the end of this process, you collect a credit card number from the customer and then display a final confirmation page asking the user to review the order and okay it. The page shows the items ordered and presents item quantities as pop-up menus to enable the customer to make final adjustments. It also contains the user's credit card number in a hidden field. That way, when the user submits the form to confirm the order, you can get all the information you need to process the order by extracting the parameters from the form. For example, if I'm ordering three boxes of light bulbs, the confirmation page you present to me may include a form that looks something like this (for brevity, I've omitted fields for information such as shipping address):

```
<form method="post" action="http://www.snake.net/cgi-perl/order_confirm.pl">
<input type="hidden" name="credit_card" value="012345678901">
<input type="hidden" name="item1" value="light bulbs">
Light bulbs (box):
<select name="quantity">
<option value="1">1</option>
```

continues

continued

```
<option value="2">2</option>
<option value="3" selected>3</option>
<option value="4">4</option>
</select>
<input type="submit" name="choice" value="Confirm">
</form>
```

If I want to subvert your application so that you send me a hundred boxes of light bulbs and bill someone else for them, here's the procedure I follow:

- I save the confirmation page displayed in my browser to a file on my local disk.

- I open the file in a text editor, and then modify it by changing the credit_card field value to a different number (perhaps one that I've stolen from someone else). I also add an option to the quantity pop-up menu for 100 units and select it:

```
<form method="post" action="http://www.snake.net/cgi-perl/order_confirm.pl">
<input type="hidden" name="credit_card" value="109876543210">
<input type="hidden" name="item1" value="light bulbs">
Light bulbs (box):
<select name="quantity">
<option value="1">1</option>
<option value="2">2</option>
<option value="3">3</option>
<option value="4">4</option>
<option value="100" selected>100</option>
</select>
<input type="submit" name="choice" value="Confirm">
</form>
```

- I save the file, reload it into my browser, and select the Submit button to send the form back to your application.

- Your application processes my order. I get 100 boxes of light bulbs, and somebody else gets the bill.

What I've just described is one way an application can be attacked, but it's by no means the only way. A script may find itself invoked from entirely unexpected sources, and being fed input that bears no relation to what it expects. If I want to send you bad information, the preceding example discusses one way I can break the relationship between the form an application sends and the form it gets back. But I don't have to modify a form you send me; I can write my own form and point it at your script. Furthermore, although I'd include fields with the same names as the parameters your application expects to receive, I don't need to use the same types of fields you use in your own form. If I make them text-input fields, I can submit any value whatsoever for any parameter. For example, I need not go through the trouble of actually running your `order_confirm.pl` application to get to the confirmation page. I can write a simple Web page containing a form that looks like this:

```
<form method="post" action="http://www.snake.net/cgi-perl/order_confirm.pl">
Credit card number:
<input type="text" name="credit_card">
Item:
<input type="text" name="item1">
Quantity:
<input type="text" name="quantity">
<input type="submit" name="choice" value="Confirm">
</form>
```

This form points to your script and it has the same field names as a legitimate form generated by your application. But the contents are fully editable directly from my browser window. I can select any item, in any quantity, and bill it to someone else. All I have to do is load this page into my browser, fill in the fields, press the Submit button, and the contents of the form get sent to your script. In this case, I'm forcing your script to process the contents of my form—a form over which you have no control and about which you can make no assumptions.

The implication of this is that no type of form element affords any measure of protection at all. You may as well consider all fields in any form you generate as completely editable, because in fact anyone can write an attack form that treats them that way. (You might even say that the real danger posed by hidden fields and list fields is that form designers come to think their values are safe from tampering and can be used safely.)

Form input need not come even from a form at all. "Form input" really is just data encoded in a particular way and sent to your Web server. Anyone can write a script that encodes false information so that it appears to originate from a form, then opens a connection to your Web server to invoke your script and shoves the information at it. Writing a program to generate information that looks like a form submission is one way to make it easier to perform automated attacks. There's no need to fill in a form manually; just run the program repeatedly.

In summary, the preceding discussion illustrates several principles to keep in mind when you're writing applications that process form input:

- There is no necessary relationship between the form you send to a client and the form you get back.

- There is no necessary relationship between the type of form elements you use to collect information and the way the information actually is collected. Don't think that hidden fields or structured fields that provide a fixed set of options offer any guarantee of integrity on the values you'll get back.

- Your application may normally expect to be invoked by forms that it generates itself, but other people can point their own forms at your script, or invoke it without using a form at all.

Responding to User Input

Given the extent of the potential for subversion of input by users, should you just throw up your hands and declare that it's not worth trying to write any applications at all? Well, no. The point is not that you should fall into deep despair. The point is that if you want to enforce some constraints on the values of form elements, but you're not willing to trust the client (and there is little reason that you should), you need to enforce the constraints yourself on the server side *after* the form has been submitted. You can't trust what you get from the client, so you must validate the values of all fields for which you expect a particular kind of information.

In some cases, not much verification may be needed. For example, if you have a search form with a `sex` field represented by a pop-up menu containing values of `male` and `female`, you probably won't care much if someone hacks the form to submit a silly value such as `bookcase`. All that will accomplish is to ensure that the query makes no sense and returns no records. No harm done. Other kinds of information are relatively free format and require little or no validation. If you're collecting comments for a guestbook, you may care only whether the value is empty. If you're collecting names as well, it may not matter whether the user puts in the correct name. (Besides, if users can't be counted on to supply their own name correctly, you certainly have no way of doing so for them.) If you're running a poll and the user modifies your form to cast a vote for a non-existent candidate, it's likely that the query to update the tally will affect no records, with the result that the vote simply is discarded.

In other cases, however, validation of user input is extremely important to make sure that values are in the expected format. For example, if a field value is supposed to look like an email address, telephone number, Zip code, or credit card number, you'll want to perform some kind of pattern match. We've developed a few functions like this in earlier chapters to help check values (such as `strip_non_digits()` and `looks_like_email()`). To augment these, you'll probably write your own arsenal of validation functions suited to the type of information you collect. You may also want to check length, not just content. (You can include a `maxlength` parameter in a text field, but that's easily bypassed, so you should not assume any value submitted really is within the legal length.)

Validation is particularly important when you're using input to construct queries that change the contents of your database. You want the modifications to be legal ones that make sense. Suppose you have a form-based application for updating employee records by applying a percentage pay raise to them. You'll want to verify that the raise is valid each time a form is submitted. (If you have a form element with percent increase values of 2, 4, 6, 8, and 10, make sure the user really submitted one of those values to prevent the user from giving raises of 50 or 100 percent to friends.)

> ### Does Client-Side Validation Improve Form Integrity?
>
> Some applications use client-side validation to check field contents before a form is returned to the server. If you have a field into which the user must enter a number, for example, you can include JavaScript code that checks the value and pops up an alert if the value is bad. This technique also has the benefit of reducing the number of round trips to the server for invalid values. That sounds helpful, and there's no particular reason not to use such techniques.
>
> However, be sure to recognize that they can only reduce the likelihood of receiving malformed input from the client, not eliminate it. Some browsers don't handle JavaScript at all. But even for those that do, client-side validation cannot be trusted as authoritative. It is an additional check that helps honest users, but is no barrier to malicious ones. There's little you can do to be sure the client hasn't subverted the form to remove the validity-checking code. JavaScript can be hacked just like HTML, or the user can disable JavaScript entirely in the browser preferences. It's still necessary to validate the input yourself on the server side.

Detecting Form Tampering

You may not be able to keep a user from illegitimately modifying the contents of a form, but you can construct the form so that tampering is detectable. For example, if you have a hidden field containing a record ID number that you expect to come back with exactly the same value you sent to the client, you can add a checksum.

This doesn't prevent the user from changing the value, but it does enable you to detect such attempts. If in addition you want to prevent the user from being able to see the original field value, you can encrypt it. These techniques are illustrated later in the chapter (see the section "Writing a Secure Application").

For fields such as pop-up menus or check boxes that present a specific list of options to the user, you can detect tampering by making sure that the value returned to your application corresponds to a value that actually was present in the form that you sent to the client. This means the form generation and validation components of your application must agree about the set of legal values. That is pretty easy if you're processing forms using methods such as those described in Chapter 6, "Automating the Form-Handling Process." For example, to present a set of radio buttons corresponding to the elements of an ENUM column my_enum in a table my_table, you can get the information you need from the table description. Suppose the column is defined like this:

```
my_enum ENUM('value a','value b','value c')
```

The definition can be used to generate a form element. To generate a set of radio buttons, you might do something like this:

```
$tbl_info = WebDB::TableInfo->get ($dbh, "my_table");
@members = $tbl_info->members ("my_enum");
print radio_group (-name => "my_enum", -values => \@members);
```

To verify values that users submit, use the column description again:

```
$tbl_info = WebDB::TableInfo->get ($dbh, "my_table");
@members = $tbl_info->members ("my_enum");
$val = param ("my_enum");
$legal = defined ($val) && grep (/^$val$/i, @members);
```

`$legal` will be true if the value of the `my_enum` field is one of those listed in the `my_enum` column description, false otherwise.

Handling User Input Safely for Query Construction

After you've checked the input presented to your application by the user to be sure that it makes sense, are you done? Is the information safe to use? The answer to that question is, "Safe for what?" If you're going to use the input to issue database queries, you must still be careful about how you construct the queries. For example, you might collect search parameters to use in a SELECT statement, or you might store form information by issuing an INSERT statement. In all such cases, you must ensure that clients cannot submit information (either mistakenly or maliciously) that causes the query to be malformed. At best, your statement will just fail with a syntax error, but certain types of input can have serious unintended consequences unless you take steps to prevent them. A SELECT that normally selects just a few rows may select an entire table if constructed incorrectly, leading to excessive server resource consumption or Web server failure. If a client can produce such a result, your machine can be tied up to such an extent that the input serves effectively as a denial-of-service attack. Worse yet, a query may destroy data. For example, a malformed DELETE or UPDATE query can change many more rows than you intend.

To prevent these problems, you must encode information into your queries properly to ensure that you don't generate malformed SQL or queries that do something other than what you want. As it happens, you already know how to do this. Throughout the earlier chapters, we've been using placeholders or `quote()` to make sure that data values are properly encoded when they are added to a query string. I haven't said all that much about why we should do this, other than to make sure that characters such as quotes or backslashes are escaped properly; now it's time to discuss how failure to encode values can really hurt you.

Suppose you run a Web site for an organization that maintains a descriptive profile of members and allows members to edit or delete their own profile using a form-based Web application. The application keeps track of the record being edited using an ID number stored in a hidden field. When a form is submitted, you collect the ID value and put it in a variable `$id`. If the user request is to delete the record, you might construct the DELETE statement like this by inserting the value of `$id` directly into the query string:

```
$dbh->do ("DELETE FROM my_table WHERE id = $id");
```

That's fine as long as the application is used legitimately for its intended purpose. Suppose, however, that a user hacks the form to supply an `id` value such as "`1 OR id !=
1`"; in that case, the query becomes:

```
DELETE FROM my_table WHERE id = 1 OR id != 1
```

That query is true for every record, so it completely empties the table. (Whoops! I hope you had a backup.) This illustrates that if you don't treat user input with the proper respect, people can attack your database through your own Web applications.

In this particular instance, you might have detected the hack attempt by testing the `id` parameter to make sure its value really is a number. But sometimes field values are free format and content checks can't be applied so readily. To make sure an input value doesn't get treated as anything other than a single data value in the query string, you should reference it using a placeholder:

```
$dbh->do ("DELETE FROM my_table WHERE id = ?", undef, $id);
```

Alternatively, use the `quote()` method:

```
$dbh->do ("DELETE FROM my_table WHERE id = " . $dbh->quote ($id));
```

Either way, the attacker's input is encoded safely into the query string, which ends up looking like this:

```
DELETE FROM my_table WHERE id = '1 OR id != 1'
```

MySQL will perform a string-to-number conversion on the `id` comparison value to produce the value 1. The result is that the query affects only the record with an ID of 1, not every record in the table. (This does not help you detect whether the user actually did modify the form—it just limits the damage. Form modification detection and prevention is covered in the later section "Writing a Secure Application.")

The preceding example shows how a user might attempt to damage your database by causing records to be changed or lost. A similar attack can be used in search contexts. If you have a record-retrieval application that solicits an `id` value for the `my_table` table, you might construct and execute the query like this:

```
$sth = $dbh->prepare ("SELECT * FROM my_table WHERE id = $id");
$sth->execute ();
while (my $ref = $sth->fetchrow_hashref ())
{
    # display record here ...
}
$sth->finish ();
```

Here, too, if the user submits an `id` value such as "`1 OR id != 1`", and you put it directly into the query string, you end up with a statement that doesn't do what you want:

```
SELECT * FROM my_table WHERE id = 1 OR id != 1
```

This query retrieves the entire contents of the table, causing your database and Web servers to devote more computing resources to processing the query than you intend. Input like this can be used as the basis for a denial-of-service attack that causes your machine to spend so much time doing useless work processing bogus queries that it cannot respond effectively to legitimate client requests. The solution, just as with the preceding DELETE query, is to change the code to use placeholders or quote(). The placeholder version looks like this:

```
$sth = $dbh->prepare ("SELECT * FROM my_table WHERE id = ?");
$sth->execute ($id);
while (my $ref = $sth->fetchrow_hashref ())
{
    # display record here ...
}
$sth->finish ();
```

Using quote(), the code looks like this:

```
$id = $dbh->quote ($id);
$sth = $dbh->prepare ("SELECT * FROM my_table WHERE id = $id");
$sth->execute ();
while (my $ref = $sth->fetchrow_hashref ())
{
    # display record here ...
}
$sth->finish ();
```

Placeholders and quote() do have their limitations; they can be used only for data values. For other query elements, they're inapplicable and you must verify the values yourself. These include the following types of information:

- **Database, table, or column names.** These are commonly used as form elements in database-browsing applications. For example, you might provide a pop-up menu containing a list of table names for the user to choose from.

- **Comparison operators.** You might use a form such as the following one that enables the user to specify an operator to be applied to a price value in a search query:

```
print start_form (-action => url ()),
    "Find records where the price is", br (),
    radio_group (-name => "operator",
                -values => [ "<", "=", ">" ],
                -labels => {
                    "<" => "less than",
                    "=" => "equal to",
                    ">" => "greater than"}),
    br (), " the following value: ", br (),
    textfield (-name => "price"),
    end_form ();
```

- **Function names.** Suppose you have an application that enables the user to apply a functional transform to a column of data values from a table, using a query like this:

```
SELECT x, function_name(x) AS y FROM my_table
```

The application would construct the SELECT query, but you might allow the user to choose the function name by means of a pop-up menu in a form like this:

```
print start_form (-action => url ()),
    "Pick a function name: ",
    popup_menu (-name => "func_name",
               -values => [ "SQRT", "EXP", "LOG", "SIN", "COS" ]),
    end_form ();
```

In each of these cases, you must check for yourself that submitted values are valid. For database, table, or column names, verify that the name is legal. For the operator or function name examples, make sure the value that comes back from the user is one you actually provided as a choice.

File Upload Issues

Uploaded files are another kind of user input. CGI.pm stores each uploaded file in a temporary directory on the Web server host, and then deletes it after your script terminates. (This is why you must copy the file somewhere else if you want it to exist beyond the lifetime of your script.) CGI.pm's default file upload behavior includes two aspects that may present problems under some circumstances:

- **File visibility.** All scripts run by the Web server normally run with the same file system access privileges unless you take steps to ensure otherwise. Therefore, any script can see temporary files created by another script if they happen to be running at the same time. This won't be a problem if you're the only one who can install Web scripts to be executed by the server, but if multiple users can do so and you don't trust them all, you may have cause for concern.

- **File size.** It's possible for a user to upload a huge file that fills up the file system where the temporary file directory is located. Although the file will be deleted when the script terminates, that doesn't help other programs that try to write to the file system while the upload is in progress.

You can address these problems by setting CGI.pm configuration variables, which are located in the initialize_globals() routine of the CGI.pm source. To change them, you'll need to edit the installed version of CGI.pm.[1] Three variables are relevant to file uploads:

---

1. If you do this, remember that you'll need to make your changes again each time you install a new version of CGI.pm.

- `$PRIVATE_TEMPFILES` controls whether temporary upload files are private to the script that creates them. By default, this variable is 0 (false), so files are visible to other Web scripts that run at the same time. If you set this to a true value (such as 1), CGI.pm immediately deletes the temporary file after opening it. This is a UNIX idiom that causes the file's name to disappear from the file system (thus rendering it unavailable to other processes) but still be available to your script through the open file handle. (As you might guess from the preceding sentence, setting this variable to true has no effect under Windows.) If you do enable `$PRIVATE_TEMPFILES`, be aware that this causes the CGI.pm function `tmpFileName()` to stop working. That function returns the name of the uploaded file, but the private file mechanism causes that name to be gone by the time you'd call `tmpFileName()`. Normally, this shouldn't be a problem because your script still has access to the file through the file handle. The CGI.pm documentation deprecates use of `tmpFileName()`, anyway.

- `$POST_MAX` controls the maximum size of uploaded files. The default value is −1 (no limit); set it to a positive value to constrain file sizes to that many bytes.

- `$DISABLE_UPLOADS` controls whether file uploads are allowed at all. By default, the value is false; set it to true to prevent uploads.

If you edit the CGI.pm source to enable these restrictions globally, scripts that need to override them can do so on an individual basis. Suppose you set the variables in CGI.pm as follows to allow uploads but make temporary files private and limited to one kilobyte in size:

```
$DISABLE_UPLOADS = 0;      # allow uploads
$PRIVATE_TEMPFILES = 1;    # make temporary files private
$POST_MAX = 1024;          # limit file size to 1KB
```

A script can make files public (perhaps so it can use `tmpFileName()`) and set the maximum posting size to 1 megabyte by resetting the variables like this:

```
$CGI::PRIVATE_TEMPFILES = 0;     # files not private
$CGI::POST_MAX = 1024 * 1024;    # limit size to 1MB
```

If `$PRIVATE_TEMPFILES` is enabled globally, a script can disable it only for its own temporary files. In other words, another user's script cannot gain access to your script's temporary files by setting the variable false. That's small comfort, though. If you save the temporary file somewhere more permanent, the permanent file may be visible to any other Web script that knows where to look, whether the script was written by you or by someone else. The reason for this is explained in the section "Dangers from Other Users with Apache Access."

Using *$POST_MAX* To Limit Text Field Input

The $POST_MAX variable actually applies not just to a single uploaded file, but to the combined size of all the elements in a form. Therefore, you can set this variable to keep people from pasting huge amounts of junk into text fields, too.

Dangers Presented by Local Users

The preceding section describes security issues that relate primarily to problems with client users on the remote end of connections to your Web server. However, there are other users you should be concerned about, too. For example, if your Web site runs on a multiple-user operating system such as UNIX and other people have the ability to install Web scripts, there are certain exploits to which you are exposed. First, we'll discuss general issues relating to file system access by other users—in particular, access that may be gained through scripts run by Apache. Then we'll cover issues that pertain more specifically to the MySQL server.

Dangers from Other Users with Apache Access

Your general goal with Apache is that it should do the things you want it to, but not anything else. Unfortunately, in a multiple-user situation, other people want Apache to do things, too, and you cannot control their actions. This in itself might not be a problem, except for one thing: Scripts run by Apache have Apache's file system access privileges, no matter who they were written by or who they are owned by. You might write a Web script expecting it to have your own privileges when run under Apache, but that's not how it works. Apache runs with the privileges associated with a specific user and group, and so do any scripts that it executes. This gives all users who can install scripts in the Web tree a certain equivalence. Even if you set the permissions on your Web-related directories and files to keep me out when I'm logged in as me, they still must be accessible to Apache. (Otherwise, Apache wouldn't be able to serve your pages or run your scripts.) If I can install a script for the server to execute, it will have Apache's privileges when it runs and thus be able to access any of your Web files. This means that under Apache, I may as well be you for all intents and purposes, because your scripts and mine have the same privileges and my scripts can access anything your scripts can access.

This privilege equivalence of scripts that Apache runs leads to potential problems in the following ways:

- **Scripts can read files.** For files such as HTML documents that are intended to be served to the public by Apache anyway, that is not a problem. However, script file system access is not limited to HTML documents; it also includes the source code for your scripts and libraries, and files in which you might store sensitive information. You probably don't want just anyone reading those files. For example, the ability to read the source code of your scripts might allow another user to figure out interesting exploits to mount against you.

- **Scripts can write files.** Someone else can create (or remove!) files in your Web directories if you don't protect them properly.

- **Scripts can open connections to database servers.** If your scripts read a file to get a MySQL username and password, my scripts can read that file, too. That allows me to open a connection using your MySQL name and password to access your databases. (Put another way, this means you have no secrets from me; your databases are effectively public information.)

Ideally, you will have complete control over your Web server and be the only one with access to it. When you are the only user on your machine, you have fewer file system access issues to be concerned about.[2] To the extent that other people have accounts on your system and have access to the Web or database servers, you have to consider how much trust you're willing to extend. (That's why full control is ideal; when you have control, you don't need to have trust.) There are at least two important things that should be true before you trust other users who have accounts on the same machine as you:

- You're confident they won't deliberately attack your information.
- You're confident about their competence to write secure programs, rather than insecure ones that allow someone else to attack your information.

Some multiple-user situations may be acceptable. A group of developers who all trust each other and are the only ones with server access may be collaborating on a Web-based project and sharing a single server without any problems.

A less acceptable—and very possibly *unacceptable*—scenario occurs when a Web server is shared by people with disparate interests and purposes. Examples are academic departments that provide a shared server to handle Web accounts for students and staff, or ISPs that provide Web-hosting accounts using the same server for multiple customers. These scenarios can be very dangerous. Suppose you get an account with an ISP that provides Web hosting. As part of this service, you get your own domain name `your-dom.com` and a `cgi-bin` directory owned by you and into which you can install scripts for Apache to execute when clients request URLs of this form:

```
http://www.your-dom.com/cgi-bin/script.pl
```

Now if I want to attack you, here's how I do it. I get an account with this same ISP, which gives me my own domain `my-dom.com` and `cgi-bin` directory and sets them up to be handled by the same server that handles your account. (Such accounts are often billed as "virtual servers," but in this case, that means nothing more than "your own domain name, hosted on a server that handles a bunch of other people's domain names.")

---

2. That's not to say that there are *no* file system issues. For example, you'll still want to run Apache under user and group IDs that differ from yours. Then make your Web directories, scripts, and files owned by you and readable to Apache but not writable by Apache. This helps prevent remote exploits that attempt to cause the Web server to create or destroy files on the server host.

You can probably set the access permissions on your Web-related directories so that I cannot just log in on the server host and access them directly. However, you must make those directories and their contents available to Apache, and that's all the access I require to create a security breach. I have my own `cgi-bin` directory, so I just put a script `breach.pl` there and have Apache execute it by requesting it from my browser like this:

```
http://www.my-dom.com/cgi-bin/breach.pl
```

`breach.pl` need not be complex or clever. The following listing shows a short implementation that opens a file and displays its contents over the Web. As shown here, `breach.pl` is set to display itself, but I can easily change that by modifying the value of `$file` to point at one of your files:

```perl
#! /usr/bin/perl -w
# breach.pl - illustrate a security breach by showing how a Web script
# can display the contents of other Web server-accessible files.

use strict;
use CGI qw(:standard escapeHTML);

# Set $file to the name of the file you want the script to display.
# The setting below causes the script to display its own source code.

my $file = "breach.pl";

print header (), start_html (-title => "Security Breach", -bgcolor => "white");

if (!open (IN, $file))
{
    print p (escapeHTML ("Cannot open $file: $!"));
}
else
{
    print p (escapeHTML ("Contents of $file:"));
    print "<pre>\n";
    print escapeHTML ($_) while defined ($_ = <IN>);
    print "</pre>\n";
    close (IN);
}

print end_html ();

exit (0);
```

When Apache executes my script, it runs under the same user and group IDs as Apache itself, so I can access your files. How will you stop me? (Or more to the point, ask your service provider how you can stop me.)

Of course, you can mount this same kind of attack against me, too. Unless we trust each other, this arrangement is just a little too cozy. Unfortunately, it's also rather common, and the dangers of this scenario seem not to be very widely appreciated. Note that the problem is not that a single Apache server can handle requests for multiple domains. That's a powerful and important feature. The problem arises from the use of this feature to have the same server handle domains for different people with incompatible interests. (After all, if I own several domains, I can use the same server for all of them without putting myself in danger, because I'm not likely to attack myself.)

A shared server can be a source of problems even in the absence of any intent by its users to mistreat each other. All it takes to place everyone at risk is for one person to install a script with an inadvertent security problem that allows an outside attacker to gain access to or destroy information on the server machine.

Security is one of those "only as good as the weakest link" things; what's the competence level of the other people with whom you share a server? Are you comfortable with that?

mod_perl in a Shared Environment

If you're running a server that is enabled to run mod_perl, you definitely don't want to be operating in a shared-server environment with other untrusted users:

- mod_perl scripts can affect the environment in which later scripts run. Malicious scripts can do this deliberately, and poorly written scripts may do it accidentally, but the effect can be the same. (ISPs often won't provide mod_perl in their servers; this is one reason why.)

- The mod_perl initialization file is read during the Apache startup process, while Apache is still running as root. Anyone with access to this file effectively has root access. (For example, you can use the initialization file to start up another process that runs as root and that can do whatever you want.)

Limiting Access by Other Users

It's pretty clear from the preceding discussion that you shouldn't run your server as root, because then Web scripts run as root, and anyone who can install a Web script can gain complete access to do anything at all.

To run Apache with the privileges of an ordinary account, use the User and Group directives in the httpd.conf file. For example, to run Apache with the privileges of the user wwwusr and the group wwwgrp, use these directives:

```
User wwwusr
Group wwwgrp
```

The server starts up as root during the system startup process, and then changes the effective user and group IDs to those listed in the configuration file before it starts handling requests. (Naturally, httpd.conf itself should be accessible only to a trusted administrator, otherwise other users may be able to change the User line from wwwusr to root and you'll have no security at all.)

Running Apache as an ordinary user limits the damage it can do, but does not eliminate the problem of other users installing Web scripts that may place your information in danger. Apache version 2.xx provides a general solution to the privilege equivalence problem by allowing specific user and group IDs to be associated with each virtual host. The server can handle requests for you at www.your-dom.com under your user and group IDs, and requests for me at www.my-dom.com under my user and group IDs. This improves server security because it allows you to make your Web scripts and documents accessible only to yourself; that way, other people who share the server can't write scripts that access your files directly. However, Apache 2.xx is not yet in wide use (it just went from alpha to beta as I write), so most sites still run 1.3.xx. In the meantime, other options for running scripts owned by different users under different user IDs include the following:

- If the Apache suEXEC feature is available, you can use it to run scripts under your own user ID. This enables you to protect sensitive files so that they cannot be accessed by anyone else's scripts. The cost is some degradation of performance. In addition, suEXEC cannot be used for any application that requires mod_perl, with which it is incompatible. suEXEC also has its own security implications, so you should read its documentation carefully before using it:

    http://www.apache.org/docs/suexec.html

- You can get your own server. If you're using an ISP, investigate whether that ISP can provide an independent server. The hardware version of this solution involves putting you on your own machine, which can be pricey. A less expensive alternative is the software virtual server, in which the resources of a machine are logically partitioned so as to appear to be multiple separate physical machines. Users in one server cannot access the files in another server, because processes in each partition run under completely independent user and group IDs. ISPs that provide this type of service rightly point out its security advantages over the kind of "virtual server" that really is only a shared server providing separate domain names. Many ISPs don't like to partition their machines as true virtual servers, though, because the number of server processes becomes a linear function of the number of customers and represents a greater drain on system resources than using shared servers. Therefore, although a virtual server is less expensive than a separate physical machine, it may cost you more than an account on a shared server. Can you afford it? That depends. Can you afford to have your databases be public information, the way they are on a shared server? Ask your ISP what measures are provided to prevent your resources from being accessed illegitimately by other customers. If you don't receive a satisfactory answer, you may need to consider another provider.

- If you cannot prevent other people from reading your Web-related files, you should at least try to to prevent people from writing them. Make sure the files are owned by you and located in a directory owned by you. Then change into the directory and turn off the group-write and world-write permissions on the directory and everything under it:

```
% chmod -R go-w .
```

For more information about Apache security, a good place to start is, not surprisingly, the security section of the Apache manual:

```
http://www.apache.org/docs/misc/security_tips.html
```

Script Location Issues

You may or may not want to keep your Web scripts private from other local users, but you should always keep remote users from looking at them. Whenever possible, put your scripts in directories that are outside the Apache document tree. Directories such as `cgi-bin` or `cgi-perl` should not be located anywhere under the document root, because an Apache misconfiguration can allow scripts in the document tree to be retrieved as plain text. If a script contains information such as a MySQL username and password, they'll be visible in plain view. (If you can't keep the script itself out of the document tree, at least encapsulate the database connection call in a library routine and put the library outside the tree.) Exposure of a script's source code may also allow hackers to see how to exploit it (for example, to obtain more information from your database than you intend or to mount denial-of-service attacks) if despite your best efforts the script has a security flaw. Keeping your scripts out of the document tree helps prevent these problems.

MySQL Server Access Issues

All access to database information managed by MySQL goes through the MySQL server, which requires each client to supply a name and password. At least, that's what's supposed to happen. Tables in databases are stored in files, so one possible exploit is to bypass the server entirely and access those files directly. Other problems are MySQL accounts that have not been assigned passwords, or stolen names and passwords. And, just as with Apache, you should limit the powers of the MySQL server by not running it as `root`. The following instructions illustrate how to enforce some MySQL protection. You'll likely need to run some of the commands shown here as `root`, because they involve changing file ownerships.

Let's start with the easiest thing first: Run the MySQL server as an ordinary user, not as `root`. The following instructions describe how to do this. (Before you follow them, you should bring down the server.)

If you want to use an account named `mysqlusr`, specify the account name in the `[mysqld]` group of the systemwide MySQL options file `/etc/my.cnf`:

```
[mysqld]
user=mysqlusr
```

You should also protect `/etc/my.cnf` so that it can be modified only by `root`:

```
# chown root /etc/my.cnf
# chmod 644 /etc/my.cnf
```

The file needs to be world-readable because other unprivileged programs may need read access.

Next, protect the MySQL data directory and its contents by limiting access only to `mysqlusr`. If the data directory is `/usr/local/mysql/var`, protect it like this:

```
# chown -R mysqlusr /usr/local/mysql/var
# chmod -R go-rwx /usr/local/mysql/var
```

If you restrict access to the data directory as just described so that its contents are available only to your MySQL server, you will have a problem if the server's UNIX domain socket file is located in that directory. (The symptom is that local client connections to `localhost` will stop working because they no longer can access the socket.) To deal with this, your best bet is to recompile MySQL to place the socket file in a different location. If this is not an option (perhaps you installed MySQL using a binary distribution or from RPM files), open up the data directory enough that client programs can connect to the socket file:

```
# chmod go+rx /usr/local/mysql/var
```

This has the disadvantage that, although it allows MySQL client programs to access the socket file, other users can also run `ls` to get a listing of the data directory. Because databases hosted by the MySQL server correspond to directories in the data directory, this enables people to find out what databases are available. If you start the server with the `--skip-show-database` option to restrict people from using the SHOW DATABASES statement, the ability to run `ls` on the data directory represents an end run around that restriction.

After making the preceding modifications, bring the server back up:

```
# safe_mysqld &
```

The server starts up as `root`, then finds the user line in the `/etc/my.cnf` option file and changes its user ID to run as `mysqlusr`.

To protect your server against unauthorized users connecting to it, make sure each MySQL account has a password. To find any that do not, connect to the server as your MySQL `root` user to access the `mysql` database and run this query:

```
mysql> SELECT * FROM user WHERE Password = '';
```

If the query returns any rows, the corresponding accounts are insecure and you'll probably want to remove them or assign passwords to them. (There may be some exceptions. You might, for example, set up a no-password account for use in log file rotation scripts such that the account has only the RELOAD privilege and no access to actual database information. Such accounts should be few and are best allowed to connect only from localhost.)

Are There Other MySQL Superusers?

Earlier in this chapter, we discussed the file system privilege problems that arise if other users have access to Apache. A similar issue comes up with the MySQL server. If other users have MySQL accounts with global (superuser) privileges for the databases managed by the server, your information is accessible to them. Ideally, you should be the only one with such privileges.

Personal MySQL option files used only by yourself can and should be protected. For example, your personal scripts might read connection parameters from the .my.cnf file in your home directory. Make sure no one but you can read this file by using either of the following commands:

```
% chmod 600 .my.cnf
% chmod go-rwx .my.cnf
```

On the other hand, preventing other users from stealing MySQL account names and passwords stored in option files that are accessible to Apache can be a difficult problem to solve. As discussed earlier in "Dangers from Other Users with Apache Access," your best option is to operate in an environment with no other Apache users or with only trusted users. If you have parameters stored in a file used by Web scripts, the file can be set to be readable only by yourself and Apache. One way to do this is to have the file be owned by you with group ownership set to the group that Apache runs in. If that group is wwwgrp, the commands to set the ownerships and mode look like this:

```
# chown paul filename
# chgrp wwwgrp filename
# chmod g-w,o-rwx filename
```

The mode setting revokes group-write permission for Apache, and all world-access permissions. This won't keep out people who can install Web scripts, but it will at least prevent everybody else from reading the file.

MySQL accounts that are used by Web scripts should have only the privileges they require. In particular, the FILE privilege gives a MySQL user great power; don't grant it to any account that you use in your Web scripts for connecting to MySQL, at least not without a good reason. The privilege allows a user to read any file on the database host that the MySQL server can read, and allows the user to cause the server to create files on the host in any directory for which the server has write access. This power can be used to hijack information that you may not want leaking out over the Web, or to alter the operation of your system. The potential for damage is multiplied greatly if you run the server as root; this is one of the reasons to run it as an ordinary user. There may be applications that require the FILE privilege, but make sure you understand the implications before granting it.

For more information about MySQL security, consult the MySQL Reference Manual or a text on MySQL that discusses MySQL administration.

Network Access and Client Privacy Protection

Web applications, based as they are on networking, are subject to dangers from wire-tapping or snooping. It's bad enough when wiretapping actually involves wires, but with wireless networking on the rise, it may be possible for an attacker to join your network just by wandering into your vicinity with a suitable receiver and transmitter. (Two things you can do to reduce the risk are to require a password before access to the network is allowed and to turn on encryption of wireless traffic.)

Information sent over the network may be intercepted by a third party, inspected, and used for various forms of mischief such as masquerading as someone else or mounting replay attacks. Stolen names and passwords can be used later to forge an identity. Captured data can be replayed by sending it to the Web server for processing again. (You didn't really intend to submit 317 individual orders for a dozen self-sealing stem bolts? Maybe you ordered once and someone else replayed your order 316 times.)

In a Web environment, the most obvious source of network traffic is the information that travels between your Web server and remote clients. Your basic tool for protecting these connections is encryption. This can be done by enabling support for SSL (the Secure Sockets Layer protocol) in your Web server, at least for clients that also support SSL.[3] Connections between the Web server and MySQL may also provide a network-based point of exposure. To protect information that passes between Apache and MySQL, you have a couple of options. If you run Apache and MySQL on the same host, you can keep information between the two from traveling over the network by having your Web scripts specify the hostname `localhost` when connecting to MySQL server. Then the connections will not use TCP/IP connections that are subject to eavesdropping. They will use UNIX domain sockets or the loopback interface, for which traffic is not routed onto the Internet. If you run Apache and MySQL on separate hosts, you can use SSH port-forwarding to create a secure tunnel. (MySQL includes direct support for establishing SSL connections from version 3.23.9 and on, but this capability is not yet available from within DBI scripts.)

For some applications, another network information channel may be involved. For example, an e-commerce application might set up a connection between Apache and a vendor with whom you have a merchant account for handling credit card transactions. This kind of channel normally will be encrypted for security.

Information on how SSL works, how to use it for setting up secure connections for your Web clients, and how to create secure connections to the MySQL server are covered in the following sections of this chapter. The topic of connecting to merchant account vendors is covered in Chapter 10, "E-Commerce Applications."

---

3. For example, versions of the `lynx` browser prior to 2.8.3 do not support secure connections, and even for recent versions, SSL support is optional.

Dangers of Password Fields

One type of input field you can use in forms is the password field. (With CGI.pm, these are produced using the password_field() call.) Password fields pose a kind of security risk, but not because of anything the client does. The danger occurs from Web developers being lulled into thinking that password fields are secure in any way. They aren't. The browser shows bullets or asterisks rather than the characters the user actually enters into the field, but that provides only an illusion of security. Other people may not be able to look over the user's shoulder to see the characters in the browser window, but the password is sent over the network to the Web server as unencrypted plain text. If the connection is wiretapped, the password will be just as visible as any other information in the form. If you really need to protect the password from snooping, use a secure connection.

Do You Have a Privacy Policy?

It's important not only to take steps to ensure your clients' privacy, but also to make sure they know you take their privacy seriously. You may put a lot of effort into addressing security issues, but if visitors can't tell that you're doing so, they may have a nagging sense of unease about using your site or divulging personal or confidential information to you. A simple measure you can take to make your users aware of your efforts is a prominent link to a privacy statement in which you set out for your visitors the efforts you're taking to protect their information. If you use cookies to associate users with session information, you can explain why the cookies you use are not dangerous to them. You can point out that you use secure connections where necessary to ensure confidentiality of sensitive or private information. You can also explain to customers that you're not going to engage in practices such as selling their names to other people (assuming you're not going to). The TRUSTe Web site (http://www.truste.com/) is a good place to visit for helpful information about privacy guidelines.

The Basis for Secure Web Connections

A client requests a secure connection to the Web server in a very simple way, by using a URL that begins with https rather than with http. The first example below illustrates how to request a normal connection and the second how to request a secure connection:

```
http://www.snake.net/
https://www.snake.net/
```

When the server receives a secure-connection request, the server and client engage in some negotiation, the result of which is an encrypted channel over which to exchange information in a safe way. A typical visible sign of this on the client end is the appearance in the browser window of an icon showing a padlock in locked state.

Secure Web connections are implemented using SSL (https means "HTTP over SSL", the Secure Sockets Layer protocol). This protocol uses public key encryption to establish a connection in which only the parties involved know the key required to decrypt traffic that flows over the connection. This keeps out untrusted third parties.

SSL connections also enable the client to verify the server's authenticity based on the server's digital certificate. This protects the client by preventing site spoofing—one site posing as another to fool the client into submitting private information.

Public key cryptography is based on key pairs. The keys are related in such a way that data encrypted using one key can be decrypted only with the other key. The key owner keeps one key secret (the private key), but makes the other available to anyone that wants it (the public key). For example, if you want to send me a private message, I send you my public key. You use the key to encrypt the message and send me the result. If your message is intercepted by an eavesdropper, it doesn't matter, because the message can be decrypted only by my private key, which only I know. (Obviously, it's extremely important to protect the private key so that no one else can access it. Anyone who comes into possession of a private key can use it to decrypt traffic obtained by wiretapping.)

One problem with the preceding scenario is that you don't necessarily know that I'm me. Someone else might be posing as me, trying to trick you into sending some interesting bit of information. This imposter would send you a public key and claim it's mine, when in reality it may be just the complement of the imposter's secret key. In a Web context, this scam takes the form of a fake Web site setting itself up to appear to be some other site. This is where digital certificates come in. If I'm running a Web server, my certificate verifies my identity so that you can trust me when I say who I am. Possession of a digital certificate (also known as the server ID) indicates that the organization running the Web server has satisfied the authorization procedure for a certificate authority, which is a trusted third party (generally a company such as VeriSign or Thawte). The server's digital certificate contains the information such as the following:

- The Web server host name
- The server owner's name and identification information
- The server's public key
- The certificate authority's digital certificate
- The time period over which the certificate is valid

With the preceding background in mind, we're in a position to discuss what actually happens behind the scenes when a client requests a secure connection to the Web server:

1. The client issues a request that begins with `https`.

2. The server responds by sending the client its digital certificate to assure the client that the server is in fact who it says it is, rather than an imposter setting itself up as someone else.

3. The client checks the credentials in the certificate to verify the server's authenticity. Browsers such as those from Netscape and Microsoft ship with a list of certificate authorities that they trust, so the browser checks the server certificate against this list to see whether it was issued by a recognized authority. If not, the browser engages the user in a dialog that allows the user to examine the contents of the certificate and to decline or accept the certificate.

4. If the certificate is accepted, the browser generates a secret key to use for encrypting connection traffic. This secret is known as the session key, and it has two important properties: It is very difficult to guess, and it will be known only to the client and the server.

5. The client must transmit the session key to the server, but protect it so that no one else can intercept the key and figure it out. To do this, the client extracts the server's public key from the server's certificate and uses it to encrypt the session key before sending it to the server.

6. The server receives the encrypted session key and decrypts it using its own private key. Only the server knows this key, so at this point, only the client and server know the session key. All further traffic between the two is encrypted using this key for the duration of the session. The session key ensures that any information sent between the client and server is encrypted with some unique value that cannot be guessed by attackers. An attacker might wiretap the connection, but the content will appear to be gibberish due to the encryption, and cannot be interpreted without the session key.

You can set up your own digital server certificate to use for testing. When you're ready to obtain a "real" certificate, there are many certificate authority companies to choose from. (The Apache-SSL home page at `http://www.apache-ssl.org/` lists several.) You should visit the Web sites of a few of these vendors; they're good sources for a great deal of helpful information. Of course, the content of those sites also includes a certain amount of promotional hype. Here's an interesting claim from one of these vendors, extolling how easy it is to enable secure communications: "Because SSL is built into all major browsers and Web servers, simply installing a digital certificate, or Server ID, enables SSL capabilities." That statement glosses over the fact that although Apache is *the* major Web server, the default Apache configuration includes no SSL support, so installing a certificate will do nothing. You can recompile the server to take advantage of SSL, but the procedure isn't necessarily so trivial as the claim makes it sound. You'll need to check your installation to see whether SSL capabilities are already present. (For example, OpenBSD ships an SSL-enabled version of Apache, and SSL can be turned on by starting `httpd` with the `-DSSL` command-line option or by using `apachectl startssl`.) If not, you'll need to do a little work. The next section provides some guidelines for doing this.

Should Secure Connections Be the Default?

If secure connections keep information private, why not just use them all the time? For one thing, secure connections have greater computational requirements. They put a lot more load on your server, so you don't want to use them indiscriminately. Another factor to consider is that applications have differing security requirements, and not all applications need an encrypted connection. A script that displays public information probably won't need much in the way of special security treatment. On the other hand, if the application involves money or sensitive personal information such as a credit card number, that's a clue that you should give more than average attention to security.

Clients Can Provide Credentials, Too

When a client issues a request for a secure connection, the server provides a certificate as proof of its identity. Servers can also ask clients to authenticate themselves. This is based on the use of client digital certificates (see, for example, `http://www.verisign.com/clientauth/`). VeriSign says that more than a million people have digital IDs. That sounds like a lot, but it's actually just a small fraction of the Web-browsing population. Still, expect to see the popularity of client certificates increase in the future, because digital certificates enable you to dispense with your passwords and hold promise for unifying the authentication process across multiple sites. They can also be useful in situations such as when a company issues certificates to employees for the purpose of accessing its internal servers.

Using Secure Connections

To provide secure Web connections for visitors to your site, you must have a Web server that has SSL support built in. If your version of Apache is currently enabled for SSL, you just need to make sure your server certificate and key files are set up and that the file `httpd.conf` is configured the way you want it; see "Configuring Apache for SSL Support." Otherwise, you can recompile Apache to allow secure connections, or use a related version such as Apache-SSL. Another possibility is to use one of the commercial servers with SSL such as Raven (Covalent) or Stonghold. The latter approach might be preferable if you want someone else to do the work of building the server. The Web sites for these server vendors are

```
http://www.covalent.net/
http://www.c2net.com/
```

There are other commercial vendors, too; you may want to do further research for comparison.

If you elect to configure Apache yourself, you'll need source distributions for Apache and for `mod_ssl`, the Apache module that provides support for SSL connections. You will also need to install OpenSSL if you don't already have it, because `mod_ssl` actually uses OpenSSL to do much of its work. If you don't have OpenSSL, check to see whether you have SSLeay. If you do, you can use it rather than OpenSSL. SSLeay is the original name of what is now OpenSSL, although some of its commands are named and invoked differently.

If you want to use Apache-SSL rather than Apache, you won't need mod_ssl, but you'll still need OpenSSL. The Web sites for the various components just mentioned can be visited at the following locations:

```
http://www.apache.org/
http://www.apache-ssl.org/
http://www.modssl.org/
http://www.openssl.org/
```

A Sample *mod_ssl* Installation Procedure

I don't want to turn this chapter into an installation manual, but installation of mod_ssl is not always completely obvious, so you may find it helpful to see an example. The following sequence of commands are those I used on a system running Red Hat Linux 7.0. (These particular commands will almost certainly be different for your machine, so be sure to read carefully the installation instructions included with each component you plan to install.) The example assumes that you've already obtained the source distributions for any components you need and that they're all located under a common parent directory. If you use a different layout, some of the pathnames shown in the commands will need adjustment. The make install commands may need to be run as root.

If you do not already have OpenSSL installed on your system, configure, build, and install it from the main OpenSSL source directory. The following commands install it under the /usr/local/ssl directory:

```
% ./config --prefix=/usr/local/ssl
% make
% make test
% make install
```

Then move into the mod_ssl source tree and configure it:

```
% ./configure \
    --with-apache=../apache_1.3.19 \
    --with-ssl=/usr/local/ssl \
    --enable-shared=ssl \
    --disable-rule=SSL_COMPAT \
    --with-crt=$PWD/pkg.sslcfg/server.crt \
    --with-key=$PWD/pkg.sslcfg/server.key
```

The configure command installs the mod_ssl files into the Apache source tree. That means you don't need to run make in the mod_ssl directory; when you compile Apache, mod_ssl will be built automatically. The --with-ssl option indicates the base directory of the installed OpenSSL; the option shown in the preceding command indicates that OpenSSL is installed under /usr/local/ssl. If you want to point mod_ssl at the OpenSSL source tree, you can do that instead; the following command has a --with-ssl option that points to the OpenSSL tree located at ../openssl-0.9.6:

```
% ./configure \
    --with-apache=../apache_1.3.19 \
    --with-ssl=../openssl-0.9.6 \
    --enable-shared=ssl \
    --disable-rule=SSL_COMPAT \
    --with-crt=$PWD/pkg.sslcfg/server.crt \
    --with-key=$PWD/pkg.sslcfg/server.key
```

If you do use an OpenSSL source distribution when configuring mod_ssl, the configure command still expects to find the OpenSSL binaries under the directory indicated by the --with-ssl option. Therefore, before running configure in the mod_ssl directory, you should configure and build OpenSSL in ../openssl-0.9.6, but *do not* run make clean there.

mod_ssl patches the source for Apache to extend its programming interface. The implication of this is that you'll not only need to rebuild Apache, but also any additional modules you use that aren't part of the Apache source tree. If you build DSO versions of the mod_perl and mod_php modules, for example, they'll need to be recompiled as well. We'll get to this shortly.

After running the configure command in the mod_ssl source directory, change into the Apache source directory and run make to recompile Apache. As this operation completes, it should display some information about building a server digital certificate and key files:

```
Before you install the package you now should prepare the SSL
certificate system by running the 'make certificate' command.
For different situations the following variants are provided:

% make certificate TYPE=dummy    (dummy self-signed Snake Oil cert)
% make certificate TYPE=test     (test cert signed by Snake Oil CA)
% make certificate TYPE=custom   (custom cert signed by own CA)
% make certificate TYPE=existing (existing cert)
        CRT=/path/to/your.crt [KEY=/path/to/your.key]
```

To build a new certificate, use one of the first three make certificate commands shown here (the first is the simplest). The certificate won't be "genuine" in the sense of having been issued by a trusted certificate authority, but it's good enough for testing purposes. After creating the certificate, install Apache:

```
% make install
```

If this is not your initial Apache installation, you may find that make install doesn't modify your already-installed httpd.conf file or module files. It might also fail to replace some of the programs already installed in the Apache bin directory. In this case, you can move the originals to a different location and run the installation command again. Then you can compare the new configuration files with the originals and merge in any local changes that you want to retain.

As noted earlier, the configuration command for mod_ssl modifies the Apache source code to use an extended API (EAPI). This changes the Apache programming interface not just for mod_ssl, but for other Apache modules. You'll need to recompile any such modules you use that are built outside the Apache source tree, such as external DSO modules. If you use DSO versions of mod_perl and mod_php, for example, you'll have to rebuild them. Ideally, this should be just a matter of reconfiguring the modules using the same configuration commands you used originally. DSO modules are built with the help of the apxs utility that is part of the Apache distribution. The new version of apxs that you've just installed should report the correct compiler flags to let the configuration commands for your DSO modules know about the presence of mod_ssl and the need to compile with the -DEAPI flag that is needed for the extended API. For example, I configure mod_perl using this command:

```
% perl Makefile.PL \
    USE_APXS=1 \
    WITH_APXS=/usr/local/apache/bin/apxs \
    EVERYTHING=1
```

For mod_php (PHP 4), I use this command:

```
% ./configure \
    --with-mysql=/usr/local/mysql \
    --with-apxs=/usr/local/apache/bin/apxs \
    --enable-track-vars
```

In both cases, the configuration command runs the new version of apxs, which reports the proper flags indicating that mod_ssl is available and that the extended API is to be used. After configuring each module, rebuild and reinstall it.

Configuring Apache for SSL Support

At this point, you should have an Apache server that has mod_ssl support built in, as well as certificate and key files that the server can use to set up secure connections with clients. Now you must modify httpd.conf to reflect how you want mod_ssl to operate. You may find that the make install command for Apache put several SSL-related directives in your configuration file already; if so, it probably won't be necessary to do much here other than look through the file and check that all the settings seem reasonable.

This section describes some of the configuration directives you'll need to use. What I hope to do here is provide enough information that you can set up a working system, and make it easier for you to assimilate the more complete documentation about configuration directives that you'll find in the reference chapter of the mod_ssl manual. The discussion here shows representative examples only; the mod_ssl manual contains more extensive information and additional examples. (If you're using Apache-SSL rather than Apache and mod_ssl, you should consult the Apache-SSL documentation, because the SSL directives for that server differ somewhat from those for mod_ssl.)

First, tell Apache about the `mod_ssl` module by listing it in the configuration file with `LoadModule`. For UNIX, the directive might look like this:

```
LoadModule ssl_module modules/libssl.so
```

For Windows, the module name is different:

```
LoadModule ssl_module modules/ApacheModuleSSL.dll
```

The actual pathname to your module files under the server root directory may be somewhat different; adjust the `LoadModule` directive to match. (For example, it's common under UNIX for module files to be installed in a directory named `libexec` rather than `modules`.) You may also need an `AddModule` directive:

```
AddModule mod_ssl.c
```

The server needs to listen on an additional port because SSL connections are not handled on the default port. Normally the HTTP and HTTPS ports are 80 and 443; to tell the server to pay attention to these ports, use `Listen` directives (if you use different port numbers, make the appropriate substitutions):

```
Listen 80
Listen 443
```

You'll also need to modify your network routing configuration to allow inbound traffic on port 443 if you're behind a firewall or a router that currently blocks that port. Otherwise, you'll test your SSL configuration on your internal network and it will work fine, but connections to the server from outside your network will fail.

Enable the SSL engine:

```
SSLEngine on
```

The argument must be `on` or `off`. You will probably want to use this directive inside `<VirtualHost>` blocks. Otherwise, it applies globally and the server will expect all connections to be secure; that is, the server no longer will understand normal non-SSL URLs! At a minimum, enable SSL within a generic virtual host block like this one:

```
<VirtualHost _default_:443>
SSLEngine on
</VirtualHost>
```

If you use a more complex virtual hosting setup, associate SSL directives with each virtual host for which you want to enable SSL capabilities. For example, you can place `SSLEngine` directives within `<VirtualHost>` blocks to selectively enable or disable SSL processing for individual hosts. Other directives described in the rest of this section that are commonly used on a host-specific basis include the locations of key files, allowable cipher types, or log file locations.

Tell the server where its private key and digital certificate files are:

```
SSLCertificateKeyFile conf/ssl.key/server.key
SSLCertificateFile conf/ssl.crt/server.crt
```

These pathnames are typical defaults; make sure they match your setup. SSLCertificateFile can be used twice if you have both RSA-based and DSA-based certificates.

List the cipher types that the client can negotiate. I usually find that the Apache make install step installs a directive such as this in my httpd.conf file (see the mod_ssl manual for a list of all the cipher types and how to construct the list):

```
SSLCipherSuite ALL:!ADH:!EXPORT56:RC4+RSA:+HIGH:+MEDIUM:+LOW:+SSLv2:+EXP:+eNULL
```

mod_ssl can use a connection cache so that successive secure requests from the same client need not all engage in the entire authentication and key generation process. On the first request, the server assigns the SSL session a unique identifier that the client can present on subsequent requests to minimize overhead. The server remembers these IDs in a cache, which is controlled by several directives. OpenSSL itself caches session information for a single server process, so in an environment such as Windows where there is only one child httpd process, you need not enable the mod_ssl cache at all:

```
SSLSessionCache none
```

In an environment such as UNIX in which several child httpd processes may be running, successive requests from a single client may be served by different children. In this case, the mod_ssl cache allows the child processes to communicate with each other to determine whether a given client has already set up a secure session. The SSLSessionCache directive specifies the type of cache mechanism to use and SSLSessionCacheTimeout controls how long session information is maintained in the cache. For example, to use a DBM hash file to hold cache entries and maintain them for 5 minutes (300 seconds), use these directives:

```
SSLSessionCache dbm:logs/ssl_cache
SSLSessionCacheTimeout 300
```

The SSLMutex directive determines how Apache creates a lock for operations that child httpd processes must perform in a mutually exclusive way. Under Windows, you must use a semaphore mutex mechanism:

```
SSLMutex sem
```

That may also work under UNIX if your platform supports it. A more portable alternative is to use a file:

```
SSLMutex file:logs/ssl_mutex
```

OpenSSL generates random numbers at server startup time and when a new SSL connection is established. SSLRandomSeed controls how the generator is seeded. The builtin seeding source is always available and can be used in both contexts:

```
SSLRandomSeed startup builtin
SSLRandomSeed connect builtin
```

However, `builtin` is not necessarily a very good source of seeding information at server startup time, so you may want to use another source in the `startup` context. Another common seeding source is the `/dev/random` device:

```
SSLRandomSeed startup file:/dev/random
SSLRandomSeed connect file:/dev/random
```

On some systems, `/dev/urandom` is a better choice than `/dev/random`. But before you decide to use either one, you should read the `mod_ssl` manual's discussion of the `SSLRandomSeed` directive, because there can be significant problems with either device if used improperly. The manual gives other choices for such cases. You can specify multiple seeding sources by listing multiple `SSLRandomSeed` directives for either context in the configuration file.

If you want to log SSL connections, name the log file using `SSLLog` and the amount of information you want using `SSLLogLevel`. The levels are (in increasing order of verbosity) `none`, `error`, `warn`, `info`, `trace`, and `debug`. Here's an example:

```
SSLLog logs/ssl.log
SSLLogLevel info
```

`mod_ssl` logs errors to the general Apache error log as well, so there's no need for a special SSL log if you're interested only in error information.

You may find it necessary to compensate for broken browsers. A common problem is that some versions of Internet Explorer cannot connect to secure pages properly unless you include the following directive to modify how `mod_ssl` communicates with them:

```
SetEnvIf User-Agent ".*MSIE.*" \
    nokeepalive ssl-unclean-shutdown downgrade-1.0 force-response-1.0
```

A couple of options related to access control that may interest you are `SSLRequireSSL` and `SSLRequire`. `SSLRequireSSL` is used to deny access to particular directories or virtual hosts unless the client accesses their contents using `https` URLs. `SSLRequire` is similar but provides more general condition-based testing. You can use it to grant or deny access based on factors such as URLs, time of day, browser type, or CGI variables. If you want to use `SSLRequire` to check CGI variables that contain SSL information, you'll need to use the `SSLOptions` directive that configures miscellaneous `mod_ssl` options. One of the options it provides is `StdEnvVars`, which causes extra SSL-related variables to be added to the CGI environment in which scripts run. You can see the effect of the `StdEnvVars` option using the `perltest.pl` script that was discussed in Chapter 3, "Improving Performance with `mod_perl`." If you have that script installed in your `cgi-perl` directory, turn on `StdEnvVars` for that directory like this:

```
<Directory /usr/local/apache/cgi-perl/>
    SSLOptions +StdEnvVars
</Directory>
```

Then invoke the script using insecure and secure connections to see the difference between the output; in the latter case, you'll see a lot of variables that have names beginning with SSL_:

```
http://www.snake.net/cgi-perl/perltest.pl
https://www.snake.net/cgi-perl/perltest.pl
```

Check the mod_ssl manual for more complete information about SSLRequireSSL, SSLRequire, and SSLOptions.

If you want to, you can set up the server so that it can be run either with or without SSL support. To do this, enclose SSL directives in conditional blocks that look like this:

```
<IfDefine SSL>
# SSL directives here
</IfDefine>
```

For example:

```
<IfDefine SSL>
    Listen 80
    Listen 443
</IfDefine>
```

By using conditional blocks, you can enable SSL support by defining the SSL symbol on the httpd command line when you start up Apache. The next section describes how to do this.

Starting Apache with SSL Support Enabled

After you've modified httpd.conf, check your changes for errors, bring Apache down if no errors are reported, and then bring it back up with SSL support enabled. The commands you use to do this depend on whether you placed SSL-related directives within conditional blocks (<IfDefine SSL>). If you didn't use conditional blocks, use these commands, which are no different from those you'd normally use:

```
# apachectl configtest
# apachectl stop
# apachectl start
```

If you did use conditional blocks to enable SSL support, you'll need to pass the -DSSL command-line option to httpd to test the configuration:

```
# httpd -t -DSSL
```

apachectl configtest doesn't work for this because it doesn't pass -DSSL to httpd. To restart the server after stopping it, either of the following commands should work:

```
# apachectl startssl
# httpd -DSSL
```

If you use conditional blocks and you want Apache to start up by default with SSL enabled at system boot time, you'll also need to modify your startup procedure. (For example, if you have an httpd script in an /etc/rc.d/init.d or /etc/init.d directory that invokes `apache`, you'll need to change it to add the `-DSSL` flag.) If you enabled SSL support in the configuration file unconditionally, no changes to the startup procedure are required.

After your server is running and listening to port 443, try to establish a connection to your server's home page using `https` in the URL:

```
https://www.snake.net/
```

If you're using your own self-signed server certificate, your browser probably will present a series of dialog boxes complaining about the certificate. Just go ahead and accept the certificate anyway. Then you should see your site's home page, as well as a lock icon at the bottom of the browser window displayed in its locked state. The complaints occur because the certificate does not originate from a recognized certificate authority and browsers warn their users when they connect to a server that doesn't provide a certificate from a known source. The connection will still work, but clients who don't understand why this happens will be suspicious, which is completely antithetical to the assurance you're trying to provide by using secure connections! You can get a commercial certificate so that your visitors can connect without warnings. Some of the vendors provide free trial versions that you can use for testing and evaluation purposes before investing in a for-pay certificate. Visit their Web sites for information about the trial versions and for the procedure to follow to obtain an official certificate.

It's likely that when you start Apache with SSL support enabled, you'll be prompted to supply the passphrase for the server's private key file. This happens because the server's private key is encrypted and protected with a password for additional security, but it's not very convenient if you normally plan to start Apache at system startup time automatically. (If your server reboots while you're not around, the startup process will stop at the point where it launches Apache until you enter the private key password.) You can remove the encryption from the key file so that you don't have to supply the password each time Apache starts—but be aware that if you do so, and someone gains access to the key file, your security will be compromised.

To create an unencrypted version of the key file, first back up the encrypted version, then create a new version without the password and make sure no one but `root` can access it. You can do this using the following commands, assuming the file is named `server.key` and is located in the `ssl.key` directory under `/usr/local/apache/conf`. When prompted for the PEM passphrase, enter your server key password.

```
# cd /usr/local/apache/conf/ssl.key
# cp server.key server.key.orig
# openssl rsa -in server.key.orig -out server.key
read RSA key
Enter PEM pass phrase:
writing RSA key
# chmod 400 server.key server.key.orig
```

Setting Up Secure MySQL Connections

If your Apache and MySQL servers are running on the same host, you can have your scripts connect to MySQL using the host name `localhost` rather than the host's domain name. Then, traffic over the connection will be routed through the software loopback interface rather than onto any physical network. On the other hand, if the servers run on different hosts, traffic between your Web scripts and MySQL has to go over a network and may be subject to eavesdropping. To protect against this, you can use SSH (secure shell) to forward MySQL traffic from your programs over an encrypted channel to the MySQL server.

Normally, a client such as the `mysql` program or a DBI script connects to the MySQL server and talks to it directly. When you use SSH to forward the connection, the client program connects instead to a local SSH process running on the same machine. The local SSH process then sends traffic over an encrypted connection to a remote SSH process running on the database host. The remote SSH process contacts the MySQL server on your behalf. Traffic from the server back to the client program gets routed in the other direction over this same encrypted connection. What this means is that instead of unencrypted traffic flowing between MySQL and its clients over the network where anyone with a sniffer can intercept it, that traffic is encrypted and protected from eavesdropping.

This section describes how to implement secure MySQL connections by setting up SSH forwarding. To get this to work, you must have SSH installed on both the Web and database hosts. You must also configure your scripts to connect to the local SSH forwarder running on the Web host, rather than directly to the MySQL server on the database host. (If your scripts open a connection to MySQL by calling a library routine, this is easy—just change that routine.) The instructions here assume you have OpenSSH installed on each host and that you have a version recent enough to support SSH protocol version 2. You can use other SSH implementations, but the commands may be somewhat different than those shown here.[4]

For this discussion, assume that the Web and database hosts are named `www.snake.net` and `db.snake.net`, and that there is an account for a user named `paul` on each host. You should substitute your own login name and host names, of course. I'll show the sequence of steps needed to set up a forwarding connection, but if you're already using SSH (for example, as an alternative to Telnet), you may already have performed some of the earlier parts of the sequence.

---

4. An alternative to SSH is Stunnel, which sets up encrypted tunnels between hosts using OpenSSL. See `http://stunnel.mirt.net/` and `http://www.stunnel.org/`.

First, you'll need to generate your encryption keys if you don't already have them. To generate private and public key files, run this command on the Web server host www.snake.net:

```
% ssh-keygen -t dsa
Generating public/private dsa key pair.
Enter file in which to save the key (/u/paul/.ssh/id_dsa):
Created directory '/u/paul/.ssh'.
Enter passphrase (empty for no passphrase): SomePassPhrase
Enter same passphrase again: SomePassPhrase
Your identification has been saved in /u/paul/.ssh/id_dsa.
Your public key has been saved in /u/paul/.ssh/id_dsa.pub.
The key fingerprint is:
cb:9e:ac:3d:80:32:bc:bf:cf:87:59:5e:60:33:c6:25 paul@www.snake.net
```

This creates a directory named .ssh in your home directory and writes files there named id_dsa and id_dsa.pub to hold your private and public keys. The command uses -t dsa to specify DSA-type encryption. You can use -t rsa to specify RSA encryption instead, in which case the files will be named id_rsa and id_rsa.pub. (If your version of ssh-keygen doesn't support the -t option, try ssh-keygen -d.) Then log in on the database server host db.snake.net and run the ssh-keygen command there, too. This will ensure that the .ssh directory is set up and has the proper permissions on both hosts.

Next, copy your public key file id_dsa.pub (or id_rsa.pub) from www.snake.net and append it to the authorized_keys2 file in the .ssh directory on db.snake.net. (If authorized_keys2 doesn't exist, create it.) Make sure that authorized_keys2 is owned by you and has mode 600. If it doesn't belong to you or it doesn't have a restrictive access mode, SSH will probably assume that it's been compromised by an outside user and refuse to use it.

After you've installed your public key on db.snake.net, try using the ssh program to log in from www.snake.net to db.snake.net:

```
% ssh -2 db.snake.net
Enter passphrase for key '/u/paul/.ssh/id_dsa':
```

Enter your passphrase to log in, and then log out again. (The first time you run this command, ssh may present you with a dialog about establishing the authenticity of the remote host. Once you add that host to the list of known hosts, the dialog won't be presented again.)

If you want to be able to use ssh in the other direction (that is, to log in from db.snake.net to www.snake.net), copy your public key on db.snake.net to the authorized_keys2 file on www.snake.net. (It's a good idea to do this, because it starts you moving toward SSH and away from Telnet, which is a notoriously insecure protocol.)

Now you should be able to set up a forwarding process. Try running the following command on www.snake.net:

```
% ssh -2 -N -f -L 3307:localhost:3306 db.snake.net
Enter passphrase for key '/u/paul/.ssh/id_dsa':
```

The final argument of this command, db.snake.net, specifies the host to which the connection should be forwarded. The -L option specifies a local forwarder; the command sets up a local SSH process to listen on port 3307, and a counterpart remote SSH process that forwards to its own local port 3306 (which is the port that MySQL listens to). Note that localhost:3306 in the -L option is interpreted by the *remote* SSH process; therefore, it refers to port 3306 on db.snake.net. The other arguments have meanings as follows:

- -2 specifies SSH protocol version 2; this is needed because the command also uses -N, which isn't supported by version 1.
- -N says that we just want to forward traffic. Without this argument, ssh expects you to specify a command to be executed on the remote host.
- -f causes ssh to run in the background.

Test the forwarder by trying to connect through it to the MySQL server. You can do this using the mysql program. Suppose you normally connect to MySQL from www.snake.net by running this command:

```
% mysql -h db.snake.net -p -u webdev webdb
Enter password: webdevpass
```

To use the forwarder instead, connect to local port 3307 like this:

```
% mysql -h 127.0.0.1 -P 3307 -p -u webdev webdb
Enter password: webdevpass
```

What's happening here is that the ssh command has set up a local process on www.snake.net that is waiting for connections to port 3307. When you run mysql with the -h 127.0.0.1 and -P 3307 arguments, it connects to that process, which sends traffic over a secure connection to the counterpart remote SSH process running on db.snake.net. The remote SSH sends the traffic to port 3306 on its own host, where the MySQL server is listening. This completes the connection between the mysql program on www.snake.net and the MySQL server on db.snake.net.

When connecting through the forwarder, it's important to use 127.0.0.1 rather than the host name localhost, even though in most contexts the two are synonymous. MySQL programs interpret localhost as having a special meaning of "connect to the local server using a UNIX domain socket if possible." Using the IP number explicitly requests a TCP/IP connection.

The SSH forwarder can be used by your DBI scripts, too. Suppose you currently connect to MySQL like this:

```
$dbh = DBI->connect ("DBI:mysql:host=db.snake.net;database=webdb",
                     "webdev", "webdevpass", {PrintError => 0, RaiseError => 1});
```

Change that to connect to port 3307 on the local host (here, too, it's important to use
127.0.0.1 rather than localhost for the host value):

```
$dbh = DBI->connect ("DBI:mysql:host=127.0.0.1;port=3307;database=webdb",
                     "webdev", "webdevpass", {PrintError => 0, RaiseError => 1});
```

You can also set up a forwarder by starting it from db.snake.net. This is called a
remote forwarder. ("Remote" is relative to the host on which the clients run.) To ini-
tiate a forwarding process from db.snake.net, make sure you've installed your public
key from that host into authorized_keys2 on www.snake.net. Then kill the SSH lis-
tener on www.snake.net if it's still running and run this command on db.snake.net:

```
% ssh -2 -N -f -R 3307:localhost:3306 www.snake.net
Enter passphrase for key '/u/paul/.ssh/id_dsa':
```

This command involves the same two hosts as the previous ssh command, but uses
-R rather than -L to specify that the direction of the forwarding is reversed, relative
to the host from which you run the command. After starting this forwarder on
db.snake.net, you should be able to connect to the MySQL server from
www.snake.net using the same command as when you're running a local forwarder:

```
% mysql -h 127.0.0.1 -P 3307 -p -u webdev webdb
Enter password: webdevpass
```

The preceding procedure shows how to start an SSH forwarder manually. If you want
to set up a forwarding connection automatically at system boot time, there are some
additional issues to consider:

- You need to add a step for invoking the forwarding process during the system
  startup sequence.
- You don't want ssh to issue any password prompts. You may not be around to
  answer them, and you don't want the startup sequence to hang because of that.
  This can be done by using a private key that doesn't have any passphrase. That
  means you should run the forwarder from a restricted account that doesn't allow
  logins.

The general procedure for setting up a special forwarding account is as follows:

- Pick an account name to use and create accounts with that name on both the
  Apache and MySQL server hosts.
- Log in to each host under the new account name and run ssh-keygen to generate the private and public key files. However, when you're prompted for the
  passphrase, just press Return. This will allow ssh to be run without having to
  specify a password. Then install the public key file from each host into the
  .ssh/authorized_keys2 file on the other.
- Try logging in using ssh from one host to the other under the new account
  name to make sure there's no password prompt.

- Change the account shell on both hosts to `/bin/false`. This will disallow logins, but still allow forwarding.

- Modify the system startup process of one of the hosts to create an SSH forwarder. You can use `su` or `sudo` to run the command under the user ID for your forwarding account.

Writing a Secure Application

In the preceding part of this chapter, we've surveyed a number of security problems and discussed techniques for dealing with them. In this section, we'll write an application that uses several of these methods to show how they apply in practice. The basic scenario is somewhat like one of those presented in Chapter 7, "Performing Searches," where we wrote a couple of applications to display a staff directory consisting of records that describe individual staff members. The primary focus for those applications was on the presentation of read-only information from the directory. Here, we'll use a similar table that contains information about the people listed in it, but we'll be more concerned about providing write access, and doing so in a secure manner: We'll allow users to update their own record over the Web using a browser. This goal is deceptively modest, because although it sounds almost trivial, implementing it in a secure way actually involves a number of issues:

- Unauthorized users must be kept out. Only people who are listed in the table should be able to use the application. We can achieve this by using a login step that requires people to identify themselves before the application will cooperate by presenting an editing form containing the appropriate record. The application also will generate a session ID for authorized users. When the editing form is submitted, the session ID is a user's proof of having logged in, because you can't acquire a valid session ID otherwise.

- People who have successfully logged in must be given access only to their own record and not allowed to trick the application into updating the wrong record. We can accomplish this by including the record ID in the editing form, but encoded in such a way that we can detect tampering. Also, because the application generates UPDATE statements based on user input, we'll need to thwart attempts at entering input intended to cause the application to create SQL that does something other than we intend. This is done through proper use of placeholders.

- Third parties should not be able to eavesdrop on network traffic generated by the login and editing phases to steal passwords or to intercept and modify information submitted by legitimate users. To handle this, we can use a secure connection between each user and the application.

Setting Up the Table

We'll use a table called `bio` that contains descriptive (biographical) information about each person listed in it. The table lists the username and password of the person who "owns" each record; to gain access to the record, that person must authenticate by supplying both values at login time. The final piece of information included in the table is the user's email address. This is useful because a common problem with passwords is that people forget them. If we have email addresses, we can mail forgotten passwords to their owners. (This feature also has the salutary effect of reducing the number of "I forgot my password, can you tell me what it is?" messages that the application administrator receives!) The `bio` table looks like this:

```
CREATE TABLE bio
(
    id          INT UNSIGNED NOT NULL AUTO_INCREMENT PRIMARY KEY,
    username    CHAR(20) BINARY NOT NULL,   # user name and password
    UNIQUE (username),
    password    CHAR(20) BINARY NOT NULL,
    email       CHAR(50) NOT NULL,
    bio         CHAR(255) NOT NULL           # biographical information
)
```

Notice that the `username` and `password` columns are declared as `BINARY`; this is done to make them case sensitive. `CHAR` columns normally are not case sensitive, which results in less strict matching. That is often useful, but not for authentication purposes. It isn't very secure to allow a password of `ABC` to be matched not only by `ABC`, but also by `abc`, `Abc`, and so forth.

Obviously, the `bio` table is quite minimal. It doesn't even have a column for the user's real name. I'm keeping the table simple because the emphasis here is on the application's security aspects, not its ability to present fancy display or editing pages.

To initialize the table, use an `INSERT` statement such as the following one. The passwords are the usernames backward, which is convenient for testing, but of course not a good idea in general:

```
INSERT INTO bio (username,password,email,bio)
    VALUES
        ('Dopey','yepoD','dopey@snake.net','I\'m a dwarf'),
        ('Mickey','yekciM','mickey@snake.net','I\'m a mouse'),
        ('George','egroeG','president@whitehouse.gov','I\'m a president'),
        ('Paul','luaP','paul@snake.net','Awaiting further instructions')
```

Now we can proceed to write an application `edit_bio.pl` that enables users listed in the table to log in and edit their biographical information. The implementation requires that you have session support set up as described in Chapter 8, "Session Management," because it uses the `sessions` table and the `WebDB::Session` module developed in that chapter.

Overall Application Flow

The edit_bio.pl application will operate as follows. When you first invoke it, it presents a login page as a gateway that you have to get past to gain access to your record. The page contains a form containing username and password fields and buttons labeled Log In and Email Password. If you can't remember your password, you can fill in just the username and select the Email Password button. The application will look for a record that matches your username, and then mail the password to your address as listed in that record. Otherwise, to identify yourself, fill in both fields and select the Log In button. If the name and password match a record in the bio table, the application proceeds to the editing stage.

After you log in, the application generates a unique session ID and presents an editing form initialized with the contents of your record. The form will contain editable fields for your email address and biographical information, and also include the session ID and record ID in the form as a hidden field. The session ID is proof that you've logged in and the record ID indicates which record you're editing. To modify your record, edit the fields appropriately and select the Update button. The application applies the changes to your record and displays the result in a confirmation page that contains a Continue Editing button in case you want to make further changes, and a Log Out button if you're finished.

Preventing Session and Record ID Tampering

In the editing form sent to the browser, edit_bio.pl includes the session ID for the client to use as proof of passing the login stage, and the record identifier to indicate which record is being edited. However, these values must be protected to keep the user from modifying them and gaining access to another person's record. To accomplish this, edit_bio.pl uses both checksums and encryption:

- A checksum is calculated from the session and record identifiers; this checksum becomes part of the form sent to the client. It helps prevent mischief, because if the user were to modify the session or record ID, a new checksum calculated from the submitted values won't match the checksum in the form. (A mismatch indicates that the user modified either the IDs or the checksum. It doesn't really matter which; either way, edit_bio.pl will reject the form.)

- A weakness of checksums is that if an attacker can guess your algorithm for calculating them, it's still possible to modify the form as follows: pick ID values to substitute for the real ones, then run them through the algorithm and use the result to replace the checksum, too. edit_bio.pl would never know the difference. To make this kind of attack more difficult, we'll encrypt the checksum and the session and record identifiers. This adds another layer of protection, because an attacker must perform a successful decryption first before attempting to tamper with the values. In addition, we'll incorporate a key value into the checksum and encryption operations; the attacker must also know this key to "break the code."

The use of a key presents its own problem: How do you keep it secret? I'll take the expedient route here of writing the key literally into the text of the script. Remote clients cannot view the script to see the key, but remember that if you're sharing a Web server with other people, your scripts are readable to them (see "Dangers from Other Users with Apache Access"). With access to your script's source code, these users also have access to your checksum and encryption algorithms as well.

edit_bio.pl performs checksumming and encryption/decryption using a pair of functions, encode() and decode(), that complement each other. encode() takes an argument list consisting of data values to be processed and produces an encrypted string that contains the values along with a checksum calculated from them. To encode a session ID $sess_id and record ID $id, use the function like this:

```
$secret_stuff = encode ($sess_id, $id);
```

The result will become the value of a hidden field named secret_stuff in the editing form. When the user returns the form, we can unpack the value to recover the session and record IDs. In the meantime, while the user has access to the form, the value is protected against tampering.

To verify the integrity of a submitted form, we pass the value of the secret_stuff parameter to decode(). This function takes an encrypted string and decrypts it to recover the original data values and the associated checksum. It verifies the values against the checksum to make sure they weren't modified, and returns the values as an array if they're okay, or an empty array to signal tampering:

```
($sess_id, $id) = decode ($secret_stuff) or die "Hey, I smell trouble\n";
```

The Perl CPAN offers a number of Perl modules for computing checksums and for performing encryption. Visit the security and encryption area of the Perl CPAN to look through the possibilities. The ones I've chosen are extremely simple to use. edit_bio.pl uses Digest::MD5 to compute checksums. You give it your input values and it grinds them up and spits out a checksum based on them. To perform encryption, edit_bio.pl uses Crypt::CBC (cipher block chaining) in conjunction with Crypt::Blowfish. As usual, you can use perldoc to read module documentation:

```
% perldoc Digest::MD5
% perldoc Crypt::CBC
% perldoc Crypt::Blowfish
```

To use the modules in our edit_bio.pl script, we must include the appropriate use statements:

```
use Digest::MD5;
use Crypt::CBC;
use Crypt::Blowfish;
```

Then we can implement encode() as follows. It combines the input values with a key that only edit_bio.pl knows to produce a checksum, and then encrypts the checksum along with the values and returns the result as a string of hexadecimal digits:

```
sub encode
{
my @val = @_;
my $key = "This is the key value";
my $md = Digest::MD5->new ();
my $cipher = Crypt::CBC->new ($key, "Blowfish");
my $checksum;

    $md->add (join ("", $key, @val));
    $checksum = $md->hexdigest ();
    return ($cipher->encrypt_hex (join (":", $checksum, @val)));
}
```

encode() uses a colon (':') as the delimiter between the checksum and the data values in constructing the string to be encrypted, so that they can be separated later by decode(). This is not a good choice if any of your values might contain a colon, but all of the ones we're using are drawn from the set of hexadecimal digits, so we're safe.

The decode() function decrypts the enciphered string to recover the checksum and the data values, and then runs the checksum algorithm on the values to verify their integrity. A match between the new checksum and the one in the encrypted string indicates that no attempt was made to modify the information, in which case decode() returns the original data values. Otherwise, it returns an empty list to indicate tampering:

```
sub decode
{
my $ciphertext = shift;
my $key = "This is the key value";
my $md = Digest::MD5->new ();
my $cipher = Crypt::CBC->new ($key, "Blowfish");
my ($checksum, $checksum2);
my @val;

    ($checksum, @val) = split (/:/, $cipher->decrypt_hex ($ciphertext));
    $md->add (join ("", $key, @val));
    $checksum2 = $md->hexdigest ();
    return (@val) if $checksum eq $checksum2;    # everything's okay
    return ();                                   # looks like tampering
}
```

If you want to calculate checksums using a module such as Digest::HMAC_MD5 or Digest::HMAC_SHA1 rather than Digest::MD5, the interfaces for all three are very similar. Just include the appropriate use statement, and alter the new() call slightly. For example, to use Digest::HMAC_SHA1, include this statement:

```
use Digest::HMAC_SHA1;
```

Then create the message digest object in `encode()` and `decode()` like this:

```
my $md = Digest::HMAC_SHA1->new ($key);
```

As just shown, `Crypt::Blowfish` is one encryption module that works with
`Crypt::CBC`, but there are others, such as `Crypt::DES` and `Crypt::IDEA`. You may in fact
find it necessary to use one of these alternatives. I've had mixed results installing the
various modules on different versions of UNIX, so if you have trouble installing
`Crypt::Blowfish`, try one of the others and modify `edit_bio.pl` to use it.

> **Checksums and Encryption Are Not Only for Form Data**
>
> The techniques described in this section to protect information in hidden fields are not limited to form
> data. You can also use checksums and encryption with information that you send to clients in URLs or in
> cookies.

Main Dispatch Logic

The main part of the script implements the application logic by checking the conditions with the strictest requirements first, and falling back to less restrictive conditions
as necessary:

- If the user is logged in (that is, if a valid session ID is present), we're already in
  the middle of presenting an editing session. The actions available to the user are
  Update to submit changes, Continue Editing to return to the editing form, and
  Log Out to quit.
- If no session ID is found, but the `choice` parameter is present, the user just
  submitted the login form. The actions here might be Log In or Email Password.
- Failing both of the preceding conditions, just present the login page.

Following this logic, the main part of the script looks like this:

```
use strict;
use lib qw(/usr/local/apache/lib/perl);
use CGI qw(:standard escape escapeHTML);
use Mail::Sendmail;
use Digest::MD5;
use Crypt::CBC;
use Crypt::Blowfish;
use WebDB;
use WebDB::Session;

my $sess_id;                                # session ID
my $sess_ref;                               # reference to session record
my $id;                                     # bio record ID
my $choice = lc (param ("choice"));         # any button user may have selected
my $page;                                   # contents of page to be displayed
```

continues

continued

```
# Extract the encoded session and record identifiers.  If they're present,
# make sure the session record is valid.  If these checks are successful,
# the user has passed the login phase and is editing a bio record.

if (defined (param ("secret_stuff"))
    && (($sess_id, $id) = decode (param ("secret_stuff"))))
{
    # Use open_with_expiration() so we get undef if the session has expired.
    $sess_ref = WebDB::Session->open_with_expiration (undef, $sess_id);
}

if (defined ($sess_ref))              # user is already logged in
{
    # Shove IDs into environment for other functions to find
    param (-name => "sess_id", -value => $sess_id);
    param (-name => "id", -value => $id);

    if ($choice eq "update")              # submit changes
    {
        $page .= submit_changes ();
    }
    elsif ($choice eq "continue editing")   # do some more editing
    {
        $page .= continue_editing ();
    }
    elsif ($choice eq "log out")              # user wants to quit
    {
        $page .= p ("Good bye.");
        $sess_ref->delete ();                  # destroy session
        undef ($sess_ref);
    }
    else
    {
        $page .= escapeHTML ("Logic error: unknown choice: $choice");
    }
    $sess_ref->close () if defined ($sess_ref);
}
elsif ($choice eq "log in")              # user wants to log in
{
    $page .= start_editing ();
}
elsif ($choice eq "email password")     # user requested password
{
    $page .= email_password ();
}
else                                      # present the login page
{
    $page .= login_page ();
}
```

```
print header (),
        start_html (-title => "Edit Biographical Information",
                    -bgcolor => "white"),
        $page,
        end_html ();
```

Presenting the Login Page

The initial login page that the user sees is generated by the login_page() function:

```
sub login_page
{
my $page;

    $page .= start_form (-action => url ())
            . p ("Please log in. If you cannot remember your password,\n"
                . "enter your user name and select Email Password to\n"
                . "have your password sent to you via email.")
            . p ("User name:")
            . textfield (-name => "username")
            . p ("Password:")
            . textfield (-name => "password")
            . br () . br ()
            . submit (-name => "choice", -value => "Log In")
            . " "
            . submit (-name => "choice", -value => "Email Password")
            . end_form ();
        return ($page);
}
```

If the user has forgotten the password and selects the Email Password button to receive it by email, edit_bio.pl invokes email_password(), which expects to find a username in the form contents. This function uses the name to look up the email address and the password, generates a message, and mails it to the user:

```
sub email_password
{
my ($dbh, $page);
my ($username, $email, $password);

    # Make sure username is present in the login form

    $username = WebDB::trim (param ("username"));
    if ($username eq "")
    {
        $page .= p ("Error: You must supply a username.")
                . login_page ();
        return ($page);
    }
```

continues

continued

```
                # Look for a matching record in the bio table

                $dbh = WebDB::connect ();
                ($email, $password) = $dbh->selectrow_array (
                            "SELECT email, password FROM bio WHERE username = ?",
                            undef, $username);
                $dbh->disconnect ();
                if (!defined ($email))        # no matching record found
                {
                    $page .= p ("Error: Invalid username or no email address\n"
                                . "available; cannot mail password.")
                            . login_page ();
                    return ($page);
                }

                # Mail the password and indicate the status of the attempt

                my %mail = (    # hash containing mail message information
                        From    => $email,
                        To      => $email,
                        Subject => "Your bio record password",
                        Message => "Your password is: $password\n"
                );
                if (sendmail (%mail))
                {
                    $page .= p (escapeHTML ("Password has been mailed to $email."));
                }
                else
                {
                    $page .= p (escapeHTML ("An error occurred sending mail to $email."));
                }

                return ($page);
            }
```

edit_bio.pl will send the password only to the address listed in the record. It does *not*
allow users to specify the address where they'd like the password sent. That would
enable anyone to get any password just by guessing a valid username.

If the user enters both the name and password into the login form and selects Log
In, start_editing() uses the name to look up the user's record, checks the password
to make sure it's correct, then initializes the session and presents the entry form:

```
sub start_editing
{
my ($dbh, $sth, $bio_ref, $sess_ref, $page);
my ($username, $password);

    # Make sure username and password are present in the form
```

```
$username = WebDB::trim (param ("username"));
$password = WebDB::trim (param ("password"));
if ($username eq "" || $password eq "")
{
    $page .= p ("Error: You must supply bot a username and password.")
            . login_page ();
    return ($page);
}

# Look for a matching record in the bio table.

$dbh = WebDB::connect ();
$sth = $dbh->prepare (
            "SELECT * FROM bio
            WHERE username = ? AND password = ?");
$sth->execute ($username, $password);
$bio_ref = $sth->fetchrow_hashref ();
$sth->finish ();
$dbh->disconnect ();
if (!defined ($bio_ref))    # no matching record found
{
    $page .= p ("Error: Login failed; username or password were invalid.")
            . login_page ();
    return ($page);
}

# Generate a session record with a lifetime of 24 hours.  Put the
# session ID and the contents of the bio record into the script
# environment for editing_form() to find.

if (!defined ($sess_ref = WebDB::Session->open (undef, undef)))
{
    $page .= p ("Error: could not create session ID")
            . login_page ();
    return ($page);
}
$sess_ref->expires ($sess_ref->now () + 60 * 60 * 24);
param (-name => "sess_id", -value => $sess_ref->session_id ());
foreach my $key (keys (%{$bio_ref}))
{
    param (-name => $key, -value => $bio_ref->{$key});
}
$page .= editing_form ();
$sess_ref->close ();                  # done with session; close it

return ($page);
}
```

Presenting the Editing Page

The editing_form() function generates the form that enables the user to make changes. It encodes the session and record IDs to protect them and places the result in the hidden secret_stuff field, displays the username as static text, and the email address and biographical information values as editable text. The form includes an Update button for submitting changes, as well as a Log Out button so the user can quit without changing anything:

```
sub editing_form
{
my $secret_stuff;
my $page;

    $secret_stuff = encode (param ("sess_id"), param ("id"));
    $page .= start_form (-action => url ())
            . p ("Please edit your record to make the desired changes,\n"
                . "then select Update (or Log Out to cancel changes).")
            . hidden (-name => "secret_stuff",
                        -value => $secret_stuff, -override => 1)
            . hidden (-name => "username",
                        -value => param ("username"), -override => 1)
            . p (escapeHTML ("User name:" . param ("username")))
            . p ("Email address:")
            . textfield (-name => "email")
            . p ("Biographical information:")
            . textarea (-name => "bio", -rows => 3, -columns => 80)
            . br () . br ()
            . submit (-name => "choice", -value => "Update")
            . " "
            . submit (-name => "choice", -value => "Log Out")
            . end_form ();
        return ($page);

}
```

Confirming the User's Changes

After the user submits the editing form, submit_changes() is called to update the corresponding record in the database. We don't need to check the integrity of the session or record IDs—that's already been done by the main part of the script, which invokes decode() to check the values before submit_changes() gets called. (You can try hacking the form to make sure that edit_bio.pl refuses to cooperate with you if you change the value of the secret_stuff field. It should notice the tampering and throw you back to the login page.)

```
sub submit_changes
{
my $sess_id = param ("sess_id");
```

```
my $id = param ("id");
my $email = WebDB::trim (param ("email"));
my $bio = WebDB::trim (param ("bio"));
my $secret_stuff;
my $dbh;
my $page;

    # The only validation is to make sure the email
    # field contains a valid address.

    if ($email eq "" || !WebDB::looks_like_email ($email))
    {
        $page .= p ("Error: The email field must be filled in with\n"
                    . "a valid address")
                    . editing_form ();
        return ($page);
    }

    $dbh = WebDB::connect ();
    $dbh->do ("UPDATE bio SET email = ?, bio = ? WHERE id = ?",
                            undef, $email, $bio, $id);
    $dbh->disconnect ();

    $secret_stuff = encode ($sess_id, $id);
    $page .= p ("Your record has been updated. The new values are:")
            . table (
                Tr (
                    td ("Email address:"),
                    td (escapeHTML ($email))
                ),
                Tr (
                    td ("Biographical information:"),
                    td (escapeHTML ($bio))
                )
            )
            . start_form (-action => url ())
            . p ("Select Continue Editing to make further changes,\n"
                . "Log Out to quit.")
            . hidden (-name => "secret_stuff",
                        -value => $secret_stuff, -override => 1)
            . submit (-name => "choice", -value => "Continue Editing")
            . " "
            . submit (-name => "choice", -value => "Log Out")
            . end_form ();
    return ($page);
}
```

When submit_changes() extracts parameter values from its environment, it uses trim() to trim off any extra whitespace from the values entered into the form by the user. It doesn't use trim() for the session or record ID values; the dispatch code placed those into the environment after extracting them from the hidden secret_stuff field, so they are usable as is.

The confirmation page generated by submit_changes() contains a Continue Editing button should the user decide to make more changes to the record. The function continue_editing() handles this case. It's somewhat similar to start_editing(), but doesn't create a session ID because there is already a session in place. It also knows the ID of the record to look up, so there's no need to solicit the username and password again.

```perl
sub continue_editing
{
my ($dbh, $sth, $bio_ref, $page);

    # Look for the current record in the bio table.

    $dbh = WebDB::connect ();
    $sth = $dbh->prepare ( "SELECT * FROM bio WHERE id = ?");
    $sth->execute (param ("id"));
    $bio_ref = $sth->fetchrow_hashref ();
    $sth->finish ();
    $dbh->disconnect ();
    if (!defined ($bio_ref))    # no matching record found (shouldn't happen)
    {
        $page .= p ("Error: Could not retrieve your record.")
                  . login_page ();
        return ($page);
    }

    # Put the contents of the bio record into the script
    # environment for editing_form() to find.

    foreach my $key (keys (%{$bio_ref}))
    {
        param (-name => $key, -value => $bio_ref->{$key});
    }
    $page .= editing_form ();

    return ($page);
}
```

Making the Session Secure

Thus far, we've made sure that unauthorized users cannot gain access to the application, by means of a login page. We've also protected the session and record IDs from tampering to ensure that once logged in, a user can't modify someone else's record. Our final safeguard will be to protect the user's privacy from eavesdroppers by allowing the entire session from login to logout to be performed over a secure connection. Assuming your Web server is set up to support SSL (as described in "Using Secure

Connections") and that the user's browser also understands SSL, a secure connection can be provided quite easily. We can just require that the user invoke the script using `https` rather than `http` when requesting the `edit_bio.pl` script:

```
https://www.snake.net/cgi-perl/edit_bio.pl
```

This requires no changes to `edit_bio.pl` at all. The user gets a secure connection and we don't have to do any work. But it's not really a very good idea to rely on clients remembering to invoke the script using `https` and not `http`.[5] What are our options here for helping the user? One possibility is to put an `SSLRequire` directive in the Apache configuration file to prevent the script from being run unless the URL begins with `https`.[6] However, that approach probably is not very helpful. It keeps a user from using a non-secure connection, but doesn't tell the user what do instead. Another possibility is to have `edit_bio.pl` check for itself when the user first connects whether the connection is secure. If not, the login page can offer the option of logging in securely, in the form of a link that points to the login page but that begins with `https`. This is easy to do with a small modification to `login_page()`. At the end of that function, you'll find a line like this:

```
return ($page);
```

To change the function to offer a secure login, add the following code just before the `return` statement:

```
# If the user isn't logging in over a secure connection,
# offer the option of doing so.
if (!defined ($ENV{HTTPS}))
{
    my $url = url ();
    $url =~ s/^http:/https:/i; #http -> https
    $page .= p ("Note: you are about to log in over an insecure\n"
                . "connection. To log in securely, select\n"
                . a ({-href => $url}, "this link") . ".");
}
```

The code here uses the fact that `mod_ssl` defines the `HTTPS` environment variable if the connection is secure. If the connection is insecure, we construct a secure URL that begins with `https` rather than with `http`. (The pattern match and substitution operations use the `i` modifier for a non-case-sensitive test because the URL might begin with `HTTP`, `Http`, or some other lettercase variation.) Then we generate a paragraph containing warning message and offer a link that uses the secure URL.

---

5. Try asking several Web users sometime if they've ever even noticed that secure connections use `https`.

6. If you want to try this, see the `mod_ssl` manual for information about the capabilities that `SSLRequire` offers you.

After you make this change to the script, invoke it using a URL that begins with http to make sure it properly detects the non-secure connection and offers you the secure login link. Then select the link to verify that you get a secure connection.

The preceding change to login_page() offers users a secure login option by modifying the URL to begin with https. Does that mean we need to modify other parts of the script to generate URLs that begin with https, too? No. If the user follows the secure link, subsequent URLs produced by the script are generated in relation to that link and thus also will begin with https.

Our application draws on several of the techniques discussed earlier in the chapter. It includes methods for preventing the client from connecting without authenticating, for preventing the connected client from illegitimately modifying information, and for preventing third parties from snooping. At this point, I'm willing to say that I believe edit_bio.pl to be reasonably secure from several kinds of attack, both from outsiders attempting to gain unauthorized access and from authorized users attempting to modify someone's record other than their own. Of course, the trouble with saying something like that is that I may have made some boneheaded mistake or oversight that renders the application insecure. If so, I'm sure some reader will be delighted (perhaps a little *too* delighted!) to point that out. If that reader is you, please let me know. When it comes to security, it's better to know about a problem so that it can be fixed than not to know about it and have someone silently exploit it.

Suggested Modifications

The application enables users to request their password by email if they can provide the username in the login form. But if a person can't even remember the correct username, there's a problem. To handle this, add some descriptive text to the login page that indicates how to contact the application administrator in the event of such problems.

Allow the user to change the password in the editing form. If you implement this by presenting a password field so that onlookers can't gawk at the browser window to see what the user is typing, you should probably present *two* fields and require that they match. Otherwise, it's very easy for the user to make a mistake and end up with a password different from what was intended.

Store the record ID in the session record on the server side rather than on the client side in a hidden field. Then you only have to perform checksumming and encrypting on a single value (the session ID).

Transmit the session ID using a cookie rather than in a hidden field. This doesn't eliminate the need to prevent tampering (users can modify cookie contents), but it does allow an editing session to be resumed if the user accidentally closes the editing window. Is this good or bad?

The passwords in the bio table are stored as plain text, so anyone with SELECT access to the table can find out all the passwords easily. Can you prevent this by encrypting the passwords? (Some of the possibilities here include MySQL's

PASSWORD(), ENCRYPT(), MD5(), ENCODE(), and DECODE() functions.) Does your solution break the application's capability to mail passwords to record owners? That is, does the encryption method offer reversibility? If it is reversible, is the encryption reversible *only* by the application? Will your solution work if some other MySQL user has UPDATE access to the bio table?

In this chapter, we've covered a number of security issues that present themselves when you develop Web applications, as well as techniques for preventing security breaches. One area for which security generally has a very high priority is e-commerce, because such applications quite often involve private or sensitive information or financial transactions. In Chapter 10, "E-Commerce Applications," we'll put some of these techniques for addressing security and privacy concerns to use in contexts that engage users in commercial interaction.

10

E-Commerce Applications

MANY PEOPLE PREFER SHOPPING IN PERSON or over the telephone to shopping online, but electronic commerce (e-commerce) is increasingly popular, and those who'd rather go online to conduct business tend to want to do as much as possible that way. Therefore, if you're thinking about running an e-commerce Web site, it's also worth thinking about providing services other than just a shopping cart. One way to define an e-commerce site is indeed as a site devoted to selling things, but there is a larger picture to keep in mind. Just as business in general is about more than just "making the sale," so too e-commerce Web sites can allow customers to do more than click Add To Cart buttons. Your Web server is capable of much more than that. You can use it to

- Provide information about your company. Give the customer a sense of familiarity with your organization and help the customer become more willing to do business. You can tell visitors about your company mission, how you can benefit them, and why they should do business with you.

- Make your product catalog available online, including specifications, pricing, and perhaps other information such as what the product is good for and why the customer should purchase it. Send email notifications when items arrive in inventory that match customer interests.

- Sell products by enabling customers to select items and pay for them. Let customers know when out-of-stock items arrive in inventory. Allow customers to track the progress of an order.

- Provide customer support, both before and after a sale. Offer an online help desk, technical support, or other general assistance. Help customers register products, return items, or resolve problems with defective items. Enable visitors to sign up for newsletters or product updates.

- Provide other general information, such as a privacy policy or warranty information.

- Gather customer feedback via surveys, forms, or polls. Ask your customers what they think about you or your site.

As you look through this list, you'll notice that it's not just customers who can use your Web site. For example, putting your product catalog online also benefits sales staff by making it available to them out in the field, and order-tracking capabilities can be used by help desk staff who are assisting customers.

Different e-commerce sites implement different combinations of these functions. Some sites that exist only for marketing purposes provide information about a company, its products, and services, and are designed to tell you only enough that you can call or write for more information. Or they may assist you in finding local dealers for a product. A selling site is designed for immediate sales; it provides information to help the customer come to a decision and make a purchase on the spot. Clearly, e-commerce can be a complex area, and a single chapter isn't going to be a comprehensive treatment. However, this chapter will provide some essential background information and get you going with enough material that you'll easily come up with lots of ideas for creating your own e-commerce applications. In addition, you already know many techniques you can use, because several of the activities you might engage in on your site have been touched on earlier. In Chapter 5, "Writing Form-Based Applications," we wrote a product registration application. Chapter 7, "Performing Searches," discussed techniques that can be applied to e-commerce situations such as product inventory searches. In Chapter 8, "Session Management," we saw ways to track information as users move around your site, which can be helpful for implementing shopping carts or remembering customer preferences. Chapter 9, "Security and Privacy Issues," covered use of secure connections, such as you might set up before asking customers to divulge personal information or credit card numbers.

The discussion in this chapter is framed almost entirely in terms of commercial activities, but several of the concepts described here apply in other ways. For example, shopping cart techniques aren't limited just to things that people pay for. The underlying idea is simple: allow a user to select items, and remember what's been chosen. A cart is commonly used to keep track of items that you're selling, but you can turn the concept completely around and keep track of items that you're giving away. (In this day and age, it's not impossible to imagine a Web-based interface to a non-profit food pantry operation.) The chapter also discusses how to perform transactions in MySQL—that is, how to group a set of SQL statements so they succeed as a unit or else are undone if any of them fail. For example, your order fulfillment department may mark an item on an order as having been added to a customer's shipping container and at the same time decrement the inventory count for that item in your product catalog. Both operations should take place in tandem so that if one fails, the effect of the other is rolled back or reverted. This kind of problem is common in commercial applications but arises in other contexts as well. Another technique shown here that you may want to adapt for purposes other than e-commerce is a method for presenting pages generated by different scripts within a common framework so that they have a similar overall appearance. You can use this technique to produce thematic consistency for a site.

The Place of a Database in E-Commerce

A Web server is clearly essential for an e-commerce Web site, but in most cases a database is no less important. Although the database need not be involved in all aspects of your site (your privacy policy or warranty information statement may be provided as static pages, for example), it's difficult to run an effective site of any complexity without using a database in some capacity. Many of the services supported by e-commerce sites involve the customer directly, but the utility of a database extends beyond that to other areas as well. A database allows you to

- Store your product catalog so that customers and staff can browse through it or perform searches on it.
- Store and process orders submitted by customers.
- Store product registrations, comments, questions, or survey results.
- Maintain customer and supplier lists so that you can send out notices of product updates or changes in ordering policies.
- Generate reports of all kinds. Query inventory levels for items in the product catalog to determine which need to be reordered; summarize customer orders for a sales report; summarize orders to suppliers for an expense report.

Should You Use MySQL for E-Commerce?

What database should you use for your site? In particular, should you use MySQL for e-commerce applications? It's only fair to tell you that some people say "no," some of them quite emphatically.[1] However, you should also know that objections to using MySQL for e-commerce have been based largely on the lack of support for transactions in older versions. Prior to version 3.23.17, MySQL had no transaction support.

---

1. `http://openacs.org/philosophy/why-not-mysql.html` provides some interesting, if occasionally rabid, reading on this topic.

That's no longer true, so transaction-based objections to MySQL as an e-commerce engine have little force. Naturally, you should use the database that works best for you; I encourage you to run your own tests and evaluations. If you're running your own server, you should be able to upgrade to a recent version of MySQL if necessary to perform such evaluations. If a separate service provider hosts your site, you're more likely to have an older version. Providers tend not to upgrade very often, to avoid surprising their customers; therefore, you may need to ask your provider for a more recent version of MySQL if you need transaction support. Note also that even for recent versions, transaction support may not have been configured in; be sure your server was built to include transactional capabilities. Transactions are discussed further in "Performing Transactions" later in this chapter.

Setting Up a Virtual Storefront

The rest of this chapter is devoted to setting up a small site that serves as the e-commerce base for a fictitious company, PseudEcom Corporation,[2] and that implements several of the functions listed in the chapter introduction. In this section, we'll design a storefront home page that provides general information about the site and points to its other major areas. Then we'll cover implementation of those areas in the sections to follow.

A helpful and informative home page is important for making a good first impression on people who arrive at that page when they first visit your site. However, it's also important to realize that many people won't reach you that way. Your site undoubtedly will be indexed by search engines (whether or not you explicitly request it), and most of the time these engines will take people to pages other than your home page. For example, people looking for a particular product may find a reference in a search engine that jumps them directly to a page that displays an item from your product catalog.

Don't make the mistake of thinking that you have any control over how people come into your site. Instead, plan in advance to handle this issue by providing good navigation aids on every page. At a minimum, each page should have a link to your home page, but you can also provide links to other major site areas. A useful technique for assisting visitors is to put a standard navigation area on each page. This provides a consistent point of reference that helps them move about. It also allows users to gain a sense of familiarity with your site more quickly. That's a good thing because it helps your visitors feel at home. Other standard page layout features can be used, such as a company logo to help brand pages with a common look or identity, or a copyright notice to make your legal department happy. You can also include a "for testing purposes only" notice during development, and then remove it when the site goes live.

---

2. PseudEcom = pseudo (fake) e-com, pronounced SOO-de-com.

In a script-based environment, standard layout elements can be implemented different ways. For example, you could write a function that produces these elements and invoke it from all parts of your scripts that produce pages. Another approach (the one we'll use) is to generate the main content of each page in memory as a string. Then, when you reach the end of the script and you're ready to display the page to the client, you can pass the string to a function that adds the standard page elements (or "boilerplate"). One advantage of using a script to produce boilerplate is that you're not limited to producing static standard elements. For example, you can include banner ads as part of your page layout and choose the advertisement to show at page display time.

For the PseudEcom site, the standard "look" divides pages into four sections—the company name to the upper left, a navigation panel containing links to major site areas down the left side of the page, a small message area along the top, and the rest of the page devoted to the main content area. The PseudEcom home page shown in Figure 10.1 demonstrates this layout.

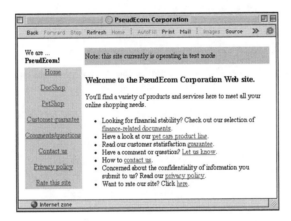

Figure 10.1   PseudEcom home page.

As you can see from the figure, the main areas supported by the PseudEcom site and listed on the home page are as follows:

- Two shopping areas, one for financial assistance documents and one for the oh-so-essential pet-care items you need to keep those little loved ones happy. (If you were building your own site, you'd probably integrate your product lines into a single interface. The PseudEcom site involves two separate applications to illustrate different approaches to online sales.)
- The customer satisfaction guarantee.
- A way for customers to submit comments or feedback or to ask questions.

- Company contact information.
- The company privacy policy.
- A "rate this site" poll to solicit customer opinions.

Implementation of these various site functions varies quite a bit in complexity. Some of them (statements of policy, for example) are quite simple, the shopping applications are the most complex, and the others lie somewhere between.

Because the page boilerplate is generated on-the-fly, every page on the PseudEcom site is produced by a script, even the storefront home page that serves as the entryway to the site. This script, `store.pl`, shows visitors what's available and provides access to its services:

```perl
#! /usr/bin/perl -w
# store.pl - Present general PseudEcom Corporation home page

use strict;
use lib qw(/usr/local/apache/lib/perl);
use CGI qw(:standard escape escapeHTML);
use WebDB;
use WebDB::PseudEcom;

my $page = h3 ("Welcome to the PseudEcom Corporation Web site.")
        . p ("You'll find a variety of products and services here to\n"
          . "meet all your online shopping needs.")
        . ul (
        li ("Looking for financial stability? Check out our selection of\n"
          . get_doc_shop_link ("finance-related documents")
          . "."),
        li ("Have a look at our\n"
          . get_pet_shop_link ("pet-care product line")
          . "."),
        li ("Read our customer statisfaction\n"
          . get_satisfaction_link ("guarantee")
          . "."),
        li ("Have a comment or question?\n"
          . get_feedback_link ("Let us know")
          . "."),
        li ("How to\n"
          . get_contact_link ("contact us")
          . "."),
        li ("Concerned about the confidentiality of information you\n"
          . "submit to us? Read our\n"
          . get_privacy_link ("privacy policy")
          . "."),
        li ("Want to rate our site? Click\n"
          . get_rating_link ("here")
          . ".")
        );
```

```
$page = add_boilerplate ($page);    # add standard page elements

print header (),
       start_html (-title => "PseudEcom Corporation", -bgcolor => "white"),
       $page,
       end_html ();

exit (0);
```

This script does little more than present a bit of introductory welcome text, followed by a list of the site's services. The items in this list provide links to the same parts of the site as the navigation panel that lies along the left edge of each PseudEcom page, but the associated text is more descriptive. (The get_*xxx*_link() routines used in creating the list are functions that generate hyperlinks to the major site areas. These functions are located in WebDB::PseudEcom, a module that provides support routines for PseudEcom scripts; it's described in the next section.) After generating the main page content and saving it in the $page variable, store.pl calls add_boilerplate() to embed the content within the standard page layout elements, and then displays the result.

Support Routines

The WebDB::PseudEcom support module provides access to functions that are used in common by the scripts that implement the PseudEcom site. The module source file PseudEcom.pm can be found in the WebDB directory of the book's webdb source distribution. Copy it to a WebDB directory that is under some directory in your Perl script search path. (This is similar to the way the WebDB::TableInfo and WebDB::Poll modules were installed in Chapter 6, "Automating the Form-Handling Process." See that chapter for further information about module installation.)

The WebDB::PseudEcom module file begins with a package statement naming the module and some use statements referencing the other modules that it requires. That's much like the other modules we've written up to this point. However, the module also does something we haven't done before—it uses Exporter to export the names of some of its functions as public routines. This allows any of these functions to be invoked without naming the package. That is, a function f() can be called as just f() rather than as WebDB::PseudEcom::f().[3] The initial part of WebDB::PseudEcom looks like this:

```
package WebDB::PseudEcom;

# Arrange to export the "public" function names

require Exporter;
@ISA = qw(Exporter);
@EXPORT = qw(
```

continues

---

3. Should we have taken this same approach of exporting names from the modules that we wrote earlier in the book?

continued

```
            get_url_prefix
            get_home_link
            get_doc_shop_link
            get_pet_shop_link
            get_contact_link
            get_satisfaction_link
            get_privacy_link
            get_feedback_link
            get_rating_link
            get_card_type_list
            get_card_exp_month_list
            get_card_exp_year_list
            add_boilerplate
            fatal_error
    );

    use strict;
    use lib qw(/usr/local/apache/lib/perl);
    use CGI qw(:standard escape escapeHTML);
    use WebDB;
```

Most of the `WebDB::PseudEcom` module is devoted to uninteresting functions that generate URLs or hyperlinks to the major site areas. These encapsulate the details of the site layout into a functional interface to make it easier to rearrange the site if you like. (You might not want to use the same layout as the one that I show in this chapter.) However, these functions also are somewhat mindless to write, so I won't show them all. The following routine, `get_home_link()`, is a representative example. It returns a string that contains a hyperlink pointing to `store.pl`, the home page script:

```
    sub get_home_link
    {
    my $label = shift;

        return (get_link (get_url ("store.pl"), $label));
    }
```

You can see how `get_home_link()` is used by looking back at the source for `store.pl`, which also shows instances for most of the other link generators. To see how these functions are written (as well as other helper routines such as `get_link()` and `get_url()`), have a look at the `PseudEcom.pm` source file.

Another support routine is `add_boilerplate()`, the function that adds standard layout elements to a page. It uses a 2×2 table to divide the page into quadrants and places the main page content in the lower-right section:

```
    sub add_boilerplate
    {
    my $page = shift;

        return (table (Tr (
                # upper left corner
                td ("We are ..." . br () . strong ("PseudEcom!")),
```

```
            td (),                                  # spacer column
            # message at top of page
            td ({-bgcolor => "silver"},
                "Note: this site currently is operating in test mode")
        ),
        Tr (td ({-colspan => "3"})),                # spacer row
        Tr (
            # navigation panel
            td ({-bgcolor => "lightblue",
                    -align => "center", -valign => "top"},
                    get_home_link ("Home")
                    . br () . br ()
                    . get_doc_shop_link ("DocShop")
                    . br () . br ()
                    . get_pet_shop_link ("PetShop")
                    . br () . br ()
                    . get_satisfaction_link ("Customer guarantee")
                    . br () . br ()
                    . get_feedback_link ("Comments/questions")
                    . br () . br ()
                    . get_contact_link ("Contact us")
                    . br () . br ()
                    . get_privacy_link ("Privacy policy")
                    . br () . br ()
                    . get_rating_link ("Rate this site")
                    ),
            td (),                                  # spacer column
            # main page content
            td ({-align => "left", -valign => "top"}, $page)
    )));
}
```

add_boilerplate() is used by all the PseudEcom scripts to produce pages. Therefore, if you want to modify the overall appearance of the site, this is the routine to tinker with. The boilerplate function is even used by fatal_error(), a WebDB::PseudEcom utility routine that places error message text within the standard boilerplate when terminal conditions occur:

```
sub fatal_error
{
my $msg = shift;
my $page;

    $page .= p ("An error has occurred.")
            . p (escapeHTML ($msg))
            . p ("Return to the PseudEcom " . get_home_link ("home page"));
    print header (),
            start_html (-title => "PseudEcom Corporation",
                        -bgcolor => "white"),
            add_boilerplate ($page),
            end_html ();
    exit (0);
}
```

Other functions in this module file are discussed as the need arises. For example, the module includes routines that help generate fields for collecting credit card information. These are covered when we implement the first shopping application.

Configuring Apache to Recognize the Site

Where should the storefront home page script `store.pl` go? For this chapter, I'll just assume that you install `store.pl` in the `cgi-perl` directory and invoke it the usual way:

```
http://www.snake.net/cgi-perl/store.pl
```

On the other hand, if your entire server will be devoted to e-commerce functions, it's likely you'd want the script to be invoked whenever a user enters into a browser nothing more than your domain name or the most likely guess for your home page:

```
http://www.snake.net/
http://www.snake.net/index.html
```

When Apache sees either URL, normally it will expect to serve a page named `index.html` from the top level of your document tree. If you want it to execute `store.pl` instead, you can "trap" these URLs and map them onto the storefront script using redirection directives in the Apache configuration file. For example, if `store.pl` is installed in the `cgi-perl` directory, the following two directives will accomplish this:

```
RedirectMatch ^/$ http://www.snake.net/cgi-perl/store.pl
RedirectMatch ^/index.html$ http://www.snake.net/cgi-perl/store.pl
```

If your site is not devoted entirely to e-commerce functions, you may want to segregate the PseudEcom "store" as a separate area of the site, for example, to be accessed through URLs that begin like this:

```
http://www.snake.net/store/...
```

In this case, you'll need to make different adjustments to your Apache configuration.

Whichever way you configure your site, at this point you should install the `WebDB::PseudEcom` module and the `store.pl` script, and then invoke the latter to try it out. It should present a page in your browser that resembles Figure 10.1, although none of the links except the "Home" link will work yet, because we haven't yet implemented any of the other areas of the site. That's covered in the following sections.

Presenting Static Library Pages

Now we can begin implementing other parts of the site to go along with the storefront page. Let's take care of the easiest thing first, which is to present the areas that consist of static information. These include the privacy policy, the customer satisfaction guarantee, and the contact information pages. The main content for these pages is static, but they need to have boilerplate added to give them the "site look." We'll implement display for static pages like these by setting up a page library and writing a simple page processor static.pl. To present any page that has a main content area containing static HTML, the processor reads the library file containing the content, adds the boilerplate, and sends the result to the client. static.pl looks like this:

```perl
#! /usr/bin/perl -w
# static.pl - Handle a PseudEcom site "static" page.

# Read the requested page from the library directory, add the standard
# boilerplate, and send the result to the client.

use strict;
use lib qw(/usr/local/apache/lib/perl);
use IO::File;
use CGI qw(:standard);
use WebDB;
use WebDB::PseudEcom;

# Change this pathname as necessary for your site
my $static_page_dir = "/usr/local/apache/lib/htfiles";

my $page;

my $page_name = WebDB::trim (param ("page"));
$page_name ne ""
    or fatal_error ("No page was requested; invocation error");
$page_name = $static_page_dir . "/" . $page_name;

my $fh = new IO::File ($page_name)
    or fatal_error ("Could not open $page_name");

{   # undefine local copy of input separator to disable it
    local $/;
    undef $/;
    $page .= <$fh>;     # slurp entire file
}

undef $fh;          # close file

print header (),
        start_html (-title => "PseudEcom Corporation", -bgcolor => "white"),
        add_boilerplate ($page),
        end_html ();

exit (0);
```

The library files need not be stored in the Apache document tree. They just need to be in a location where the page processor can read them. As distributed, static.pl assumes the files are installed in /usr/local/apache/lib/htfiles. (You can find these files in the ecom/htfiles directory of the webdb distribution. Copy them where you want and, if necessary, adjust the pathname to them in the static.pl script.)

Library pages can be as simple or as complex as you like. For example, the customer satisfaction guarantee can be stated quite briefly:

```
<h3>PseudEcom's Customer Satisfaction Guarantee</h3>
<p>
We guarantee that you will be delighted with any product you purchase from us.
</p>
<p>
If you are not, we offer the following simple policy:
You keep the product and we will keep the money.
</p>
<p>
No questions asked!
</p>
```

Extending the Library Pages

Our static pages are written as HTML that is processed without interpretation. This has certain limitations. For example, if you need to include in a library page a link to some other area of the site, you could hardwire the link in, but then it would become invalid should you rearrange the site. An alternative approach would be to treat the HTML library pages as templates rather than as uninterpreted text. You could include special markers in the page that the page processor can recognize and convert to the proper links on-the-fly when the page is served. Then if you rearrange the site, you need only update the link-generation functions in the WebDB::PseudEcom module. If you want to use templates without writing your own template processor, take a look at Perl modules such as Text::Template and HTML::Mason.

An Online Document Sales Application

A few areas of the PseudEcom site are functional now. Customers can visit the home page, and they can select the links that present policy statements or contact information. Let's proceed on to our next application, one that implements our first online shopping scenario. The situation we'll use for this application is that we are in possession of a wealth of wonderful information guaranteed to produce financial prosperity and security and that customers can have access to—for a price, of course. This application, doc_shop.pl, delivers the information in the form of PDF documents. It works in several stages:

- Initially, doc_shop.pl presents a catalog of product offerings—a list of the documents we have for sale. The user chooses the documents that look interesting, and then selects the Check Out button.

- The checkout page displays the items that were chosen so that the user can review the order. It also presents a billing information form containing fields for name, email address, and credit card information. (No shipping address is needed because we'll deliver the documents electronically.) The user fills in the billing form and selects Submit Order.

- When `doc_shop.pl` receives the billing information, it charges the user's credit card (don't get excited; we're going to fake this part), and then displays a page containing an order confirmation number and hyperlinks to each of the purchased documents. These links enable the customer to download the documents, although each one will be tied to a password to discourage people from downloading documents without paying for them. We'll also send the customer an email message containing the order information as a more permanent record of the transaction.

What Information Should You Ask for, and When?

`doc_shop.pl` first determines what the customer wants to order, and then asks for billing information. There's no logical reason you couldn't ask for the billing information first, but there are a couple of practical reasons not to. First, if the visitor doesn't purchase anything, we won't need billing information and will have wasted the visitor's time by requiring it. Second, it's best not to make people identify themselves or provide sensitive information until you really need such information, because people don't like it when you do that. If you require a credit card number before allowing customers into the shopping area, for example, they'll become suspicious of your motives. (If I have to provide a card number, only to find that you don't have the goods in which I'm interested, I may assume you're a fraudulent site set up solely for the purpose of capturing numbers. I will never visit you again.)

To avoid alienating your customers, here's a good principle to follow: Provide information *to* your customers as they request it, but require information *from* them only as you need it and not before. Think of it this way: You don't want to stop your customers at the door—you want them to come in and look around.

`doc_shop.pl` begins with a preamble that implements its overall logic like this:

```perl
#! /usr/bin/perl -w
# doc_shop.pl - Present document-shopping activity

use strict;
use lib qw(/usr/local/apache/lib/perl);
use CGI qw(:standard escape escapeHTML);
use Mail::Sendmail;
use Business::CreditCard;
use Digest::MD5;
use WebDB;
use WebDB::PseudEcom;

my $dbh = WebDB::connect ();
my $page = h3 ("The PseudEcom Doc Shop");

# Dispatch to proper action based on user selection

my $choice = lc (param ("choice")); # get choice, lowercased
```

```
if ($choice eq "")                     # initial invocation
{
    $page .= display_catalog ($dbh);
}
elsif ($choice eq "check out")        # user is ready to check out
{
    $page .= display_billing_form ($dbh);
}
elsif ($choice eq "submit order")   # record the order, deliver goods
{
    $page .= close_order ($dbh);
}
else
{
    $page .= p (escapeHTML ("Logic error, unknown choice: $choice"));
}

$dbh->disconnect ();

print header (),
        start_html (-title => "PseudEcom Corporation", -bgcolor => "white"),
        add_boilerplate ($page),
        end_html ();
```

That doesn't look very complicated, but of course it's just the tip of the iceberg. The application implementation involves several issues:

- **Product catalog presentation.** For this application, the catalog is small and we can display the entire product line in a single page for the user to browse. Later, we'll build an application that uses a more extensive catalog for which we'll provide a search interface. When you allow browsing or searching over multiple pages, you need some way to remember what items have been ordered so far, and that means a shopping cart. The simpler catalog is convenient as a starting point because we can get away without writing a cart.

- **Collecting and processing billing information.** We'll allow payment by credit card, so we'll need to solicit card information from the customer, and we'll also need to set up a secure connection.

- **Transactions.** Orders will be recorded using two tables. One (doc_order) lists general order and customer information; the other (doc_item) lists each item in the order. It would not be good to update only one table if the update to the other failed for some reason. We want all updates for a given order to succeed as a unit, which means we need to use transactions to make sure that partial updates get rolled back.

- **Order delivery.** doc_shop.pl uses electronic delivery, so we need not determine any shipping charges. Electronic delivery also eliminates any need to keep track of item quantities, at least for this scenario. After all, after a user has downloaded a PDF file, it can be printed multiple times at will. (For other types of downloads, you'd probably want to associate quantities with items ordered. If you were selling software titles, you might allow multiple-unit purchases and issue separate serial numbers for each unit of a given title.)

Setting Up the Tables

`doc_shop.pl` requires three tables. One contains the catalog items, and the other two are used to record orders that we receive from customers. We'll also need to store the PDF files somewhere. We could store them in the database, the same way we managed image data in Chapter 5, "Writing Form-Based Applications," and in Chapter 7, "Performing Searches." Or we could store just the document names in the database and store the documents in the file system. To demonstrate this alternative, that's the approach `doc_shop.pl` takes.

The catalog table `doc_catalog` looks like this:

```
CREATE TABLE doc_catalog
(
    # document ID, title, price, and filename
    doc_id      BIGINT UNSIGNED NOT NULL AUTO_INCREMENT PRIMARY KEY,
    title       VARCHAR(60) NOT NULL,
    price       DECIMAL(10,2) NOT NULL,
    filename    VARCHAR(40) NOT NULL
)
```

`doc_id` is the unique document identifier. `title` provides a descriptive title that we'll display for customers in the catalog page to indicate what the document is about. `price` is the selling price. (Its type, `DECIMAL(10,2)`, provides 10 digit values with 2 decimal places of accuracy—well suited to monetary values.) `filename` indicates where to find the PDF document. We'll store all the documents in a single library directory, so this value need only be the basename of the file within that directory. An `INSERT` statement to create some sample records in the `doc_catalog` table looks like this:

```
INSERT INTO doc_catalog (title,price,filename)
    VALUES
        ('Make Money Fast!',20.00,'fast.pdf'),
        ('Double Your Money in 5 Minutes',15.00,'double5.pdf'),
        ('The Secret of Financial Success',19.95,'secret.pdf'),
        ('How To Be Tax Free',25.00,'tax-free.pdf')
```

That's only part of the job of initializing the catalog, because we also must install the PDF documents that the catalog refers to. For `doc_shop.pl`, we'll use the same library directory where we store the static HTML pages that are processed by `static.pl` (that is, `/usr/local/apache/lib/htfiles`). Sample documents corresponding to those named in the `INSERT` statement just shown can be found in the `ecom/htfiles` directory of the `webdb` distribution; move into that directory and copy the PDF files to the library directory where `doc_shop.pl` expects to find them. If you want to install the files in a different directory, change the path name near the beginning of `doc_shop.pl`. (You'll also need to change another script, `serve_doc.pl`, to match.)

If you want to add other documents to the catalog, add a record for each one to the doc_catalog table and copy the corresponding PDF file to the library directory. Similarly, to remove a document, delete the doc_catalog record and remove the file. Compared to the technique of storing documents in the database, this is more cumbersome because each action involves a database operation and a file system operation. On the other hand, storing the documents in the file system does have some advantages. To replace a document, for example, you can just flop a new one on top of it. Thus, each approach has its own pros and cons.

Note that although we stored images in the database in earlier chapters and PDF documents in the file system here, we could just as well have done things the other way around. There is no inherent property of images, documents, or, indeed, any other kind of data that constrains you to using one method or the other.

To store orders received from customers, doc_shop.pl uses two tables:

```
CREATE TABLE doc_order
(
    order_id    BIGINT NOT NULL AUTO_INCREMENT PRIMARY KEY,
    order_date  DATE NOT NULL,              # date of order
    order_amt   DECIMAL(10,2) NOT NULL,     # total cost
    auth_id     VARCHAR(10) NOT NULL,       # transaction authorization
    cust_name   VARCHAR(40) NOT NULL,       # customer name
    cust_email  VARCHAR(60) NOT NULL        # customer email address
) TYPE = BDB

CREATE TABLE doc_item
(
    order_id    BIGINT UNSIGNED NOT NULL,   # order number
    doc_id      BIGINT UNSIGNED NOT NULL,   # document number
    price       DECIMAL(10,2) NOT NULL,     # price paid
    password    CHAR(32) NOT NULL,          # item password (for downloading)
    UNIQUE (order_id, doc_id)
) TYPE = BDB
```

doc_order contains general information about each order; there will be one record in this table per order. doc_item will contain one row per order for each document purchased. The order_id and item_id columns indicate the order the record belongs to and which document was ordered. The price column shows how much the customer paid for it. (We record the price here in the doc_item table because otherwise we wouldn't be able to determine how much customers paid for each document if we happened to change the prices in the doc_catalog table.) The password column contains a value that the customer must present to download the document after paying for it. The column is a CHAR(32) because we'll generate passwords that are 32-character strings. (The passwords will be created using the Digest::MD5 module, which is why the preamble of doc_shop.pl includes a use Digest::MD5 statement.)

The CREATE TABLE statements for the order storage tables include something we haven't used before—a TYPE clause at the end. This indicates that the doc_order and doc_item tables should be created using a specific table type, rather than whatever the default type happens to be. BDB is a type that supports transactions, which we'll require later when updating both order tables at the same time. (I'm using BDB tables here because, although other kinds of transaction-capable tables may be available, BDB tables were the first such to be included in MySQL, and therefore the most likely to be present in your version. To use a different transactional table type, substitute an appropriate clause for the TYPE = BDB part of the CREATE TABLE statements. If your version of MySQL doesn't have transaction support, you should remove TYPE = BDB from the statements entirely.)

Presenting the Document Catalog

The first thing that doc_shop.pl does for the customer is present the list of documents we have for sale. The display_catalog() function handles this. It selects the items from the doc_catalog table and presents them as a table that shows the document ID, description, and price. It also displays a check box next to each item that the customer can use to select documents.

```perl
sub display_catalog
{
my $dbh = shift;
my ($sth, @row, $page, $url);

    push (@row, Tr (
            th ("Select"),
            th ("Item No."),
            th ("Document Title"),
            th ("Price (USD)")
        ));
    $sth = $dbh->prepare ("SELECT * FROM doc_catalog ORDER BY doc_id");
    $sth->execute ();
    while (my $ref = $sth->fetchrow_hashref ())
    {
        my $item_no = "item_" . $ref->{doc_id};
        push (@row, Tr (
                # explicitly give checkbox no label
                td (checkbox (-name => $item_no, -label => "")),
                td (escapeHTML ($ref->{doc_id})),
                td (escapeHTML ($ref->{title})),
                td ({-align => "right"},
                    escapeHTML (sprintf ("%.2f", $ref->{price})))
            ));
    }
    $sth->finish ();
```

continues

continued

```
# present a secure link for the Check Out button
($url = url ()) =~ s/^http:/https:/i;
$page .= p ("Please select the documents you wish to purchase,\n"
            . "then select Check Out.")
        . start_form (-action => $url)
        . table (@row)
        . submit (-name => "choice", -value => "Check Out")
        . end_form ();

    return ($page);
}
```

The check boxes presented in the catalog page are individual fields. They do *not* form a group; each one corresponds to a specific document. The check boxes are given names of the form item_*n*, where *n* is the doc_id value for the associated document. This makes it easy to identify the relevant parameters when the customer submits the form. Note that the check box labels are explicitly set to the empty string. If we don't specify any labels at all, the check box names will be displayed as the labels, which is not what we want.

The document selection form includes an action parameter that begins with https so that when the customer submits the form, a secure connection will be set up for collecting the billing information in the next stage. This way, the customer can see that we're going to protect any information that we ask for. (If you don't have your server set up for secure connections yet, this https link won't work. For testing, you can modify the script to use the unaltered value of url(), but that's not a good idea for production applications.)

Collecting Billing Information

After the user indicates which document or documents to purchase and selects the Check Out button on the catalog page, doc_shop.pl proceeds to the checkout stage, implemented using the display_billing_form() function. This routine first determines which items were chosen by the customer. If nothing was selected, display_billing_form() says so and redisplays the catalog page. Otherwise, it presents a table showing the selected items and the total order cost, along with a form for collecting billing information. This form also contains the item IDs as hidden fields so that we'll be able to determine which documents to charge the user for when the billing form is submitted:

```
sub display_billing_form
{
my $dbh = shift;
my (@id, $order_info, $page);

    # Find field names of the form item_n and extract n
    # from each to determine which items were selected.
```

```perl
@id = grep (s/^item_//, param ());
if (!@id)
{
    $page .= p ("You didn't choose any items.");
    $page .= display_catalog ($dbh);
    return ($page);
}

# fetch information for the selected documents from the catalog and
# format it into a table for display to the customer

$order_info = fetch_catalog_items ($dbh, @id);

$page .= p ("You chose these item(s):");
$page .= format_items_html ($order_info);

$page .= p ("Please provide your name, email address, and\n"
            . "credit card information, then select Submit Order.");

$page .= start_form (-action => url ());

# add item IDs as hidden fields

foreach my $id (@id)
{
my $item_no = "item_" . $id;

    $page .= hidden (-name => $item_no, -value => $id, -override => 1);
}

$page .= table (
            Tr (
                td ("Your name (as listed on card):"),
                td (textfield (-name => "cust_name", -size => "40"))
            ),
            Tr (
                td ("Email address:"),
                td (textfield (-name => "cust_email", -size => "60"))
            ),
            Tr (
                td ("Credit card type:"),
                td (popup_menu (-name => "card_type",
                                -values => get_card_type_list ()))
            ),
            Tr (
                td ("Credit card number:"),
                td (textfield (-name => "card_number", -size => "30"))
            ),
            Tr (
                td ("Expiration date (month, year):"),
                td (popup_menu (-name => "card_exp_month",
```

continues

continued

```
                                        -values => get_card_exp_month_list ())
                      . popup_menu (-name => "card_exp_year",
                                        -values => get_card_exp_year_list ()))
            )
         )
         . br ()
         . submit (-name => "choice", -value => "Submit Order")
         . end_form ();

      return ($page);
   }
```

To generate the first part of the page that displays the items that the customer selected, `display_billing_form()` needs to extract the item ID values from the order form the user submitted (the form generated by `display_catalog()`). These IDs were encoded using field names such as `item_14` for document 14, so we can get the item numbers by looking for fields with names of that form and stripping off the initial `item_` prefix:

```
@id = grep (s/^item_//, param ());
```

After we know the item numbers, we can retrieve information for them from the `doc_catalog` table to use in formatting the order information. This information is obtained by calling `fetch_catalog_items()`, which takes a database handle and a list of document IDs. It returns a structure containing an array of item records and the total cost of the items:

```
sub fetch_catalog_items
{
my ($dbh, @id) = @_;
my ($sth, $info);

   return undef unless @id;     # no ID values were passed

   $info = {};
   $info->{item} = []; # array for item hashrefs

   $sth = $dbh->prepare (
               "SELECT * FROM doc_catalog WHERE doc_id IN("
               . join (",", ("?") x @id)
               . ") ORDER BY doc_id");
   $sth->execute (@id);
   $info->{total_price} = 0;
   while (my $ref = $sth->fetchrow_hashref ())
   {
       push (@{$info->{item}}, $ref);
       $info->{total_price} += $ref->{price};
   }
   $sth->finish ();

   return undef unless @{$info->{item}};   # none of the IDs were valid

   return ($info);
}
```

The `fetch_catalog_items()` routine uses MySQL's `IN()` function to avoid looking up records one at a time. For example, if the user has selected items 3, 14, and 22, the query to retrieve them looks like this:

```
SELECT * FROM doc_catalog WHERE doc_id IN(3,14,22) ORDER BY doc_id
```

`IN()` takes a variable number of arguments, which is convenient because we might be looking for variable numbers of documents. However, we can't use a fixed query string because the string must contain one placeholder per document. (Placeholders represent single data values, so we can't use one placeholder to represent a list of values.) For example, to retrieve three records, we need a query string that looks like this:

```
SELECT * FROM doc_catalog WHERE doc_id IN(?,?,?) ORDER BY doc_id
```

To create the proper query for the general case, we need to know how many IDs there are. That's available as the value of `@id`, which in a scalar context returns the number of elements in the array. Then we can use the value to construct a comma-separated list of placeholder characters like this:

```
join (",", ("?") x @id)
```

The `x n` operator, when applied to a list, concatenates the list *n* times to produce another list, and `join` produces a string consisting of the list elements separated by commas. The resulting list of placeholders can be placed into the `IN()` call to construct a query string that expects the proper number of ID values, which we supply by passing `@id` to `execute()` after preparing the query.

After `display_billing_form()` calls `fetch_catalog_items()` to get the item information, it invokes `format_order_html()` to format that information for display to the customer:

```
sub format_items_html
{
my $order_info = shift;
my @row;

    push (@row, Tr (
            th ("Item No."),
            th ("Document Title"),
            th ("Price (USD)")
        ));

    foreach my $ref (@{$order_info->{item}})
    {
        push (@row, Tr (
                td (escapeHTML ($ref->{doc_id})),
                td (escapeHTML ($ref->{title})),
                td ({-align => "right"},
                    escapeHTML (sprintf ("%.2f", $ref->{price})))
```

continues

continued

```
                    ));
    }

    push (@row, Tr (
            td (""),
            td ("Total Price"),
            td ({-align => "right"},
                escapeHTML (sprintf ("%.2f", $order_info->{total_price})))
        ));

    return (table (@row));
}
```

Following the formatted order information, `display_billing_form()` presents a form to solicit credit card information. The form includes several fields that are constructed using helper routines from the `WebDB::PseudEcom` module. These functions return array references pointing to the proper lists of values for the pop-up menus used to specify the credit card type and expiration month and year:

```
sub get_card_type_list
{
    return ([ "Visa", "MasterCard", "American Express", "Discover" ]);
}

sub get_card_exp_month_list
{
    return ([ "01", "02", "03", "04", "05", "06",
            "07", "08", "09", "10", "11", "12" ]);
}

sub get_card_exp_year_list
{
my $year = (localtime (time ()))[5] + 1900;

    # list 10 successive years, beginning with current year
    return ([ map { $year + $_ } (0 .. 9) ]);
}
```

Closing the Order and Delivering the Documents

After the customer provides the credit card information and submits the billing information form, we have everything we need to close the order and to provide the documents that the customer selected. For `doc_shop.pl`, this process begins by extracting and checking the contents of the billing form. If the information looks reasonable, we issue an authorization request to charge the customer's credit card, store the order in the database, and provide the customer with a final copy of the order (both in a browser window and by email):

```perl
sub close_order
{
my $dbh = shift;
my ($billing_info, $order_info, $card_info, $auth_id);
my (@id, @error);
my $page;

    ($billing_info, @error) = get_billing_info ();

    # determine which items were ordered by checking the hidden
    # "item_n" fields, then retrieve the corresponding catalog entries

    @id = grep (s/^item_//, param ());
    if (!@id)
    {
        push (@error, "No items are present in the order");
    }
    else
    {
        $order_info = fetch_catalog_items ($dbh, @id)
            or push (@error, "No valid items are present in the order");
    }

    # If validation errors occurred, say what they were and redisplay
    # billing information page so user can correct them

    if (@error)
    {
        @error = map { escapeHTML ($_) } @error;
        $page .= p ("Please correct the following problem(s)")
                . ul (li (\@error));
        $page .= display_billing_form ($dbh);
        return ($page);
    }

    # Package credit card information into a hash
    # for use in the authorization request

    $card_info = {};
    $card_info->{card_type} = $billing_info->{card_type};
    $card_info->{card_number} = $billing_info->{card_number};
    $card_info->{card_exp_month} = $billing_info->{card_exp_month};
    $card_info->{card_exp_year} = $billing_info->{card_exp_year};
    $card_info->{cust_name} = $billing_info->{cust_name};
    $card_info->{total_price} = $order_info->{total_price};
```

continues

continued

```
$order_info->{auth_id} = issue_authorization_request ($card_info);
if (!$order_info->{auth_id})
{
    $page .= p ("Sorry, credit card authorization failed.\n"
                . "Please make sure your credit card information\n"
                . "in the form below is correct.");
    $page .= display_billing_form ($dbh);   # redisplay page
    return ($page);
}

# Once we have the authorization ID, we'll work with that;
# the credit card number is no longer needed.

delete ($card_info->{card_number});

# Store the order in the database (after loading into $order_info
# any remaining billing information that needs to be stored).
# Perform all statements involved in the database update as a
# transaction.

$order_info->{cust_name} = $billing_info->{cust_name};
$order_info->{cust_email} = $billing_info->{cust_email};

$dbh->{AutoCommit} = 0;     # disable auto-commit mode
eval
{
    store_order ($dbh, $order_info) and $dbh->commit ();
};
if ($@)                     # transaction failed, abort and notify user
{
    $dbh->rollback ();
    $dbh->disconnect ();
    fatal_error ("Sorry, could not store order in database");
}
$dbh->{AutoCommit} = 1;     # restore auto-commit mode

# Generate the confirmation page and email message

$page .= gen_confirmation_page ($order_info);
$page .= send_confirmation_email ($order_info);

return ($page);
}
```

Validation of the billing form is handled by get_billing_info(), which returns two kinds of information: a reference to a hash containing the various billing form fields, and an error message array. The array will be non-empty if any errors occurred:

```
sub get_billing_info
{
my $billing_info = {};
my @error;

    $billing_info->{cust_name} = WebDB::trim (param ("cust_name"));
    $billing_info->{cust_email} = WebDB::trim (param ("cust_email"));
    $billing_info->{card_type} = WebDB::trim (param ("card_type"));
    $billing_info->{card_number} = WebDB::trim (param ("card_number"));
    $billing_info->{card_exp_month} = WebDB::trim (param ("card_exp_month"));
    $billing_info->{card_exp_year} = WebDB::trim (param ("card_exp_year"));

    $billing_info->{cust_name} ne ""
        or push (@error, "Name must be filled in");
    WebDB::looks_like_email ($billing_info->{cust_email})
        or push (@error, "You must supply a valid email address");

    # card type and expiration values must be in corresponding lists
    # of legal values
    grep (/^$billing_info->{card_type}$/, @{get_card_type_list ()})
        or push (@error, "The credit card type is invalid");
    grep (/^$billing_info->{card_exp_month}$/, @{get_card_exp_month_list ()})
        or push (@error, "The credit card expiration month is invalid");
    grep (/^$billing_info->{card_exp_year}$/, @{get_card_exp_year_list ()})
        or push (@error, "The credit card expiration year is invalid");
    # get rid of spaces, dashes, etc. from card number
    $billing_info->{card_number} =
            WebDB::strip_non_digits ($billing_info->{card_number});
    validate ($billing_info->{card_number})
        or push (@error, "The credit card number is invalid");

    return ($billing_info, @error)
}
```

Most of the validation performed by get_billing_info() is fairly routine. The customer name must be non-blank and the email address must look like a valid address. The credit card type and expiration date values are checked to make sure that they're present in the value lists that were used to generate the fields in the first place. The expiration year value returned from the card_exp_year field will be four digits long. If your authorization service wants two digits only, modify the billing form or use the following expression to modify the value returned from it. The modulo operation (% 100) takes the two least significant digits and the sprintf() call makes sure there is a leading zero if the result is less than 10:

```
$card_exp_year = sprintf ("%02d", $card_exp_year % 100);
```

To check the credit card number, we call `validate()`, which is a function from the `Business::CreditCard` module. It performs a checksum test on the number to make sure it's not bogus or mistyped.[4] Before checking the number, we strip it of any non-digit characters. (The `validate()` function allows non-digits, but your authorization service may not.)

After `close_order()` invokes `get_billing_info()`, it extracts the list of document ID numbers to determine which documents were selected. (These were placed in the form as hidden values by the `display_billing_form()` function.) Including the IDs as unprotected values in the form may seem to be insecure. Can the customer hack the form? Yes. Will that accomplish anything? No. When the billing information is submitted, we'll look up the prices of the IDs listed in the form's hidden fields. If the customer changed the ID list, all that will happen is that the bill will be generated based on the modified list. It certainly won't trick us into giving away any free merchandise. Try it yourself by hacking the form to see what happens. (Of course, if you're not convinced by this reasoning, there's nothing to stop you from protecting the list using checksum and encryption techniques such as were discussed in Chapter 9, "Security and Privacy Issues." Far be it from me to discourage paranoia!)

The final section of `close_order()` calls several other functions to authorize the credit transaction, store the order, and send information to the customer. These routines are described in the next few sections.

Getting a Credit Authorization

The part of `close_order()` that issues the authorization request looks "official" in that it sets up information to be sent to the authorization service, issues the request, and takes action according to the result of the request:

```
# Package credit card information into a hash
# for use in the authorization request

$card_info = {};
$card_info->{card_type} = $billing_info->{card_type};
$card_info->{card_number} = $billing_info->{card_number};
$card_info->{card_exp_month} = $billing_info->{card_exp_month};
$card_info->{card_exp_year} = $billing_info->{card_exp_year};
$card_info->{cust_name} = $billing_info->{cust_name};
$card_info->{total_price} = $order_info->{total_price};

$order_info->{auth_id} = issue_authorization_request ($card_info);
if (!$order_info->{auth_id})
{
    $page .= p ("Sorry, credit card authorization failed.\n"
            . "Please make sure your credit card information\n"
            . "in the form below is correct.");
    $page .= display_billing_form ($dbh);   # redisplay page
    return ($page);
}
```

---

4. This test is described further in "Credit Card Processing." If you need a number to use for testing the application, try `1000 0000 0000 0008`.

```
# Once we have the authorization ID, we'll work with that;
# the credit card number is no longer needed.

delete ($card_info->{card_number});
```

But the version of `issue_authorization_request()` in `doc_shop.pl` is really nothing more than a fake "stub" routine that ignores its argument and returns the same transaction ID each time it's invoked:

```
sub issue_authorization_request
{
my $card_info = shift;

    return ("123456");
}
```

The specific details involved in handling these requests will depend on your authorization service, so you'd have to replace `issue_authorization_request()` with a routine that conforms to your service's conventions. See "Collecting Payment Information" later in the chapter for an overview of this process.

Performing Transactions

If the credit authorization request succeeds, we can store the order in the database. However, recall that `doc_shop.pl` is going to use two tables to store order information (`doc_order` and `doc_item`). We want them to be updated together, but it's possible that the updates will succeed for one table and fail for the other. This would leave the tables in an inconsistent state. The way to handle this is to use a transaction—a set of statements that succeed or fail as a unit.

MySQL and DBI Transaction Syntax

To execute a group of statements as a transaction, you must manipulate MySQL's statement committal mode. By default, MySQL runs in auto-commit mode: changes produced by individual statements are committed to the database immediately as soon as they execute. (In other words, it's as if a `COMMIT` statement implicitly follows each statement.) DBI also runs in auto-commit mode by default.

MySQL's commit mode is affected by the following two SQL statements:

```
SET AUTOCOMMIT = 0          # disable auto-commit
SET AUTOCOMMIT = 1          # enable auto-commit
```

While auto-commit is disabled, you begin a transaction with `BEGIN` and end it with `COMMIT`, like this:

```
BEGIN
INSERT INTO table1 ...
INSERT INTO table2 ...
COMMIT
```

If an error occurs during the transaction, you can roll back the effect of all its constituent statements by issuing a ROLLBACK statement.

Unfortunately, the preceding syntax isn't necessarily portable to other transaction-capable databases, which may use somewhat different SQL statements from what MySQL uses. To deal with this problem, DBI provides a transaction abstraction for better portability. To turn auto-commit mode on or off from within a DBI script, set the AutoCommit attribute of your database handle:

```
$dbh->{AutoCommit} = 0;      # disable auto-commit
$dbh->{AutoCommit} = 1;      # enable auto-commit
```

To execute a multiple-statement transaction with auto-commit disabled, issue the statements, and then invoke commit() to commit the statements as a group:

```
$dbh->do ("INSERT INTO table1 ...");
$dbh->do ("INSERT INTO table2 ...");
$dbh->commit ();
```

(Another way to end a successful transaction is to set the AutoCommit attribute true again; this causes commit() to be called automatically for any pending transaction.) If an error occurs during the transaction, invoke the rollback() method to abort it.

The effect of closing a database handle while a transaction is pending is undefined in DBI, so be sure to commit transactions yourself before disconnecting from the database server.

Requirements for Transaction Support

Transaction support in DBI requires transaction capabilities in the underlying database. For MySQL, transactions appeared in version 3.23.17. However, the 3.23.xx series wasn't declared stable until version 3.23.28, so it's best to use a release at least that recent.

You also need to use table types that support transactions, and not all types do (for example, ISAM and MyISAM tables do not). The CREATE TABLE statements that were shown earlier set up the doc_order and doc_item table as BDB tables, one of the applicable types. BDB (Berkeley DB) tables are based on work contributed by Sleepycat. Depending on your version of MySQL, other transaction-capable table types may be available to you as well, such as InnoDB tables, contributed by InnoBase, and Gemini tables, contributed by NuSphere. (The Gemini work is in beta at the moment, but should be ready by the time you read this.) Consult the MySQL manual to see what table types are available for performing transactions in current releases.

Finally, you'll need a version of DBD::mysql (the MySQL-specific DBI driver) at least as recent as 1.2216 if you want to use the DBI transaction abstraction. Older versions of the driver cannot handle transactions using the standard DBI mechanism (setting the AutoCommit attribute has no effect). In this case, to control transactional behavior, you'll have to issue SET AUTOCOMMIT, BEGIN, COMMIT, and ROLLBACK statements directly.

Storing Document Orders Using Transactions

The `store_order()` routine takes the order information and stores it in the `doc_order` and `doc_item` tables. This routine simply issues the requisite INSERT statements necessary to store an order, blissfully unaware of anything having to do with transactions. The real work of setting up transactional behavior takes place in `close_order()`, from which `store_order()` is called:

```
$dbh->{AutoCommit} = 0;      # disable auto-commit mode
eval
{
    store_order ($dbh, $order_info) and $dbh->commit ();
};
if ($@)                      # transaction failed, abort and notify user
{
    $dbh->rollback ();
    $dbh->disconnect ();
    fatal_error ("Sorry, could not store order in database");
}
$dbh->{AutoCommit} = 1;      # restore auto-commit mode
```

This section of code first disables auto-commit behavior. Then it calls `store_order()` within an `eval` block so that errors can be trapped. If `store_order()` executes successfully, the SQL statements issued by it are committed using `commit()`. If `store_order()` fails, an exception is raised and the error is returned in the `$@` variable. In that case, we call `rollback()` to cancel the transaction and inform the user of the problem.

This code is written based on the assumption that DBI catches errors automatically and triggers an exception if one occurs. Otherwise, the `commit()` call will execute even if a statement fails—which of course defeats the purpose of using a transaction in the first place! You can ensure the proper behavior by disabling `PrintError` and enabling `RaiseError`.

If your version of MySQL doesn't have transaction support and you can't upgrade, you can change the preceding section of code by substituting the following statements instead:

```
if (!store_order ($dbh, $order_info))
{
    $dbh->disconnect ();
    fatal_error ("Sorry, could not store order in database");
}
```

However, if you do this and failure occurs in the middle of a transaction, you may end up with `doc_order` records that have no corresponding `doc_item` records. You can use the following query to test for this condition:

```
SELECT doc_order.*
FROM doc_order LEFT JOIN doc_item USING (order_id)
WHERE doc_item.order_id IS NULL
```

If the query produces any rows, they represent failed attempts to store order information that didn't succeed in updating both tables.

The function that actually stores rows into the two order tables, store_order(), looks like this:

```
sub store_order
{
my ($dbh, $order_info) = @_;

    # add one record to the doc_order table

    $dbh->do ("INSERT INTO doc_order
                (order_date,order_amt,auth_id,cust_name,cust_email)
                VALUES(CURRENT_DATE,?,?,?,?)",
                undef,
                $order_info->{total_price},
                $order_info->{auth_id},
                $order_info->{cust_name},
                $order_info->{cust_email});

    # order_id is the AUTO_INCREMENT value from the preceding INSERT statement
    $order_info->{order_id} = $dbh->{mysql_insertid};

    # add one record to the doc_item table for each document ordered; use
    # the order_id value to tie the records to the corresponding doc_order
    # record

    foreach my $ref (@{$order_info->{item}})
    {
        # generate password for the document, store it in the item record,
        # and use it to construct the URL for downloading the document
        my $password = get_rand_pass ();
        $ref->{url} = get_url_prefix () # need full URL path here!
                        . sprintf ("serve_doc.pl?order=%s;doc=%s;password=%s",
                                    escape ($order_info->{order_id}),
                                    escape ($ref->{doc_id}),
                                    escape ($password));
        $dbh->do ("INSERT INTO doc_item
                    (order_id,doc_id,price,password)
                    VALUES(?,?,?,?)",
                        undef,
                        $order_info->{order_id},
                        $ref->{doc_id},
                        $ref->{price},
                        $password);
    }
}
```

As it stores the doc_item record for each document, store_order() creates the password that must be supplied by the customer to obtain the document. These passwords are random 32-character MD5-based strings. The gen_rand_pass() routine that creates passwords uses a random number, the current time, and the current process ID as sources of randomness:[5]

```
sub get_rand_pass
{
my $md = Digest::MD5->new ();

    $md->add (rand ());              # add random number
    $md->add (localtime (time ())); # add current time
    $md->add ($$);                   # add current process ID
    return ($md->hexdigest ());
}
```

store_order() also generates the URL to be used for downloading each document and stores it in the order information structure. These URLs are used later when we tell the customer how to obtain the documents. (The serve_doc.pl script named in the URLs is described in the next section.) The URLs are absolute rather than relative. Although relative links would work for a browser page, the URLs will also be used in the mail message we send to the customer. Absolute URLs are needed in that context.

Providing the Documents for Download

We've finally arrived at the part the customer is interested in: getting the documents. We provide these by presenting a browser page containing a link for each document the customer ordered. We'll also email a copy of the links because the customer might accidentally close the browser window—thus causing the links to disappear!

close_order() invokes gen_confirmation_page() to generate the final order information in HTML format for browser display and send_confirmation_email() to create and send the corresponding email message in plain text format:

```
sub gen_confirmation_page
{
my $order_info = shift;
my $page;

    $page .= p ("Thank you for ordering from PseudEcom.")
            . p (escapeHTML ("Order number: $order_info->{order_id}"))
            . p (escapeHTML ("Order authorization ID: $order_info->{auth_id}"))
            . format_items_html ($order_info)
            . p ("To download your documents, use the following links:");

    foreach my $ref (@{$order_info->{item}})
    {
```
continues

---

5. The current process ID by itself is not necessarily unique if you're running in a mod_perl environment because a given script may be executed several times by the same httpd process.

continued

```perl
        $page .= p ("Document $ref->{doc_id}: "
                        . a ({-href => $ref->{url}}, escapeHTML ($ref->{title})));
    }

    $page .= p ("A copy of this information also will be mailed to you at\n"
                    . escapeHTML ($order_info->{cust_email}) . ".");

    return ($page);
}

sub send_confirmation_email
{
my $order_info = shift;
my $formatted_items = format_items_text ($order_info);
my %mail = (
        From    => "black-hole\@localhost", # YOU SHOULD CHANGE THIS!
        To      => $order_info->{cust_email},
        Subject => "Your PseudEcom document order",
        Message => ""
);
my $page;

        $mail{Message} = <<EOF;
Thank you for ordering from PseudEcom.

Order number: $order_info->{order_id}
Order authorization ID: $order_info->{auth_id}

$formatted_items

To download your documents, use the following links:

EOF

    foreach my $ref (@{$order_info->{item}})
    {
        $mail{Message} .= "Document $ref->{doc_id} ($ref->{title}):\n"
                        . "$ref->{url}\n";
    }

    sendmail (%mail)
        or $page .= p (escapeHTML ("Oops, failure sending mail to $mail{To}"));

    return (defined ($page) ? $page : "");
}
```

The `format_order_html()` function used by `gen_confirmation_page()` has already been shown. `format_order_text()`, used by `send_confirmation_email`, is much the same, so I won't show it here.

Each URL sent to the customer to be used for downloading a document includes the order and document numbers and the document-specific password:

```
http://.../serve_doc.pl?order=order_id;doc=doc_id;password=xxx
```

Aside from some code to check the document password, the serve_doc.pl script that handles document downloading is fairly similar in principle to serve_image.pl, a script written for transferring images in Chapter 5. The only real difference is that we generate a different set of headers to send prior to the request data. These headers are

- A Content-Type: header with a value of application/pdf.

- A Content-Length: header; the value is the size of the file containing the PDF document.

- A Content-Disposition: header to let the browser know the document filename. (Whether the browser actually saves the file or just displays it is subject to client user preferences that are beyond our control.)

serve_doc.pl looks like this:

```perl
#! /usr/bin/perl -w
# serve_doc.pl - Serve a PDF file from the document shop

# The document should be requested using a URL of the form:
#   .../serve_doc.pl?order=order_num;doc=doc_num;password=xxx
# order_num and doc_num are the order and document ID values, and
# xxx is the document password.

use strict;
use lib qw(/usr/local/apache/lib/perl);
use IO::File;
use CGI qw(:standard);
use WebDB;
use WebDB::PseudEcom;

# Change this pathname as necessary for your site
my $pdf_lib_dir = "/usr/local/apache/lib/htfiles";

my $order_id = param ("order");
my $doc_id = param ("doc");
my $password = param ("password");

(defined ($order_id) && defined ($doc_id) && defined ($password))
    or fatal_error ("Invocation error: required parameters are missing");

my $dbh = WebDB::connect ();
# Make sure customer ordered this document and knows the password
$dbh->selectrow_array (
                "SELECT doc_id FROM doc_item
                WHERE order_id = ? AND doc_id = ? AND password = ?",
                undef, $order_id, $doc_id, $password)
```

continues

continued

```
        or fatal_error ("Document password mismatch");
    # Look up document's file name
    my $file_name = $dbh->selectrow_array (
                        "SELECT filename FROM doc_catalog WHERE doc_id = ?",
                        undef, $doc_id);
    fatal_error ("No file with ID $doc_id found") unless defined ($file_name);
    $dbh->disconnect ();

    # Open the document and transfer it as a PDF download.
    # Print the request headers, then the file's content.

    my $path_name = $pdf_lib_dir . "/" . $file_name;
    my $fh = new IO::File ($path_name)
        or fatal_error ("Could not open $file_name");
    print header (-type => "application/pdf",
                    -Content_Length => (-s $fh),     # size of file
                    -Content_Disposition => "attachment; filename = $file_name");
    my $data;
    print $data while read ($fh, $data, 1024);
    undef $fh;            # close file

    exit (0);
```

PDF Documents Need No Conversion

PDF is a platform-neutral format, so we can transfer PDF documents as is with no interpretation or conversion to a different format. I'm pointing this out to make a plea: *Don't* take platform-neutral documents and convert them to platform-specific form. For example, PDF, Word, and Excel documents all can be opened perfectly well in native format on either Mac OS or Windows machines. But here in Wisconsin, some state government agencies do a strange thing with such documents: They package them inside executable .exe installer programs that can be run only under Windows. It's insane to turn a multiple-platform document into something that can be opened only on a single platform.

Suggested Modifications

Add a Revise Order button to the checkout page so that the user can return to the initial document selection page. This handles cases where the user notices upon reaching the checkout page that the order isn't correct.

serve_doc.pl isn't particularly helpful to the customer if an error occurs. Add some text to any error pages it prints to provide the customer with a URL or other contact information for reaching the customer service department. Alternatively, add an option so users can avoid download operations altogether by requesting that documents be delivered as email attachments.

The email address that we collect in the billing form is needed for sending order confirmation messages, but could be useful in other ways. Add a check box to the form that enables customers to indicate whether they'd like to receive notices when new documents are available. Then use the `doc_order` table to create a mailing list so that you can issue such notices.

Collecting Payment Information

For the `doc_shop.pl` application, we pretty quickly skipped over the part that showed what to do with credit card information that we obtain from customers. Let's return to the topic of payment and discuss the issue in more detail.

When you sell something, you want to be paid for it, so it's necessary to arrange for collection of information that allows you to assess the proper charges to the customer. Most people who shop online prefer to pay by credit card rather than by some other method, so that's the most common means by which business is transacted over the Internet. It's also the method this section concentrates on, though we'll also survey other payment methods briefly.

Credit Card Processing

If you want to accept credit cards, you need a merchant account with a financial institution such as your bank. This account allows you to engage in credit card transactions, but does not in itself necessarily have anything to do with online ordering. To conduct credit card transactions electronically over the Internet, you'll also need an account with an authorization service. (If you're a large company, you might be able to deal directly with your bank for this, but more typically you'll use a service that handles transactions on behalf of many banks.)

A merchant account isn't free; the cost typically is tied to the volume of business you conduct. As a merchant, you receive only part of the purchase price if the customer pays by credit card, because the bank through which you have your merchant account extracts a percentage of each sale. The merchant account may also involve other costs, such as signup fees or annual fees. Given this obvious disadvantage in terms of revenue loss, do you gain anything by contracting for services that allow you to accept credit card payments? Perhaps. Given that more online consumers prefer to pay by credit card than by any other method, you're likely to lose sales if you don't provide this capability.

The conditions you'll have to meet to obtain a merchant account are something you should discuss with your bank. You'll also need to contact an authorization service that will help you implement online credit transactions; the authorization procedure for this will be specific to the vendor, so make sure the interface software will work with your system. (It's no good for the service vendor to provide software for Windows NT if you're using a UNIX server, or vice versa.)

How Credit Card Transactions Work

When a credit card purchase takes place, it involves the following parties:

- The customer making the purchase
- The merchant selling the merchandise
- The customer's card issuer
- The merchant's bank
- The bank network

Processing the transaction can involve many steps, several of which take place behind the scenes and require exchanges of information over the bank network to assess the customer's creditworthiness and to obtain permission to make a charge against the customer's account. For our purposes, the process can be boiled down to these essential elements:

- The customer gives us a credit card number to pay for an order.
- We send to the authorization service a credit authorization request that contains the card number and any other information the service requires.
- The authorization service processes the request and sends back either a rejection or an authorization ID for the transaction.

If the request results in a rejection, you inform the customer that the purchase cannot be completed ("sorry, please contact your card issuer"). Otherwise, the authorization ID gives you permission to charge the customer's account. However, actually debiting the account (the "capture" stage) is in many cases deferred a bit. If you charge immediately for an item that is backordered or that cannot be sent right away, customers tend not to like it. Therefore, it's common to defer capture until you're ready to ship the order.

In practice, authorization request rejections are rare, due to the amount of time that would be necessary to perform more thorough checks on the customer's credit status at the time of the transaction. Apparently the business policy is that more money stands to be lost by making customers wait than by incurring a somewhat higher risk of credit card fraud. Still, authorization failure does occur—even for people with good credit, as I've had occasion to discover. I once went through a period during which I purchased a significant amount of electronic equipment. After several days' worth of making multiple purchases, I discovered that my card no longer worked. Attempts to use it to make purchases failed because authorization requests were denied at the store I was visiting. It turned out that the credit card company had noticed the unusual number of electronics purchases. Stolen cards are often used to buy items in that category, and because the pattern of charges arriving for my account didn't fit my usual buying habits, the card company turned my card off until I called to inquire what was happening. Was the card company protecting me as a consumer? I doubt it. Consumers aren't liable for purchases made on stolen cards. The company was attempting to cut its own fraud-related losses through analysis of purchase patterns and identification of unusual events that are likely to be illegitimate. Of course, if you're a merchant, this benefits you by reducing the incidence of fraudulent purchases by customers for which you might otherwise be liable.

Collecting Credit Card Information

When you present a form containing fields for gathering credit card information, you'll typically collect at least the following values:

- The name on the card
- The card type (Visa, MasterCard, American Express, and so forth)
- The card number
- The card expiration month and year

Some cards also have a card security code (or card verification number). Visa and MasterCard use a three-digit value on the back of the card; American Express cards have a four-digit number on the front. It's a little more inconvenient for the customer to provide this code in addition to the regular part of the credit card number, but it has the potential to reduce card fraud to some extent, so it's information that you might want to collect. Your authorization service will use the security code if you submit one.

Address verification service (AVS) may be another option available to you. This involves checking whether a street address provided by the customer matches the address listed on file for the account by the card issuer. If your authorization service offers AVS, you may want to ask the customer for an address, even if you don't need it to deliver your product. (For example, we needed no such address for `doc_shop.pl` to perform order delivery because documents were provided electronically.)

The card type and expiration date can be presented with structured elements, such as pop-up menus, so that the user need not enter any keystrokes. (For example, the expiration date can be represented using one pop-up containing the values 1 to 12 for the month, and another containing year values for the next 10 years or so.) On the other hand, the card number has to be entered manually, which can be a source of error. To lessen this possibility, you can perform a preliminary test that validates the number and helps catch customer typos immediately. This helps you minimize the number of requests to your authorization service (and thus, perhaps the fees you pay).

The validation test is based on the fact that credit card numbers are constructed such that the final digit serves as a check digit—that is, a checksum calculated from the card number should yield a result equal to the final digit. This was instituted as a guard against errors made by keystroke operators submitting card numbers into data entry programs, but the same test helps catch mistakes made by customers ordering online. The check digit serves the same purpose as the checksum technique we used in

Chapter 9 to encode session and record identifiers: It allows changes to the original data value to be detected. The changes can be inadvertent (as with a keystroke error entering a credit card number) or deliberate (as with a user attempting to hack a form); either way, the checksum or check digit help ensure data integrity.

There's nothing secret about the credit card number check digit algorithm; it's a published standard (ISO 2894). The algorithm is not very complicated and it's relatively easy to write an implementation.[6] But it's even easier to use a module that can perform the test for you, such as `Business::CreditCard`. This module has a `validate()` function that takes a credit card argument and returns true or false to indicate whether the number passes the check digit test:

```
use Business::CreditCard;

if (validate ($card_number))
{
    print "It's good\n";
}
else
{
    print "It's bad\n";
}
```

The check digit test is useful for weeding out obvious bad numbers or numbers that customers have entered incorrectly, but it doesn't tell you whether there actually is any card with a particular number. You still must submit the number to an authorization service to find out whether the number is creditworthy. In other words, the preliminary check is useful for reducing the number of requests that you issue to your authorization service, but cannot replace the service. If someone is intent on defrauding you, they'll most certainly know how to generate a card number that passes the check digit test. If you deliver orders based on that number without checking it with the authorization service first, who'll be left holding the bag for the cost? You.

Obtaining Credit Card Authorizations

Authorization requests for credit card transactions can be issued a couple of ways:

- With remote mode authorization, you present a link to the authorization service from your ordering page. The customer follows this link, provides credit card information to the service to obtain an authorization ID, and then returns to your site and submits the order along with the ID.

- With local mode authorization, the customer presents the card information directly to you, and you contact the authorization service to obtain the authorization ID on the customer's behalf.

---

6. For a description of the algorithm, one source is Garfinkel and Spafford (see Appendix B, "References and Further Reading").

The first may be somewhat simpler for you to implement, but the second is more convenient for the customer. In any case, the specific details of the authorization procedure depend on your particular service. Recall that doc_shop.pl used a generic stub routine to generate authorization IDs. You'd need to replace it with one that follows your vendor's conventions. Depending on the authorization service you have, you might be able to use one of the Perl modules that facilitate authorization requests, such as the following:

```
Apache::iNcom
Apache::iNcom::CartManager
Business::OnlinePayment
Business::OnlinePayment::AuthorizeNet
Business::OnlinePayment::CardStream
```

In other cases, the vendor may provide a suitable module that you can integrate into your applications.

Protecting Credit Card Information

When you need to perform a transaction that requires a credit card number, observe the following security precautions to protect customer information:

- When you reach the point in the ordering process where you need to request sensitive customer information, switch to a secure connection with the client's browser so that the information is not transmitted in the clear.

- When you receive the credit card number, don't store it in the database. Connect to your authorization server (over a secure channel, of course) and give them the number. If the transaction is approved, the service will store the card number for you; let *them* worry about keeping it secure. Refer to the order from that point on using the authorization ID that the service gives you. If you store the credit card number in a database and your site gets hacked, you could compromise your customer data. Store the authorization ID instead and use it for any further dealings involving the order.

Is it Dangerous To Send Credit Card Numbers Over an Insecure Connection?

Credit card information normally is collected over a secure connection, but not always. Just how dangerous is it to send credit card numbers in the clear over the Internet? That's difficult to tell exactly, but it's certainly more likely that a bad guy will try to hack a site that stores thousands of card numbers than to attempt to steal individual numbers with a network sniffer. For this reason, the risks of credit card theft during order submission may be overstated, compared to the risks involved with using your card other ways. Is it really more secure to use your card over the telephone or in person? If you call in an order over a cordless phone, it's possible that your call may be picked up by an outside party. And what's to stop a clerk in a store from using the information on the store copy of your credit slip? Nevertheless, despite these risks (which may mean that sending a card number over the Internet is actually less risky than other means of conducting credit card transactions), many consumers are reluctant to provide a card number online, especially if it's not evident that you're using a secure connection. So take the trouble to set up a secure channel. Then, to address the concerns of customers who are still hesitant, you can provide alternative means of payment. These are surveyed in the next section, "Other Payment Options."

Other Payment Options

Credit card payment is convenient for e-commerce because it can be done completely online, and authorization (or rejection) can be obtained immediately. However, other methods can be used, particularly for situations where deferred payment is acceptable. Some of these may help you obtain orders from people who are uneasy about submitting their credit card number over the Internet:

- The order page displayed by your application is a convenient means of presenting all the item information together in one place. You can take advantage of this even for customers who don't want to submit the order online. Allow the customer to print the order page and fax it in, to mail it by post, or even to call in the order over the telephone and read off the contents of the order page to your customer service representative. Enabling your site for these options need not involve much more than putting a notice somewhere on the ordering pages pointing out that such options are available and acceptable.

- You can allow the customer to submit the order online but pay offline later. To do this, accept the order and provide to the customer in response a confirmation page that displays the order number and the telephone number of your customer service department. The customer calls up later, gives the order number as a reference, and provides payment information over the phone. (This option can be carried out by fax or mail, as well.) Consider putting an expiration period on outstanding orders if you separate order submission and collection of billing information this way. It's not unknown for customers to change their mind about an order—or even to forget that they purchased anything!

- You can arrange to send the customer an invoice. This is appropriate mainly for business customers with whom you have long-term relationships. Generally, you'll require a customer account number, a purchase order number, and contact information so that you can verify the order before processing it. You might also want to use a login stage so that customers must authenticate to gain access to your ordering system.

- If you don't want orders to go directly into your database without being examined first, you can transmit them to your order processing department using email messages. Obviously, with this method, it's best to encrypt the contents of the message.

A Cart-Based Sales Application

The doc_shop.pl application that was developed earlier in the chapter handled a shopping situation simple enough to allow us to avoid dealing with issues such as managing a shopping cart or creating a mechanism for presenting a large catalog in smaller portions. In this section, we'll deal with another shopping scenario that requires those capabilities. The application is called pet_shop.pl, because it provides access to a catalog of items that relate to keeping your pets happy, healthy, well-groomed, and so forth. When you first invoke `pet_shop.pl`, it presents a page showing a list of product categories and a set of links across the top that provide access to the various functions of the application (see Figure 10.2):

- Browse presents a category-based catalog browsing page (the same page that you see initially). Selecting a category name takes you to a page that lists the items in that category. Each item includes an Add Item link for adding the item to your order. The product catalog is too large to display in a single page; the browsing interface is one way the application allows you to view the catalog in sections.

- Search takes you to a form you can use to look up items by keyword. This is another interface to the product catalog.

- View Cart shows the current contents of your order. If you want to delete items, you can do so from this page.

- Check Out begins the order-submission process by presenting a page that solicits a shipping address and billing information. The page also displays the cart so that you can delete items if you want.

- Cancel terminates the shopping session. The order expires if you don't complete it within a reasonable amount of time, but this operation explicitly forces the order to be jettisoned immediately.

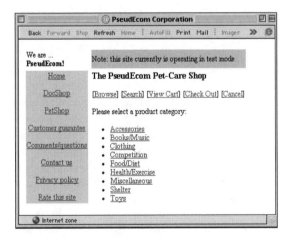

Figure 10.2   The `pet_shop.pl` main page.

Catalog Presentation Issues

A general goal of online catalog presentation is to make it easy for customers to find product offerings so they can select and purchase them. If you offer only a few products, you can list them all on a single page (as we did for doc_shop.pl earlier in the chapter). That won't work for pet_shop.pl, because the catalog is larger and therefore not easily usable in single-page form. This has two important implications:

- We need a mechanism for presenting the catalog in sections. One option is to present a browseable interface that divides the catalog into categories, subcategories, and so forth. Another is to provide a search interface so that users can specify directly what they're looking for. pet_shop.pl gives customers the choice of looking through the catalog either way.

- Because the catalog is presented in sections, customers typically view products across multiple pages. That means we must implement a shopping cart so that items selected from different pages can be remembered.

A browsing interface can be implemented by treating the product catalog as a tree. At the top level, you present an index page containing links for general categories. These take the customer to more specific index pages, finally leading to "leaf" pages that list product descriptions. Two general principles govern the index navigation and item display functions of such an interface:

- Don't make the user go through too many index page levels to get to leaf pages. The fewer steps it takes to reach an item description, the better.

- Don't overwhelm the user by presenting too many items on a single leaf page. The fewer items there are, the easier a page is to understand.

Unfortunately, these principles conflict. If you subdivide your catalog into smaller sections to make leaf pages easier to understand, you'll often end up using more levels in the browse tree. Conversely, reducing the number of index levels in the tree generally is achieved at the cost of increasing the number of items per leaf page. With your own product catalogs, you'll likely need to do some experimenting to find a good balance between these opposing principles. For the catalog used by pet_shop.pl, we'll implement a simple two-level browse tree with a top-level index page that lists general product categories, and a leaf page for each category that lists items in that category.

Our other interface to the pet-care catalog uses a search mechanism. This is based on a form with a text field for entering keywords and radio buttons for selecting "all words" or "any word" matches. One problem here is that with a large enough catalog, it's possible for a search to match many, many items. What should we do in that case? Two options are to use a LIMIT clause to constrain the size of the result set, or to present the result over multiple pages. A multiple-page display is probably better because the customer can get at all the relevant information. In the interests of space and simplicity, pet_shop.pl uses the LIMIT clause method. However, to give the customer somewhat more control, the search form includes a field for controlling the maximum number of records to show. By default, this will be set to a small value (10), but the user can set it higher if desired. (For information on presenting multiple-page search results, see Chapter 7.)

Setting Up the Tables

pet_shop.pl uses several tables. The pet_catalog table holds the product catalog:

```
CREATE TABLE pet_catalog
(
    item_id     BIGINT UNSIGNED NOT NULL AUTO_INCREMENT PRIMARY KEY,
    description VARCHAR(60) NOT NULL,    # item description
    category    VARCHAR(40) NOT NULL,    # item category
    price       NUMERIC(10,2) NOT NULL   # unit price
)
```

item_id is the unique item identifier, description says what the item is, category indicates the general category the item falls into, and price lists the item unit cost.

Two tables are used to store orders received from customers. pet_order records general order and customer information, and pet_item records individual items in each order:

```
CREATE TABLE pet_order
(
    order_id    BIGINT NOT NULL AUTO_INCREMENT PRIMARY KEY,
    order_date  DATE NOT NULL,           # date of order
    order_amt   DECIMAL(10,2) NOT NULL,  # total cost
    auth_id     VARCHAR(10) NOT NULL,    # transaction authorization
    cust_name   VARCHAR(40) NOT NULL,    # customer name
    cust_email  VARCHAR(40) NOT NULL,    # customer email address
    street      VARCHAR(40),             # shipping address
    city        VARCHAR(40),
    state       CHAR(2),
    zip         VARCHAR(10)
) TYPE = BDB

CREATE TABLE pet_item
(
    order_id    BIGINT UNSIGNED NOT NULL,    # order number
    item_id     BIGINT UNSIGNED NOT NULL,    # item number
    qty         INT UNSIGNED NOT NULL,       # item quantity
    price       NUMERIC(10,2) NOT NULL,      # unit price
    UNIQUE (order_id, item_id)
) TYPE = BDB
```

The doc_shop.pl application also used two tables for recording orders, but the tables used by pet_shop.pl contain somewhat different information. For one thing, pet-care items can't be delivered electronically, so we need the customer's shipping address to tell where to send each order. Also, it's possible that customers might want to order items in quantities greater than one, so the pet_item table contains a qty column.

Just as with the order-recording tables used for doc_shop.pl, you should remove TYPE = BDB from the CREATE TABLE statements if your version of MySQL does not include transaction support.

The final two tables used by pet_shop.pl are lookup tables. One, pet_category, contains all the possible categories into which items can be classified:

```
CREATE TABLE pet_category
(
    category    VARCHAR(40) NOT NULL
)
```

This table is the source for the category names presented in the browsing interface to the product catalog. (It relates to the catalog in that the category column value stored in each pet_catalog record should match some value in the pet_category table.) The other lookup table, us_state, contains state abbreviations and names. It will be used to generate a pop-up menu for the state field in the shipping address part of the billing form:

```
CREATE TABLE us_state
(
    abbrev  CHAR(2),        # state abbreviation
    name    CHAR(30)        # state name
)
```

The webdb distribution contains data files you can use to populate the pet_catalog, pet_category, and us_state tables. To load these files into the database, move into the ecom directory of the distribution. Then, after you've created the tables, issue the following commands from the mysql program:

```
% mysql webdb
mysql> LOAD DATA LOCAL INFILE 'pet_catalog.txt' INTO TABLE pet_catalog;
mysql> LOAD DATA LOCAL INFILE 'pet_category.txt' INTO TABLE pet_category;
mysql> LOAD DATA LOCAL INFILE 'us_state.txt' INTO TABLE us_state;
```

Alternatively, use the mysqlimport command-line utility:

```
% mysqlimport --local webdb pet_catalog.txt
% mysqlimport --local webdb pet_category.txt
% mysqlimport --local webdb us_state.txt
```

Tracking the Customer's Selections

Before discussing how the general application logic works, it's worth having a look at some of the support routines—in particular, the mechanism for keeping track of what the user wants to buy. pet_shop.pl uses a shopping cart to remember items as the user selects them. The cart is based on server-side session-based storage so that we don't have to send all the information back and forth with each page.[7] The only thing we'll

---

7. pet_shop.pl requires that you have session support set up for using the WebDB::Sessions module described in Chapter 8, "Session Management."

send to the client is a session ID. As discussed in Chapter 8, we could store this in a hidden field, in the URL, or in a cookie. pet_shop.pl uses a cookie, which means that even if a customer visits another area of the site (or even some other site altogether) and then returns to the pet shopping area, the application will remember the order.

The shopping cart implementation is relatively simple. A cart is maintained as a hash that consists of elements indexed by item ID values. Each element contains information about an item such as the price, description, and the quantity the customer wants. We track the cart using a reference to the hash, so initializing a new cart amounts to nothing more than this:

```
$cart_ref = {};
```

To perform manipulations on cart contents, we'll use two routines, add_item() and delete_item(). The add_item() function increments the item quantity if the item is already in the cart. Otherwise, it looks up the item in the pet_catalog table and uses the information it finds there to create a new cart entry. Because add_item() might need to perform database lookups, it takes a database handle argument in addition to the cart reference and item ID:

```
sub add_item
{
my ($dbh, $cart_ref, $item_id) = @_;

    # If the item isn't already in the cart, look it up from the database
    # and store it in the cart as a new entry with a quantity of zero.
    if (!exists ($cart_ref->{$item_id}))
    {
        my $sth = $dbh->prepare ("SELECT * FROM pet_catalog
                                  WHERE item_id = ?");
        $sth->execute ($item_id);
        my $item_ref = $sth->fetchrow_hashref ();
        $sth->finish ();
        return if !defined ($item_ref); # this shouldn't happen...
        $cart_ref->{$item_id} = {}; # create new entry, indexed by item ID
        $cart_ref->{$item_id}->{description} = $item_ref->{description};
        $cart_ref->{$item_id}->{price} = $item_ref->{price};
        $cart_ref->{$item_id}->{qty} = 0;
    }
    ++$cart_ref->{$item_id}->{qty};      # increment item quantity
}
```

delete_item() removes the item from the cart:

```
sub delete_item
{
my ($cart_ref, $item_id) = @_;

    delete ($cart_ref->{$item_id});
}
```

To convert the contents of the cart to HTML for display to the user, we call
format_cart_html(). The arguments are a reference to the cart itself and a flag indicating whether to include Delete links in the display that enable the customer to remove
items from the cart. format_cart_html() is used while the customer is shopping (in
which case the second argument is true), and also for presenting the confirmation
page at the end of the shopping session. (In which case, the argument is false, because
at that point the order has been stored for processing and cannot be changed).

```perl
sub format_cart_html
{
my ($cart_ref, $show_links) = @_;
my $total_price = 0;
my @row;

    if (!keys (%{$cart_ref}))
    {
        return (p ("Shopping cart is empty."));
    }

    push (@row, Tr (
                th (""),
                th ("Item"),
                th ("Quantity"),
                th ("Description"),
                th ("Unit Price"),
                th ("Price")
            ));
    foreach my $item_id (sort (keys (%{$cart_ref})))
    {
        my $item_ref = $cart_ref->{$item_id};
        my $total_item_price = $item_ref->{qty} * $item_ref->{price};
        $total_price += $total_item_price;
        # generate a link allowing the item to be deleted from the cart
        my $url = sprintf ("%s?choice=delete;item_id=%s",
                        url (), escape ($item_id));
        push (@row, Tr (
                ($show_links
                    ? td (a ({-href => $url}, "Delete"))
                    : td ("")),
                td (escapeHTML ($item_id)),
                td (escapeHTML ($item_ref->{qty})),
                td (escapeHTML ($item_ref->{description})),
                td ({-align => "right"},
                    escapeHTML (sprintf ("%.2f", $item_ref->{price}))),
                td ({-align => "right"},
                    escapeHTML (sprintf ("%.2f", $total_item_price)))
            ));
    }
    push (@row, Tr (
                td ({-colspan => "3"}, ""),
```

```
            td ({-colspan => "2"}, "Total"),
            td ({-align => "right"},
                escapeHTML (sprintf ("%.2f", $total_price)))
        ));

    return (table (@row));
}
```

A similar function `format_cart_text()` does the same thing, but produces plain text. (It's needed for sending email to the customer after the order has been submitted.) This routine is very similar to `format_cart_html()`, so I won't show it here.

We'll also need to retrieve the cart from the session record when `pet_shop.pl` begins and store it back into the session when the script ends. These are trivial operations:

```
$cart_ref = $sess_ref->attr ("cart");    # retrieve cart
$sess_ref->attr ("cart", $cart_ref);     # store cart
```

The cart helps us remember a customer's selections, but we don't necessarily want to remember them forever—perhaps the customer leaves the PseudEcom site without completing the order and never comes back! To cause the cart to expire, we'll assign an appropriate expiration date to both the session in which the cart is stored and the cookie with which the session is associated. That way the browser will expire the cookie on the client side, and we can set up one of the session expiration scripts described in Chapter 8 to remove dead shopping sessions periodically on the server side.

As a concession to the customer who might shop somewhat slowly or who is interrupted by some other activity, we won't constrain the total shopping session time to one hour. Instead, `pet_shop.pl` uses a "rolling horizon" expiration technique—that is, each time the customer invokes the application, the session expiration date is reset to an hour from the *current* time. Thus, as long as the customer continues to shop (even if slowly), the session remains active.

Presenting the Shopping Session

The initial part of `pet_shop.pl` sets up the variables needed for tracking the user's actions. First, it checks whether a session is already in progress. If not, it creates one. Then it sets the lifetime of the session to an hour and creates a cookie (also with a lifetime of an hour) to send to the client. It also extracts the current contents of the shopping cart from the session. (For a new session, there won't be any cart, in which case the script initializes a new one.) The preamble of `pet_shop.pl` that sets up these tracking variables looks like this:

```
my $cookie;        # cookie to hold session ID
my $sess_id;       # session ID
my $sess_ref;      # reference to session record
my $cart_ref;      # reference to shopping cart
```

continues

continued

```
# Look for the cookie containing the session ID and read the
# corresponding session record.  (Use open_with_expiration() so that
# if the session exists but is too old, it'll be expired automatically.)

if (defined ($sess_id = cookie ("pet_shop")))
{
    $sess_ref = WebDB::Session->open_with_expiration (undef, $sess_id);
}

# If no session was found (or it was too old), create a new one.

if (!defined ($sess_ref))
{
    defined ($sess_ref = WebDB::Session->open (undef, undef))
        or fatal_error ("Cannot create session to track shopping activity");
}

# Set the session and the cookie to have a lifetime of 60 minutes.
# (Setting this each invocation implements rolling-horizon expiration.)

$sess_ref->expires ($sess_ref->now () + 3600);   # 3600 seconds = 60 minutes
$cookie = cookie (-name => "pet_shop",
                    -value => $sess_ref->session_id (),
                    -path => url (-absolute => 1),
                    -expires => "+1h");          # expire in one hour

# Extract the shopping cart from the session; if there wasn't one yet,
# initialize it.

if (!defined ($cart_ref = $sess_ref->attr ("cart")))
{
    # cart is a reference to a hash of item records indexed by item ID
    $cart_ref = {};
}
```

At this point the cookie, session, and shopping cart are set up and ready to go, and pet_shop.pl connects to the database and prepares for page generation by setting up some initial page content:

```
my $dbh = WebDB::connect ();

my $page = h3 ("The PseudEcom Pet-Care Shop");
my $std_links = get_std_links ();   # standard page links
my $redisplay_previous = 0;
```

These statements create the page title and a set of standard page links that let the customer invoke the various operations the application is capable of performing (browsing, searching, displaying the cart, and so forth).[8] These links normally go across the top of the page, but we don't add them to the page just yet, because some actions the user may take terminate the shopping session and the links no longer will apply. (If the customer cancels the order or submits the order, for example, the shopping session terminates and there's no need for the links. The dispatch code for such actions undefines $std_links to prevent them from being displayed.)

The $redisplay_previous variable is used to tell the application when it needs to redisplay the previous page (the one the user was just looking at) rather than a new one. This variable is set true for operations that add or delete items from the shopping cart. For example, if the customer submitted a search and is viewing a result page showing the matching items, clicking an Add Item link will add the corresponding item, and then cause pet_shop.pl to rerun the search to show the same results page again. This way the customer doesn't have to click the Back button to return to the result page, or enter the search parameters again manually.

Next, pet_shop.pl determines what action to perform, based on the value of the choice parameter. I'll show the dispatch logic that implements these actions, and then discuss the cases in more detail. Because the dispatch code is rather long and ungainly, you probably should just skim through this listing initially and then refer back to it as you read the discussion that follows:

```
# Dispatch to proper action based on user selection

my $choice = lc (param ("choice")); # get choice, lowercased

if ($choice eq "")                   # initial invocation
{
    # default page is the category browse list
    $page .= get_category_list ($dbh);
}
elsif ($choice eq "browse")          # show browse page
{
    if (!defined (param ("cat")))
    {
        # show category browse list
        $page .= get_category_list ($dbh);
    }
    else
    {
        # show items-in-category browse list
        $page .= get_category_items ($dbh, param ("cat"));
    }
}
elsif ($choice eq "search")          # display search form/perform search
```

continues

---

8. get_std_links() isn't shown here; it's simply the concatenation of several hyperlink-generating statements.

continued

```
{
    $page .= search_catalog ($dbh);
}
elsif ($choice eq "view")            # display shopping cart
{
    $page .= format_cart_html ($cart_ref);
}
elsif ($choice eq "checkout")        # customer is ready to check out
{
    $page .= display_billing_form ($dbh, $cart_ref);
}
elsif ($choice eq "submit order")    # customer submitted the order
{
    my ($status, $str) = close_order ($dbh, $cart_ref);
    if ($status)
    {
        # the order was stored properly: tell the browser to destroy
        # the cookie; destroy the session
        $cookie = cookie (-name => "pet_shop",
                          -value => $sess_ref->session_id (),
                          -path => url (-absolute => 1),
                          -expires => "-1h");
        $sess_ref->delete ();
        undef $sess_ref;

        # this is the final page of the session; no standard links needed
        undef $std_links;
    }

    # if no error occurred, $str contains the confirmation page;
    # otherwise, it contains the billing form to redisplay
    $page .= $str;
}
elsif ($choice eq "cancel")          # customer wants to quit
{
    # tell the browser to destroy the cookie; destroy the session
    $cookie = cookie (-name => "pet_shop",
                      -value => $sess_ref->session_id (),
                      -path => url (-absolute => 1),
                      -expires => "-1h");
    $sess_ref->delete ();
    undef $sess_ref;

    # this is the final page of the session; no standard links needed
    undef $std_links;

    $page .= p ("Your shopping session has been terminated.")
            . p (a ({-href => url ()}, "Start over"));
}
elsif ($choice eq "add")             # add item to shopping cart
{
```

```
    add_item ($dbh, $cart_ref, param ("item_id"));
    $redisplay_previous = 1;    # display previous page
}
elsif ($choice eq "delete")          # delete item from shopping cart
{
    delete_item ($cart_ref, param ("item_id"));
    $redisplay_previous = 1;    # display previous page
}
else
{
    $page .= p (escapeHTML ("Logic error, unknown choice: $choice"));
}
```

Presenting the Catalog Interfaces

The first few cases of the dispatch code present the browsing and search interfaces to the product catalog. The top-level browsing page is generated by get_category_list(). It contains a list of category names, each of which is linked to a leaf page that displays items in the corresponding category:

```
sub get_category_list
{
my $dbh = shift;
my ($cat_name_ref, @link, $page);

    # get the product category names
    $cat_name_ref = WebDB::get_lookup_values (
                        $dbh,
                        "SELECT category FROM pet_category ORDER BY category");

    # Generate links to pages for each category
    foreach my $cat_name (@{$cat_name_ref})
    {
        push (@link, get_browse_link ($cat_name, $cat_name));
    }

    if (@link)
    {
        $page .= p ("Please select a product category:")
                . ul (li (\@link));
    }
    else
    {
        $page .= p ("Hmm ... someone forgot to load the category table!");
    }

    return ($page);
}
```

The get_lookup_values() routine used here was described in Chapter 6, "Automating the Form-Handling Process." It returns a reference to the array of values returned from the lookup table named in the query. Each value is passed to get_browse_link() to generate a link to a leaf page. If the category name is "Toys," for instance, get_browse_link() generates a hyperlink that looks like this:

```
<a href="pet_shop.pl?choice=browse;cat=Toys">Toys</a>
```

If the customer selects one of these links, the dispatch code calls get_category_items() to look up items in the category and produce a table showing information about each item:

```
sub get_category_items
{
my ($dbh, $cat_name) = @_;
my ($sth, $page);

    $sth = $dbh->prepare ("SELECT * FROM pet_catalog
                            WHERE category = ? ORDER BY description");
    $sth->execute ($cat_name);
    $page = get_product_table ($sth);

    if ($page)
    {
        $page = p ("Items in product category:\n" . escapeHTML ($cat_name))
                . $page;
    }
    else
    {
        # if the category is empty, say so and show the category list again
        $page .= p ("There are no items in this product category:\n"
                    . escapeHTML ($cat_name));
        $page .= get_category_list ($dbh);
    }

    return ($page);
}
```

get_category_items() calls get_product_table() to do most of its work. (This latter function will be described shortly.) If it turns out there aren't any items in the category, we display the category list again immediately so the customer doesn't have to click the Browse link to get to it.

When the customer wants to specify a search or submits a search, pet_shop.pl invokes search_catalog(). This function presents a new search form and, if a search was just submitted, runs a catalog query and displays the results:

```
sub search_catalog
{
my $dbh = shift;
my $sth;
my @condition;      # conditions for WHERE clause
```

```perl
my @placeholder;    # values for placeholders
my ($where, $limit);
my $page;

    # Put the search form at the top of the page.  Use GET method so
    # that search parameters appear on the URL when the user submits the
    # form (otherwise redirecting back to this page won't work when user
    # selects an "Add Item" link).

    $page .= start_form (-action => url (), -method => "GET")
        . table (
            Tr (
                td ("Keywords:"),
                td (textfield (-name => "keywords", -size => "60"))
            ),
            Tr (
                td (""),
                td (radio_group (-name => "match_type",
                                 -values => [ "all", "any" ],
                                 labels => {
                                     "all" => "Match all words",
                                     "any" => "Match any word"
                                 }))
            ),
            Tr (
                td ("Max. items to show:"),
                td (popup_menu (-name => "limit",
                                -values => [ "10", "25", "50", "75", "100" ]))
            )
        )
        . br ()
        . submit (-name => "choice", -value => "Search")
        . end_form ();

    # Get keywords to look for, bust up into individual words,
    # construct LIKE tests for each of them, and join with the proper
    # boolean according to the match_type parameter.

    my $val = WebDB::trim (param ("keywords"));
    # if no keywords were entered, just display the form
    return ($page) if $val eq "";

    $page .= p (escapeHTML ("Search keywords: $val"));

    my @word = split (/\s+/, $val);
    $val = lc (param ("match_type"));
    my $bool_op = "AND";    # determine boolean connective (default = AND)
    $bool_op = "AND" if $val eq "all";
    $bool_op = "OR" if $val eq "any";
    # create one test per word; join tests with $bool_op;
    # enclose entire string in parentheses
```

continues

continued

```
push (@condition,
       "("
       . join (" $bool_op ", ("description LIKE ?") x @word)
       . ")");
# convert each word xxx to %xxx% before adding to @placeholder
push (@placeholder, map { "%$_%" } @word);

# construct WHERE clause listing the keyword conditions
$where = "WHERE " . join (" AND ", @condition) if @condition;
$where = "" unless $where;

# determine maximum number of items to show;
# default is 10 if $limit looks suspicious
$limit = WebDB::trim (param ("limit"));
$limit = 10 if $limit !~ /^\d+$/ || $limit > 100;

$sth = $dbh->prepare ("SELECT * FROM pet_catalog
                      $where
                      ORDER BY category, description
                      LIMIT $limit");
$sth->execute (@placeholder);

my $table = get_product_table ($sth);
$page .= ($table ? $table : p ("No items were found."));

return ($page);
}
```

search_catalog() generates the search form using the GET method rather than POST. This is done so that the form parameters will be included in the URL when the user submits a search. Then when the search result is displayed, if the user selects Add Item for one of the items, we can examine the HTTP_REFERER environment variable to find out how to redisplay the proper result page by running the search again. If we generate the form using POST, the referring URL won't include the parameters, and we'd have to add them ourselves. (You can see this for yourself by changing the script to use POST rather than GET.)

Much of the code for constructing the keyword search query is similar to that used by the res_search2.pl script developed in Chapter 7. See the section "Searching for Keywords in Text" in that chapter for further discussion.

Like get_category_items(), search_catalog() prepares and executes a query and then calls get_product_table() to do the work of producing the item table. The latter routine takes the statement handle, fetches the records, and formats them. Each item in the table includes a link that enables the customer to add the item to the shopping cart:

```
sub get_product_table
{
my $sth = shift;
my @row;

    while (my $ref = $sth->fetchrow_hashref ())
    {
        # generate a link allowing the item to be added to the cart
        my $url = sprintf ("%s?choice=add;item_id=%s",
                            url (), escape ($ref->{item_id}));
        push (@row, Tr (
                    td (a ({-href => $url}, "Add Item")),
                    td (escapeHTML ($ref->{item_id})),
                    td (""),    # spacer
                    td (escapeHTML ($ref->{description})),
                    td ({-align => "right"},
                        escapeHTML (sprintf ("%.2f", $ref->{price})))
                ));
    }
    $sth->finish ();

    return undef unless @row;        # no items?

    unshift (@row, Tr (              # put header row at beginning
                th (""),
                th ("Item No."),
                th (""),    # spacer
                th ("Description"),
                th ("Price")
            ));

    return (table (@row));
}
```

Displaying the Shopping Cart

The View Cart link takes the customer to a page that lists the shopping cart. The display is generated by format_cart_html(), a routine that was shown earlier. Each entry in the cart display contains a Delete link for removing the item from the cart.

Checking Out

The final stage in creating an order is reached when the customer has finished shopping and selects Check Out from the top of the page. pet_shop.pl sets up a secure connection and proceeds to the checkout page. This page displays the contents of the shopping cart for the customer to review, a form for collecting shipping and billing information, and a Submit Order button. When the customer fills in the form and selects Submit Order, pet_shop.pl stores the order and terminates the session.

As it happens, most of the machinery in `pet_shop.pl` for gathering billing information, storing the order, and presenting the confirmation page to the customer is quite similar to the code that performs these actions in `doc_shop.pl`. Consequently, I'm not going to discuss this process for `pet_shop.pl` at all. You can check the source for the two scripts to see the nature of the differences, such as they are.

Canceling the Order

The Cancel link terminates the shopping session. It's implemented by destroying the session; the effect is to delete the shopping cart entirely. Also, to cause the browser to forget the session ID value, we tell it to delete the cookie containing that identifier.

Modifying the Shopping Cart

The dispatch logic contains two cases for adding items to and deleting items from the shopping cart. These actions are handled by `add_cart()` or `delete_cart()`, two routines that already have been shown. The notable thing about these cases is that they both enable `$redisplay_previous` to tell `pet_shop.pl` to display the page the user just came from, instead of generating a new page.

Finishing Up

After executing the dispatch code, `pet_shop.pl` saves the contents of the shopping cart as necessary, disconnects from the database, and displays the page constructed during dispatch execution:

```perl
# If session hasn't been destroyed, store the shopping
# cart back into it and close it.

my $cart_count = 0;
if (defined ($sess_ref))
{
    # count the number of items in the cart for use
    # below as a bit of feedback for the user
    foreach my $item_id (sort (keys (%{$cart_ref})))
    {
        my $item_ref = $cart_ref->{$item_id};
        $cart_count += $item_ref->{qty};
    }
    $sess_ref->attr ("cart", $cart_ref);
    $sess_ref->close ();
}

$dbh->disconnect ();

# Add/Delete operations set $redisplay_previous to cause
# the page the user just came from to be redisplayed.  referer()
# contains the value of the HTTP_REFERER environment variable and
# redirect() generates Status: and Location: redirection headers.
```

```
if ($redisplay_previous)
{
    print redirect (referer ());
    exit (0)
}

# Add the standard links if they haven't been suppressed;
# add the cart item count as well

if (defined ($std_links))
{
    $page = p ($std_links . " (items in cart: $cart_count)")
            . $page;
}

print header (-cookie => $cookie),
        start_html (-title => "PseudEcom Corporation", -bgcolor => "white"),
        add_boilerplate ($page),
        end_html ();
```

Suggested Modifications

Present a note "this application requires cookies to be enabled in your browser" when a customer first invokes pet_shop.pl. (You can detect this condition by the absence of the session ID cookie.) If your visitor has cookies turned on, the message will appear only once per shopping session. If cookies are turned off, the customer's browser will never return a cookie to the application and pet_shop.pl will present the message every time it's invoked. But that's what you want; the customer gets a constant reminder that the application requires a condition that isn't being met.

The pet_shop.pl application allows only one item to be added to the cart at a time. Modify the pages that display Add Item links to include quantity fields so that the customer can specify quantities explicitly.

Modify the search form to add a pop-up menu that lists product categories so that customers can limit searches to a single category. (Remember to include an "All" or "Any" item so that users can still search all categories.)

The search form contains a limit field, enabling the customer to specify a limit on the number of hits displayed in search result pages. This value is carried from page to page as long as the customer moves between pages that display the search form, but is lost otherwise. Modify pet_shop.pl to remember the limit in the session record so that it can be preserved uniformly across all pages presented by the application.

pet_shop.pl doesn't include any image-display capabilities, but it's not a bad idea to present pictures of your products if you have them; people often like to see what they're buying. Add the capability of displaying text and images on the same page, based on the techniques discussed in Chapter 5 and Chapter 7.

If a customer searches for an item that is out of stock, provide an option for requesting an email notification when the item is back in stock. (To do this, you'd need to add some machinery for maintaining current inventory stock levels, of course.)

If you select an Add Item link on a page that displays items from the catalog, the link changes to the "visited-link" color in your browser when the page is redisplayed. However, if you then delete the item and revisit a page that displays the item, the Add Item link continues to display in the visited-link color, even though the item no longer is in the cart. This might be a source of confusion to customers. Change the application to present the links for adding and deleting items in such a way that it doesn't matter whether these links have been followed.

Completing the Site

This section describes the two remaining applications that must be implemented to complete the PseudEcom e-commerce Web site. One (feedback.pl) enables customers to ask questions or make comments using a free text form. The other (site_rating.pl) solicits customer opinions about the site itself using a poll.

Collecting Feedback and Questions

The feedback.pl script presents a form so that visitors can express concerns or submit comments to PseudEcom. The form contains fields for the customer name and email address (both optional; we won't require them to identify themselves unless they want to), and a field for the comment itself. We'll also include a pop-up menu that the customer can use to categorize the comments, which may be helpful for routing submissions to the appropriate support personnel. The feedback table on which the application is based contains columns corresponding to these fields:

```
CREATE TABLE feedback
(
    id          BIGINT UNSIGNED NOT NULL AUTO_INCREMENT PRIMARY KEY,
    date        DATE NOT NULL,                  # when comment was submitted
    name        VARCHAR(60),                    # customer name
    email       VARCHAR(60),                    # customer email address
    category    ENUM('Question','Comment',      # comment type
                'Complaint','Accolade',
                'Problem with product',
                'Other'),
    comment     TEXT                            # text of comment
)
```

The table also contains an id column so each comment has a unique identifier, and a date column for recording when comments were submitted. comment is a TEXT column rather than CHAR or VARCHAR, because the application enables users to submit comments that are more than 255 characters long.

The `feedback.pl` script is as follows:

```perl
#! /usr/bin/perl -w
# feedback.pl - Collect customer feedback

use strict;
use lib qw(/usr/local/apache/lib/perl);
use CGI qw(:standard escapeHTML);
use WebDB;
use WebDB::TableInfo;
use WebDB::PseudEcom;

my $dbh = WebDB::connect ();
my $page = h3 ("PseudEcom Customer Feedback Page");

# Dispatch to proper action based on user selection

my $choice = lc (param ("choice")); # get choice, lowercased

if ($choice eq "")                  # initial invocation
{
    $page .= generate_form ($dbh);
}
elsif ($choice eq "submit")         # a comment was submitted
{
    $page .= save_comment ($dbh);
}
else
{
    $page .= p (escapeHTML ("Logic error, unknown choice: $choice"));
}

$dbh->disconnect ();

print header (),
      start_html (-title => "PseudEcom Corporation", -bgcolor => "white"),
      add_boilerplate ($page),
      end_html ();

exit (0);

# ------------------------------------------------------------------------

# Generate the comment form

sub generate_form
{
my $dbh = shift;
my ($tbl_info, @category, $page);
```

continues

continued

```
        # Generate the "type of comment" popup based on the ENUM
        # values that are legal for the category column
        $tbl_info = WebDB::TableInfo->get ($dbh, "feedback");
        @category = $tbl_info->members ("category");

        $page .= p ("Please use the following form to tell us who you are\n"
                    . "(optional) and what you'd like us to know.")
                  . p ("If you'd like a response to your comment, be sure\n"
                    . "to include a valid email address. Thank you.");

        $page .= start_form (-action => url ())
              . table (
                  Tr (
                      td ("Your name:" . br () . "(optional)"),
                      td (textfield (-name => "name", size => "60"))
                  ),
                  Tr (
                      td ("Email address:" . br () . "(optional)"),
                      td (textfield (-name => "email", size => "60"))
                  ),
                  Tr (
                      td ("Type of comment:"),
                      td (popup_menu (-name => "category",
                                      -values => \@category))
                  ),
                  Tr (
                      td ({-valign => "top"}, "Comment:"),
                      td (textarea (-name => "comment",
                                    -rows => "5", -cols => "60"))
                  ),
              )
              . br () . br ()
              . submit (-name => "choice", -value => "Submit")
              . end_form ();

    return ($page);
}


# Store the contents of the comment form in the database.  This routine
# does the bare minimum of validation -- none!

sub save_comment
{
my $dbh = shift;
my ($stmt, $val, @placeholder, $page);

    $stmt = "date = CURRENT_DATE";
    foreach my $param_name ("name", "email", "category", "comment")
    {
        $val = WebDB::trim (param ($param_name));
```

```
        next if $val eq "";              # skip empty fields
        $stmt .= "," if $stmt;           # put commas between assignments
        $stmt .= $param_name . " = ?";   # add column name, placeholder
        push (@placeholder, $val);       # save placeholder value
    }
    $stmt = "INSERT INTO feedback SET $stmt";   # complete the statement
    $dbh->do ($stmt, undef, @placeholder);      # save the comment

    $page .= p ("Thank you for your comment.");

    return ($page);
}
```

The `save_comment()` routine doesn't validate submitted comment forms at all. You might want to add a few rudimentary checks, such as making sure that the comment field is not blank and that the email address is valid if it's not blank.

As written, this application files away comments in the database, but does nothing else with them. Without any further action on your part, the comments will just sit there forever. That might help PseudEcom come to resemble large faceless corporations that appear not to respond in any way to customer concerns, but presumably if you implement an information-gathering application such as `feedback.pl`, you do so in order to use the information for some purpose. For example, you might set up a `cron` job that runs each day, looks for comments submitted the previous day, and forwards them to someone in charge of customer relations. Or, you could modify `feedback.pl` itself to generate an email alert to a responsible party each time it stores a record in the `feedback` table.

Asking Visitors To Rate the Site

Our final application presents a poll that asks customers to rate the PseudEcom Web site. It illustrates one way to use the `WebDB::Poll` module in an e-commerce context. (This module was developed in Chapter 6 along with the `poll` and `poll_candidate` tables that it uses. If you haven't already created these tables, check that chapter for instructions.)

First, we need to set up the poll by adding information to the proper polling tables:

```
INSERT INTO poll (name,title,question,begin_date)
    VALUES('PseudEcom rating','Rate the PseudEcom Web site',
           'How well do you like our Web site?',NOW())
INSERT INTO poll_candidate (id,seq,name,label)
    VALUES
        (LAST_INSERT_ID(),1,'like-lot','Like it a lot'),
        (LAST_INSERT_ID(),2,'like-little','Like it a little'),
        (LAST_INSERT_ID(),3,'neutral','I\'m neutral'),
        (LAST_INSERT_ID(),4,'dislike-little','Dislike it a little'),
        (LAST_INSERT_ID(),5,'dislike-lot','Dislike it a lot'),
        (LAST_INSERT_ID(),5,'bogus','It\'s completely bogus')
```

Then we write a short script, site_rating.pl, that presents the poll and records responses. The script is really just a slight variation on the poll.pl script from Chapter 6. It's modified to suppress the link that enables users to see the current voting results (this is an "internal use only" poll) and to embed the polling form within the standard PseudEcom page boilerplate:

```perl
#! /usr/bin/perl -w
# site_rating.pl - Present poll for customers to rate the PseudEcom site

use strict;
use lib qw(/usr/local/apache/lib/perl);
use CGI qw(:standard escape escapeHTML);
use WebDB;
use WebDB::Poll;
use WebDB::PseudEcom;

my $dbh = WebDB::connect ();
my $poll = WebDB::Poll->new ($dbh, "PseudEcom rating");
$poll or fatal_error ("Sorry, poll is not available");
$poll->{results_link} = 0;       # turn off "current results" link
my $page = h3 (escapeHTML ($poll->{data}->{title}));

# Dispatch to proper action based on user selection

my $choice = lc (param ("choice")); # get choice, lowercased

if ($choice eq "")                                    # initial invocation
{
    $page .= $poll->generate_form ();
}
elsif ($choice eq lc ($poll->{data}->{submit_title}))   # a vote was submitted
{
    # tally vote, but ignore return value (we don't report errors)
    $poll->tally_vote (param ("candidate"));
    $page .= p ("Thanks for your input.");
}
else
{
    $page .= p (escapeHTML ("Logic error, unknown choice: $choice"));
}

$dbh->disconnect ();

print header (),
        start_html (-title => "PseudEcom Corporation", -bgcolor => "white"),
        add_boilerplate ($page),
        end_html ();

exit (0);
```

To see the current results from the poll, run this query:

```
mysql> SELECT poll_candidate.label, poll_candidate.tally
    -> FROM poll, poll_candidate
    -> WHERE poll.name = 'PseudEcom Rating' and poll.id = poll_candidate.id
    -> ORDER BY poll_candidate.seq;
+-----------------------+-------+
| label                 | tally |
+-----------------------+-------+
| Like it a lot         |    41 |
| Like it a little      |   112 |
| I'm neutral           |    90 |
| Dislike it a little   |    78 |
| Dislike it a lot      |    19 |
| It's completely bogus |   493 |
+-----------------------+-------+
```

Suggested Site-Wide Modifications

Several of the earlier sections describing the scripts that implement the PseudEcom site have suggested modifications that pertain to individual applications. This section suggests some changes that are more general and affect the operation of the site as a whole.

Modify the boilerplate routine `add_boilerplate()` to indicate whether the customer currently has a pet shop session open, and to report the number of items in the shopping cart if so. This serves as a reminder that the customer has some unfinished business to take care of—that is, to complete the ongoing purchase and send us some money!

You can use your storefront to provide your customers with access to information that is not actually stored on your site. For example, if you want customers to be able to see current stock quotes for your company or for related companies of interest, you can include links that point to one of the stock market sites and trigger quote displays.

In Chapter 5, "Writing Form-Based Applications," we wrote a script for collecting product registrations (`prod_reg.pl`). That was a standalone application. What would it take to integrate it into the PseudEcom site? For example, to make sure the pages that `prod_reg.pl` presents use the same boilerplate and have the same look as other site pages, what changes would you need to make? More generally, what design principles can you identify that should be followed to make an application integrate more easily into the PseudEcom Web site?

Final Thoughts

The PseudEcom site is complete now. It includes several kinds of applications typical of e-commerce sites, and most of them are based on MySQL. The site is presented in a way that displays pages using a consistent appearance and that allows visitors to navigate the site easily. In addition, the site's appearance and layout are controlled largely by library routines, so other areas can be added to the site relatively easily to extend it. It's up to you to decide what kind of applications you might want to add. If they involve a database (and they're likely to), so much the better—MySQL will help you accomplish your goals.

Obtaining Software

THIS BOOK DISCUSSES HOW TO WRITE LOTS of applications, but you certainly won't
want to type in all the source code yourself. Instead, you should download the source
distribution that contains the application scripts, support files for setting up the associated
database tables, and sample data. These are known collectively as the webdb distribution
(because the database used in the book is named webdb), and may be found at:

```
http://www.kitebird.com/mysql-perl/
```

To use this distribution, you need to have a certain amount of other software installed
already. Some software is required before you can do anything at all, and some is necessary only for the applications written in certain parts of the book. This
appendix indicates what you need and where to get it.

Many of the packages listed are Perl modules. To find out whether a given module
is installed already, try to read its documentation using the perldoc command. For
example, to read the documentation for the DBI or DBD::mysql modules, try these
commands:

```
% perldoc DBI
% perldoc DBD::mysql
```

If a perldoc command produces no information about a module, the module isn't
installed. (And if perldoc can't be found, you'll need to install Perl itself.)

Required Software

This section lists the software components you must have installed to use this book, and the Web sites where you can get them. You may find many of them already available, particularly if you have an account with an ISP that offers Web-hosting services to its customers. There are three major required components:

- MySQL (http://www.mysql.com/)

   The MySQL database management system underlies almost all the applications in this book. I used the MySQL 3.23.xx series to write the applications, but most of them should work without modification under 3.22.xx version as well. (There are a few exceptions, such as applications that require transactions; transaction support is not present in MySQL 3.22.xx.)

- Perl (http://www.perl.com/, http://www.activestate.com/)

   The Perl programming language—you should have Perl 5.005 or newer or some scripts in this book may not work properly. Under UNIX, Perl will almost certainly already be installed. Under Windows, you can use ActiveState Perl.

- Apache (http://www.apache.org/)

   The Apache Web server. Any recent version should be suitable.

You also need several Perl modules: CGI.pm, DBI, and DBD::mysql. (Note that DBD::mysql is packaged in the module named Msql-Mysql-modules.) If you want to perform transaction processing at the DBI abstraction level, you'll need DBD::mysql version 1.2216 or newer. All these modules, as well as those listed in "Optional Software," can be obtained from the CPAN (Comprehensive Perl Archive Network), a valuable resource at http://cpan.perl.org/ that contains lots of useful Perl software. Under Windows, use ActiveState's PPM (Perl Package Manager) tool to install modules that are not included in the standard ActiveState distribution.

NuSphere (http://www.nusphere.com/) provides an easy-to-use package that installs all the required components for you. It's a convenient way to get going, and it works under Linux, Solaris, and Windows.[1]

Optional Software

If you plan to run your Web scripts under mod_perl, visit http://perl.apache.org/ for distributions and instructions.

Many of the scripts in this book use additional Perl modules besides those listed in the previous section. Some of these modules (such as IO::File or Time::Local) should be present in the standard Perl distribution. Others may not be installed and you'll need to obtain them:

---

1. Disclaimer! I work for NuSphere. (But I *do* think it's a nice installer.)

- `Business::CreditCard`

  This module contains routines for checking credit card numbers. It's used in Chapter 10, "E-Commerce Applications."

- `Crypt::CBC`

  A cryptography module used for encryption in Chapter 9, "Security and Privacy Issues." This module isn't used by itself; you'll need another subsidiary module to go along with it, such as `Crypt::Blowfish`, `Crypt::DES`, or `Crypt::IDEA`.

- `Digest::MD5`, `Digest::HMAC_MD5`, `Digest::HMAC_SHA1`

  Modules for generating checksums, as discussed in Chapter 9, "Security and Privacy Issues."

- `Apache::Session`

  Needed to provide session support for applications in Chapter 8, "Session Management," and some applications in the following chapters.

- `Image::Magick`

  Used to produce image thumbnails in Chapter 5, "Writing Form-Based Applications." If you install the C source distribution of ImageMagick, it may install the `Image::Magick` Perl module for you.

- `Mail::Sendmail`

  Gives scripts the capability to send email. It doesn't use the UNIX `sendmail` program, so it works under Windows, too, and is useful for generating mail on a cross-platform basis.

Several scripts in this book are written with the intent that they be run under the UNIX `cron` job-scheduling mechanism. For Windows, a free version of `cron` is available at:

```
http://members.nbci.com/kalab/cron.htm
```

Other Windows schedulers that may be suitable can be obtained at:

```
http://www.simplythebest.net/schedule.html
```

Installing Software

Sometimes you can find prebuilt versions of the components you need. This is so particularly under Linux, for which distributions tend to be available in RPM (RedHat Package Manager) format. Using prebuilt packages can be more convenient if you don't want to mess around running a lot of build commands, but compiling from source has the advantage that you can put things where you want them, instead of where someone else assumes you want them. (A warning: For MySQL, RedHat's own RPMs tend to be somewhat broken. If you've installed one of these, I recommend uninstalling it by running `rpm -e mysql` and then installing RPMs obtained from the

MySQL site instead. Make sure you get all the RPM files you need; the full set includes server, client, and development RPMs.)

If you're building from source, then with the exception of the Perl modules, installation procedures for the various pieces of software used in this book vary. You'll need to read and follow the instructions for each component. For mod_perl especially, note the many INSTALL.* files in the main distribution directory. Read them, pick the one that offers a recipe that looks most likely to suit your system, and follow its instructions.

For Perl, most modules can be built and installed using the following sequence of commands (you'll likely need to run the make install command as root):

```
% perl Makefile.PL
% make
% make test
% make install
```

Alternatively, you may find it more convenient to download, build, and install modules using Perl's CPAN module in interactive mode. (This too may need to be run as root.) Here's an example:

```
% perl -MCPAN -e shell
cpan> install Mail::Sendmail
```

With ActiveState Perl under Windows, use the PPM tool to obtain and install Perl modules:

```
C:\> ppm
PPM> install Mail::Sendmail
Install package 'Mail::Sendmail?' (y/N): y
```

B

References and Further Reading

THE FOLLOWING REFERENCES PROVIDE ADDITIONAL information about the software used in this book and the topics it discusses. These fall into two categories: Books and Online Resources. (By the way, "online" doesn't necessarily mean "a page or two." Several of the Web sites include online manuals that easily would qualify for listing under "Books" were they printed out.) You can also find instructions for joining mailing lists at several of the sites. These are often useful for asking questions and obtaining information, and several of the lists also have archives that are available in searchable form.

Books

For some of these topics, other books are available; those listed here are the ones I happen to like best or find most useful.

HTML & XHTML: The Definitive Guide (4th Edition), by Chuck Musciano and Bill Kennedy. Sebastopol, CA: O'Reilly & Associates (2000).

Mastering Regular Expressions, by Jeffrey E. F. Friedl. Sebastopol, CA: O'Reilly & Associates (1997).

MySQL, by Paul DuBois. Indianapolis, IN: New Riders (1999). Companion Web site: `http://www.kitebird.com/mysql-book/`

Official Guide to Programming with CGI.pm, by Lincoln Stein. New York, NY: Wiley Computer Publishing (1998). Companion Web site: `http://www.wiley.com/comp-books/stein/source.html`

Professional Apache, by Peter Wainwright. Birmingham, UK: Wrox Press, Inc. (1999).

Programming the Perl DBI, by Alligator Descartes and Tim Bunce. Sebastopol, CA: O'Reilly & Associates (2000).

Programming Perl (3rd Edition), by Larry Wall, Tom Christiansen, and Jon Orwant. Sebastopol, CA: O'Reilly & Associates (2000).

SSH, The Secure Shell: The Definitive Guide, by Daniel J. Barrett and Richard E. Silverman. Sebastopol, CA: O'Reilly & Associates (2001). Companion Web site: `http://www.snailbook.com/`

Web Security & Commerce, by Simson Garfinkel with Gene Spafford. Sebastopol, CA: O'Reilly & Associates (1997).

Writing Apache Modules with Perl and C, by Lincoln Stein and Doug MacEachern. Sebastopol, CA: O'Reilly & Associates (1999). Companion Web site: `http://www.modperl.com/`

Online Resources

`http://cpan.perl.org/`, the Comprehensive Perl Archive Network, source for all kinds of Perl software.

`http://dbi.perl.org/`, home for DBI and DBI-related software.

`http://hoohoo.ncsa.uiuc.edu/cgi/`, the Common Gateway Interface (CGI) specification.

`http://perl.apache.org/`, the Apache Group's `mod_perl` site. You're likely to find several areas on this site particularly useful:

- `http://perl.apache.org/guide/`, the `mod_perl` Guide.
- `http://perl.apache.org/dist/cgi_to_mod_perl.html`, hints for converting CGI scripts to run under `mod_perl`.
- `http://perl.apache.org/dist/mod_perl_traps.html`, problems to watch out for when using `mod_perl`.
- `http://perl.apache.org/stories/` and `http://perl.apache.org/tidbits.html`, case studies and testimonials.
- `http://perl.apache.org/tuning/`, the `mod_perl` performance-tuning guide; tips for helping Apache run better.

`http://stein.cshl.org/WWW/software/CGI/`, the online CGI.pm documentation.

`http://www.apache.com/`, the primary Apache site.

`http://www.ics.uci.edu/pub/ietf/http/rfc2109.txt`, RFC 2109, the document describing the specification for cookie-based state management.

`http://www.modssl.org/`, the `mod_ssl` site.

`http://www.mysql.com/`, the home of MySQL. The MySQL Reference Manual (the official MySQL documentation) is available here. (It's also included with MySQL source distributions, which are available at this site as well.)

`http://www.openssh.org/`, the OpenSSH Web site.

`http://www.securityfocus.com/`, the SecurityFocus site; it hosts several security-related mailing lists and maintains an archive of security alerts and fixes.

`http://www.truste.com/`, the TRUSTe site; a good source of information about protection of client privacy.

Index

G

H

K-L

HOW TO CONTACT US

VISIT OUR WEB SITE

WWW.NEWRIDERS.COM

On our web site, you'll find information about our other books, authors, tables of contents, and book errata. You will also find information about book registration and how to purchase our books, both domestically and internationally.

EMAIL US

Contact us at: **nrfeedback@newriders.com**

- If you have comments or questions about this book
- To report errors that you have found in this book
- If you have a book proposal to submit or are interested in writing for New Riders
- If you are an expert in a computer topic or technology and are interested in being a technical editor who reviews manuscripts for technical accuracy

Contact us at: **nreducation@newriders.com**

- If you are an instructor from an educational institution who wants to preview New Riders books for classroom use. Email should include your name, title, school, department, address, phone number, office days/hours, text in use, and enrollment, along with your request for desk/examination copies and/or additional information.

Contact us at: **nrmedia@newriders.com**

- If you are a member of the media who is interested in reviewing copies of New Riders books. Send your name, mailing address, and email address, along with the name of the publication or web site you work for.

BULK PURCHASES/CORPORATE SALES

If you are interested in buying 10 or more copies of a title or want to set up an account for your company to purchase directly from the publisher at a substantial discount, contact us at 800-382-3419 or email your contact information to corpsales@pearsontechgroup.com. A sales representative will contact you with more information.

WRITE TO US

New Riders Publishing
201 W. 103rd St.
Indianapolis, IN 46290-1097

CALL/FAX US

Toll-free (800) 571-5840
If outside U.S. (317) 581-3500
Ask for New Riders
FAX: (317) 581-4663

VOICES THAT MATTER

WWW.NEWRIDERS.COM

RELATED NEW RIDERS TITLES

ISBN: 0735709211
800 pages
US $49.99

MySQL

Paul DuBois

MySQL teaches readers how to use the tools provided by the MySQL distribution, by covering installation, setup, daily use, security, optimization, maintenance, and troubleshooting. It also discusses important third-party tools, such as the Perl DBI and Apache/PHP interfaces that provide access to MySQL.

ISBN: 0735710430
368 pages
US $45.00

Advanced Linux Programming

CodeSourcery, LLC

An in-depth guide to programming Linux from the most recognized leaders in the Open Source community, this book is the ideal reference for Linux programmers who are reasonably skilled in the C programming language and who are in need of a book that cover the Linux C library (glibc).

ISBN 0735710910
416 pages
US $34.99

Python Essential Reference, Second Edition

David Beazley

Python Essential Reference, Second Edition, concisely describes the Python programming language and its large library of standard modules—collectively known as the Python programming environment. It is arranged into four major parts. First, a brief tutorial and introduction is presented, then an informal language reference covers lexical conventions, functions, statements, control flow, datatypes, classes, and execution models. The third section covers the Python library, and the final section covers the Python C API that is used to write Python extensions. This book is highly focused and clearly provides the things a reader needs to know to best utilize Python.

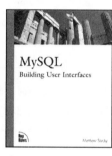

ISBN: 073571049X
656 pages
US $49.99

MySQL: Building User Interfaces

Matthew Stucky

A companion to *MySQL*, this book teaches readers to make decisions on how to provide a robust and efficient database solution for any enterprise. The author presents valuable insight from his experience with differe companies with varying needs ar sizes. This is the only book available that covers GTK+ and data base accessibility.

ISBN: 0735711143
500 pages
US $44.99

Perl for the Web

Chris Radcliff

This book provides the tools an principles needed to design a high-performance, dynamic Wel site using Perl. Special attention given to templates, integration, and load testing. Topics covered include the need for speed, document management with templates and embedded Perl, faster performance using persistent Perl, good Web coding style, faster database access from Perl, and pairing XML with Perl for content management and B2B communication.

Solutions from experts you know and trust.

www.informit.com

New Riders has partnered with **InformIT.com** to bring technical information to your desktop. Drawing on New Riders authors and reviewers to provide additional information on topics you're interested in, **InformIT.com** has free, in-depth information you won't find anywhere else.

- **Master the skills you need, when you need them**

- **Call on resources from some of the best minds in the industry**

- **Get answers when you need them, using InformIT's comprehensive library or live experts online**

- **Go above and beyond what you find in New Riders books, extending your knowledge**

As an **InformIT** partner, **New Riders** has shared the wisdom and knowledge of our authors with you online. Visit **InformIT.com** to see what you're missing.

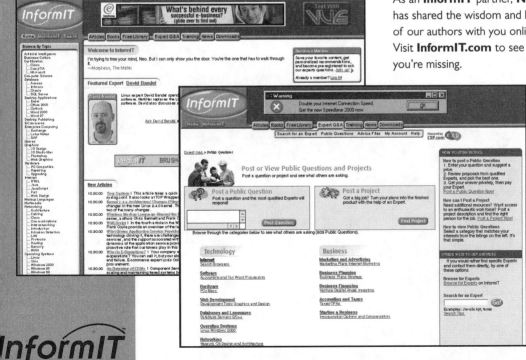

Love

Need me.

Treasure me.

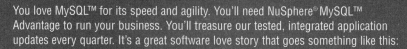

Colophon

The ruined castle on the cover of this book, captured by photographer David Toase, is that of Denbigh Castle, Denbighshire, Wales. The name Denbigh is Welsh for "little fort." Built in the thirteenth century by Henry de Lacy, Earl of Lincoln, the castle served as part of Edward I's campaigns against the Welsh.[1] Denbigh Castle sits on a steep hill above the town of Denbigh. Its triple-towered Great-Gatehouse is considered one of its most unique features. It is also noted for its town walls, which at almost two-thirds of a mile long, connect to the castle. It is believed that the castle was held under siege during both the War of the Roses and the English Civil War.

This book was written using vi and groff, then converted to XML DocBook format and exported through Jade to rtf. It was laid out in QuarkXPress. The font used for the body text is Bembo and MCPdigital. It was printed on 50# Husky Offset Smooth paper at VonHoffman Graphics, Inc. in Owensville, Missouri. Prepress consisted of PostScript computer-to-plate technology (filmless process). The cover was printed at Moore Langen Printing in Terre Haute, Indiana, on 12pt, coated on one side.

---

1. http://www.wales-calling.com/castles/denbigh-castle.htm